ZB

SPELLING CONNECTIONS

The Right Connections, The Right Results!

Author, J. Richard Gentry, Ph.D.

Spelling **and** Thinking

Spelling **and** Vocabulary

Spelling **and** Reading

Spelling **and** Writing

www.zaner-bloser.com

The Right Connections ▷ The Right Results

Students Succeed

Every unit in the Student Edition makes the important connections needed to help students learn more, retain more, and transfer more of their spelling know-how to their daily work.

Teachers Succeed

The Teacher Edition provides complete, step-by-step lesson plans, time management tools, and activities for different learning styles to help busy teachers plan the level and pace of instruction. A special *Word Sort CD-ROM* is included.

Teacher Resource Book

Provides teachers with a full range of spelling support in one convenient book of reproducibles.

Transparencies

Show students how to make important spelling connections with transparencies that reinforce the lessons in each unit.
- Student Writing Models
- Writing Prompts
- Word Lists
- Proofreading Every Day

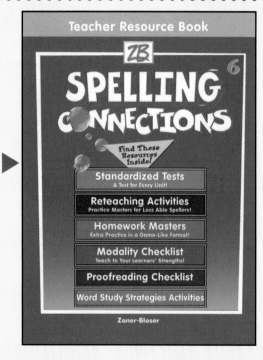

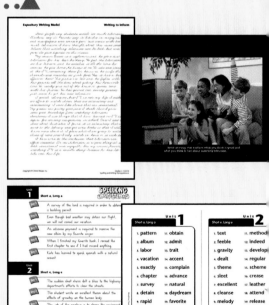

The Right Connections ▸ The Right Results

FOR SPELLING SUCCESS!

Thinking, Vocabulary, Reading, and Writing.

Home Spelling Practice Book

This book of reproducible letters keeps parents up-to-date with student progress and offers additional practice activities.

Practice Book for Grammar, Usage, and Mechanics

Provides additional spelling word practice while teaching grammar, usage, and mechanics skills.

Audiotape

Provides dictation sentences for pretests and posttests.

Spelling Support for Second Language Learners

Offers vocabulary practice and teaching strategies.

Support Software

The *Spelling Connections* CD-ROM includes options for interactive spelling and word-search activities and games.

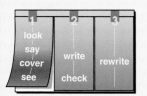

Flip Folder

A ready-made flip folder saves time and offers a fun and effective way to practice spelling.

The Right Connections ⟩ The Right Results

CONNECTIONS FOR

Spelling Connections helps

CONNECTIONS TO VOCABULARY

Systematic and explicit instruction helps students learn and apply words in meaningful context.

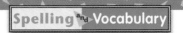

Spelling **and** Vocabulary

Synonyms
Write a spelling word that is a synonym for each word.
1. lawful   4. normal   6. middle
2. opponent   5. substance   7. tag
3. useful

Word Structure
8. Write the spelling word that has the /oo/ sound spelled **eu**.
9. Write the spelling word that has the /oo/ sound spelled **u**.
10. Write the spelling word that begins with the consonant digraph **ch**.
11.–12. Change the first letter in **national** and in **funnel**. Write the spelling words.

Antonyms
Write the spelling words that complete the meaning.
13. **Tie** is to **untie** as **pleasant** is to ____.
14. **Whole** is to **piece** as **complete** is to ____.

USING THE Dictionary

When you pronounce a word that has more than one syllable, you emphasize one syllable more than the others. The dictionary uses dark type and a symbol called a **stress mark** (') to indicate which syllable to emphasize.
15.–20. Write the spelling words ending in /ənt/ that are pronounced with the stress on the first syllable.

63

CONNECTIONS TO THINKING

Word lists are presented in both manuscript and cursive for easier reading.

Spelling words are presented in complete sentences and used in context to underscore meaning.

Practice activities and spelling strategies help students develop mastery of spelling words.

Unit **10**
/ə/ in Final Syllables

Spelling **and** Thinking

READ THE SPELLING WORDS

1.	unpleasant	*unpleasant*	Washing a pan is an **unpleasant** task.
2.	absent	*absent*	She was **absent** from school today.
3.	practical	*practical*	His **practical** answer surprised us.
4.	neutral	*neutral*	You can take sides, but I am **neutral**.
5.	turbulent	*turbulent*	The ocean was **turbulent** from a storm.
6.	rival	*rival*	We will play our **rival** in today's game.
7.	rational	*rational*	He gave us a **rational** explanation.
8.	instant	*instant*	I saw the rainbow for only an **instant**.
9.	talent	*talent*	She is known for her musical **talent**.
10.	partial	*partial*	He gave only a **partial** answer.
11.	label	*label*	The **label** says the tie is made of silk.
12.	legal	*legal*	He asked a lawyer for **legal** advice.
13.	cruel	*cruel*	It is **cruel** to leave the dog alone.
14.	distant	*distant*	She seemed shy and **distant** at first.
15.	tunnel	*tunnel*	The truck stalled in the **tunnel**.
16.	typical	*typical*	Her **typical** day begins with a jog.
17.	channel	*channel*	The boat sailed through the **channel**.
18.	ignorant	*ignorant*	He was **ignorant** of the game rules.
19.	central	*central*	I live in the **central** part of the state.
20.	material	*material*	The new **material** was delivered today.

SORT THE SPELLING WORDS

1.–9. Write the words that have the /əl/ sound spelled **al**.
10.–13. Write the words that have the /əl/ sound spelled **el**.
14.–16. Write the words that have the /ənt/ sound spelled **ent**.
17.–20. Write the words that have the /ənt/ sound spelled **ant**.

REMEMBER THE SPELLING STRATEGY

Remember that the **schwa** sound (/ə/) often occurs in unstressed final syllables. Think about how /ə/ is spelled in the final syllable in **legal**, **label**, **talent**, and **distant**.

62

Using the Dictionary section develops skills and provides experience in using spelling resources.

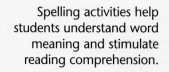

SPELLING SUCCESS!

students make important connections for real spelling success.

CONNECTIONS TO READING

Spelling activities help students understand word meaning and stimulate reading comprehension. ▶▶

Students quickly use and apply what they know while learning reading comprehension strategies. ◀◀

Spelling and Reading

unpleasant	absent	practical	neutral	turbulent
rival	rational	instant	talent	partial
label	legal	cruel	distant	tunnel
typical	channel	ignorant	central	material

Solve the Analogies Write a spelling word to complete each analogy.

1. **Angry** is to **pleased** as **present** is to _____.
2. **Famous** is to **unknown** as **educated** is to _____.
3. **Arrive** is to **depart** as **near** is to _____.
4. **Low** is to **high** as **slow** is to _____.
5. **Wind** is to **fierce** as **water** is to _____.
6. **Quiet** is to **calm** as **useful** is to _____.

Complete the Sentences Write a spelling word to complete each sentence.

7. This painting demonstrates his remarkable _____.
8. Switzerland remained _____ during two world wars.
9. The _____ joke hurt his feelings.
10. He was so angry that he was not behaving in a _____ way.
11. It is not _____ to park here so you will get a ticket.
12. Read the _____ before you buy the product.
13. I watch the morning news on another _____.

Complete the Paragraph Write spelling words from the box to complete the paragraph.

Building a __14.__ in the 1920s was a difficult and __15.__ task. Every day, __16.__ progress was made toward the goal. A __17.__ problem was preventing soft __18.__ from sliding into the hole as workers dug. Often two __19.__ digging crews worked from opposite sides. They met in the __20.__ area known as the "hole through."

typical
rival
unpleasant
tunnel
partial
material
central

64

CONNECTIONS TO WRITING

Writing

Tools and activities help students apply correct spelling to their own writing. ▶▶

Students learn the writing process while actively transferring spelling skills to their own writing efforts. ▶▶

_____ ly in this paragraph. Write the

Proofreading Marks	
≡	Make a capital.
/	Make a small letter.
∧	Add something.
ℒ	Take out something.
⊙	Add a period.
¶	New paragraph
SP	Spelling error

al talent for business. During _____ Strauss sold canvas for tents. _____ er needed heavy-duty pants, _____ tion. He used some of his _____ er, Strauss replaced the _____ called denim. He changed the nuetral color of the denim by dyeing it a dark blue. Customers were parcial to this softer, darker fabric. Strauss's pants, or Levi's, were an instent hit.

 Write a Paragraph _Descriptive Writing_

Every paragraph has a main idea, which is stated in the topic sentence. The other sentences in the paragraph support or develop that central idea. Write a paragraph that describes something.

• Write about something that you have done or someone else has done.
• Follow the form used in the proofreading sample.

Use as many spelling words as you can.

Proofread Your Writing During ▶ Editing

Proofread your writing for spelling errors as part of the editing stage in the writing process. Be sure to check each word carefully. Use a dictionary to check spelling if you are not sure.

Writing Process

Prewriting
⇩
Drafting
⇩
Revising
⇩
Editing
⇩
Publishing

 65

The Right Connections ▷ **The Right Results**

ZB VOCABULARY CONNECTIONS

Spelling **and** Thinking

Spelling **and** Vocabulary

Spelling **and** Reading

Spelling **and** Writing

Vocabulary study improves scores on achievement tests and learning outcomes in all the content areas. Vocabulary connection activities ensure vocabulary growth and understanding.

Unit 10 enrichment

VOCABULARY CONNECTIONS

Strategy Words

Review Words: /ə/ in Final Syllables

Write words from the box to complete this thank-you note.

| angel | final | incident | loyal | pleasant |

Dear Lucy,

You were an __1.__ to come to my rescue last night when I had a flat tire. You even helped me through the __2.__ of the empty gas tank. You are a __3.__ friend indeed. I promise you that that was the __4.__ episode in my adventures. Our next occasion together will be more __5.__

Your grateful friend,
Dave

Preview Words: / / in Final Syllables

Write the word from the box that completes each sentence.

| apparent | diesel | equidistant | confidential | ordinal |

6. Most trucks have a ___ engine.
7. Something that is private is ___.
8. Something that is easily understood is ___.
9. If the store is a mile from each of our homes, it is ___ from our homes.
10. First, second, and third are examples of ___ numbers.

66

Content Words

Math: Proportions

Write the word from the box that completes each sentence.

| equivalent | ratio | invert | reciprocal | proportion |

1. Twelve inches are ___ to one foot.
2. The ___ of ⁴/₃ is ³/₄.
3. If you ___ ¹/₄, the result is ⁴/₁.
4. The size of things in comparison to each other refers to ___.
5. The ___ of 2 to 3 is ²/₃.

Social Studies: Debate

Write the words from the box that complete the paragraph.

| debate | opinion | disagreement | panelist | logical |

Jurors __6.__ the issues that have been discussed during a trial. A jury __7.__ must form his or her own __8.__ and make __9.__ decisions based on what the jury learned during the trial. Any major __10.__ must be solved among the jurors before their verdict is delivered.

Apply the Spelling Strategy

Circle the letters that spell the /əl/ or the /ənt/ sound in the final syllable of four of the Content Words you wrote.

Word Study

Prefixes

The prefix **equi-** came from a Latin form, **aequi-**, that meant "even, same." Things that are **equivalent** are the same or equal. Write the Strategy Word that has this prefix and means "equally far apart."

67

Connections to Strategy Words

Reinforce each spelling strategy with additional words above and below grade level.

Connections to Content Words

Help students relate the spelling strategy to important content-area words.

Word Study

Word study practice provides an in-depth look at words and encourages spelling development.

Z6

The Right Connections ▶ The Right Results

EXTRA CONNECTIONS
to Spelling and Writing

In addition to proofreading and writing in every unit, *Spelling Connections* offers a wide array of extra resources to help students transfer good spelling to their writing.

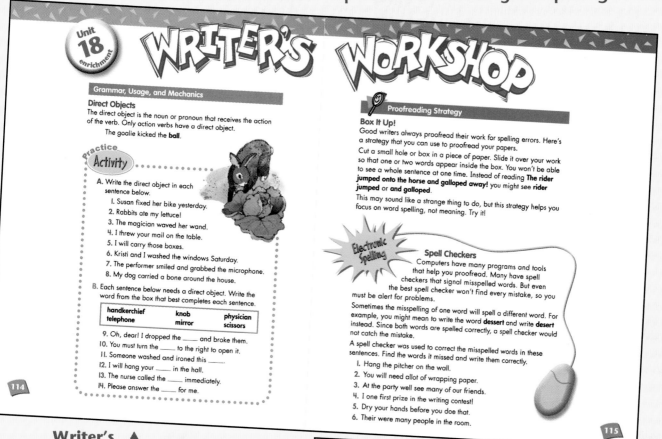

Unit 18 enrichment

WRITER'S WORKSHOP

Grammar, Usage, and Mechanics

Direct Objects

The direct object is the noun or pronoun that receives the action of the verb. Only action verbs have a direct object.

The goalie kicked the **ball**.

Practice Activity

A. Write the direct object in each sentence below.

1. Susan fixed her bike yesterday.
2. Rabbits ate my lettuce!
3. The magician waved her wand.
4. I threw your mail on the table.
5. I will carry those boxes.
6. Kristi and I washed the windows Saturday.
7. The performer smiled and grabbed the microphone.
8. My dog carried a bone around the house.

B. Each sentence below needs a direct object. Write the word from the box that best completes each sentence.

| handkerchief | knob | physician |
| telephone | mirror | scissors |

9. Oh, dear! I dropped the _____ and broke them.
10. You must turn the _____ to the right to open it.
11. Someone washed and ironed this _____.
12. I will hang your _____ in the hall.
13. The nurse called the _____ immediately.
14. Please answer the _____ for me.

114

Proofreading Strategy

Box It Up!

Good writers always proofread their work for spelling errors. Here's a strategy that you can use to proofread your papers.

Cut a small hole or box in a piece of paper. Slide it over your work so that one or two words appear inside the box. You won't be able to see a whole sentence at one time. Instead of reading **The rider jumped onto the horse and galloped away!** you might see **rider jumped** or **and galloped**.

This may sound like a strange thing to do, but this strategy helps you focus on word spelling, not meaning. Try it!

Electronic Spelling

Spell Checkers

Computers have many programs and tools that help you proofread. Many have spell checkers that signal misspelled words. But even the best spell checker won't find every mistake, so you must be alert for problems.

Sometimes the misspelling of one word will spell a different word. For example, you might mean to write the word **dessert** and write **desert** instead. Since both words are spelled correctly, a spell checker would not catch the mistake.

A spell checker was used to correct the misspelled words in these sentences. Find the words it missed and write them correctly.

1. Hang the pitcher on the wall.
2. You will need allot of wrapping paper.
3. At the party well see many of our friends.
4. I one first prize in the writing contest!
5. Dry your hands before you doet that.
6. Their were many people in the room.

115

Writer's Workshop pages are found in every **Assessment and Review Unit.**

Three valuable resources are found in the back of the Student Edition.
• Thesaurus
• Dictionary
• Writer's Handbook

▶▶

Writing Thesaurus

Spelling Dictionary

WRITER'S HANDBOOK Contents

Home Spelling Practice Book

This book of reproducibles keeps parents informed of student progress.

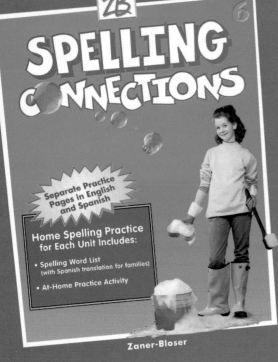

Reproducible pages feature notes to home, additional spelling practice, and fun activities for parents and children to do together.

Home Spelling Practice Book

ZB

SPELLING CONNECTIONS

Separate Practice Pages in English and Spanish

Home Spelling Practice for Each Unit Includes:

- Spelling Word List (with Spanish translation for families)
- At-Home Practice Activity

Zaner-Bloser

Unit **4**

Home Spelling Practice

Short o, Long o

Dear Family,
Ask your child to write the spelling words correctly on the blank lines. As you work with your child to practice this week's spelling words, try the following activity.

A Good Place to Start Encourage your child to write a beginning to this story ...ing:

...ackie climbed into ...back seat, she ...ed and whispered, ... call when I get ...e. Remember, we ...ed not to tell ... anyone about the ...s. Besides, no one ...d believe it."

1. profit
2. oppose
3. bronze
4. video
5. constant
6. approach
7. pose
8. associate
9. contact
10. opportunity
11. positive
12. donate
13. stereo
14. beyond
15. charcoal
16. notice
17. opposite
18. emotion
19. project
20. respond

English reproducible page shown.

Each reproducible page presents word lists in English, or English with Spanish translations.

Unit **4**

Práctica de ortografía para el hogar

Short o, Long o

Querida familia:
Pida a su hijo(a) que escriba correctamente en las líneas en blanco las palabras para deletrear de esta semana. Al practicar estas palabras con su hijo(a), prueben el siguiente ejercicio.

Un buen lugar para empezar
Animen a su hijo o hija a escribir el principio de un cuento que terminaría así:

As Jackie climbed into the back seat, she turned and whispered, "I'll call when I get home. Remember, we agreed not to tell anyone about the caves. Besides, no one would believe it."

(Mientras se sentaba en el asiento de atrás, Jackie se volteó y murmuró:—Te llamaré cuando llegue a casa. Acuérdate de que prometimos no contarle a nadie sobre las cuevas. Además, nadie lo creería.)

1. profit — beneficio; provecho
2. oppose — oponer
3. bronze — bronce
4. video — vídeo
5. constant — constante
6. approach — acercamiento; acercarse
7. pose — pose; posar
8. associate — asociado; asociar
9. contact — contacto; ponerse en contacto con
10. opportunity — oportunidad
11. positive — positivo
12. donate — donar; dar
13. stereo — estéreo; tocadiscos
14. beyond — más allá
15. charcoal — carbón
16. notice — noticia; aviso
17. opposite — opuesto; contrario
18. emotion — emoción
19. project — proyecto; projectar
20. respond — responder

15

Spanish reproducible page shown.

The Right Connections > The Right Results

ASSESSMENT CONNECTIONS

Spelling **and** Thinking

Spelling **and** Vocabulary

Spelling **and** Reading

Spelling **and** Writing

Focused Study and Review

Assessment tools help teachers monitor student progress so they can effectively plan and manage overall classroom instruction and activities.

Transfer spelling skills to writing with these activities!!!

Assessment activities determine how well students can apply strategies and word patterns to new words.

▶▶

Review activities help students practice their spelling of words taught in previous units.

▼
▼

Unit 18
Review Units 13–17

Assessment and Review

Assessment
Units 13–17

Each Assessment Word in the box fits one of the spelling strategies you have studied over the past five weeks. Read the spelling strategies. Then write each Assessment Word under the unit number it fits.

Unit 13 _____
1.–4. The **f** sound (/**f**/) can be spelled in different ways: **f** in **faint**, **ff** in **baffle**, and **ph** in **phone**.

Unit 14 _____
5.–8. The /**z**/ sound can be spelled: **z** as in **freeze**, **s** as in **phase**, and **ss** as in **scissors**. The /**zh**/ sound can be spelled **s** and is often followed by **ual** (usual) or **ion** (vision).

Unit 15 _____
9.–12. The suffixes **-ed** and **-ing** can be added to some base words to form new words. In other words, the final consonant is doubled when **-ed** or **-ing** is added.

Unit 16 _____
13.–16. Some words have more consonant letters than consonant sounds. If a consonant is not pronounced, it is considered silent: **k** in **knob** and **b** in **tomb**.

Unit 17 _____
17.–20. Double consonants usually represent a single sound: **banner, mirror**.

scuffle
illusion
patrolling
dumb
glossary
intellect
salve
patrolled
dispose
gopher
chef
hazel
frightened
knelt
surround
suggest
knead
frightening
hazy
fatal

Review — Unit 13: /r/ Spelled f, ff, ph

effort	fulfill	physician	sophomore	faint
difficult	phone	offer		phrase	officer

Write a spelling word for each clue.
1. another word for doctor
2. last year's freshman
3. person in a position of authority

Use spelling words to complete each sentence.
4.–5. I will make an _____ to _____ your wish.
6. It took me an hour to solve that _____ math problem.
7.–9. The _____ was too _____ to hear on the _____.
10. I will sell it if you will make me a fair _____.

Review — Unit 14: Consonant Sounds /z/, /zh/

optimism	scissors	usual	conclusion	amaze
leose	pause	husband	visitor	television

Write the spelling word that matches the definition.
11. a person who visits
12. a tool that cuts
13. the end
14. a male spouse
15. to surprise or astonish
16. to stop briefly
17. routine
18. a hopeful disposition
19. to bother by making jokes or gestures
20. a set that receives images and sounds

Review — Unit 15: Suffixes -ed, -ing

directed	complaining	differed	admitting	directing
resulted	profiting	remained	remaining	permitted

Write the spelling word that is the opposite of the word or words given.
1. praising
2. refused to allow
3. agreed
4. losing money
5. departed
6. denying
7. took orders
8. departing
9. following orders
10. had no effect

Review — Unit 16: Silent Consonants

aisle	column	knowledge	handkerchief	knob
palm	numb	kneel	solemn	autumn

Write the spelling word that completes each sentence.
11. The knight was forced to _____ before his captors.
12. After walking in the snow, my toes became _____.
13. He wore a tie and carried a matching _____.
14. The runner placed the baton firmly in the _____ of her teammate's hand.
15. It is a lovely day and quite warm for _____.
16. It was a sad and _____ ceremony.
17. We have seats in section A, _____ 13.
18. He writes a _____ for the daily newspaper.
19. I tried to open the cabinet door, but the _____ fell off.
20. Ask Sally who has a lot of _____ about that topic.

Review — Unit 17: Double Consonants

connect	occasion	possess	recess	announce
terrible	mirror	horrible	success	accident

Write a spelling word for each clue.
1. This is a good part of the school day.
2. This is an event that wasn't planned.
3. Look in this to see yourself.
4. When you join two things, you do this to them.
5. When an event goes very well, it is this.
6. This is a particular event or happening.
7.–8. These words might describe a wicked monster.
9. If you own a bicycle, you could say this about owning it.
10. If you tell something, you do this to it.

GAME — Spelling Study Strategy

Spelling TIC-TAC-TOE

Practicing spelling words can be fun if you make it into a game. Play this game with a partner.

1. Both you and your partner write spelling words on lists. Trade lists.
2. Draw a tic-tac-toe board on a piece of paper. Decide who will use **O** and who will use **X**.
3. Ask your partner to call the first word on your spelling list to you. Spell it out loud. If you spell it correctly, make an **X** or an **O** on the tic-tac-toe board. If you misspell the word, ask your partner to spell it out loud for you. You miss your turn.
4. Now you call a word from your partner's spelling list.
5. Keep playing until one of you makes a tic-tac-toe. Keep starting over until you have both practiced all your spelling words.

Spelling ᵃⁿᵈ Thinking

Spelling ᵃⁿᵈ Vocabulary

Spelling ᵃⁿᵈ Reading

Spelling ᵃⁿᵈ Writing

At the Start of the Year and at the End of the Year

Two survey tests (Form A and Form B) are included at the back of this Teacher Edition. (See pages T345–T346.) The words on these tests were chosen from the basic word lists in each *Spelling Connections* Student Edition. A dictation sentence for each word is also provided.

The words on these tests appear in the order in which they appear in the program, unit by unit. However, beginning and ending units were eliminated. Thus, in Grade 1, words were chosen from Units 9 through 33, and in Grades 2 through 8, words were chosen from Units 5 through 34.

Either Form A or Form B may be administered at the beginning of the year and the other form administered at the end of the year. A comparison of these scores will help measure students' annual spelling progress.

Weekly Pretest

The pretest is a valuable part of spelling instruction and helps students target spelling words they do not know.

To administer the pretest each week, use the **Pretest Sentences** in the Teacher Edition for each unit. Follow this procedure for each word:

1. Say the spelling word.
2. Read the context sentence aloud.
3. Say the word again.
4. Remind the students to write the word to the best of their ability.

For students who need to study fewer words, pretest only those words on the shorter, **Alternate Word List**. Words on this list and accompanying context sentences are marked with a pink star.

It is important that each student self-check his or her pretest. (You may wish to use the **Word List Transparency** provided for each unit in the *Spelling Connections Transparency Book* to display the word list and help the students check their pretests.) Page 256 in the Student Edition details the steps for taking and checking a pretest. You may wish to use this page as a basis for a mini-lesson to teach students correct procedures for taking and checking a pretest.

The Unit Test

Spelling Connections provides three testing options for the weekly unit test.

Option 1: One Spelling Word Per Sentence

Pink stars indicate words on the **Alternate Word List**. This option can be administered in the same way as the pretest.

Option 2: Multiple Spelling Words Per Sentence

If you choose this option, ask students to write the entire sentence. In this way, you can check students' knowledge of the spelling words within a larger context. You may wish to ask the students to underline the spelling words within the sentence.

Option 3: Standardized Test

A reproducible standardized test for each unit is provided in the *Teacher Resource Book*. This option tests students' ability to identify correct spellings within a standardized test format.

The Right Connections ⟩ The Right Results

Assessment and Review Units

Every sixth unit is an **Assessment and Review Unit**. These units provide unique opportunities to measure students' understanding of targeted spelling strategies.

The first page of each **Assessment and Review Unit** presents a list of **Assessment Words** that the students have not encountered in the previous five units. These words do, however, represent the various spelling strategies the students have studied. **Assessment Words** may be used in one of two ways:

- Students may complete the **Assessment** activity on the student page. This activity challenges students to match each **Assessment Word** to a relevant spelling strategy. For example, students might match **ink** and **tank** to the spelling strategy about final consonant clusters.

- The **Assessment Words** may be administered as a spelling test. (Context sentences are provided in the Teacher Edition.) This pretest will help you assess how well students apply targeted spelling strategies to spell new words.

Either use helps you assess students' understanding of the spelling strategies they have encountered in the previous five units. Students can then use the **Review** activities in the remainder of the unit as reteaching tools to relearn spelling strategies they have not yet mastered.

A posttest consisting of targeted words from the **Assessment and Review Unit** completes the assessment options in each **Assessment and Review Unit**.

SPELLING AND WRITING

Spelling and Thinking

Spelling and Vocabulary

Spelling and Reading

Spelling and Writing

Spelling and Handwriting

Any teacher who has attempted to correct an illegible spelling test knows that handwriting and spelling are related. A child with poor handwriting may very well know how to spell words correctly, but poor handwriting may not allow him or her to communicate that knowledge on a written test. In fact, improved legibility may boost spelling test scores by as much as twenty percent!

To help students improve their handwriting, each developmental *Spelling Connections* unit includes a **One-Minute Handwriting Hint** in the Teacher Edition. Each hint relates handwriting to word features in the spelling unit (e.g., the correct joining for the letter **r** might be featured in a unit targeting r-controlled vowels). Each **One-Minute Handwriting Hint** can be the basis of a mini-lesson to boost your students' legibility.

Personal Spelling Journals

A personal spelling journal provides valuable assistance in helping students become confident, independent spellers. Follow these steps to help your students take advantage of this powerful learning tool:

Make the Journal

First, ask students to dedicate a spiral notebook (or a portion of a notebook) to the spelling journal. Tell them to label two consecutive pages with the letter **A**, the next two pages with **B**, and so on until they have pages for each letter of the alphabet. (They may wish to devote only a single page to letters that do not commonly begin words, such as **X**.) Tell students that they will use these pages to write words they want to learn how to spell that begin with each letter.

Find the Words

Words should be added to the journal from three basic sources: unit tests, student writing, and student reading.

- After each unit test, ask the students to write the words they missed on the test in their spelling journals.

- Explain to students that you will mark misspelled words with a green pen when you review their writing. Words marked in green should be written (spelled correctly, of course) in the spelling journal. Students should also add words that others, such as peer editors, have identified as misspelled in their writing.

- Encourage students to write words they encounter in their reading (and may wish to use in their writing) in their spelling journals.

Check the Spelling

Remind students to make sure that all words entered in the spelling journal are spelled correctly. A periodic review of each student's spelling journal can correct any errors and also offer insight into the kinds of words students add on their own.

The Right Connections > **The Right Results**

The Writing Process

Spelling Connections recognizes that spelling is for writing. But although spelling may be for writing, spelling is not the first aspect of writing students should address as they work through the writing process to create a written work.

To help students understand the writing process, as well as the place of correct spelling within that process, *Spelling Connections* provides an overview of the writing process on page 258 in the Student Edition.

This overview is accompanied by a range of writing prompts within four different writing modalities: narrative, persuasive, expository, and descriptive. These writing prompts will fit nicely within your classroom's broader writing curriculum.

In addition to the information in the **Writer's Handbook,** each *Spelling Connections* developmental unit concludes with a proofreading activity and a related writing prompt in one of the four modalities. These activities, as well as the restatement of the steps of the writing process within each unit, allow students to implement the writing process on a regular basis.

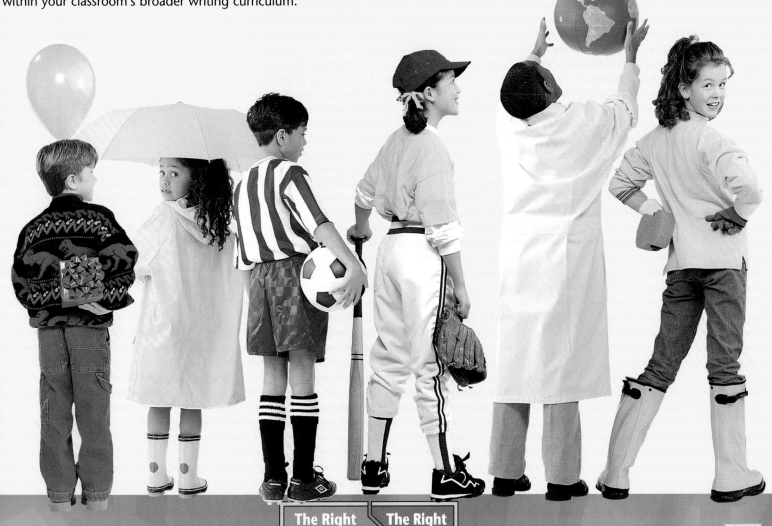

The Right Connections > The Right Results

RESEARCH

A Conversation With J. Richard Gentry, Ph.D.

About the Author:
J. Richard Gentry,
Ph.D.

In addition to writing the popular books **Spel...Is a Four-Letter Word, Teaching Kids to Spell, My Kid Can't Spell!,** and **The Literacy Map,** Dr. Gentry continues to conduct workshops that have helped thousands of school districts throughout the United States adopt better practices for spelling instruction. A popular speaker at educational conferences nationwide, Dr. Gentry has spent much of his entire, successful career finding better ways to teach spelling.

I myself am a struggling speller. I have a personal record of 252 scores of 100 on the Friday spelling test, but I've always struggled with spelling in my own writing. I know what it's like for a child who scores 100 on the Friday test, but the following week misspells those very same words in his own writing. Spelling is complex. There are many better ways to learn spelling than memorizing a list of words.

Dr. Gentry began his career as a classroom teacher. Later, he earned his Ph.D. in Reading Education from the University of Virginia and served as professor of elementary education and reading at Western Carolina University, where he directed the reading center. As a result of his spelling research and educational experience, he has become a well-known authority on how spelling ability develops and how it contributes to a child's writing and overall literacy development.

Spelling Connections provides the curriculum and resources you need to deliver effective, explicit, research-based instruction in spelling. Over 25 years of spelling research and research synthesis have contributed to the success and effectiveness of *Spelling Connections.* No other program offers the extensive research perspective outlined below. *Spelling Connections* is not about trends, fads, or gimmicks: It is solidly grounded in research.

How does this research-based program differ from other methods of teaching spelling?

Spelling Connections is based on a comprehensive, consolidated synthesis of research underscoring the fact that learning to spell is complex. Any contention that spelling ability is gained easily, either by memorizing, learning rules, recycling "high use" writing words, focusing on writing and teaching spelling in use, or "catching" spelling from reading, is **NOT** supported by research. The research base for *Spelling Connections* covers a spectrum of spelling issues and practices and reflects the complexity of spelling as well as the important connection of spelling to reading and writing.

Is it necessary to teach spelling explicitly or is there a more effective way for children to learn word-specific knowledge?

There are two competing theories regarding instructional approaches for spelling acquisition (Allal, 1997). The first calls for specific instruction in spelling, and *Spelling Connections* fits into this category. The other stance calls for integrating spelling in writing and reading instruction. There is little or no empirical research base for the latter theory (Allal, 1997). While the aim of that approach—to teach spelling within the context of communication—might seem

desirable, **research has not come forth to support abandoning explicit instruction** and simply integrating spelling into the teaching of reading and writing. The assumption that extensive reading and writing, perhaps with some strategic intervention, will lead students to function well with this skill has a long-standing history of NOT being supported by research. In an important synthesis of research in spelling entitled "Learning to Spell in the Classroom," Allal reports, "Approaches integrating spelling acquisition in text production do not yet constitute a well-recognized option validated by long-term empirical research in the classroom" (1997, p. 145). It makes sense to pay attention to research! Before Smith inaccurately theorized that children learn to spell by reading (1998), spelling researcher Margaret Peters published findings from spelling research and admonished, "A great many children do not manage to 'catch' spelling as they read" (1985, p. 25).

That being said, complex issues are rarely black and white. We have learned much from attempts to teach spelling within the authentic context of communication, and there are, indeed, functional, social, and contextual advantages to **CONNECTING** spelling to writing and reading. These advantages include increasing reading vocabulary and fluency, as well as developing proofreading skills and better spelling habits in writing. We would not have you teach spelling in isolation. Rather, we have made powerful connections to reading and writing in every unit.

I tried word lists before. Why weren't they effective?

Spelling researcher Allal writes, "Study of word lists is very widespread in elementary schools, but many teachers do not apply the principles that assure instructional effectiveness" (1997, p. 136). Practices that lead to problems include no individualization, badly designed exercises, developmentally inappropriate words, words that aren't relevant to writing, too many worksheets, and testing words with no teaching at all. Even though we anchor our program with word lists, we have worked hard to make sure you avoid the pitfalls of bad practice. For example, *Spelling Connections* provides options for differentiating instruction and the word list. Our word list is thoroughly researched, and all words were carefully selected with the developmental appropriateness of the type and timing of instruction in mind. We provide research-based study strategies and activities, and we have carefully designed exercises relevant to the learner and connections to writing and reading. This ensures that the skills learned will be reinvested in reading and writing situations.

How were words chosen for each *Spelling Connections* word list?

The spelling words and the way they are organized for study are vital to a good spelling program. Common sense tells us a spelling program must teach the words that students use in their writing (E. Horn, 1960; Hollingsworth, 1965; T.D. Horn, 1969; Graves, 1981; Smith and Ingersoll, 1984). A good spelling program will identify these words by using both studies of children's writings (Rinsland, 1945; Smith and Ingersoll, 1984) and studies that note how often particular words appear in print (Thorndike and Lorge, 1944; Kucera and Francis, 1967; Carroll et al., 1971; Fry et al., 1985). Other considerations should include the word's degree of difficulty, universality, permanence, and application to other areas of the curriculum.

We conducted the most thorough word analysis ever accomplished to develop the word lists in *Spelling Connections*. In all, 22 published word lists and vocabulary studies were analyzed.

The result was a list of more than 7,800 words in five important categories: Basic Words, Content Words, Strategy Words, Challenge Words, and Assessment Words. Following is a detailed summary of the word study done for *Spelling Connections*.

Writing Level
The words that students learn to spell should be the same words that they use in their writing. We consulted all the important recent analyses of students' written vocabulary, including Smith and Ingersoll's landmark 1984 study. In addition, we compared modern lists with classic lists such as Rinsland's to determine the enduring importance, permanency, and frequency of each word in students' writing.

Reading Level
Spelling Connections helps students build their writing vocabularies with words they know from their reading. To find out when students might encounter a word in their reading, we consulted lists of words found in children's and adults' reading material. These lists helped determine whether to include a word on the list, and if so, in which grade to place it.

Spelling Proficiency Level
Spelling proficiency is a measure of how difficult it is to spell a word and is based on how many students can spell the word correctly at a particular grade level. Spelling proficiency is an important clue to the grade level at which a word would best be taught. Rather than rely on obsolete data, we developed our own proficiency list based on the most current word usage.

Other Criteria
Additional data helped determine how and when words should be presented for study. Gates' list of "Spelling Difficulties in 3876 Words" identified the common misspellings of many words. Several lists helped determine spelling "demons" and the most frequently misspelled words in each elementary grade. The BORN (Barbe-O'Rourke-Nault) word list was used to determine which words are no longer in common use.

How can I be sure words are presented at the appropriate grade level?

Research provides clear evidence that spelling should be taught systematically (T.D. Horn, 1969). The right words must be presented at the right time. Because spelling growth is a developmental process, the organization of words and their placement makes a difference in how easily students learn to spell them. The *Spelling Connections* word list is organized according to principles set forth by linguistic, cognitive, and developmental theory.

- Early in a spelling curriculum (Grades K–2) emphasis should be placed on the alphabetic principle, i.e., how letters correspond to sounds.
- At the third and fourth grade levels, emphasis should be placed on structural patterns, visual patterns, and relationships of letters within words (Henderson and Templeton, 1986; Read, 1986). Sound-by-sound spellings become secondary to visual coding.
- Fifth and sixth grade children spell new words by comparing them to known words. At this stage, instruction must focus on word derivations, vocabulary study, and spellings related by meaning.
- Mature spellers should focus on how spelling is related to meaning and word derivation (Henderson and Templeton, 1986), as well as known words (Marsh et al., 1980).

Is it important to organize words by spelling patterns?

Presenting words by patterns or relationships helps students learn and retain the words (Read and Hodges, 1982). The patterns should cause students to focus on word similarities rather than differences. When students see patterns or relationships, they find it easier to learn new information (Bloom, 1956). When words are grouped to show common structural characteristics or letter patterns, students can see relationships.

In addition, word lists should be organized to help students perceive the elements of meaning as well as the words' visual elements. For example, **sign, signal,** and **signature**

share both meaning and visual similarities. Word lists that take into account both similarities aid analogical reasoning, which enables students to learn new words by perceiving their similarities to known words. This strategy is especially important to the mature speller (Marsh et al., 1980). By organizing word lists according to a visual principle, *Spelling Connections* aids analogical reasoning, spelling retention, and the visualization of correct spellings.

Which works best—memorization of lists or analysis of spelling patterns by word sorting and other exercises—or should you teach spelling rules?

Spelling Connections includes all of the above with correct balance. In a comprehensive review of spelling research, Graham (1983) validated the use of word lists to anchor the spelling program in a structured approach "planned, modified, and monitored on the basis of assessment information" (Graham, 1983, p. 563, reported in Allal, 1997, p. 135). Graham outlined five research-based principles in his synthesis:

1. Do use word lists but not arbitrary lists. Construct lists to reflect words and patterns likely to be used by writers at developmentally appropriate grade levels and to teach a few key rules.
2. Pretest and have students self-correct.
3. Teach students to use a research-based word study technique. Our look-say-see-write-check technique is directly based on a method Horn validated (Horn, 1954).
4. Use the "test-study-test" cycle.
5. Use spelling games and other alternative activities to increase motivation and to take advantage of the social context of learning.

Each of these research-based strategies has been built into *Spelling Connections*. In addition, we bring to you our knowledge and balance of research to highlight other important aspects of methodology. For example, we considered the merits of text dictation as a pedagogical tool. Even though we didn't find empirical studies to validate its use (Allal, 1997), we recognized the merits of dictation (i.e., spelling words are not always isolated) and included two dictation options.

Is learning to spell a developmental process? What does the research say about that?

Spelling is not just a matter of acquiring habits. Spelling develops (Read, 1986). A large body of research on developmental spelling has provided a better understanding of the spelling process and how it is acquired (Read, 1975; Gentry, 1977; Henderson and Beers, 1980; Read, 1986).

Instruction in *Spelling Connections* reflects the most recent understandings of children's developing cognitive and linguistic strategies for spelling.

The program acknowledges that "creative" or "developmental" spelling is the result of a valid thinking process and enhances early spelling development. It also enables students to apply what they have learned about spelling in their writing. The long-standing but antiquated view that spelling is memorization is replaced with the view that spelling is a complex cognitive process.

Learning to spell is systematic and orderly. It progresses in stages, much like learning to speak does. Several developmental stages have been identified at the early levels of spelling (Gentry, 1977, 1982; Beers, 1974; Henderson and Beers, 1980; Read, 1986).

Early on, children create "words" by stringing together random letters (Gentry, 1977). Next, they recognize that letters represent sounds. They segment language by producing phonetic spelling, i.e., spelling sound by sound (Beers, 1974; Read, 1975; Gentry, 1982). When spelling is influenced by reading and formal spelling instruction, simple and concrete spelling strategies give way to complex abstract representation.

At least four stages of developmental spelling are illustrated in Gentry's discussion of a child who progresses from **precommunicative** (Stage 1) spelling (in which invented spellings lack letter-sound correspondence), to **semiphonetic** spellings (Stage 2) which partially map letters to sounds, to **phonetic** spellings (Stage 3) which completely map the letters to the sounds of words, to **transitional** spellings (Stage 4) which show conventions of English spelling and the influence of a visual-coding strategy (Gentry, 1987).

The new *Spelling Connections for Kindergarten* incorporates the latest research on developmental aspects of learning to spell and its relationship to the development of emerging readers and writers. *Spelling Connections for Kindergarten* gives credence to the research that validates the use of developmental spelling (Gentry, 1997; Snow, Burns, & Griffin, 1998; International Reading Association, 1998). Not only do we explicate the research base for developmental spelling (which is now considered best practice), we show teachers how to lead young students to move from lower to higher stages even as they learn correct spellings. This is groundbreaking work for a basal spelling program using the cutting edge sociocognitive framework for writing instruction inspired by the research of Vygotsky (1978) and clearly articulated in new research showing how instruction leads development (Brodrova and Leong, 1998; Gentry, in press). We are proud to be the leader in bringing this methodology into classrooms. Our primary program will be a force in leading children to knowledge of sounds and letters, phonemic awareness, and phonics, and it will promote children's learning and fluency in both reading and writing.

In addition, all levels of *Spelling Connections* give credence to other research-based principles set forth by linguistic, cognitive, and developmental theory, paying meticulous attention, for example, to the types of word sorts that are most likely to be developmentally appropriate at a particular grade level (Henderson, 1985; Templeton, 1981; Marsh, 1980; Zutell, 1998; Morris and Brown, in press; Gentry, in press).

The Right Connections > The Right Results

Does *Spelling Connections* include word sorting?

Word sorting is one of the key research-based strategies in our program. Research shows that when the speller takes into account the position, environment, and stress of the phoneme-grapheme in a word, the spelling is often predictable by rule (Hanna, Hanna, Hodges, & Rudorf, 1966). Sorting helps the speller recognize the probability that a certain spelling pattern is the best choice.

Studies focusing on spelling patterns have definitely guided the construction of this spelling program. We recognize that spelling knowledge is much more than memorization. Rather, it is a manifestation of all knowledge of how the English spelling system works, progressively acquired through a multiplicity of reading and writing activities including word sorting (Templeton, 1991; Zutell, 1998).

Word sorting activities in *Spelling Connections* go beyond rote memorization and allow students to acquire concepts about how the system of English works, such as recognizing the consonant-vowel-consonant-**silent e** pattern. Research firmly backs the instructional power of word sorting because sorts are multi-modal (visual, auditory, kinesthetic, tactile), manipulative, collaborative, and accessible for modeling and demonstration (Zutell, 1998). The new *Spelling Connections Word Sort CD-ROM* allows students to take full advantage of the word sorts incorporated into *Spelling Connections*.

Why do some students make 100% on the test but later misspell the same words in their writing?

Spelling Connections doesn't just assess for memorization in Assessment and Review Units (Grades 2–8), it tests comparable words that fit the patterns or concepts being reviewed. By asking students to spell words not previously studied, we are able to assess deeper spelling knowledge and provide the help each learner needs.

Word Studies Consulted in Compiling the *Spelling Connections* Word List

The American Heritage Word Frequency Book, Carroll et al. (1971)

"*The Barbe, O'Rourke, Nault (BORN) Word List,*" Barbe et al. (1987)

"A Basic Core for Writing," Fitzgerald (1951)

Basic Elementary Reading Vocabularies, Harris and Jacobson (1972)

A Basic Vocabulary of Elementary School Children, Rinsland (1945)

The Basic Writing Vocabulary, Horn (1927)

Canadian Word Lists and Instructional Techniques, Thomas (1974)

Computational Analysis of Present-Day American English, Kucera and Francis (1967)

"High-Frequency Word List for Grades 3 through 9," Walker (1979)

Instant Words, Fry et al. (1985)

The Living Word Vocabulary, Dale and O'Rourke (1981)

"Nault Content Words" (Grades 1–8), Nault (1988)

The New Iowa Spelling Scale, Green (1954)

"100 Words Most Often Misspelled by Children in the Elementary Grades," Johnson (1950)

Phoneme-Grapheme Correspondence as Cues to Spelling Improvement, Hanna et al. (1966)

Spelling Difficulties in 3876 Words, Gates (1937)

The Teacher's Word Book of 30,000 Words, Thorndike and Lorge (1944)

3000 Instant Words, 2nd ed., Sakiey and Fry (1984)

"220 Basic Sight Words," Dolch (1939)

"2000 Commonest Words for Spelling," Dolch (1942)

Written Vocabulary of Elementary School Children, Hillerich (1978)

Written Vocabulary of Elementary School Pupils, Ages 6–14, Smith and Ingersoll (1984)

Selected Bibliography
Complete bibliography can be found at www.zaner-bloser.com.

Allal, L. (1997). Learning to spell in the classroom, in C.A. Perfetti, L. Rieben, & M. Fayol (Eds.), *Learning to Spell* (pp. 237–269). London: Lawrence Erlbaum Associates.

Gentry, J.R. (1977). *A study of the orthographic strategies of beginning readers.* Unpublished doctoral dissertation, University of Virginia, Charlottesville.

Gentry, J.R. (1982). An analysis of developmental spelling in GNYS at WRK. *The Reading Teacher,* 36, 192–200.

Gentry, J.R. (1997). *My Kid Can't Spell.* Portsmouth, NH: Heinemann.

Gentry, J.R. (2000a). A retrospective on invented spelling and a look forward. *The Reading Teacher,* 54(3), 318–332.

Gentry, J.R. (2000b). *The Literacy Map: Guiding Children to Where They Need to Be (K–3).* New York: Mondo.

Gentry, J.R. (2002). *The Literacy Map: Guiding Children to Where They Need to Be (4–6).* New York: Mondo.

Graham, S. (1983). Effective spelling instruction. *The Elementary School Journal,* 83, 560–567.

International Reading Association, (1998). Learning to read and write: Developmentally appropriate practices for young children. *The Reading Teacher,* 52, 193–214.

Paulesu, E., J.F. Demonet, F. Fazio, E. McCrory, V. Chanoine, N. Brunswick, S.F. Cappa, G. Cossu, M. Habib, C.D. Frith & U. Frith. (2001). Dyslexia: Cultural diversity and biological unity. *Science,* Vol. 291, No. 5511, March 16, 2001.

Peters, M.L. (1985). *Spelling: Caught or Taught?* London: Routledge & Kegan Paul.

Snow, C., M.W. Burns, and P. Griffin. (1998). *Preventing Reading Difficulties in Young Children.* Washington, DC: National Academy Press.

Vygotsky, L.S. (1978). *Mind and Society: The Development of Higher Mental Processes.* Cambridge, MA: Harvard University Press. (Original work published in 1930, 1933, 1935.)

Spelling and Thinking

Spelling and Vocabulary

Spelling and Reading

Spelling and Writing

Games and Word Sorts

Practicing spelling words, in a focused manner, can make students more fluent spellers. But in order to remain effective, practice must be lively and engaging. A variety of practice options can help students maintain a fresh attitude toward practicing their spelling words.

Pages from the *Spelling Connections Word Sort CD-ROM,* included with this Teacher Edition, may be printed and duplicated to allow you and your students to physically manipulate words that are being sorted.

Each **Assessment and Review Unit** in *Spelling Connections* includes the directions for an alternative practice option. This option is either a partner activity, which often has a game like format, or a suggestion for sorting spelling words in a way that students have not encountered previously. Students can use these games to practice any spelling list, and the word sorts provide alternate ways of thinking about and grouping words.

Flip Folder

Making the Flip Folder

The **Flip Folder** can provide another way for students to practice their spelling words. Ready-made **Flip Folders** are available from Zaner-Bloser. To make your own **Flip Folder,** simply use a standard (8½" x 11") manila file folder. Follow these steps:

- Place the file folder on a table in front of you. Turn the folder so that the edge of the folder with the tab is facing you.
- Draw two vertical lines to divide the top of the folder into three equal sections. Cut along these lines to the fold. You should have three equal flaps that remain joined to the back of the folder at the fold.
- Write "Look–Say–Cover–See" on the first flap, "Write–Check" on the middle flap, and "Rewrite" on the third flap. The folder is ready for spelling practice.

Using the Flip Folder

Duplicate the **Flip Folder Practice Master** in the back of the *Teacher Resource Book.* Each student who is using a **Flip Folder** will need a fresh copy of the **Flip Folder Practice Master** each week. Students should copy the words they wish to study in the first column of the practice sheet.

Students follow these steps to practice each word with the **Flip Folder:**

1. **Look** at the word.
   Say the word out loud.
   Cover the word.
   See (in your mind) how the word is spelled.
2. **Write** the word in the second column.
   Check your spelling by comparing what you have written with the correct spelling in the first column.
3. **Rewrite** the word in the third column.

The Right Connections ▷ **The Right Results**

ZB
SPELLING CONNECTIONS

J. Richard Gentry, Ph.D.

6

Series Author

J. Richard Gentry, Ph.D.

Editorial Development: Cottage Communications

Art and Production: PC&F

Photography: George C. Anderson: cover, pages 1, 4, 6, 7, 254, 255, 256, 257; The Stock Market: p. 270 © 93 Kunio Owaki, p. 273 © 93 David Chalk, p. 286 © 97 Don Mason, p. 295 © 97 Arthur Beck, p. 297 © Roy Morsch, p. 312 © 98 Ronnie Kaufman, p. 313 © 94 Mug Shots; Tony Stone Images: p. 269 © Julian Calder, p. 271 © David Maisel, p. 272 © David Harry Stewart, p. 275 © John Millar, p. 279 © Brian Stablyk, p. 282 © Bruce Forster, p. 283 © Tom Bean, p. 285 © Laurence Dutton, p. 289 © Mark Wagner, p. 294 © Manoj Shah, p. 296 © Alejandro Balaguer, p. 309 © Vince Streano, p. 311 © Jon Gray; Corbis Bettmann ©: p. 277, p. 278, p. 284 © Kelly-Mooney Photography, p. 287 Dimitri Iundt, TempSport, p. 290 Schenectady Museum, Hall of Electrical, p. 291 Kevin Fleming, p. 293 James Marshall, p. 300 Historical Picture Archive, p. 301 Kevin R. Morris, p. 305 Mike Zens, p. 306 Gianni Dagli Orti, p. 307 Richard Hamilton Smith, p. 308; Artville ©: p. 276, p. 292, p. 310

Illustrations: Laurel Aiello: pages 106, 227, 248; Dave Blanchette: pages 15, 82, 130; Len Ebert: pages 10, 23, 33, 39, 40, 41, 42, 57, 75, 76, 78, 87, 95, 111, 112, 114, 148, 149, 150, 182, 183, 184, 219, 220, 221, 222; Tom Elliot: pages 73, 77, 103, 127, 147, 181; Ruth Flanigan: pages 11, 17, 29, 35, 47, 53, 59, 65, 71, 83, 89, 101, 107, 119, 125, 131, 137, 143, 197; Rusty Fletcher: pages 173, 209; Collin Fry: pages 155, 161; Bill Ogden: pages 16, 28, 34, 45, 52, 64, 88, 94, 100, 129, 142, 154, 160, 189, 190, 196; Remy Simard: pages 167, 171, 191, 203, 215; George Ulrich: pages 172, 179, 208

The following references were used in the development of the **Word Study** activities included on the **Vocabulary Connections** pages in each developmental spelling unit:

Ayto, John. *Arcade Dictionary of Word Origins: The Histories of More Than 8,000 English-Language Words*. New York: Arcade Publishing, Little, Brown, and Company, 1990.

Barnhart, Robert K., ed. *The Barnhart Dictionary of Etymology: The Core Vocabulary of Standard English*. New York: The H.W. Wilson Company, 1988.

Makkai, Adam, ed. *A Dictionary of American Idioms*. New York: Barron's Educational Series, Inc., 1987.

Rheingold, Howard. *They Have a Word for It: A Lighthearted Lexicon of Untranslatable Words and Phrases*. Los Angeles: Jeremy P. Tarcher, Inc., 1988.

Terban, Marvin. *Time to Rhyme: A Rhyming Dictionary*. Honesdale, PA: Wordsong, Boyds Mills Press, 1994.

ISBN: 0-7367-2071-5

Zaner-Bloser, Inc., P.O. Box 16764, Columbus, Ohio 43216-6764 (1-800-421-3018)
www.zaner-bloser.com
Printed in the United States of America

Contents

3

4

5

Spelling Study Strategy

Look ➡ Say ➡ Cover ➡ See ➡ Write ➡ Check

1 **Look** at the word.

2 **Say** the letters in the word. Think about how each sound is spelled.

3 **Cover** the word with your hand or close your eyes.

4 **See** the word in your mind. Spell the word to yourself.

5 **Write** the word.

6 **Check** your spelling against the spelling in the book.

7

Basic Spelling List

pattern	obtain
album	admit
labor	trait
vacation	accent
exactly	complain
chapter	advance
survey	natural
detain	daydream
rapid	favorite
cancel	behave

Strategy Words

Review
brand	grayer
claim	locate
disobey	

Preview
anagram	entertain
caption	mistake
display	

Content Words

Fine Arts: Sculpture
chisel	woodcut
sculptor	marble
engraving	

Science: Astronomy
crater	terrain
module	meteorite
lunar	

Individual Needs

Challenge Words
adequate	ancestor
elastic	exclaim
container	complaint

Alternate Word List ★
pattern	complain
vacation	natural
exactly	daydream
rapid	favorite
admit	behave

★ For students who need to study fewer Basic Spelling words

T8A

MATERIALS

Student Edition
Pages 8–13
Challenge Activities, p. 224

Teacher Edition
Pages T8A–T13
Challenge Activities, p. T224

Teacher Resource Book
Unit 1 Homework Master
Unit 1 Practice Masters
Flip Folder Practice Master
Unit 1 Test Master

Home Spelling Practice Book
Unit 1 Home Spelling Practice
(English or Spanish)

Other *Spelling Connections* Resources
- Audiotape, Grade 6
- Practice Book for Grammar, Usage, and Mechanics, Grade 6
- Spelling Support for Second Language Learners, Grade 6
- Support Software on CD-ROM
- Transparency Book, Grade 6
- Word Sort CD-ROM, Grade 6

OBJECTIVES

Spelling and Thinking
Students will
- **read** the spelling words in list form and in context.
- **sort** the spelling words according to the **short a** sound and the **long a** sound spelled **a, ai, ay, a-consonant-e,** and **ey.**
- **read** and remember this week's spelling strategy.

Spelling and Vocabulary
Students will
- **replace** words in a sentence with spelling words that have the same or nearly the same meaning.
- **substitute** word parts to create spelling words.
- **use** dictionary guide words to locate spelling words.

Spelling and Reading
Students will
- **complete** sentences using spelling words.
- **solve** analogies using spelling words.
- **complete** a paragraph with spelling words.

Spelling and Writing
Students will
- **proofread** a journal entry.
- **use** the writing process to write a journal entry.
- **proofread** their writing.

MEETING INDIVIDUAL NEEDS
Learning Styles

 Visual

Form teams of eight to ten players each. Pronounce a spelling word. The first player on each team writes the word on a sheet of paper and then passes the paper to the next player. That player checks the word, rewrites it if necessary, and then writes the next word pronounced. The paper is passed on until each player has had a turn. The team with the most nearly perfect paper wins.

 Auditory

To play "Spello," give each student some paper squares and a grid six squares across and three squares down. The students randomly write a spelling word in each square. As you say each spelling word, the students spell the word aloud in unison and cover the word on their grids. The student who first covers a row of words and calls out "Spello!" is the winner.

 Kinesthetic

Divide a piece of oaktag into twenty sections. Write a spelling word in each section. Make twenty vowel-pattern cards: ten cards with **a** in a closed syllable (as in **admit**), four cards with **ai**, one with **ey**, one with **ay**, three with **a** in an open syllable (as in **labor**), and one with **a-consonant-e**. Give three students a set of different colored paper squares. Shuffle the vowel-pattern cards. One player draws a card, finds a word on the oaktag board with the spelling for the /ă/ or /ā/, says the word, and then spells it. If correct, the player covers the word with a paper square. After all the words are covered, count the colored squares to tally the score.

Hands-On Practice
All students will benefit from practicing with a **Flip Folder**. See page Z18.

Language and Cultural Differences

Some students may have difficulty hearing the **short a** and **long a** sounds because of regional pronunciation differences or language backgrounds that do not include the sound. In Spanish, for example, the **long a** sound is spelled **e**, and there are no short vowel sounds. To help the students recognize the different vowel sounds, have them print each spelling of the /ă/ and /ā/ on an index card. As you pronounce each word, have the students hold up the card(s) representing that spelling of the **short a** or **long a** sound. Point out that a word may contain more than one /ă/ or /ā/. Then, have the students write the spelling words and underline the **short a** and **long a** sounds.

MANAGING INSTRUCTION

3–5 Day Plan		Average	Below Average	Above Average
Day 1	**Day 1**	Pretest Spelling Mini-Lesson, p. T8 Spelling and Thinking, p. 8	Pretest Spelling Mini-Lesson, p. T8 Spelling and Thinking, p. 8	Pretest Spelling and Thinking, p. 8
	Day 2	Spelling and Vocabulary, p. 9	Spelling and Vocabulary, p. 9 (or) Unit 1 Practice Master, A and B	Spelling and Vocabulary, p. 9 Spelling and Reading, p. 10
Day 2	**Day 3**	Spelling and Reading, p. 10	Spelling and Reading, p. 10 (or) Unit 1 Practice Master, C and D	Challenge Activities, p. 224
	Day 4	Spelling and Writing, p. 11 Unit 1 Homework Master	Spelling and Writing, p. 11	Spelling and Writing, p. 11 Unit 1 Homework Master
Day 3	**Day 5**	Weekly Test	Weekly Test	Weekly Test
Vocabulary Connections (pages 12 and 13) may be used anytime during this unit.				

Objectives

Spelling and Thinking

Students will

• **read** the spelling words in list form and in context.
• **sort** the spelling words according to the **short a** sound and the **long a** sound spelled **a, ai, ay, a-consonant-e,** and **ey.**
• **read** and remember this week's spelling strategy.

UNIT PRETEST

Use **Pretest Sentences** below. Refer to the self-checking procedures on student page 256. You may wish to use the **Unit 1 Word List Overhead Transparency** as part of the checking procedure.

TEACHING THE STRATEGY

Spelling Mini-Lesson

Write **rapid, labor, behave, daydream, trait,** and **survey** on the board. Ask a volunteer to read each word aloud.

Ask students what they notice about the **a** vowel sound. (Short a is heard in rapid; long a is in the other words.) Ask volunteers to circle letters that spell /ă/ and /ā/ in these words. (/ă/: a [rapid]; /ā/: a [labor], ai [trait], ay [daydream], ey [survey], a-consonant-e [behave])

Review the difference between an open syllable and a closed syllable. (An open syllable ends with a vowel sound; a closed syllable ends with a consonant sound.) Ask students for examples of words with an open syllable and a closed syllable. Point out that **a** spells the **long a** sound in an open syllable in words like **vacation.**

Explain that while two vowel letters may combine to make the **long a** sound, there is only one spelling pattern for the **short a** sound: **a** in a closed syllable, as in **admit.**

Invite volunteers to write each remaining spelling word under a word with the matching sound and spelling pattern, e.g., all **short a** words would go under **rapid.**

Ask a volunteer to read **Remember the Spelling Strategy** on page 8.

Order of answers may vary.
short a
1. p**a**ttern ★
2. **a**lbum
3. ex**a**ctly ★
4. ch**a**pter
5. r**a**pid ★
6. c**a**ncel
7. **a**dmit ★
8. **a**ccent
9. **a**dvance
10. n**a**tural ★
long a spelled a, ai, ay
11. l**a**bor
12. v**a**cation ★
13. det**ai**n
14. obt**ai**n
15. tr**ai**t
16. compl**ai**n ★
17. d**ay**dream ★
18. f**a**vorite ★
long a spelled a-consonant-e, ey
19. beh**a**ve ★
20. surv**ey**

8

Spelling and **Thinking**

READ THE SPELLING WORDS

1. pattern	*pattern*	The leaves formed a colorful **pattern**.
2. album	*album*	He arranged his pictures in an **album**.
3. labor	*labor*	Scrubbing the floor was difficult **labor**.
4. vacation	*vacation*	We delayed our summer **vacation**.
5. exactly	*exactly*	The book cost **exactly** five dollars.
6. chapter	*chapter*	I have read the first **chapter**.
7. survey	*survey*	The engineer will **survey** the land.
8. detain	*detain*	I must not **detain** you any longer.
9. rapid	*rapid*	The rain caused a **rapid** river current.
10. cancel	*cancel*	They might **cancel** the soccer game.
11. obtain	*obtain*	You must **obtain** a permit to park here.
12. admit	*admit*	This ticket will **admit** one person.
13. trait	*trait*	His sense of humor is his best **trait**.
14. accent	*accent*	She speaks with a British **accent**.
15. complain	*complain*	They often **complain** about the service.
16. advance	*advance*	The team will **advance** to the next level.
17. natural	*natural*	He has **natural** artistic ability.
18. daydream	*daydream*	You must try not to **daydream** in class.
19. favorite	*favorite*	They played my **favorite** song.
20. behave	*behave*	I am trying to teach my dog to **behave**.

SORT THE SPELLING WORDS

1.–10. Write the words with the **short a** sound.
11.–18. Write the words that spell **long a** as **a, ai,** or **ay.**
19.–20. Write the words that spell **long a** as **a-consonant-e** or **ey.**
Circle the letters that spell the **short a** sound or **long a** sound.

REMEMBER THE SPELLING STRATEGY

Remember that the **short a** sound in **rapid** is spelled **a.** The **long a** sound is spelled **a** in **labor, ai** in **trait, ay** in **daydream, a-consonant-e** in **behave,** and **ey** in **survey.**

Pretest Sentences (See procedures on pages Z10–Z11.)

★ 1. Anaka is choosing a **pattern** for a dress she will make.
2. My mother keeps pictures of our family in a photo **album**.
3. The difficult task required thoughtful planning and hard **labor**.
★ 4. This summer, we will spend part of our **vacation** at the beach.
★ 5. The identical twins look **exactly** alike.
6. The last **chapter** of the book was the most exciting.
7. The company took a **survey** to find out if people liked the product.
8. To **detain** means to hold back.
★ 9. Traveling by airplane is a **rapid** means of transportation.
10. Because it rained, we had to **cancel** our picnic.
11. How can I **obtain** a free pass for the museum?
★12. When Alonso makes a mistake, he will always **admit** it.
13. Sharon's eyes are her outstanding physical **trait**.
14. I enjoy hearing a person speak English with a Spanish **accent**.
★15. Bob always finds something to **complain** about.
16. The winners of the tennis match will **advance** to the semifinals.
★17. We must protect our **natural** resources.
★18. One of my favorite adventures happened in a **daydream**.
★19. Strawberries and cream is my **favorite** dessert.
★20. The boys were quiet in the library, since they knew how to **behave**.

Spelling and Vocabulary

Word Meanings

Write the spelling word that could best replace each underlined word or words.

1. The fabric has a floral design.
2. She speaks with a French style of speech.
3. I must not delay you with my questions.
4. I need to call off today's appointment.
5. This job requires hours of hard work.
6. You must get a permit to park here.
7. Never express feelings of unhappiness about life.

Word Analysis

Change the underlined part of each word to write a spelling word.

8. daylight
9. surprise
10. become
11. after
12. submit
13. advice

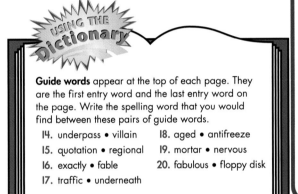

Guide words appear at the top of each page. They are the first entry word and the last entry word on the page. Write the spelling word that you would find between these pairs of guide words.

14. underpass • villain
15. quotation • regional
16. exactly • fable
17. traffic • underneath
18. aged • antifreeze
19. mortar • nervous
20. fabulous • floppy disk

Word Meanings
1. pattern
2. accent
3. detain
4. cancel
5. labor
6. obtain
7. complain

Word Analysis
8. daydream
9. survey
10. behave
11. chapter
12. admit
13. advance

Using the Dictionary
14. vacation
15. rapid
16. exactly
17. trait
18. album
19. natural
20. favorite

9

Developing Oral Language Skills

Remind students that proper pronunciation of words can be an important factor in correct spelling. In a word like **natural,** it is important to pronounce all three syllables when thinking about the spelling. A careless pronunciation will result in the loss of the vowel sound in the second syllable.

MEETING INDIVIDUAL NEEDS

Providing More Help

To aid students in identifying the **short a** and **long a** patterns, have them write a spelling word that matches the pattern in each row.

1. answer, atom, grand (rapid, pattern, accent, album, cancel, chapter, natural, admit, advance, exactly)
2. brain, chain, praise (trait, obtain, detain, complain)
3. radio, paper, flavor (labor, favorite, vacation)
4. chase, became, wave (behave)
5. way, holiday, spray (daydream)
6. hey, grey, they (survey)

★Students who need to study fewer words should use the **Alternate Word List.** This list is starred on page T8 in the Teacher Edition. The **Unit 1 Practice Masters** (*Teacher Resource Book*) provide additional practice with these words.

Unit 1 Practice Masters

Name ____

Practice Master Unit 1

| 1. rapid | 3. natural | 5. exactly | 7. vacation | 9. daydream |
| 2. pattern | 4. admit | 6. favorite | 8. behave | 10. complain |

A. Write the spelling words in alphabetical order.

1. _____
2. _____
3. _____
4. _____
5. _____
6. _____
7. _____
8. _____
9. _____
10. _____

B. Write the spelling word that belongs in each sentence.

1. Sixth graders always ____ politely.
2. Shelia was lost in a pleasant ____ of the past summer.
3. I have to ____ that it's great being back in school.
4. The ____ setting of tall pines and flowing streams was very peaceful.
5. The park is ____ three blocks from home.

Objectives

Spelling and Reading

Students will
- **complete** sentences using spelling words.
- **solve** analogies using spelling words.
- **complete** a paragraph with spelling words.

Complete the Sentences
1. cancel
2. pattern
3. daydream
4. obtain
5. detain
6. accent
7. complain
8. labor

Solve the Analogies
9. natural
10. chapter
11. survey
12. album
13. advance
14. vacation

Complete the Paragraph
15. trait
16. favorite
17. exactly
18. rapid
19. admit
20. behave

Spelling and Reading

pattern	album	labor	vacation	exactly
chapter	survey	detain	rapid	cancel
obtain	admit	trait	accent	complain
advance	natural	daydream	favorite	behave

Complete the Sentences Write the spelling word that completes each sentence.
1. Please _____ my magazine subscription.
2. His vegetables grow in a neat _____ of rows.
3. Sheila was lost in a long _____ about last summer.
4. Dan mixed the paints to _____ an unusual shade of red.
5. We should not _____ them any longer than we must.
6. You speak with a beautiful Spanish _____.
7. He tries to compliment people rather than _____ about them.
8. Jenny likes to do heavy physical _____.

Solve the Analogies Write a spelling word to complete each analogy.
9. **Easy** is to **difficult** as **artificial** is to _____.
10. An **act** is to a **play** as a _____ is to a **book**.
11. **Recall** is to **remember** as **examine** is to _____.
12. A **recipe** is to a **cookbook** as a **photo** is to an _____.
13. **Finish** is to **complete** as **progress** is to _____.
14. **Work** is to a **job** as **relax** is to a _____.

Complete the Paragraph Write the spelling words from the box to complete the paragraph.

Friendliness is the most desirable ___15.___ a dog can have. Of all the dogs along my mail route, Daisy is my ___16.___. Every day, she waits for me in ___17.___ the same spot. The ___18.___ wagging of her tail tells me how happy she is to see me. I must ___19.___ that Daisy may ___20.___ this way because of the treat I give her.

| behave |
| exactly |
| rapid |
| trait |
| favorite |
| admit |

10

MEETING INDIVIDUAL NEEDS

Providing More Challenge

Challenge Words and **Challenge Activities** for Unit 1 appear on page 224. **Challenge Word Test Sentences** appear on page T224.

Unit 1 Challenge Activities

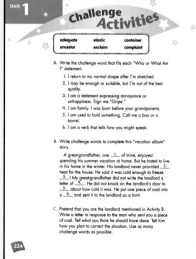

Weekly Test Options

Option 1:
One Spelling Word Per Sentence
(See procedures on pages Z10–Z11.)

1. Please teach me to speak French without an American **accent**.
★ 2. Do you **admit** that you hurt her feelings?
3. He is certain to **advance** in his chosen career.
4. I enjoy looking at the pictures in my family's photo **album**.
★ 5. We remembered to **behave** at the concert.
6. The argument led them to **cancel** their plans.
7. Have you read the last **chapter** of the book?
★ 8. He wanted to **complain,** but he had to accept the rules.
★ 9. I create a pleasant **daydream** whenever I'm unhappy.
10. Don't **detain** me, as I'm already late.
★11. The color in my new sweater matches my skirt **exactly**.
★12. Her **favorite** sport is baseball.
13. The reward for your **labor** is reaching your goal.

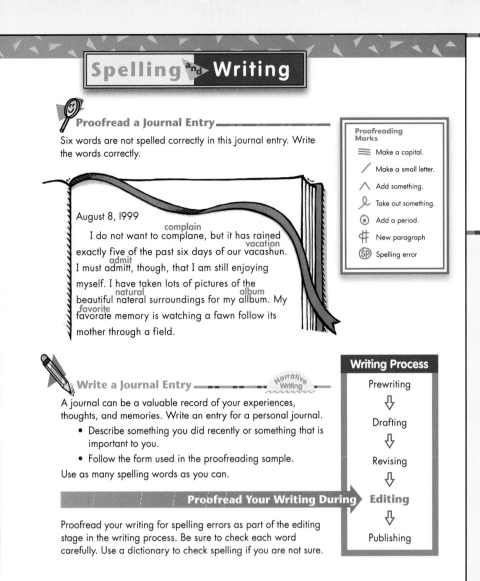

Spelling and Writing

Proofread a Journal Entry

Six words are not spelled correctly in this journal entry. Write the words correctly.

August 8, 1999

    complain
    I do not want to complane, but it has rained
                  vacation
exactly five of the past six days of our vacashun.
  admit
I must admitt, though, that I am still enjoying
myself. I have taken lots of pictures of the
    natural   album
beautiful nateral surroundings for my allbum. My
 favorite
favorate memory is watching a fawn follow its
mother through a field.

Proofreading Marks

≡ Make a capital.
/ Make a small letter.
∧ Add something.
ℰ Take out something.
⊙ Add a period.
⌗ New paragraph
⟨SP⟩ Spelling error

Write a Journal Entry

Narrative Writing

A journal can be a valuable record of your experiences, thoughts, and memories. Write an entry for a personal journal.

- Describe something you did recently or something that is important to you.
- Follow the form used in the proofreading sample.

Use as many spelling words as you can.

Proofread Your Writing During →

Proofread your writing for spelling errors as part of the editing stage in the writing process. Be sure to check each word carefully. Use a dictionary to check spelling if you are not sure.

Writing Process

Prewriting
⇩
Drafting
⇩
Revising
⇩
Editing
⇩
Publishing

11

Objectives

Spelling and Writing

Students will
- **proofread** a journal entry.
- **use** the writing process to write a journal entry.
- **proofread** their writing.

Using the Writing Process

Before assigning **Write a Journal Entry** in this unit, see pages 258–259 in the Student Edition for a complete review of the writing process and additional writing assignments. You may also wish to refer to pages Z12–Z13 in the Teacher Edition.

Keeping a Spelling Journal

Encourage students to record the words they misspelled on the weekly test in a personal spelling journal. These words may be recycled for future study. Students may also wish to include words from their writing. See pages Z12–Z13 in the Teacher Edition for more information.

★14. His **natural** ability to draw made him a skilled artist.
15. She needed to **obtain** paints and paper for art class.
★16. We used a simple **pattern** to make a kite.
★17. The **rapid** motion of the train was frightening.
18. Have you answered the question on the **survey**?
19. His kindness is his best **trait**.
★20. We will go to the mountains on our **vacation**.

Option 2:
Multiple Spelling Words Per Sentence
(See procedures on pages Z10–Z11.)

1. We will **complain** if you **detain** us any longer.
2. The girl's speech **pattern** was unusual due to her **accent**.
3. A **survey** showed a **rapid** growth of **natural** resources.
4. Do you **admit** that you did not **behave** well at the party?
5. We began to **daydream** about our **vacation** far in **advance** of the day we left.
6. How did you **obtain** that rare photo **album**?
7. The station is going to **cancel** my **favorite** program.
8. The last **chapter** of the book is about **labor** practices.
9. His honesty is **exactly** the right **trait** for a businessman.

Option 3:
Standardized Test
(See *Teacher Resource Book,* Unit 1.)

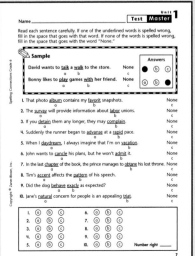

**Unit 1
Test Master**

T11

Objectives

Strategy Words

Students will

- **review** words studied previously that are related to the spelling strategy.
- **preview** unknown words that are related to the spelling strategy.

Remind the students that the **Strategy Words** are related to the spelling patterns they have studied in this unit. The **Review Words** are below grade level, and the **Preview Words** are above grade level. You may wish to use the following sentences to introduce the words in context.

Review Words:
Words From Grade 5

1. Each **brand** of cereal has a special location in the store.
2. Did he **claim** the prize?
3. The motorist did not **disobey** the traffic signal.
4. The artist used a **grayer** shade than I would have chosen.
5. Please **locate** the cities on this map.

Preview Words:
Words From Grade 7

6. The word <u>cares</u> is an **anagram** for <u>races</u>.
7. The **caption** was left off the picture.
8. Our committee was supposed to create a **display** in the window.
9. The band will **entertain** at the football game.
10. We found a **mistake** in the recipe.

Review Words
1. brand
2. grayer
3. locate
4. claim
5. disobey

Preview Words
6. caption
7. entertain
8. mistake
9. display
10. anagram

Unit 1 enrichment

VOCABULARY CONNECTIONS

Strategy Words

Review Words: Short a, Long a

Write a word from the box to complete each sentence.

brand	claim	disobey	grayer	locate

1. Try this new _____ of cereal.
2. His hair is a little _____ than it was when I met him several years ago.
3. I am trying to _____ his town on this map.
4. Please _____ your prize by midnight tonight.
5. If you _____ the traffic laws of this town, you will get a ticket.

Preview Words: Short a, Long a

Write the word from the box that matches each clue.

anagram	caption	display
entertain	mistake	

6. This is a short explanation for a picture in a book, magazine, or newspaper.
7. A comedian might stand on a stage to do this for an audience.
8. You might apologize for this.
9. An athlete might do this with her trophies.
10. **Tap** and **pat** are examples of this word puzzle.

12

Unit 1 Homework Master

Unit 1 RECAP

You may wish to assign the **Unit 1 Homework Master** (*Teacher Resource Book,* Unit 1) as a fun way to recap the spelling words.

Homework Master Unit 1

Name _____

Write each spelling word that you unscramble.

1. niated	____	6. tiart	____
2. mubla	____	7. robal	____
3. larutan	____	8. timda	____
4. lecnac	____	9. retpahc	____
5. niatbo	____	10. dipar	____

Note the letters that stand for long **a**. Write the spelling word that fits each shape.

Write the spelling words that complete the sentences.

1. The stress on a syllable is called an ____.
2. To go forward means to ____.
3. To make a paper snowflake, use this ____.
4. The book that you like best is your ____.
5. To get the best results, follow this recipe ____.
6. I am teaching the puppy to ____.

T12

Content Words

Fine Arts: Sculpture

Write the word from the box that fits each definition.

chisel	sculptor	engraving	woodcut	marble

1. a person who carves figures
2. an engraved block of wood to print from
3. the art of cutting designs into a surface
4. a hard rock made from limestone
5. a metal tool with a sharp edge

Science: Astronomy

Write the words from the box to complete the paragraph.

crater	module	lunar	terrain	meteorite

On July 20, 1969, astronauts were about to set foot on the moon for the first time. Neil Armstrong and Buzz Aldrin climbed into the landing __6.__ They guided their vehicle toward the __7.__ surface, narrowly missing a deep __8.__ The two men explored the moon's rugged and dusty __9.__ Unless a __10.__ hits that area of the moon, their footprints will probably last for millions of years.

Apply the Spelling Strategy

Circle the letters that spell the **long a** sound in three of the Content Words you wrote.

Word Study

Word Roots

The old Latin word, **terra,** meant "earth" or "land." Terra cotta is a kind of pottery, or earthenware. Write the Content Word that has the root **terra.**

13

Fine Arts: Sculpture
1. sculptor
2. woodcut
3. engr(a)ving
4. marble
5. chisel

Science: Astronomy
6. module
7. lunar
8. cr(a)t(e)r
9. terr(ai)n
10. meteorite

Word Roots
1. terrain

Objectives

Content Words

Students will
- **expand** vocabulary with content-related words.
- **relate** the spelling strategy to words outside the basic spelling list.
- **understand** a word root and find it in a word.

Content Words

Fine Arts: Sculpture

Use these sentences to introduce the words and their meanings.

1. The woodcarver used a **chisel** to carve larger pieces of wood.
2. The **sculptor** made her statue from a large block of stone.
3. The **engraving** was done locally.
4. The students carved designs on one side of a block to make the **woodcut**.
5. The white columns were **marble**.

Science: Astronomy

Use these sentences to introduce the words and their meanings.

6. The pictures showed a large **crater** on the moon.
7. Astronauts use a **module** for a moon landing.
8. During a **lunar** eclipse the moon is obscured.
9. The **terrain** was quite rugged and hard to drive over.
10. We could see the **meteorite** as it entered Earth's orbit.

Note: The **long a** sound in **engraving** and **crater** is actually spelled by the **vowel-consonant-e** pattern evident in **crate** and **engrave**.

Word Study

Word Roots

Point out that a **word root** is a word or word part from which other words are made. Word roots for English words often come from Latin or Greek. Understanding word roots can help students build their vocabulary.

Unit 2 Home Spelling Practice

Spanish

English

MANAGING INSTRUCTION

Looking Ahead to Unit 2

To save time, you may wish to duplicate the **Unit 2 Home Spelling Practice** now. (See *Home Spelling Practice Book*, Unit 2.)

T13

Basic Spelling List

text	method
feeble	indeed
gravity	develop
dealt	regular
theme	scheme
sleet	crease
excellent	leather
cleanse	attend
melody	release
employee	meadow

Strategy Words

Review

beneath	memory
expect	needle
homestead	

Preview

activities	league
extreme	newsreel
headline	

Content Words

Language Arts: Genres

autobiography	
journal	novel
serial	trilogy

Health: First Aid

artery	tourniquet
pressure	emergency
bleed	

Individual Needs

Challenge Words

definite	prevent
velvet	cheetah
appeal	charity

Alternate Word List ★

melody	scheme
method	leather
indeed	attend
develop	release
regular	meadow

★ For students who need to study fewer Basic Spelling words

MATERIALS

Student Edition
Pages 14–19
Challenge Activities, p. 225

Teacher Edition
Pages T14A–T19
Challenge Activities, p. T225

Teacher Resource Book
Unit 2 Homework Master
Unit 2 Practice Masters
Flip Folder Practice Master
Unit 2 Test Master

Home Spelling Practice Book
Unit 2 Home Spelling Practice
(English or Spanish)

Other *Spelling Connections* Resources
• Audiotape, Grade 6
• Practice Book for Grammar, Usage, and Mechanics, Grade 6
• Spelling Support for Second Language Learners, Grade 6
• Support Software on CD-ROM
• Transparency Book, Grade 6
• Word Sort CD-ROM, Grade 6

OBJECTIVES

Spelling and Thinking

Students will
• **read** the spelling words in list form and in context.
• **sort** the spelling words according to **short e** and **long e** sounds and spelling patterns.
• **read** and remember this week's spelling strategy.

Spelling and Vocabulary

Students will
• **match** word meaning clues with spelling words.
• **identify** initial and final sounds in spelling words.
• **decode** dictionary respellings to identify spelling words and their stressed syllables.

Spelling and Reading

Students will
• **identify** spelling words that complete a series of meaning-related words.
• **solve** analogies using spelling words.
• **complete** sentences using spelling words.

Spelling and Writing

Students will
• **proofread** a play description.
• **use** the writing process to write a play description.
• **proofread** their writing.

MEETING INDIVIDUAL NEEDS
Learning Styles

 Visual

Write each spelling word on a separate 3" × 5" card. On the back of each card, write **short e** or **long e** to describe the vowel sound in the word. When a word has more than one /ĕ/ or /ē/, make a card for each occurrence of the sound. Place the cards facedown. One student says a spelling word, writes it, and then turns over a card that may be the one on which the word is written. If it is, the student keeps the card. If it is not, the card is placed facedown again. Either way, the next player has a turn. Whoever collects the most cards wins the game.

 Auditory

Use the word cards and game strategy of the visual activity, but also have the students spell the word aloud as they write it.

 Kinesthetic

Use the word cards of the visual activity. Place the cards facedown on the chalk tray. Divide the class into two teams. Pronounce a word. A student from each team comes to the tray to locate the correct card. The first player to find the word scores a point. Both players then spell the word aloud and write it. The game continues until all the cards have been used.

Hands-On Practice
All students will benefit from practicing with a **Flip Folder**. See page Z18.

Language and Cultural Differences

The /ĕ/ and /ē/ sounds may be difficult for some students to hear and spell due to regional pronunciations or language backgrounds that do not include the sounds or that spell them differently. For example, in Spanish, the letter **i** is used for a sound similar to the **long e** sound in English.

Write the spelling words on the chalkboard. Ask volunteers to use the words in sentences or to define them.

Pronounce each word, asking students to repeat it in unison after you. Point out the various ways in which the **long e** and **short e** sounds are spelled. In each spelling word, underline the letters that spell the /ĕ/ and /ē/. Have the students copy and underline the words in the same way.

MANAGING INSTRUCTION

3–5 Day Plan		Average	Below Average	Above Average
Day 1	**Day 1**	Pretest Spelling Mini-Lesson, p. T14 Spelling and Thinking, p. 14	Pretest Spelling Mini-Lesson, p. T14 Spelling and Thinking, p. 14	Pretest Spelling and Thinking, p. 14
	Day 2	Spelling and Vocabulary, p. 15	Spelling and Vocabulary, p. 15 (or) Unit 2 Practice Master, A and B	Spelling and Vocabulary, p. 15 Spelling and Reading, p. 16
Day 2	**Day 3**	Spelling and Reading, p. 16	Spelling and Reading, p. 16 (or) Unit 2 Practice Master, C and D	Challenge Activities, p. 225
	Day 4	Spelling and Writing, p. 17 Unit 2 Homework Master	Spelling and Writing, p. 17	Spelling and Writing, p. 17 Unit 2 Homework Master
Day 3	**Day 5**	Weekly Test	Weekly Test	Weekly Test

Vocabulary Connections (pages 18 and 19) may be used anytime during this unit.

Objectives

Spelling and Thinking

Students will
- **read** the spelling words in list form and in context.
- **sort** the spelling words according to **short e** and **long e** sounds and spelling patterns.
- **read** and remember this week's spelling strategy.

UNIT PRETEST

Use **Pretest Sentences** below. Refer to the self-checking procedures on student page 256. You may wish to use the **Unit 2 Word List Overhead Transparency** as part of the checking procedure.

TEACHING THE STRATEGY

Spelling Mini-Lesson

Write /ĕ/ and /ē/ on the board. Remind the students that these are the dictionary symbols for **short e** and **long e**.

Ask for a volunteer to read the spelling list aloud. Ask students to decide whether each word has a **short e** or **long e** vowel sound and to write the word in the appropriate column. (**Note:** Employee and **melody** belong in both columns.)

Ask them if all the words on each list share the same spelling pattern. (no) Invite volunteers to circle letters that spell the **short e** sound in the first list (e, ea) and letters that spell **long e** in the second list. (ee, ea, e-consonant-e, y)

Explain that a vowel digraph is two vowel letters written together that make one vowel sound. Examples of vowel digraphs are /ĕ/ spelled **ea** and /ē/ spelled **ee** or **ea**. Ask the students to identify words on the list that include a vowel digraph.

Read **Remember the Spelling Strategy** on page 14.

Order of answers may vary.

short e and long e
1. ⓔmployeⓔ
2. mⓔlodⓨ ★

short e
3. tⓔxt
4. dⓔⓐlt
5. ⓔxcellent
6. clⓔanse
7. mⓔthod ★
8. devⓔlop ★
9. rⓔgular ★
10. lⓔⓐther ★
11. attⓔnd ★
12. mⓔⓐdow ★

long e
13. feⓔble
14. gravitⓨ
15. thⓔmⓔ
16. sleⓔt
17. indeⓔd ★
18. schⓔmⓔ ★
19. crⓔⓐse
20. relⓔⓐse ★

1.	text	*text*	We revised the speechwriter's **text**.
2.	feeble	*feeble*	Grandpa is **feeble** but has a sharp mind.
3.	gravity	*gravity*	The pull of **gravity** gives us weight.
4.	dealt	*dealt*	He **dealt** with his problem with courage.
5.	theme	*theme*	The **theme** of my report is earthquakes.
6.	sleet	*sleet*	The cold air changed the rain to **sleet**.
7.	excellent	*excellent*	She has an **excellent** attendance record.
8.	cleanse	*cleanse*	Be sure to **cleanse** the wound carefully.
9.	melody	*melody*	He was humming a familiar **melody**.
10.	employee	*employee*	The new **employee** arrived at work early.
11.	method	*method*	We are trying a new cooking **method**.
12.	indeed	*indeed*	She is **indeed** a very bright woman.
13.	develop	*develop*	A storm might **develop** overnight.
14.	regular	*regular*	The **regular** price has been reduced.
15.	scheme	*scheme*	She has a **scheme** for making money.
16.	crease	*crease*	He ironed the **crease** in his pants.
17.	leather	*leather*	The shoes are made of genuine **leather**.
18.	attend	*attend*	Hundreds will **attend** tonight's lecture.
19.	release	*release*	I will **release** the name of the winner.
20.	meadow	*meadow*	Plant life abounds in the **meadow**.

1.–2. Write the words with both the **short e** and the **long e** sounds.

3.–12. Write the other words with the **short e** vowel sound.

13.–20. Write the other words with the **long e** vowel sound.

Circle the letters that spell the **short e** sound or the **long e** sound.

Remember that the **short e** sound is spelled **e** in **text** and **ea** in **dealt**. The **long e** sound is spelled **ee** in **sleet**, **ea** in **crease**, **e-consonant-e** in **theme**, and **y** in **gravity**.

14

Pretest Sentences (See procedures on pages Z10–Z11.)

1. Please look up the names of the planets in your science **text**.
2. After the surgery, Joe felt **feeble**.
3. Earth attracts other bodies by a force called **gravity**.
4. Benji **dealt** the play money to each game player.
5. What is the **theme** of your essay?
6. The **sleet** on the road made driving dangerous.
7. Luna received an **excellent** grade for her science report.
8. Use this detergent to **cleanse** the dirty towels.
★ 9. While Carl sang the words, we hummed the **melody**.
10. The new **employee** was introduced to the other office workers.
★11. What **method** did you use to solve the puzzle?
★12. When Sue asked if she could help, her father said, "Yes, **indeed**."
★13. It takes time and effort to **develop** good study skills.
★14. Our **regular** teacher was absent from class.
★15. Our class presented a **scheme** for raising money.
16. Sam folded the newspaper, making a thick **crease**.
★17. The horseman wore **leather** boots.
★18. Will you be able to **attend** the meeting on Friday?
★19. The bird might fly away if you **release** it from its cage.
★20. Wildflowers grew in the **meadow**.

Spelling and Vocabulary

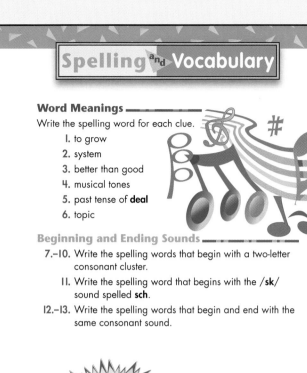

Word Meanings
Write the spelling word for each clue.

1. to grow
2. system
3. better than good
4. musical tones
5. past tense of **deal**
6. topic

Beginning and Ending Sounds

7.–10. Write the spelling words that begin with a two-letter consonant cluster.

11. Write the spelling word that begins with the /**sk**/ sound spelled **sch**.

12.–13. Write the spelling words that begin and end with the same consonant sound.

USING THE Dictionary

An accent mark follows a boldface syllable. This marks the syllable that is stressed when it is pronounced. Write the spelling words for the dictionary respellings. Underline the stressed syllable in each word.

14. /lĕ**th**′ ər/
15. /**mĕd**′ ō/
16. /ĕm **ploi**′ ē/
17. /ə **tĕnd**′/
18. /**fē**′ bəl/
19. /ĭn **dēd**′/
20. /rĭ **lēs**′/

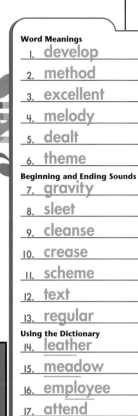

Word Meanings
1. develop
2. method
3. excellent
4. melody
5. dealt
6. theme

Beginning and Ending Sounds
7. gravity
8. sleet
9. cleanse
10. crease
11. scheme
12. text
13. regular

Using the Dictionary
14. leather
15. meadow
16. employee
17. attend
18. feeble
19. indeed
20. release

15

MEETING INDIVIDUAL NEEDS
Providing More Help

To aid the students in learning the correct spelling patterns, have them write the spelling words that share the vowel pattern in each set of words below.

1. breath, breakfast, meant (dealt, meadow, cleanse, leather)
2. contest, sent, tenth (excellent, text, method, regular, attend, develop)
3. unlucky, vanity, cavity (melody, gravity)
4. concrete, recede, complete (theme, scheme)
5. defeat, least, weave (crease, release)
6. breeze, cheese, needle (sleet, feeble, indeed, employee)

★Students who need to study fewer words should use the **Alternate Word List**. This list is starred on page T14 in the Teacher Edition. The **Unit 2 Practice Masters** (*Teacher Resource Book*) provide additional practice with these words.

Unit 2 Practice Masters

Name _____

Practice **Master** Unit **2**

| 1. method | 3. attend | 5. meadow | 7. indeed | 9. scheme |
| 2. regular | 4. develop | 6. leather | 8. release | 10. melody |

A. Write the spelling words in alphabetical order.

1. ___   6. ___
2. ___   7. ___
3. ___   8. ___
4. ___   9. ___
5. ___   10. ___

B. Write the spelling word that goes with each clue.

1. to let loose _____
2. to grow _____
3. usual _____
4. system _____

C. Write the spelling word that belongs in each group.

1. silk, cotton, denim, _____
2. normal, average, usual, _____
3. pasture, field, grassland, _____
4. let go, set free, let fly, _____
5. music, tune, tones, _____

9

Practice **Master** Unit **2**

| indeed | scheme |
| release | melody |

s hidden in the puzzle. Circle

l	a	r	g	c
e	l	o	d	y
a	t	h	e	r
s	e	s	w	a
e	e	d	i	t
p	c	b	e	x
d	o	f	k	p

10

Objectives

Spelling and Reading

Students will
- **identify** spelling words that complete a series of meaning-related words.
- **solve** analogies using spelling words.
- **complete** sentences using spelling words.

One-Minute Handwriting Hint

The undercurve beginning of the lowercase **e** must be wide to allow room for the loop and slant stroke. Be sure to keep the loop open or the letter will look like an **i**.

WIDE → *e* ↗ LOOP

Legible handwriting can boost spelling scores by as much as 20%.

Complete the Sequences
1. meadow
2. sleet
3. regular
4. employee
5. feeble

Solve the Analogies
6. leather
7. melody
8. release
9. cleanse
10. excellent
11. scheme
12. dealt

Complete the Sentences
13. gravity
14. attend
15. method
16. develop
17. crease
18. theme
19. text
20. indeed

Spelling and Reading

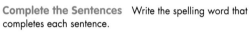

text	feeble	gravity	dealt	theme
sleet	excellent	cleanse	melody	employee
method	indeed	develop	regular	scheme
crease	leather	attend	release	meadow

Complete the Sequences   Write a spelling word to complete each sequence.

1. field, pasture, grassland, _____
2. hail, rain, snow, _____
3. normal, usual, ordinary, _____
4. worker, laborer, attendant, _____
5. weak, frail, shaky, _____

Solve the Analogies   Write a spelling word to complete each analogy.

6. **Sweater** is to **wool** as **belt** is to _____.
7. **Painting** is to **color** as **music** is to _____.
8. **Argue** is to **agree** as **restrain** is to _____.
9. **Dirt** is to **smudge** as **soap** is to _____.
10. **Foolish** is to **wise** as **poor** is to _____.
11. **Devise** is to **plan** as **concoct** is to _____.
12. **Meet** is to **met** as **deal** is to _____.

Complete the Sentences   Write the spelling word that completes each sentence.

13. The force of _____ made rocks roll down the hill.
14. We would like you to _____ tonight's meeting.
15. Electronic mail is a fairly new _____ of communication.
16. This tiny bud will _____ into an enormous flower.
17. Fold the paper and cut the design along the _____.
18. Modern art is the _____ of the lecture series.
19. I found the answer on page five of the _____.
20. The play was _____ enjoyable.

16

MEETING INDIVIDUAL NEEDS

Providing More Challenge

Challenge Words and **Challenge Activities** for Unit 2 appear on page 225. **Challenge Word Test Sentences** appear on page T225.

Unit 2 Challenge Activities

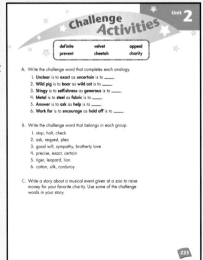

Weekly Test Options

Option 1:

One Spelling Word Per Sentence
(See procedures on pages Z10–Z11.)

★ 1. The sisters **attend** daily piano classes after school.
2. The cook must **cleanse** her hands often.
3. Be careful not to **crease** the paper.
4. The blow he was **dealt** made his head ache.
★ 5. Children grow and **develop** at different rates.
6. The **employee** tries to assist the boss whenever possible.
7. The sky was so clear that the view was **excellent**.
8. That **feeble** animal can hardly walk.
9. The force that keeps us on Earth is **gravity**.
★10. She is **indeed** proud of her fine singing ability.
★11. She never wore her **leather** boots in rainy weather.
★12. He sat in the **meadow** and read a book.
★13. I like the **melody** of that song better than the lyrics.
★14. We all used the same **method** to solve the puzzle.
★15. The **regular** school day is about six hours long.
★16. The doctor will **release** the patient from the hospital.

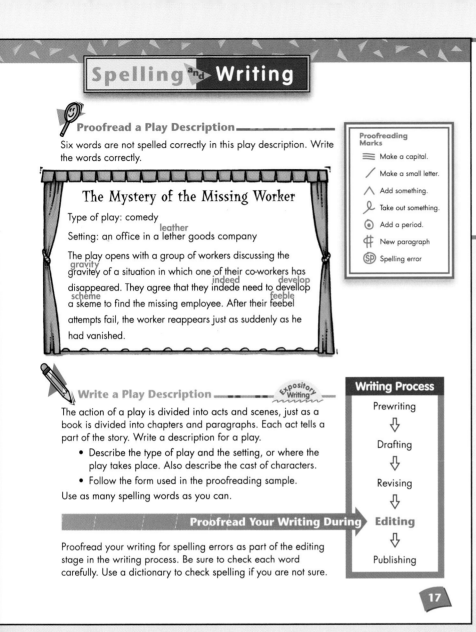

Spelling and Writing

Proofread a Play Description

Six words are not spelled correctly in this play description. Write the words correctly.

The Mystery of the Missing Worker

Type of play: comedy

Setting: an office in a lether goods company
leather

The play opens with a group of workers discussing the *gravity* gravety of a situation in which one of their co-workers has disappeared. They agree that they *indeed* indede need to *develop* devellop a *scheme* skeme to find the missing employee. After their *feeble* feebel attempts fail, the worker reappears just as suddenly as he had vanished.

Proofreading Marks

≡ Make a capital.
/ Make a small letter.
∧ Add something.
ℓ Take out something.
⊙ Add a period.
⌗ New paragraph.
ⓢⓟ Spelling error

Write a Play Description

Expository Writing

The action of a play is divided into acts and scenes, just as a book is divided into chapters and paragraphs. Each act tells a part of the story. Write a description for a play.

- Describe the type of play and the setting, or where the play takes place. Also describe the cast of characters.
- Follow the form used in the proofreading sample.

Use as many spelling words as you can.

Proofread Your Writing During

Proofread your writing for spelling errors as part of the editing stage in the writing process. Be sure to check each word carefully. Use a dictionary to check spelling if you are not sure.

Writing Process

Prewriting
⇩
Drafting
⇩
Revising
⇩
Editing
⇩
Publishing

17

Objectives

Spelling and Writing

Students will
- **proofread** a play description.
- **use** the writing process to write a play description.
- **proofread** their writing.

Using the Writing Process

Before assigning **Write a Play Description,** see pages 258–259 in the Student Edition for a complete review of the writing process and additional writing assignments. You may also wish to refer to pages Z12–Z13 in the Teacher Edition.

Keeping a Spelling Journal

Encourage students to record the words they misspelled on the weekly test in a personal spelling journal. These words may be recycled for future study. Students may also wish to include words from their writing. See pages Z12–Z13 in the Teacher Edition for more information.

★17. What **scheme** do you have to get all your work done?
18. As the snow fell, it turned to **sleet**.
19. Read the next chapter in your science **text**.
20. What is the **theme** of the article you are reading?

Option 2:
Multiple Spelling Words Per Sentence
(See procedures on pages Z10–Z11.)

1. The **theme** of the **text** is the nature of **gravity**.
2. The **feeble** old horse was kept in the **meadow**.
3. Each **employee** must **attend** all company meetings.
4. **Sleet** and rain may stain a **leather** jacket.
5. What **method** will you use to **release** the animal from the trap?
6. The dishonest **scheme dealt** a blow to the company.
7. This is **indeed** a beautiful **melody**.
8. Don't remove the **crease** when you **cleanse** my pants.
9. The gym instructor will **develop** an **excellent regular** program of activity for you.

Option 3:
Standardized Test
(See *Teacher Resource Book,* Unit 2.)

**Unit 2
Test Master**

T17

Objectives

Strategy Words

Students will
- **review** words studied previously that are related to the spelling strategy.
- **preview** unknown words that are related to the spelling strategy.

VOCABULARY CONNECTIONS

⊳Strategy Words⊲

Remind the students that the **Strategy Words** are related to the spelling patterns they have studied in this unit. The **Review Words** are below grade level, and the **Preview Words** are above grade level. You may wish to use the following sentences to introduce the words in context.

Review Words:
Words From Grade 5

1. I kept my arms **beneath** the warm quilts.
2. Did you **expect** an answer today?
3. The museum built a replica of my grandparents' **homestead**.
4. My favorite **memory** is about a day I saw a musical by Gilbert and Sullivan.
5. Was there a **needle** in that haystack?

Preview Words:
Words From Grade 7

6. My favorite **activities** at school are band and volleyball.
7. Ralph made an **extreme** effort to do his best.
8. The **headline** in the paper made us feel proud of our city.
9. My mother plays golf in a **league**.
10. We studied the **newsreel** for information about early space flights.

Review Words
1. needle
2. memory
3. homestead
4. beneath
5. expect

Preview Words
6. headline
7. league
8. activities
9. newsreel
10. extreme

⊳Strategy Words⊲

Review Words: Short e, Long e

Write the words from the box to complete the paragraph.

beneath	expect	homestead
memory	needle	

With a __1.__ and thread, Abigail had captured the __2.__ of the old family __3.__ in Kansas. Her quilt now hangs on the wall in the historical society. A description of the quilt is __4.__ it. I __5.__ that everyone who sees the quilt admires it.

Preview Words: Short e, Long e

Write the word from the box that matches each clue.

activities	extreme	headline
league	newsreel	

6. This appears on the front page of a newspaper.
7. Sports teams might come together to form this.
8. Plan a lot of these to keep a group of two-year-olds busy all day.
9. This would show motion pictures of news events.
10. This could describe the heat of the desert.

18

Unit 2 RECAP

You may wish to assign the **Unit 2 Homework Master** (*Teacher Resource Book, Unit 2*) as a fun way to recap the spelling words.

Unit 2 Homework Master

Name _____

Homework Master Unit **2**

Read down, across, backwards, and diagonally to find spelling words in the puzzle. Circle each spelling word.

```
a p t c l o s e l p a i n t f d
d l m i l m e a t t e n d r e d
e a e x c e l l e n t p l a t e
v n e e z e a a x u h e c y t l
e e c a f e i n t p e m e h c s
l m e t h o d g s i m t u b t a
o o m a l e d r f e e b l e w n
p o l e v e n a r a l u g e r d
c l s e l a m v a i s y a w l a
h o l i c o e i c n e s a e r c
a d e a l t d t t d a n c i n g
i n e m p l o y e e s a e l e r
n o t e o w o d a e m i w s a w
m r e h t a e l a d a f l a m e
```

Now write the spelling words in alphabetical order.

1. _____ 11. _____
2. _____ 12. _____
3. _____ 13. _____
4. _____ 14. _____
5. _____ 15. _____
6. _____ 16. _____
7. _____ 17. _____
8. _____ 18. _____
9. _____ 19. _____
10. _____ 20. _____
12.

Content Words

Language Arts: Genres

Write the word from the box that fits each definition.

autobiography	journal	serial	novel	trilogy

1. a record of the events in your day
2. the story of your life
3. a series of three related plays, operas, or novels
4. a story that is published one part at a time
5. a long work of fiction

Health: First Aid

Write the words from the box to complete the paragraph.

artery	pressure	bleed	tourniquet	emergency

After the accident, the __6.__ team immediately set to work.
First they checked the victim's blood __7.__. They tied a __8.__
around his arm so that the wound would not continue to __9.__.
Fortunately, the broken glass had missed an __10.__ in his arm.
He will be released from the hospital today.

Apply the Spelling Strategy

Circle the five Content Words you wrote that spell the **long e** sound **ee** or **y**.

Word Study

Spelling Changes Over Time

For a long time, **catalog** and **dialog** were spelled **catalogue** and **dialogue**. Over time, the silent letters started to be dropped, and currently both spellings are accepted. Write a related Strategy Word whose spelling may also change over time.

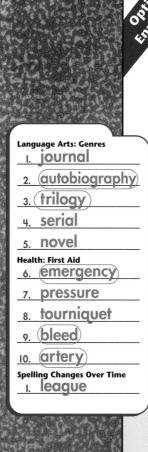

Language Arts: Genres
1. journal
2. autobiography
3. trilogy
4. serial
5. novel

Health: First Aid
6. emergency
7. pressure
8. tourniquet
9. bleed
10. artery

Spelling Changes Over Time
1. league

19

Unit 3 Home Spelling Practice

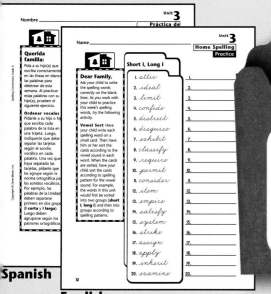

Spanish

English

MANAGING INSTRUCTION

Looking Ahead to Unit 3

To save time, you may wish to duplicate the **Unit 3 Home Spelling Practice** now. (See *Home Spelling Practice Book,* Unit 3.)

Objectives

Content Words

Students will
- **expand** vocabulary with content-related words.
- **relate** the spelling strategy to words outside the basic spelling list.
- **understand** that the spelling of a word can change over time.

Content Words

Language Arts: Genres

Use these sentences to introduce the words and their meanings.

1. I read an **autobiography** of Truman.
2. Keep the words that you misspelled in a **journal**.
3. A story about the Revolutionary War was a four-part **serial** on TV.
4. My favorite **novel** was written by Maya Angelou.
5. I have read the first two books of the **trilogy**.

Health: First Aid

Use these sentences to introduce the words and their meanings.

6. He checked his pulse by placing his fingers over an **artery** on his wrist.
7. She applied **pressure** to the wound.
8. Did the wound **bleed**?
9. A **tourniquet** needs to be applied carefully to stop bleeding.
10. I handled the **emergency** because of the class I took in first aid.

Word Study

Spelling Changes Over Time

Help the students understand that language is never static. Words and spelling patterns change and evolve over time as new spellings are accepted and become part of the written language.

Basic Spelling List

attic	consider
ideal	item
limit	empire
confide	satisfy
district	system
disguise	strike
exhibit	assign
classify	apply
require	inherit
permit	examine

Strategy Words

Review

arrive	signs
bicycle	simplify
digit	

Preview

admire	hinder
alliance	resign
byline	

Content Words

Language Arts: Genres

legend	ballad
fable	short story
myth	

Social Studies: Petroleum

derrick	tanker
platform	pipeline
petroleum	

Individual Needs

Challenge Words

categorize	glimpse
hibernate	citrus
logic	inhabit

Alternate Word List ★

attic	item
limit	system
disguise	strike
exhibit	assign
consider	examine

★ For students who need to study fewer Basic Spelling words

MATERIALS

Student Edition
Pages 20–25
Challenge Activities, p. 226

Teacher Edition
Pages T20A–T25
Challenge Activities, p. T226

Teacher Resource Book
Unit 3 Homework Master
Unit 3 Practice Masters
Flip Folder Practice Master
Unit 3 Test Master

Home Spelling Practice Book
Unit 3 Home Spelling Practice
(English or Spanish)

Other *Spelling Connections* Resources
- Audiotape, Grade 6
- Practice Book for Grammar, Usage, and Mechanics, Grade 6
- Spelling Support for Second Language Learners, Grade 6
- Support Software on CD-ROM
- Transparency Book, Grade 6
- Word Sort CD-ROM, Grade 6

OBJECTIVES

Spelling and Thinking

Students will
- **read** the spelling words in list form and in context.
- **sort** the spelling words according to **short i** and **long i** sounds and spelling patterns.
- **read** and remember this week's spelling strategy.

Spelling and Vocabulary

Students will
- **change** noun forms into verb forms.
- **replace** words in a sentence with spelling words with the same or nearly the same meaning.
- **decode** dictionary re-spellings of two-syllable words and divide these words into syllables.

Spelling and Reading

Students will
- **solve** analogies using spelling words.
- **complete** sentences using spelling words.
- **complete** a paragraph with spelling words.

Spelling and Writing

Students will
- **proofread** a science fiction story.
- **use** the writing process to write a science fiction story.
- **proofread** their writing.

MEETING INDIVIDUAL NEEDS
Learning Styles

 Visual

Have the students look for the spelling words in old magazines or newspapers. Have them cut out each spelling word that they find, glue the word on paper, and write the word beside the printed version.

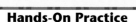

Hands-On Practice
All students will benefit from practicing with a **Flip Folder**. See page Z18.

 Auditory

Ask the students to write short nonsense rhymes using the spelling words. Example:

At the costume **exhibit** a man in **disguise** was ordered to **limit** the cost of supplies.

Ask the students to read their poems to the class. Have the other students name the spelling words used in the poems and spell them.

 Kinesthetic

Divide a game board into twenty sections. Mark the "Start" and "Finish." Write each spelling word on a card. Stack the cards facedown. Have two to four students play at a time. The first player asks the player on his or her right to spell the word on the top card. If correct, the speller moves a marker the number of spaces equal to the number of syllables in the word. If incorrect, the marker remains in place. The game continues until all have reached the "Finish."

Language and Cultural Differences

The **long i** and **short i** sounds may be difficult for some students to hear and spell due to regional pronunciations or language backgrounds that do not include the sounds or that spell them differently. For example, in Spanish, the letter **i** is used for a sound similar to the **long e** sound in English. A more likely cause of spelling difficulty, however, is that students must remember several spelling patterns for the **long i** sound. In Spanish, each vowel sound is generally represented by one letter.

First, write the spelling words on the chalkboard. Ask the students to tell something about the meaning of each word. Clarify and expand the students' definitions.

Next, write each spelling word on a 3" × 5" card. Hand out the cards to the students. Let them take turns holding up their word cards and calling out the words. After the student pronounces the spelling word, use the word in a sentence. Then ask the students to write the word and check for correct spelling by looking at the card the student is holding.

MANAGING INSTRUCTION

3–5 Day Plan		Average	Below Average	Above Average
Day 1	**Day 1**	Pretest Spelling Mini-Lesson, p. T20 Spelling and Thinking, p. 20	Pretest Spelling Mini-Lesson, p. T20 Spelling and Thinking, p. 20	Pretest Spelling and Thinking, p. 20
	Day 2	Spelling and Vocabulary, p. 21	Spelling and Vocabulary, p. 21 (or) Unit 3 Practice Master, A and B	Spelling and Vocabulary, p. 21 Spelling and Reading, p. 22
Day 2	**Day 3**	Spelling and Reading, p. 22	Spelling and Reading, p. 22 (or) Unit 3 Practice Master, C and D	Challenge Activities, p. 226
	Day 4	Spelling and Writing, p. 23 Unit 3 Homework Master	Spelling and Writing, p. 23	Spelling and Writing, p. 23 Unit 3 Homework Master
Day 3	**Day 5**	Weekly Test	Weekly Test	Weekly Test
Vocabulary Connections (pages 24 and 25) may be used anytime during this unit.				

Objectives

Spelling and Thinking

Students will
- **read** the spelling words in list form and in context.
- **sort** the spelling words according to **short i** and **long i** sounds and spelling patterns.
- **read** and remember this week's spelling strategy.

UNIT PRETEST

Use **Pretest Sentences** below. Refer to the self-checking procedures on student page 256. You may wish to use the **Unit 3 Word List Overhead Transparency** as part of the checking procedure.

TEACHING THE STRATEGY

Spelling Mini-Lesson

Write the following words on the board: **attic, limit, district, exhibit, permit, consider, system, inherit,** and **examine.** Have students read through this list. Ask, "Do these words have the **long i** sound or the **short i** sound?" (short i) Ask a volunteer to circle the letter that spells the **short i** sound in each word. (i, as in limit; y, as in system)

Write **ideal, confide, disguise, classify, require, item, empire, satisfy, strike, assign,** and **apply** on the board. Ask a volunteer to circle the letter(s) that spells the **long i** sound. (i, as in item; i-consonant-e, as in strike; y, as in classify) Students may note that **disguise** and **satisfy** have both the **long i** and **short i** sounds.

Review that, usually, final **silent e** in a **vowel-consonant-e** spelling pattern signals that the vowel before the consonant is long. Challenge students to find the word on the list that is an exception to this guideline and to explain why it is an exception. (examine; i-consonant-e is pronounced as short i) Some students may note that **examine** begins with a **short i** sound spelled **e.**

Explain that **long i** can be spelled **i** in either an open or closed syllable. An open syllable ends with a vowel sound (e.g., **item**). A closed syllable ends with a consonant sound (e.g., **assign**). Point out that **long i** spelled **y** usually occurs at the end of a word.

Order of answers may vary.
short i and long i

1. disguise ★
2. satisfy

short i

3. attic ★
4. limit ★
5. district
6. exhibit ★
7. permit
8. consider ★
9. system ★
10. inherit
11. examine ★

long i

12. ideal
13. confide
14. classify
15. require
16. item ★
17. empire
18. strike ★
19. assign ★
20. apply

20

Spelling and Thinking

READ THE SPELLING WORDS

1.	attic	*attic*	I found the old clothes in the **attic**.
2.	ideal	*ideal*	The weather is **ideal** for sailing.
3.	limit	*limit*	The speed **limit** is forty miles an hour.
4.	confide	*confide*	I **confide** my worries to my friend.
5.	district	*district*	The school **district** covers five miles.
6.	disguise	*disguise*	He tried to **disguise** his handwriting.
7.	exhibit	*exhibit*	The art will be on **exhibit** for a month.
8.	classify	*classify*	Librarians **classify** novels as literature.
9.	require	*require*	Laws will **require** the use of seat belts.
10.	permit	*permit*	We will **permit** you to leave at noon.
11.	consider	*consider*	I **consider** him to be an expert on cars.
12.	item	*item*	She had one **item** in her grocery cart.
13.	empire	*empire*	The **empire** fell in the fifth century.
14.	satisfy	*satisfy*	We try to **satisfy** all of our customers.
15.	system	*system*	The bank installed a new alarm **system**.
16.	strike	*strike*	The workers voted to begin the **strike**.
17.	assign	*assign*	Your teacher will **assign** your seats.
18.	apply	*apply*	I decided to **apply** for the job.
19.	inherit	*inherit*	The baby might **inherit** your blue eyes.
20.	examine	*examine*	The detective will **examine** the evidence.

SORT THE SPELLING WORDS

1.–2. Write the words with both the **short i** and **long i** sounds.

3.–11. Write the other words that have the **short i** vowel sound.

12.–20. Write the other words that have the **long i** vowel sound.

Circle the letters that spell the **short i** sound or **long i** sound.

REMEMBER THE SPELLING STRATEGY

Remember that the **short i** sound is spelled **i** in **permit** and **y** in **system**. The **long i** sound is spelled **i** in **item**, **i-consonant-e** in **strike**, and **y** in **satisfy**.

Pretest Sentences (See procedures on pages Z10–Z11.)

★ 1. I enjoy looking at the old things stored in the **attic**.
  2. Mr. Webster chose Hawaii as the **ideal** place to vacation.
★ 3. Levar wishes his teachers would **limit** homework assignments.
  4. Jeff will often **confide** a secret to a close and trusted friend.
  5. Who is the superintendent of your school **district**?
★ 6. No one at the costume party knew her in that **disguise**.
★ 7. The students' handicrafts were on **exhibit** in a glass case.
  8. What animals besides alligators would you **classify** as reptiles?
  9. This task will **require** courage and skill.
  10. Will your parents **permit** you to attend the evening concert?
★11. Did you **consider** all the risks before you made your decision?
★12. Each student will bring in one **item** for the display.
  13. An emperor usually controls an **empire**.
  14. A glass of cold water will **satisfy** my thirst.
★15. Scientists prefer to use the metric **system** of measurement.
★16. A **strike** can stop the factory from producing bicycles.
★17. My teacher will surely **assign** the next chapter for homework.
  18. Can you **apply** any math rules to this science problem?
  19. Did you **inherit** your father's artistic talent?
★20. The board wants to **examine** the plans for a new gymnasium.

Spelling and Vocabulary

Word Structure

Change each of these nouns into verbs to write a spelling word.

1. consideration
2. classification
3. examination
4. requirement
5. limitation

Word Meanings

Write the spelling word that could best replace each underlined word or words.

6. He tried to <u>conceal</u> his voice on the phone.
7. You forgot to buy one <u>article</u> on the list.
8. The artist's works are on <u>public display</u> at the museum.
9. Be sure to <u>put on</u> the paint with a thick brush.
10. He ate, and ate, but he could not <u>put an end to</u> his hunger.
11. The coach is using a new <u>way of doing something</u>.
12. She will <u>receive</u> a clock from her grandfather.
13. The weather was <u>perfect</u> for the race.
14. There was a lightning <u>hit</u> in our neighborhood.

Using the Dictionary

Syllable division often occurs between two consonants. Write the spelling words for the dictionary respellings. Draw a line between the syllables. Underline the consonants that come immediately before and after the syllable division.

15. /kən **fīd′**/
16. /**ĕm′** pīr/
17. /ə **sīn′**/
18. /**ăt′** ĭk/
19. /**dĭs′** trĭkt/
20. /pər **mĭt′**/

Word Structure

1. consider
2. classify
3. examine
4. require
5. limit

Word Meanings

6. disguise
7. item
8. exhibit
9. apply
10. satisfy
11. system
12. inherit
13. ideal
14. strike

Using the Dictionary

15. con/fide
16. em/pire
17. as/sign
18. at/tic
19. dis/trict
20. per/mit

21

Objectives

Spelling and Vocabulary

Students will

- **change** noun forms into verb forms.
- **replace** words in a sentence with spelling words with the same or nearly the same meaning.
- **decode** dictionary respellings of two-syllable words and divide these words into syllables.

Developing Oral Language Skills

Practice listening to and pronouncing the **short a, short e,** and **short i** sounds. Use three-letter words such as **pat, pet,** and **pit; sat, set,** and **sit;** and **bat, bet,** and **bit.** Have one student write a series of five three-letter words that contain **short a, short e,** and **short i** in random order. This student then gives his or her paper to another student. The second student reads the words aloud. A third student then attempts to repeat the words and spell them correctly.

MEETING INDIVIDUAL NEEDS

Providing More Help

Write two headings on the chalkboard: **short i** and **long i.** Then write the spelling words under the appropriate heading, pronouncing them as you do this. Ask the students to circle the letters that spell each /ĭ/ or /ī/ sound. Have them pronounce the words, emphasizing the **i** sounds. Finally, have them copy the list and circle the vowels that represent each **i** sound.

★Students who need to study fewer words should use the **Alternate Word List**. This list is starred on page T20 in the Teacher Edition. The **Unit 3 Practice Masters** (*Teacher Resource Book*) provide additional practice with these words.

Unit 3 Practice Masters

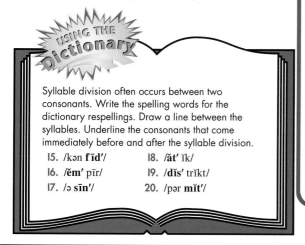

Name _____   Practice **Master** Unit **3**

| 1. limit | 3. system | 5. examine | 7. item | 9. disguise |
| 2. attic | 4. exhibit | 6. consider | 8. strike | 10. assign |

A. Fill in missing vowels to form spelling words. Write the words.

1. __ ss __ gn _____
2. __ t __ m _____
3. c __ ns __ d __ r _____
4. l __ m __ t _____
5. __ tt __ c _____
6. __ xh __ b __ t _____
7. s __ st __ m _____
8. __ x __ m __ n __ _____
9. str __ k __ _____
10. d __ sg __ __ s __ _____

B. Write the spelling word that goes with each definition.

1. to appoint _____
2. a method _____
3. space under a roof _____
4. to conceal _____
5. to hit sharply _____
6. a separate article _____

Practice **Master** Unit **3**

| item | disguise |
| strike | assign |

...ing words.

The letters **i** or **y** are given in ...letters to find the Mystery

T21

Objectives

Spelling and Reading
Students will
- **solve** analogies using spelling words.
- **complete** sentences using spelling words.
- **complete** a paragraph with spelling words.

One-Minute Handwriting Hint

Be sure to pause after the first stroke of the lowercase **i**. Pull the slant stroke to the baseline. Dot the letter directly above the slant stroke.

DOT → ⟋ PAUSE

Legible handwriting can boost spelling scores by as much as 20%.

Spelling and Reading

Solve the Analogies
1. exhibit
2. attic
3. satisfy
4. empire
5. confide

Complete the Sentences
6. inherit
7. assign
8. examine
9. district
10. item
11. system
12. strike
13. apply
14. disguise

Complete the Paragraph
15. ideal
16. classify
17. permit
18. limit
19. require
20. consider

attic	ideal	limit	confide	district
disguise	exhibit	classify	require	permit
consider	item	empire	satisfy	system
strike	assign	apply	inherit	examine

Solve the Analogies Write a spelling word to complete each analogy.
1. **Help** is to **aid** as **display** is to ____.
2. **Down** is to **up** as **basement** is to ____.
3. **Argue** is to **agree** as **disappoint** is to ____.
4. **President** is to **nation** as **emperor** is to ____.
5. **Idea** is to **suggest** as **secret** is to ____.

Complete the Sentences Write spelling words to complete the sentences.
6. Children ____ traits from their parents.
7. I will ____ your homework for tomorrow.
8. Always ____ the evidence before drawing a conclusion.
9. The voters in this ____ approved the new school.
10. I read an interesting ____ in the newspaper.
11. The heart is part of the circulatory ____.
12. The clock should ____ midnight soon.
13. You can ____ your math knowledge to the science project.
14. No one recognized the man with the ____.

Complete the Paragraph Write spelling words from the box to complete the paragraph.

The __15.__ science fiction story includes scientific facts. Even so, librarians __16.__ science fiction as fiction, not as science. If you write science fiction, __17.__ your imagination to soar. Do not feel that you should __18.__ the time to the present. These stories do not __19.__ that the setting be on Earth. You should __20.__ all possibilities for your story.

limit
require
ideal
classify
permit
consider

22

MEETING INDIVIDUAL NEEDS
Providing More Challenge

Challenge Words and **Challenge Activities** for Unit 3 appear on page 226. **Challenge Word Test Sentences** appear on page T226.

Unit 3 Challenge Activities

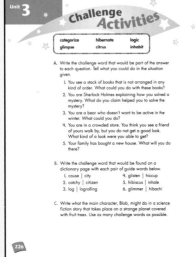

Weekly Test Options

Option 1:
One Spelling Word Per Sentence
(See procedures on pages Z10–Z11.)

1. Dad wants to **apply** for that new job.
★ 2. Did your teacher **assign** any homework during vacation?
★ 3. All of my old things are in the **attic**.
4. Would you **classify** this book as nonfiction?
5. He likes to **confide** in his sister.
★ 6. Always **consider** the rights of others before you act.
★ 7. He wore an elephant costume as a **disguise** for the party.
8. What is the name of the school in that **district**?
9. That company is run like an **empire**.
★10. The doctor wants to **examine** her throat.
★11. Did you enjoy the **exhibit** on space travel?
12. This is an **ideal** meal for an outing.
13. She will **inherit** his fishing pole when he leaves.
★14. Write the name of each **item** you plan to buy.
★15. She has to **limit** her activity because of her illness.

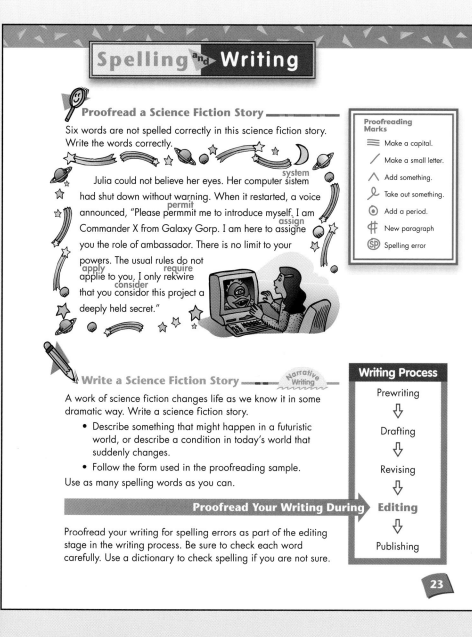

Spelling and Writing

Proofread a Science Fiction Story

Six words are not spelled correctly in this science fiction story. Write the words correctly.

system
Julia could not believe her eyes. Her computer sistem had shut down without warning. When it restarted, a voice

permit
announced, "Please permmit me to introduce myself. I am Commander X from Galaxy Gorp. I am here to assigne

assign
you the role of ambassador. There is no limit to your

apply   require
powers. The usual rules do not applie to you. I only rekwire

consider
that you considor this project a deeply held secret."

Proofreading Marks

≡ Make a capital.
/ Make a small letter.
∧ Add something.
⍭ Take out something.
⊙ Add a period.
New paragraph.
SP Spelling error

Write a Science Fiction Story

Narrative Writing

A work of science fiction changes life as we know it in some dramatic way. Write a science fiction story.

- Describe something that might happen in a futuristic world, or describe a condition in today's world that suddenly changes.
- Follow the form used in the proofreading sample.

Use as many spelling words as you can.

Proofread Your Writing During ➤ Editing

Proofread your writing for spelling errors as part of the editing stage in the writing process. Be sure to check each word carefully. Use a dictionary to check spelling if you are not sure.

Writing Process

Prewriting
⇩
Drafting
⇩
Revising
⇩
Editing
⇩
Publishing

23

16. I will not **permit** you to swim in the river.
17. This kite will **require** a strong wind to fly it.
18. I **satisfy** my love for music by playing the piano.
★19. The umpire called a **strike** and our side was out.
★20. How this **system** works is a mystery to me.

Option 2:
Multiple Spelling Words Per Sentence
(See procedures on pages Z10–Z11.)

1. The son of the king will **inherit** the **empire** someday.
2. Did you **examine** and **classify** each **item** in the **exhibit**?
3. Each teacher will **consider** how to **assign** students to the new **district** program.
4. Did you **apply** for a **permit** to fish in the lake?
5. She created a **disguise** from clothes in the **attic**.
6. The new **system** is **ideal** and will **satisfy** everyone.
7. You must **limit** the number of people you **confide** in.
8. If the workers go on **strike,** the boss will **require** them to stay outside.

Option 3:
Standardized Test
(See *Teacher Resource Book*, Unit 3.)

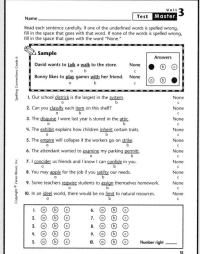

Unit 3 Test Master

T23

Objectives

Strategy Words

Students will
- **review** words studied previously that are related to the spelling strategy.
- **preview** unknown words that are related to the spelling strategy.

VOCABULARY CONNECTIONS

Strategy Words

Remind the students that the **Strategy Words** are related to the spelling patterns they have studied in this unit. The **Review Words** are below grade level, and the **Preview Words** are above grade level. You may wish to use the following sentences to introduce the words in context.

Review Words:
Words From Grade 5

1. We plan to **arrive** early for the launching of the spacecraft.
2. Is this your **bicycle**?
3. What is the place value of the **digit** 5 in the number 50?
4. These **signs** were printed to help guide guests to the launching.
5. To **simplify** the process, we developed a chart.

Preview Words:
Words From Grade 7

6. I **admire** people who are kind to others.
7. The United States has formed an **alliance** with countries who belong to the United Nations.
8. His **byline** appeared under the article describing the space program.
9. We can't allow the interruption to **hinder** our progress.
10. When the project is completed, she plans to **resign**.

Review Words
1. simplify
2. bicycle
3. signs
4. digit
5. arrive

Preview Words
6. alliance
7. hinder
8. byline
9. resign
10. admire

Strategy Words

Review Words: Short i, Long i

Write words from the box to complete the paragraph.

| arrive | bicycle | digit | signs | simplify |

This year we are trying to __1.__ the rules of the __2.__ race. The route of the race through town will be clearly marked. Along the route, volunteers will hold __3.__ with two- __4.__ numbers on them. These signs will indicate the number of kilometers left in the race. When you __5.__ at the finish line, someone will hand you a card with your time.

Preview Words: Short i, Long i

Write the word from the box that matches each clue.

| admire | alliance | byline | hinder | resign |

6. Marriage is an example of this.
7. Heavy snow could do this to road travel.
8. This tells you the author of a newspaper article.
9. You might do this if you were unhappy with your job.
10. After you finish a painting, you might stand back and do this.

24

Unit 3 RECAP

You may wish to assign the **Unit 3 Homework Master** (*Teacher Resource Book*, Unit 3) as a fun way to recap the spelling words.

Unit 3 Homework Master

Name _____

Homework Master Unit 3

Complete each puzzle with spelling words. The letters **i**, **i-e**, or **y** are given in each word as a clue. The letters circled in each puzzle form another spelling word. Unscramble these letters and write the word on the line.

Add and subtract letters to change the words below into spelling words. Write the spelling words.

1. constant – tant + lid – l + er =
2. symbol – mbol + stem =
3. cloud – oud + grass – gr + ify =
4. return – turn + qus – s + ire =
5. as + spk – pk + igs – s + n =
6. satin – in + is + fy =
7. conduct – duct + fidget – get + e =

T24

Content Words

Language Arts: Genres

Write a word from the box to complete each sentence.

legend	fable	myth	ballad	short story

1. A narrative poem set to music is a _____.
2. The _____ told how Zeus's anger caused lightning.
3. The story of King Arthur and his knights is an English _____.
4. A _____ is a brief story in which animals are the main characters.
5. A short piece of fiction is called a _____.

Social Studies: Petroleum

Write the words from the box to complete the paragraph.

derrick	platform	petroleum	tanker	pipeline

Oil, or __6.__, is often found under the ocean. A steel or concrete __7.__ provides a stable structure, and the drilling and pumping equipment is attached to the __8.__. The oil is brought ashore by an underwater __9.__ or an oil __10.__.

Apply the Spelling Strategy

Circle the letters that spell the **short i** or the **long i** sound in three of the Content Words you wrote.

Word Study

Word History

This Strategy Word can mean "a finger" or "any whole number below ten." What's the connection? Numbers less than ten can be counted on the fingers! Write the Strategy Word.

25

Language Arts: Genres
1. ballad
2. myth
3. legend
4. fable
5. short story

Social Studies: Petroleum
6. petroleum
7. platform
8. derrick
9. pipeline
10. tanker

Word History
1. digit

Objectives

Content Words

Students will
- **expand** vocabulary with content-related words.
- **relate** the spelling strategy to words outside the basic spelling list.
- **understand** the history of the word **digit**.

Content Words

Language Arts: Genres

Use these sentences to introduce the words and their meanings.
1. Do you know a **legend** about Washington and the cherry tree.
2. The **fable** pointed out the dangers of not being truthful.
3. The **myth** we read explained how the world was created.
4. I couldn't remember the words, so I hummed the **ballad**.
5. The **short story** held our attention.

Social Studies: Petroleum

Use these sentences to introduce the words and their meanings.
6. The **derrick** lifted a huge weight.
7. The woman stood on the **platform** to control the heavy machinery.
8. **Petroleum** was pumped from the ground.
9. The **tanker** transported the liquid to the factory.
10. The **pipeline** across Alaska can be damaged by extremely cold weather.

Word Study

Word History

Remind students that a word history, or **etymology,** traces the origin of a word and the development of its meaning. Etymologies are shown after the entry word in most dictionaries.

Unit 4 Home Spelling Practice

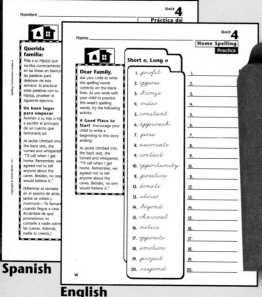

Spanish

English

MANAGING INSTRUCTION

Looking Ahead to Unit 4

To save time, you may wish to duplicate the **Unit 4 Home Spelling Practice** now. (See *Home Spelling Practice Book,* Unit 4.)

Basic Spelling List

profit	positive
oppose	donate
bronze	stereo
video	beyond
constant	charcoal
approach	notice
pose	opposite
associate	emotion
contact	project
opportunity	respond

Strategy Words

Review

colonist	promise
loaves	slope
Ohio	

Preview

oval	trophy
monotone	toxic
pronto	

Content Words

Language Arts: Periodicals

brochure	catalog
periodical	publication
pamphlet	

Science: The Environment

conservation	fertilizer
depletion	topsoil
erosion	

Individual Needs

Challenge Words

focus	commotion
melodious	congress
devote	monument

Alternate Word List ★

video	beyond
constant	notice
approach	opposite
opportunity	project
positive	respond

★ For students who need to study fewer Basic Spelling words

T26A

MATERIALS

Student Edition
Pages 26–31
Challenge Activities, p. 227

Teacher Edition
Pages T26A–T31
Challenge Activities, p. T227

Teacher Resource Book
Unit 4 Homework Master
Unit 4 Practice Masters
Flip Folder Practice Master
Unit 4 Test Master

Home Spelling Practice Book
Unit 4 Home Spelling Practice
(English or Spanish)

Other *Spelling Connections* Resources
- Audiotape, Grade 6
- Practice Book for Grammar, Usage, and Mechanics, Grade 6
- Spelling Support for Second Language Learners, Grade 6
- Support Software on CD-ROM
- Transparency Book, Grade 6
- Word Sort CD-ROM, Grade 6

OBJECTIVES

Spelling and Thinking
Students will
- **read** the spelling words in list form and in context.
- **sort** the spelling words according to **short o** and **long o** sounds and spelling patterns.
- **read** and remember this week's spelling strategy.

Spelling and Vocabulary
Students will
- **identify** spelling words that complete a series of meaning-related words.
- **use** sound and letter patterns to identify spelling words.
- **decode** dictionary respellings of spelling words with the same etymology.

Spelling and Reading
Students will
- **solve** analogies using spelling words.
- **use** context clues to complete sentences with spelling words.
- **replace** words in a paragraph with spelling words that have the same or nearly the same meaning.

Spelling and Writing
Students will
- **proofread** a description for a CD cover.
- **use** the writing process to write a description for a CD cover.
- **proofread** their writing.

MEETING INDIVIDUAL NEEDS
Learning Styles

 Visual

Make four columns on the chalkboard. Label them: 1) the **short o** sound; 2) the **long o** sound in an open syllable (i.e., a syllable that ends with a vowel); 3) the **long o** sound spelled **oa;** and 4) the **long o** sound spelled by the **o-consonant-e** pattern. Ask volunteers to write the spelling words under the appropriate headings. Make sure the students use the correct spellings.

 Auditory

Divide the class into four groups. To each group, assign one of the spellings of the /ŏ/ or /ō/ outlined in the visual activity. Have the students close their eyes as you read the spelling words. Tell the students to raise their hands when they hear a word that has the sound and spelling pattern assigned to their group.

 Kinesthetic

Play a form of "Charades" by dividing the class into two teams. Assign the spelling words with the /ŏ/ to one team, and the spelling words with the /ō/ to the other. Write each spelling word on a separate piece of paper. Then have pairs of team members take turns selecting one of the other team's words and acting out the word. The opposite team must not only guess the word, but must also spell it correctly.

> **Hands-On Practice**
> All students will benefit from practicing with a **Flip Folder**. See page Z18.

Language and Cultural Differences

Some students may have difficulty with the **long** and **short o** sounds because of regional pronunciation differences or language backgrounds that do not include the sound. For example, Spanish-speaking students may have some difficulty, since in the Spanish language /ō/ is always represented by the single letter **o.**

Write the word **video** on the chalkboard. Underline the letter **o.** Ask the students what spelling sound and pattern the letter **o** represents. (the long o sound in an open syllable at the end of a word) Follow this procedure to highlight the patterns that spell the **long o** sound. Use the word **oppose** to illustrate /ō/ in the **o-consonant-e** pattern, the word **charcoal** to illustrate /ō/ spelled **oa,** and the word **emotion** to illustrate /ō/ in an open syllable within a word.

MANAGING INSTRUCTION

3–5 Day Plan		Average	Below Average	Above Average
Day 1	**Day 1**	Pretest Spelling Mini-Lesson, p. T26 Spelling and Thinking, p. 26	Pretest Spelling Mini-Lesson, p. T26 Spelling and Thinking, p. 26	Pretest Spelling and Thinking, p. 26
	Day 2	Spelling and Vocabulary, p. 27	Spelling and Vocabulary, p. 27 (or) Unit 4 Practice Master, A and B	Spelling and Vocabulary, p. 27 Spelling and Reading, p. 28
Day 2	**Day 3**	Spelling and Reading, p. 28	Spelling and Reading, p. 28 (or) Unit 4 Practice Master, C and D	Challenge Activities, p. 227
	Day 4	Spelling and Writing, p. 29 Unit 4 Homework Master	Spelling and Writing, p. 29	Spelling and Writing, p. 29 Unit 4 Homework Master
Day 3	**Day 5**	Weekly Test	Weekly Test	Weekly Test

Vocabulary Connections (pages 30 and 31) may be used anytime during this unit.

Objectives

Spelling and Thinking

Students will
- **read** the spelling words in list form and in context.
- **sort** the spelling words according to **short o** and **long o** sounds and spelling patterns.
- **read** and remember this week's spelling strategy.

UNIT PRETEST

Use **Pretest Sentences** below. Refer to the self-checking procedures on student page 256. You may wish to use the **Unit 4 Word List Overhead Transparency** as part of the checking procedure.

TEACHING THE STRATEGY

Write the following words on the board: **profit, bronze, constant, contact, opportunity, positive, beyond, opposite, project,** and **respond.** Ask a volunteer to read the list. Ask, "Do these words have the **short o** sound or the **long o** sound?" (short o) Ask a volunteer to circle the letter that spells the **short o** sound in each word. (o)

Repeat the process for the following words: **oppose, video, approach, pose, associate, donate, stereo, charcoal, notice,** and **emotion.** Ask a volunteer to circle the letter(s) that spells the **long o** sound in each word. (o, as in donate and stereo; oa, as in charcoal; o-consonant-e, as in pose)

Remind the students that **vowel-consonant-e** usually signals a long vowel sound before the consonant. Challenge them to find exceptions to this guideline on this week's list involving **i-consonant-e.** (positive, opposite, notice)

Read **Remember the Spelling Strategy** on page 26.

Note: Video and **stereo** have interesting word histories that you may wish to share with the students.
- **Video** comes from the Latin word meaning "I see."
- **Stereo** is the shortened form of **stereophonic. Stereophonic** comes from two Greek words: **stereos,** meaning "solid," and **phone,** meaning "sound."

Order of answers may vary.
short o
1. profit
2. bronze
3. constant ★
4. contact
5. opportunity ★
6. positive ★
7. beyond ★
8. opposite ★
9. project ★
10. respond ★
long o
11. video ★
12. associate
13. donate
14. stereo
15. notice ★
16. emotion
o-consonant-e
17. oppose
18. pose
oa
19. approach ★
20. charcoal

READ THE SPELLING WORDS

1.	profit	*profit*	The store made a **profit** from the sale.
2.	oppose	*oppose*	The mayor will **oppose** the new highway.
3.	bronze	*bronze*	The lamp base is made of solid **bronze.**
4.	video	*video*	I watched a **video** about dog training.
5.	constant	*constant*	His **constant** humming was annoying.
6.	approach	*approach*	Slow down as you **approach** the light.
7.	pose	*pose*	The photographer asked us to **pose.**
8.	associate	*associate*	She consulted her business **associate.**
9.	contact	*contact*	I use the Internet to **contact** friends.
10.	opportunity	*opportunity*	I cannot pass up this **opportunity.**
11.	positive	*positive*	She is **positive** that she saw them.
12.	donate	*donate*	He will **donate** the proceeds to charity.
13.	stereo	*stereo*	The **stereo** speakers are ten feet apart.
14.	beyond	*beyond*	We drove **beyond** our destination.
15.	charcoal	*charcoal*	He sketched the portrait in **charcoal.**
16.	notice	*notice*	She did not **notice** the missing cookies.
17.	opposite	*opposite*	We stood on **opposite** sides of the room.
18.	emotion	*emotion*	He did not cry or show any **emotion.**
19.	project	*project*	The class **project** is nearly done.
20.	respond	*respond*	They did not **respond** to my phone call.

SORT THE SPELLING WORDS

1.–10. Write the words that spell **short o** as **o.**
11.–16. Write the words that spell **long o** as **o.**
17.–18. Write the words that spell **long o** as **o-consonant-e.**
19.–20. Write the words that spell **long o** as **oa.**

REMEMBER THE SPELLING STRATEGY

Remember that the **short o** sound in **bronze** is spelled **o.** The **long o** sound is spelled **o** in **notice, o-consonant-e** in **pose,** and **oa** in **approach.**

26

Pretest Sentences (See procedures on pages Z10–Z11.)

1. Our successful book sale makes a **profit** every year.
2. Will you agree to these plans, or will you **oppose** them?
3. The athlete received a **bronze** medal for third place.
★ 4. The **video** on the old TV set was often distorted.
★ 5. Young children seem to be in **constant** motion as they play.
★ 6. The timid child was afraid to **approach** the store Santa Claus.
7. Mom asked me to **pose** for a photograph on my birthday.
8. I always **associate** monkeys with bananas.
9. When the bike you ordered arrives, I will **contact** you.
★10. Our class may have the **opportunity** to visit the state capitol.
★11. Juanita was **positive** all her answers were correct.
12. Can you **donate** one hour of your time to this project?
13. The sound was much clearer on the new **stereo** system.
★14. I could not swat the fly because it flew **beyond** my reach.
15. The **charcoal** must be hot so the steak will cook properly.
★16. Did you **notice** the cost of admission to the circus?
★17. *Strong* is the **opposite** of *weak.*
18. At the game, the fans showed their **emotion** with cheers.
★19. Please describe the science **project** you have made.
★20. The teacher asked Tien to **respond** to the next question.

Spelling and Vocabulary

Word Groups

Write a spelling word to complete each sequence.

1. connect, communicate, _____
2. reaction, feeling, _____
3. answer, reply, _____
4. steady, continual, _____
5. chance, occasion, _____
6. connect, correlate, _____
7. give, provide, _____
8. past, farther, _____
9. announcement, report, _____

Sound and Letter Patterns

10.–13. Write the spelling words that begin with a two-letter consonant cluster.

14.–15. Write the spelling words that begin or end with **ch**.

16. Write the spelling word that begins like **voice** and ends in two long vowel sounds.

USING THE Dictionary

A dictionary entry provides the history or origin of some words. This is called **etymology**. Four of the spelling words trace back to the Latin word **ponere**, meaning "to put or place." Write the spelling words for the dictionary respellings of these four words.

17. /ə pōz′/
18. /pŏz′ ĭ tĭv/
19. /ŏp′ ə zĭt/
20. /pōz/

Word Groups
1. contact
2. emotion
3. respond
4. constant
5. opportunity
6. associate
7. donate
8. beyond
9. notice

Sound and Letter Patterns
10. profit
11. bronze
12. stereo
13. project
14. approach
15. charcoal
16. video

Using the Dictionary
17. oppose
18. positive
19. opposite
20. pose

27

Developing Oral Language Skills

Help students work in teams using dictionaries to develop three- or four-word sentences that contain words beginning with **short o** or **long o** sounds. Have them take turns reading these sentences to the rest of the class. A sample sentence might be "Oceans hold odd opportunities." Have a volunteer read the sentence aloud, write the sentence on the chalkboard, and underline the letters that spell the **short o** or **long o** sounds.

MEETING INDIVIDUAL NEEDS

Providing More Help

For students who need help in hearing the **short o** and **long o** sounds, use the pairs of words below. First, pronounce both words together. Then pronounce one word at a time and have the students clap after you say the word that has either the /ō/ or /ŏ/. Then repeat with the same word pairs. This time have the students stand up when you pronounce a word that has the /ō/.

1. ship, **shop**
2. **explode**, shame
3. **stone**, shape
4. clap, **notice**
5. friend, **foam**
6. try, **pole**

★Students who need to study fewer words should use the **Alternate Word List**. This list is starred on page T26 in the Teacher Edition. The **Unit 4 Practice Masters** (*Teacher Resource Book*) provide additional practice with these words.

Unit 4 Practice Masters

Name _____
Practice Master 4

1. constant 3. beyond 5. positive 7. opportunity 9. approach
2. project 4. respond 6. opposite 8. notice 10. video

A. Fill in the missing vowels to form spelling words. Write the words.

1. n __ tice _____
2. vid __ __ _____
3. bey __ nd _____
4. __ pportunity _____
5. c __ nstant _____
6. appr __ __ ch _____
7. p __ sitive _____
8. resp __ nd _____
9. __ pp __ site _____
10. pr __ ject _____

B. Write the spelling words in alphabetical order.

1. _____ 6. _____
2. _____ 7. _____
3. _____ 8. _____
4. _____ 9. _____
5. _____ 10. _____

Objectives

Spelling and Reading

Students will
- **solve** analogies using spelling words.
- **use** context clues to complete sentences with spelling words.
- **replace** words in a paragraph with spelling words that have the same or nearly the same meaning.

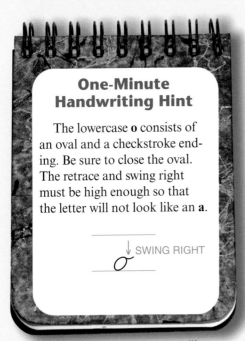

One-Minute Handwriting Hint

The lowercase **o** consists of an oval and a checkstroke ending. Be sure to close the oval. The retrace and swing right must be high enough so that the letter will not look like an **a**.

↓ SWING RIGHT

Legible handwriting can boost spelling scores by as much as 20%.

Solve the Analogies
1. opportunity
2. profit
3. emotion
4. charcoal
5. associate

Complete the Sentences
6. stereo
7. contact
8. beyond
9. opposite
10. approach
11. respond
12. constant

Complete the Paragraph
13. project
14. bronze
15. positive
16. donate
17. oppose
18. notice
19. pose
20. video

28

Spelling and Reading

profit	oppose	bronze	video	constant
approach	pose	associate	contact	opportunity
positive	donate	stereo	beyond	charcoal
notice	opposite	emotion	project	respond

Solve the Analogies   Write a spelling word to complete each analogy.

1. **Fame** is to **stardom** as **chance** is to _____.
2. **Defeat** is to **victory** as **loss** is to _____.
3. **Regret** is to **mistake** as **feel** is to _____.
4. **White** is to **snow** as **black** is to _____.
5. **Opponent** is to **rival** as **co-worker** is to _____.

Complete the Sentences   Write a spelling word to complete each sentence.

6. The live concert was reproduced in _____.
7. The school needs to know whom to _____ in an emergency.
8. We walked two blocks _____ the park.
9. My reaction to the book was the _____ of his.
10. You will recognize the building as you _____ it.
11. Please _____ to the invitation by Friday.
12. We heard the _____ roar of the waterfall.

Complete the Paragraph   Write the spelling words that could replace the boldfaced words in the paragraph.

Spectators at the race asked the chairman to **direct** his voice [13.] when he announced the winner of the **metal** trophy. [14.] The winner said she was **certain** that she would **give** the prize money to the [15.] [16.] animal shelter. The chairman did not **resist** her request. [17.] He asked the racers to **pay attention to** the woman with the camera and [18.] **hold their expression** for her. [19.] He also invited them to watch the **taped recording** of the race. [20.]

MEETING INDIVIDUAL NEEDS

Providing More Challenge

Challenge Words and **Challenge Activities** for Unit 4 appear on page 227. **Challenge Word Test Sentences** appear on page T227.

Unit 4 Challenge Activities

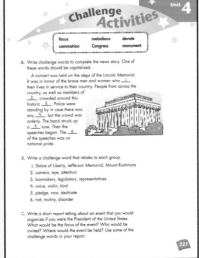

Weekly Test Options

Option 1:
One Spelling Word Per Sentence
(See procedures on pages Z10–Z11.)

★ 1. We are traveling westward and will soon **approach** Montana.
2. He is my close friend and **associate**.
★ 3. Do you think we will ever travel **beyond** the stars?
4. The meat was cooking over the **charcoal** fire.
★ 5. She is my **constant** companion.
6. One way to get in **contact** with a friend is to write a letter.
7. I liked the **bronze** statue in the museum best of all.
8. We always **donate** our old clothes to those in need.
9. Love is a powerful **emotion**.
★10. I hope you will **notice** the lovely roses.
★11. We had an **opportunity** to go sailing.
12. Dad is sure to **oppose** those plans.
★13. The **opposite** of forget is remember.
14. I will **pose** before the stone wall.

Spelling and Writing

 Proofread a Description for a CD Cover

Six words are not spelled correctly in this description for a CD cover. Write the words correctly.

The Groovie Brothers' Greatest Hits

respond
Ben and Joe Groovie responde to their fans
with this medley of their most popular songs. Ben
project   *beyond*
said that although the prodgect went beyond the
opportunity
six-month completion date, it was a rare oportunity
for the two brothers to sing together again. They
donate   *profit*
plan to donait the prophit from the sales of the home
video to charity.

Proofreading Marks

≡	Make a capital.
/	Make a small letter.
∧	Add something.
ℒ	Take out something.
⊙	Add a period.
⊹	New paragraph
⒮⒫	Spelling error

✏️ **Write the Description for a CD Cover** *Descriptive Writing*

A musical CD cover is designed to capture your interest. Write the description for a CD.

- Describe the musicians and their music.
- What is special about the music?
- Follow the form used in the proofreading sample.

Use as many spelling words as you can.

Proofread Your Writing During →

Proofread your writing for spelling errors as part of the editing stage in the writing process. Be sure to check each word carefully. Use a dictionary to check spelling if you are not sure.

Writing Process

Prewriting
⇓
Drafting
⇓
Revising
⇓
Editing
⇓
Publishing

29

★15. Are you **positive** that this will be included on the test?
16. A concert will **profit** the school in many ways.
★17. Do you think his **project** will win the contest?
★18. How did the patient **respond** to the treatment?
19. Her **stereo** system is broken.
★20. We must not touch Dad's **video** camera.

Option 2:
Multiple Spelling Words Per Sentence
(See procedures on pages Z10–Z11.)

1. Our **video** player includes a **stereo** sound system.
2. I **oppose** asking her business **associate** to **donate** money to the **project**.
3. They have an **opportunity** to **profit** from her **approach**.
4. In the **pose** of the woman in **bronze**, the artist captured a strong **emotion**.
5. There is a **constant contact** between the two sisters.
6. Did you **notice** a car on the **opposite** side of the street?
7. Are you **positive, beyond** all doubt, that this is true?
8. How did she **respond** to the **charcoal** drawing?

Option 3:
Standardized Test
(See *Teacher Resource Book,* Unit 4)

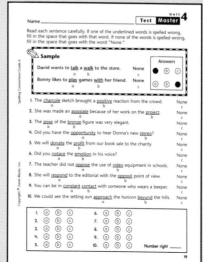

Unit 4 Test Master

Objectives

Strategy Words

Students will
- **review** words studied previously that are related to the spelling strategy.
- **preview** unknown words that are related to the spelling strategy.

VOCABULARY CONNECTIONS

▶Strategy Words◀

Remind the students that the **Strategy Words** are related to the spelling patterns they have studied in this unit. The **Review Words** are below grade level, and the **Preview Words** are above grade level. You may wish to use the following sentences to introduce the words in context.

Review Words:
Words From Grade 5

1. One **colonist** was chosen as leader of the group.
2. Mother bought three **loaves** of bread at the grocery store.
3. I have a friend who lives in **Ohio**.
4. Did you **promise** that you would write to him?
5. The steep **slope** of this hill makes it fun for sledding in the winter.

Preview Words:
Words From Grade 7

6. Our new track forms an **oval** around the football field.
7. The **monotone** of the speaker's voice put us to sleep.
8. Mother said, "Please come **pronto**."
9. Our team worked hard to win the championship **trophy**.
10. The bottle was marked **toxic,** so we kept it out of reach of my younger brother.

Review Words
1. colonist
2. Ohio
3. loaves
4. slope
5. promise

Preview Words
6. pronto
7. monotone
8. trophy
9. toxic
10. oval

▶Strategy Words◀

Review Words: Short o, Long o

Write words from the box to complete the paragraph.

colonist	loaves	Ohio	promise	slope

It was May of 1787. The __1.__ and his family were settling in a part of the country that would later become the state of __2.__. Just a few __3.__ of bread remained at the end of the long trip. They built a log cabin on a __4.__ overlooking their newly cleared farmland. Their future held much __5.__.

Preview Words: Short o, Long o

Write the word from the box that matches each clue.

oval	monotone	pronto	trophy	toxic

6. It is an informal way of saying **immediately**.
7. It begins with **mono**, which means "one" or "single."
8. This goes to the winner of the race.
9. It is a synonym for **poisonous**.
10. An egg has this shape.

30

Unit 4 RECAP

You may wish to assign the **Unit 4 Homework Master** (*Teacher Resource Book*, Unit 4) as a fun way to recap the spelling words.

Unit 4 Homework Master

Name _____

Some vowel letters are missing from the words. Write the missing letter or letters in each word.

stere ____   appr ____   ch ____ bey ____ nd
br ____ nze   resp ____ nd   ass ____ ciate
charc ____ l   em ____ tion   opp ____ s ____
d ____ nate   n ____ tice   c ____ nstant
p ____ s   vide ____   pr ____ fit
p ____ sitive   pr ____ ject
____ pportunity

Now write the completed words in alphabetical order.

1. ____   7. ____   13. ____
2. ____   8. ____   14. ____
3. ____   9. ____   15. ____
4. ____   10. ____   16. ____
5. ____   11. ____   17. ____
6. ____   12. ____   18. ____

Write a sentence using the words **contact** and **opposite**.

_____

20

◄Content Words►

Language Arts: Periodicals

Write the word from the box that fits each clue.

brochure periodical pamphlet catalog publication

1. It begins with a /k/ sound spelled **c**.
2. It has a **long e** sound spelled **i**.
3. It has an /f/ sound spelled **ph**.
4. It has an /sh/ sound spelled **ch**.
5. It ends like **vacation**.

Science: The Environment

Write the words from the box to complete the paragraph.

conservation depletion erosion fertilizer topsoil

Imagine you woke up and found that all the surface layer of earth, or __6.__, had washed away. Heavy rain can cause __7.__ of unprotected land. A loss of vegetation will result in a __8.__ of the soil's basic components. Using __9.__ can help restore the loss, but it can be harmful to our water supply. We must create __10.__ laws that will protect all our valuable resources.

Apply the Spelling Strategy

Circle the letters that spell the **short o** or the **long o** sound in five of the Content Words you wrote.

◄Word Study►

Words From Native American Languages

The Iroquois used a word for a certain large river far south of Lake Erie. It meant "something great." Later, the same word was used to name a state bordering this river. Write the Strategy Word that came from this Iroquois history.

31

Language Arts: Periodicals
1. catal(o)g
2. peri(o)dical
3. pamphlet
4. br(o)chure
5. publication

Science: The Environment
6. t(o)psoil
7. er(o)sion
8. depletion
9. fertilizer
10. c(o)nservation

Words From Native American Languages
1. Ohio

Objectives

Content Words

Students will
- **expand** vocabulary with content-related words.
- **relate** the spelling strategy to words outside the basic spelling list.
- **understand** that some words are borrowed from other languages.

◄Content Words►

Language Arts: Periodicals

Use these sentences to introduce the words and their meanings.

1. The **brochure** came from the famous hotel.
2. My favorite **periodical** is *Time*.
3. We asked for a **pamphlet** on dogs.
4. This **catalog** gives us many choices.
5. The **publication** date is at the front of the book.

Science: The Environment

Use these sentences to introduce the words and their meanings.

6. We are learning better methods of **conservation** every day.
7. The **depletion** of natural resources is a worry.
8. Wind and water cause **erosion**.
9. Farmers add **fertilizer** to replenish lost nutrients in the soil.
10. Good **topsoil** is vital to plants.

◄Word Study►

Words From Native American Languages

The names of many places in the United States trace their origins to Native American languages. Challenge students to suggest other place names, besides **Ohio,** that have come into English from Native American languages. Possibilities include both **Chicago** and **Illinois**.

Unit 5 Home Spelling Practice

Spanish

English

MANAGING INSTRUCTION

Looking Ahead to Unit 5

To save time, you may wish to duplicate the **Unit 5 Home Spelling Practice** now. (See *Home Spelling Practice Book,* Unit 5.)

MATERIALS

Student Edition
Pages 32–37
Challenge Activities, p. 228

Teacher Edition
Pages T32A–T37
Challenge Activities, p. T228

Teacher Resource Book
Unit 5 Homework Master
Unit 5 Practice Masters
Flip Folder Practice Master
Unit 5 Test Master

Home Spelling Practice Book
Unit 5 Home Spelling Practice
(English or Spanish)

Other *Spelling Connections* Resources
- Audiotape, Grade 6
- Practice Book for Grammar, Usage, and Mechanics, Grade 6
- Spelling Support for Second Language Learners, Grade 6
- Support Software on CD-ROM
- Transparency Book, Grade 6
- Word Sort CD-ROM, Grade 6

Basic Spelling List

stubborn	smudge
computer	custody
customer	bugle
contribute	confuse
budge	acute
barbecue	insult
union	suffer
dispute	punish
community	accuse
uniform	result

Strategy Words

Review

amuse	unit
discuss	value
publish	

Preview

commute	tuxedo
culprit	unison
mutual	

Content Words

Fine Arts: Canvas, Pen, and Thread

pigment	hue
mural	etching
tapestry	

Science: Measurement

capacity	velocity
volume	mass
dimensions	

Individual Needs

Challenge Words

confusion	continual
strenuous	punishment
substance	sculpture

Alternate Word List ★

stubborn	community
computer	confuse
customer	suffer
contribute	punish
barbecue	result

★ For students who need to study fewer Basic Spelling words

OBJECTIVES

Spelling and Thinking
Students will
- **read** the spelling words in list form and in context.
- **sort** the spelling words according to **short u** and **long u** sounds and spelling patterns.
- **read** and remember this week's spelling strategy.

Spelling and Vocabulary
Students will
- **identify** spelling words that complete a series of meaning-related words.
- **supply** the missing syllables to write spelling words.
- **use** word origins to identify spelling words.

Spelling and Reading
Students will
- **use** context clues to complete sentences.
- **solve** analogies using spelling words.
- **complete** a paragraph using spelling words.

Spelling and Writing
Students will
- **proofread** a list of rules.
- **use** the writing process to write a list of rules.
- **proofread** their writing.

MEETING INDIVIDUAL NEEDS

Learning Styles

Visual

Write each spelling word on a separate piece of paper and fold the paper in half, with the word inside. On the chalkboard make two columns—one labeled **the short u sound** and the other labeled **the long u sound**. Have the students take turns choosing a paper with a spelling word and writing that word under the appropriate heading on the chalkboard.

Hands-On Practice
All students will benefit from practicing with a **Flip Folder**. See page Z18.

Auditory

As you read the spelling words aloud, have the students listen carefully to the difference between the **short u** and **long u** sounds. Then read the spelling words again, but this time have the students clap once after each word that contains the /ŭ/ and twice after each word that contains the /yōō/.

Kinesthetic

Let students choose a partner. Have each pair write five spelling words with /ŭ/ and five spelling words with /yōō/ on 3" × 5" cards. (Students should write one word per card.) Then have them write ten words with neither /ŭ/ or /yōō/ on cards.

The goal is to collect all cards with either /ŭ/ or /yōō/. Five cards are dealt to each player. The rest are placed face-down. The first player draws a card and discards another. The other player can pick up that card or draw a card before discarding. Play continues until one player gets all five cards with the /ŭ/ or /yōō/.

Language and Cultural Differences

The /yōō/ and the /ŭ/ may be difficult for some students to hear and spell due to regional pronunciations or language backgrounds that do not include these sounds or that spell them differently. If the students have trouble pronouncing the spelling words, first make sure they know what the words mean. Have volunteers make up sentences using the words, or explain the meanings of

the words yourself. Expand or clarify the students' definitions as necessary.

Next, ask the students to look at how each word is spelled as you write it on the chalkboard. Underline the appropriate vowel(s) in each word. Pronounce each word and have the students repeat it in unison.

MANAGING INSTRUCTION

3–5 Day Plan		Average	Below Average	Above Average
Day 1	**Day 1**	Pretest Spelling Mini-Lesson, p. T32 Spelling and Thinking, p. 32	Pretest Spelling Mini-Lesson, p. T32 Spelling and Thinking, p. 32	Pretest Spelling and Thinking, p. 32
	Day 2	Spelling and Vocabulary, p. 33	Spelling and Vocabulary, p. 33 (or) Unit 5 Practice Master, A and B	Spelling and Vocabulary, p. 33 Spelling and Reading, p. 34
Day 2	**Day 3**	Spelling and Reading, p. 34	Spelling and Reading, p. 34 (or) Unit 5 Practice Master, C and D	Challenge Activities, p. 228
	Day 4	Spelling and Writing, p. 35 Unit 5 Homework Master	Spelling and Writing, p. 35	Spelling and Writing, p. 35 Unit 5 Homework Master
Day 3	**Day 5**	Weekly Test	Weekly Test	Weekly Test
Vocabulary Connections (pages 36 and 37) may be used anytime during this unit.				

Objectives

Spelling and Thinking

Students will
- **read** the spelling words in list form and in context.
- **sort** the spelling words according to **short u** and **long u** sounds and spelling patterns.
- **read** and remember this week's spelling strategy.

UNIT PRETEST

Use **Pretest Sentences** below. Refer to the self-checking procedures on student page 256. You may wish to use the **Unit 5 Word List Overhead Transparency** as part of the checking procedure.

TEACHING THE STRATEGY

Spelling Mini-Lesson

Write this sentence on the board:
> The United States of America was the result of the union of the thirteen original colonies.

Ask a volunteer to identify the word in the sentence with the **short u** sound spelled **u**. (result) Ask another volunteer to identify the words with the **long u** sound. (union, United)

Write **result** on the board under /ŭ/ and **union** and **United** under /yōō/. Remind the students that these are the dictionary symbols for the **short u** and **long u** sounds.

Encourage volunteers to write each spelling word in the column that matches the **u** vowel sound in that word. Ask the students to identify the spelling patterns used to spell each sound. (Short u is spelled u. Long u is spelled u, as in union; ue, as in barbecue; and u-consonant-e, as in acute.)

Ask the students to identify the base words in **computer** and **community**. (compute, commune) Explain that **long u** in **computer** and **community** is derived from the **u-consonant-e** pattern in the base words.

Read **Remember the Spelling Strategy** on page 32.

T32

Spelling and Thinking

Order of answers may vary.

short u
1. stubborn ★
2. customer ★
3. budge
4. smudge
5. custody
6. insult
7. suffer ★
8. punish ★
9. result ★

long u
10. computer ★
11. union
12. community ★
13. uniform
14. bugle

u-consonant-e and ue
15. contribute ★
16. barbecue ★
17. dispute
18. confuse ★
19. acute
20. accuse

 32

READ THE SPELLING WORDS

1.	stubborn	*stubborn*	The **stubborn** man will not move.
2.	computer	*computer*	Our files are on the **computer**.
3.	customer	*customer*	The **customer** waited in line.
4.	contribute	*contribute*	I will **contribute** to the charity.
5.	budge	*budge*	We could not **budge** the heavy rock.
6.	barbecue	*barbecue*	I will serve chicken at the **barbecue**.
7.	union	*union*	The first colonies formed a **union**.
8.	dispute	*dispute*	The company settled the **dispute**.
9.	community	*community*	We planned a **community** picnic.
10.	uniform	*uniform*	All officers will wear a **uniform**.
11.	smudge	*smudge*	The paint will **smudge** if it is wet.
12.	custody	*custody*	The thief is in police **custody**.
13.	bugle	*bugle*	You will hear the **bugle** at dawn.
14.	confuse	*confuse*	Too many details will **confuse** us.
15.	acute	*acute*	A bad sprain causes **acute** pain.
16.	insult	*insult*	His thoughtless comments **insult** her.
17.	suffer	*suffer*	Some people **suffer** from back pain.
18.	punish	*punish*	We had to **punish** our puppy once.
19.	accuse	*accuse*	Do not **accuse** me of laziness.
20.	result	*result*	The game **result** was announced.

SORT THE SPELLING WORDS

1.–9. Write the spelling words with the **short u** sound.

10.–14. Write the words with the **long u** sound spelled **u**.

15.–20. Write the words with the **long u** sound spelled **u-consonant-e** or **ue**.

REMEMBER THE SPELLING STRATEGY

Remember the **short u** sound in **result** is spelled **u**. The **long u** sound is spelled **u** in **union**, **u-consonant-e** in **acute**, and **ue** in **barbecue**.

Pretest Sentences (See procedures on pages Z10–Z11.)

★ 1. He is very **stubborn**, and he always wants his own way.

★ 2. I like to do my math homework on my **computer**.

★ 3. Mr. Chapman treated each **customer** with courtesy.

★ 4. I was asked to **contribute** my time to the school fair.

5. The camel would not **budge**, though its owner tugged.

★ 6. To me, chicken tastes best with **barbecue** sauce.

7. The United States is a **union** of individual states.

8. The neighbors had a **dispute** about that section of land.

★ 9. The **community** in which I live has many restaurants.

10. The nurse wore a white **uniform**.

11. I got a **smudge** of chalk dust on my sweater.

12. The keys to the building are in the **custody** of Ms. Nugent.

13. Felisa learned how to play a trumpet and a **bugle**.

★14. Did my directions **confuse** you or help you?

15. Because I ate too much, the pains in my stomach were **acute**.

16. When you talk about a person, make a kind remark, not an **insult**.

★17. No one wants to see another person **suffer** in pain.

★18. Do not **punish** a puppy harshly for making a mistake.

19. I will not **accuse** anyone of taking my pen until I search for it.

★20. Did you hear the **result** of the election?

Spelling and Vocabulary

Word Groups

Write a spelling word to complete each group.

1. trumpet, horn, _____
2. safekeeping, care, _____
3. picnic, cookout, _____
4. difficult, inflexible, _____
5. discipline, reprimand, _____
6. mark, smear, _____
7. blame, criticize, _____
8. outcome, effect, _____
9. argue, debate, _____
10. baffle, puzzle, _____
11. keyboard, monitor, _____
12. move, advance, _____

Letters and Syllables

Add the missing syllable and write a spelling word.

13. con_ _ _ _ute   15. suf_ _ _   17. _ _sult
14. _ _ _tomer   16. a_ _ _ _

USING THE Dictionary

A dictionary often provides the history or origin of a word. Write the spelling words that have these similar origins.

18. From Latin **unus,** and **forma,** meaning "shape."
19. From Latin **unus** meaning "one."
20. From Latin **communis,** meaning "common."

Word Groups
1. bugle
2. custody
3. barbecue
4. stubborn
5. punish
6. smudge
7. accuse
8. result
9. dispute
10. confuse
11. computer
12. budge

Letters and Syllables
13. contribute
14. customer
15. suffer
16. acute
17. insult

Using the Dictionary
18. uniform
19. union
20. community

33

Objectives

Spelling and Vocabulary

Students will
- **identify** spelling words that complete a series of meaning-related words.
- **supply** the missing syllables to write spelling words.
- **use** word origins to identify spelling words.

Developing Oral Language Skills

Ask a volunteer to say each spelling word and transpose the sound of **u,** i.e., if the sound is **long u,** pronounce it as a **short u** and vice-versa. So, **stubborn** would be pronounced /stūbrn/. The students should call out the correct pronunciation and spelling as soon as they know it.

MEETING INDIVIDUAL NEEDS

Providing More Help

On the chalkboard, write the headings **the long u sound** and **the short u sound**. Write each syllable of each spelling word on a flash card. For instance, **uniform** would have three cards: **u, ni, form**. Put the cards for each word in random order on the chalkboard ledge and ask a volunteer to arrange the cards so that they form a spelling word. Then have another volunteer write the spelling word on the chalkboard under the proper heading.

★Students who need to study fewer words should use the **Alternate Word List**. This list is starred on page T32 in the Teacher Edition. **The Unit 5 Practice Masters** (*Teacher Resource Book*) provide additional practice with these words.

Unit 5 Practice Masters

Objectives

Spelling and Reading

Students will

- **use** context clues to complete sentences.
- **solve** analogies using spelling words.
- **complete** a paragraph using spelling words.

One-Minute Handwriting Hint

There are two undercurve slant motions in the lowercase **u.** Be sure to pause after the two undercurves. The two slant strokes should be parallel.

PAUSES

Legible handwriting can boost spelling scores by as much as 20%.

Complete the Sentences

1. smudge
2. insult
3. custody
4. stubborn
5. punish
6. barbecue

Solve the Analogies

7. community
8. uniform
9. bugle
10. customer
11. computer
12. acute
13. confuse

Complete the Paragraph

14. union
15. suffer
16. contribute
17. budge
18. accuse
19. result
20. dispute

Spelling and Reading

stubborn	computer	customer	contribute	budge
barbecue	union	dispute	community	uniform
smudge	custody	bugle	confuse	acute
insult	suffer	punish	accuse	result

Complete the Sentences Write spelling words to complete the sentences.

1. The ink left a _____ on the paper.
2. I did not mean to _____ you with my critical remark.
3. The parents have joint _____ of the children.
4. He was too _____ to listen to my explanation.
5. I hope they will not _____ me for being late.
6. We will hold the _____ in spite of the rain.

Solve the Analogies Write a spelling word to complete each analogy.

7. **Country** is to **nation** as **neighborhood** is to _____.
8. **Actor** is to **costume** as **officer** is to _____.
9. **Painting** is to **brush** as **music** is to _____.
10. **Hospital** is to **patient** as **store** is to _____.
11. **Photographer** is to **camera** as **programmer** is to _____.
12. **Safe** is to **dangerous** as **mild** is to _____.
13. **Depart** is to **arrive** as **clarify** is to _____.

Complete the Paragraph Write the spelling words from the box that complete the paragraph.

Members of the postal __14.__ were willing to __15.__ the consequences of a strike. The workers said they would __16.__ some of their pay, but the employers refused to __17.__. Each side was eager to __18.__ the other of unfair practices. The __19.__ of this __20.__ is that we are still waiting to receive our mail.

accuse
dispute
budge
contribute
union
suffer
result

34

MEETING INDIVIDUAL NEEDS

Providing More Challenge

Challenge Words and **Challenge Activities** for Unit 5 appear on page 228. **Challenge Word Test Sentences** appear on page T228.

Unit 5 Challenge Activities

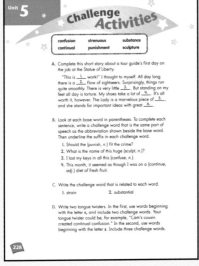

Weekly Test Options

Option 1:
One Spelling Word Per Sentence

(See procedures on pages Z10–Z11.)

1. Did he **accuse** you of having a messy desk?
2. The student had an **acute** sense of direction.
★ 3. In summer we always cook outdoors on a **barbecue**.
4. He did not **budge** when his alarm went off.
5. We could hear the sound of a **bugle** playing far away.
★ 6. Our **community** holds a music festival every year.
★ 7. A **computer** has many fascinating uses.
★ 8. Do not **confuse** me by telling me so many things at once.
★ 9. Will you **contribute** some useful items to our street fair?
10. The puppy was put in the **custody** of its new owners.
★11. The **customer** bought flowers from the florist.
12. Their argument turned into a full-scale **dispute**.
13. That **insult** hurt his feelings.
★14. Would you like to discuss the **result** of your work?
15. The mother wiped the **smudge** off her child's face.

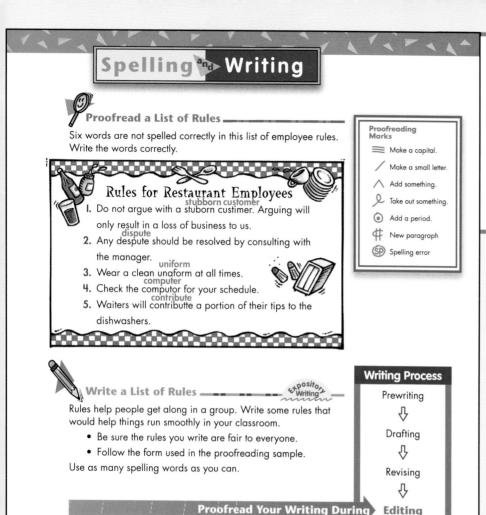

Spelling and Writing

Proofread a List of Rules

Six words are not spelled correctly in this list of employee rules. Write the words correctly.

Rules for Restaurant Employees

1. Do not argue with a stuborn custimer. Arguing will
   only result in a loss of business to us.
   stubborn customer
2. Any despute should be resolved by consulting with
   the manager.
   dispute
3. Wear a clean unaform at all times.
   uniform
4. Check the computor for your schedule.
   computer
5. Waiters will contributte a portion of their tips to the
   dishwashers.
   contribute

Proofreading Marks

≡ Make a capital.
/ Make a small letter.
∧ Add something.
⌇ Take out something.
⊙ Add a period.
New paragraph
SP Spelling error

Write a List of Rules

Expository Writing

Rules help people get along in a group. Write some rules that
would help things run smoothly in your classroom.
- Be sure the rules you write are fair to everyone.
- Follow the form used in the proofreading sample.
Use as many spelling words as you can.

Writing Process

Prewriting
⇩
Drafting
⇩
Revising
⇩
Editing
⇩
Publishing

Proofread Your Writing During → **Editing**

Proofread your writing for spelling errors as part of the editing
stage in the writing process. Be sure to check each word
carefully. Use a dictionary to check spelling if you are not sure.

35

Objectives

Spelling and Writing
Students will
- **proofread** a list of rules.
- **use** the writing process to write a list of rules.
- **proofread** their writing.

Using the Writing Process

Before assigning **Write a List of Rules,** see pages 258–259 in the Student Edition for a complete review of the writing process and additional writing assignments. You may also wish to refer to pages Z12–Z13 in the Teacher Edition.

Keeping a Spelling Journal

Encourage students to record the words they misspelled on the weekly test in a personal spelling journal. These words may be recycled for future study. Students may also wish to include words from their writing. See pages Z12–Z13 in the Teacher Edition for more information.

★16. Try not to be **stubborn,** and you will get along well.
★17. In summer, many people **suffer** from the heat.
★18. When I do not try to do my best, I only **punish** myself.
19. What color are your school **uniforms**?
20. The football players formed a **union**.

Option 2:
Multiple Spelling Words Per Sentence
(See procedures on pages Z10–Z11.)

1. Our **community** will **contribute** to the **barbecue**.
2. Will you **punish** the **stubborn** boy if he does not play his **bugle** for the audience?
3. The **customer** asked which **computer** to buy.
4. Her **uniform** had a big **smudge** across the front.
5. What was the **result** of the long **dispute**?
6. She seems to **suffer** from an **acute** pain in her head.
7. It is an **insult** to **accuse** someone of evil.
8. The lawyer would not **budge** from his stand in the **custody** case.
9. The **union** leader seemed to **confuse** the members.

Option 3:
Standardized Test
(See *Teacher Resource Book,* Unit 5.)

**Unit 5
Test Master**

Objectives

Strategy Words

Students will
- **review** words studied previously that are related to the spelling strategy.
- **preview** unknown words that are related to the spelling strategy.

Unit 5 enrichment

VOCABULARY CONNECTIONS

►Strategy Words◄

Remind the students that the **Strategy Words** relate to the spelling patterns they have studied in this unit. The **Review Words** are below grade level, and the **Preview Words** are above grade level. You may wish to use the following sentences to introduce the words in context.

Review Words:
Words From Grade 5

1. I really believe this book will **amuse** you.
2. Please **discuss** this with your parents.
3. They hope to **publish** the book soon.
4. We will study fractions in the next math **unit**.
5. Do you realize the **value** of a good education?

Preview Words:
Words From Grade 7

6. His **commute** to work takes thirty minutes.
7. Who was the **culprit** that damaged the door?
8. We have a **mutual** friend in Texas.
9. His father wore a **tuxedo** to the wedding.
10. When asked if they wanted a story, the children responded, "Yes," in **unison**.

Review Words
1. discuss
2. publish
3. value
4. amuse
5. unit

Preview Words
6. mutual
7. tuxedo
8. unison
9. commute
10. culprit

►Strategy Words◄

Review Words: Short u, Long u

Write words from the box to complete the letter.

| amuse | discuss | publish | unit | value |

Dear Editor,

I would like to __1.__ a recent article. I wonder why you __2.__ material like this, since it appears to have no __3.__. Perhaps your intent is to __4.__ the reader. Well, you can decrease the number of copies to print by a __5.__ of one, because I have canceled my subscription.

Sincerely,

I. M. Annoyed

Preview Words: Short u, Long u

Write the word from the box that matches each clue.

| commute | culprit | mutual | tuxedo | unison |

6. My friend and I have many _____ interests.
7. He rented a _____ to wear to the wedding.
8. The musical group sang in _____.
9. She has a one-hour _____ to work.
10. The fingerprints led us to the _____.

36

Unit 5 RECAP

You may wish to assign the **Unit 5 Homework Master** (*Teacher Resource Book*, Unit 5) as a fun way to recap the spelling words.

Unit 5 Homework Master

Name _____

Homework Master Unit 5

Decode the spelling words by replacing each letter with the letter that comes before it in the alphabet.

Example: d-v-t-u-p-e-z *custody*

1. v o j p o
c b s c f d v f
2. t n v e h f
3. v o j g p s n
4. t v g g f s
5. d p o u s j c v u f
6. q v o j t i
7.

8. d p n n v o j u z
d p n q v u f s
9. t v v c c p s o
10. b d d v t f
11. d p o g v t f
12. e j t q v u f
13. d v t u p n f s
14.

Five spelling words are hidden in these puzzles. Begin at the arrows. Move across, down, and up to find the letters that spell each word. Write the spelling words.

a	e	b
c	g	u
u	l	d
t	e	g

1. _____
2. _____
3. _____

i	e	r
n	s	f
o	u	l
d	g	t

4. _____
5. _____

24

Content Words

Fine Arts: Canvas, Pen, and Thread

Write a word from the box to complete each sentence.

pigment	mural	tapestry	hue	etching

1. We hung the woven _____ on the wall.
2. **Color** is a synonym for _____.
3. The wall is decorated with a painted _____.
4. The artist added green _____ to the paint.
5. An _____ is a design made from a metal plate.

Science: Measurement

Write the word from the box that matches each clue.

capacity	volume	dimensions	velocity	mass

6. This is the amount of space an object occupies.
7. The weight of an object can change, but this will always stay the same.
8. These are the measurements of length, width, and height.
9. This is the rate at which an object moves in a specific direction.
10. This is the amount that something can hold.

Apply the Spelling Strategy

Circle the letters that spell the **long u** sound **ue** or **u-consonant-e** in two of the Content Words you wrote.

Word Study

Toponyms

A **toponym** is a word that comes from the name of a certain place. The **canary,** a bright yellow songbird, was named for its home in the Canary Islands. Write the Strategy Word for a formal men's suit that came from the name of the town in New York where this suit was first worn.

37

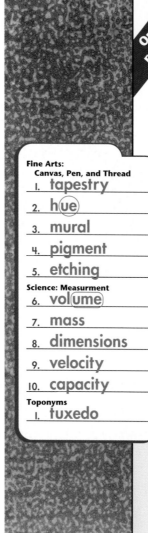

Fine Arts:
Canvas, Pen, and Thread
1. tapestry
2. hue
3. mural
4. pigment
5. etching

Science: Measurment
6. volume
7. mass
8. dimensions
9. velocity
10. capacity

Toponyms
1. tuxedo

Objectives

Content Words

Students will
- **expand** vocabulary with content-related words.
- **relate** the spelling strategy to words outside the basic spelling list.
- **understand** and identify a toponym.

Content Words

Fine Arts:
Canvas, Pen, and Thread

Use these sentences to introduce the words and their meanings.
1. The **pigment** used in the painting was a good match.
2. Our class project was to complete the **mural** on the wall.
3. The **tapestry** hanging in the museum was very old and fragile.
4. It was difficult to decide which **hue** would best match the carpet.
5. The **etching** on the silver was done by my cousin.

Science Words: Measurement

Use these sentences to introduce the words and their meanings.
6. The **capacity** of the stadium is 45,000 people.
7. We have learned formulas to measure the **volume** of different objects.
8. What are the **dimensions** of the room?
9. The meteorologist measured the **velocity** of the wind.
10. How much energy would it take to move a **mass** weighing 100 pounds?

Word Study

Toponyms

Challenge students to name other possible toponyms (e.g., **cheddar cheese** is named for the town of Cheddar, England, and **hamburger** comes from Hamburg, Germany). Can they coin a toponym related to the name of their city or town?

Unit 6 Home Spelling Practice

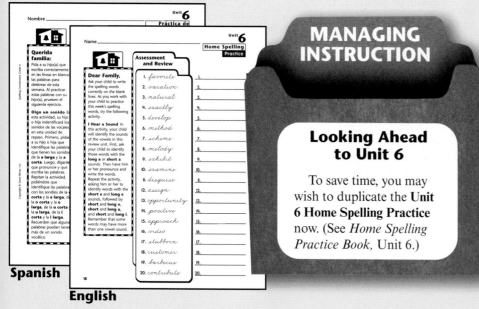

Spanish

English

MANAGING INSTRUCTION

Looking Ahead to Unit 6

To save time, you may wish to duplicate the **Unit 6 Home Spelling Practice** now. (See *Home Spelling Practice Book,* Unit 6.)

Assessment Words

estate	granite
treasury	retreat
critic	besides
oatmeal	popular
secure	deduct
cue	bundle
patrol	polish
specify	wheeze
plenty	cactus
praise	despise

Review Words

Unit 1
favorite*	pattern
vacation*	admit
natural*	behave
exactly*	daydream
rapid	complain

Unit 2
develop*	attend
method*	meadow
scheme*	leather
melody*	indeed
regular	release

Unit 3
exhibit*	attic
examine*	system
disguise*	consider
assign*	item
limit	strike

Unit 4
opportunity*	project
positive*	beyond
approach*	opposite
video*	notice
constant	respond

Unit 5
stubborn*	result
customer*	confuse
barbecue*	punish
contribute*	computer
suffer	community

* Posttest sentences and the **Unit 6 Test Master** test these words. Students review all words listed.

MATERIALS

Student Edition
Pages 38–43

Teacher Edition
Pages T38A–T43

Teacher Resource Book
Flip Folder Practice Master
Unit 6 Test Master

Home Spelling Practice Book
Unit 6 Home Spelling Practice
(English or Spanish)

Other *Spelling Connections* Resources
• Transparency Book, Grade 6

OBJECTIVES

Spelling and Assessment
Students will
• **assess** their spelling success by matching new words to the spelling strategies presented in Units 1–5.
• **connect** new words to the spelling strategies in Units 1–5.
• **write** new words that relate to the spelling strategies taught in Units 1–5.

Spelling and Review
Students will
• **review** and practice the spelling strategies and words in Units 1–5.
• **learn** an alternative spelling study strategy.

Spelling and Writing
Students will
• **review** the types of sentences and their parts.
• **compose** a descriptive piece of writing that describes a local place.
• **learn** a proofreading strategy.
• **understand** the importance of using correct spelling in a search engine.
• **proofread** for frequently misspelled words.

MEETING INDIVIDUAL NEEDS
Learning Styles

 Visual

Form teams of eight to ten players each. Pronounce a spelling word. The first player on each team writes the word on a sheet of paper and then passes the paper to the next player. That player checks the word, rewrites it if necessary, and then writes the next word pronounced. The paper is passed on until each player has had a turn. The team with the most correct answers wins.

Hands-On Practice
All students will benefit from practicing with a **Flip Folder**. See page Z18.

 Auditory

Give each student some paper squares and a grid six squares across and three squares down. The students will use these to play "Spello." The students write a spelling word in each square. As you say each spelling word, the students spell the word aloud in unison and cover the word on their grids. The student who first covers a row of words and calls out "Spello!" is the winner.

 Kinesthetic

Divide a piece of oak-tag into 10 sections. Write one of these sounds, in random order, in each section: **short a, long a, short e, long e, short i, long i, short o, long o, short u, long u**. On pieces of colored paper, write spelling words with a variety of the targeted vowel sounds. Form teams and give each team a set of words on the same color paper. Have one team at a time put each of their words on the section that corresponds to the vowel sound or sounds of the word.

Language and Cultural Differences

The same or very similar English sounds might be spelled consistently in other ways in other languages. In the Spanish language, each vowel sound is generally represented by only one letter. In Spanish, the **long a** sound is always spelled with the letter **e**. The letters **ay** and **ai** are used to spell the **long i** sound. The sound most similar to **long e** in English is spelled with the letter **i** in Spanish. In Spanish, the **long o** sound is always spelled with the letter **o**. Another factor is that in Spanish the final **e** is most often pronounced as a **long a** sound, so the **vowel-consonant-e** patterns can present difficulties for Spanish-speaking students.

Help students clarify their understanding of the meanings of the spelling words by using word cards. Pronounce each word clearly. Have students repeat the word. Use the word in a sentence. Then have students write each word and check their spelling by comparing their writing with the word cards.

MANAGING INSTRUCTION

3–5 Day Plan		Average	Below Average	Above Average
Day 1	**Day 1**	Assessment: Units 1–5, p. 38 (Option 1 or 2, p. T38)	Assessment: Units 1–5, p. 38 (Option 1 or 2, p. T38)	Assessment: Units 1–5, p. 38 (Option 1 or 2, p. T38)
	Day 2	Review: Units 1 and 2, p. 39	Review: Units 1 and 2, p. 39	Review: Units 1 and 2, p. 39 Review: Units 3 and 4, p. 40
Day 2	**Day 3**	Review: Units 3 and 4, p. 40	Review: Units 3 and 4, p. 40	Review: Unit 5, p. 41 Spelling Study Strategy, p. 41
	Day 4	Review: Unit 5, p. 41 Spelling Study Strategy, p. 41	Review: Unit 5, p. 41 Spelling Study Strategy, p. 41	Writer's Workshop, pages 42–43
Day 3	**Day 5**	Weekly Test, Option 1 or 2, p. T41	Weekly Test, Option 1 or 2, p. T41	Weekly Test, Option 1 or 2, p. T41

Writer's Workshop (pages 42 and 43) may be used anytime during this unit.

Objectives

Spelling and Assessment

Students will

- **assess** their spelling success by matching new words to the spelling strategies presented in Units 1–5.
- **connect** new words to the spelling strategies in Units 1–5.
- **write** new words that relate to the spelling strategies taught in Units 1–5.

Order of answers may vary.

Unit 1
1. estate
2. praise
3. granite
4. cactus

Unit 2
5. treasury
6. specify
7. plenty
8. retreat
9. wheeze

Unit 3
10. critic
11. besides
12. despise

Unit 4
13. oatmeal ▲
14. patrol
15. popular
16. polish ▲

Unit 5
17. secure
18. cue
19. deduct
20. bundle

Unit 6

Review Units 1–5

Assessment and Review

Assessment Units 1–5

Each Assessment Word in the box fits one of the spelling strategies you have studied over the past five weeks. Read the spelling strategies. Then write each Assessment Word under the unit number it fits.

Unit 1
1.–4. The **short a** sound in **rapid** is spelled **a**. The **long a** sound is spelled **a** in **labor**, **ai** in **trait**, **ay** in **daydream**, a-consonant-e in **behave**, and **ey** in **survey**.

Unit 2
5.–9. The **short e** sound is spelled **e** in **text** and **ea** in **dealt**. The **long e** sound is spelled **ee** in **sleet**, **ea** in **crease**, e-consonant-e in **theme**, and **y** in **gravity**.

Unit 3
10.–12. The **short i** sound is spelled **i** in **permit** and **y** in **system**. The **long i** sound is spelled **i** in **item**, i-consonant-e in **strike**, and **y** in **satisfy**.

Unit 4
13.–16. The **short o** sound in **bronze** is spelled **o**. The **long o** sound is spelled **o** in **notice**, o-consonant-e in **pose**, and **oa** in **approach**.

Unit 5
17.–20. The **short u** sound in **result** is spelled **u**. The **long u** sound is spelled **u** in **union**, u-consonant-e in **acute**, and **ue** in **barbecue**.

estate
treasury
critic
oatmeal
secure
cue
patrol
specify
plenty
praise
granite
retreat
besides
popular
deduct
bundle
polish
wheeze
cactus
despise

38

ASSESSMENT: UNITS 1–5

Option 1

Assessment Option 1 is the test that appears in the Student Edition on page 38. You may wish to have students take this test to determine their ability to recognize the spelling strategy in each unit and to match words not previously taught to that strategy. **Assessment Option 1** also serves as additional review and practice.

▲ Words designated with this symbol include more than one of the targeted spelling strategies. The answer key has placed them according to the most obvious spelling emphasis. However, if a student places a word in another category, and the word fits that generalization, accept that response. Remember, the objective is to place each word with any appropriate spelling generalization.

Option 2

Assessment Option 2 is a dictation test using the sentences on page T39. This test assesses students' ability to spell words not previously taught but that are exemplars of a spelling strategy. This test more specifically assesses students' ability to apply the spelling knowledge they have learned.

In either assessment test option, the words are identified by unit in the Teacher Edition. You may wish to index those misspelled words to the review exercises that follow in this unit. Determine which units students need to review and use the additional unit exercises found in this **Assessment and Review Unit** for reteaching the skill in a more focused way.

T38

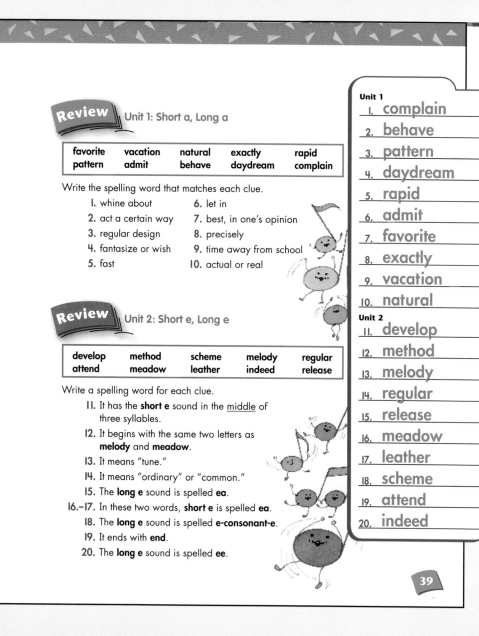

Review Unit 1: Short a, Long a

| favorite | vacation | natural | exactly | rapid |
| pattern | admit | behave | daydream | complain |

Write the spelling word that matches each clue.

1. whine about
2. act a certain way
3. regular design
4. fantasize or wish
5. fast
6. let in
7. best, in one's opinion
8. precisely
9. time away from school
10. actual or real

Review Unit 2: Short e, Long e

| develop | method | scheme | melody | regular |
| attend | meadow | leather | indeed | release |

Write a spelling word for each clue.

11. It has the **short e** sound in the <u>middle</u> of three syllables.
12. It begins with the same two letters as **melody** and **meadow**.
13. It means "tune."
14. It means "ordinary" or "common."
15. The **long e** sound is spelled **ea**.
16.–17. In these two words, **short e** is spelled **ea**.
18. The **long e** sound is spelled **e-consonant-e**.
19. It ends with **end**.
20. The **long e** sound is spelled **ee**.

Unit 1
1. complain
2. behave
3. pattern
4. daydream
5. rapid
6. admit
7. favorite
8. exactly
9. vacation
10. natural

Unit 2
11. develop
12. method
13. melody
14. regular
15. release
16. meadow
17. leather
18. scheme
19. attend
20. indeed

39

Objectives

Spelling and Review
Students will
• **review** and practice the spelling strategy and words in Unit 1.
• **review** and practice the spelling strategy and words in Unit 2.

Assessing Progress: The Spelling Journal

If your students have been keeping a personal spelling journal, a periodical review of these journals can be a rich assessment tool. Students should include the words they have misspelled from each unit spelling test. They should also be encouraged to write the words they consistently misspell in their own writing and content-area words that present a challenge. Being able to discriminate the words in their everyday writing whose spelling they need to master is a powerful spelling skill.

Pretest Sentences: Assessment Words

(See procedures on pages Z10–Z11.)

1. A white fence surrounded the entire huge **estate**.
2. How much money is left in the **treasury**?
3. The movie **critic** thinks this film is the best of the year.
4. I like raisins in my breakfast **oatmeal**.
5. We felt safe and **secure** in our warm house.
6. Shout "Surprise!" when I give the **cue**.
7. It is no longer necessary to **patrol** the halls.
8. Please **specify** which pizza toppings you want.
9. There are **plenty** of seats still available for the concert.
10. There was great **praise** for the performance.
11. The town founder's face is carved in **granite**.
12. If you hear the whistle, **retreat** to the storm shelter.
13. Who is going **besides** you and me?
14. She is the most **popular** player on the team.
15. If you pick the wrong word, we will **deduct** points from your score.
16. You may pick up your **bundle** of newspapers early in the morning.
17. I need some black shoe **polish** for these boots.
18. The old machine began to cough and **wheeze** loudly.
19. Be careful not to get too close to the thorns on this **cactus**.
20. I **despise** having to repeat everything I say.

Objectives

Spelling and Review

Students will
- **review** and practice the spelling strategy and words in Unit 3.
- **review** and practice the spelling strategy and words in Unit 4.

Unit 3
1. examine
2. exhibit
3. assign
4. disguise
5. strike
6. item
7. system
8. consider
9. limit
10. attic

Unit 4
11. positive
12. approach
13. video
14. project
15. beyond
16. opposite
17. respond
18. notice
19. constant
20. opportunity

 Unit 3: Short i, Long i

exhibit	examine	disguise	assign	limit
attic	system	consider	item	strike

Write the spelling word that completes each sentence.

1. Let the doctor _____ the cut on your arm.
2. That was a wonderful art _____!
3. Did the director _____ the play parts yet?
4. No one will know you with that funny _____.
5. The umpire has called one ball and one _____.
6. Put a check beside the first _____ on the list.
7. Our new public address _____ has been installed.
8. I hope you will _____ voting for me.
9. There is a _____ of two on the number you can buy.
10. The old photos are kept in a box up in the _____.

 Unit 4: Short o, Long o

opportunity	positive	approach	video	constant
project	beyond	opposite	notice	respond

Change the underlined part of these words to write spelling words.

11. pos<u>sible</u>
12. <u>re</u>proach
13. <u>vis</u>ion
14. pro<u>duce</u>
15. be<u>side</u>
16. com<u>posite</u>
17. res<u>pect</u>
18. no<u>tion</u>
19. in<u>stant</u>
20. com<u>munity</u>

 40

Bulletin Board Idea

Book Jackets

Create (or copy) book jackets for the following types of books: modern novel, adventure, biography, autobiography, humor, journal, mystery, historical novel, and science fiction. Color the jackets in bright colors and attach them to the bulletin board. Next to each book jacket attach a piece of theme paper on which you have written the type of book as a heading. Ask students to write titles of books, in the appropriate categories, that they have read and enjoyed and would recommend to others. You may also want to have them write paragraphs promoting their favorite books and/or draw pictures illustrating them. If you do, place these on the bulletin board.

Review Unit 5: Short u, Long u

stubborn	customer	barbecue	contribute	suffer
result	confuse	punish	computer	community

Write spelling words to complete the paragraph.

   This year we had a street fair in our __1.__. The businesses agreed to __2.__ something. The John's Ribs store made their delicious __3.__ to sell. Each paying __4.__ bought tokens to use. The tokens were different sizes so that we wouldn't __5.__ them. Mr. Hempstead kept track of all the sales on his __6.__. We were pleased with the __7.__ of the fair. We decided not to __8.__ ourselves in the future by trying our old fund-raising methods. We wouldn't __9.__ any more by going door to door asking for money. Even the most __10.__ residents agreed that the fair was a great idea.

Unit 5

1. community
2. contribute
3. barbecue
4. customer
5. confuse
6. computer
7. result
8. punish
9. suffer
10. stubborn

 **Spelling Study Strategy**

Spelling Capture

Swap spelling lists with a partner. On a sheet of paper, make five rows of dots with five dots in each row. Decide who is Player 1 and who is Player 2.

Player 2 says the first word on Player 1's list, and Player 1 spells the word. If it's correct, Player 1 uses a pencil to connect any two dots that are side by side. If Player 1 misspells the word, no dots are connected. Player 2 spells the misspelled word aloud correctly. Then it's Player 2's turn to spell the first word on his or her list.

Continue to take turns, spelling the next word on each list. Each time a player connects two dots to make a square, that player writes initials in the square. That square is "captured." The player who has the most initialed squares at the end of the game wins.

41

Objectives

Spelling and Review

Students will
• **review** and practice the spelling strategy and words in Unit 5.
• **learn** an alternative spelling study strategy.

Learning an Alternative Spelling Study Strategy

   Students should always have a number of study strategies to draw from when it comes to learning their spelling words. **Spelling Capture** is a partner game that makes practicing spelling fun to do. Encourage students to remember this spelling study strategy and to consider using it with any list they need to study and learn.

Weekly Test Options

Option 1:
One Spelling Word Per Sentence
(See procedures on pages Z10–Z11.)

1. The **customer** bought a bunch of flowers.
2. His **natural** ability to draw made him a skilled artist.
3. We will take a **vacation** in May.
4. Children grow and **develop** at different rates.
5. We learned a **method** for solving the puzzle.
6. What **scheme** have you come up with?
7. Did your teacher **assign** any homework?
8. Her **favorite** sport is baseball.
9. He wore an elephant costume as a **disguise**.
10. My sweater matches my skirt **exactly**.
11. Did you enjoy the **exhibit** on space travel?
12. We had an **opportunity** to go sailing.
13. I am **positive** this will be on the test.
14. The doctor wants to **examine** her throat.
15. The plane will soon **approach** the airport.
16. In summer we always **barbecue** outdoors.
17. I like the **melody** of that song better than the lyrics.
18. Will you **contribute** some items to our sale?
19. Try not to be **stubborn** so that you will get along well with others.
20. We mustn't touch Dad's **video** camera.

Option 2:
Standardized Test

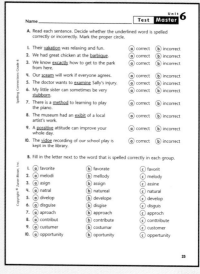

Unit 6 Test Master

(See *Teacher Resource Book,* Unit 6.)

Objectives

Spelling and Writing

Students will

• **review** the types of sentences and their parts.

• **compose** a descriptive piece of writing that describes a local place. (See **Spelling and the Writing Process** below.)

A

1. declarative
2. interrogative
3. exclamatory
4. interrogative
5. imperative
6. declarative
7. imperative

B

8. Daydreams
9. you (understood)
10. Leather
11. Julia
12. you (understood)
13. Customers
14. Vacation

42

Grammar, Usage, and Mechanics

Sentences and Their Parts

There are four kinds of sentences: declarative (ones that tell), interrogative (ones that ask), imperative (ones that command), and exclamatory (ones that show strong feeling).

Every sentence has a subject and a predicate. The simple subject tells whom or what the sentence is about. The simple predicate tells what the subject is, has, or does. In a command, the subject is often not named. It is understood to be **you,** the person being spoken to.

Practice Activity

A. Write **declarative, interrogative, imperative,** or **exclamatory** to show what kind of sentence each is.

1. Kelly's video was played for the class.
2. Who left this sweater on the chair?
3. What an awful storm that was!
4. Is Mrs. Garcia your neighbor?
5. Call everyone on the team.
6. The new pet store opens today.
7. Watch out for the broken glass.

B. Write the subject of each sentence.

8. Daydreams filled my head.
9. Call home after school.
10. Leather lasts longer than cloth.
11. Julia spotted a comet.
12. Notice that player in the back.
13. Customers complained about the noise.
14. Vacation ended too soon.

Descriptive Writing **Spelling and the Writing Process**

You may wish to use this writing assignment to help students master the writing process. For other writing ideas, see pages 258–259 in the Student Edition.

Explain that students will write a detailed riddle in which they describe a familiar place for classmates.

Prewriting Hint: You may wish to help students plan their writing by recommending the following chart. Have them replicate the chart, filling in the columns with details about the place.

Location	school
Obvious or Important Features	bookcases, carts, tables
Details About Features	

Revising Hint: Remind students that when they revise what they have written they should organize their descriptions in a logical order. You may wish to suggest that they first try spatial order.

WORKSHOP

Proofreading Strategy

One at a Time!

Good writers always proofread their writing for spelling mistakes. Here's a strategy you can use to proofread your papers.

Look for one kind of mistake at a time. First, skim your paper and look at any word endings. Then, look for words that contain **ie** or **ei**. Go through again and check contractions.

This may sound like a lot of work, but it's not. You do not read many words each time. Instead, you focus on a small group each time. You look for particular problems. Try it!

Electronic Spelling

Search Engines

Search engines are wonderful tools. They help you find information on the Internet, in encyclopedias, and in many programs. To use them, you simply type a word or phrase. However, you have to be sure you type this word or phrase correctly. A search engine can't guess what you are looking for; it can only look.

Some words are often misspelled by many people. Some have silent letters or double consonants. Others may just be hard to remember. If you are unsure of a word's spelling, look it up.

Look at these frequently misspelled words, which are often used in searches. Which are misspelled here? Write them correctly. Write **OK** if a name is correct.

1. sistem
2. community
3. exibit
4. examin
5. project
6. vidio

Electronic Spelling

1. system
2. OK
3. exhibit
4. examine
5. OK
6. video

43

Unit 7 Home Spelling Practice

Spanish

English

MANAGING INSTRUCTION

Looking Ahead to Unit 7

To save time, you may wish to duplicate the **Unit 7 Home Spelling Practice** now. (See *Home Spelling Practice Book*, Unit 7.)

Objectives

Spelling and Writing

Students will
- **learn** a proofreading strategy.
- **understand** the importance of using correct spellings in a search engine.
- **proofread** for frequently misspelled words.

Using Proofreading Strategies

Students are often unaware that there are a variety of approaches to proofreading their own writing. Building a repertory of strategies is important to improving students' writing and editing skills.

Spelling and Technology

The advent of word processing, computer protocols, and the Internet has actually increased, not lessened, the pressure on users to be better, more aware spellers. Spell checkers, for example, create circumstances in which the ability to discriminate between an acceptable and unacceptable spelling is a critical skill. A homophone substitution, a correct spelling of the wrong word, an inadvertent word omission—these are examples of situations in computer usage that require a deeper understanding of spelling principles and a more adroit proofreading capability. It may be worthwhile to underscore this increased need as a whole-class discussion after students finish this unit's **Electronic Spelling** activity.

Basic Spelling List

aptitude	could've
understood	should've
intrude	through
routine	goodness
proof	approve
neighborhood	bulletin
would've	conclude
cushion	introduce
fluid	teaspoon
tablespoon	assume

Strategy Words

Review

foolish	solution
good-bye	woodwind
goulash	

Preview Words

bamboo	pollutant
boutique	pursuit
footage	

Content Words

Social Studies: The Caribbean

Caribbean	tropics
sunset	lagoon
coral	

Social Studies: International Relations

diplomat	enlist
rumor	quota
protect	

Individual Needs

Challenge Words

renewal	distribute
juvenile	supreme
supermarket	bulldozer

Alternate Word List ★

understood	through
routine	goodness
proof	bulletin
neighborhood	introduce
cushion	assume

★ For students who need to study fewer Basic Spelling words

MATERIALS

Student Edition
Pages 44–49
Challenge Activities, p. 229

Teacher Edition
Pages T44A–T49
Challenge Activities, p. T229

Teacher Resource Book
Unit 7 Homework Master
Unit 7 Practice Masters
Flip Folder Practice Master
Unit 7 Test Master

Home Spelling Practice Book
Unit 7 Home Spelling Practice
(English or Spanish)

Other *Spelling Connections* Resources
• Audiotape, Grade 6
• Practice Book for Grammar, Usage, and Mechanics, Grade 6
• Spelling Support for Second Language Learners, Grade 6
• Support Software on CD-ROM
• Transparency Book, Grade 6
• Word Sort CD-ROM, Grade 6

OBJECTIVES

Spelling and Thinking

Students will
• **read** the spelling words in list form and in context.
• **sort** the spelling words according to /o͞o/ and /o͝o/ sounds.
• **read** and remember this week's spelling strategy.

Spelling and Vocabulary

Students will
• **write** spelling words to complete a series of meaning-related words.
• **distinguish** spelling words by their structure.
• **use** a thesaurus to find synonyms for words.

Spelling and Reading

Students will
• **solve** analogies using spelling words.
• **complete** sentences using spelling words.
• **complete** a paragraph using spelling words.

Spelling and Writing

Students will
• **proofread** a friendly letter.
• **use** the writing process to write a friendly letter.
• **proofread** their writing.

MEETING INDIVIDUAL NEEDS
Learning Styles

Visual

Draw a football field on poster board. Place a marker on the 50-yard line. Divide the class into two teams. Say a spelling word for each student on Team A to write. Have someone on Team B check the spelling. If all spell a word correctly, move the football ten yards. Continue until someone misspells a word or scores a touchdown. If Team A misspells a word, and everyone on Team B spells the word correctly, the ball is moved ten yards toward their goal, and Team B continues spelling.

Auditory

Have the students play "Spelling Football" as described in the visual activity. Make this addition: Before the students write the spelling word, have one student on the team spell the word aloud.

Kinesthetic

Have the students play "Spelling Football" as described in the visual activity. Make these additions: Have the students imagine that they are in the cheering section of the game. Give each student one blue and one red card. As a student on the team spells the word aloud, the others hold up the red card when they hear the /o͞o/ and call out the sound; they hold up the blue card and call out the sound when they hear the /o͞o/.

Hands-On Practice
All students will benefit from practicing with a **Flip Folder**. See page Z18.

Language and Cultural Differences

The **long oo** sound and the **short oo** sound may be difficult for some students to hear and spell due to regional pronunciations or language backgrounds that do not include these sounds or that spell them differently. However, the more likely cause of difficulty is that the students must remember several different spelling patterns for these two sounds.

Pronounce each spelling word and review its meaning. Then have the students divide their papers into two columns, one with the **long oo** heading, the other with the **short oo** heading. Write the same headings on the chalkboard. Call out the spelling words one at a time. Have a volunteer write the word on the chalkboard in the appropriate column and underline the letter(s) that spell the vowel sound. Have the students copy the columns of spelling words on their papers.

MANAGING INSTRUCTION

3–5 Day Plan		Average	Below Average	Above Average
Day 1	**Day 1**	Pretest Spelling Mini-Lesson, p. T44 Spelling and Thinking, p. 44	Pretest Spelling Mini-Lesson, p. T44 Spelling and Thinking, p. 44	Pretest Spelling and Thinking, p. 44
	Day 2	Spelling and Vocabulary, p. 45	Spelling and Vocabulary, p. 45 (or) Unit 7 Practice Master, A and B	Spelling and Vocabulary, p. 45 Spelling and Reading, p. 46
Day 2	**Day 3**	Spelling and Reading, p. 46	Spelling and Reading, p. 46 (or) Unit 7 Practice Master, C and D	Challenge Activities, p. 229
	Day 4	Spelling and Writing, p. 47 Unit 7 Homework Master	Spelling and Writing, p. 47	Spelling and Writing, p. 47 Unit 7 Homework Master
Day 3	**Day 5**	Weekly Test	Weekly Test	Weekly Test
Vocabulary Connections (pages 48 and 49) may be used anytime during this unit.				

Objectives

Spelling and Thinking

Students will
- **read** the spelling words in list form and in context.
- **sort** the spelling words according to /o͞o/ and /o͝o/ sounds.
- **read** and remember this week's spelling strategy.

UNIT PRETEST

Use **Pretest Sentences** below. Refer to the self-checking procedures on student page 256. You may wish to use the **Unit 7 Word List Overhead Transparency** as part of the checking procedure.

TEACHING THE STRATEGY

Spelling Mini-Lesson

Write **soon, group, reduce, foot, should,** and **full** on the board. Read each word aloud; ask the students to pronounce it after you.

Explain that two different sounds are emphasized in this unit's spelling words, and that each sound can be spelled in different ways. One sound is the vowel sound in **soon, group, junior,** and **reduce.** Write /o͞o/ over these words and remind students that this is the dictionary symbol for this vowel sound. The other sound is the vowel sound in **foot, should,** and **full.** Write /o͝o/ above these words. Encourage students to repeat the words to hear the difference in vowel sounds.

Ask volunteers to identify the different spellings of /o͞o/ (oo, ou, u, u-consonant-e) and the different spellings of /o͝o/. (oo, ou, u)

Spelling and Thinking

Order of answers may vary.

/o͞o/
1. apt**i**t**u**de
2. intr**u**de
3. r**ou**tine ★
4. pr**oo**f ★
5. fl**u**id
6. tablesp**oo**n
7. thr**ou**gh ★
8. appr**o**v**e**
9. concl**u**de
10. introd**u**ce ★
11. teasp**oo**n
12. ass**u**me ★

/o͝o/
13. underst**oo**d ★
14. neighborh**oo**d ★
15. w**ou**ld've
16. c**u**shion ★
17. c**ou**ld've
18. sh**ou**ld've
19. g**oo**dness ★
20. b**u**lletin ★

READ THE SPELLING WORDS

1. aptitude	*aptitude*	He has an **aptitude** for languages.
2. understood	*understood*	I **understood** the reason for the rule.
3. intrude	*intrude*	We should not **intrude** on a meeting.
4. routine	*routine*	The car is here for a **routine** checkup.
5. proof	*proof*	We have **proof** that Pluto exists.
6. neighborhood	*neighborhood*	I just moved to this **neighborhood**.
7. would've	*would've*	I **would've** helped you make dinner.
8. cushion	*cushion*	The **cushion** is comfortable.
9. fluid	*fluid*	Your car is low on engine **fluid**.
10. tablespoon	*tablespoon*	Add a **tablespoon** of flour.
11. could've	*could've*	I **could've** helped you clean up.
12. should've	*should've*	You **should've** attended the meeting.
13. through	*through*	Walk **through** the door on the left.
14. goodness	*goodness*	His **goodness** is known to everyone.
15. approve	*approve*	Do you **approve** of the new rules?
16. bulletin	*bulletin*	A **bulletin** warned us to stay inside.
17. conclude	*conclude*	I will **conclude** my speech with a joke.
18. introduce	*introduce*	I want to **introduce** you to my family.
19. teaspoon	*teaspoon*	Add a **teaspoon** of salt to the mix.
20. assume	*assume*	I **assume** you brought your umbrella.

SORT THE SPELLING WORDS

1.–12. Write the words with the /o͞o/ vowel sound spelled **oo, ou, u,** or **vowel-consonant-e**. Circle the letters that spell this vowel sound.

13.–20. Write the words with the /o͝o/ vowel sound spelled **oo, ou,** or **u**. Circle the letters that spell this vowel sound.

REMEMBER THE SPELLING STRATEGY

Remember that the /o͞o/ sound is spelled **oo** in **proof**, **ou** in **routine**, **u** in **fluid**, and **vowel-consonant-e** in **assume**. The /o͝o/ sound is spelled **oo** in **goodness**, **ou** in **could've**, and **u** in **bulletin**.

44

Pretest Sentences (See procedures on pages Z10–Z11.)

1. An **aptitude** test measures interest and ability.
★ 2. The teacher asked if we **understood** the directions.
3. It is impolite to **intrude** upon another's privacy.
★ 4. Some jobs involve variety, while others are **routine**.
★ 5. Do you have **proof** this book bag is yours?
★ 6. My **neighborhood** has many apartment buildings.
7. I **would've** liked to have seen you yesterday, but I was busy studying for a test.
★ 8. The soft **cushion** makes this chair very comfortable.
9. A liquid is sometimes called a **fluid**.
10. We measured the liquid with a **tablespoon**.
11. We **could've** gone to the movies if we had had enough money.
12. We **should've** called to say we would be late.
★13. We walked **through** the park instead of around it.
★14. Everyone loved her for her **goodness**.
15. Will you please **approve** our plans for the school play?
★16. I received a **bulletin** about free vaccinations.
17. After reviewing the evidence, what will the jury **conclude**?
★18. Let me **introduce** you to my brother.
19. This recipe calls for one-fourth **teaspoon** of vanilla.
★20. I can **assume** that red and yellow will produce orange.

Spelling and Vocabulary

Word Groups

Write a spelling word to complete each group.

1. schedule, system, _____
2. pillow, buffer, _____
3. kindness, decency, _____
4. news report, notice, _____
5. water, liquid, _____
6. guarantee, evidence, _____
7. accept, suppose, _____

Word Structure

8.–10. Write the spelling words that are contractions.

11. Write the spelling word that ends in the suffix **-hood**.

12.–13. Write the spelling words that are compound words and that name units of measure.

14. Write the spelling word that ends in silent **gh**.

15. Write the spelling word that is the verb form of the noun **introduction**.

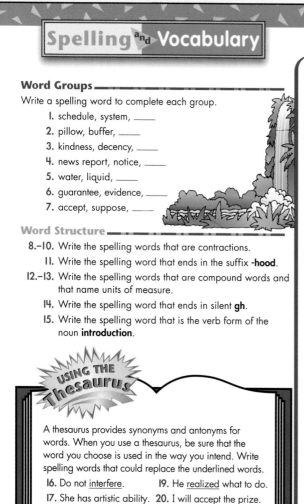

USING THE Thesaurus

A thesaurus provides synonyms and antonyms for words. When you use a thesaurus, be sure that the word you choose is used in the way you intend. Write spelling words that could replace the underlined words.

16. Do not <u>interfere</u>.
17. She has artistic <u>ability</u>.
18. We will <u>finish</u> at noon.
19. He <u>realized</u> what to do.
20. I will <u>accept</u> the prize.

Word Groups
1. routine
2. cushion
3. goodness
4. bulletin
5. fluid
6. proof
7. assume

Word Structure
8. would've
9. could've
10. should've
11. neighborhood
12. tablespoon
13. teaspoon
14. through
15. introduce

Using the Thesaurus
16. intrude
17. aptitude
18. conclude
19. understood
20. approve

45

Objectives

Spelling and Vocabulary

Students will
- **write** spelling words to complete a series of meaning-related words.
- **distinguish** spelling words by their structure.
- **use** a thesaurus to find synonyms for words.

Developing Oral Language Skills

Have students work in pairs. The first student asks a question that includes one of the words from the spelling list. For example, the student might ask, "Have you seen my **tablespoon**?" The second student answers the question. The answer must also include a spelling word, but the spelling word must not contain the same vowel sound. For example, the second student might answer, "I put it on the **cushion**."

MEETING INDIVIDUAL NEEDS

Providing More Help

To aid the students in making sound-spelling associations, have them write the words in each group that have the /o͞o/ or /o͝o/ sound:

1. **proof, tablespoon,** mercy
2. **teaspoon,** fact, **intrude**
3. taste, **routine, assume**
4. cereal, **could've, goodness**
5. **through, fluid,** sand
6. **conclude,** parade, **introduce**

★Students who need to study fewer words should use the **Alternate Word List**. This list is starred on page T44 in the Teacher Edition. The **Unit 7 Practice Masters** (*Teacher Resource Book*) provide additional practice with these words.

Unit 7 Practice Masters

Name _____

Practice Master Unit **7**

1. proof 3. through 5. introduce 7. understood 9. bulletin
2. routine 4. assume 6. goodness 8. neighborhood 10. cushion

A. Unscramble the letters to form and write the spelling words.

1. s h o n u c i _____
2. r e u n i t o _____
3. h o g h t r u _____
4. m s a e s u _____
5. f r o p o _____
6. d u t d e o r n s o _____

7. When you meet someone for the first time you **dutroecni** yourself.

B. Write the spelling word that goes with each group.

1. announcement, news report, _____ _____
2. evidence, guarantee, _____ _____
3. pillow, soft pad, _____ _____
4. system, schedule, _____ _____
5. kindness, thoughtfulness, _____ _____
6. present, bring in, _____ _____

26

Practice Master Unit **7**

understood   bulletin
neighborhood cushion

each definition.

within larger words. Write the spelling

27

T45

Objectives

Spelling and Reading

Students will
- **solve** analogies using spelling words.
- **complete** sentences using spelling words.
- **complete** a paragraph using spelling words.

One-Minute Handwriting Hint

When joining **o** to **o**, be sure to swing wide and close the **o**, or the joining will look like **oc**.

↓ SWING WIDE

Legible handwriting can boost spelling scores by as much as 20%.

Solve the Analogies

1. aptitude
2. cushion
3. fluid
4. conclude
5. understood
6. goodness
7. could've

Complete the Sentences

8. should've
9. tablespoon
10. routine
11. would've
12. intrude
13. assume

Complete the Paragraph

14. through
15. bulletin
16. neighborhood
17. proof
18. introduce
19. teaspoon
20. approve

Spelling and Reading

aptitude	understood	intrude	routine
proof	neighborhood	would've	cushion
fluid	tablespoon	could've	should've
through	goodness	approve	bulletin
conclude	introduce	teaspoon	assume

Solve the Analogies   Write a spelling word to complete each analogy.

1. **Progress** is to **growth** as **talent** is to _____.
2. **Bed** is to **pillow** as **chair** is to _____.
3. **Rock** is to **solid** as **water** is to _____.
4. **Inhale** is to **exhale** as **start** is to _____.
5. **Break** is to **broke** as **understand** is to _____.
6. **Weak** is to **weakness** as **good** is to _____.
7. **They will** is to **they'll** as **could have** is to _____.

Complete the Sentences   Write spelling words to complete the sentences.

8. You _____ seen the surprised look on his face.
9. A _____ is equal to three teaspoons.
10. His morning _____ begins with a long walk.
11. I know you _____ enjoyed the play last night.
12. She did not want to _____ on our conversation.
13. I am not certain, but I _____ he will be here.

Complete the Paragraph   Write spelling words from the box to complete the paragraph.

Chef Fidelia shares her recipes __14.__ a weekly __15.__. Her crowded __16.__ restaurant is __17.__ of her good cooking. Chef Fidelia tries to __18.__ one new dish a week to her menu. When asked about her trade secrets, Chef Fidelia says, "I simply add a __19.__ of this and a pinch of that." Townspeople enthusiastically __20.__ of this new restaurant.

neighborhood
proof
bulletin
teaspoon
through
approve
introduce

46

MEETING INDIVIDUAL NEEDS

Providing More Challenge

Challenge Words and **Challenge Activities** for Unit 7 appear on page 229. **Challenge Word Test Sentences** appear on page T229.

Unit 7 Challenge Activities

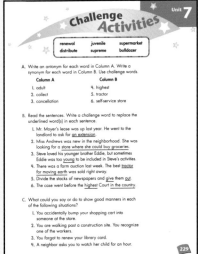

Weekly Test Options

Option 1:
One Spelling Word Per Sentence
(See procedures on pages Z10–Z11.)

1. Did your parents **approve** of your new haircut?
2. She has a special **aptitude** for math.
★ 3. I **assume** that you will be home by supper time.
★ 4. We read about the event in the news **bulletin**.
5. What did the student **conclude** in her report?
6. I **could've** used your help, but you were not here.
★ 7. He pushed the **cushion** away and sat on the hard bench.
8. Please put a **tablespoon** of oil on the salad.
9. She poured the green **fluid** into the sink.
★10. The **goodness** of the king was known to all.
★11. Please **introduce** me to your friends.
12. The rule in our house is not to **intrude** upon each other's privacy.
★13. Is there a park in your **neighborhood**?
★14. Do you have **proof** that someone took your book?
★15. Her habits had now become **routine**.

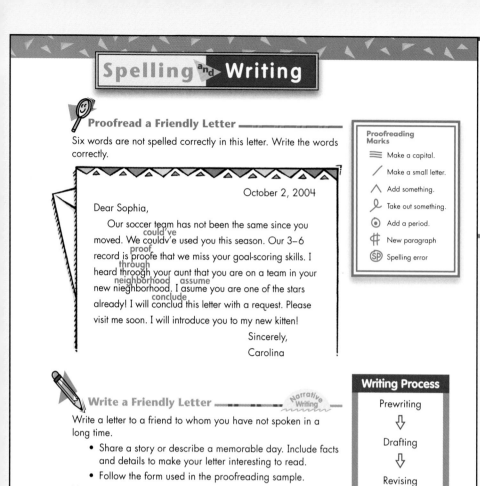

Spelling and Writing

Proofread a Friendly Letter

Six words are not spelled correctly in this letter. Write the words correctly.

October 2, 2004

Dear Sophia,

Our soccer team has not been the same since you moved. We couldv'e *could've* used you this season. Our 3–6 record is proofe *proof* that we miss your goal-scoring skills. I heard throogh *through* your aunt that you are on a team in your new nieghborhood *neighborhood*. I asume *assume* you are one of the stars already! I will conclud *conclude* this letter with a request. Please visit me soon. I will introduce you to my new kitten!

Sincerely,
Carolina

Proofreading Marks

≡ Make a capital.
/ Make a small letter.
∧ Add something.
ℒ Take out something.
⊙ Add a period.
New paragraph
SP Spelling error

Write a Friendly Letter

Narrative Writing

Write a letter to a friend to whom you have not spoken in a long time.

- Share a story or describe a memorable day. Include facts and details to make your letter interesting to read.
- Follow the form used in the proofreading sample.

Use as many spelling words as you can.

Proofread Your Writing During → **Editing**

Proofread your writing for spelling errors as part of the editing stage in the writing process. Be sure to check each word carefully. Use a dictionary to check spelling if you are not sure.

Writing Process

Prewriting
⇩
Drafting
⇩
Revising
⇩
Editing
⇩
Publishing

47

Objectives

Spelling and Writing

Students will
- **proofread** a friendly letter.
- **use** the writing process to write a friendly letter.
- **proofread** their writing.

Using the Writing Process

Before assigning **Write a Friendly Letter,** see pages 258–259 in the Student Edition for a complete review of the writing process and additional writing assignments. You may also wish to refer to pages Z12–Z13 in the Teacher Edition.

Keeping a Spelling Journal

Encourage students to record the words they misspelled on the weekly test in a personal spelling journal. These words may be recycled for future study. Students may also wish to include words from their writing. See pages Z12–Z13 in the Teacher Edition for more information.

---

16. You **should've** been more careful not to awaken the baby.
★17. Dad drove the car **through** the park.
★18. We **understood** the terms of the agreement.
19. Use one level **teaspoon** of baking powder in the batter.
20. I **would've** been on time if the bus had not been late.

Option 2:
Multiple Spelling Words Per Sentence
(See procedures on pages Z10–Z11.)

1. We **would've understood** the **routine** if we had had more time to practice.
2. Don't **assume** that you may **intrude** whenever you want.
3. Let me **introduce** you to the others in the **neighborhood.**
4. I **could've** fallen asleep on that soft **cushion.**
5. Does the recipe call for one **tablespoon** or one **teaspoon** of **fluid?**
6. We **should've** read the **bulletin** with more care.
7. His **goodness** often helps him **through** tough times.
8. This test score is **proof** of your high **aptitude.**
9. I **conclude** that our teacher will **approve** this report.

Option 3:
Standardized Test
(See *Teacher Resource Book,* Unit 7.)

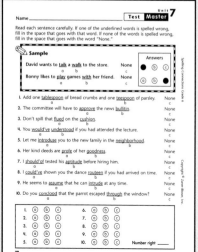

Unit 7
Test Master

T47

Objectives

Strategy Words

Students will
• **review** words studied previously that are related to the spelling strategy.
• **preview** unknown words that are related to the spelling strategy.

Optional Enrichment

VOCABULARY CONNECTIONS

►Strategy Words◄

Remind the students that the **Strategy Words** are related to the spelling patterns they have studied in this unit. The **Review Words** are below grade level, and the **Preview Words** are above grade level. You may wish to use the following sentences to introduce the words in context.

Review Words:
Words From Grade 5

1. It is **foolish** not to do your best.
2. We said **good-bye** as we were driving away.
3. My grandfather makes great **goulash**.
4. Did they find a **solution** to the problem?
5. A clarinet is a **woodwind** instrument.

Preview Words:
Words From Grade 7

6. She likes to use a **bamboo** fishing pole.
7. We bought the scarf at a **boutique** in the mall.
8. He used most of the **footage** in the video camera on wild animals.
9. Any **pollutant** in the water can cause a bad taste.
10. Keep up your **pursuit** of excellence.

Review Words
1. goulash
2. foolish
3. solution
4. woodwind
5. good-bye

Preview Words
6. bamboo
7. pollutant
8. pursuit
9. boutique
10. footage

►Strategy Words◄

Review Words: Vowels /o͞o/, /o͝o/

Write a word from the box to complete each sentence.

foolish	good-bye	goulash	solution	woodwind

1. He ordered the homemade beef _____.
2. It would be _____ to go out in the cold without your coat.
3. I think I have the _____ to your problem.
4. He plays the bassoon in the _____ section of the city's orchestra.
5. She abruptly said _____ and left.

Preview Words: Vowels /o͞o/, /o͝o/

Write the word from the box that matches each clue.

bamboo	boutique	footage	pollutant	pursuit

6. This is the panda bear's favorite food.
7. Exhaust from cars is an example of this.
8. This is a hobby, an interest, or a high-speed chase.
9. This is a small and fashionable shop.
10. This is the length or amount of motion picture film.

48

Unit **7** RECAP

You may wish to assign the **Unit 7 Homework Master** (*Teacher Resource Book,* Unit 7) as a fun way to recap the spelling words.

Unit 7 Homework Master

Content Words

Social Studies: The Caribbean

Write the word from the box that matches each clue.

Caribbean	sunset	coral	tropics	lagoon

1. the region of the earth near the equator
2. a shallow body of water
3. an arm of the Atlantic Ocean between Central and South America
4. the time when the sun disappears in the west
5. a hard substance formed by skeletons of tiny sea animals

Social Studies: International Relations

Write the words from the box to complete the paragraph.

diplomat	rumor	protect	enlist	quota

A __6.__ was spreading among the immigrants that the president was going to restrict their __7.__ of persons entering the country. The president decided to __8.__ help. He appointed a __9.__ to assure the immigrants that every effort would be made to __10.__ their rights.

Apply the Spelling Strategy

Circle the letters that spell the /o͞o/ or /o͝o/ sound in two of the Content Words you wrote.

Word Study

Words From Other Languages

This Strategy Word came from a Hungarian term for a kind of stew made by herdsmen while they were pasturing their animals. Write the Strategy Word.

49

Social Studies: The Caribbean
1. tropics
2. lagoon
3. Caribbean
4. sunset
5. coral

Social Studies: International Relations
6. rumor
7. quota
8. enlist
9. diplomat
10. protect

Words From Other Languages
1. goulash

Objectives

Content Words

Students will
- **expand** vocabulary with content-related words.
- **relate** the spelling strategy to words outside the basic spelling list.
- **understand** that some words are borrowed from other languages.

Content Words

Social Studies: The Caribbean

Use these sentences to introduce the words and their meanings.
1. We cruised on the **Caribbean** Sea.
2. The **sunset** was the most beautiful I had ever seen.
3. We could see the **coral** reef beneath the water.
4. Millions of types of plants are found in the **tropics**.
5. Alligators were seen in the **lagoon**.

Social Studies: International Relations

Use these sentences to introduce the words and their meanings.
6. He served as a **diplomat** in Mexico.
7. We should not rely on **rumor** when dealing with others.
8. We try to **protect** our interests when we meet with other countries.
9. These people will **enlist** in the United States Army.
10. A **quota** can limit the number of immigrants into a country.

Word Study

Words From Other Languages

As people have moved to America from other countries, the English language has grown by absorbing new words from the languages of the newcomers. Challenge students to suggest other words from other languages. These might include **pizza** (Italian), **taco** (Mexican Spanish), and **sushi** (Japanese).

Unit 8 Home Spelling Practice

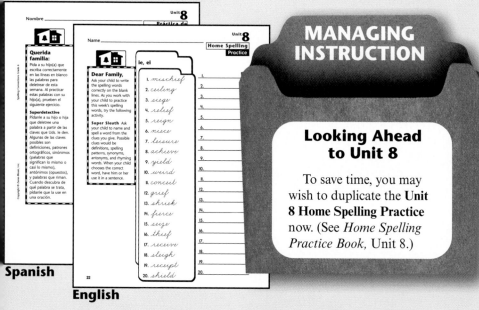

Spanish

English

MANAGING INSTRUCTION

Looking Ahead to Unit 8

To save time, you may wish to duplicate the **Unit 8 Home Spelling Practice** now. (See *Home Spelling Practice Book,* Unit 8.)

Basic Spelling List

mischief	conceit
ceiling	grief
siege	shriek
relief	fierce
reign	seize
niece	thief
leisure	receive
achieve	sleigh
yield	receipt
weird	shield

Strategy Words

Review
chiefs	protein
midfield	weight
pierce	

Preview
achieving	mischievous
believable	briefly
fierceness	

Content Words

Science: Radios
amplitude	reverberate
receiver	loudness
decibel	

Health: Skin
dermis	dermatologist
hygiene	complexion
epidermis	

Individual Needs

Challenge Words
overview	surveillance
fiendish	deceit
chiefly	piercing

Alternate Word List★
mischief	shriek
ceiling	fierce
relief	seize
niece	thief
leisure	receive

★ For students who need to study fewer Basic Spelling words

T50A

MATERIALS

Student Edition
Pages 50–55
Challenge Activities, p. 230

Teacher Edition
Pages T50A–T55
Challenge Activities, p. T230

Teacher Resource Book
Unit 8 Homework Master
Unit 8 Practice Masters
Flip Folder Practice Master
Unit 8 Test Master

Home Spelling Practice Book
Unit 8 Home Spelling Practice (English or Spanish)

Other *Spelling Connections* Resources
- Audiotape, Grade 6
- Practice Book for Grammar, Usage, and Mechanics, Grade 6
- Spelling Support for Second Language Learners, Grade 6
- Support Software on CD-ROM
- Transparency Book, Grade 6
- Word Sort CD-ROM, Grade 6

OBJECTIVES

Spelling and Thinking
Students will
- **read** the spelling words in list form and in context.
- **sort** the spelling words according to the **ie** and **ei** spelling patterns.
- **read** and remember this week's spelling strategy.

Spelling and Vocabulary
Students will
- **write** spelling words to complete a series of meaning-related words.
- **write** rhyming words to complete sentences.
- **use** dictionary guide words to locate spelling words.

Spelling and Reading
Students will
- **solve** analogies using spelling words.
- **complete** sentences using spelling words.
- **complete** a paragraph with spelling words.

Spelling and Writing
Students will
- **proofread** a story.
- **use** the writing process to write a story.
- **proofread** their writing.

MEETING INDIVIDUAL NEEDS
Learning Styles

 Visual

Each student writes each spelling word on a separate piece of paper and puts the papers in an envelope. Divide the class into pairs of students. Have the partners take turns drawing a slip of paper out of each other's envelope. One partner then pronounces the word, and the other writes it. If the word is spelled correctly, the slip of paper is discarded. If the word is misspelled, the student studies the word and returns it to the envelope. The object of the game is to empty both envelopes.

 Auditory

Divide the class into two teams. Pronounce a spelling word for one team to spell. One student spells the word aloud. If the word is spelled correctly, the team scores a point. If the word is spelled incorrectly, a member of the other team tries to spell the word. If this time the word is spelled correctly, the second team scores the point and also has a chance to spell the next word. Continue the game until all the words have been correctly spelled.

 Kinesthetic

Make a rectangular shape on the floor with tape. Mark off twenty blocks. Write each spelling word on a sheet of construction paper, leaving the vowels out. Tape one word paper in each block. The first player stands on a line a few feet from the form and tosses a penny. The student must spell the word on which the penny lands. The student scores one point for each correct answer. Continue the game until all the words have been correctly spelled.

> **Hands-On Practice**
> All students will benefit from practicing with a **Flip Folder**. See page Z18.

Language and Cultural Differences

The /ē/ sound in Spanish is spelled by the letters **i** or **y**. Spanish-speaking students may therefore have some difficulty spelling words that contain the /ē/ sound spelled **ie** or **ei**.

Make two columns on the chalkboard, one headed with **ie,** the other with **ei**. Call out the spelling words in random order and have volunteers write each word in the appropriate columns and then pronounce the word.

MANAGING INSTRUCTION

3–5 Day Plan		Average	Below Average	Above Average
Day 1	**Day 1**	Pretest Spelling Mini-Lesson, p. T50 Spelling and Thinking, p. 50	Pretest Spelling Mini-Lesson, p. T50 Spelling and Thinking, p. 50	Pretest Spelling and Thinking, p. 50
	Day 2	Spelling and Vocabulary, p. 51	Spelling and Vocabulary, p. 51 (or) Unit 8 Practice Master, A and B	Spelling and Vocabulary, p. 51 Spelling and Reading, p. 52
Day 2	**Day 3**	Spelling and Reading, p. 52	Spelling and Reading, p. 52 (or) Unit 8 Practice Master, C and D	Challenge Activities, p. 230
	Day 4	Spelling and Writing, p. 53 Unit 8 Homework Master	Spelling and Writing, p. 53	Spelling and Writing, p. 53 Unit 8 Homework Master
Day 3	**Day 5**	Weekly Test	Weekly Test	Weekly Test
Vocabulary Connections (pages 54 and 55) may be used anytime during this unit.				

Objectives

Spelling and Thinking

Students will
- **read** the spelling words in list form and in context.
- **sort** the spelling words according to the **ie** and **ei** spelling patterns.
- **read** and remember this week's spelling strategy.

UNIT PRETEST

Use **Pretest Sentences** below. Refer to the self-checking procedures on student page 256. You may wish to use the **Unit 8 Word List Overhead Transparency** as part of the checking procedure.

TEACHING THE STRATEGY

Spelling Mini-Lesson

Write **grief, mischief, receive,** and **neighbor** on the chalkboard.

Use the words on the board to explain that the spelling patterns for **ie** and **ei** have different pronunciations:
- **ie** is usually pronounced with the **long e** sound (as in **grief**) but can be pronounced with the **short i** sound (as in **mischief**);
- **ei** can be pronounced as **long e** (as in **receive**) or as **long a** (as in **neighbor**).

Read **Remember the Spelling Strategy** on page 50. Tell the students to use these guidelines for remembering how to spell words that have the **ie** or **ei** pattern.

Point out that there are exceptions to the guidelines. Encourage the students to check the spelling list for possible exceptions. They may know other exceptions as well. Write these exceptions from the spelling list on the board: **leisure, seize, weird.** Other exceptions include **either, Fahrenheit, height, neither, seizure, sheik, protein, counterfeit, forfeit, foreign, species, financier.** Discuss why each word is an exception.

Ask a volunteer to read the spelling list aloud. Discuss word meanings as needed.

Order of answers may vary.

ie
1. mischief ★
2. siege
3. relief ★
4. niece ★
5. achieve
6. yield
7. grief
8. shriek ★
9. fierce ★
10. thief ★
11. shield

ei
12. ceiling ★
13. reign
14. leisure ★
15. weird
16. conceit
17. seize ★
18. receive ★
19. sleigh
20. receipt

50

Spelling and Thinking

READ THE SPELLING WORDS

1.	mischief	*mischief*	A puppy often gets into **mischief**.
2.	ceiling	*ceiling*	Paint was peeling from the **ceiling**.
3.	siege	*siege*	The town was under **siege** for two months.
4.	relief	*relief*	It was a **relief** to have the test over.
5.	reign	*reign*	The queen's **reign** lasted for fifty years.
6.	niece	*niece*	His **niece** is in sixth grade.
7.	leisure	*leisure*	He spends his **leisure** time fishing.
8.	achieve	*achieve*	She will try to **achieve** good grades.
9.	yield	*yield*	The driver slowed down at the **yield** sign.
10.	weird	*weird*	I thought the movie had a **weird** ending.
11.	conceit	*conceit*	His **conceit** caused him to lose friends.
12.	grief	*grief*	Her sad expression revealed her **grief**.
13.	shriek	*shriek*	We heard her **shriek** with laughter.
14.	fierce	*fierce*	The **fierce** wind blew the door open.
15.	seize	*seize*	At the signal, **seize** the ball and run.
16.	thief	*thief*	The police caught the **thief** in the act.
17.	receive	*receive*	You will **receive** the letter in the mail.
18.	sleigh	*sleigh*	The horse pulled the **sleigh** down the path.
19.	receipt	*receipt*	The sales clerk handed her the **receipt**.
20.	shield	*shield*	The hat will **shield** you from the rain.

SORT THE SPELLING WORDS

1.–11. Write the words that have the **ie** spelling pattern. Circle this vowel combination in the words you write.

12.–20. Write the words that have the **ei** spelling pattern. Circle this vowel combination in the words you write.

REMEMBER THE SPELLING STRATEGY

Remember this rhyme can often help you decide when to use **ie** and when to use **ei**: Use **i** before **e**, except after **c**, or when sounded as **a**, as in **neighbor** and **weigh**.

Pretest Sentences (See procedures on pages Z10–Z11.)

★ 1. My frisky cat is always getting into **mischief**.
★ 2. Paint was falling from the **ceiling** of the old house.
  3. Julio recovered after a long **siege** of illness.
★ 4. When I heard the good news, I felt great **relief**.
  5. The king was a successful leader and had a long **reign**.
★ 6. My mother's **niece** is my first cousin.
★ 7. How do you spend your **leisure** time?
  8. Michael works hard to **achieve** his goals.
  9. A **yield** sign directs drivers to allow oncoming traffic to go first.
  10. Jan made that **weird** costume from a box and a lamp shade.
  11. A person who is very proud may be accused of **conceit**.
  12. Her sad expression showed that she was filled with **grief**.
★13. I was so frightened by the horror that I wanted to **shriek**.
★14. We were frightened by the tiger's **fierce** growl.
★15. He tried to **seize** the paper before the breeze blew it away.
★16. The word **thief** is a synonym for robber.
★17. In a few days you should **receive** the postcard I sent you.
  18. Have you ever ridden in a horse-drawn **sleigh**?
  19. Did the salesperson give you a **receipt** for your purchase?
  20. Sunglasses **shield** your eyes from the rays of the sun.

Spelling and Vocabulary

Word Groups

Write a spelling word to complete each sequence.

1. sorrow, sadness, _____
2. trouble, misconduct, _____
3. free time, rest, _____
4. submit, give up, _____
5. grasp, grab, _____
6. realize, reach, _____
7. strange, unusual, _____
8. robber, burglar, _____
9. wild, violent, _____
10. rule, govern, _____

Ending Sounds

Write a spelling word that fits each sentence. The spelling word will rhyme with the underlined word.

11. Dropping at her <u>feet</u> was the grocery store _____.
12. Causing the candidate's <u>defeat</u> was his annoying _____.
13. The boards will <u>creak</u>, and the children will _____.
14. He cut a <u>piece</u> of cake and gave it to his _____.
15. They piled the <u>hay</u> into the wooden _____.
16. The knight in the <u>field</u> was protected by his _____.

Dictionary **guide words** help you find a word easily. The guide words appear at the top of the page and are the first entry word and the last entry word on a page. Write the spelling word that you would find between each of these pairs of guide words.

17. quotation • regional
18. regular • rival
19. candidate • CEO
20. secondary • skyscraper

Word Groups

1. grief
2. mischief
3. leisure
4. yield
5. seize
6. achieve
7. weird
8. thief
9. fierce
10. reign

Ending Sounds

11. receipt
12. conceit
13. shriek
14. niece
15. sleigh
16. shield

Using the Dictionary

17. receive
18. relief
19. ceiling
20. siege

51

Objectives

Spelling and Vocabulary

Students will
• **write** spelling words to complete a series of meaning-related words.
• **write** rhyming words to complete sentences.
• **use** dictionary guide words to locate spelling words.

Developing Oral Language Skills

Have students write a sentence using one of the spelling words. Then ask one student to read his or her sentence to the class, leaving out the spelling word. The first student able to determine the spelling word that was omitted from the sentence gets to read the next sentence.

MEETING INDIVIDUAL NEEDS

Providing More Help

This activity will help the students in understanding the **ei / ie** spelling patterns. Write the spelling words on the chalkboard, omitting the **ei** or **ie** letters in each word. Ask volunteers to take turns telling what the words are and filling in the blanks.

★Students who need to study fewer words should use the **Alternate Word List**. This list is starred on page T50 in the Teacher Edition. The **Unit 8 Practice Masters** (*Teacher Resource Book*) provide additional practice with these words.

Unit 8 Practice Masters

Name _____

Practice Master **Unit 8**

| 1. niece | 3. shriek | 5. mischief | 7. ceiling | 9. seize |
| 2. thief | 4. relief | 6. fierce | 8. receive | 10. leisure |

A. Three words in each row follow the same spelling pattern. Write the word that is different.

1. field, seize, shield, wield _____
2. receive, mischief, conceit, receipt _____
3. receive, thief, siege, shriek _____
4. leisure, conceit, seize, fierce _____

B. Write the spelling word you would find between these guide words.

1. reliable | relieve _____
2. legend | lemon _____
3. nation | notice _____
4. casual | channel _____
5. text | traffic _____
6. shelf | sleet _____

C. A sentence may be declarative, exclamatory, imperative, or interrogative. Write the spelling words missing from the sentences below. Then write what type of sentence each is.

1. Now _____ the opportunity. _____
2. Our playful puppy is full of _____. _____
3. How I enjoy my _____ time! _____
4. Did you _____ the package? _____

30

Practice Master **Unit 8**

ceiling   seize
receive   leisure

Letters are given to get you

T51

Spelling and Reading

Students will
- **solve** analogies using spelling words.
- **complete** sentences using spelling words.
- **complete** a paragraph with spelling words.

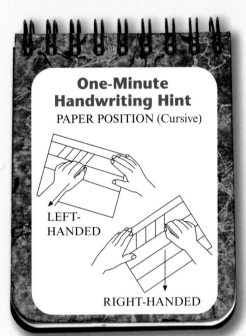

One-Minute Handwriting Hint
PAPER POSITION (Cursive)

LEFT-HANDED

RIGHT-HANDED

Legible handwriting can boost spelling scores by as much as 20%.

Spelling and Reading

mischief	ceiling	siege	relief	reign
niece	leisure	achieve	yield	weird
conceit	grief	shriek	fierce	seize
thief	receive	sleigh	receipt	shield

Solve the Analogies Write a spelling word to complete each analogy.

1. **President** is to **term** as **king** is to _____.
2. **Wheel** is to **car** as **runner** is to _____.
3. **Brother** is to **sister** as **nephew** is to _____.
4. **Delight** is to **joy** as **sorrow** is to _____.
5. **House** is to **roof** as **room** is to _____.
6. **Construct** is to **destroy** as **give** is to _____.

Solve the Analogies
1. reign
2. sleigh
3. niece
4. grief
5. ceiling
6. receive

Complete the Sentences Write a spelling word to complete each sentence.

7. I cannot return the shirt without the _____.
8. You should _____ the opportunity to see the movie.
9. She enjoys painting in her _____ time.
10. It is good to have confidence but not _____.
11. The package arrived safely, to my great _____.
12. I know she will _____ with delight at the news.
13. The shadows made _____ figures on the wall.
14. Police apprehended the _____ outside the bank.

Complete the Sentences
7. receipt
8. seize
9. leisure
10. conceit
11. relief
12. shriek
13. weird
14. thief

Complete the Paragraph Write spelling words from the box to complete the paragraph.

There are many legends about noble knights of medieval times who traveled the land defending the helpless against __15.__ intruders. With only their sword and __16.__, they were able to __17.__ noble deeds, preventing the __18.__ of a castle. Other stories tell of daring knights who forced robbers to __19.__ their weapons, keeping them from causing further harm and __20.__.

| siege |
| achieve |
| yield |
| fierce |
| shield |
| mischief |

Complete the Paragraph
15. fierce
16. shield
17. achieve
18. siege
19. yield
20. mischief

52

MEETING INDIVIDUAL NEEDS

Providing More Challenge

Challenge Words and **Challenge Activities** for Unit 8 appear on page 230. **Challenge Word Test Sentences** appear on page T230.

Unit 8 Challenge Activities

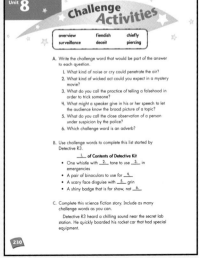

Unit 8 ★ Challenge Activities

overview | fiendish | chiefly
surveillance | deceit | piercing

A. Write the challenge word that would be part of the answer to each question.
1. What kind of noise or cry could penetrate the air?
2. What kind of wicked act could you expect in a mystery movie?
3. What do you call the practice of telling a falsehood in order to trick someone?
4. What might a speaker give in his or her speech to let the audience know the broad picture of a topic?
5. What do you call the close observation of a person under suspicion by the police?
6. Which challenge word is an adverb?

B. Use challenge words to complete this list started by Detective R3.
___1___ of Contents of Detective Kit
- One whistle with __2__ tone to use for __3__ in emergencies
- A pair of binoculars to use for __4__
- A scary face disguise with __5__ grin
- A shiny badge that is for show, not __6__

C. Complete this science fiction story. Include as many challenge words as you can.
Detective R3 heard a chilling sound near the secret lab station. He quickly boarded his rocket car that had special equipment.

230

Weekly Test Options

Option 1:
One Spelling Word Per Sentence
(See procedures on pages Z10–Z11.)

1. What goal do you expect to **achieve** by working hard?
★ 2. The **ceiling** of the old house was made of tin.
3. His **conceit** makes others dislike him.
★ 4. The **fierce** animal made a hissing sound.
5. She could feel only **grief** at the sad news.
★ 6. He likes to write stories in his **leisure** time.
★ 7. Little children often get into **mischief**.
★ 8. My uncle has only one **niece**.
9. Save the **receipt** in case you need to return the item.
★10. Did you **receive** the package yet?
11. The king's **reign** lasted for eighteen years.
★12. It was a **relief** to know that she was not hurt.
★13. **Seize** my hat before it blows away!
14. The tent will **shield** us from the rain.

Spelling and Writing

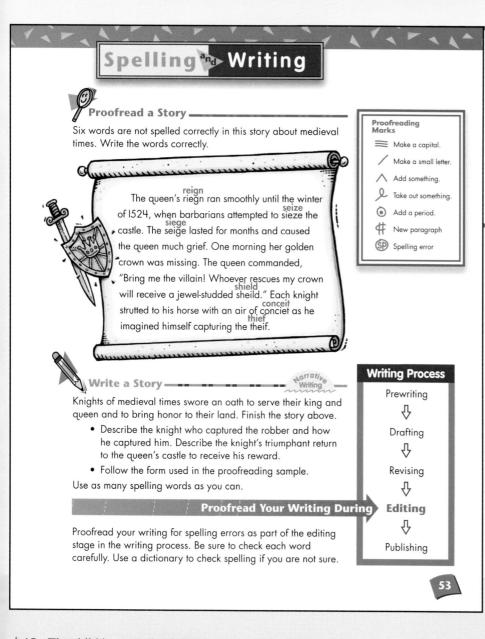

Proofread a Story

Six words are not spelled correctly in this story about medieval times. Write the words correctly.

reign
The queen's riegn ran smoothly until the winter of 1524, when barbarians attempted to **seize** the castle. The **siege** lasted for months and caused the queen much grief. One morning her golden crown was missing. The queen commanded, "Bring me the villain! Whoever rescues my crown will receive a jewel-studded **shield**." Each knight strutted to his horse with an air of **conceit** as he imagined himself capturing the **thief**.

Proofreading Marks

≡ Make a capital.
/ Make a small letter.
∧ Add something.
℘ Take out something.
⊙ Add a period.
⌗ New paragraph.
SP Spelling error

Write a Story

Narrative Writing

Knights of medieval times swore an oath to serve their king and queen and to bring honor to their land. Finish the story above.

- Describe the knight who captured the robber and how he captured him. Describe the knight's triumphant return to the queen's castle to receive his reward.
- Follow the form used in the proofreading sample.

Use as many spelling words as you can.

Proofread Your Writing During → Editing

Proofread your writing for spelling errors as part of the editing stage in the writing process. Be sure to check each word carefully. Use a dictionary to check spelling if you are not sure.

Writing Process

Prewriting
⇩
Drafting
⇩
Revising
⇩
Editing
⇩
Publishing

53

Objectives

Spelling and Writing
Students will
- **proofread** a story.
- **use** the writing process to write a story.
- **proofread** their writing.

Using the Writing Process

Before assigning **Write a Story,** see pages 258–259 in the Student Edition for a complete review of the writing process and additional writing assignments. You may also wish to refer to pages Z12–Z13 in the Teacher Edition.

Keeping a Spelling Journal

Encourage students to record the words they misspelled on the weekly test in a personal spelling journal. These words may be recycled for future study. Students may also wish to include words from their writing. See pages Z12–Z13 in the Teacher Edition for more information.

★ 15. The child let out a loud **shriek** in the scary movie.
16. The island was under **siege** from a nearby country.
17. We could see the tracks of the **sleigh** in the snow.
★ 18. The **thief** ran away with my money.
19. The **weird** sounds made us think we were in danger.
20. The farmer got a good **yield** from his second planting.

Option 2:
Multiple Spelling Words Per Sentence
(See procedures on pages Z10–Z11.)

1. The **thief** wanted to **seize** my watch, but I ran away.
2. During his **reign** the city was under **siege**.
3. The **fierce** look of the tiger made us **shriek** with fear.
4. It was a **relief** to **achieve** our goal at last.
5. My **niece** likes to ride in a **sleigh** in the snow during her **leisure** time.
6. The man who fixed the **ceiling** gave my mother a **receipt** marked paid.
7. It is not always possible to **shield** yourself from **grief**.
8. Do not **yield** to **mischief** or **conceit**.
9. Did you **receive** the same **weird** message I did?

Option 3:
Standardized Test
(See *Teacher Resource Book,* Unit 8.)

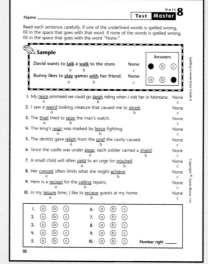

Unit 8 Test Master

Objectives

Strategy Words

Students will
- **review** words studied previously that are related to the spelling strategy.
- **preview** unknown words that are related to the spelling strategy.

Optional Enrichment

Unit 8 enrichment

VOCABULARY CONNECTIONS

►Strategy Words◄

Remind the students that the **Strategy Words** are related to the spelling pattern they have studied in this unit. The **Review Words** are below grade level, and the **Preview Words** are above grade level. You may wish to use the following sentences to introduce the words in context.

Review Words:
Words From Grade 5
1. The three boys were elected **chiefs** of their cabins.
2. He caught the ball in **midfield**.
3. The sharp needle can **pierce** the heavy cloth.
4. **Protein** is a needed body nutrient.
5. The **weight** limit of the bridge was posted.

Preview Words:
Words From Grade 7
6. She likes **achieving** high scores on her tests.
7. The science fiction story seemed **believable**.
8. We were aware of the **fierceness** of the wild animals.
9. The **mischievous** children were punished for their deeds.
10. The movie was only shown **briefly** in our town.

Review Words
1. pierce
2. protein
3. midfield
4. weight
5. chiefs

Preview Words
6. achieving
7. mischievous
8. fierceness
9. believable
10. briefly

►Strategy Words◄

Review Words: ie, ei

Write a word from the box that matches each clue.

chiefs	midfield	pierce
	protein	weight	

1. This is what a nail might do to a tire.
2. Meat, milk, eggs, and some beans have this.
3. This is the middle of the field.
4. This would decrease if you were on the moon.
5. This is what you would call two fire department leaders.

Preview Words: ie, ei

Write words from the box to complete the movie review.

achieving	believable	fierceness
	mischievous	briefly	

In this, his first attempt at directing a movie, David Parker seems to be __6.__ near perfection. In his playful and __7.__ way, Parker weaves reality with fiction, combining the __8.__ of battle scenes with touching moments. The result is a __9.__ story that even I found convincing. Pausing only __10.__ to enjoy his success, Parker is already planning his next movie.

54

Unit 8 RECAP

You may wish to assign the **Unit 8 Homework Master** (*Teacher Resource Book,* Unit 8) as a fun way to recap the spelling words.

Unit 8 Homework Master

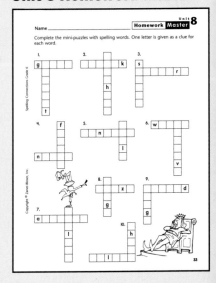

Content Words

Science: Radios

Write a word from the box that matches each clue.

| amplitude receiver decibel reverberate loudness |

1. part of a radio that picks up signals
2. a unit used for measuring the intensity of sounds
3. to sound again
4. the distance between the highest and lowest point of a sound wave
5. the volume of a sound

Health: Skin

Write the words from the box that complete the paragraph.

| dermis hygiene epidermis dermatologist complexion |

Dr. Wong is a __6.__. She told me that proper __7.__ is the key to keeping my __8.__ healthy. She says the skin has layers. The __9.__, or outer layer, suffers the most wear and tear. The __10.__, the layer just below the outer layer, contains the structures that allow the skin to sweat.

Apply the Spelling Strategy

Circle the **ie** or **ei** spelling pattern in two of the Content Words you wrote.

Word Study

Eponyms

An **eponym** is a word that comes from someone's name. For example, the **leotard** was named after Jules Leotard, a trapeze artist. Write the Content Word that was formed by adding the old Latin term for "ten" to part of Alexander Graham Bell's name.

55

Science: Radios
1. rec(ei)ver
2. decibel
3. reverberate
4. amplitude
5. loudness

Health: Skin
6. dermatologist
7. hyg(ie)ne
8. complexion
9. epidermis
10. dermis

Eponyms
1. decibel

Objectives

Content Words

Students will
- **expand** vocabulary with content-related words.
- **relate** the spelling strategy to words outside the basic spelling list.
- **understand** and identify an eponym.

Content Words

Science: Radios

Use these sentences to introduce the words and their meanings.

1. The **amplitude** of the radio was included in the instruction book.
2. The **receiver** on our TV needed to be replaced.
3. The **decibel** level of our new CD player is more than we needed.
4. We could hear the sound **reverberate** throughout the house.
5. The **loudness** was unpleasant.

Health: Skin

Use these sentences to introduce the words and their meanings.

6. Nerve endings and blood vessels are contained in the **dermis** of the skin.
7. **Hygiene** helps keep us healthy.
8. The **epidermis** is the outermost layer of skin.
9. The **dermatologist** warned against too much exposure to the sun.
10. He tried many soaps in order to improve his **complexion**.

Word Study

Eponyms

Challenge students to name other eponyms they know (e.g., the **teddy bear** was named for President Theodore Roosevelt, the **Morse code** after Samuel Morse, and the **braille** system of writing for Louis Braille). Point out that if they do something to become famous, a word could be named after them!

Unit 9 Home Spelling Practice

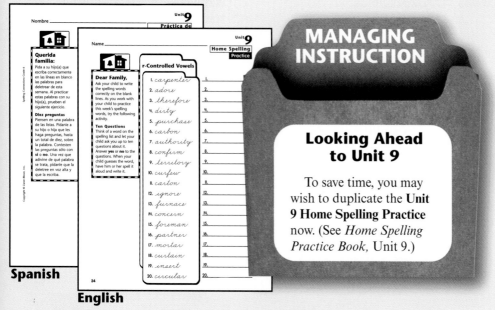

Spanish

English

MANAGING INSTRUCTION

Looking Ahead to Unit 9

To save time, you may wish to duplicate the **Unit 9 Home Spelling Practice** now. (See *Home Spelling Practice Book,* Unit 9.)

Basic Spelling List

carpenter	carton
adore	ignore
therefore	furnace
dirty	concern
purchase	foreman
carbon	partner
authority	mortar
confirm	curtain
territory	insert
curfew	circular

Strategy Words

Review
birthmark	murmur
carpet	service
fortune	

Preview
awareness	furthermore
affirm	refer
endorse	

Content Words

Fine Arts: Music
castanets	timpani
percussion	marimba
chimes	

Science: Respiratory System
cartilage	trachea
respiratory	inhale
exhale	

Individual Needs

Challenge Words
nursery	departure
garment	porcelain
dormitory	formation

Alternate Word List ★
carpenter	ignore
therefore	concern
dirty	partner
purchase	curtain
carton	circular

★ For students who need to study fewer Basic Spelling words

MATERIALS

Student Edition
Pages 56–61
Challenge Activities, p. 231

Teacher Edition
Pages T56A–T61
Challenge Activities, p. T231

Teacher Resource Book
Unit 9 Homework Master
Unit 9 Practice Masters
Flip Folder Practice Master
Unit 9 Test Master

Home Spelling Practice Book
Unit 9 Home Spelling Practice (English or Spanish)

Other *Spelling Connections* Resources
- Audiotape, Grade 6
- Practice Book for Grammar, Usage, and Mechanics, Grade 6
- Spelling Support for Second Language Learners, Grade 6
- Support Software on CD-ROM
- Transparency Book, Grade 6
- Word Sort CD-ROM, Grade 6

OBJECTIVES

Spelling and Thinking
Students will
- **read** the spelling words in list form and in context.
- **sort** the spelling words according to **r-controlled** vowel sounds.
- **read** and remember this week's spelling strategy.

Spelling and Vocabulary
Students will
- **write** spelling words to complete a group of meaning-related words.
- **distinguish** spelling words by their structure.
- **use** a dictionary to find base words and their part of speech.

Spelling and Reading
Students will
- **write** spelling words that answer questions.
- **complete** sentences using spelling words.
- **complete** a paragraph using spelling words.

Spelling and Writing
Students will
- **proofread** a paragraph.
- **use** the writing process to write a paragraph showing contrast.
- **proofread** their writing.

MEETING INDIVIDUAL NEEDS
Learning Styles

 Visual

Have two teams line up across the room from each other. Call out a spelling word. A member of each team races to the chalkboard and writes the word. The speller then runs back and touches the next speller on the team as you call out another spelling word. Continue the game until all of the spelling words have been written. Have the students on one team check and correct the other team's spelling. A team scores five points for each word spelled correctly.

 Auditory

Divide the class into two teams. For each team, draw a large tree with bare branches on poster board. Pronounce a spelling word aloud. The first player on Team A pronounces the word and spells it aloud. Others on Team A write the word and then check each other's spelling. Each student who spells the word correctly receives a leaf to put on Team A's tree. Then it is Team B's turn to spell a word. The teams take turns until all of the spelling words have been spelled. The team whose tree has the most leaves is the winner.

 Kinesthetic

Have a spelling race. Designate "start" and "finish" points on the floor. Call out a word for each student to spell aloud in turn. If a student spells a word correctly, he or she takes one 12-inch step toward the finish line. The first student to cross the finish line is the winner.

> **Hands-On Practice**
> All students will benefit from practicing with a **Flip Folder**. See page Z18.

Language and Cultural Differences

The **r**-controlled vowel sound-symbol associations may be difficult for some students to make because of regional pronunciations or language backgrounds that do not include the sounds. For example, Spanish-speaking students may tend to trill the **r** in the /är/ and the /ôr/ and may have difficulty with the /ûr/, which does not exist in Spanish. In addition, in some English dialects the **r** sound with **r**-controlled vowels is not pronounced. Although exact pronunciation is not essential for correct spelling, some students are likely to need extra practice with the spelling words for this unit.

MANAGING INSTRUCTION

3–5 Day Plan		Average	Below Average	Above Average
Day 1	**Day 1**	Pretest Spelling Mini-Lesson, p. T56 Spelling and Thinking, p. 56	Pretest Spelling Mini-Lesson, p. T56 Spelling and Thinking, p. 56	Pretest Spelling and Thinking, p. 56
	Day 2	Spelling and Vocabulary, p. 57	Spelling and Vocabulary, p. 57 (or) Unit 9 Practice Master, A and B	Spelling and Vocabulary, p. 57 Spelling and Reading, p. 58
Day 2	**Day 3**	Spelling and Reading, p. 58	Spelling and Reading, p. 58 (or) Unit 9 Practice Master, C and D	Challenge Activities, p. 231
	Day 4	Spelling and Writing, p. 59 Unit 9 Homework Master	Spelling and Writing, p. 59	Spelling and Writing, p. 59 Unit 9 Homework Master
Day 3	**Day 5**	Weekly Test	Weekly Test	Weekly Test

Vocabulary Connections (pages 60 and 61) may be used anytime during this unit.

Objectives

Spelling and Thinking

Students will
• **read** the spelling words in list form and in context.
• **sort** the spelling words according to **r**-controlled vowel sounds.
• **read** and remember this week's spelling strategy.

UNIT PRETEST

Use **Pretest Sentences** below. Refer to the self-checking procedures on student page 256. You may wish to use the **Unit 9 Word List Overhead Transparency** as part of the checking procedure.

TEACHING THE STRATEGY

Spelling Mini-Lesson

Write **insert, dirty,** and **curtain** on the chalkboard. Read each word aloud. Ask the students which sound these words have in common. (the r-controlled vowel, /ûr/) Write /**ûr**/ on the board and tell them that this is the dictionary respelling for this vowel sound. Ask a volunteer to circle letters that spell /**ûr**/. (er in insert, ir in dirty, ur in curtain)

Write **carton, therefore, adore,** and **territory** on the board. Ask, "Do these words all have the same **r**-controlled vowel sound?" (no) Ask students to listen for the difference in the **r**-controlled vowel sound in each word. Write /**är**/ next to **carton,** /**âr**/ next to **there** in **therefore,** /**ôr**/ next to **adore** and **territory.** Remind them that these are the dictionary respellings for these **r**-controlled vowel sounds.

Explain that vowel sounds are controlled by **r** only in accented syllables. Write the dictionary respelling of **carpenter** (/kär′ pən tər/) on the board. Explain that the accented first syllable has the **r**-controlled vowel sound; the last syllable is pronounced /**tər**/ because it is not accented.

Find **therefore** in the **Spelling Dictionary.** Discuss the fact that **therefore** has a primary accent on the first syllable and a secondary accent on the second syllable. So, there is an **r**-controlled vowel sound in each syllable.

Read **Remember the Spelling Strategy** on page 56.

T56

Order of answers may vary.

/ûr/
1. dirty ★
2. purchase ★
3. confirm
4. curfew
5. furnace
6. concern ★
7. curtain ★
8. insert
9. circular ★

/är/
10. carpenter ★
11. carbon
12. carton ★
13. partner ★

/är/ and /ôr/
14. therefore ★

/ôr/
15. adore
16. authority
17. territory
18. ignore ★
19. foreman
20. mortar

56

READ THE SPELLING WORDS

1.	carpenter	*carpenter*	The **carpenter** repaired the door frame.
2.	adore	*adore*	I know that they **adore** seafood.
3.	therefore	*therefore*	It is raining; **therefore,** the game is off.
4.	dirty	*dirty*	Please leave your **dirty** shoes at the door.
5.	purchase	*purchase*	She made a ten-dollar **purchase.**
6.	carbon	*carbon*	Charcoal has **carbon** in it.
7.	authority	*authority*	He is an **authority** on birds.
8.	confirm	*confirm*	Call the airline to **confirm** your flight.
9.	territory	*territory*	This **territory** is used for agriculture.
10.	curfew	*curfew*	The teenagers have a ten o'clock **curfew.**
11.	carton	*carton*	The **carton** broke, and the books fell out.
12.	ignore	*ignore*	You should **ignore** his rude remark.
13.	furnace	*furnace*	Check the **furnace** before winter arrives.
14.	concern	*concern*	My main **concern** is for your safety.
15.	foreman	*foreman*	The **foreman** asked us to work overtime.
16.	partner	*partner*	He is my **partner** in science class.
17.	mortar	*mortar*	A mason puts **mortar** between bricks.
18.	curtain	*curtain*	She chose a heavy fabric for the **curtain.**
19.	insert	*insert*	First **insert** the ticket in the slot.
20.	circular	*circular*	The house has a wide **circular** staircase.

SORT THE SPELLING WORDS

1.–9. Write the words that spell the /**ûr**/ sound **er, ir,** or **ur.**
10.–13. Write the words that spell the /**är**/ sound **ar.**
14. Write the word that spells the /**âr**/ sound **er** and the /**ôr**/ sound **ore.**
15.–20. Write the other words that spell the /**ôr**/ sound **or** or **ore.**

REMEMBER THE SPELLING STRATEGY

Remember that **r**-controlled vowel sounds can be spelled in different ways, including /**ûr**/ spelled **er, ir,** and **ur;** /**är**/ spelled **ar;** /**âr**/ spelled **er;** and /**ôr**/ spelled **or** and **ore.**

Pretest Sentences (See procedures on pages Z10–Z11.)

★ **1.** This cabinet was built by a skilled **carpenter.**
2. I **adore** the decorations in that shop window.
★ **3.** I know that you are right; **therefore,** I agree.
★ **4.** His shoes were **dirty** because he was playing in the mud.
★ **5.** What will you **purchase** with your birthday money?
6. Archaeologists use radioactive **carbon** to learn the age of bones.
7. Jamal was given the **authority** to check the tests.
8. I hope that the reports do not **confirm** this bad news.
9. The **territory** along the equator is tropical in climate.
10. Jack's parents gave him a nine o'clock **curfew.**
★**11.** The family stored the old books in a cardboard **carton.**
★**12.** We tried to **ignore** the noise, but it disturbed our sleep.
13. When our **furnace** broke down, we had no heat for a week.
★**14.** The change in the schedule will **concern** everyone.
15. The **foreman** is in charge of fifty people.
★**16.** Will you be my **partner** and work with me on this assignment?
17. A mixture for holding bricks together is called **mortar.**
★**18.** Will one wide **curtain** be enough to cover that window?
19. You can buy a newspaper if you **insert** two quarters in the machine.
★**20.** The **circular** driveway created an elegant approach to the house.

Spelling and Vocabulary

Related Words

Write a spelling word to complete each group.

1. box, package, crate, _____
2. worry, distress, anxiety, _____
3. area, region, zone, _____
4. filthy, unclean, soiled, _____
5. builder, woodworker, cabinetmaker, _____
6. tin, lead, silicon, _____
7. heater, radiator, boiler, _____
8. glue, sealant, filler, _____
9. shade, blinds, drapes, _____
10. supervisor, boss, manager, _____
11. deadline, time limit, _____
12. avoid, disregard, _____

Word Analysis

Change the underlined part of each word to write a spelling word.

13. thereafter   15. purpose
14. community   16. particular

USING THE Dictionary

Write the spelling word that is the base word of each word below. Write the part of speech after each word you write.

17. adorable, adj.   19. partnership, n.
18. confirmation, n.   20. insertion, n.

◆ ◆ ◆

Dictionary Check Be sure to check your answers in your **Spelling Dictionary**.

Related Words
1. carton
2. concern
3. territory
4. dirty
5. carpenter
6. carbon
7. furnace
8. mortar
9. curtain
10. foreman
11. curfew
12. ignore

Word Analysis
13. therefore
14. authority
15. purchase
16. circular

Using the Dictionary
17. adore, v.
18. confirm, v.
19. partner, n.
20. insert, v.

57

Developing Oral Language Skills

Do a word sort by syllable. Write the following headings on the chalkboard: **two syllables, three syllables, more than three syllables**. Have a student read a spelling word aloud and call on a classmate to write the word under the proper heading. When finished listing the words, ask volunteers to say each word aloud again and to draw a line between the syllables. Finally, ask the students to note the spelling of each syllable and to circle those syllables that contain the **r**-controlled vowel sound.

MEETING INDIVIDUAL NEEDS
Providing More Help

To aid the students in understanding **r**-controlled vowel sounds, pronounce the spelling words and write them on the chalkboard. After you write each word, have the students write it on paper. Ask a volunteer to circle the **r**-controlled vowel in the word on the chalkboard, and have the students circle the vowel on their papers. Pronounce the word again, heavily emphasizing the accented syllable—**car′** pen ter, **part′** ner.

★Students who need to study fewer words should use the **Alternate Word List**. This list is starred on page T56 in the Teacher Edition. The **Unit 9 Practice Masters** (*Teacher Resource Book*) provide additional practice with these words.

Unit 9 Practice Masters

Name _____   Practice **Master** 9

| 1. carton | 3. partner | 5. dirty | 7. ignore | 9. curtain |
| 2. carpenter | 4. concern | 6. circular | 8. therefore | 10. purchase |

A. Write the spelling words in alphabetical order.

1. _____
2. _____
3. _____
4. _____
5. _____
6. _____
7. _____
8. _____
9. _____
10. _____

B. Write the spelling word that goes with each group.

1. box, package, crate, _____   _____
2. builder, woodworker, cabinetmaker, _____   _____
3. buy, acquire, obtain, _____   _____
4. unclear, filthy, impure, _____   _____
5. companion, associate, co-owner, _____   _____

34

Practice **Master** 9

ignore   curtain
therefore   purchase

Objectives

Spelling and Reading

Students will
- **write** spelling words that answer questions.
- **complete** sentences using spelling words.
- **complete** a paragraph using spelling words.

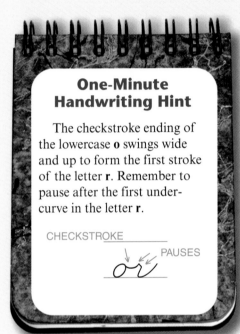

One-Minute Handwriting Hint

The checkstroke ending of the lowercase **o** swings wide and up to form the first stroke of the letter **r**. Remember to pause after the first under-curve in the letter **r**.

CHECKSTROKE

PAUSES

Legible handwriting can boost spelling scores by as much as 20%.

Spelling and Reading

carpenter	adore	therefore	dirty	purchase
carbon	authority	confirm	territory	curfew
carton	ignore	furnace	concern	foreman
partner	mortar	curtain	insert	circular

Answer the Questions Write the spelling word that answers each question.

1. What pattern of motion does a windmill have?
2. What do you call a cardboard milk container?
3. What kind of paper was once used to make copies?
4. What requires someone to be home before dark?
5. What mixture is made with cement, sand, and water?
6. What does a customer do in a store?
7. Who works side by side with someone else?

Complete the Meaning Write a spelling word to complete each sentence.

8. To open the box, _____ the key and turn.
9. He dumped the _____ laundry into the washer.
10. We are late; _____, we should walk fast.
11. An ornithologist is an _____ on birds.
12. I will ask him to play a song that I _____.
13. The director signaled me to open the _____ on the stage.
14. Much of the _____ in northern Africa is desert.

Complete the Paragraph Write spelling words from the box to complete the paragraph.

The ___15.___ of the construction project gathered his crew to express his ___16.___. He wanted to ___17.___ that the house would be completed on time. The ___18.___ had finished the framing. The ___19.___ had been installed. The crew was prepared to ___20.___ the rainy weather and work until the job was done.

furnace
concern
foreman
confirm
carpenter
ignore

Answer the Questions
1. circular
2. carton
3. carbon
4. curfew
5. mortar
6. purchase
7. partner

Complete the Meaning
8. insert
9. dirty
10. therefore
11. authority
12. adore
13. curtain
14. territory

Complete the Paragraph
15. foreman
16. concern
17. confirm
18. carpenter
19. furnace
20. ignore

58

MEETING INDIVIDUAL NEEDS

Providing More Challenge

Challenge Words and **Challenge Activities** for Unit 9 appear on page 231. **Challenge Word Test Sentences** appear on page T231.

Unit 9 Challenge Activities

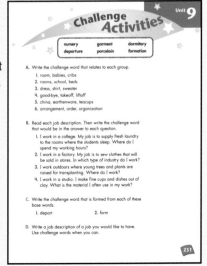

Weekly Test Options

Option 1:
One Spelling Word Per Sentence

(See procedures on pages Z10–Z11.)

1. All living things contain some **carbon**.
★ 2. That garden bench was built by a **carpenter**.
★ 3. Here is a small **carton** for your cards and letters.
★ 4. A ring is **circular**.
5. Do not forget to **insert** your letter in the envelope.
6. We will try to **confirm** that these reports are true.
7. The stores closed before the **curfew**.
★ 8. The **curtain** was raised as the play started.
★ 9. How did your clothes get so **dirty**?
10. Bricks and **mortar** make a strong wall.
11. The automatic **furnace** turns itself on and off.
12. My dad is the **foreman** at the factory.
13. The President has the **authority** to appoint judges.
★14. You cannot **ignore** the errors in the report.
★15. Your mother's **concern** is that you eat a healthy diet.

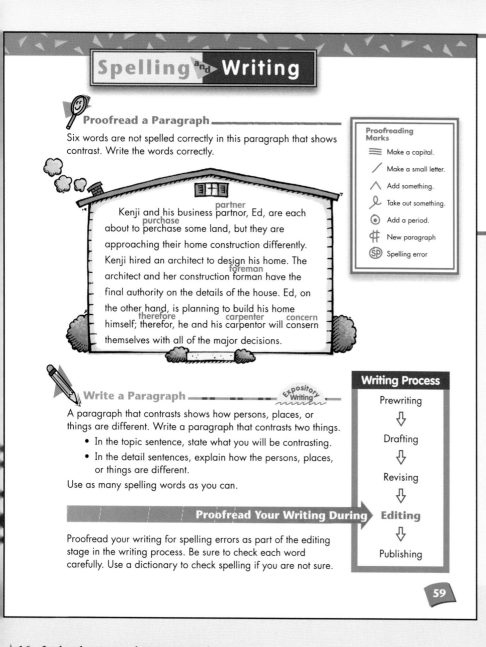

Spelling and Writing

Proofread a Paragraph

Six words are not spelled correctly in this paragraph that shows contrast. Write the words correctly.

Kenji and his business partnor, Ed, are each *partner* about to perchase some land, but they are *purchase* approaching their home construction differently. Kenji hired an architect to design his home. The architect and her construction forman have the *foreman* final authority on the details of the house. Ed, on the other hand, is planning to build his home himself; therefor, he and his carpentor will consern *therefore* *carpenter* *concern* themselves with all of the major decisions.

Proofreading Marks

≡ Make a capital.
/ Make a small letter.
∧ Add something.
℘ Take out something.
⊙ Add a period.
⌗ New paragraph
ⓈⓅ Spelling error

Write a Paragraph
Expository Writing

A paragraph that contrasts shows how persons, places, or things are different. Write a paragraph that contrasts two things.

• In the topic sentence, state what you will be contrasting.
• In the detail sentences, explain how the persons, places, or things are different.

Use as many spelling words as you can.

Proofread Your Writing During → Editing

Proofread your writing for spelling errors as part of the editing stage in the writing process. Be sure to check each word carefully. Use a dictionary to check spelling if you are not sure.

Writing Process

Prewriting
⇩
Drafting
⇩
Revising
⇩
Editing
⇩
Publishing

59

Objectives

Spelling and Writing

Students will
• **proofread** a paragraph.
• **use** the writing process to write a paragraph showing contrast.
• **proofread** their writing.

Using the Writing Process

Before assigning **Write a Paragraph,** see pages 258–259 in the Student Edition for a complete review of the writing process and additional writing assignments. You may also wish to refer to pages Z12–Z13 in the Teacher Edition.

Keeping a Spelling Journal

Encourage students to record the words they misspelled on the weekly test in a personal spelling journal. These words may be recycled for future study. Students may also wish to include words from their writing. See pages Z12–Z13 in the Teacher Edition for more information.

★16. Is that boy your dance **partner**?
★17. I will use the money to **purchase** some furniture.
18. My cat thinks that our yard is her **territory**.
★19. Her decision is logical and **therefore** appeals to me.
20. "I **adore** that baby!" she exclaimed.

Option 2:
Multiple Spelling Words Per Sentence
(See procedures on pages Z10–Z11.)

1. The **foreman** used his **authority** to **purchase** new uniforms for the **carpenter**.
2. The workers built a brick and **mortar** wall around the **territory**.
3. The new **furnace** was **circular** in shape.
4. **Carbon** paper can make your hands **dirty**.
5. Please **insert** the **curtain** into that **carton**.
6. The mayor's **concern** led her to set up a **curfew** for one week.
7. This letter will **confirm** that he is to be made a **partner** in the business.
8. I **adore** you; **therefore**, please do not **ignore** me.

Option 3:
Standardized Test
(See *Teacher Resource Book,* Unit 9.)

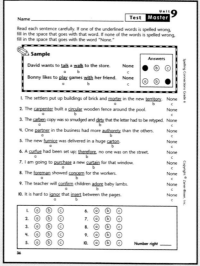

**Unit 9
Test Master**

T59

Objectives

Strategy Words

Students will
- **review** words studied previously that are related to the spelling strategy.
- **preview** unknown words that are related to the spelling strategy.

Optional Enrichment

VOCABULARY CONNECTIONS

Strategy Words

Remind the students that the **Strategy Words** are related to the spelling patterns they have studied in this unit. The **Review Words** are below grade level, and the **Preview Words** are above grade level. You may wish to use the following sentences to introduce the words in context.

Review Words:
Words From Grade 5

1. His **birthmark** was a family characteristic.
2. My family selected the **carpet** on our living room floor.
3. It is our good **fortune** to live in a democracy.
4. There was a low **murmur** in the crowd as news of his arrival spread.
5. Serving in the military is a **service** to our country.

Preview Words:
Words From Grade 7

6. The teacher's **awareness** of the problem prevented many hurt feelings.
7. The nurse will **affirm** that this illness is not contagious.
8. The famous baseball player will **endorse** this brand of shoes.
9. The president stated, **furthermore,** that we would be sure to begin on time.
10. I will **refer** to many books while doing research for my report.

Review Words
1. birthmark
2. murmur
3. service
4. fortune
5. carpet

Preview Words
6. endorse
7. refer
8. furthermore
9. awareness
10. affirm

Strategy Words

Review Words: r-Controlled Vowels

Write a word from the box to match each definition.

birthmark	carpet	fortune	murmur	service

1. a mark on the body since birth
2. say something in a low voice
3. the act of helping others
4. the good or bad luck that comes to someone
5. a heavy covering for a floor

Preview Words: r-Controlled Vowels

Write words from the box that complete this letter to an editor.

awareness	affirm	endorse	furthermore	refer

Dear Editor:

Regarding tomorrow's election, I would like to __6.__ Julio Flores for governor. For proof of his skill, you need only __7.__ to his excellent performance as attorney general. And __8.__, his __9.__ of the needs of the people of our state serves to __10.__ his ability to lead.

Sincerely,

Mun Sook Kim

Mun Sook Kim
Middletown

60

Unit 9 RECAP

You may wish to assign the **Unit 9 Homework Master** (*Teacher Resource Book,* Unit 9) as a fun way to recap the spelling words.

Unit 9 Homework Master

Name _____

Use the code to write your spelling words. Unscramble the first five letters in circles to find the spelling word that answers the first riddle. Use the other circled letters to answer the second riddle.

| ☆ -ar | △ -er | ▲ -ir | □ -or | ● -ur |

1. t △ rit □ y
2. c ☆ b o n
3. c o n f ▲ m
4. c ● t a i n
5. c ▲ c u l ☆
6. c ☆ t o n
7. i g n □ e
8. d ▲ t y
9. c ☆ p e n t △
10. c o n c △ n
11. p □ t n △
12. t h △ e f □ e
13. m □ t ☆
14. f ● n a c e
15. c ● f e w
16. p ● c h a s e

What can cause a draft if you leave it ajar? _____

If five men don't show up for a baseball team, what will there be?

a ___ ___ ___ ___ ___ ___ ___ ___ ___ team

37

▼Content Words▼

Fine Arts: Music

Write the word from the box that matches each clue.

castanets	percussion	chimes	timpani	marimba

1. instrument that makes bell-like sounds
2. a large xylophone
3. instruments that are struck to produce sounds
4. Spanish dancer's instrument
5. kettledrums

Science: Respiratory System

Write the word from the box that completes each sentence.

cartilage	respiratory	exhale	trachea	inhale

6. The _____ system controls breathing.
7. Your joints have _____ to protect the bones from wear and tear.
8. When you _____, your lungs expand.
9. The windpipe is another name for the _____.
10. When you breathe out, you _____ carbon dioxide.

Apply the Spelling Strategy

Not all vowels followed by **r** are **r**-controlled. The vowel must be in the same syllable as the **r** and affected by the **r** in pronunciation. Circle the letters that spell the **r**-controlled vowel sound in two of the Content Words you wrote.

▼Word Study▼

Onomatopoeia

Onomatopoeia means that a word sounds like what it names. **Chuckle, chirp, groan,** and **moo** are examples of onomatopoeia. Write the Strategy Word that shows onomatopoeia.

Fine Arts: Music
1. chimes
2. marimba
3. percussion
4. castanets
5. timpani

Science: Respiratory System
6. respirat(or)y
7. c(ar)tilage
8. inhale
9. trachea
10. exhale

Onomatopoeia
1. murmur

61

Objectives

Content Words

Students will
- **expand** vocabulary with content-related words.
- **relate** the spelling strategy to words outside the basic spelling list.
- **understand** onomatopoeia and identify simple onomatopoeic words.

▼Content Words▼

Fine Arts: Music

Use these sentences to introduce the words and their meanings.
1. The rhythm of the **castanets** helped set a mood for the Spanish dancers.
2. There was a special practice for the **percussion** instruments of the band.
3. We could hear the soft **chimes** as we walked through the chapel.
4. The beat of the **timpani** added a new sound to the music.
5. I was excited to have been chosen to play the **marimba**.

Science: Respiratory System

Use these sentences to introduce the words and their meanings.
6. The **cartilage** in his knee was damaged in the accident.
7. We studied the **respiratory** system.
8. When we breathe out, we **exhale**.
9. Our **trachea** carries air to our lungs.
10. When we breathe in, we **inhale**.

▼Word Study▼

Onomatopoeia

Teach the word **onomatopoeia** to the students, and help them pronounce it: ŏn' ə-măt' ə-pē' ə. Challenge students to name other words that show onomatopoeia (e.g., **chirp, buzz,** and **thud**).

Unit 10 Home Spelling Practice

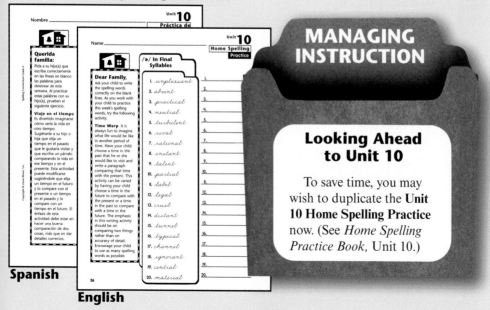

Spanish

English

MANAGING INSTRUCTION

Looking Ahead to Unit 10

To save time, you may wish to duplicate the **Unit 10 Home Spelling Practice** now. (See *Home Spelling Practice Book*, Unit 10.)

Basic Spelling List

unpleasant	label
absent	legal
practical	cruel
neutral	distant
turbulent	tunnel
rival	typical
rational	channel
instant	ignorant
talent	central
partial	material

Strategy Words

Review
angel	loyal
final	pleasant
incident	

Preview
apparent	equidistant
confidential	ordinal
diesel	

Content Words

Math: Proportions
equivalent	reciprocal
ratio	proportion
invert	

Social Studies: Debate
debate	panelist
opinion	logical
disagreement	

Individual Needs

Challenge Words
hysterical	cordial
interval	frequent
jovial	inhabitant

Alternate Word List★
practical	tunnel
instant	typical
talent	ignorant
label	central
distant	material

★ For students who need to study fewer Basic Spelling words

MATERIALS

Student Edition
Pages 62–67
Challenge Activities, p. 232

Teacher Edition
Pages T62A–T67
Challenge Activities, p. T232

Teacher Resource Book
Unit 10 Homework Master
Unit 10 Practice Masters
Flip Folder Practice Master
Unit 10 Test Master

Home Spelling Practice Book
Unit 10 Home Spelling Practice
(English or Spanish)

Other *Spelling Connections* Resources
- Audiotape, Grade 6
- Practice Book for Grammar, Usage, and Mechanics, Grade 6
- Spelling Support for Second Language Learners, Grade 6
- Support Software on CD-ROM
- Transparency Book, Grade 6
- Word Sort CD-ROM, Grade 6

OBJECTIVES

Spelling and Thinking
Students will
- **read** the spelling words in list form and in context.
- **sort** the spelling words according to /ə/ sounds and spelling patterns.
- **read** and remember this week's spelling strategy.

Spelling and Vocabulary
Students will
- **write** spelling words that are synonyms for given words.
- **distinguish** spelling words by their structure.
- **use** antonym relationships to identify spelling words.
- **use** stress in pronunciation to identify spelling words.

Spelling and Reading
Students will
- **solve** analogies using spelling words.
- **complete** sentences using spelling words.
- **complete** a paragraph using spelling words.

Spelling and Writing
Students will
- **proofread** a paragraph.
- **use** the writing process to write a descriptive paragraph.
- **proofread** their writing.

MEETING INDIVIDUAL NEEDS
Learning Styles

 Visual

Divide the class into pairs of students. One partner pronounces a spelling word while the other writes it on the chalkboard. The first student then checks the spelling. Misspelled words should be written correctly. The pairs continue, trading places, until they have spelled all the words correctly.

 Auditory

Divide the class into two teams to play "Word Baseball." Pronounce a spelling word to the team member at bat. A student who spells the word correctly scores a hit. A student who misspells the word strikes out, and the next team member tries to spell the word. Continue until the team has three outs; then the other team takes a turn.

 Kinesthetic

Give each student some cold cooked spaghetti noodles, toothpicks, and sheets of construction paper. Have the students form the letters of a spelling word on the paper. After they have spelled a word with spaghetti, have the students write the word on another piece of paper. Other materials that could be used include felt scraps and string.

Hands-On Practice
All students will benefit from practicing with a **Flip Folder**. See page Z18.

Language and Cultural Differences

The /ə/ + l and /ən/ + t sounds may be difficult for Spanish-speaking students to hear because these sounds do not occur in Spanish. Exact pronunciation is not essential to spelling, however, if the student has an opportunity to associate word meaning with the visual sequence of letters.

Write the spelling words on the board, clearly pronouncing each word and emphasizing the stressed syllables. Write the words that have the final /ə/ + l in one color, and the words that have the final /ən/ + t sound in a different color. Have the students copy the spelling words from the board, using two different colors.

MANAGING INSTRUCTION

3–5 Day Plan		Average	Below Average	Above Average
Day 1	**Day 1**	Pretest Spelling Mini-Lesson, p. T62 Spelling and Thinking, p. 62	Pretest Spelling Mini-Lesson, p. T62 Spelling and Thinking, p. 62	Pretest Spelling and Thinking, p. 62
	Day 2	Spelling and Vocabulary, p. 63	Spelling and Vocabulary, p. 63 (or) Unit 10 Practice Master, A and B	Spelling and Vocabulary, p. 63 Spelling and Reading, p. 64
Day 2	**Day 3**	Spelling and Reading, p. 64	Spelling and Reading, p. 64 (or) Unit 10 Practice Master, C and D	Challenge Activities, p. 232
	Day 4	Spelling and Writing, p. 65 Unit 10 Homework Master	Spelling and Writing, p. 65	Spelling and Writing, p. 65 Unit 10 Homework Master
Day 3	**Day 5**	Weekly Test	Weekly Test	Weekly Test
Vocabulary Connections (pages 66 and 67) may be used anytime during this unit.				

Objectives

Spelling and Thinking

Students will
- **read** the spelling words in list form and in context.
- **sort** the spelling words according to /ə/ sounds and spelling patterns.
- **read** and remember this week's spelling strategy.

UNIT PRETEST

Use **Pretest Sentences** below. Refer to the self-checking procedures on student page 256. You may wish to use the **Unit 10 Word List Overhead Transparency** as part of the checking procedure.

TEACHING THE STRATEGY

Spelling Mini-Lesson

Write **legal** and **label** on the board. Ask a volunteer to pronounce each word. Ask, "Do you hear any difference in how the second syllable is pronounced in each word?" (no)

Circle **al** and **el** in these words and point out that both endings are pronounced the same: **schwa + l.** Write /ə/ on the chalkboard and remind students that this is the symbol for the **schwa** sound. This sound is very much like **short u** and can occur in unaccented syllables.

Encourage students to brainstorm other words that end in **al** or **el.** Write them on the chalkboard and determine if they also include /ə/ + l.

Write **distant** and **talent** on the board and repeat the process for /ən/ + t.

Discuss the fact that words whose final syllables include the schwa sound can be difficult to spell because any vowel can spell the schwa sound. Encourage students to come up with mnemonic devices, or sayings, to help them remember how to spell words that are difficult for them. For example, "There is an <u>ant</u> in **ignorant**" could help them remember how to spell **ignorant.** Discuss other possible mnemonics.

Read **Remember the Spelling Strategy** on page 62.

Order of answers may vary.

al
1. practical ★
2. neutral
3. rival
4. rational
5. partial
6. legal
7. typical ★
8. central ★
9. material ★

el
10. label ★
11. cruel
12. tunnel ★
13. channel

ent
14. absent
15. turbulent
16. talent ★

ant
17. unpleasant
18. instant ★
19. distant ★
20. ignorant ★

62

Spelling and Thinking

READ THE SPELLING WORDS

1. unpleasant	*unpleasant*	Washing a pan is an **unpleasant** task.
2. absent	*absent*	She was **absent** from school today.
3. practical	*practical*	His **practical** answer surprised us.
4. neutral	*neutral*	You can take sides, but I am **neutral.**
5. turbulent	*turbulent*	The ocean was **turbulent** from a storm.
6. rival	*rival*	We will play our **rival** in today's game.
7. rational	*rational*	He gave us a **rational** explanation.
8. instant	*instant*	I saw the rainbow for only an **instant.**
9. talent	*talent*	She is known for her musical **talent.**
10. partial	*partial*	He gave only a **partial** answer.
11. label	*label*	The **label** says the tie is made of silk.
12. legal	*legal*	He asked a lawyer for **legal** advice.
13. cruel	*cruel*	It is **cruel** to leave the dog alone.
14. distant	*distant*	She seemed shy and **distant** at first.
15. tunnel	*tunnel*	The truck stalled in the **tunnel.**
16. typical	*typical*	Her **typical** day begins with a jog.
17. channel	*channel*	The boat sailed through the **channel.**
18. ignorant	*ignorant*	He was **ignorant** of the game rules.
19. central	*central*	I live in the **central** part of the state.
20. material	*material*	The new **material** was delivered today.

SORT THE SPELLING WORDS

1.–9. Write the words that have the /əl/ sound spelled **al.**

10.–13. Write the words that have the /əl/ sound spelled **el.**

14.–16. Write the words that have the /ənt/ sound spelled **ent.**

17.–20. Write the words that have the /ənt/ sound spelled **ant.**

REMEMBER THE SPELLING STRATEGY

Remember that the **schwa** sound (/ə/) often occurs in unstressed final syllables. Think about how /ə/ is spelled in the final syllable in **legal, label, talent,** and **distant.**

Pretest Sentences (See procedures on pages Z10–Z11.)

1. Because of pesky flies, our picnic was **unpleasant.**
2. John is never **absent** from school.
★ 3. A headband is a **practical** way to keep your hair in place.
4. Sarah would neither agree nor disagree, so she was **neutral.**
5. The forecaster predicted strong gusts of wind and **turbulent** weather.
6. The cheers stopped when the **rival** team scored a basket.
7. Remain calm and you will find a **rational** solution to your problem.
★ 8. This camera develops the picture in an **instant.**
★ 9. Dion is a skilled athlete, but my special **talent** is art.
10. That page has only a **partial** listing of today's events.
★11. The directions are printed on the **label.**
12. Since there are no signs, it is a **legal** parking space.
13. Aretha was never **cruel** to animals.
★14. Can you hear the **distant** sound of an airplane?
★15. We drove into a **tunnel** carved right through a mountain.
★16. It is a **typical** reaction for a dog to bark at strangers.
17. Which **channel** do you prefer to watch on television?
★18. Do you believe that a horse is a smart or an **ignorant** animal?
★19. The theme of the story is its **central** idea.
★20. What **material** will you choose to work with for your art project?

Spelling and Vocabulary

Synonyms

Write a spelling word that is a synonym for each word.

1. lawful	4. normal	6. middle
2. opponent	5. substance	7. tag
3. useful		

Word Structure

8. Write the spelling word that has the /o͞o/ sound spelled **eu**.
9. Write the spelling word that has the /o͞o/ sound spelled **u**.
10. Write the spelling word that begins with the consonant digraph **ch**.
11.–12. Change the first letter in **national** and in **funnel**. Write the spelling words.

Antonyms

Write the spelling words that complete the meaning.

13. **Tie** is to **untie** as **pleasant** is to _____.
14. **Whole** is to **piece** as **complete** is to _____.

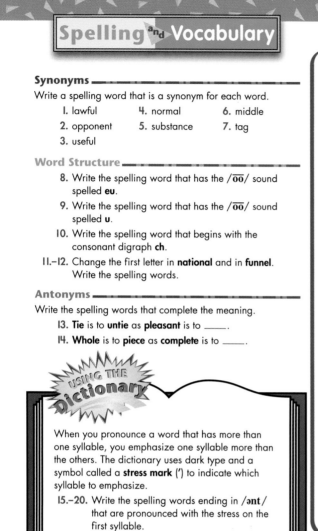

USING THE Dictionary

When you pronounce a word that has more than one syllable, you emphasize one syllable more than the others. The dictionary uses dark type and a symbol called a **stress mark** (′) to indicate which syllable to emphasize.

15.–20. Write the spelling words ending in /ənt/ that are pronounced with the stress on the first syllable.

Synonyms
1. legal
2. rival
3. practical
4. typical
5. material
6. central
7. label

Word Structure
8. neutral
9. cruel
10. channel
11. rational
12. tunnel

Antonyms
13. unpleasant
14. partial

Using the Dictionary
15. absent
16. turbulent
17. instant
18. talent
19. distant
20. ignorant

63

Objectives

Spelling and Vocabulary

Students will
• **write** spelling words that are synonyms for given words.
• **distinguish** spelling words by their structure.
• **use** antonym relationships to identify spelling words.
• **use** stress in pronunciation to identify spelling words.

Developing Oral Language Skills

Have students practice pronouncing the spelling words with three or more syllables, first in isolation, then in an original sentence. Have the class listen to be sure each syllable is clearly pronounced.

MEETING INDIVIDUAL NEEDS

Providing More Help

This activity will aid the students in understanding the schwa sound in unstressed syllables at the ends of words. In each row below, two words have the /ə/ in an unaccented syllable. Read each group of words aloud and ask the students to write the words that have the /ə/.

rational, neutral, bloom	**central,** glove, **rival**
channel, frown, **tunnel**	lampshade, **instant, ignorant**
kindred, **talent, absent**	radio, **cruel, label**

★Students who need to study fewer words should use the **Alternate Word List**. This list is starred on page T62 in the Teacher Edition. The **Unit 10 Practice Masters** (*Teacher Resource Book*) provide additional practice with these words.

Unit 10 Practice Masters

Name_____ Practice **Master** Unit **10**

| 1. central | 3. typical | 5. label | 7. talent | 9. instant |
| 2. material | 4. practical | 6. tunnel | 8. distant | 10. ignorant |

A. Unscramble the letters to form spelling words. Write the words.

1. b e l l a _____
2. y a p i l c t _____
3. r i m a a l t e _____
4. n e l n u t _____
5. s t n n i a t _____
6. r e t a l c n _____

B. The underlined words are synonyms for spelling words. Write the spelling words.

1. The driver was <u>unaware</u> that the tank was leaking. _____
2. A sticky <u>substance</u> was draining out of the truck. _____
3. The <u>characteristic</u> response was to step on the brakes. _____
4. This was not <u>useful</u> due to heavy traffic. _____

C. Write the spelling word that goes with each definition.

1. a special ability _____
2. far away or long ago _____
3. a passage beneath the ground _____
4. not having knowledge _____
5. a short time _____
6. near the middle _____

38

Practice **Master** Unit **10**

| talent | instant |
| distant | ignorant |

Down
1. long ago or far away
2. at or near the center
3. silk, wool, or cotton

39

Objectives

Spelling and Reading

Students will
- **solve** analogies using spelling words.
- **complete** sentences using spelling words.
- **complete** a paragraph using spelling words.

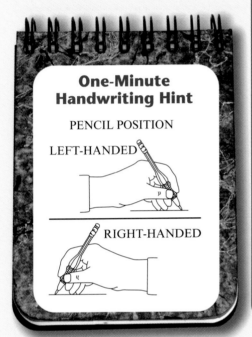

One-Minute Handwriting Hint

PENCIL POSITION

LEFT-HANDED

RIGHT-HANDED

Legible handwriting can boost spelling scores by as much as 20%.

---

unpleasant	absent	practical	neutral	turbulent
rival	rational	instant	talent	partial
label	legal	cruel	distant	tunnel
typical	channel	ignorant	central	material

Solve the Analogies

1. absent
2. ignorant
3. distant
4. instant
5. turbulent
6. practical

Complete the Sentences

7. talent
8. neutral
9. cruel
10. rational
11. legal
12. label
13. channel

Complete the Paragraph

14. tunnel
15. unpleasant
16. partial
17. typical
18. material
19. rival
20. central

Solve the Analogies Write a spelling word to complete each analogy.

1. **Angry** is to **pleased** as **present** is to _____.
2. **Famous** is to **unknown** as **educated** is to _____.
3. **Arrive** is to **depart** as **near** is to _____.
4. **Low** is to **high** as **slow** is to _____.
5. **Wind** is to **fierce** as **water** is to _____.
6. **Quiet** is to **calm** as **useful** is to _____.

Complete the Sentences Write a spelling word to complete each sentence.

7. This painting demonstrates his remarkable _____.
8. Switzerland remained _____ during two world wars.
9. The _____ joke hurt his feelings.
10. He was so angry that he was not behaving in a _____ way.
11. It is not _____ to park here so you will get a ticket.
12. Read the _____ before you buy the product.
13. I watch the morning news on another _____.

Complete the Paragraph Write spelling words from the box to complete the paragraph.

Building a __14.__ in the 1920s was a difficult and __15.__ task. Every day, __16.__ progress was made toward the goal. A __17.__ problem was preventing soft __18.__ from sliding into the hole as workers dug. Often two __19.__ digging crews worked from opposite sides. They met in the __20.__ area known as the "hole through."

typical
rival
unpleasant
tunnel
partial
material
central

64

MEETING INDIVIDUAL NEEDS

Providing More Challenge

Challenge Words and **Challenge Activities** for Unit 10 appear on page 232. **Challenge Word Test Sentences** appear on page T232.

Unit 10 Challenge Activities

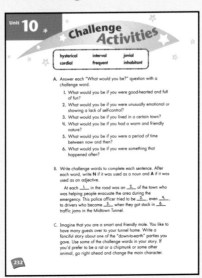

Weekly Test Options

Option 1:
One Spelling Word Per Sentence

(See procedures on pages Z10–Z11.)

1. Were you **absent** from class yesterday?
★ 2. We had to mail the package from the **central** station.
3. Our favorite program is on this **channel**.
4. This is only a **partial** list of your spelling words.
5. Do not be **cruel** to that animal!
★ 6. We could hear the **distant** sound of music.
★ 7. Jason has **talent** as an actor.
8. Squeaking brakes make an **unpleasant** noise.
★ 9. No one was **ignorant** of the school rules.
★10. Tell me the **instant** you hear the news.
★11. Every morning, he reads the **label** on the cereal box.
12. The farmer made **legal** claim to the land.
13. There must be a **rational** solution to this mystery.
★14. The jacket was made of a thick **material**.
15. Try to remain **neutral** when your friends disagree.
★16. She has a **practical** reason for everything she does.

Spelling and Writing

Proofread a Paragraph

Six words are not spelled correctly in this paragraph. Write the words correctly.

> Levi Strauss had a special talent for business. During the gold rush of the 1850s, Strauss sold canvas for tents. Knowing that the tipical [typical] miner needed heavy-duty pants, Strauss had a practicle [practical] solution. He used some of his canvas to stitch overalls. Later, Strauss replaced the canvas with a new materiel [material] called denim. He changed the nuetral [neutral] color of the denim by dyeing it a dark blue. Customers were parcial [partial] to this softer, darker fabric. Strauss's pants, or Levi's, were an instent [instant] hit.

Proofreading Marks

≡ Make a capital.
/ Make a small letter.
∧ Add something.
ℓ Take out something.
⊙ Add a period.
⌗ New paragraph.
SP Spelling error

Write a Paragraph

Descriptive Writing

Every paragraph has a main idea, which is stated in the topic sentence. The other sentences in the paragraph support or develop that central idea. Write a paragraph that describes something.

- Write about something that you have done or someone else has done.
- Follow the form used in the proofreading sample.

Use as many spelling words as you can.

Proofread Your Writing During → **Editing**

Proofread your writing for spelling errors as part of the editing stage in the writing process. Be sure to check each word carefully. Use a dictionary to check spelling if you are not sure.

Writing Process

Prewriting
⇩
Drafting
⇩
Revising
⇩
Editing
⇩
Publishing

65

---

17. **Turbulent** air currents made the plane ride rough.
18. That team is our constant **rival**.
★19. It is **typical** for friends to spend time together.
★20. Father drove the car through the **tunnel**.

Option 2:
Multiple Spelling Words Per Sentence
(See procedures on pages Z10–Z11.)

1. We could hear **distant** thunder as the **turbulent** storm approached.
2. It is not **typical** for her **rival** to be **absent** from meetings.
3. The **label** will list the kinds of **material** used to make the dress.
4. It is **ignorant** to be **unpleasant** or **cruel** to others.
5. It is more **practical** to take the **tunnel** than the bridge.
6. His **talent** gained **instant** approval.
7. A **neutral** judge and a **rational** jury are **central** to our **legal** system.
8. This is a **partial** list of the programs on this **channel**.

Option 3:
Standardized Test
(See *Teacher Resource Book,* Unit 10.)

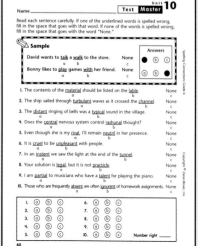

Unit 10 Test Master

T65

Objectives

Strategy Words

Students will
- **review** words studied previously that are related to the spelling strategy.
- **preview** unknown words that are related to the spelling strategy.

Strategy Words

Remind the students that the **Strategy Words** are related to the spelling patterns they have studied in this unit. The **Review Words** are below grade level, and the **Preview Words** are above grade level. You may wish to use the following sentences to introduce the words in context.

Review Words:
Words From Grade 5

1. Mother said I was an **angel** because I was so good.
2. This is the **final** test on the chapter.
3. Did you inform the teacher of the **incident** on the playground?
4. Jennifer is a **loyal** baseball fan.
5. It was a very **pleasant** day for a picnic.

Preview Words:
Words From Grade 7

6. It was **apparent** that he had studied because he did well on the test.
7. The **diesel** engine was used in the truck.
8. The North and South Poles are **equidistant** from the Equator.
9. The **confidential** report was locked in the cabinet.
10. When we put things in order, we use **ordinal** numbers.

Unit 10 enrichment

Review Words
1. angel
2. incident
3. loyal
4. final
5. pleasant

Preview Words
6. diesel
7. confidential
8. apparent
9. equidistant
10. ordinal

Strategy Words

Review Words: /ə/ in Final Syllables

Write words from the box to complete this thank-you note.

angel	final	incident	loyal	pleasant

Dear Lucy,

　　You were an __1.__ to come to my rescue last night when I had a flat tire. You even helped me through the __2.__ of the empty gas tank. You are a __3.__ friend indeed. I promise you that that was the __4.__ episode in my adventures. Our next occasion together will be more __5.__.

　　　　　　　　Your grateful friend,
　　　　　　　　Dave

Preview Words: /ə/ in Final Syllables

Write the word from the box that completes each sentence.

apparent	diesel	equidistant
confidential	ordinal	

6. Most trucks have a _____ engine.
7. Something that is private is _____.
8. Something that is easily understood is _____.
9. If the store is a mile from each of our homes, it is _____ from our homes.
10. **First, second,** and **third** are examples of _____ numbers.

66

Unit 10 RECAP

You may wish to assign the **Unit 10 Homework Master** (*Teacher Resource Book,* Unit 10) as a fun way to recap the spelling words.

Unit 10 Homework Master

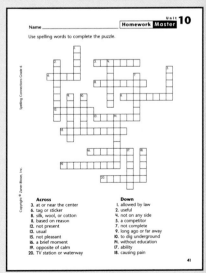

Content Words

Math: Proportions

Write the word from the box that completes each sentence.

equivalent	ratio	invert	reciprocal	proportion

1. Twelve inches are _____ to one foot.
2. The _____ of $^4/_3$ is $^3/_4$.
3. If you _____ $^1/_4$, the result is $^4/_1$.
4. The size of things in comparison to each other refers to _____.
5. The _____ of 2 to 3 is $^2/_3$.

Social Studies: Debate

Write the words from the box that complete the paragraph.

debate	opinion	disagreement	panelist	logical

Jurors __6.__ the issues that have been discussed during a trial. A jury __7.__ must form his or her own __8.__ and make __9.__ decisions based on what the jury learned during the trial. Any major __10.__ must be solved among the jurors before their verdict is delivered.

Apply the Spelling Strategy

Circle the letters that spell the /əl/ or the /ənt/ sound in the final syllable of four of the Content Words you wrote.

Word Study

Prefixes

The prefix **equi-** came from a Latin form, **aequi-**, that meant "even, same." Things that are **equivalent** are the same or equal. Write the Strategy Word that has this prefix and means "equally far apart."

67

Math: Proportions
1. equival(ent)
2. reciproc(al)
3. invert
4. proportion
5. ratio

Social Studies: Debate
6. debate
7. panelist
8. opinion
9. logic(al)
10. disagreem(ent)

Prefixes
1. equidistant

Objectives

Content Words

Students will
- **expand** vocabulary with content-related words.
- **relate** the spelling strategy to words outside the basic spelling list.
- **understand** how a prefix can affect the meaning of a word.

Content Words

Math: Proportions

Use these sentences to introduce the words and their meanings.

1. What is the **equivalent** of a dollar in English money?
2. Combine the liquids at a **ratio** of two cups of milk to one cup of water.
3. **Invert** the pail to empty it.
4. Their friendship was based on a **reciprocal** respect.
5. A large **proportion** of the class received a good grade.

Social Studies: Debate

Use these sentences to introduce the words and their meanings.

6. We watched the presidential **debate**.
7. We asked the principal's **opinion** about our project.
8. The **disagreement** occurred because of a misunderstanding.
9. Chantelle was chosen as a **panelist** on the committee.
10. A **logical** choice was to study.

Word Study

Prefixes

Help students understand that a **prefix** is a word part that is placed or "fixed" before a word (thus, "prefix") and changes the meaning of the word. Challenge students to identify other prefixes with which they are familiar (e.g., **un-, re-, dis-**).

Unit 11 Home Spelling Practice

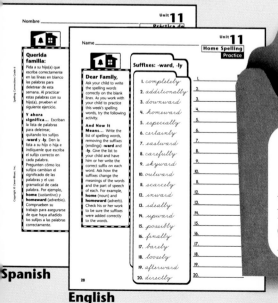

Spanish

English

Looking Ahead to Unit 11

To save you time, you may wish to duplicate the **Unit 11 Home Spelling Practice** now. (See *Home Spelling Practice Book,* Unit 11.)

Suffixes: -ward, -ly
1. completely
2. additionally
3. downward
4. homeward
5. especially
6. certainly
7. eastward
8. carefully
9. skyward
10. outward
11. scarcely
12. inward
13. ideally
14. upward
15. possibly
16. finally
17. barely
18. loosely
19. afterward
20. directly

Dear Family,
Ask your child to write the spelling words correctly on the blank lines. As you work with your child to practice this week's spelling words, try the following activity.

And Now It Means... Write the list of spelling words, removing the suffixes (endings) **-ward** and **-ly**. Give the list to your child and have him or her write the correct suffix on each word. Ask how the suffixes change the meanings of the words and the part of speech of each. For example, **home** (noun) and **homeward** (adverb). Check his or her work to be sure the suffixes were added correctly to the words.

Querida familia:
Pida a su hijo(a) que escriba correctamente en las líneas en blanco las palabras para deletrear de esta semana. Al practicar estas palabras con su hijo(a), prueben el siguiente ejercicio.

Y ahora significa... Escriban la lista de palabras para deletrear, quitando los sufijos **-ward** y **-ly**. Den la lista a su hijo o hija e indíquenle que escriba el sufijo correcto en cada palabra. Pregunten cómo los sufijos cambian el significado de las palabras y el uso gramatical de cada palabra. Por ejemplo, **home** (sustantivo) y **homeward** (adverbio). Comprueben su trabajo para asegurarse de que haya añadido los sufijos a las palabras correctamente.

MANAGING INSTRUCTION

Basic Spelling List

completely	scarcely
additionally	inward
downward	ideally
homeward	upward
especially	possibly
certainly	finally
eastward	barely
carefully	loosely
skyward	afterward
outward	directly

Strategy Words

Review
backward	westward
biweekly	forward
proudly	

Preview
accurately	initially
economically	usually
historically	

Content Words

Math: Geometry
congruent	transversal
perpendicular	
parallel	linear

Social Studies: International Relations
accord	blockade
regional	sanction
ally	

Individual Needs

Challenge Words
frontward	practically
politely	perfectly
actively	vigorously

Alternate Word List ★
completely	upward
downward	finally
especially	barely
certainly	loosely
carefully	afterward

★ For students who need to study fewer Basic Spelling words

T68A

MATERIALS

Student Edition
Pages 68–73
Challenge Activities, p. 233

Teacher Edition
Pages T68A–T73
Challenge Activities, p. T233

Teacher Resource Book
Unit 11 Homework Master
Unit 11 Practice Masters
Flip Folder Practice Master
Unit 11 Test Master

Home Spelling Practice Book
Unit 11 Home Spelling Practice
(English or Spanish)

Other *Spelling Connections* Resources
- Audiotape, Grade 6
- Practice Book for Grammar, Usage, and Mechanics, Grade 6
- Spelling Support for Second Language Learners, Grade 6
- Support Software on CD-ROM
- Transparency Book, Grade 6
- Word Sort CD-ROM, Grade 6

OBJECTIVES

Spelling and Thinking
Students will
- **read** the spelling words in list form and in context.
- **sort** the spelling words according to the suffixes **-ward** and **-ly**.
- **read** and remember this week's spelling strategy.

Spelling and Vocabulary
Students will
- **replace** words in a sentence with spelling words with the same or nearly the same meaning.
- **identify** spelling words that are antonyms.
- **add** a suffix to base words to form spelling words.

Spelling and Reading
Students will
- **solve** analogies using spelling words.
- **complete** sentences using spelling words.
- **complete** a paragraph using spelling words.

Spelling and Writing
Students will
- **proofread** a paragraph.
- **use** the writing process to write a set of directions.
- **proofread** their writing.

MEETING INDIVIDUAL NEEDS
Learning Styles

 Visual

As you pronounce each spelling word, have a student write the word on the chalkboard while the others write the word on paper. If necessary, correct the spelling of the word on the chalkboard. Then have all of the students check the spelling of the words on their papers.

 Auditory

Have the students play "What's My Word?" Each student chooses and writes a spelling word that he or she will describe. Then each student in turn gives the other students a clue about the chosen word. The clue can be about the meaning of the word, or can be related to the spelling pattern of the word. Those students who want to guess the word raise their hands. When the word is identified, each student writes the word on his or her paper. Each player who guesses a word and spells it correctly scores one point.

 Kinesthetic

Give each student about one hundred toothpicks. Allow the students ten minutes to arrange the toothpicks to form as many of the spelling words as possible. When a word is formed, its spelling must be confirmed as correct by a second student. Then both students write the word on their papers.

Hands-On Practice
All students will benefit from practicing with a **Flip Folder.** See page Z18.

Language and Cultural Differences

In Spanish, the /ē/ is represented by the letter **i.** Because the suffix **-ly** is pronounced with the /ē/, it may present a spelling problem for Spanish-speaking students. Remind the students that in English the /ē/ sound may be spelled in a variety of ways. Write **actively, shortly,** and **suitably** on the chalkboard and explain that in the suffix **-ly,** the /ē/ sound is spelled with the letter **y.**

The words that have the suffix **-ward** may be difficult for some students to spell because the letter **a** in the suf-

fix is a schwa sound. The spelling of the **-ward** suffix is often confused with the spelling of **word.**

On the chalkboard create two columns, one with the heading **-ward,** and the other with the heading **-ly.** Write the base words from which the spelling words were formed under the appropriate suffix headings. Have the students write the correct suffix at the end of each word.

MANAGING INSTRUCTION

3–5 Day Plan		Average	Below Average	Above Average
Day 1	Day 1	Pretest Spelling Mini-Lesson, p. T68 Spelling and Thinking, p. 68	Pretest Spelling Mini-Lesson, p. T68 Spelling and Thinking, p. 68	Pretest Spelling and Thinking, p. 68
	Day 2	Spelling and Vocabulary, p. 69	Spelling and Vocabulary, p. 69 (or) Unit 11 Practice Master, A and B	Spelling and Vocabulary, p. 69 Spelling and Reading, p. 70
Day 2	Day 3	Spelling and Reading, p. 70	Spelling and Reading, p. 70 (or) Unit 11 Practice Master, C and D	Challenge Activities, p. 233
	Day 4	Spelling and Writing, p. 71 Unit 11 Homework Master	Spelling and Writing, p. 71	Spelling and Writing, p. 71 Unit 11 Homework Master
Day 3	Day 5	Weekly Test	Weekly Test	Weekly Test
Vocabulary Connections (pages 72 and 73) may be used anytime during this unit.				

Objectives

Spelling and Thinking

Students will
- **read** the spelling words in list form and in context.
- **sort** the spelling words according to the suffixes **-ward** and **-ly**.
- **read** and remember this week's spelling strategy.

UNIT PRETEST

Use **Pretest Sentences** below. Refer to the self-checking procedures on student page 256. You may wish to use the **Unit 11 Word List Overhead Transparency** as part of the checking procedure.

TEACHING THE STRATEGY

Spelling Mini-Lesson

Write **upward** on the chalkboard. Circle the suffix **-ward**, explaining that it means "direction or tendency." Discuss the meaning of **upward** and how the meaning of the word relates to the base word **up** and the suffix **-ward**.

Repeat the procedure with **carefully,** explaining that **-ly** means "in a specific manner." Note that when a word ends in a consonant, **-ly** can be added without changing the spelling of the base word.

Write **completely** and **possibly** on the board. Use these words to explain that:
- The suffix **-ly** is added directly to most words that end in a **silent e** without changing the spelling of the base word.
- When an adjective that ends in **able** or **ible** (e.g., **possible**) is changed to an adverb by adding **-ly**, the final **le** is dropped before adding the suffix.

Write the remaining spelling words on the board. Ask students to write the base word next to each spelling word. Discuss how the meaning of each base word changed when the suffix was added.

Point out that words that end in the suffixes **-ward** and **-ly** are usually adverbs, words that describe verbs.

Read **Read Remember the Spelling Strategy** on page 68.

Order of answers may vary.

-ward
1. downward ★
2. homeward
3. eastward
4. skyward
5. outward
6. inward
7. upward ★
8. afterward ★

-ly, base word changed
9. possibly

-ly
10. completely ★
11. additionally
12. especially ★
13. certainly ★
14. carefully ★
15. scarcely
16. ideally
17. finally ★
18. barely ★
19. loosely ★
20. directly

68

READ THE SPELLING WORDS

1.	completely	*completely*	The food is **completely** gone.
2.	additionally	*additionally*	He is, **additionally,** a skilled artist.
3.	downward	*downward*	This **downward** path leads to a pond.
4.	homeward	*homeward*	Seeing the storm, we headed **homeward.**
5.	especially	*especially*	He is **especially** fond of spaghetti.
6.	certainly	*certainly*	I am **certainly** happy that you are home.
7.	eastward	*eastward*	The storm is moving **eastward.**
8.	carefully	*carefully*	Please open the package **carefully.**
9.	skyward	*skyward*	We looked **skyward** to see the plane.
10.	outward	*outward*	Fire laws say doors must open **outward.**
11.	scarcely	*scarcely*	I have **scarcely** finished my breakfast.
12.	inward	*inward*	These windows open **inward.**
13.	ideally	*ideally*	This is **ideally** the best place to meet.
14.	upward	*upward*	The wind carried the balloons **upward.**
15.	possibly	*possibly*	She is **possibly** the best soccer player.
16.	finally	*finally*	They **finally** arrived at midnight.
17.	barely	*barely*	I have **barely** started my homework.
18.	loosely	*loosely*	Place the flowers **loosely** in the vase.
19.	afterward	*afterward*	I will answer your question **afterward.**
20.	directly	*directly*	You should go **directly** to the bus.

SORT THE SPELLING WORDS

1.–8. Write the spelling words that end in **-ward**.

9. Write the spelling word in which the spelling of the base word changed when the suffix **-ly** was added.

10.–20. Write the spelling words that end in **-ly** with no changes to the spelling of the base word.

REMEMBER THE SPELLING STRATEGY

Remember that the suffix **-ward** means "direction" or "tendency." The suffix **-ly** means "in a specific manner." These suffixes are added to base words to form adverbs.

Pretest Sentences (See procedures on pages Z10–Z11.)

- ★ 1. Carmen has finished her homework **completely**.
- 2. Please wash the car this week and, **additionally,** wax it.
- ★ 3. Press **downward** on the handle to open the door.
- 4. Are you **homeward** bound?
- ★ 5. My aunt is an **especially** friendly person.
- ★ 6. Your party plans sound great, and we will **certainly** attend.
- 7. The wind was blowing in an **eastward** direction.
- ★ 8. She **carefully** placed the glass vase on the table.
- 9. If you want to see the rainbow, look **skyward**.
- 10. The **outward** push of his arm almost knocked me over.
- 11. We were **scarcely** in the house when the phone rang.
- 12. The door swung **inward** toward the kitchen.
- 13. **Ideally** the game should begin exactly at noon.
- ★14. We moved slowly **upward** on the crowded stairs.
- 15. Could this good news **possibly** be true?
- ★16. We **finally** came to the end of our journey.
- ★17. The airplane was **barely** visible through the clouds.
- ★18. His shoelaces were tied **loosely**.
- ★19. We went to the movies and **afterward** took a walk in the park.
- 20. When school is over, please come **directly** home.

Spelling and Vocabulary

Word Replacement

Write the spelling word that could replace the underlined word or words in each sentence.

1. I in particular enjoyed the ice skating.
2. We promised that we would come home immediately after school.
3. You, moreover, have earned a second award.
4. She cautiously drove down the narrow street.
5. And, lastly, I would like to thank my good friends.
6. We thought that you could perhaps help us.
7. The car at the top of the hill rolled toward a lower place.
8. The stock market is headed toward a higher position.

Antonyms

Write a spelling word that is an antonym for each word.

9. westward   11. doubtfully   13. beforehand
10. tightly   12. partially

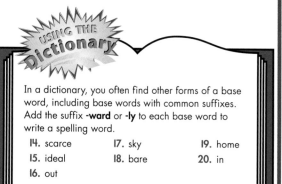

USING THE Dictionary

In a dictionary, you often find other forms of a base word, including base words with common suffixes. Add the suffix **-ward** or **-ly** to each base word to write a spelling word.

14. scarce   17. sky   19. home
15. ideal   18. bare   20. in
16. out

Word Replacement

1. especially
2. directly
3. additionally
4. carefully
5. finally
6. possibly
7. downward
8. upward

Antonyms

9. eastward
10. loosely
11. certainly
12. completely
13. afterward

Using the Dictionary

14. scarcely
15. ideally
16. outward
17. skyward
18. barely
19. homeward
20. inward

 69

Objectives

Spelling and Vocabulary

Students will

- **replace** words in a sentence with spelling words with the same or nearly the same meaning.
- **identify** spelling words that are antonyms.
- **add** a suffix to base words to form spelling words.

Developing Oral Language Skills

The word **finally** (/fī′ nə lē/) is sometimes misspelled because the second syllable is omitted when the word is pronounced. Write **finally** on the chalkboard. Have students pronounce **finally** and note whether they pronounce the word as two syllables or three syllables. If it is pronounced as a two-syllable word, have them practice saying the word as a three-syllable word. Repeat the activity using the words **additionally, especially, carefully,** and **ideally.** Note any syllables that are omitted in pronunciation.

MEETING INDIVIDUAL NEEDS

Providing More Help

Write the base words of the spelling words on the chalkboard. Have students take turns going up to the chalkboard and adding the right ending, either **-ly** or **-ward,** to form the spelling word. Remind the students that one word drops **le** from the base before **-ly** is added.

★Students who need to study fewer words should use the **Alternate Word List.** This list is starred on page T68 in the Teacher Edition. The **Unit 11 Practice Masters** (*Teacher Resource Book*) provide additional practice with these words.

Unit 11 Practice Masters

Name _____

Practice Master Unit **11**

1. upward   3. afterward   5. certainly   7. completely   9. carefully
2. downward   4. barely   6. loosely   8. finally   10. especially

A. The **Incorrect** suffixes have been added to these words. Write the spelling words correctly.

1. downly _____
2. looseward _____
3. afterly _____
4. especialward _____
5. uply _____
6. finalward _____

B. Write the spelling word that is an antonym for each word.

1. upward _____
2. tightly _____
3. doubtfully _____
4. before _____
5. carelessly _____

42

Practice Master Unit **11**

completely   carefully
finally   especially

for each word.

the words.

◯ = -ly

43

Objectives

Spelling and Reading

Students will
- **solve** analogies using spelling words.
- **complete** sentences using spelling words.
- **complete** a paragraph using spelling words.

One-Minute Handwriting Hint

The checkstroke ending of the lowercase **w** retraces and then swings wide to form the top of the letter **a**.

FORM TOP OF **a** ↓

Legible handwriting can boost spelling scores by as much as 20%.

Solve the Analogies
1. directly
2. afterward
3. loosely
4. skyward
5. certainly
6. completely
7. scarcely

Complete the Sentences
8. upward
9. homeward
10. inward
11. outward
12. ideally

Complete the Paragraph
13. downward
14. especially
15. barely
16. additionally
17. eastward
18. carefully
19. finally
20. possibly

Spelling and Reading

completely	additionally	downward	homeward
especially	certainly	eastward	carefully
skyward	outward	scarcely	inward
ideally	upward	possibly	finally
barely	loosely	afterward	directly

Solve the Analogies Write a spelling word to complete each analogy.

1. **Frantically** is to **fearfully** as **honestly** is to _____.
2. **Past** is to **future** as **beforehand** is to _____.
3. **Quietly** is to **softly** as **freely** is to _____.
4. **Back** is to **backward** as **sky** is to _____.
5. **Capable** is to **capably** as **certain** is to _____.
6. **Easily** is to **smoothly** as **entirely** is to _____.
7. **Silent** is to **silently** as **scarce** is to _____.

Complete the Sentences Write a spelling word to complete each sentence.

8. We looked _____ toward the decorated ceiling.
9. After a long time away from his family, he headed _____.
10. The boat sprung a leak, and water rushed _____.
11. From _____ appearances, she seems confident and capable.
12. The store is _____ located near several apartments.

Complete the Paragraph Write spelling words from the box to complete the paragraph.

The pilot looked __13.__ toward the field below. This was going to be an __14.__ difficult landing because of the fog. He could just __15.__ make out the field. There was, __16.__, a strong wind from the west and heading __17.__. The people in the control tower helped the pilot as he __18.__ guided the small plane toward the runway. When he __19.__ landed, he said to his co-pilot that this was __20.__ his toughest landing yet.

| carefully |
| downward |
| eastward |
| finally |
| barely |
| possibly |
| especially |
| additionally |

70

MEETING INDIVIDUAL NEEDS

Providing More Challenge

Challenge Words and **Challenge Activities** for Unit 11 appear on page 233. **Challenge Word Test Sentences** appear on page T233.

Unit 11 Challenge Activities

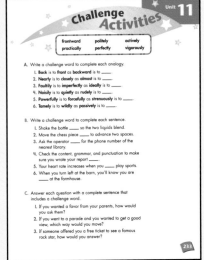

Weekly Test Options

Option I:
One Spelling Word Per Sentence
(See procedures on pages Z10–Z11.)

1. State your age and, **additionally,** your date of birth.
★ 2. Go to the store first and **afterward** to the park.
★ 3. We could **barely** see her in the crowd.
★ 4. She carried the baby **carefully,** not wanting to wake him.
★ 5. You will **certainly** enjoy this game.
★ 6. Do not stop until you have finished **completely.**
7. He walked **directly** home after the meeting.
★ 8. The paper floated **downward** to the street.
9. The train runs **eastward** along the route.
★10. I am **especially** interested in this event.
★11. His work was **finally** over for the day.
12. The soldiers marched **homeward** after the battle.
13. **Ideally** the train will arrive on time.
14. He pushed the gate **inward** to open it.
★15. She wrapped the string **loosely** around the books.

T70

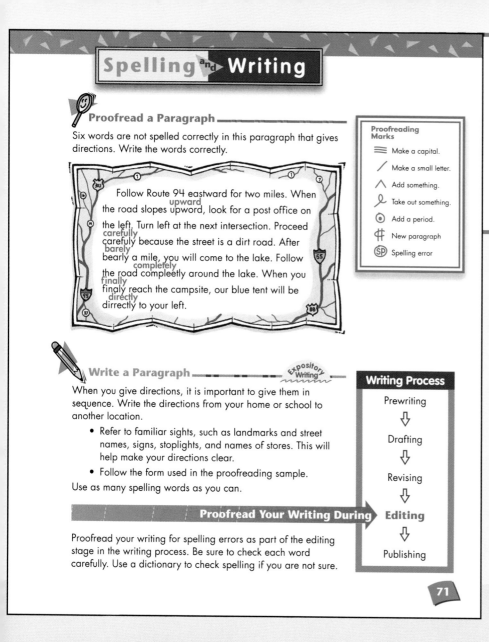

Spelling and Writing

Proofread a Paragraph

Six words are not spelled correctly in this paragraph that gives directions. Write the words correctly.

> Follow Route 94 eastward for two miles. When the road slopes *upward*, look for a post office on the left. Turn left at the next intersection. Proceed *carefully* because the street is a dirt road. After *barely* a mile, you will come to the lake. Follow the road *completely* around the lake. When you *finally* reach the campsite, our blue tent will be *directly* to your left.

Proofreading Marks

≡ Make a capital.
/ Make a small letter.
∧ Add something.
✎ Take out something.
⊙ Add a period.
New paragraph
SP Spelling error

Write a Paragraph

Expository Writing

When you give directions, it is important to give them in sequence. Write the directions from your home or school to another location.

- Refer to familiar sights, such as landmarks and street names, signs, stoplights, and names of stores. This will help make your directions clear.
- Follow the form used in the proofreading sample.

Use as many spelling words as you can.

Proofread Your Writing During → Editing

Proofread your writing for spelling errors as part of the editing stage in the writing process. Be sure to check each word carefully. Use a dictionary to check spelling if you are not sure.

Writing Process

Prewriting
⇩
Drafting
⇩
Revising
⇩
Editing
⇩
Publishing

71

Objectives

Spelling and Writing
Students will
- **proofread** a paragraph.
- **use** the writing process to write a set of directions.
- **proofread** their writing.

Using the Writing Process

Before assigning **Write a Paragraph,** see pages 258–259 in the Student Edition for a complete review of the writing process and additional writing assignments. You may also wish to refer to pages Z12–Z13 in the Teacher Edition.

Keeping a Spelling Journal

Encourage students to record the words they misspelled on the weekly test in a personal spelling journal. These words may be recycled for future study. Students may also wish to include words from their writing. See pages Z12–Z13 in the Teacher Edition for more information.

---

16. The door opened **outward** to let me in.
17. Could you **possibly** help me with this?
18. Her voice was so soft I could **scarcely** hear her.
★19. They moved the heavy piano **upward** step by step.
20. The kite flew **skyward** on the wind.

Option 2:
Multiple Spelling Words Per Sentence
(See procedures on pages Z10–Z11.)

1. The plane rose **skyward,** taking us **homeward**.
2. You **certainly** tied this ribbon **loosely**.
3. He could **barely** move his arm **upward**.
4. That door can swing **inward** and, **additionally, outward**.
5. She held the baby **especially carefully**.
6. **Possibly** because he was ill, he could **scarcely** understand the book he read and **afterward** remembered none of it.
7. The train **finally** headed **eastward** on the journey home.
8. The rain fell **directly downward**.
9. **Ideally,** we will be **completely** finished in an hour.

Option 3:
Standardized Test
(See *Teacher Resource Book,* Unit 11.)

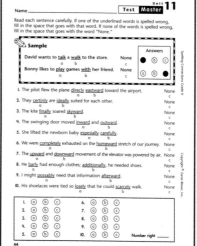

Unit 11 Test Master

T71

Objectives

Strategy Words

Students will
- **review** words studied previously that are related to the spelling strategy.
- **preview** unknown words that are related to the spelling strategy.

VOCABULARY CONNECTIONS

►Strategy Words◄

Remind the students that the **Strategy Words** are related to the spelling patterns they have studied in this unit. The **Review Words** are below grade level, and the **Preview Words** are above grade level. You may wish to use the following sentences to introduce the words in context.

Review Words:
Words From Grade 5
1. We stepped **backward** to avoid the traffic.
2. This paper comes **biweekly**.
3. The class **proudly** displayed their work.
4. We studied the **westward** movement of the pioneers in history class.
5. The lady stepped **forward** to receive her reward.

Preview Words:
Words From Grade 7
6. My mother **accurately** predicted that it would rain.
7. This stock is **economically** very sound.
8. **Historically,** immigrants came to America from many countries.
9. **Initially,** we asked that our tickets be mailed.
10. They **usually** celebrated birthdays with cake and ice cream.

Review Words
1. proudly
2. forward
3. westward
4. backward
5. biweekly

Preview Words
6. initially
7. economically
8. usually
9. historically
10. accurately

►Strategy Words◄

Review Words: Suffixes -ward, -ly

Write words from the box to complete this announcement.

backward	biweekly	proudly	westward	forward

We at *On the Road* __1.__ announce our latest travel magazine. We are moving __2.__ toward our goal of being the leader in the latest travel information. This time we are moving __3.__ from the Midwest to Utah and beyond. We do this without a __4.__ glance. Order your __5.__ subscription today.

Preview Words: Suffixes -ward, -ly

Write a word from the box to complete each sentence.

accurately	economically	historically
	initially	usually

6. He was _____ reluctant to speak before such a large group, but later he did it easily.
7. The country has increased its exports; it is striving to be _____ independent.
8. He is late today, but he _____ arrives at work by seven o'clock.
9. The 1700s was _____ a period of great change in our country.
10. She described the accident _____ in every detail.

72

Unit 11 RECAP

You may wish to assign the **Unit 11 Homework Master** (*Teacher Resource Book,* Unit 11) as a fun way to recap the spelling words.

Unit 11 Homework Master

Name _____

Homework **Master** Unit **11**

Use the code to write your spelling words.

| ☆ = -ward | ☾ = -ly |

1. after ☆ _____
2. complete ☾ _____
3. direct ☆ _____
4. sky ☆ _____
5. loose ☾ _____
6. down ☆ _____
7. ideal ☾ _____
8. home ☆ _____
9. final ☾ _____
10. especial ☾ _____
11. in ☆ _____
12. certain ☾ _____
13. bare ☾ _____
14. up ☆ _____
15. scarce ☾ _____
16. out ☆ _____
17. additional ☾ _____
18. careful ☾ _____

Answer each question with a spelling word that has not been used as yet on this page.

1. If a classmate asked you if all your answers on this page are correct, what might your one-word answer be?

2. If you got up early to see the sunrise, which direction would you look?

45

Content Words

Math: Geometry

Write a word from the box to complete each sentence.

congruent	perpendicular	linear
transversal		parallel

1. When two lines meet to form right angles, they are _____.
2. Two triangles the same size and shape are _____.
3. Lines that never meet are called _____ lines.
4. The base word of _____ is **line**.
5. A line that intersects two or more other lines is a _____.

Social Studies: International Relations

Write the words from the box that complete the news item.

accord	regional	ally	blockade	sanction

The nation joined with its __6.__ to establish a __7.__ against the country that had broken the peace __8.__ The __9.__ of the harbor will remain in place until all __10.__ neighbors are satisfied that the demands are being met.

Apply the Spelling Strategy

Circle the five Content Words you wrote that could have an **-ly** ending added to them.

Word Study

Shades of Meaning

When words mean almost but not quite the same thing, we say they have different **shades of meaning**. **Huge, big,** and **giant** all refer to something of a large size. Write the Content Word whose shade of meaning fits with these words: **friend, companion, pal, ____.**

Math: Geometry
1. perpendicular
2. congruent
3. parallel
4. linear
5. transversal

**Social Studies:
International Relations**
6. ally
7. sanction
8. accord
9. blockade
10. regional

Shades of Meaning
1. ally

73

Objectives

Content Words

Students will
- **expand** vocabulary with content-related words.
- **relate** the spelling strategy to words outside the basic spelling list.
- **understand** and identify words with different shades of meaning.

Content Words

Math: Geometry

Use these sentences to introduce the words and their meanings.
1. **Congruent** angles match exactly.
2. The sides of the house are **perpendicular** to the ground.
3. The **linear** lines of the roof gave a solid appearance to the house.
4. The **transversal** lines of latitude intersect with longitude lines.
5. The edges of the board are **parallel**.

Social Studies: International Relations

Use these sentences to introduce the words and their meanings.
6. The two parties signed an **accord** to stop the hostilities.
7. Due to **regional** weather patterns, we planned our vacation early.
8. The principal is our **ally**.
9. Ships will **blockade** the port.
10. Did the leader **sanction** the law?

Word Study

Shades of Meaning

Help students recognize that words with different shades of meaning are "near-synonyms." Emphasize that learning how these shades of meaning differ can help students select words that reflect just the meaning they want in their writing.

Unit 12 Home Spelling Practice

Spanish

English

MANAGING INSTRUCTION

Looking Ahead to Unit 12

To save time, you may wish to duplicate the **Unit 12 Home Spelling Practice** now. (See *Home Spelling Practice Book,* Unit 12.)

T73

Assessment Words

crooked	rooster
mantelpiece	infield
sworn	original
torrent	yearly
windward	hardly
simply	gravel
pennant	archery
swirl	fiend
outfield	prune
gloomy	mercury

Review Words

Unit 7
through*	assume
bulletin*	understood
introduce*	goodness
neighborhood*	
proof	cushion
routine	

Unit 8
niece*	shriek
receive*	relief
mischief*	fierce
leisure*	ceiling
thief	seize

Unit 9
carton*	partner
circular*	concern
purchase*	dirty
therefore*	ignore
carpenter	curtain

Unit 10
ignorant*	label
typical*	instant
material*	tunnel
practical*	talent
central	distant

Unit 11
finally*	upward
certainly*	completely
especially*	downward
afterward*	loosely
carefully	barely

* Posttest sentences and the **Unit 12 Test Master** test these words. Students review all words listed.

MATERIALS

Student Edition
Pages 74–79

Teacher Edition
Pages T74A–T79

Teacher Resource Book
Flip Folder Practice Master
Unit 12 Test Master

Home Spelling Practice Book
Unit 12 Home Spelling Practice
(English or Spanish)

Other *Spelling Connections* Resources
• Transparency Book, Grade 6

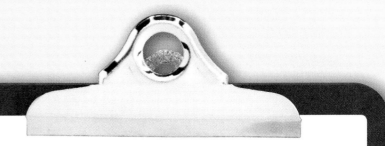

OBJECTIVES

Spelling and Assessment
Students will
• **assess** their progress in understanding the spelling strategies and patterns taught in Units 7–11.
• **connect** new words to the spelling strategies in Units 7–11.
• **write** new words that relate to the spelling strategies taught in Units 7–11.

Spelling and Review
Students will
• **review** the spelling strategy and words taught in Units 7–11.
• **learn** an alternative spelling study strategy.

Spelling and Writing
Students will
• **review** prepositions and prepositional phrases.
• **compose** a descriptive piece of writing that tells about some day when life changed.
• **learn** a proofreading strategy.
• **understand** the importance of correct spellings of acronyms used on computers.
• **proofread** for misspelled acronyms.

MEETING INDIVIDUAL NEEDS
Learning Styles

 Visual

To play "Spelling Football," draw a football field on poster board. Place a marker on the 50-yard line. Form two teams of students. Pronounce a spelling word. Ask each student on one team to write the word. Have a player on the other team check the spelling. If all have spelled the word correctly, move the football ten yards toward the first team's goal. If a team member misspells a word and everyone on the other team spells the word correctly, the ball is advanced ten yards to the other goal, and this team continues spelling. After a touchdown, the ball is placed on the 50-yard line.

 Auditory

Have the students play "Spelling Football" with this addition: Before the students write the spelling word, have one student on the team spell the word aloud.

 Kinesthetic

Make a rectangular form on the floor with tape. Mark off twenty blocks. Write four spelling words from each of Units 7–11 on a sheet of construction paper. Leave out the letters that illustrate the spelling strategies. Tape one sheet in each block. The first player stands on a line a few feet from the form and tosses a penny. The student must spell the word on which the penny lands. The student scores one point for each correct answer. Continue the game until all the words have been correctly spelled.

Write other sets of words and retape them to the blocks to provide more practice.

 Hands-On Practice

All students will benefit from practicing with a **Flip Folder**. See page Z18.

Language and Cultural Differences

The sounds in this group of units may be difficult for some students to hear and spell because of regional pronunciations or language backgrounds that do not include these sounds or that spell them differently. However, the more likely cause of difficulty is that students must remember several different spelling patterns for the sounds.

Review the spelling words in groups according to the spelling strategies of the units. Pronounce each spelling word and review its meaning. Then have students write the word. Ask a volunteer to write the word on the chalkboard and say aloud the spelling of the focus element.

MANAGING INSTRUCTION

3–5 Day Plan		Average	Below Average	Above Average
Day 1	**Day 1**	Assessment: Units 7–11, p. 74 (Option 1 or 2, p. T74)	Assessment: Units 7–11, p. 74 (Option 1 or 2, p. T74)	Assessment: Units 7–11, p. 74 (Option 1 or 2, p. T74)
	Day 2	Review: Units 7 and 8, p. 75	Review: Units 7 and 8, p. 75	Review: Units 7 and 8, p. 75 Review: Units 9 and 10, p. 76
Day 2	**Day 3**	Review: Units 9 and 10, p. 76	Review: Units 9 and 10, p. 76	Review: Unit 11, p. 77 Spelling Study Strategy, p. 77
	Day 4	Review: Unit 11, p. 77 Spelling Study Strategy, p. 77	Review: Unit 11, p. 77 Spelling Study Strategy, p. 77	Writer's Workshop, pages 78–79
Day 3	**Day 5**	Weekly Test, Option 1 or 2, p. T77	Weekly Test, Option 1 or 2, p. T77	Weekly Test, Option 1 or 2, p. T77
Writer's Workshop (pages 78 and 79) may be used anytime during this unit.				

Assessment and Review

Objectives

Spelling and Assessment

Students will

- **assess** their progress in understanding the spelling strategies and patterns taught in Units 7–11.
- **connect** new words to the spelling strategies in Units 7–11.
- **write** new words that relate to the spelling strategies taught in Units 7–11.

Unit 7
1. crooked
2. gloomy
3. rooster
4. prune

Unit 8
5. mantelpiece
6. outfield
7. infield
8. fiend

Unit 9
9. sworn
10. torrent ▲
11. swirl
12. hardly ▲
13. archery
14. mercury

Unit 10
15. pennant
16. original
17. gravel

Unit 11
18. windward
19. simply
20. yearly

Assessment / Units 7–11

Each Assessment Word in the box fits one of the spelling strategies you have studied over the past five weeks. Read the spelling strategies. Then write each Assessment Word under the unit number it fits.

Unit 7 _____
1.–4. The /o͞o/ sound is spelled **oo** in **proof**, **ou** in **routine**, **u** in **fluid**, and vowel-consonant-e in **assume**. The /o͝o/ sound is spelled **oo** in **goodness**, **ou** in **could've**, and **u** in **bulletin**.

Unit 8 _____
5.–8. This rhyme can often help you decide when to use **ie** and when to use **ei**: Use **i** before **e**, except after **c**, or when sounded as **a**, as in **neighbor** and **weigh**.

Unit 9 _____
9.–14. The **r**-controlled vowel sounds can be spelled in different ways, including /ûr/ spelled **er, ir,** and **ur**; /är/ spelled **ar**; /âr/ spelled **er**; and /ôr/ spelled **or** and **ore**.

Unit 10 _____
15.–17. The **schwa** sound (/ə/) often occurs in unstressed final syllables. Think about how /ə/ is spelled in the final syllable in **legal, label, talent,** and **distant**.

Unit 11 _____
18.–20. The suffix **-ward** means "direction" or "tendency." The suffix **-ly** means "in a specific manner." These suffixes are added to base words to form adverbs.

Assessment Words
crooked
mantelpiece
sworn
torrent
windward
simply
pennant
swirl
outfield
gloomy
rooster
infield
original
yearly
hardly
gravel
archery
fiend
prune
mercury

74

ASSESSMENT: UNITS 7–11

Option 1

Assessment Option 1 is the test that appears in the Student Edition on page 74. You may wish to have students take this test to determine their ability to recognize the spelling strategy in each unit and to match words not previously taught to that strategy. **Assessment Option 1** also serves as additional review and practice.

 Words designated with this symbol include more than one of the targeted spelling strategies. The answer key has placed them according to the most obvious spelling emphasis. However, if a student places a word in another category, and the word fits that generalization, accept that response. Remember, the objective is to place each word with any appropriate spelling generalization.

Option 2

Assessment Option 2 is a dictation test using the sentences on page T75. This test assesses students' ability to spell words not previously taught but that are exemplars of a spelling strategy. This test more specifically assesses students' ability to apply the spelling knowledge they have learned.

In either assessment test option, the words are identified by unit in the Teacher Edition. You may wish to index those misspelled words to the review exercises that follow in this unit. Determine which units students need to review and use the additional unit exercises found in this **Assessment and Review Unit** for reteaching the skill in a more focused way.

Review Unit 7: Vowels /ōō/, /o͝o/

| through | bulletin | introduce | neighborhood | proof |
| routine | assume | understood | goodness | cushion |

Write the spelling words that complete the paragraph.

This week our local __1.__ association sent out a __2.__ about a picnic. The new mayor wanted to __3.__ himself in person, so he took the notices to every house. He was __4.__ with the job by noon. We can __5.__ he got to every house, but there is no __6.__ of that. Deliveries are not part of his usual __7.__, but we have __8.__ that this is a new kind of mayor. We hope it's a sign of his generosity and __9.__ and that he has a good __10.__ for each of his shoes!

Review Unit 8: ie, ei

| niece | receive | mischief | leisure | thief |
| shriek | relief | fierce | ceiling | seize |

Write the spelling words by adding the missing letters.

11. n __ __ ce
12. misch __ __ f
13. th __ __ f
14. shr __ __ k
15. rel __ __ f

16. f __ __ rce
17. rec __ __ ve
18. c __ __ ling
19. s __ __ ze
20. l __ __ sure

Unit 7
1. neighborhood
2. bulletin
3. introduce
4. through
5. assume
6. proof
7. routine
8. understood
9. goodness
10. cushion

Unit 8
11. niece
12. mischief
13. thief
14. shriek
15. relief
16. fierce
17. receive
18. ceiling
19. seize
20. leisure

75

Objectives

Spelling and Review

Students will
• **review** and practice the spelling strategy and words in Unit 7.
• **review** and practice the spelling strategy and words in Unit 8.

Assessing Progress: The Spelling Journal

If your students have been keeping a personal spelling journal, a periodical review of these journals can be a rich assessment tool. Students should have included the words they have misspelled from each unit spelling test. They should also be encouraged to write the words they consistently misspell in their own writing and content-area words that present a challenge. Being able to discriminate the words in their everyday writing whose spelling they need to master is a powerful spelling skill.

Pretest Sentences: Assessment Words

(See procedures on pages Z10–Z11.)

1. One line is straight, but the other is **crooked**.
2. Mother hung a mirror over the **mantelpiece**.
3. I have **sworn** to keep your secret.
4. A great **torrent** of rain suddenly stopped our game.
5. This is the **windward** side of the island.
6. I **simply** cannot agree with you.
7. Our team won the **pennant** last year.
8. The wind made the leaves on the ground **swirl**.
9. The ball flew far into the **outfield**.
10. The clouds made the day seem **gloomy**.
11. Did you hear the **rooster** crow at dawn?
12. The **infield** players watched the runner on base.
13. This bike still has the **original** tires.
14. The Halloween party is a **yearly** event.
15. I **hardly** know where to begin.
16. The car moved slowly down the **gravel** road.
17. I'll use my new bow for the **archery** lesson.
18. His wicked laugh made him seem like a **fiend**.
19. The fruit salad has a banana and a **prune** in it.
20. This old thermometer is filled with **mercury**.

Objectives

Spelling and Review

Students will
- **review** and practice the spelling strategy and words in Unit 9.
- **review** and practice the spelling strategy and words in Unit 10.

Unit 9
1. purchase
2. carpenter
3. partner
4. carton
5. curtain
6. ignore
7. therefore
8. dirty
9. concern
10. circular

Unit 10
11. central
12. practical
13. ignorant
14. label
15. distant
16. instant
17. tunnel
18. material
19. typical
20. talent

 Review Unit 9: r-Controlled Vowels

| carton | circular | purchase | therefore | carpenter |
| partner | concern | dirty | ignore | curtain |

Write a spelling word that completes each group.

1. buy, acquire, _____
2. builder, roofer, _____
3. helper, co-worker, _____
4. box, package, _____
5. drape, shutter, _____
6. neglect, overlook, _____
7. so, then, _____
8. soiled, dusty, _____
9. care, interest, _____
10. round, ring-shaped, _____

Review Unit 10: /ə/ in Final Syllables

| ignorant | typical | material | practical | central |
| label | instant | tunnel | talent | distant |

Replace the underlined letters with one or more letters to write a spelling word.

11. cent<u>er</u>
12. practi<u>ce</u>
13. ignor<u>e</u>
14. lab<u>or</u>
15. distan<u>ce</u>
16. inst<u>ead</u>
17. <u>f</u>unnel
18. <u>s</u>erial
19. typ<u>ist</u>
20. <u>de</u>scent

76

Bulletin Board Idea

The World of Words

Create a bulletin board display around the concept of etymologies. (It can last for the entire year.) The title of the display is "Where in the World Do Words Come From?" Place this title in large letters across the top of the bulletin board, and pin a large map of the world under the title.

You will need 3" × 5" cards, string, and pins for this activity. Have the students, working together, print one spelling word, with its etymology, on each card. The card is then pinned to the edge of the bulletin board. A pin is placed in the country in which the word originated, and a piece of string is attached to that pin to connect it to the appropriate word card. For this activity,

you may want to use only those spelling words whose origins are given in the spelling book. Or, you may decide to have the students trace the origins of all the spelling words, assigning various students to the task of looking up the origins of the spelling words in each unit. These students then prepare word cards and attach them to the bulletin board and the appropriate countries on the map. If you follow the latter course, you will have to take down cards from time to time to make room for new ones. Store the "retired" cards in a box for ready reference throughout the year.

finally	certainly	especially	afterward	carefully
upward	completely	downward	loosely	barely

Form spelling words by adding **-ward** or **-ly** to the underlined word in each sentence.

1. <u>After</u> we went to the movies.
2. She moved <u>down</u> to the bottom of the slide.
3. Joe climbed <u>up</u> to the top of the stairs.
4. You are <u>certain</u> welcome to come with us.
5. He was <u>especial</u> happy to see his grandfather.
6. We <u>final</u> finished the examination!
7. We <u>careful</u> dusted around the glass figurines.
8. We <u>bare</u> had time to catch the bus.
9. They tied the ribbon <u>loose</u> around the kitten's neck.
10. He is <u>complete</u> finished with his homework.

Unit 11

1. Afterward
2. downward
3. upward
4. certainly
5. especially
6. finally
7. carefully
8. barely
9. loosely
10. completely

WORD SORT Spelling Study Strategy

noun

Sorting by Parts of Speech

Sorting words is a good way to help you practice your spelling words. Here is a way to sort the spelling words with a partner.

1. Make four columns on a piece of paper and write **noun, verb, adjective, adverb** at the top of the columns. Write a sample word in each column. For example, you could write **proof** under **noun**, **adore** under **verb**, **distant** under **adjective**, and **completely** under **adverb**.
2. Have a partner write a spelling word on the list. Help your partner decide whether the word is in the right list.
3. Take turns filling in the columns.

verb

77

Objectives

Spelling and Review

Students will
• **review** and practice the spelling strategy and words in Unit 11.
• **learn** an alternative spelling strategy.

Learning an Alternative Spelling Study Strategy

Students should always have a number of study strategies to draw from when it comes to learning their spelling words. **Sorting by Parts of Speech** is a fun way of differentiating between words and reviewing basic parts of speech. Encourage students to remember this spelling study strategy and to consider using it with any appropriate list they need to study and learn.

Weekly Test Options

Option 1:
One Spelling Word Per Sentence
(See procedures on pages Z10–Z11.)

1. It is **ignorant** to be cruel to others.
2. We heard the news in the **bulletin**.
3. I need money to **purchase** furniture.
4. The jacket was made of a thick **material**.
5. He likes to write stories in his **leisure** time.
6. She has a **practical** reason for going home.
7. Please **introduce** me to your friends.
8. Go to the store first and to the park **afterward**.
9. Did you **receive** the package yet?
10. Dad drove the car **through** the park.
11. A ring is **circular**.
12. Little children often get into **mischief**.
13. Is there a park in your **neighborhood**?
14. Her decision is logical and **therefore** appeals to me.
15. My uncle has only one **niece**.
16. Here is a **carton** for your letters.
17. You should **certainly** enjoy this game.
18. I am **especially** interested in this event.
19. His work was **finally** over for the day.
20. It is **typical** for friends to spend a great deal of time together.

Unit 12 Test Master

(See *Teacher Resource Book,* Unit 12.)

Option 2:
Standardized Test

Name _____ **Test Master** Unit **12**

A. Read each sentence. Decide whether the underlined word is spelled correctly or incorrectly. Mark the proper circle.

1. She peered <u>through</u> the fence. ⓐ correct ⓑ incorrect
2. The <u>bulitin</u> was posted on the wall. ⓐ correct ⓑ incorrect
3. Please <u>interduce</u> me to Salina. ⓐ correct ⓑ incorrect
4. The park in our <u>neighborhood</u> is big. ⓐ correct ⓑ incorrect
5. Jane is my father's <u>niece</u> and my cousin. ⓐ correct ⓑ incorrect
6. You will <u>recieve</u> the package today. ⓐ correct ⓑ incorrect
7. Watch this kitten get into <u>mischeif</u>. ⓐ correct ⓑ incorrect
8. We enjoy our <u>leisure</u> time. ⓐ correct ⓑ incorrect
9. The <u>carton</u> was filled with sponges. ⓐ correct ⓑ incorrect
10. A glass helps you draw a <u>circular</u> pattern. ⓐ correct ⓑ incorrect

B. Fill in the letter next to the word that is spelled correctly in each group.

1. ⓐ therefor ⓑ therefore ⓒ therfore
2. ⓐ perchase ⓑ purchas ⓒ purchase
3. ⓐ ignorant ⓑ ignorent ⓒ ignornt
4. ⓐ materal ⓑ matirial ⓒ material
5. ⓐ tipical ⓑ typical ⓒ tipycal
6. ⓐ practical ⓑ practicle ⓒ practial
7. ⓐ certenly ⓑ curtainly ⓒ certainly
8. ⓐ especialy ⓑ especially ⓒ especialy
9. ⓐ finally ⓑ finiley ⓒ finaly
10. ⓐ afterwerd ⓑ afterwood ⓒ afterward

46

Spelling Connections Grade 6

Copyright © Zaner-Bloser, Inc.

T77

Objectives

Spelling and Writing

Students will

- **review** prepositions and prepositional phrases.
- **compose** a descriptive piece of writing that tells about some day when life changed. (See **Spelling and the Writing Process** below.)

Optional Enrichment

Unit **12** enrichment

WRITER'S

Grammar, Usage, and Mechanics

Prepositions and Prepositional Phrases

A preposition relates a word in a sentence to a noun or pronoun that follows it. This noun or pronoun is the object of the preposition. The preposition, its object, and the words in between make a prepositional phrase.

The cat sleeps <u>under</u> the <u>bed</u>.

preposition   object of the preposition

Practice Activity

A. Write the preposition in each sentence below.

1. Birds flew around the trees.
2. The package on the table is yours.
3. The rocket blasted into space.
4. The puppies in the window look so cute!
5. Under the branches I found a tunnel.
6. Dancers wandered through the building.
7. Clouds gathered above our heads.

B. Complete the sentences by adding an object of the preposition. Try to use spelling words you reviewed.

8. Several families moved into our _____.
9. I found a quarter under the middle _____!
10. Hang that lamp from the _____.
11. Return the hammer to the _____.
12. I am standing with my nephew and _____.
13. We placed the blankets inside a big _____.
14. Is there a window behind that thick _____?

A

1. around
2. on
3. into
4. in
5. Under
6. through
7. above

B
Answers for numbers 8 through 14 may vary. Possible answers are provided.

8. neighborhood
9. cushion
10. ceiling
11. carpenter
12. niece
13. carton
14. curtain

78

Descriptive Writing

Spelling and the Writing Process

You may wish to use this writing assignment to help students master the writing process. For other writing ideas, see pages 258–259 in the Student Edition.

Explain that students will write a true story about a day that changed their lives in some way. The audience might include parents and classmates.

Prewriting Hint: You may wish to help students plan their writing by recommending the chart on this page. Have them replicate the chart, filling in the columns with specific details that they remember.

Life Before	What Happened That Day	Life Afterward
I was bored every August	I went to computer camp	

Revising Hint: Remind students that when they revise what they have written they should try to paint a word picture of the important day for readers. Encourage them to close their eyes and try to picture the scene, people, and events.

WORKSHOP

 Proofreading Strategy

Circle and Check

Good writers always proofread their writing for spelling errors. Here's a strategy you can use to proofread your papers.

Instead of reading your paper the regular way, look at just the first three or four words. Are they spelled correctly? If you are sure that they are correct, go on and check the next three or four words. If you are not sure of the spelling of a word, circle it and keep going. Look at your whole paper this way—one small group of words at a time.

When you finish, get a dictionary and check the spelling of all the circled words. Looking up several words at once is faster than looking them up one by one. It's also easier. Try it!

Electronic Spelling

Electronic Spelling	
1.	FAQ
2.	OK
3.	WAIS
4.	OK
5.	HTTP
6.	OK

Internet Addresses and Terms

You have to tell computers what you want. You do this by typing and clicking. However, you must spell your requests correctly or a computer cannot find what you are looking for.

Some terms are made up from the initial letters of words. For example, the **www** in many Internet addresses stands for **world wide web**. Study these terms:

BBS	**B**ulletin **B**oard **S**ervice
FAQ	**F**requently **A**sked **Q**uestions
HTTP	**H**yper**t**ext **T**ransfer **P**rotocol
URL	**U**niform **R**esource **L**ocator
WAIS	**W**ide **A**rea **I**nformation **S**erver

Which of the following are misspelled? Write them correctly. Write **OK** if a term is correct.

1. FQA 2. BBS 3. WIAS 4. URL 5. HTPT 6. WAIS

79

Unit 13 Home Spelling Practice

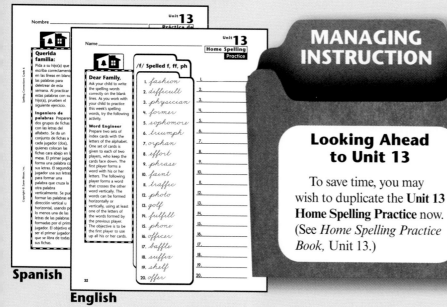

Spanish

English

/f/ Spelled f, ff, ph

1. fashion
2. difficult
3. physician
4. former
5. sophomore
6. triumph
7. orphan
8. effort
9. phrase
10. faint
11. traffic
12. photo
13. golf
14. fulfill
15. phone
16. officer
17. baffle
18. suffix
19. shelf
20. offer

MANAGING INSTRUCTION

Looking Ahead to Unit 13

To save time, you may wish to duplicate the **Unit 13 Home Spelling Practice** now. (See *Home Spelling Practice Book,* Unit 13.)

Objectives

Spelling and Writing
Students will
- **learn** a proofreading strategy.
- **understand** the importance of correct spellings of acronyms used on computers.
- **proofread** for misspelled acronyms.

Using Proofreading Strategies

Students are often unaware that there are a variety of approaches to proofreading their own writing. Building a repertory of strategies is important to improving students' writing and editing skills.

Spelling and Technology

The advent of word processing, computer protocols, and the Internet has actually increased, not lessened, the pressure on users to be better, more aware spellers. Spell checkers, for example, create circumstances in which the ability to discriminate between an acceptable and an unacceptable spelling is a critical skill. A homophone substitution, a correct spelling of the wrong word, an inadvertent word omission— these are examples of situations in computer usage that require a deeper understanding of spelling principles and a more adroit proofreading capability. It may be worthwhile to underscore this increased need as a whole-class discussion after students finish this unit's **Electronic Spelling** activity.

Basic Spelling List

fashion	traffic
difficult	photo
physician	golf
former	fulfill
sophomore	phone
triumph	officer
orphan	baffle
effort	suffix
phrase	shelf
faint	offer

Strategy Words

Review
beliefs	famous
buffalo	phosphorus
coffee	

Preview
affinity	manifest
enforce	phonics
folio	

Content Words

Fine Arts: Photography
film	tripod
shutterbug	photograph
lens	

Social Studies: Government
amendment	suffrage
patriot	nominate
candidate	

Individual Needs

Challenge Words
finalist	fantastic
tariff	sheriff
offense	phobia

Alternate Word List ★
difficult	faint
physician	fulfill
sophomore	phone
effort	officer
phrase	offer

★ For students who need to study fewer Basic Spelling words

MATERIALS

Student Edition
Pages 80–85
Challenge Activities, p. 234

Teacher Edition
Pages T80A–T85
Challenge Activities, p. T234

Teacher Resource Book
Unit 13 Homework Master
Unit 13 Practice Masters
Flip Folder Practice Master
Unit 13 Test Master

Home Spelling Practice Book
Unit 13 Home Spelling Practice
(English or Spanish)

Other *Spelling Connections* Resources
- Audiotape, Grade 6
- Practice Book for Grammar, Usage, and Mechanics, Grade 6
- Spelling Support for Second Language Learners, Grade 6
- Support Software on CD-ROM
- Transparency Book, Grade 6
- Word Sort CD-ROM, Grade 6

OBJECTIVES

Spelling and Thinking
Students will
- **read** the spelling words in list form and in context.
- **sort** the spelling words according to the /f/ sound and spelling patterns.
- **read** and remember this week's spelling strategy.

Spelling and Vocabulary
Students will
- **write** spelling words to complete a group of words.
- **replace** words in sentences with spelling words with the same or nearly the same meaning.
- **use** the **Spelling Dictionary** to learn the etymology of spelling words.

Spelling and Reading
Students will
- **solve** analogies using spelling words.
- **complete** sentences using spelling words.
- **complete** a paragraph using spelling words.

Spelling and Writing
Students will
- **proofread** a dialogue.
- **use** the writing process to write a dialogue.
- **proofread** their writing.

MEETING INDIVIDUAL NEEDS
Learning Styles

 Visual

Divide the class into two teams. Each team lines up to form a spelling chain. Pronounce a word. The first player on each team writes the first letter of the word on a sheet of paper and passes the paper to the second player. That player adds the second letter of the word. Play continues until the word has been spelled. The next player checks the accuracy of the spelling, makes any corrections, and then writes the word on the chalkboard. The first team to write the word correctly scores one point. Play continues until all the spelling words have been spelled.

 Auditory

Write all the spelling words on the chalkboard. Give the definition of one spelling word. Have a volunteer spell aloud the word that matches the definition. Then erase that word and have the students write it at their desks as the volunteer again spells the word aloud.

 Kinesthetic

Divide the class into three groups. Give one group the spelling words that have /f/ spelled **f**; to another group give the words that have /f/ spelled **ff**; to the third group give the words that have /f/ spelled **ph**. Have each group act out the meanings of three of their spelling words or use their bodies to form the letters of each of the three spelling words. The students in the other two groups guess which word is being acted out or spelled.

> **Hands-On Practice**
> All students will benefit from practicing with a **Flip Folder**. See page Z18.

Language and Cultural Differences

Some students may have difficulty with these sound-symbol associations because of regional pronunciations or language backgrounds that do not include the sounds or the variant spelling patterns. In Spanish, for example, the **ph** digraph does not exist, except in rare words borrowed from ancient Greek. The double **ff** spelling may also be a problem for Spanish-speaking students, for whom a single letter usually represents a consonant sound. There are some double consonants in Spanish, but they represent special sounds. In English, the second letter of a double consonant is rarely articulated in oral language, but it does function as a syllable marker in written language.

MANAGING INSTRUCTION

3–5 Day Plan		Average	Below Average	Above Average
Day 1	**Day 1**	Pretest Spelling Mini-Lesson, p. T80 Spelling and Thinking, p. 80	Pretest Spelling Mini-Lesson, p. T80 Spelling and Thinking, p. 80	Pretest Spelling and Thinking, p. 80
	Day 2	Spelling and Vocabulary, p. 81	Spelling and Vocabulary, p. 81 (or) Unit 13 Practice Master, A and B	Spelling and Vocabulary, p. 81 Spelling and Reading, p. 82
Day 2	**Day 3**	Spelling and Reading, p. 82	Spelling and Reading, p. 82 (or) Unit 13 Practice Master, C and D	Challenge Activities, p. 234
	Day 4	Spelling and Writing, p. 83 Unit 13 Homework Master	Spelling and Writing, p. 83	Spelling and Writing, p. 83 Unit 13 Homework Master
Day 3	**Day 5**	Weekly Test	Weekly Test	Weekly Test
Vocabulary Connections (pages 84 and 85) may be used anytime during this unit.				

Objectives

Spelling and Thinking

Students will
- **read** the spelling words in list form and in context.
- **sort** the spelling words according to the **/f/** sound and spelling patterns.
- **read** and remember this week's spelling strategy.

UNIT PRETEST

Use **Pretest Sentences** below. Refer to the self-checking procedures on student page 256. You may wish to use the **Unit 13 Word List Overhead Transparency** as part of the checking procedure.

TEACHING THE STRATEGY

Spelling Mini-Lesson

Write **golf, baffle,** and **phrase** on the chalkboard. Ask a volunteer to pronounce each word and circle the letter or letters that spell the **f** sound. (f, ff, ph)

Write **/f/** on the board and point out that this is the dictionary respelling of the sound commonly associated with **f.**

Write **phone, photo, physician, orphan, sophomore,** and **triumph** on the board. Explain that most words that spell **/f/** with **ph** come from Greek. **Phone** (short for **telephone**), **photo** (short for **photograph**), **orphan, sophomore,** and **phrase** all come from Greek. Remind the students that **ph** is a **consonant digraph,** i.e., a set of letters used together to spell a single sound.

Read through the spelling list. Encourage students to generate mnemonics, or sayings, to help them remember the spellings of words that are difficult for them. For example, "There is a <u>fort</u> in **effort**" may help a student remember the double f in **effort.**

Conclude by reading **Remember the Spelling Strategy** on page 80.

Spelling and Thinking

Order of answers may vary.

f
1. fashion
2. former
3. faint ★
4. golf
5. fulfill ★
6. shelf

ff
7. difficult ★
8. effort ★
9. traffic
10. officer ★
11. baffle
12. suffix
13. offer ★

ph
14. physician ★
15. sophomore ★
16. triumph
17. orphan
18. phrase ★
19. photo
20. phone ★

READ THE SPELLING WORDS

1. fashion	*fashion*	Long skirts are in **fashion** today.
2. difficult	*difficult*	Cleaning up after a storm is **difficult**.
3. physician	*physician*	She plans to see a **physician** today.
4. former	*former*	The mayor is a **former** basketball star.
5. sophomore	*sophomore*	Max is a **sophomore** in high school.
6. triumph	*triumph*	The win was a **triumph** for our team.
7. orphan	*orphan*	The **orphan** was taken in by a family.
8. effort	*effort*	Running several miles requires **effort**.
9. phrase	*phrase*	I am fond of the **phrase** "Less is more."
10. faint	*faint*	He was feeling **faint** after the race.
11. traffic	*traffic*	She listened to the **traffic** report.
12. photo	*photo*	He asked me if I had a current **photo**.
13. golf	*golf*	They played on a public **golf** course.
14. fulfill	*fulfill*	You can **fulfill** all of your dreams.
15. phone	*phone*	He kept me on the **phone** for an hour.
16. officer	*officer*	The **officer** on duty inquired about us.
17. baffle	*baffle*	The story seems to **baffle** everyone.
18. suffix	*suffix*	A **suffix** is added to the end of a word.
19. shelf	*shelf*	We keep the blender on the top **shelf**.
20. offer	*offer*	I had to turn down her generous **offer**.

SORT THE SPELLING WORDS

1.–6. Write the words that have the **/f/** sound spelled **f**.

7.–13. Write the words that have the **/f/** sound spelled **ff**.

14.–20. Write the words that have the **/f/** sound spelled **ph**.

REMEMBER THE SPELLING STRATEGY

Remember that the **f** sound (**/f/**) can be spelled in different ways: **f** in **faint**, **ff** in **baffle**, and **ph** in **phone**.

80

Pretest Sentences (See procedures on pages Z10–Z11.)

1. Continue in this **fashion** until you have finished the job.
★ 2. Sometimes an idea is **difficult** to understand.
★ 3. It takes years of medical training to become a **physician**.
4. His **former** teammate is now a rival.
★ 5. The second year of high school is called the **sophomore** year.
6. Our team came home in **triumph** after taking first place.
7. Since her parents are no longer living, the **orphan** lives with her married sister.
★ 8. To be successful, you must put more **effort** into your work.
★ 9. Sometimes just a short **phrase** can have great meaning.
★10. There was a **faint** smell of perfume in the air.
11. We were caught in a terrible **traffic** jam.
12. This is a wonderful **photo** of you.
13. **Golf** is a difficult sport to master.
★14. To **fulfill** your goal, you usually must have a detailed plan and follow it.
★15. Do you prefer to use a dial or push-button **phone**?
★16. The **officer** gave the troops the command to march.
17. When instructions are poorly written, they really **baffle** me.
18. A **suffix** often changes the meaning of a word.
19. Please put this box on that **shelf**.
★20. Will you **offer** to help with the decorations for the party?

Spelling ᴬⁿᵈ Vocabulary

Word Groups
Write a spelling word to complete each group of words.

1. hard, laborious, _____
2. victory, success, _____
3. attempt, struggle, _____
4. weak, dim, _____
5. cars, highways, _____
6. clubs, green, _____
7. platform, storage, _____
8. senior, junior, _____
9. affix, prefix, _____
10. nurse, dentist, _____

Word Meanings
Write the spelling word that could replace the underlined word in each sentence.

11. This <u>picture</u> would look nice in an oval frame.
12. The computer problem might <u>puzzle</u> him at first.
13. The chairperson has another <u>plan</u> to suggest.
14. The inventor was able to <u>express</u> his ideas clearly.
15. You can <u>form</u> a lovely wreath out of dried flowers.
16. The <u>previous</u> owner of the house built the addition.

The **etymology** of a word traces the origin of the word back to the language from which it came. Write a spelling word for each etymology.

17. From Greek **phone**, meaning "sound."
18. From Latin **officium**, meaning "service."
19. From Greek **orphanos**, meaning "without parents."
20. From Old English **ful**, meaning "full," and **fyllan**, meaning "to fill."

Word Groups
1. **difficult**
2. **triumph**
3. **effort**
4. **faint**
5. **traffic**
6. **golf**
7. **shelf**
8. **sophomore**
9. **suffix**
10. **physician**

Word Meanings
11. **photo**
12. **baffle**
13. **offer**
14. **phrase**
15. **fashion**
16. **former**

Using the Dictionary
17. **phone**
18. **officer**
19. **orphan**
20. **fulfill**

 81

81

Objectives

Spelling and Vocabulary
Students will
- **write** spelling words to complete a group of words.
- **replace** words in sentences with spelling words with the same or nearly the same meaning.
- **use** the **Spelling Dictionary** to learn the etymology of spelling words.

Developing Oral Language Skills

Write **sophomore** on the chalkboard. Have students pronounce **sophomore** and note whether they pronounce the word as two syllables or three syllables. If it is pronounced as a two-syllable word, have them practice saying the word as a three-syllable word. Remind students that words like **sophomore** (/sŏf′ ə môr′/ or /sŏf′ môr/) may cause spelling problems because the second syllable is weak or disappears entirely when the word is pronounced.

MEETING INDIVIDUAL NEEDS

Providing More Help

Write the following sets of words on the chalkboard. Have volunteers circle the word that is spelled correctly.

1. bafle **baffle** baphle
2. **effort** efort ephort
3. ffoto foto **photo**
4. opher ofer **offer**
5. **faint** phaint ffaint
6. orfan **orphan** orffan

★Students who need to study fewer words should use the **Alternate Word List**. This list is starred on page T80 in the Teacher Edition. The **Unit 13 Practice Masters** (*Teacher Resource Book*) provide additional practice with these words.

Unit 13 Practice Masters

Name _____

Practice Master Unit **13**

| 1. faint | 3. effort | 5. offer | 7. phone | 9. physician |
| 2. fulfill | 4. difficult | 6. officer | 8. phrase | 10. sophomore |

A. The letters **f**, **ff**, or **ph** are missing in the spelling words. Fill in the missing letters. Write the words.

1. di _____ icult _____
2. so _____ omore _____
3. _____ rase _____
4. _____ aint _____
5. _____ one _____
6. o _____ er _____

B. These words are misspelled. Write the spelling words correctly.

1. fiscian _____
2. ofer _____
3. oficer _____
4. fullfil _____
5. efort _____
6. frase _____

C. Write the spelling word that matches the etymology or word origin.

1. from Greek **sophos**, meaning "wise," and **moros**, meaning "foolish"
2. from Old French **fisique**, meaning "medical"
3. from Old English **ful**, meaning "full," and **fyllan**, meaning "to fill"

1. _____
2. _____
3. _____

47

Practice Master Unit **13**

phone   physician
phrase   sophomore

48

T81

Spelling and Reading

Students will
- **solve** analogies using spelling words.
- **complete** sentences using spelling words.
- **complete** a paragraph using spelling words.

One-Minute Handwriting Hint

Correct slant is achieved by positioning the paper correctly, pulling the slant strokes in the proper direction, and shifting your paper as the writing progresses. To check slant, draw lines through the slant strokes of the letters. All the lines should slant forward and be parallel.

Legible handwriting can boost spelling scores by as much as 20%.

Spelling ᵃⁿᵈ Reading

Solve the Analogies

1. physician
2. phone
3. photo
4. sophomore
5. suffix
6. golf
7. baffle

Complete the Sentences

8. shelf
9. officer
10. orphan
11. traffic
12. former
13. fashion

Complete the Paragraph

14. faint
15. difficult
16. fulfill
17. phrase
18. effort
19. offer
20. triumph

82

fashion	difficult	physician	former	sophomore
triumph	orphan	effort	phrase	faint
traffic	photo	golf	fulfill	phone
officer	baffle	suffix	shelf	offer

Solve the Analogies Write a spelling word to complete each analogy.

1. **School** is to **teacher** as **hospital** is to ____.
2. **Write** is to **pencil** as **speak** is to ____.
3. **Painter** is to **painting** as **photographer** is to ____.
4. **Fourth** is to **senior** as **second** is to ____.
5. **Before** is to **after** as **prefix** is to ____.
6. **Boxer** is to **boxing** as **golfer** is to ____.
7. **Conceal** is to **hide** as **bewilder** is to ____.

Complete the Sentences Write a spelling word to complete each sentence.

8. We will need an extra ____ for all of these books.
9. The police ____ asked us if we needed help.
10. As an ____, the young man longed to have a family.
11. Because of the ____ jam, he was late to work.
12. We have vacationed in the mountains and near the ocean, but we prefer the ____.
13. You make quite a ____ statement with those shoes.

Complete the Paragraph Write spelling words from the box to complete the paragraph.

Aisha was exhausted and felt __14.__ as she came off the basketball court after a __15.__ third quarter. Her team was about to __16.__ their goal of achieving a winning season. The __17.__ that came to her mind was "success takes __18.__." She knew that Coach Grassi would __19.__ to put someone else in so that she could rest. But Aisha wanted to be out on the court to see her team eventually __20.__.

| phrase |
| triumph |
| difficult |
| faint |
| fulfill |
| effort |
| offer |

MEETING INDIVIDUAL NEEDS

Providing More Challenge

Challenge Words and **Challenge Activities** for Unit 13 appear on page 234. **Challenge Word Test Sentences** appear on page T234.

Unit 13 Challenge Activities

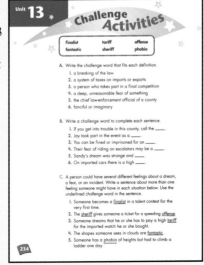

Weekly Test Options

Option 1:
One Spelling Word Per Sentence
(See procedures on pages Z10–Z11.)

1. His weird ideas **baffle** me.
★ 2. Baseball is a **difficult** game to play.
★ 3. Make an **effort** to do your best work.
★ 4. What did you **offer** to bring to the class festival?
★ 5. The **officer** called the meeting to order.
★ 6. There was a **faint** sound of music in the room.
7. He likes to dress in the latest **fashion**.
8. My **former** neighbor moved to another city.
★ 9. Call me on the **phone** if you need to get in touch with me.
★10. You must try to **fulfill** your own desires.
11. Have you ever played a round of **golf**?
12. That young child is an **orphan**.
13. I would like to keep this **photo** of you.
★14. That song title soon became a common **phrase**.
★15. That woman is our family **physician**.
16. I keep my books on a high **shelf**.

Spelling and Writing

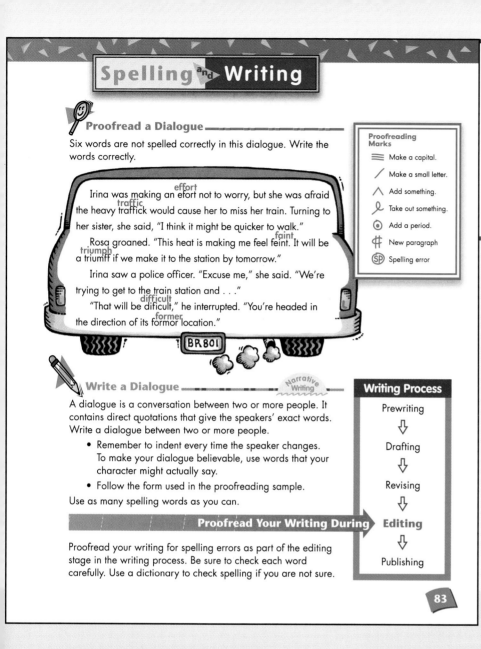

Proofread a Dialogue

Six words are not spelled correctly in this dialogue. Write the words correctly.

effort
Irina was making an efort not to worry, but she was afraid
traffic
the heavy traffick would cause her to miss her train. Turning to
her sister, she said, "I think it might be quicker to walk."

Rosa groaned. "This heat is making me feel feint. It will be
faint
triumph
a triumff if we make it to the station by tomorrow."

Irina saw a police officer. "Excuse me," she said. "We're
trying to get to the train station and . . ."
difficult
"That will be dificult," he interrupted. "You're headed in
the direction of its formor location."
former

BR 801

Proofreading Marks

≡ Make a capital.
/ Make a small letter.
∧ Add something.
⌒ Take out something.
⊙ Add a period.
⌗ New paragraph
ⓈⓅ Spelling error

Write a Dialogue

Narrative Writing

A dialogue is a conversation between two or more people. It contains direct quotations that give the speakers' exact words. Write a dialogue between two or more people.

- Remember to indent every time the speaker changes. To make your dialogue believable, use words that your character might actually say.
- Follow the form used in the proofreading sample.

Use as many spelling words as you can.

Writing Process

Prewriting
⇩
Drafting
⇩
Revising
⇩
Editing
⇩
Publishing

Proofread Your Writing During → **Editing**

Proofread your writing for spelling errors as part of the editing stage in the writing process. Be sure to check each word carefully. Use a dictionary to check spelling if you are not sure.

83

Objectives

Spelling and Writing

Students will
- **proofread** a dialogue.
- **use** the writing process to write a dialogue.
- **proofread** their writing.

Using the Writing Process

Before assigning **Write a Dialogue,** see pages 258–259 in the Student Edition for a complete review of the writing process and additional writing assignments. You may also wish to refer to pages Z12–Z13 in the Teacher Edition.

Keeping a Spelling Journal

Encourage students to record the words they misspelled on the weekly test in a personal spelling journal. These words may be recycled for future study. Students may also wish to include words from their writing. See pages Z12–Z13 in the Teacher Edition for more information.

★**17.** She will be a **sophomore** when she is fifteen years old.
18. The teacher asked me to name a common **suffix**.
19. There is always too much **traffic** on that road.
20. The team's victory was a **triumph** for the whole country.

Option 2:
Multiple Spelling Words Per Sentence
(See procedures on pages Z10–Z11.)

1. The **physician** made every **effort** to help the boy.
2. The new **officer** was asked to direct **traffic**.
3. That beautiful woman is a **former fashion** model.
4. The store has a special **offer** with the purchase of **golf** clubs.
5. It is **difficult** to learn how to use that **suffix**.
6. The **orphan** was so thin that we thought she would **faint**.
7. The **sophomore** team scored a **triumph** in that game.
8. I kept her **photo** on the **shelf** above my bed.
9. Do you understand the meaning of that **phrase** or does it **baffle** you?
10. Will you **fulfill** your promise to **phone** him?

Option 3:
Standardized Test
(See *Teacher Resource Book*, Unit 13.)

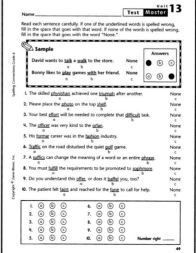

Unit 13 Test Master

T83

Objectives

Strategy Words

Students will
• **review** words studied previously that are related to the spelling strategy.
• **preview** unknown words that are related to the spelling strategy.

VOCABULARY CONNECTIONS

Unit 13 enrichment

Optional Enrichment

Strategy Words

Remind the students that the **Strategy Words** relate to the spelling patterns they have studied in this unit. The **Review Words** are below grade level, and the **Preview Words** are above grade level. You may wish to use the following sentences to introduce the words in context.

Review Words:
Words From Grade 5

1. His **beliefs** were based on the things he remembered about his family.
2. We saw **buffalo** grazing in open fields during our travels.
3. Could you smell the **coffee** brewing?
4. My uncle became **famous** as an expert cook.
5. The decorations on my wall glowed in the dark because of the **phosphorus** that was added to the paint.

Preview Words:
Words From Grade 7

6. Men have an **affinity** for dogs as pets.
7. We must **enforce** the rules in order to have good school environment.
8. He removed the **folio** from his briefcase.
9. **Manifest** destiny was the colonists' early belief that their land should grow and prosper.
10. The study of **phonics** helps us learn to pronounce words.

Review Words
1. buffalo
2. phosphorus
3. famous
4. coffee
5. beliefs

Preview Words
6. affinity
7. enforce
8. phonics
9. folio
10. manifest

Strategy Words

Review Words: /f/ Spelled f, ff, ph

Write a word from the box to match each clue.

beliefs	buffalo	coffee	famous	phosphorus

1. the bison of North America
2. used in fertilizers and detergents
3. a synonym for **prominent**
4. a drink that comes from the beanlike seeds of a tropical tree
5. strong opinions about something

Preview Words: /f/ Spelled f, ff, ph

Write a word from the box to complete each of these sentences.

affinity	enforce	folio	manifest	phonics

6. Our golden retriever has an _____ for people, especially children.
7. It was the officer's job to _____ the speed limits in the county.
8. The study of sounds and letters is called _____.
9. A _____ can be a leaf in a manuscript or the page number printed on a page in a book.
10. The jury took note of the clear and _____ error emphasized by the attorney.

84

Unit 13 RECAP

You may wish to assign the **Unit 13 Homework Master** (*Teacher Resource Book,* Unit 13) as a fun way to recap the spelling words.

Unit 13 Homework Master

Homework Master Unit 13

Name _____

The letters **f, ff,** or **ph** are missing in the words. Fill in the letters. Then write the complete words on the lines.

1. or ___ ___ an _____
2. shel ___ _____
3. ___ ormer _____
4. ___ ___ ysician _____
5. di ___ icult _____
6. so ___ ___ omore _____
7. ___ ___ rase _____
8. ___ aint _____
9. ___ ___ one _____
10. tra ___ ic _____
11. su ___ ___ ix _____

The following words are misspelled. Rewrite the words correctly on the lines.

1. foto _____
2. bafle _____
3. phashion _____
4. ofer _____
5. oficer _____
6. fulffill _____
7. triumf _____
8. efort _____

50

◤ Content Words ◢

Fine Arts: Photography

Write the words from the box that complete the paragraph.

film	shutterbug	lens	tripod	photograph

Eurie is a __1.__ who never misses an opportunity to take a __2.__. She usually uses high-speed __3.__ to capture action shots. To steady her camera, she attaches it to a __4.__. When everything is set, she adjusts the camera __5.__ and shoots.

Social Studies: Government

Write the words from the box that complete the paragraph.

amendment	patriot	candidate
suffrage	nominate	

Women in the early 1900s had to overcome great opposition to gain __6.__, or the right to vote. In 1920, the nineteenth __7.__ to the Constitution was passed. This provided women with the right to __8.__ and vote for the __9.__ of their choice. Every woman __10.__ had worked hard toward this goal.

Apply the Spelling Strategy

Circle the letters that spell the /**f**/ sound in three of the Content Words you wrote.

◤ Word Study ◢

Words in Other Languages

Words in several other languages are very similar to this Strategy Word. For example, in Russian, it's **kofe;** in Spanish, it's **café;** and in Swedish, it's **kaffe.** Write the Strategy Word.

Fine Arts: Photography
1. shutterbug
2. photogra(ph)
3. (f)ilm
4. tripod
5. lens

Social Studies: Government
6. suf(f)rage
7. amendment
8. nominate
9. candidate
10. patriot

Words in Other Languages
1. coffee

85

Optional Enrichment

Objectives

Content Words

Students will
- **expand** vocabulary with content-related words.
- **relate** the spelling strategy to words outside the basic spelling list.
- **understand** that some words are similar in a variety of languages.

◤ Content Words ◢

Fine Arts: Photography

Use these sentences to introduce the words and their meanings.
1. We bought extra **film.**
2. We called him a **shutterbug** because of his strong interest in photography.
3. Did you scratch the camera **lens**?
4. To get a good steady picture, the photographer used a **tripod.**
5. This is a **photograph** of my mother.

Social Studies: Government

Use these sentences to introduce the words and their meanings.
6. The **amendment** to the club's constitution was introduced.
7. He has always been a true **patriot.**
8. Will you be a **candidate** for the office of vice president?
9. Women's **suffrage** was a long battle.
10. I will **nominate** him if he asks me.

◤ Word Study ◢

Words in Other Languages

Point out to students that some words are similar in many languages throughout the world. An awareness of this relationship will help students develop their vocabulary.

Unit 14 Home Spelling Practice

Spanish

English

MANAGING INSTRUCTION

Looking Ahead to Unit 14

To save time, you may wish to duplicate the **Unit 14 Home Spelling Practice** now. (See *Home Spelling Practice Book,* Unit 14.)

Basic Spelling List

magazine	vision
pessimism	browse
conclusion	usual
optimism	freeze
television	visual
amaze	scissors
cruise	arise
casual	pause
husband	visitor
phase	tease

Strategy Words

Review

trousers	clause
crackers	measures
dramatize	

Preview

applause	version
corsage	xylophone
positively	

Content Words

Math: Multiplication

multiplier	divisibility
factoring	multiples
multiplicand	

Social Studies: Citizenship

excel	patriotism
citizenship	national
ceremony	

Individual Needs

Challenge Words

drizzle	amusing
disaster	mayonnaise
excursion	pleasurable

Alternate Word List ★

conclusion	usual
optimism	scissors
television	pause
amaze	visitor
husband	tease

★ For students who need to study fewer Basic Spelling words

MATERIALS

Student Edition
Pages 86–91
Challenge Activities, p. 235

Teacher Edition
Pages T86A–T91
Challenge Activities, p. T235

Teacher Resource Book
Unit 14 Homework Master
Unit 14 Practice Masters
Flip Folder Practice Master
Unit 14 Test Master

Home Spelling Practice Book
Unit 14 Home Spelling Practice
(English or Spanish)

Other *Spelling Connections* Resources
- Audiotape, Grade 6
- Practice Book for Grammar, Usage, and Mechanics, Grade 6
- Spelling Support for Second Language Learners, Grade 6
- Support Software on CD-ROM
- Transparency Book, Grade 6
- Word Sort CD-ROM, Grade 6

OBJECTIVES

Spelling and Thinking
Students will
- **read** the spelling words in list form and in context.
- **sort** the spelling words according to /z/ and /zh/ sounds and spelling patterns.
- **read** and remember this week's spelling strategy.

Spelling and Vocabulary
Students will
- **write** spelling words to complete a series of meaning-related words.
- **change** parts of words to write spelling words.
- **relate** spelling words to their less-common definitions.

Spelling and Reading
Students will
- **solve** analogies using spelling words.
- **complete** sentences using spelling words.
- **complete** a paragraph using spelling words.

Spelling and Writing
Students will
- **proofread** a persuasive paragraph.
- **use** the writing process to write a persuasive paragraph.
- **proofread** their writing.

MEETING INDIVIDUAL NEEDS
Learning Styles

 Visual

Print each spelling word on a 3" × 5" card. Cut out each letter of each word and put all the letters in a box. Have each player draw twenty letters from the box. Within five minutes, the player must form as many of the spelling words as possible using these letters. After forming each word, the player must also write the word. The winner is the student who forms the most words correctly.

 Auditory

Have an oral spelling bee with this variation: Start with all the students seated. Pronounce a spelling word for each student, who then spells the word aloud. A student who misspells a word must stand until he or she spells a word correctly.

> **Hands-On Practice**
> All students will benefit from practicing with a **Flip Folder**. See page Z18.

 Kinesthetic

Divide the class into two teams. Use the letters from the visual activity. Place the letters of each spelling word, in random order, in separate envelopes. Provide each team with a set of envelopes. Each team member takes one letter, and the members line up to spell the word. The first team to spell its word correctly scores a point. Continue in this way, with the students on the teams taking turns to spell the words.

Language and Cultural Differences

Some students may have difficulty with these sound-symbol associations because of language backgrounds that do not include the sounds or their variant spelling patterns. In Latin American Spanish, for example, the letter **z** always spells a sound similar to /**s**/.

On twenty 3" × 5" cards, write the spelling patterns for /**z**/ and /**zh**/ as these sounds are spelled in the spelling words. On three cards write "the /**z**/ sound spelled **z**"; on six cards write "the /**z**/ sound spelled by **s** followed by **silent e**"; on four cards write "the /**z**/ sound spelled **s**"; on

three cards write "the /**zh**/ sound spelled **s** followed by **ual**"; on one card write "the /**z**/ sound spelled **ss**"; and on three cards write "the /**zh**/ sound spelled **s** followed by **ion**."

Place the cards in a box. Ask a volunteer to draw a card and find a word on the spelling list that contains the same spelling pattern as that on the card. Ask the student to write that word on the board and pronounce it after you.

MANAGING INSTRUCTION

3–5 Day Plan		Average	Below Average	Above Average
Day 1	**Day 1**	Pretest Spelling Mini-Lesson, p. T86 Spelling and Thinking, p. 86	Pretest Spelling Mini-Lesson, p. T86 Spelling and Thinking, p. 86	Pretest Spelling and Thinking, p. 86
	Day 2	Spelling and Vocabulary, p. 87	Spelling and Vocabulary, p. 87 (or) Unit 14 Practice Master, A and B	Spelling and Vocabulary, p. 87 Spelling and Reading, p. 88
Day 2	**Day 3**	Spelling and Reading, p. 88	Spelling and Reading, p. 88 (or) Unit 14 Practice Master, C and D	Challenge Activities, p. 235
	Day 4	Spelling and Writing, p. 89 Unit 14 Homework Master	Spelling and Writing, p. 89	Spelling and Writing, p. 89 Unit 14 Homework Master
Day 3	**Day 5**	Weekly Test	Weekly Test	Weekly Test
Vocabulary Connections (pages 90 and 91) may be used anytime during this unit.				

Objectives

Spelling and Thinking

Students will
- **read** the spelling words in list form and in context.
- **sort** the spelling words according to /z/ and /zh/ sounds and spelling patterns.
- **read** and remember this week's spelling strategy.

UNIT PRETEST

Use **Pretest Sentences** below. Refer to the self-checking procedures on student page 256. You may wish to use the **Unit 14 Word List Overhead Transparency** as part of the checking procedure.

TEACHING THE STRATEGY

Spelling Mini-Lesson

Write **freeze, optimism,** and **visitor** on the board. Ask a volunteer to read the words aloud. Use these words to explain that the /z/ sound is spelled in different ways:

- /z/ can be spelled **z**, as in **freeze**;
- /z/ can be spelled **s** in the third syllable, especially in words like **optimism** that end in /ĭz′ əm/;
- /z/ can be spelled **s** in the first syllable of a word, as in **visitor**.

Ask students to check the spelling list to find a word in which /z/ is not spelled by **s** or **z**. (scissors) Explain that using **ss** to spell /z/ is unusual.

Write /z/ on the board. Say that this is the dictionary respelling for the sound commonly associated with **z** .

Write **usual** and **vision** on the board. Use these words to explain that /zh/ is spelled **s** when it is followed by **ual** (usual) or **ion** (vision). Explain that /zh/ is often followed by /o͞o/, as in **usual**. Write /zh/ on the board. Say that this is the dictionary respelling for this consonant sound.

Ask students to read the spelling list and identify how /z/ or /zh/ is spelled in each word. Discuss any meanings that need clarification. Encourage students to use their **Spelling Dictionary** for pronunciation or meaning.

Read **Remember the Spelling Strategy** on page 86.

Spelling and Thinking

Order of answers may vary.

/z/
1. magazi(ne)
2. pessimi(sm)
3. optimi(sm) ★
4. ama(ze) ★
5. crui(se)
6. hu(s)band ★
7. pha(se)
8. brow(se)
9. free(ze)
10. sci(ss)ors ★
11. ari(se)
12. pau(se) ★
13. vi(s)itor ★
14. tea(se) ★

/zh/
15. conclu(s)ion ★
16. televi(s)ion ★
17. ca(s)ual
18. vi(s)ion
19. u(s)ual ★
20. vi(s)ual

READ THE SPELLING WORDS

1. magazine	*magazine*	She subscribes to a sports **magazine**.
2. pessimism	*pessimism*	He is known for his gloomy **pessimism**.
3. conclusion	*conclusion*	I read the **conclusion** to the story.
4. optimism	*optimism*	Her cheerful **optimism** sees her through.
5. television	*television*	I watched a nature special on **television**.
6. amaze	*amaze*	The gymnast's ability will **amaze** you.
7. cruise	*cruise*	Ships slowly **cruise** into the harbor.
8. casual	*casual*	We wore **casual** clothes to the picnic.
9. husband	*husband*	Her **husband** works for a bus company.
10. phase	*phase*	He is going through a difficult **phase**.
11. vision	*vision*	The reading glasses improved his **vision**.
12. browse	*browse*	I will quickly **browse** through the books.
13. usual	*usual*	My **usual** lunch is yogurt and fruit.
14. freeze	*freeze*	The tender plants might **freeze**.
15. visual	*visual*	Fireworks are a bright **visual** display.
16. scissors	*scissors*	These **scissors** are not very sharp.
17. arise	*arise*	Call me if any problems **arise**.
18. pause	*pause*	There is a dramatic **pause** in the music.
19. visitor	*visitor*	He invited the **visitor** to stay for lunch.
20. tease	*tease*	Friends **tease** me about being late.

SORT THE SPELLING WORDS

1.–14. Write the words that have the /z/ sound spelled **z, s,** or **ss**. Circle the letters that spell this sound.

15.–20. Write the words that have the /zh/ sound spelled **s**. Circle the letters that spell this sound.

REMEMBER THE SPELLING STRATEGY

Remember that the /z/ sound can be spelled **z** as in **freeze**, **s** as in **phase**, and **ss** as in **scissors**. The /zh/ sound can be spelled **s** and is often followed by **ual** (usual) or **ion** (vision).

86

Pretest Sentences (See procedures on pages Z10–Z11.)

1. Rosa subscribes to a **magazine** about computers.
2. I showed my **pessimism** when I said the glass was half empty, not half full.
★ 3. What **conclusion** can you draw from these facts?
★ 4. Her **optimism** made us all believe that something good would happen.
★ 5. How much **television** do you watch each week?
★ 6. The energy we get from the sun will always **amaze** me.
7. The couple took a **cruise** on a ship going to Hawaii.
8. The dress code for the picnic will be **casual**.
★ 9. Beth's **husband** always carried their wedding picture in his pocket.
10. When a star enters the mature **phase** of its life, it is called a red giant.
11. Bert wears glasses to improve his **vision**.
12. Craig went to the library to **browse** through the books.
★13. It is **usual** for Harry to walk his dog right after dinner.
14. When you **freeze** water, it turns to ice.
15. Painting and sculpture are two of the **visual** arts.
★16. I need the **scissors** to cut this strong cord.
17. Yancy likes to **arise** at seven o'clock each morning.
★18. The speaker had to **pause** for a moment to clear his throat.
★19. The **visitor** arrived at our house exactly on time.
★20. Do not **tease** the dog, or he might bite you.

Spelling and Vocabulary

Word Groups

Write a spelling word to complete each group.

1. bother, taunt, pester, _____
2. guest, caller, company, _____
3. surprise, astonish, flabbergast, _____
4. eraser, tape, stapler, _____
5. periodical, journal, publication, _____
6. oral, auditory, tactile, _____
7. delay, break, rest, _____
8. customary, expected, normal, _____
9. hopelessness, gloom, doubt, _____

Word Analysis

Change the underlined part of each of the following words to write a spelling word.

10. <u>sun</u>rise	12. <u>con</u>ference	14. <u>op</u>tical	16. <u>cas</u>tle
11. tele<u>phone</u>	13. hus<u>tle</u>	15. free<u>dom</u>	17. <u>er</u>ase

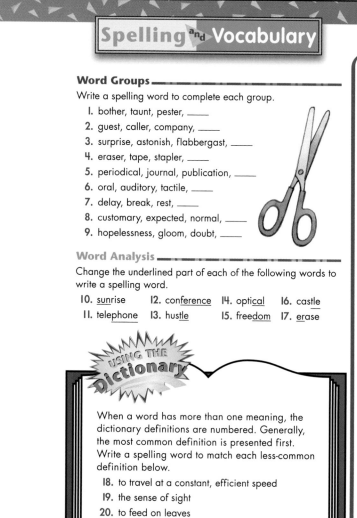

USING THE Dictionary

When a word has more than one meaning, the dictionary definitions are numbered. Generally, the most common definition is presented first. Write a spelling word to match each less-common definition below.

18. to travel at a constant, efficient speed
19. the sense of sight
20. to feed on leaves

Word Groups

1. tease
2. visitor
3. amaze
4. scissors
5. magazine
6. visual
7. pause
8. usual
9. pessimism

Word Analysis

10. arise
11. television
12. conclusion
13. husband
14. optimism
15. freeze
16. casual
17. phase

Using the Dictionary

18. cruise
19. vision
20. browse

87

Objectives

Spelling and Vocabulary

Students will
- **write** spelling words to complete a series of meaning-related words.
- **change** parts of words to write spelling words.
- **relate** spelling words to their less-common definitions.

Developing Oral Language Skills

Have students work in pairs. The first student asks a question that includes one of the words from the spelling list. For example, the student might ask, "Why do you like that **magazine**?" The second student answers the question. The answer must include a word with the /z/ or /zh/ sound. For example the second student might answer, "I get a lot of **pleasure** reading it."

MEETING INDIVIDUAL NEEDS

Providing More Help

Pass out orange and red cards made from construction paper. Read the following sets of words aloud, and tell the students to raise red cards when they hear the /z/ sound and orange cards when they hear the /zh/ sound.

1. stomach, amaze (/z/), television (/zh/)
2. magazine (/z/), visual (/zh/), store
3. husband (/z/), metallic, conclusion (/zh/)
4. ocean, freeze (/z/), usual (/zh/)
5. tease (/z/), carton, vision (/zh/)
6. casual (/zh/), grass, browse (/z/)

★Students who need to study fewer words should use the **Alternate Word List**. This list is starred on page T86 in the Teacher Edition. The **Unit 14 Practice Masters** (*Teacher Resource Book*) provide additional practice with these words.

Unit 14 Practice Masters

Name _____

Practice **Master** Unit **14**

1. amaze	3. pause	5. husband	7. scissors	9. television
2. tease	4. optimism	6. visitor	8. usual	10. conclusion

A. Write the spelling word that goes with each group.

1. brother, uncle, nephew, _____
2. staplers, paper clips, erasers, _____
3. delay, break, rest, _____
4. guest, caller, company, _____
5. radio, movie, stereo, _____

B. Read each question. Unscramble the spelling words. Write the words. Then answer each question by circling **Yes** or **No**.

1. Is a **stiivro** a guest?   Yes   No
2. Can a trapeze artist **zamea** a crowd?   Yes   No
3. Should you **espau** before crossing a street?   Yes   No
4. Are there ads on **niosivelet**?   Yes   No
5. Can **sslorssc** cut?   Yes   No
6. Can you draw a **lusioncnoc**?   Yes   No

T87

Objectives

Spelling and Reading

Students will
- **solve** analogies using spelling words.
- **complete** sentences using spelling words.
- **complete** a paragraph using spelling words.

One-Minute Handwriting Hint

The checkstroke ending of the lowercase **v** swings right and up to form the first stroke of the letter **i**. The slant stroke of the **i** is pulled to the base-line before the undercurve ending is formed.

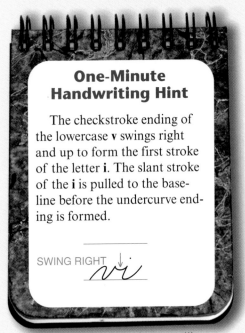

SWING RIGHT

Legible handwriting can boost spelling scores by as much as 20%.

Solve the Analogies

1. amaze
2. freeze
3. arise
4. tease
5. vision
6. cruise

Complete the Sentences

7. visitor
8. pause
9. pessimism
10. phase
11. casual
12. browse
13. television
14. husband

Complete the Paragraph

15. usual
16. visual
17. scissors
18. magazine
19. conclusion
20. optimism

Spelling and Reading

magazine	pessimism	conclusion	optimism	television
amaze	cruise	casual	husband	phase
vision	browse	usual	freeze	visual
scissors	arise	pause	visitor	tease

Solve the Analogies Write a spelling word to complete each analogy.

1. **Scare** is to **shock** as **surprise** is to _____.
2. **Chose** is to **choose** as **froze** is to _____.
3. **Won** is to **win** as **arose** is to _____.
4. **Budge** is to **move** as **pester** is to _____.
5. **Ear** is to **hearing** as **eye** is to _____.
6. **Airplane** is to **fly** as **boat** is to _____.

Complete the Sentences Write a spelling word to complete each sentence.

7. We invited our _____ to have dinner with us.
8. We will _____ for a moment before we continue the tour.
9. His _____ made everyone else gloomy too.
10. We are beginning the next _____ of the space program.
11. She made a _____ remark about meeting for lunch.
12. I like to _____ before I make a decision to buy new jeans.
13. They do not watch _____ during the week.
14. Jane's _____ gave her a ring for their anniversary.

Complete the Paragraph Write spelling words from the box to complete the paragraph.

Yesterday Julio came over to work on our report on world peace. As ⟨15.⟩, it took us a while to get to work. Mr. Rahad said that we should have a ⟨16.⟩ presentation with our oral report, so we prepared a poster. Julio borrowed my ⟨17.⟩ to cut pictures from a ⟨18.⟩. At the ⟨19.⟩ of the report, we will give reasons for our ⟨20.⟩ about world peace.

> scissors
> optimism
> visual
> magazine
> usual
> conclusion

88

MEETING INDIVIDUAL NEEDS

Providing More Challenge

Challenge Words and **Challenge Activities** for Unit 14 appear on page 235. **Challenge Word Test Sentences** appear on page T235.

Unit 14 Challenge Activities

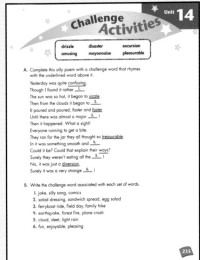

Weekly Test Options

Option 1:
One Spelling Word Per Sentence
(See procedures on pages Z10–Z11.)

★ 1. The circus acts will **amaze** the children.
2. Did you **arise** in time for breakfast at the hotel?
3. **Browse** through these items to find one that you like.
4. The doctors finished one **phase** of the treatment.
5. They wore **casual** clothes to the barbecue.
★ 6. What **conclusion** does the article draw from these events?
7. We went on a **cruise** along the coast.
8. It was so cold that we thought we would **freeze**.
★ 9. That man is a good father and **husband**.
10. Did you cut that photo out of a **magazine**?
★11. **Optimism** is the belief that good will win over evil.
★12. **Pause** for a few minutes before continuing.
13. His **pessimism** hurt his chances of winning.
★14. These **scissors** are sharp.
★15. Her mother told her not to **tease** the dog.

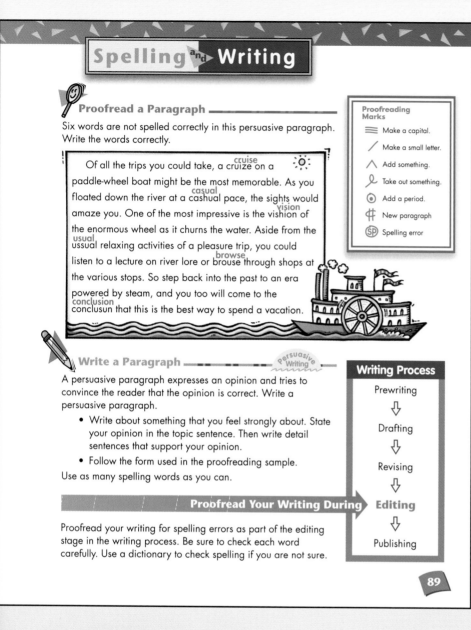

Spelling and Writing

Proofread a Paragraph

Six words are not spelled correctly in this persuasive paragraph. Write the words correctly.

Of all the trips you could take, a ~~cruize~~ cruise on a paddle-wheel boat might be the most memorable. As you floated down the river at a ~~cashual~~ casual pace, the sights would amaze you. One of the most impressive is the ~~vishion~~ vision of the enormous wheel as it churns the water. Aside from the ~~ussual~~ usual relaxing activities of a pleasure trip, you could listen to a lecture on river lore or ~~brouse~~ browse through shops at the various stops. So step back into the past to an era powered by steam, and you too will come to the ~~conclusun~~ conclusion that this is the best way to spend a vacation.

Proofreading Marks

- ≡ Make a capital.
- / Make a small letter.
- ∧ Add something.
- ℒ Take out something.
- ⊙ Add a period.
- ⌗ New paragraph.
- SP Spelling error

Write a Paragraph

persuasive Writing

A persuasive paragraph expresses an opinion and tries to convince the reader that the opinion is correct. Write a persuasive paragraph.

- Write about something that you feel strongly about. State your opinion in the topic sentence. Then write detail sentences that support your opinion.
- Follow the form used in the proofreading sample.

Use as many spelling words as you can.

Proofread Your Writing During

Proofread your writing for spelling errors as part of the editing stage in the writing process. Be sure to check each word carefully. Use a dictionary to check spelling if you are not sure.

Writing Process

Prewriting
⇩
Drafting
⇩
Revising
⇩
Editing
⇩
Publishing

89

Objectives

Spelling and Writing

Students will
- **proofread** a persuasive paragraph.
- **use** the writing process to write a persuasive paragraph.
- **proofread** their writing.

Using the Writing Process

Before assigning **Write a Paragraph**, see pages 258–259 in the Student Edition for a complete review of the writing process and additional writing assignments. You may also wish to refer to pages Z12–Z13 in the Teacher Edition.

Keeping a Spelling Journal

Encourage students to record the words they misspelled on the weekly test in a personal spelling journal. These words may be recycled for future study. Students may also wish to include words from their writing. See pages Z12–Z13 in the Teacher Edition for more information.

★16. We have two **television** sets in our house.

★17. Cereal is his **usual** breakfast.

18. With glasses, her **vision** is almost perfect.

★19. The **visitor** was happy to stay at our house.

20. His teacher used **visual** aids to teach math.

Option 2:
Multiple Spelling Words Per Sentence
(See procedures on pages Z10–Z11.)

1. The **conclusion** I have drawn will **amaze** you.
2. She and her **husband** will take a **cruise** next winter.
3. The teacher told the child to use the **scissors** to cut pictures from the **magazine**.
4. Her **optimism** must **arise** from her love of life.
5. The **visitor** to the city wanted to **browse** in all the shops.
6. There was a **pause** during the **television** program.
7. Her **vision** of the world is colored by her **pessimism**.
8. Friends sometimes **tease** each other in a **casual** way.
9. He had some **visual** problems during the worst **phase** of his illness.
10. It is **usual** to **freeze** that dessert before eating it.

Option 3:
Standardized Test
(See *Teacher Resource Book*, Unit 14.)

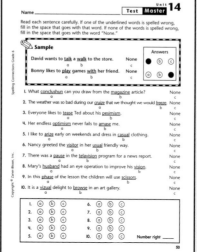

Unit 14 Test Master

T89

Objectives

Strategy Words

Students will

• **review** words studied previously that are related to the spelling strategy.

• **preview** unknown words that are related to the spelling strategy.

►Strategy Words◄

Remind the students that the **Strategy Words** relate to the spelling patterns they have studied in this unit. The **Review Words** are below grade level, and the **Preview Words** are above grade level. You may wish to use the following sentences to introduce the words in context.

Review Words:
Words From Grade 5

1. He had the **trousers** cleaned.
2. I ate **crackers** and cheese for a snack.
3. We will **dramatize** the story that is in our literature book.
4. The teacher helped me write the introductory **clause** for this compound sentence.
5. Our class discussed the safety **measures** we would need to follow.

Preview Words:
Words From Grade 7

6. The cast members appreciated the **applause** they received.
7. My sister received a **corsage** to wear to the school dance.
8. You **positively** must follow the directions carefully.
9. Which **version** of the story did you like better?
10. I took lessons to learn to play the **xylophone**.

Review Words

1. crackers
2. clause
3. trousers
4. measures
5. dramatize

Preview Words

6. xylophone
7. version
8. applause
9. positively
10. corsage

►Strategy Words◄

Review Words: Consonant Sounds /z/, /zh/

Write a word from the box to complete each of these sentences.

trousers	crackers	dramatize	clause	measures

1. He served us cheese and _____ as appetizers before dinner.
2. I have a question about the second _____ in the legal agreement.
3. He asked the tailor to shorten his new _____ at least three inches.
4. After she _____ your window, she will tell you how much fabric to buy.
5. She amuses us with the way she can _____ the most ordinary event.

Preview Words: Consonant Sounds /z/, /zh/

Write the words from the box that complete the paragraph.

applause	corsage	positively
version	xylophone	

I play the __6.__ for our community orchestra. When we played our new __7.__ of an old song, the __8.__ lasted for almost five minutes. I was __9.__ stunned. Someone even pinned a __10.__ on my dress. I felt like a celebrity!

90

Unit 14 RECAP

You may wish to assign the **Unit 14 Homework Master** (*Teacher Resource Book,* Unit 14) as a fun way to recap the spelling words.

Unit 14 Homework Master

Name _____ **Homework Master 14**

Read each question. Unscramble the spelling word. Write the spelling word correctly on the line. Then answer each question by circling **Yes** or **No**.

1. Can water **eeezfr**? _____ Yes No
2. Is a **stiivro** a guest? _____ Yes No
3. Can a trapeze artist **zaema** a crowd? _____ Yes No
4. Do you **sroebw** when you're late? _____ Yes No
5. Should you **espau** before crossing a street? _____ Yes No
6. Are there ads on **nlosivelet**? _____ Yes No
7. Can you listen to a **gamaznei**? _____ Yes No
8. Can **sslorssc** cut? _____ Yes No
9. Is the half-moon a moon **hapse**? _____ Yes No
10. Can you draw a **luslonconoc**? _____ Yes No

Add and subtract letters to form the remaining spelling words. Write the words.

1. pest – t + simple – ple + ism = _____
2. car – c + bi – b + se = _____
3. vip – p + sbo – bo + ual = _____
4. chop – ch + time – e + ism = _____
5. visit – t + only – ly = _____
6. toe – o + am – m + se = _____
7. crumb – mb + rise – r = _____
8. crib – rib + yas – y + u + al = _____
9. up – p + sum – m + al = _____
10. hurt – rt + zsb – z + and = _____

54

Content Words

Math: Multiplication

Write the words from the box that complete the paragraph.

multiplier	factoring	multiplicand
divisibility		multiples

Multiplication is one of the four basic operations of arithmetic. The __1.__ of a number can be determined by __2.__. For example, factors of 21 are 3 and 7. The numbers 3 and 7 are __3.__ of 21. In the multiplication problem 3 × 7, 3 is the __4.__, and 7 is the __5.__.

Social Studies: Citizenship

Write the words that complete the paragraph.

excel	citizenship	ceremony	patriotism	national

A special __6.__ is held to grant immigrants __7.__ in the United States. People who __8.__ at learning languages generally adjust easily to their new lives. Many new citizens quickly develop an understanding of __9.__ customs and a sense of __10.__ and pride.

Apply the Spelling Strategy

Circle the letter that spells the /z/ sound in four of the Content Words you wrote.

Word Study

Word Roots

This Strategy Word comes from a Greek root that meant "wood" and an English word for **sound**. Write the name of this musical instrument.

Math: Multiplication
1. divi(s)ibility
2. factoring
3. multiple(s)
4. multiplier
5. multiplicand

Social Studies: Citizenship
6. ceremony
7. citi(z)enship
8. excel
9. national
10. patrioti(s)m

Word Roots
1. xylophone

91

Objectives

Content Words

Students will
- **expand** vocabulary with content-related words.
- **relate** the spelling strategy to words outside the basic spelling list.
- **understand** a word root and find it in a word.

Content Words

Math: Multiplication

Use these sentences to introduce the words and their meanings.
1. In 2 × 6, 2 is the **multiplier**.
2. We will begin **factoring** fractions in the next chapter in math.
3. In 2 × 8, 8 is the **multiplicand**.
4. The **divisibility** of numbers can be checked mathematically.
5. We listed the **multiples** of ten.

Social Studies: Citizenship

Use these sentences to introduce the words and their meanings.
6. The brothers **excel** in baseball, our national sport.
7. He received his **citizenship** papers.
8. The **ceremony** was to honor outstanding members of government.
9. His **patriotism** was never doubted.
10. July Fourth is a **national** holiday.

Word Study

Word Roots

Point out that a **word root** is a word or word part from which other words are made. Word roots for English words often come from Latin or Greek. Understanding word roots can help students build their vocabulary.

Unit 15 Home Spelling Practice

Spanish

English

MANAGING INSTRUCTION

Looking Ahead to Unit 15

To save time, you may wish to duplicate the **Unit 15 Home Spelling Practice** now. (See *Home Spelling Practice Book,* Unit 15.)

Basic Spelling List

complained	resulted
permitting	admitted
remained	excelled
profiting	obtained
excelling	differing
obtaining	profited
remaining	admitting
permitted	differed
complaining	directing
directed	resulting

Strategy Words

Review
gleaming	supplying
interesting	trimmed
removed	

Preview
compelling	preferred
obliging	recurring
omitted	

Content Words

Science: Computers
debugging	programming
output	input
flow chart	

Language Arts: Linguistics
consonant	voiced
vibrate	unvoiced
linguistics	

Individual Needs

Challenge Words
discovered	discovering
satisfied	satisfying
overlapped	overlapping

Alternate Word List ★
remained	directed
profiting	resulted
remaining	admitting
permitted	differed
complaining	directing

★ For students who need to study fewer Basic Spelling words

T92A

MATERIALS

Student Edition
Pages 92–97
Challenge Activities, p. 236

Teacher Edition
Pages T92A–T97
Challenge Activities, p. T236

Teacher Resource Book
Unit 15 Homework Master
Unit 15 Practice Masters
Flip Folder Practice Master
Unit 15 Test Master

Home Spelling Practice Book
Unit 15 Home Spelling Practice
(English or Spanish)

Other *Spelling Connections* Resources
- Audiotape, Grade 6
- Practice Book for Grammar, Usage, and Mechanics, Grade 6
- Spelling Support for Second Language Learners, Grade 6
- Support Software on CD-ROM
- Transparency Book, Grade 6
- Word Sort CD-ROM, Grade 6

OBJECTIVES

Spelling and Thinking
Students will
- **read** the spelling words in list form and in context.
- **sort** the spelling words according to whether the base word changes when the suffixes **-ed** and **-ing** are added.
- **read** and remember this week's spelling strategy.

Spelling and Vocabulary
Students will
- **write** spelling words to complete a series of meaning-related words.
- **replace** words in sentences with spelling words.
- **use** the **Spelling Dictionary** to find other forms of base words.

Spelling and Reading
Students will
- **solve** analogies using spelling words.
- **complete** sentences using spelling words.
- **complete** a paragraph using spelling words.

Spelling and Writing
Students will
- **proofread** a paragraph about an event.
- **use** the writing process to write a paragraph about an event.
- **proofread** their writing.

MEETING INDIVIDUAL NEEDS
Learning Styles

 Visual

Have the students play "Affix Autos." Draw an outline of a car on poster board. From construction paper, cut out sixteen car doors. Write the base words of the spelling words (**direct, result, profit, obtain, complain, remain, differ, admit, permit, excel**) and the suffix endings (**ed, ing, t+ed, t+ing, l+ed, l+ing**) on the car doors, one word or ending to a door. Divide the class into teams or let the students play individually. Have the students place the doors on the car to form as many spelling words, or Affix Autos, as possible in a set amount of time. Have the students look carefully at each spelling word and write the word.

 Auditory

Have the students play "Affix Autos" as described in the visual activity, with these modifications: Have the students spell the word aloud after they form a spelling word. Then have them write the word on their papers, saying it aloud as they do so.

 Kinesthetic

Divide the class into groups of four. Each student takes a turn saying a spelling word aloud to the other students in the group. When the word is pronounced, these students take either of the following actions: if the word contains the suffix **-ing,** they stand and turn around once; if the word contains the suffix **-ed,** they clap their hands twice. In either case, they then write the word correctly on their papers.

> **Hands-On Practice**
> All students will benefit from practicing with a **Flip Folder**. See page Z18.

Language and Cultural Differences

The Spanish language does not include the final **ed** or **ing** sounds. Spanish-speaking students may, therefore, find it difficult to pronounce and spell words that have the **-ed** and **-ing** endings. Have these students write the base word of each spelling word, one under the other, on paper. Say each base word, and have the students write the related spelling word beside each base word.

MANAGING INSTRUCTION

3–5 Day Plan		Average	Below Average	Above Average
Day 1	**Day 1**	Pretest Spelling Mini-Lesson, p. T92 Spelling and Thinking, p. 92	Pretest Spelling Mini-Lesson, p. T92 Spelling and Thinking, p. 92	Pretest Spelling and Thinking, p. 92
	Day 2	Spelling and Vocabulary, p. 93	Spelling and Vocabulary, p. 93 (or) Unit 15 Practice Master, A and B	Spelling and Vocabulary, p. 93 Spelling and Reading, p. 94
Day 2	**Day 3**	Spelling and Reading, p. 94	Spelling and Reading, p. 94 (or) Unit 15 Practice Master, C and D	Challenge Activities, p. 236
	Day 4	Spelling and Writing, p. 95 Unit 15 Homework Master	Spelling and Writing, p. 95	Spelling and Writing, p. 95 Unit 15 Homework Master
Day 3	**Day 5**	Weekly Test	Weekly Test	Weekly Test
Vocabulary Connections (pages 96 and 97) may be used anytime during this unit.				

Objectives

Spelling and Thinking

Students will
- **read** the spelling words in list form and in context.
- **sort** the spelling words according to whether the base word changes when the suffixes **-ed** and **-ing** are added.
- **read** and remember this week's spelling strategy.

UNIT PRETEST

Use **Pretest Sentences** below. Refer to the self-checking procedures on student page 256. You may wish to use the **Unit 15 Word List Overhead Transparency** as part of the checking procedure.

TEACHING THE STRATEGY

Spelling Mini-Lesson

Write **permit, permitted; sit, sitting; profit, profited; direct, directing; tax, taxing;** and **appear, appearing** on the chalkboard. Use these words to review the guidelines for adding **-ed** and **-ing**.

- If a base word ends in one consonant preceded by one vowel and the final syllable is accented, double the consonant before adding the suffix: **permit, permitted**. One-syllable words fall into this category: **sit, sitting**.
- If a base word ends in one consonant preceded by one vowel and the final syllable is not accented, do not double the final consonant before adding the suffix: **profiting, profited**.
- If a base word ends in two consonants or with a vowel-vowel-consonant pattern, do not double the final consonant before adding the suffix: **direct, directing; appear, appearing**.
- If a base word ends in **x,** do not double the final consonant before adding the suffix: **tax, taxing**.

Write **favor, forget, prefer,** and **wonder** on the chalkboard. Ask students to listen for the accented syllable in each word and then decide how the word is spelled when **-ing** is added. (favoring, forgetting, preferring, wondering)

Read the spelling list and discuss how each word relates to a spelling guideline.

READ THE SPELLING WORDS

1.	complained	complained	He **complained** that his leg hurt.
2.	permitting	permitting	Are you **permitting** us to go now?
3.	remained	remained	The store **remained** open until six.
4.	profiting	profiting	She is **profiting** from the book sale.
5.	excelling	excelling	The team is **excelling** this season.
6.	obtaining	obtaining	He is **obtaining** his fishing license.
7.	remaining	remaining	Food is **remaining** from the picnic.
8.	permitted	permitted	Swimming is **permitted** in the lake.
9.	complaining	complaining	He is **complaining** about the heat.
10.	directed	directed	A police officer **directed** traffic.
11.	resulted	resulted	His fall **resulted** in a broken arm.
12.	admitted	admitted	I **admitted** to having lost the book.
13.	excelled	excelled	Lin **excelled** in foreign languages.
14.	obtained	obtained	He **obtained** two tickets to the play.
15.	differing	differing	We are **differing** over where to eat.
16.	profited	profited	The client **profited** from our advice.
17.	admitting	admitting	He is finally **admitting** his mistake.
18.	differed	differed	Our taste in music **differed** greatly.
19.	directing	directing	He will be **directing** the school play.
20.	resulting	resulting	Heavy rains are **resulting** in floods.

SORT THE SPELLING WORDS

1.–6. Write the spelling words in which the final consonant in the base word is doubled when **-ed** or **-ing** is added. Circle the base words.

7.–20. Write the spelling words in which the base word does not change when **-ed** or **-ing** is added. Circle the base words.

REMEMBER THE SPELLING STRATEGY

Remember that the suffixes **-ed** and **-ing** can be added to some base words to form new words. In other words, the final consonant is doubled when **-ed** or **-ing** is added.

Order of answers may vary.

final consonant doubled
1. permitting
2. excelling
3. permitted ★
4. admitted
5. excelled
6. admitting ★

no change to base word
7. complained
8. remained ★
9. profiting ★
10. obtaining
11. remaining ★
12. complaining ★
13. directed ★
14. resulted ★
15. obtained
16. differing
17. profited
18. differed ★
19. directing ★
20. resulting

92

Pretest Sentences (See procedures on pages Z10–Z11.)

1. Because of poor service, Mr. Clark **complained** to the manager.
2. Are your parents **permitting** you to go to the movies?
★ 3. After the party, only one piece of birthday cake **remained**.
★ 4. We will be **profiting** from new medical findings in years to come.
5. If she keeps **excelling** in math, she may major in it in college.
6. In order to find a job, Ms. Drew has been **obtaining** interviews.
★ 7. Are you **remaining** for refreshments or leaving after the meeting?
★ 8. The young children are not **permitted** out alone after dark.
★ 9. The farmers were **complaining** about the lack of rain.
★10. The teacher **directed** the students in the choral reading.
★11. The contest **resulted** in a tie score.
12. Larry **admitted** that he forgot to lock the front door.
13. The talented athlete **excelled** in any sport he tried.
14. We **obtained** the last two tickets to the concert.
15. Jack Sprat and his wife held **differing** views on the subject of food.
16. The school **profited** from a successful three-day carnival.
★17. The suspect is **admitting** nothing until he sees his lawyer.
★18. The results of the two separate tests **differed** greatly.
★19. The police officer at the intersection was **directing** traffic.
20. Our efforts kept **resulting** in new challenges.

Spelling and Vocabulary

Word Groups

Write a spelling word to complete each sequence.

1. getting, gaining, securing, _____
2. accused, grumbled, railed, _____
3. acknowledged, conceded, revealed, _____
4. gaining, reaping, earning, _____
5. enduring, lasting, residing, _____
6. allowing, authorizing, tolerating, _____

Word Replacement

Write spelling words that could replace the underlined words.

7. The worker was protesting about the long hours.
8. Only a few people stayed in the theater after the play.
9. The campers got a permit to pitch their tent.
10. The witness was finally confessing what he saw.
11. Swimming is not allowed in the pond.
12. I benefited from having an excellent swim coach.

USING THE Dictionary

The dictionary does not include an individual entry for every form of a word. To find a word that has a suffix, look up the base word. Write the spelling words that are formed from these base words.

result, __13.__, __14.__   excel, __17.__, __18.__
direct, __15.__, __16.__   differ, __19.__, __20.__

◆ ◆ ◆

Dictionary Check Be sure to check for the base words in your **Spelling Dictionary**.

Word Groups
1. obtaining
2. complained
3. admitted
4. profiting
5. remaining
6. permitting

Word Replacement
7. complaining
8. remained
9. obtained
10. admitting
11. permitted
12. profited

Using the Dictionary
13. resulted
14. resulting
15. directed
16. directing
17. excelled
18. excelling
19. differed
20. differing

93

Objectives

Spelling and Vocabulary

Students will
- **write** spelling words to complete a series of meaning-related words.
- **replace** words in sentences with spelling words.
- **use** the **Spelling Dictionary** to find other forms of base words.

Developing Oral Language Skills

Have students work in pairs. The first student asks a question that includes one of the words from the spelling list that ends with **-ed**. For example, the student might ask, "Have you ever **directed** a play?" The second student answers the question. The answer must change the **-ed** ending in the spelling word to **-ing**. For example, the second student might answer, "I am **directing** one next week."

MEETING INDIVIDUAL NEEDS

Providing More Help

To aid these students in understanding the suffixes **-ed** and **-ing,** list the base words of the spelling words on the chalkboard. Next to this list make two columns headed **-ing** and **-ed**. Then have volunteers go to the chalkboard and write the spelling words in the correct columns.

★Students who need to study fewer words should use the **Alternate Word List**. This list is starred on page T92 in the Teacher Edition. The **Unit 15 Practice Masters** (*Teacher Resource Book*) provide additional practice with these words.

Unit 15 Practice Masters

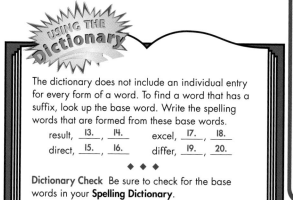

T93

Objectives

Spelling and Reading

Students will
- **solve** analogies using spelling words.
- **complete** sentences using spelling words.
- **complete** a paragraph using spelling words.

One-Minute Handwriting Hint

Be sure to close the oval of the lowercase **g** or the letter will look like **cj**. The overcurve ending crosses the slant stroke at the baseline.

g CLOSE OVAL

Legible handwriting can boost spelling scores by as much as 20%.

Solve the Analogies
1. directed
2. complained
3. admitting
4. excelling
5. differing
6. profited

Complete the Sentences
7. remaining
8. excelled
9. differed
10. profiting
11. obtaining
12. resulting
13. permitting

Complete the Paragraph
14. remained
15. permitted
16. resulted
17. complaining
18. directing
19. admitted
20. obtained

Spelling and Reading

complained	remaining	excelled	directing
obtaining	admitted	differed	excelling
profited	admitting	profiting	directed
resulted	remained	complaining	differing
permitting	permitted	obtained	resulting

Solve the Analogies   Write a spelling word to complete each analogy.
1. **Player** is to **coached** as **actor** is to _____.
2. **Inquired** is to **replied** as **praised** is to _____.
3. **Agreeing** is to **contradicting** as **denying** is to _____.
4. **Omitting** is to **including** as **failing** is to _____.
5. **Questioning** is to **replying** as **agreeing** is to _____.
6. **Bothered** is to **pestered** as **benefited** is to _____.

Complete the Sentences   Write a spelling word to complete each sentence.
7. There was not one piece of birthday cake _____.
8. Robert Frost _____ in writing poems about nature.
9. Our opinion _____ on what time the party should end.
10. Job seekers are _____ from the strong economy.
11. They are _____ a permit for their home addition.
12. His constant watering is _____ in a green lawn.
13. The principal is not _____ us to use the gym after school.

Complete the Paragraph   Write spelling words from the box to complete the paragraph.

As a result of road reconstruction, only one lane _14._ open, and trucks were not _15._ to get on the highway. These restrictions _16._ in a traffic jam during rush hour. Motorists were _17._ to a police officer who was _18._ traffic. He _19._ that this was not the best time of day for the construction, but the company had not _20._ permission to work at night.

| admitted |
| directing |
| permitted |
| obtained |
| resulted |
| remained |
| complaining |

94

MEETING INDIVIDUAL NEEDS

Providing More Challenge

Challenge Words and **Challenge Activities** for Unit 15 appear on page 236. **Challenge Word Test Sentences** appear on page T236.

Unit 15 Challenge Activities

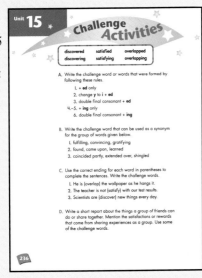

Weekly Test Options

Option 1:
One Spelling Word Per Sentence
(See procedures on pages Z10–Z11.)

1. She **admitted** that she had done something wrong.
★ 2. He seems to have a hard time **admitting** the truth.
★ 3. The twins **differed** in many ways.
4. Their **differing** ideas caused them to argue.
★ 5. The officer **directed** the busy traffic.
★ 6. Who will be **directing** the school play?
7. Because of his natural ability, he **excelled** in sports.
8. She seems to be **excelling** in math this year.
9. I **obtained** a free pass to the museum.
10. She is **obtaining** some books from the library for me.
★11. The visitor was **permitted** to see her in the hospital.
12. The coach is **permitting** us to leave early.
13. Although I **complained,** I knew Mom was right.
★14. He is always **complaining** about the unpleasant weather.
15. The company **profited** from the sale.

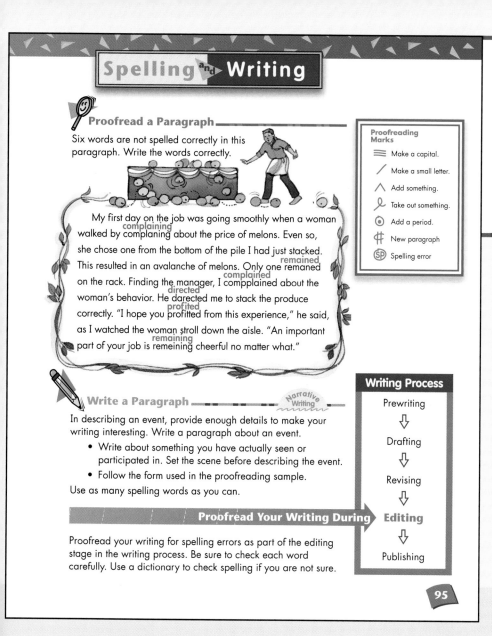

Proofread a Paragraph

Six words are not spelled correctly in this paragraph. Write the words correctly.

My first day on the job was going smoothly when a woman
complaining
walked by complaining about the price of melons. Even so,
she chose one from the bottom of the pile I had just stacked.
This resulted in an avalanche of melons. Only one remaned
remained
on the rack. Finding the manager, I compplained about the
complained
woman's behavior. He darected me to stack the produce
directed
correctly. "I hope you profited from this experience," he said,
profited
as I watched the woman stroll down the aisle. "An important
remaining
part of your job is remeining cheerful no matter what."

Proofreading Marks

≡ Make a capital.

/ Make a small letter.

∧ Add something.

℘ Take out something.

⊙ Add a period.

⌗ New paragraph

SP Spelling error

Write a Paragraph

Narrative Writing

In describing an event, provide enough details to make your writing interesting. Write a paragraph about an event.

- Write about something you have actually seen or participated in. Set the scene before describing the event.
- Follow the form used in the proofreading sample.

Use as many spelling words as you can.

Proofread Your Writing During

Proofread your writing for spelling errors as part of the editing stage in the writing process. Be sure to check each word carefully. Use a dictionary to check spelling if you are not sure.

Writing Process

Prewriting
⇩
Drafting
⇩
Revising
⇩
Editing
⇩
Publishing

95

Objectives

Spelling and Writing

Students will

- **proofread** a paragraph about an event.
- **use** the writing process to write a paragraph about an event.
- **proofread** their writing.

Using the Writing Process

Before assigning **Write a Paragraph,** see pages 258–259 in the Student Edition for a complete review of the writing process and additional writing assignments. You may wish to refer to pages Z12–Z13 in the Teacher Edition.

Keeping a Spelling Journal

Encourage students to record the words they misspelled on the weekly test in a personal spelling journal. These words may be recycled for future study. Students may also wish to include words from their writing. See pages Z12–Z13 in the Teacher Edition for more information.

★16. We are still **profiting** from her efforts.
★17. They **remained** friends even though they had argued.
★18. Kathy is **remaining** here after the race.
★19. The dispute **resulted** in a broken friendship.
  20. The heavy rains are **resulting** in floods.

Option 2:
Multiple Spelling Words Per Sentence

(See procedures on pages Z10–Z11.)

1. I **directed** my thoughts to Sam's **directing** skills.
2. Since **excelling** was so important to her, she **excelled** in everything she did.
3. He had **obtained** everything that was worth **obtaining**.
4. He **remained** in his seat for the **remaining** speeches.
5. She was **admitted** into the hospital's **admitting** room.
6. Mom **complained** about my constant **complaining**.
7. We are **permitted** to go outside, weather **permitting**.
8. My friends **differed** over things worth **differing** about.
9. Is the company **profiting** more than it **profited** last year?
10. The dispute **resulting** from his activity finally **resulted** in a positive end.

Option 3:
Standardized Test
(See *Teacher Resource Book,* Unit 15.)

**Unit 15
Test Master**

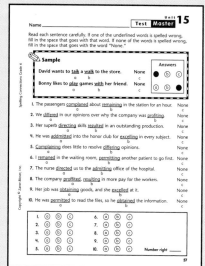

Unit 15 Test Master

Read each sentence carefully. If one of the underlined words is spelled wrong, fill in the space that goes with that word. If none of the words is spelled wrong, fill in the space that goes with the word "None."

Sample

David wants to <u>talk</u> a <u>walk</u> to the store. None
  a   b   c

Bonny likes to <u>play</u> games <u>with</u> her friend. None
  a   b   c

1. The passengers <u>complaned</u> about <u>remaining</u> in the station for an hour. None
2. We <u>differed</u> in our opinions over why the company was <u>profiting</u>. None
3. Her superb <u>directing</u> skills <u>rezulted</u> in an outstanding production. None
4. He was <u>admitted</u> into the honor club for <u>excelling</u> in every subject. None
5. <u>Complaining</u> does little to resolve <u>differing</u> opinions. None
6. I <u>remaned</u> in the waiting room, <u>permitting</u> another patient to go first. None
7. The nurse <u>directed</u> us to the <u>admitting</u> office of the hospital. None
8. The company <u>profited</u>, <u>resulting</u> in more pay for the workers. None
9. Her job was <u>obtaining</u> goods, and she <u>excelled</u> at it. None
10. He was <u>permitted</u> to read the files, so he <u>obtained</u> the information. None

Strategy Words

Students will
- **review** words studied previously that are related to the spelling strategy.
- **preview** unknown words that are related to the spelling strategy.

Optional Enrichment

Unit 15 enrichment

VOCABULARY CONNECTIONS

►Strategy Words◄

Remind the students that the **Strategy Words** relate to the spelling patterns they have studied in this unit. The **Review Words** are below grade level, and the **Preview Words** are above grade level. You may wish to use the following sentences to introduce the words in context.

Review Words:
Words From Grade 5

1. The **gleaming** lights surprised us as we watched the play.
2. She is an **interesting** person who has many hobbies.
3. I **removed** my shoes before entering the room.
4. We are **supplying** cookies for the party.
5. My father **trimmed** the shrubs, but they have grown back.

Preview Words:
Words From Grade 7

6. She felt a **compelling** urge to attend the ceremony for my brother.
7. We are **obliging** the family by doing this favor.
8. This name was **omitted** by accident.
9. We **preferred** to sit quietly because we were tired.
10. The **recurring** chorus of the music was a pleasant experience.

Review Words
1. interesting
2. removed
3. gleaming
4. supplying
5. trimmed

Preview Words
6. preferred
7. recurring
8. compelling
9. obliging
10. omitted

►Strategy Words◄

Review Words: Suffixes -ed, -ing

Write words from the box to complete the paragraph.

gleaming	interesting	removed
supplying		trimmed

Mario had created an __1.__ menu for his new restaurant. He had __2.__ some of the old furniture and waxed the floors until they were __3.__. The company __4.__ Mario with equipment had already delivered the table linens. Mario __5.__ the bushes outside the restaurant and hung the sign. He was ready for business.

Preview Words: Suffixes -ed, -ing

Write words from the box to complete the sentences.

compelling	obliging	omitted
preferred		recurring

6. Al liked baseball but _____ soccer.
7. The speaker's first point kept _____ throughout his speech.
8. The lawyer presented a very _____ argument.
9. The _____ waiter brought us water three times.
10. In her nervousness, she _____ one whole section of her speech.

96

Unit 15 RECAP

You may wish to assign the **Unit 15 Homework Master** (*Teacher Resource Book*, Unit 15) as a fun way to recap the spelling words.

Unit 15 Homework Master

Name _____

Homework Master Unit 15

Use the code to write your spelling words. Remember to double the final **t** or **l** before adding the ending on certain words.

Example: 30 cel 15 *excelling*

10 = -ed	5 = di-	9 = pro-	20 = com-	23 = per-
15 = -ing	7 = re-	11 = ob-	27 = ad-	30 = ex-

5 rect 10	9 fit 10	7 sult 15
1.	7.	13.
11 tain 15	11 tain 10	7 sult 10
2.	8.	14.
30 cel 10	7 main 15	7 main 10
3.	9.	15.
23 mit 15	5 ffer 10	23 mit 10
4.	10.	16.
9 fit 15	5 ffer 15	27 mit 15
5.	11.	17.
20 plain 15	27 mit 10	20 plain 10
6.	12.	18.

Write the spelling word that tells what the person in the picture is doing.

1. _____   2. _____

58

◢Content Words◣

Science: Computers

Write the words from the box that complete the paragraph.

| debugging output flow chart programming input |

One of the jobs of a programmer is to provide the computer with a set of instructions for problem solving. This is called __1.__. The information that programmers put into a system is __2.__. The information that a computer sends out is called __3.__. Sometimes this is in the form of a __4.__, or a diagram showing the sequence of operations. Another important job for a programmer is removing errors from, or __5.__, a program.

Language Arts: Linguistics

Write the words from the box that complete the paragraph.

| consonant vibrate linguistics voiced unvoiced |

The study of __6.__ includes understanding how the vocal system works. Saying the __7.__ letter **v** causes the vocal cords to __8.__, which in turn produces a __9.__ sound. The letter **f,** however, produces an __10.__ sound.

Apply the Spelling Strategy

Circle the suffix **-ed** or **-ing** in four of the Content Words you wrote.

◢Word Study◣

Multiple Meanings

Some words have more than one meaning. For example, **cleave** can mean "to split" or "to stick to"! Write the one Strategy Word that can have these meanings:

• cut   • decorated

97

Science: Computers
1. programm(ing)
2. input
3. output
4. flow chart
5. debugg(ing)

Language Arts: Linguistics
6. linguistics
7. consonant
8. vibrate
9. voic(ed)
10. unvoic(ed)

Multiple Meanings
1. trimmed

Objectives

Content Words

Students will
• **expand** vocabulary with content-related words.
• **relate** the spelling strategy to words outside the basic spelling list.
• **understand** that some words have more than one meaning.

◢Content Words◣

Science: Computers

Use these sentences to introduce the words and their meanings.

1. I asked the salesman about **debugging** my computer.
2. The **output** was measured in amount and accuracy.
3. It was necessary to develop a **flow chart** to complete the project.
4. He does **programming** on new computers.
5. The errors we found seemed to come from human **input**.

Language Arts: Linguistics

Use these sentences to introduce the words and their meanings.

6. We reviewed the **consonant** sounds before we began the lesson.
7. It was easy to feel our throat **vibrate** as we said the words.
8. **Linguistics** was a class being offered at my sister's college.
9. They **voiced** their disapproval.
10. Even though the disapproval was **unvoiced,** we understood.

◢Word Study◣

Multiple Meanings

Discuss the ways in which the same word can convey a variety of meanings depending on context. Encourage students to brainstorm ways in which other common words, e.g., **hand,** can have different meanings, e.g., a "pointer," as on a clock or a "crew member."

Unit 16 Home Spelling Practice

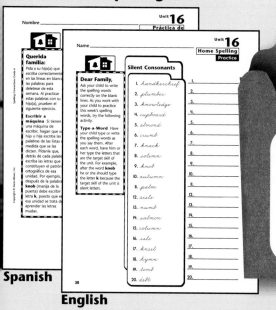

Spanish

English

T97

Basic Spelling List

handkerchief	palm
plumber	aisle
knowledge	numb
cupboard	salmon
almond	column
crumb	isle
knack	kneel
solemn	hymn
knob	tomb
autumn	debt

Strategy Words

Review
bowl	unknown
calmer	writer
knapsack	

Preview
gnarled	hustle
herb	knoll
honesty	

Content Words

Social Studies: The Law
corrupt	verdict
indict	defend
demonstrate	

Math: Geometry
decagon	trapezoid
rhombus	quadrilateral
parallelogram	

Individual Needs

Challenge Words
rhinoceros	rhubarb
symptom	subpoena
naphtha	condemn

Alternate Word List★
handkerchief	palm
knowledge	aisle
solemn	numb
knob	column
autumn	kneel

★ For students who need to study fewer Basic Spelling words

MATERIALS

Student Edition
Pages 98–103
Challenge Activities, p. 237

Teacher Edition
Pages T98A–T103
Challenge Activities, p. T237

Teacher Resource Book
Unit 16 Homework Master
Unit 16 Practice Masters
Flip Folder Practice Master
Unit 16 Test Master

Home Spelling Practice Book
Unit 16 Home Spelling Practice
(English or Spanish)

Other *Spelling Connections* Resources
- Audiotape, Grade 6
- Practice Book for Grammar, Usage, and Mechanics, Grade 6
- Spelling Support for Second Language Learners, Grade 6
- Support Software on CD-ROM
- Transparency Book, Grade 6
- Word Sort CD-ROM, Grade 6

OBJECTIVES

Spelling and Thinking
Students will
- **read** the spelling words in list form and in context.
- **sort** the spelling words according to the location of silent consonants.
- **read** and remember this week's spelling strategy.

Spelling and Vocabulary
Students will
- **identify** spelling words by using structural and meaning clues.
- **replace** words in a sentence with spelling words with the same or nearly the same meaning.
- **use** their **Writing Thesaurus** to find synonyms.

Spelling and Reading
Students will
- **solve** analogies using spelling words.
- **complete** sentences using spelling words.
- **complete** a paragraph using spelling words.

Spelling and Writing
Students will
- **proofread** a paragraph.
- **use** the writing process to write a caricature.
- **proofread** their writing.

MEETING INDIVIDUAL NEEDS
Learning Styles

 Visual

Have the students look through old magazines or newspapers to find as many spelling words as they can. Have them cut out each word, glue the word on paper, and then write the word.

 Auditory

Ask the students to write short rhymes using the spelling words. For example:

> I picked up the **crumb**
> Though my fingers felt **numb**.

Ask volunteers to read their rhymes to the class. Have the other students name the spelling words used in the rhymes and spell them aloud.

 Kinesthetic

Print each spelling word without its silent letter in black ink on a card. Print the silent letter in red on a separate card. Give each student one card—either a spelling word or a silent letter. When you say "Go," have the students take three minutes to walk around the classroom silently and match their cards. After the student who has the spelling word finds a student with the missing silent letter and the two have agreed to match their cards, both students return to their seats and silently wait for the rest of the students to finish.

Hands-On Practice
All students will benefit from practicing with a **Flip Folder**. See page Z18.

Language and Cultural Differences

These spelling words may be especially difficult for students from other language backgrounds. The Spanish language, for example, has a very consistent sound-symbol pattern. Silent letters may present a special problem in spelling for Spanish-speaking students.

To spell words with silent letters, all students, regardless of dialect or language background, must memorize certain spellings. As always, it is important to provide the students with opportunities to associate word meaning with the visual sequence of letters used in spelling.

Have the students make an illustrated dictionary for the spelling words in this unit. Assign two words to each student to define and illustrate, or allow the students to choose their words. Combine all of the students' work into one booklet.

MANAGING INSTRUCTION

3–5 Day Plan		Average	Below Average	Above Average
Day 1	**Day 1**	Pretest Spelling Mini-Lesson, p. T98 Spelling and Thinking, p. 98	Pretest Spelling Mini-Lesson, p. T98 Spelling and Thinking, p. 98	Pretest Spelling and Thinking, p. 98
	Day 2	Spelling and Vocabulary, p. 99	Spelling and Vocabulary, p. 99 (or) Unit 16 Practice Master, A and B	Spelling and Vocabulary, p. 99 Spelling and Reading, p. 100
Day 2	**Day 3**	Spelling and Reading, p. 100	Spelling and Reading, p. 100 (or) Unit 16 Practice Master, C and D	Challenge Activities, p. 237
	Day 4	Spelling and Writing, p. 101 Unit 16 Homework Master	Spelling and Writing, p. 101	Spelling and Writing, p. 101 Unit 16 Homework Master
Day 3	**Day 5**	Weekly Test	Weekly Test	Weekly Test
Vocabulary Connections (pages 102 and 103) may be used anytime during this unit.				

Objectives

Spelling and Thinking

Students will
- **read** the spelling words in list form and in context.
- **sort** the spelling words according to the location of silent consonants.
- **read** and remember this week's spelling strategy.

UNIT PRETEST

Use **Pretest Sentences** below. Refer to the self-checking procedures on student page 256. You may wish to use the **Unit 16 Word List Overhead Transparency** as part of the checking procedure.

TEACHING THE STRATEGY

Spelling Mini-Lesson

Ask students to read the spelling list aloud and to identify consonants in each word that are not pronounced.

Encourage them to develop generalizations about silent consonants. Examples include:

- The letter **k** is often silent when it appears before **n**. This combination often occurs at the beginning of a word: **knob, kneel, knack, knowledge.**
- The letter **s** may be silent when it precedes **l** inside a word: **aisle, isle.**
- The letter **b** is often silent when it follows **m** at the end of a word: **tomb, numb, crumb.** (**Note:** Plumber follows this guideline because it is formed from the archaic word, **plumb.**)
- The letter **l** is often silent when it precedes **m**: **palm, salmon, almond.**
- The letter **n** is often silent when it follows **m**: **hymn, solemn, autumn, column.**

When discussing **handkerchief** and **cupboard**, note that the silent letters (**d** in **handkerchief** and **p** in **cupboard**) are simply lost in modern pronunciations.

Read **Remember the Spelling Strategy** on page 98.

Order of answers may vary.

first consonant silent
1. knowledge ★
2. almond
3. knack
4. knob ★
5. aisle ★
6. isle
7. kneel ★

final consonant silent
8. crumb
9. solemn ★
10. autumn ★
11. numb ★
12. column ★
13. hymn
14. tomb

interior consonant silent
15. handkerchief ★
16. plumber
17. cupboard
18. palm ★
19. salmon
20. debt

98

Spelling and Thinking

READ THE SPELLING WORDS

1. handkerchief	*handkerchief*	He bought a red silk **handkerchief.**
2. plumber	*plumber*	A **plumber** repaired the leaky pipe.
3. knowledge	*knowledge*	He gained **knowledge** from books.
4. cupboard	*cupboard*	The **cupboard** is filled with cans.
5. almond	*almond*	The cookie has an **almond** flavor.
6. crumb	*crumb*	A bird pecked at the bread **crumb.**
7. knack	*knack*	He has a **knack** for cooking.
8. solemn	*solemn*	It was a very **solemn** ceremony.
9. knob	*knob*	This **knob** controls the volume.
10. autumn	*autumn*	My favorite season is **autumn.**
11. palm	*palm*	We sat in the shade of a **palm** tree.
12. aisle	*aisle*	At the movies, I prefer an **aisle** seat.
13. numb	*numb*	The cold made my hands **numb.**
14. salmon	*salmon*	The **salmon** is a freshwater fish.
15. column	*column*	Ivy will grow up the porch **column.**
16. isle	*isle*	Take a ferry to get to the **isle.**
17. kneel	*kneel*	I will **kneel** down to untie the boat.
18. hymn	*hymn*	Let's sing a **hymn** to praise nature.
19. tomb	*tomb*	That pyramid was a king's **tomb.**
20. debt	*debt*	He paid the **debt** he owed his dad.

SORT THE SPELLING WORDS

1.–7. Write the spelling words whose first consonant is silent.

8.–14. Write the spelling words with a silent final consonant.

15.–20. Write the spelling words with a silent consonant that is neither the first nor the last consonant.

REMEMBER THE SPELLING STRATEGY

Remember that some words have more consonant letters than consonant sounds. If a consonant is not pronounced, it is considered silent: **k** in **knob** and **b** in **tomb.**

Pretest Sentences (See procedures on pages Z10–Z11.)

★ 1. Jerry always has a **handkerchief** in his pocket.
2. Dad called a **plumber** to fix that leaky faucet.
★ 3. Demarco's **knowledge** of the animal kingdom is remarkable.
4. The **cupboard** was filled with cans, boxes, and jars of food.
5. That oval-shaped nut is called an **almond.**
6. The wild birds ate every **crumb** of bread.
7. Shantrice has a **knack** for saying the right thing at the right time.
★ 8. The ceremony was **solemn,** as a memorial should be.
★ 9. The **knob** was made of solid brass.
★10. **Autumn** begins in September.
★11. Hold out the **palm** of your hand, and I will put an apple in it.
★12. The bride and her father walked down the **aisle** of the church.
★13. Although I wore mittens, my fingers became **numb** from the cold.
14. A **salmon** is a tasty fish.
★15. We wrote our spelling words in a **column** for Friday's test.
16. A tiny island is called an **isle.**
★17. He had to **kneel** to plant the flowers in the yard.
18. "America the Beautiful" is a stirring **hymn.**
19. There is a **tomb** to honor the memory of the unknown soldiers.
20. Sometimes people find it difficult to pay a **debt.**

Word Clues

1. It is a homophone for **him**.

2.–3. They are homophones for **I'll**.

4. It can refer to a kind of tree or a part of your hand.

5. It ends with **er**.

6. It is a piece of cloth that you hold in your hand.

7. You do this when you get down on your knees.

8. It is a nut that grows on a tree.

9. It is a fish with pink flesh.

Word Meanings

Write a spelling word to replace the underlined word or words.

10.–11. To open the <u>cabinet</u>, turn the <u>handle</u> to the right.

12.–13. In the <u>fall</u> I will pay off my <u>financial obligation</u>.

14. I dropped a <u>little piece</u> of bread.

15. This <u>burial place</u> dates back to the twelfth century.

16. She writes a weekly <u>article</u> for the school paper.

17. He has a <u>special talent</u> for many puns.

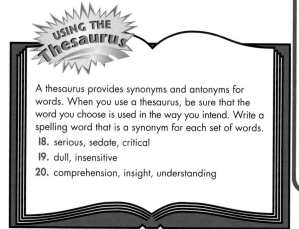

A thesaurus provides synonyms and antonyms for words. When you use a thesaurus, be sure that the word you choose is used in the way you intend. Write a spelling word that is a synonym for each set of words.

18. serious, sedate, critical

19. dull, insensitive

20. comprehension, insight, understanding

Word Clues

1. hymn
2. aisle
3. isle
4. palm
5. plumber
6. handkerchief
7. kneel
8. almond
9. salmon

Word Meanings

10. cupboard
11. knob
12. autumn
13. debt
14. crumb
15. tomb
16. column
17. knack

Using the Thesaurus

18. solemn
19. numb
20. knowledge

 99

Objectives

Spelling and Vocabulary

Students will

- **identify** spelling words by using structural and meaning clues.
- **replace** words in a sentence with spelling words with the same or nearly the same meaning.
- **use** their **Writing Thesaurus** to find synonyms.

Developing Oral Language Skills

Like most words with silent letters, the final **n** in **solemn, column, hymn,** and **autumn** is often omitted because it is not pronounced. However, students can be reminded of the silent letter if the word is associated with a related word. Write the following word pairs on the chalkboard and have students say each word pair aloud. Guide them to notice the difference between the letters and sounds they hear in each word pair.

solemnity	solemn
autumnal	autumn
columnist	column
hymnal	hymn

MEETING INDIVIDUAL NEEDS

Providing More Help

To aid the students in understanding these words with silent letters, write the following words on the board: **aisle, knob, debt, salmon, cupboard,** and **knack**. Have volunteers circle the silent consonant in each word.

★Students who need to study fewer words should use the **Alternate Word List**. This list is starred on page T98 of the Teacher Edition. The **Unit 16 Practice Masters** (*Teacher Resource Book*) provide additional practice with these words.

Unit 16 Practice Masters

Name _____ **Practice Master** Unit **16**

1. knob	3. knowledge	5. numb	7. solemn	9. column
2. kneel	4. aisle	6. palm	8. autumn	10. handkerchief

A. These words are misspelled. Write the spelling words correctly.

1. hankerchief _____   6. nob _____
2. neel _____   7. pam _____
3. ailes _____   8. solem _____
4. autum _____   9. colum _____
5. num _____   10. nowledge _____

B. Write the spelling word that belongs in each sentence.

1. When you rest on your knees, you ____. _____
2. A rounded handle can be called a ____. _____
3. All <u>knowing</u> occurs at this <u>ledge</u>. _____
4. A hairless part of the hand is the ____. _____

C. Write the spelling words in alphabetical order. Circle the silent letter in each word.

1. _____   6. _____
2. _____   7. _____
3. _____   8. _____
4. _____   9. _____
5. _____   10. _____

Practice Master Unit **16**

| | solemn | column |
| | autumn | handkerchief |

...rd for each dictionary respelling.

59

60

Objectives

Spelling and Reading

Students will
- **solve** analogies using spelling words.
- **complete** sentences using spelling words.
- **complete** a paragraph using spelling words.

One-Minute Handwriting Hint

The lowercase **m** contains three overcurve-slant motions. There is a pause after the first two overcurve-slant motions. If you write the letter carelessly, it will look like **u** or **w**.

Legible handwriting can boost spelling scores by as much as 20%.

Solve the Analogies

1. column
2. plumber
3. almond
4. hymn
5. salmon
6. solemn
7. isle

Complete the Sentences

8. autumn
9. numb
10. crumb
11. tomb
12. debt
13. knack
14. aisle
15. knowledge

Complete the Paragraph

16. knob
17. kneel
18. cupboard
19. palm
20. handkerchief

Spelling and Reading

handkerchief	plumber	knowledge	cupboard	almond
crumb	knack	solemn	knob	autumn
palm	aisle	numb	salmon	column
isle	kneel	hymn	tomb	debt

Solve the Analogies Write a spelling word to complete each analogy.

1. **Board** is to **plank** as **pillar** is to _____.
2. **Hammer** is to **carpenter** as **wrench** is to _____.
3. **Vegetable** is to **lettuce** as **nut** is to _____.
4. **Recite** is to **poem** as **sing** is to _____.
5. **Bird** is to **robin** as **fish** is to _____.
6. **Cheerful** is to **depressed** as **lively** is to _____.
7. **Ocean** is to **sea** as **island** is to _____.

Complete the Sentences Write a spelling word to complete each sentence.

8. Leaves of deciduous trees turn color in _____.
9. Her fingers felt _____ from the frigid air.
10. Norma brushed a _____ from the side of her mouth.
11. King Tut's treasures were discovered inside his _____.
12. Charles felt relieved after he paid off his _____.
13. Tasha has a _____ for always saying the right thing.
14. Fire laws prohibit anyone from sitting in the _____ at the theater.
15. Kyle has a lot of _____ about old cars.

Complete the Paragraph Write spelling words from the box to complete the paragraph.

Maria carefully turned the _16._ of the old door and tiptoed into the attic. She had to _17._ in order to peek under the wooden _18._. Suddenly, there it was in the _19._ of her hand. Wrapped in an old linen _20._ was the lost ring.

cupboard
handkerchief
knob
kneel
palm

100

MEETING INDIVIDUAL NEEDS

Providing More Challenge

Challenge Words and **Challenge Activities** for Unit 16 appear on page 237. **Challenge Word Test Sentences** appear on page T237.

Unit 16 Challenge Activities

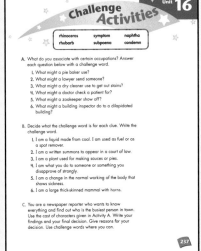

Weekly Test Options

Option 1:
One Spelling Word Per Sentence
(See procedures on pages Z10–Z11.)

★ 1. Our teacher walked up and down the **aisle** as we worked.
  2. Some foods are cooked with **almond** flavoring.
★ 3. **Autumn** is my favorite season.
★ 4. One **column** stood on each side of the stage.
  5. Only one tiny **crumb** was left on my plate.
  6. Put the dishes in the **cupboard**, please.
  7. He worked hard to pay off his **debt**.
★ 8. Wipe your eyes with my **handkerchief**.
  9. The audience sang a **hymn** to America.
 10. We went camping on a tiny **isle** in the lake.
 11. He has a **knack** for fixing things.
★12. Everyone was expected to **kneel** before the king.
★13. Turn the **knob** to open the door.
★14. How great is your **knowledge** of art?
★15. I was so **numb** that I could feel nothing.
★16. She held the bird in the **palm** of her hand.

T100

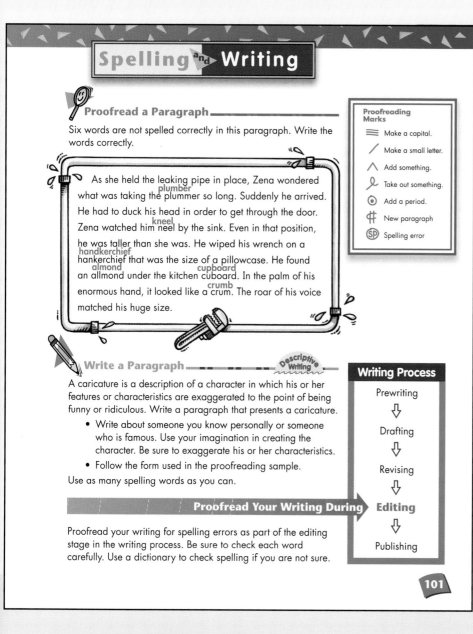

Spelling and Writing

Proofread a Paragraph

Six words are not spelled correctly in this paragraph. Write the words correctly.

As she held the leaking pipe in place, Zena wondered what was taking the plummer so long. Suddenly he arrived. He had to duck his head in order to get through the door. Zena watched him kneel by the sink. Even in that position, he was taller than she was. He wiped his wrench on a hankerchief that was the size of a pillowcase. He found an allmond under the kitchen cuboard. In the palm of his enormous hand, it looked like a crum. The roar of his voice matched his huge size.

Proofreading Marks

≡ Make a capital.
/ Make a small letter.
∧ Add something.
ℛ Take out something.
⊙ Add a period.
New paragraph
SP Spelling error

Write a Paragraph

Descriptive Writing

A caricature is a description of a character in which his or her features or characteristics are exaggerated to the point of being funny or ridiculous. Write a paragraph that presents a caricature.

- Write about someone you know personally or someone who is famous. Use your imagination in creating the character. Be sure to exaggerate his or her characteristics.
- Follow the form used in the proofreading sample.

Use as many spelling words as you can.

Proofread Your Writing During ➤ Editing

Proofread your writing for spelling errors as part of the editing stage in the writing process. Be sure to check each word carefully. Use a dictionary to check spelling if you are not sure.

Writing Process

Prewriting
⇩
Drafting
⇩
Revising
⇩
Editing
⇩
Publishing

101

Objectives

Spelling and Writing

Students will
- **proofread** a paragraph.
- **use** the writing process to write a caricature.
- **proofread** their writing.

Using the Writing Process

Before assigning **Write a Paragraph,** see pages 258–259 in the Student Edition for a complete review of the writing process and additional writing assignments. You may wish to refer to pages Z12–Z13 in the Teacher Edition.

Keeping a Spelling Journal

Encourage students to record the words they misspelled on the weekly test in a personal spelling journal. These words may be recycled for future study. Students may also wish to include words from their writing. See pages Z12–Z13 in the Teacher Edition for more information.

---

17. Has the **plumber** fixed the broken pipe?
18. **Salmon** is a very healthy food.
★ 19. The folk song had a **solemn** melody.
20. A **tomb** is a sad and quiet place.

Option 2:
Multiple Spelling Words Per Sentence
(See procedures on pages Z10–Z11.)

1. A **solemn hymn** played as the couple walked down the **aisle**.
2. Turn the **knob** on the **cupboard** door to open it.
3. Mother used **almond** paste to make the **crumb** cake.
4. The beautiful **isle** is a very restful place in **autumn**.
5. He is in **debt** because he paid so much for the **tomb**.
6. The **plumber** had a **knack** for fixing pipes.
7. The **palm** of my hand feels **numb** after holding up that **column**.
8. Put the **handkerchief** down before you **kneel** on the step.
9. The clown made believe that eating **salmon** would increase his **knowledge**.

Option 3:
Standardized Test
(See *Teacher Resource Book,* Unit 16.)

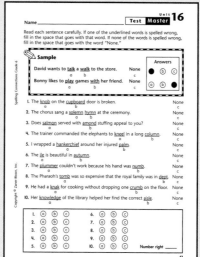

Unit 16 Test Master

T101

Objectives

Strategy Words

Students will
- **review** words studied previously that are related to the spelling strategy.
- **preview** unknown words that are related to the spelling strategy.

Optional Enrichment

Strategy Words

Remind the students that the **Strategy Words** relate to the spelling pattern they have studied in this unit. The **Review Words** are below grade level, and the **Preview Words** are above grade level. You may wish to use the following sentences to introduce the words in context.

Review Words:
Words From Grade 5

1. The **bowl** of apples was on the table.
2. He felt **calmer** after he had rested.
3. Pierre left his **knapsack** on the bus.
4. The author of this poem is **unknown**.
5. I particularly enjoyed the stories of the new **writer**.

Preview Words:
Words From Grade 7

6. The tree trunk had become **gnarled** as it grew.
7. We use plants from our **herb** garden to season our food.
8. Because of his **honesty,** he would not lie about the accident.
9. The coach told the team to **hustle** when he wanted them to do their best.
10. My neighbor calls the small hill behind his house a **knoll**.

Review Words
1. bowl
2. knapsack
3. calmer
4. unknown
5. writer

Preview Words
6. honesty
7. knoll
8. gnarled
9. herb
10. hustle

Unit 16 enrichment

VOCABULARY CONNECTIONS

Strategy Words

Review Words: Silent Consonants

Write words from the box that complete the paragraph.

bowl	calmer	knapsack	unknown	writer

Asad took a __1.__ from his __2.__ and filled it with cereal and milk. Then he grabbed his notebook and started to jot down some notes. He had been feeling much __3.__ since he had left the hectic toy store where he used to work. "I may be __4.__ now," he thought, "but someday I am going to be a successful __5.__."

Preview Words: Silent Consonants

Write words from the box that complete the paragraph.

gnarled	herb	honesty	hustle	knoll

Asad was writing an essay about truth and __6.__. He had chosen to sit on a little __7.__ overlooking the quiet valley below. He leaned against the twisted and __8.__ branch of a huge chestnut tree. Smelling a leaf of a nearby plant, he wondered if it was an __9.__. Suddenly, he realized it was getting late. He decided to __10.__ before it got dark.

102

Unit 16 RECAP

You may wish to assign the **Unit 16 Homework Master** (*Teacher Resource Book*, Unit 16) as a fun way to recap the spelling words.

Unit 16 Homework Master

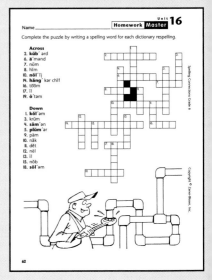

TI02

Content Words

Social Studies: The Law

Write words from the box that complete the paragraph.

corrupt	indict	demonstrate	verdict	defend

Sometimes officials are accused of being __1.__. A grand jury must determine whether or not to charge them with a crime, or __2.__ them. Lawyers __3.__ their clients and present evidence to __4.__ that their clients are not guilty. After listening to the testimony, the grand jury delivers its __5.__.

Math: Geometry

Write a word from the box that matches each clue.

decagon	rhombus	parallelogram
trapezoid	quadrilateral	

6. a geometric figure with four sides and four angles
7. a four-sided figure with opposite sides parallel
8. a geometric figure with ten sides and ten angles
9. a four-sided plane figure with opposite sides parallel and all sides equal
10. a four-sided plane figure with one pair of parallel sides

Apply the Spelling Strategy

Circle the silent consonant in two of the Content Words you wrote.

Word Study

Idioms

An **idiom** is a saying that doesn't mean what the words in it say. If you are feeling nervous, excited, or impatient, you might say you are **on edge**. Write a Strategy Word to finish this saying, which means that something is "very pleasant and easy": **it's a ____ of cherries.**

103

Social Studies: The Law
1. corrupt
2. indic(t)
3. defend
4. demonstrate
5. verdict

Math: Geometry
6. quadrilateral
7. parallelogram
8. decagon
9. r(h)ombus
10. trapezoid

Idioms
1. bowl

Unit 17 Home Spelling Practice

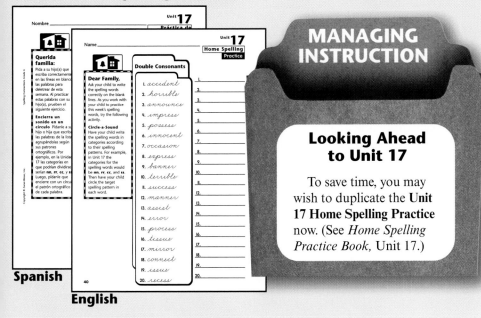

Spanish

English

Objectives

Content Words

Students will
- **expand** vocabulary with content-related words.
- **relate** the spelling strategy to words outside the basic spelling list.
- **understand** simple idiomatic expressions.

Content Words

Social Studies: The Law

Use these sentences to introduce the words and their meanings.

1. Their concern involved the **corrupt** prison.
2. The lawyer asked the court to **indict** the man suspected of burglary.
3. They **demonstrate** their belief in our system of justice by obeying laws.
4. What was the jury's **verdict**?
5. The court appointed an attorney to **defend** the prisoner.

Math: Geometry

Use these sentences to introduce the words and their meanings.

6. A **decagon** is a ten-sided figure.
7. A **rhombus** has four equal sides.
8. The **parallelogram** looked like a rectangle that had been pushed down at the top.
9. The treehouse my brother built was shaped like a **trapezoid**.
10. Any four-sided figure is a **quadrilateral**.

Word Study

Idioms

Help students understand that an **idiom** is an expression common among speakers from the same geographic area and/or culture. Learning and using idioms increases variety in students' work and makes their writing more interesting.

MANAGING INSTRUCTION

Looking Ahead to Unit 17

To save time, you may wish to duplicate the **Unit 17 Home Spelling Practice** now. (See *Home Spelling Practice Book*, Unit 17.)

Basic Spelling List

accident	success
horrible	manner
announce	assist
impress	error
possess	process
innocent	tissue
occasion	mirror
express	connect
banner	issue
terrible	recess

Strategy Words

Review

arrival	possible
cinnamon	stirrups
hiccupped	

Preview

afford	corrode
assumption	embarrass
challenge	

Content Words

Language Arts: Nouns

collective	singular
proper	possessive
plural	

Social Studies: Australia

outback	mutton
drought	grazing
paddock	

Individual Needs

Challenge Words

quizzical	rapport
irritate	possession
plummeted	propeller

Alternate Word List ★

accident	terrible
horrible	success
announce	mirror
possess	connect
occasion	recess

★ For students who need to study fewer Basic Spelling words

MATERIALS

Student Edition
Pages 104–109
Challenge Activities, p. 238

Teacher Edition
Pages T104A–T109
Challenge Activities, p. T238

Teacher Resource Book
Unit 17 Homework Master
Unit 17 Practice Masters
Flip Folder Practice Master
Unit 17 Test Master

Home Spelling Practice Book
Unit 17 Home Spelling Practice
(English or Spanish)

Other *Spelling Connections* Resources
- Audiotape, Grade 6
- Practice Book for Grammar, Usage, and Mechanics, Grade 6
- Spelling Support for Second Language Learners, Grade 6
- Support Software on CD-ROM
- Transparency Book, Grade 6
- Word Sort CD-ROM, Grade 6

OBJECTIVES

Spelling and Thinking
Students will
- **read** the spelling words in list form and in context.
- **sort** the spelling words according to double consonants.
- **read** and remember this week's spelling strategy.

Spelling and Vocabulary
Students will
- **replace** words in a sentence with spelling words.
- **substitute** one or more syllables in given words to create spelling words.
- **use** the **Spelling Dictionary** to find less common definitions of spelling words.

Spelling and Reading
Students will
- **solve** analogies using spelling words.
- **complete** sentences using spelling words.
- **complete** a paragraph using spelling words.

Spelling and Writing
Students will
- **proofread** a letter.
- **use** the writing process to write a letter.
- **proofread** their writing.

MEETING INDIVIDUAL NEEDS
Learning Styles

 Visual

Play a word-guessing game. On the chalkboard, draw a dotted line with each segment representing one letter of a spelling word. Tell the students the definition of the word. The first student in a row guesses a letter that may be in the word. If the guess is correct, the student keeps guessing. If the guess is wrong, the next student takes a turn. The student who guesses the last letter in the word takes the place of the teacher at the board, draws a dotted line to represent the letters of a spelling word, reads its definition, and continues the game.

 Auditory

Each student lists five spelling words that cause him or her difficulty. Divide the class into groups of three. Student A pronounces a word from student B's list. Student B spells the word aloud as student C writes the word. Student A checks the others' work. Each student correctly spells any misspelled word. The three continue until each has had a turn as caller, speller, and writer and their lists have been exhausted.

 Kinesthetic

Write each spelling word on the chalkboard. Pronounce each word slowly. Have the students repeat each word, clapping as they say the syllable in which they hear the double-consonant sound. Then have them write the word.

> **Hands-On Practice**
> All students will benefit from practicing with a **Flip Folder**. See page Z18.

Language and Cultural Differences

Some students may have difficulty with these spelling words because of their language backgrounds. For example, the double consonant letters **rr** represent a unique sound in Spanish. The words with double consonants can be difficult to spell because only one consonant sound is heard. On the other hand, such words as **accident** and **tissue** may present a problem because each consonant represents a different sound or the sound of a consonant digraph.

Write the spelling words on the chalkboard in syllabicated form. Pronounce them, emphasizing the stressed syllables. Have the students write the words in syllables and circle the double consonants.

MANAGING INSTRUCTION

3–5 Day Plan		Average	Below Average	Above Average
Day 1	**Day 1**	Pretest Spelling Mini-Lesson, p. T104 Spelling and Thinking, p. 104	Pretest Spelling Mini-Lesson, p. T104 Spelling and Thinking, p. 104	Pretest Spelling and Thinking, p. 104
	Day 2	Spelling and Vocabulary, p. 105	Spelling and Vocabulary, p.105 (or) Unit 17 Practice Master, A and B	Spelling and Vocabulary, p. 105 Spelling and Reading, p. 106
Day 2	**Day 3**	Spelling and Reading, p. 106	Spelling and Reading, p. 106 (or) Unit 17 Practice Master, C and D	Challenge Activities, p. 238
	Day 4	Spelling and Writing, p. 107 Unit 17 Homework Master	Spelling and Writing, p. 107	Spelling and Writing, p. 107 Unit 17 Homework Master
Day 3	**Day 5**	Weekly Test	Weekly Test	Weekly Test
Vocabulary Connections (pages 108 and 109) may be used anytime during this unit.				

Objectives

Spelling and Thinking

Students will
- **read** the spelling words in list form and in context.
- **sort** the spelling words according to double consonants.
- **read** and remember this week's spelling strategy.

UNIT PRETEST

Use **Pretest Sentences** below. Refer to the self-checking procedures on student page 256. You may wish to use the **Unit 17 Word List Overhead Transparency** as part of the checking procedure.

TEACHING THE STRATEGY

Spelling Mini-Lesson

Write **manner** and **terrible** on the chalkboard. Read these words aloud. Ask the students how many consonant sounds they hear in the middle of each word. (one) Tell the students that double consonants occur in many words and usually stand for one sound.

Write **accident** and **success** on the board. Read these words aloud. Ask the students how many consonant sounds they hear in the middle of each word. (two) Explain that when these words are pronounced, the first **c** is pronounced /**k**/ and the second **c** is pronounced /**s**/. (Students may point out that the double **s** at the end of **success** is pronounced as a single consonant sound.)

Repeat this process with **issue** and **tissue**. Guide the students to conclude that the double **s** in these words is pronounced, not as a single consonant sound, but as /**sh**/.

To reinforce that double consonants usually represent a single sound, write the remaining spelling words on the board and ask volunteers to pronounce them. You may wish to point out that double consonants are usually preceded by a short vowel sound.

Read **Remember the Spelling Strategy** on page 104.

Unit 17
Double Consonants

Spelling and Thinking

Order of answers may vary.

cc or ss
1. a(cc)ident ★
2. impre(ss)
3. po(ss)e(ss) ★
4. o(cc)asion ★
5. expre(ss)
6. su(cc)e(ss) ★
7. a(ss)ist
8. proce(ss)
9. ti(ss)ue
10. i(ss)ue
11. rece(ss) ★

rr or nn
12. ho(rr)ible ★
13. a(nn)ounce ★
14. i(nn)ocent
15. ba(nn)er
16. te(rr)ible ★
17. ma(nn)er
18. e(rr)or
19. mi(rr)or ★
20. co(nn)ect ★

READ THE SPELLING WORDS

1. accident	*accident*	I was involved in a minor car **accident**.
2. horrible	*horrible*	The skunk left a **horrible** odor.
3. announce	*announce*	They are about to **announce** the winner.
4. impress	*impress*	His knowledge will **impress** you.
5. possess	*possess*	They **possess** a large book collection.
6. innocent	*innocent*	He is **innocent** of the crime.
7. occasion	*occasion*	Tuesday will be a special **occasion**.
8. express	*express*	I would like to **express** my thanks.
9. banner	*banner*	I hung the **banner** from the railing.
10. terrible	*terrible*	He feels **terrible** about the accident.
11. success	*success*	The party was a huge **success**.
12. manner	*manner*	The students left in an orderly **manner**.
13. assist	*assist*	The salesperson said she could **assist** us.
14. error	*error*	You made one **error** on this test.
15. process	*process*	He described the filmmaking **process**.
16. tissue	*tissue*	Trace the picture on this **tissue**.
17. mirror	*mirror*	He saw his reflection in the **mirror**.
18. connect	*connect*	Now, **connect** the brace to the frame.
19. issue	*issue*	The coach will **issue** new uniforms.
20. recess	*recess*	We play basketball during **recess**.

SORT THE SPELLING WORDS

1.–11. Write the spelling words that have a double **c** or double **s**, or both. Circle these letters in the words you write.

12.–20. Write the spelling words that have a double **r** or double **n**. Circle these letters in the words you write.

REMEMBER THE SPELLING STRATEGY

Remember that double consonants usually represent a single sound: **banner, mirror**.

104

Pretest Sentences (See procedures on pages Z10–Z11.)

★ 1. Fortunately, Heather was not hurt badly in the **accident**.
★ 2. The costume included a mask with a **horrible** grin.
★ 3. The principal will **announce** the winner of the contest.
  4. I want to **impress** upon you the importance of correct spelling.
★ 5. Since I **possess** my own computer, I can complete my assignments with ease.
  6. The jury found the suspect to be **innocent**.
★ 7. On the **occasion** of her graduation, Ashanta received a watch.
  8. Did you **express** your ideas clearly in your persuasive paragraph?
  9. Our nation's flag is a **banner** of stars and stripes.
★10. The explosion to blast the rocks made a **terrible** noise.
★11. The school book fair was a great **success**.
  12. Robin's **manner** was always friendly and lighthearted.
  13. Please **assist** me by carrying some of these books.
  14. The engineer was careful not to make an **error** in her design.
  15. The doctor used a new medical **process** to treat the patient.
  16. May I have a **tissue** to wipe my eyes?
★17. Diego studied his face in a **mirror** as he tried to draw a self-portrait.
★18. The child learned how to **connect** the dots to form a picture.
  19. What **issue** in the national news have you chosen for your report?
★20. The judge called a **recess** in the trial to give the jury time to study the evidence.

Spelling and Vocabulary

Word Replacement

Write a spelling word that could replace each underlined word.

1. You should send the letter by <u>fast</u> mail.
2. Her family used to <u>own</u> a small farm.
3. He apologized for making the <u>mistake</u>.
4. The baker explained his bread-making <u>system</u>.
5. Students went outside during their morning <u>break</u>.
6. The principal will <u>distribute</u> new report cards soon.
7. He performs his job in a quiet and formal <u>way</u>.
8. She attributes her <u>achievement</u> in science to hard work.

Word Analysis

Change the underlined part of these words to write spelling words.

9. <u>hor</u>net
10. ter<u>minal</u>
11. <u>recent</u>
12. in<u>sist</u>
13. <u>octopus</u>
14. <u>actual</u>
15. <u>inspect</u>
16. imp<u>oster</u>

When a word has multiple meanings, the definitions are numbered. Often, the most common definition is first. Write a spelling word to complete each sentence. Every sentence uses a word's less-common meaning.

17. Our coach congratulated us on our _____ year.
18. He wrapped the gift in thin _____ paper.
19. People's faces often _____ their mood.
20. The butler will _____ the arrival of each guest.

Word Replacement	
1.	express
2.	possess
3.	error
4.	process
5.	recess
6.	issue
7.	manner
8.	success
Word Analysis	
9.	horrible
10.	terrible
11.	innocent
12.	assist
13.	occasion
14.	accident
15.	connect
16.	impress
Using the Dictionary	
17.	banner
18.	tissue
19.	mirror
20.	announce

Objectives

Spelling and Vocabulary

Students will
- **replace** words in a sentence with spelling words.
- **substitute** one or more syllables in given words to create spelling words.
- **use** the **Spelling Dictionary** to find less common definitions of spelling words.

Developing Oral Language Skills

Have students pronounce **terrible** and **horrible** and note whether they pronounce the words as two syllables or three syllables. If they pronounce them as two syllables, they should be reminded to pronounce the second syllable. Write **terrible** and **horrible** on the chalkboard. Remind students that words like **terrible** (/tĕr′ ə bəl/) and **horrible** (/hôr′ ə bəl/) may cause spelling problems because the second syllable is not pronounced.

MEETING INDIVIDUAL NEEDS

Providing More Help

To aid these students, write the following words on the chalkboard and have volunteers underline each correctly spelled word:

announce, anounce
mirror, miror
tisue, **tissue**
success, suces
baner, **banner**
error, eror

★Students who need to study fewer words should use the **Alternate Word List**. This list is starred on page T104 in the Teacher Edition. The **Unit 17 Practice Masters** (*Teacher Resource Book*) provide additional practice with these words.

Unit 17 Practice Masters

Name _____ **Practice Master** **Unit 17**

1. connect	3. mirror	5. terrible	7. occasion	9. success
2. announce	4. horrible	6. accident	8. recess	10. possess

A. Write the spelling word that belongs in each sentence.

1. The operator will _____ you with the main desk. _____
2. Marilyn will _____ the hockey game on the radio. _____
3. The _____ noise made us shiver with fright. _____
4. The _____ pollution made it unpleasant to go outside. _____
5. I stepped on the dog's tail by _____. _____
6. The _____ did not call for a formal introduction. _____
7. People's faces often _____ their moods. _____

B. Write the spelling word that belongs in each sentence.

1. **Know** is to **understand** as **own** is to _____. _____
2. **Echo** is to **surface** as **image** to _____. _____
3. **Yell** is to **scream** as **proclaim** is to _____. _____
4. **Anniversary** is to **event** as **birthday** is to _____. _____
5. **Horrifying** is to **horrible** as **terrifying** is to _____. _____

Practice Master **Unit 17**

occasion	success
recess	possess

63

64

Objectives

Spelling and Reading

Students will
• **solve** analogies using spelling words.
• **complete** sentences using spelling words.
• **complete** a paragraph using spelling words.

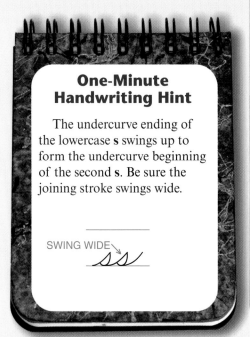
Solve the Analogies

1. mirror
2. banner
3. horrible
4. connect
5. issue
6. announce

Complete the Sentences

7. impress
8. occasion
9. possess
10. manner
11. recess
12. tissue
13. success

Complete the Letter

14. express
15. accident
16. terrible
17. innocent
18. error
19. process
20. assist

Spelling and Reading

accident	horrible	announce	impress	possess
innocent	occasion	express	banner	terrible
success	manner	assist	error	process
tissue	mirror	connect	issue	recess

Solve the Analogies Write a spelling word to complete each analogy.

1. **Echo** is to **surface** as **image** is to _____.
2. **Sign** is to **poster** as **flag** is to _____.
3. **Terror** is to **terrible** as **horror** is to _____.
4. **Donate** is to **accept** as **detach** is to _____.
5. **Assemble** is to **gather** as **distribute** is to _____.
6. **Speech** is to **present** as **news** is to _____.

Complete the Sentences Write a spelling word to complete each sentence.

7. His fine drawing will _____ you.
8. The holiday party was a happy _____.
9. They _____ many albums of photographs.
10. The waiter had a very friendly _____.
11. The judge announced a two-hour _____.
12. The scientist examined the _____ under the microscope.
13. His friends congratulated him on his _____.

Complete the Letter Write spelling words from the box to complete the letter.

Dear Mr. Greenthumb,

I would like to __14.__ my regret for the __15.__ yesterday. I feel __16.__ about cutting your prize tulips. It was an __17.__ __18.__. I know what a lengthy __19.__ it is to grow these flowers, so I would like to __20.__ you in planting some bulbs for next year.

Sincerely,
Your former gardener

innocent
accident
process
assist
express
terrible
error

106

MEETING INDIVIDUAL NEEDS

Providing More Challenge

Challenge Words and **Challenge Activities** for Unit 17 appear on page 238. **Challenge Word Test Sentences** appear on page T238.

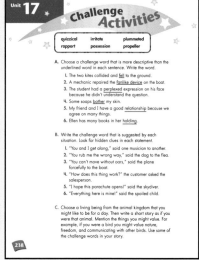

Unit 17 Challenge Activities

Weekly Test Options

Option 1:
One Spelling Word Per Sentence
(See procedures on pages Z10–Z11.)

1. The human body is made up of many kinds of **tissue**.
★ 2. Was the **accident** reported to the police?
3. Would you **assist** me in handing out the homework?
★ 4. Will you **announce** the news to the class?
5. Carry the school **banner** proudly in the parade.
★ 6. The new bridge will **connect** the two towns.
7. The cashier made a careless **error** on my receipt.
8. If we **express** our feelings openly to people we can trust, they will understand us.
★ 9. We had a **horrible** time at the party.
10. I want to **impress** Dad with my skill.
11. The **innocent** young girl was blamed for the mistake.
12. When will the next **issue** of the school magazine be published?
13. Please carry out these plans in the usual **manner**.
★14. It helps to look in a **mirror** as you comb your hair.

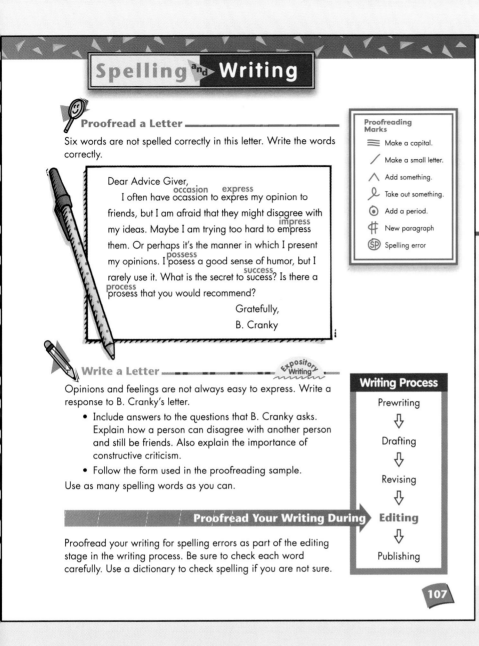

Spelling and Writing

Proofread a Letter

Six words are not spelled correctly in this letter. Write the words correctly.

Dear Advice Giver,

  I often have ocassion *(occasion)* to expres *(express)* my opinion to friends, but I am afraid that they might disagree with my ideas. Maybe I am trying too hard to empress *(impress)* them. Or perhaps it's the manner in which I present my opinions. I posess *(possess)* a good sense of humor, but I rarely use it. What is the secret to sucess *(success)*? Is there a prosess *(process)* that you would recommend?

                Gratefully,

                B. Cranky

Proofreading Marks

≡ Make a capital.
/ Make a small letter.
∧ Add something.
⸮ Take out something.
⊙ Add a period.
⌗ New paragraph
SP Spelling error

Write a Letter

Expository Writing

Opinions and feelings are not always easy to express. Write a response to B. Cranky's letter.

- Include answers to the questions that B. Cranky asks. Explain how a person can disagree with another person and still be friends. Also explain the importance of constructive criticism.
- Follow the form used in the proofreading sample.

Use as many spelling words as you can.

Proofread Your Writing During ➤ **Editing**

Proofread your writing for spelling errors as part of the editing stage in the writing process. Be sure to check each word carefully. Use a dictionary to check spelling if you are not sure.

Writing Process

Prewriting
⇩
Drafting
⇩
Revising
⇩
Editing
⇩
Publishing

107

Objectives

Spelling and Writing

Students will
- **proofread** a letter.
- **use** the writing process to write a letter.
- **proofread** their writing.

Using the Writing Process

Before assigning **Write a Letter,** see pages 258–259 in the Student Edition for a complete review of the writing process and additional writing assignments. You may wish to refer to pages Z12–Z13 in the Teacher Edition.

Keeping a Spelling Journal

Encourage students to record the words they misspelled on the weekly test in a personal spelling journal. These words may be recycled for future study. Students may also wish to include words from their writing. See pages Z12–Z13 in the Teacher Edition for more information.

★15. The Fourth of July is a joyous **occasion**.
★16. Do you **possess** the skill required to solve that problem?
  17. We will try to **process** your documents as soon as possible.
★18. We used **recess** time to plan the surprise for our teacher.
★19. She achieved great **success** as an astronaut.
★20. The **terrible** storm washed away most of the flowers.

Option 2:
Multiple Spelling Words Per Sentence
(See procedures on pages Z10–Z11.)

1. Did you paint this **banner** for a special **occasion**?
2. The teacher will soon **announce** that it is time for **recess**.
3. Will you **assist** me in carrying out this **horrible process**?
4. Does his **success impress** you?
5. I would like to **express** my views on this **issue**.
6. A child will often **possess** an **innocent manner**.
7. That was a **terrible accident** in Millville last week.
8. What kind of **tissue** can **connect** bones and tendons?
9. The **mirror** showed the tailor's **error**.

Option 3:
Standardized Test
(See *Teacher Resource Book,* Unit 17.)

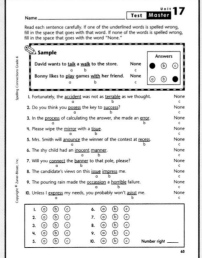

**Unit 17
Test Master**

T107

Objectives

Strategy Words

Students will
- **review** words studied previously that are related to the spelling strategy.
- **preview** unknown words that are related to the spelling strategy.

Optional Enrichment

Unit 17 enrichment

VOCABULARY CONNECTIONS

►Strategy Words◄

Review Words

1. arrival
2. hiccupped
3. possible
4. cinnamon
5. stirrups

Preview Words

6. challenge
7. afford
8. corrode
9. assumption
10. embarrass

►Strategy Words◄

Remind the students that the **Strategy Words** relate to the spelling patterns they have studied in this unit. The **Review Words** are below grade level, and the **Preview Words** are above grade level. You may wish to use the following sentences to introduce the words in context.

Review Words:
Words From Grade 5

1. Their **arrival** was expected soon.
2. I like lots of **cinnamon** on apple pie.
3. After the baby laughed, he **hiccupped**.
4. It is **possible** to do your best and still make a mistake.
5. The **stirrups** on the saddle had to be shortened before I could ride the horse.

Preview Words:
Words From Grade 7

6. My family hopes they can **afford** a vacation next summer.
7. We made the **assumption** that everyone in class had returned to the bus.
8. I make learning a personal **challenge** to do my best.
9. Moisture will cause the metal to **corrode**.
10. His policy is never to **embarrass** anyone.

Review Words: Double Consonants

Write a word from the box to complete each of these sentences.

arrival	cinnamon	hiccupped	possible	stirrups

1. The flight _____ has been delayed by an hour.
2. As a puppy, Roscoe _____ after eating his food too fast.
3. Your cheery card arrived at the best _____ time.
4. She sprinkled a little _____ on the applesauce.
5. The rider climbed onto the horse and put his feet into the _____.

Preview Words: Double Consonants

Write words from the box to complete the following paragraph.

afford	assumption	challenge	corrode	embarrass

While he struggled to start his new business, Sal had another __6.__. He could not __7.__ a new car, but the finish on his car had begun to rust and __8.__. It was his __9.__ that if he took care of his car it would last another few years. He would not allow his rusty old car to __10.__ him. In fact, he was proud of it.

108

Unit 17 RECAP

You may wish to assign the **Unit 17 Homework Master** (*Teacher Resource Book,* Unit 17) as a fun way to recap the spelling words.

Unit 17 Homework Master

Name _____   Homework **Master** 17

Use the code to write your spelling words.

w = cc	x = nn	y = rr	z = ss

1. owasion _____
2. baxer _____
3. hoyible _____
4. imprez _____
5. coxect _____
6. recez _____
7. tizue _____
8. agist _____
9. procez _____
10. eyor _____
11. awident _____
12. izue _____
13. pozez _____
14. miyor _____
15. azounce _____
16. suwez _____

To win each tic-tac-toe game, draw a ring around the three words that can be synonyms. Then write the word from the puzzle that is a spelling word.

dreadful	wonderful	severe
awful	terrible	pleasing
agreeable	delightful	unpleasant

guilty	experienced	skilled
innocent	not guilty	naive
unskilled	young	evil

print	type	way
inn	style	fashion
manner	generous	kindly

say	think	express
show	rapidly	reveal
argue	pronounce	state

66

Spelling Connections Grade 6   Copyright © Zaner-Bloser, Inc.

Content Words

Language Arts: Nouns

Write a word from the box to complete each sentence.

collective	proper	plural	singular	possessive

1. The word **family** is a _____ noun because it refers to a group as a whole.
2. The word **families** is a _____ noun; it refers to more than one person, place, or thing.
3. A _____ noun, such as **family's,** shows ownership.
4. **Child** is a _____ noun, referring to a single person, place, or thing.
5. A _____ noun, such as **Murphy,** is a formal name.

Social Studies: Australia

Write the words from the box that complete the paragraph.

outback	drought	paddock	mutton	grazing

Much of the western part of Australia is desert. The summer dry spell, or __6.__, can be severe. In the dry central plains, called the __7.__, there are huge sheep farms. People often see sheep __8.__ on grass in an enclosed area, or __9.__. Meat from these sheep is called __10.__.

Apply the Spelling Strategy

Circle the double consonants in four of the Content Words you wrote.

Word Study

Word History

This Strategy Word came from the very old English words **stirope** and **stigrap** that meant "climbing rope." Write this Strategy Word that means "special devices that support a horse rider's feet."

109

Language Arts: Nouns
1. co**ll**ective
2. plural
3. po**ss**e**ss**ive
4. singular
5. proper

Social Studies: Australia
6. drought
7. outback
8. grazing
9. pa**dd**ock
10. mu**tt**on

Word History
1. stirrups

Objectives

Content Words

Students will
- **expand** vocabulary with content-related words.
- **relate** the spelling strategy to words outside the basic spelling list.
- **understand** the history of the word **stirrups**.

Content Words

Language Arts: Nouns

Use these sentences to introduce the words and their meanings.
1. A **collective** noun refers to a group of things or people.
2. Always capitalize a **proper** noun.
3. We can form the **plural** of many words by adding **-s** or **-es**.
4. A **singular** noun can mean one person or one class.
5. We use an apostrophe to form the **possessive** of many nouns.

Social Studies: Australia

Use these sentences to introduce the words and their meanings.
6. Visit Australia's **outback**.
7. Farmers suffered poor crops because of the **drought**.
8. Horses were inside the **paddock**.
9. We ordered **mutton**.
10. We watched the sheep **grazing** near the side of the road.

Word Study

Word History

Explain to students that a word history, or **etymology,** traces the origin of a word and the development of its meaning. Etymologies are shown after the entry word in most dictionaries.

Unit 18 Home Spelling Practice

Spanish

English

MANAGING INSTRUCTION

Looking Ahead to Unit 18

To save time, you may wish to duplicate the **Unit 18 Home Spelling Practice** now. (See *Home Spelling Practice Book*, Unit 18.)

Assessment Words

scuffle	chef
illusion	hazel
patrolling	frightened
dumb	knelt
glossary	surround
intellect	suggest
salve	knead
patrolled	frightening
dispose	hazy
gopher	fatal

Review Words

Unit 13

effort*	difficult
fulfill*	phone
physician*	offer
sophomore*	phrase
faint	officer

Unit 14

optimism*	tease
scissors*	pause
usual*	husband
conclusion*	visitor
amaze	television

Unit 15

directed*	resulted
complaining*	profiting
differed*	remained
admitting*	remaining
directing	permitted

Unit 16

aisle*	palm
column*	numb
knowledge*	kneel
handkerchief*	solemn
knob	autumn

Unit 17

connect*	terrible
occasion*	mirror
possess*	horrible
recess*	success
announce	accident

* Posttest sentences and the **Unit 18 Test Master** test these words. Students review all words listed.

MATERIALS

Student Edition
Pages 110–115

Teacher Edition
Pages T110A–T115

Teacher Resource Book
Flip Folder Practice Master
Unit 18 Test Master

Home Spelling Practice Book
Unit 18 Home Spelling Practice (English or Spanish)

Other *Spelling Connections* Resources
• Transparency Book, Grade 6

OBJECTIVES

Spelling and Assessment

Students will
• **assess** their spelling success by matching new words to the spelling strategies presented in Units 13–17.
• **connect** new words to the spelling strategies in Units 13–17.
• **write** new words that relate to the spelling strategies taught in Units 13–17.

Spelling and Review

Students will
• **review** and practice the spelling strategies and words taught in Units 13–17.
• **learn** an alternative spelling study strategy.

Spelling and Writing

Students will
• **review** direct objects.
• **compose** an expository piece of writing that explains how to make something useful.
• **learn** a proofreading strategy.
• **understand** the importance of correct spelling when using a computer spell checker.
• **proofread** for misspellings that spell unintended words.

MEETING INDIVIDUAL NEEDS
Learning Styles

 Visual

Have students form two teams. Each team lines up to form a spelling chain. Pronounce a word. The first player on each team writes the first letter of the word on a sheet of paper and passes the paper to the second player. That player adds the second letter of the word. The players continue to pass the paper and add letters until the word has been spelled. The next player checks the accuracy of the spelling, makes any necessary corrections, and then writes the word on the chalkboard. The first team to write the word correctly on the chalkboard scores one point. Play continues until all the spelling words have been spelled.

 Auditory

Write spelling words on the chalkboard. Give the definition of one spelling word. Have a volunteer spell aloud the word that matches the definition, then erase that word and have the students write it at their desks as the volunteer again spells the word aloud.

 Kinesthetic

Print spelling words on 3" × 5" cards. Cut out each letter of each word. Put the letters for each word into an envelope, one word per envelope. Divide the class into two teams. Provide each team with a set of envelopes. Each team member draws one letter from the same envelope, and the members line up to spell the word. The first team to spell its word correctly scores a point. Continue in this way, with the students on the teams taking turns to spell the words.

Hands-On Practice
All students will benefit from practicing with a **Flip Folder**. See page Z18.

Language and Cultural Differences

Some students may have difficulty with these sound-symbol associations because of regional pronunciations or language backgrounds that do not include the sounds or the variant spelling patterns. In Spanish, for example, the **ph** digraph does not exist, except in rare words borrowed from ancient Greek.

Have the students make an illustrated dictionary for the spelling words. Assign two words to each student to define and illustrate, or allow the students to choose their words. Combine all the students' work into one booklet.

MANAGING INSTRUCTION

3–5 Day Plan		Average	Below Average	Above Average
Day 1	**Day 1**	Assessment: Units 13–17, p. 110 (Option 1 or 2, p. T110)	Assessment: Units 13–17, p. 110 (Option 1 or 2, p. T110)	Assessment: Units 13–17, p. 110 (Option 1 or 2, p. T110)
	Day 2	Review: Units 13 and 14, p. 111	Review: Units 13 and 14, p. 111	Review: Units 13 and 14, p. 111 Review: Units 15 and 16, p. 112
Day 2	**Day 3**	Review: Units 15 and 16, p. 112	Review: Units 15 and 16, p. 112	Review: Unit 17, p. 113 Spelling Study Strategy, p. 113
	Day 4	Review: Unit 17, p. 113 Spelling Study Strategy, p. 113	Review: Unit 17, p. 113 Spelling Study Strategy, p. 113	Writer's Workshop, pages 114–115
Day 3	**Day 5**	Weekly Test, Option 1 or 2, p. T113	Weekly Test, Option 1 or 2, p. T113	Weekly Test, Option 1 or 2, p. T113

Writer's Workshop (pages 114 and 115) may be used anytime during this unit.

Students will
- **assess** their spelling success by matching new words to the spelling strategies presented in Units 13–17.
- **connect** new words to the spelling strategies in Units 13–17.
- **write** new words that relate to the spelling strategies taught in Units 13–17.

Unit **18**
Review Units 13–17

Assessment and Review

Unit 13
1. scuffle
2. gopher
3. chef
4. fatal

Unit 14
5. illusion
6. dispose
7. hazel
8. hazy

Unit 15
9. patrolling
10. patrolled
11. frightened
12. frightening

Unit 16
13. dumb
14. salve
15. knelt
16. knead

Unit 17
17. glossary
18. intellect
19. surround
20. suggest

Assessment Units 13–17

Each Assessment Word in the box fits one of the spelling strategies you have studied over the past five weeks. Read the spelling strategies. Then write each Assessment Word under the unit number it fits.

Unit 13 _____

1.–4. The **f** sound (/f/) can be spelled in different ways: **f** in **faint**, **ff** in **baffle**, and **ph** in **phone**.

Unit 14 _____

5.–8. The /z/ sound can be spelled: **z** as in **freeze**, **s** as in **phase**, and **ss** as in **scissors**. The /zh/ sound can be spelled **s** and is often followed by **ual** (**usual**) or **ion** (**vision**).

Unit 15 _____

9.–12. The suffixes **-ed** and **-ing** can be added to some base words to form new words. In other words, the final consonant is doubled when **-ed** or **-ing** is added.

Unit 16 _____

13.–16. Some words have more consonant letters than consonant sounds. If a consonant is not pronounced, it is considered silent: **k** in **knob** and **b** in **tomb**.

Unit 17 _____

17.–20. Double consonants usually represent a single sound: **banner, mirror**.

scuffle
illusion
patrolling
dumb
glossary
intellect
salve
patrolled
dispose
gopher
chef
hazel
frightened
knelt
surround
suggest
knead
frightening
hazy
fatal

110

ASSESSMENT: UNITS 13–17

Option 1

Assessment **Option 1** is the test that appears in the Student Edition on page 110. You may wish to have students take this test to determine their ability to recognize the spelling strategy in each unit and to match words not previously taught to that strategy. **Assessment Option 1** also serves as additional review and practice.

▲ Words designated with this symbol include more than one of the targeted spelling strategies. The answer key has placed them according to the most obvious spelling emphasis. However, if a student places a word in another category, and the word fits that generalization, accept that response. Remember, the objective is to place each word with any appropriate spelling generalization.

Option 2

Assessment **Option 2** is a dictation test using the sentences on page T111. This test assesses students' ability to spell words not previously taught but that are exemplars of a spelling strategy. This test more specifically assesses students' ability to apply the spelling knowledge they have learned.

In either assessment test option, the words are identified by unit in the Teacher Edition. You may wish to index those misspelled words to the review exercises that follow in this unit. Determine which units students need to review and use the additional unit exercises found in this **Assessment and Review Unit** for reteaching the skill in a more focused way.

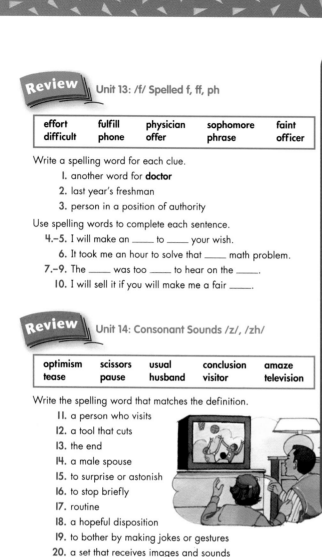

Review Unit 13: /f/ Spelled f, ff, ph

effort	fulfill	physician	sophomore	faint
difficult	phone	offer	phrase	officer

Write a spelling word for each clue.

1. another word for **doctor**
2. last year's freshman
3. person in a position of authority

Use spelling words to complete each sentence.

4.–5. I will make an ____ to ____ your wish.
6. It took me an hour to solve that ____ math problem.
7.–9. The ____ was too ____ to hear on the ____.
10. I will sell it if you will make me a fair ____.

Review Unit 14: Consonant Sounds /z/, /zh/

optimism	scissors	usual	conclusion	amaze
tease	pause	husband	visitor	television

Write the spelling word that matches the definition.

11. a person who visits
12. a tool that cuts
13. the end
14. a male spouse
15. to surprise or astonish
16. to stop briefly
17. routine
18. a hopeful disposition
19. to bother by making jokes or gestures
20. a set that receives images and sounds

Unit 13
1. physician
2. sophomore
3. officer
4. effort
5. fulfill
6. difficult
7. phrase
8. faint
9. phone
10. offer

Unit 14
11. visitor
12. scissors
13. conclusion
14. husband
15. amaze
16. pause
17. usual
18. optimism
19. tease
20. television

111

Objectives

Spelling and Review

Students will
• **review** and practice the spelling strategy and words taught in Unit 13.
• **review** and practice the spelling strategy and words taught in Unit 14.

Assessing Progress: The Spelling Journal

If your students have been keeping a personal spelling journal, a periodical review of these journals can be a rich assessment tool. Students should include the words they have misspelled from each unit spelling test. They should also be encouraged to write the words they consistently misspell in their own writing and content-area words that present a challenge. Being able to discriminate the words in their everyday writing whose spelling they need to master is a powerful spelling skill.

Pretest Sentences: Assessment Words

(See procedures on pages Z10–Z11.)

1. The officer broke up the **scuffle** on the street.
2. The magician is a master of **illusion**.
3. The police are **patrolling** the area.
4. I was so surprised that I was struck **dumb** for a second.
5. You can find that special term in the **glossary**.
6. She has the **intellect** of a true genius.
7. Rub on some **salve** to ease your sunburn.
8. The older scouts **patrolled** the camp.
9. How can we **dispose** of the waste?
10. The **gopher** scampered back into the ground when it saw us.
11. The **chef** prepared a wonderful meal.
12. The color of his eyes is **hazel**.
13. The baby was **frightened** by the loud noise.
14. She **knelt** by the car to change the tire.
15. Trees **surround** the house on all sides.
16. I **suggest** that you get to bed early tonight.
17. **Knead** the dough well before you put it in the bread pan.
18. In the dark woods, every little sound was **frightening**.
19. It was very **hazy** at that hour of the morning.
20. Alas, the accident was **fatal** for the worker.

Objectives

Spelling and Review

Students will

- **review** and practice the spelling strategy and words taught in Unit 15.
- **review** and practice the spelling strategy and words taught in Unit 16.

Unit 15

1. complaining
2. permitted
3. differed
4. profiting
5. remained
6. admitting
7. directed
8. remaining
9. directing
10. resulted

Unit 16

11. kneel
12. numb
13. handkerchief
14. palm
15. autumn
16. solemn
17. aisle
18. column
19. knob
20. knowledge

 Review Unit 15: Suffixes -ed, -ing

| directed | complaining | differed | admitting | directing |
| resulted | profiting | remained | remaining | permitted |

Write the spelling word that is the opposite of the word or words given.

1. praising
2. refused to allow
3. agreed
4. losing money
5. departed
6. denying
7. took orders
8. departing
9. following orders
10. had no effect

 Review Unit 16: Silent Consonants

| aisle | column | knowledge | handkerchief | knob |
| palm | numb | kneel | solemn | autumn |

Write the spelling word that completes each sentence.

11. The knight was forced to _____ before his captors.
12. After walking in the snow, my toes became _____.
13. He wore a tie and carried a matching _____.
14. The runner placed the baton firmly in the _____ of her teammate's hand.
15. It is a lovely day and quite warm for _____.
16. It was a sad and _____ ceremony.
17. We have seats in section A, _____ 13.
18. He writes a _____ for the daily newspaper.
19. I tried to open the cabinet door, but the _____ fell off.
20. Ask Sally who has a lot of _____ about that topic.

112

Bulletin Board Idea

Our Best Poems

Have students review the words presented in **Vocabulary Connections** in Units 13 through 17. Tell each student to select one of these words and write an acrostic poem based on it. Remind students that the initial letters of each line spell the word, while the lines of the poem must in some way relate to the meaning of the word. Have each student draw an illustration to go with the poem and/or print the poem in large, bold letters. Display the poems on the bulletin board, changing them every few days so that each student will see his or her work displayed at some time.

| connect | occasion | possess | recess | announce |
| terrible | mirror | horrible | success | accident |

Write a spelling word for each clue.

1. This is a good part of the school day.
2. This is an event that wasn't planned.
3. Look in this to see yourself.
4. When you join two things, you do this to them.
5. When an event goes very well, it is this.
6. This is a particular event or happening.
7.–8. These words might describe a wicked monster.
9. If you own a bicycle, you could say this about owning it.
10. If you tell something, you do this to it.

Unit 17
Order of answers 7 and 8 may vary.

1. recess
2. accident
3. mirror
4. connect
5. success
6. occasion
7. horrible or
8. terrible
9. possess
10. announce

GAME Spelling Study Strategy

Spelling Tic-Tac-Toe

Practicing spelling words can be fun if you make it into a game. Play this game with a partner.

1. Both you and your partner write spelling words on lists. Trade lists.
2. Draw a tic-tac-toe board on a piece of paper. Decide who will use **O** and who will use **X**.
3. Ask your partner to call the first word on your spelling list to you. Spell it out loud. If you spell it correctly, make an **X** or an **O** on the tic-tac-toe board. If you misspell the word, ask your partner to spell it out loud for you. You miss your turn.
4. Now you call a word from your partner's spelling list.
5. Keep playing until one of you makes tic-tac-toe. Keep starting over until you both have practiced all your spelling words.

113

Learning an Alternative Spelling Study Strategy

Students should always have a number of study strategies to draw from when it comes to learning their spelling words. **Spelling Tic-Tac-Toe** is a partner game that makes practicing spelling fun to do. Encourage students to remember this spelling study strategy and to consider using it with any list they need to study and learn.

Weekly Test Options

Option 1:
One Spelling Word Per Sentence
(See procedures on pages Z10–Z11.)

1. That woman is our family **physician**.
2. The twins **differed** in many ways.
3. She will soon be a **sophomore**.
4. Cereal is his **usual** breakfast.
5. The officer **directed** the busy traffic.
6. You must try to **fulfill** your obligations.
7. He is **complaining** about the delay.
8. Make an **effort** to do your best work.
9. Do not block the **aisle** with books.
10. The jury cannot reach a **conclusion** today.
11. One **column** stood on each side of the stage.
12. The Fourth of July is a joyous **occasion**.
13. The belief that things will get better soon is an example of **optimism**.
14. Dry your eyes with my **handkerchief**.
15. These **scissors** are sharp.
16. How great is your **knowledge** of art?
17. The bridge will **connect** the towns.
18. Our **recess** begins at 10 o'clock.
19. You **possess** the skill to solve the problem.
20. He has a hard time **admitting** the truth.

Option 2:
Standardized Test

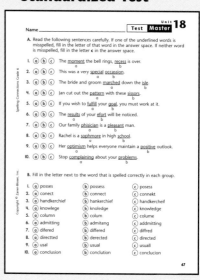

Unit 18 Test Master

(See *Teacher Resource Book,* Unit 18.)

TI13

Objectives

Spelling and Writing

Students will
• **review** direct objects.
• **compose** an expository piece of writing that explains how to make something useful. (See **Spelling and the Writing Process** below.)

A
1. bike
2. lettuce
3. wand
4. mail
5. boxes
6. windows
7. microphone
8. bone

B
9. scissors
10. knob
11. handkerchief
12. mirror
13. physician
14. telephone

Unit **18** enrichment

Grammar, Usage, and Mechanics

Direct Objects

The direct object is the noun or pronoun that receives the action of the verb. Only action verbs have a direct object.

The goalie kicked the **ball**.

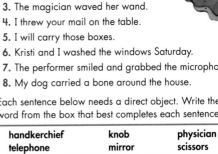

Practice Activity

A. Write the direct object in each sentence below.

1. Susan fixed her bike yesterday.
2. Rabbits ate my lettuce!
3. The magician waved her wand.
4. I threw your mail on the table.
5. I will carry those boxes.
6. Kristi and I washed the windows Saturday.
7. The performer smiled and grabbed the microphone.
8. My dog carried a bone around the house.

B. Each sentence below needs a direct object. Write the word from the box that best completes each sentence.

handkerchief	knob	physician
telephone	mirror	scissors

9. Oh, dear! I dropped the _____ and broke them.
10. You must turn the _____ to the right to open it.
11. Someone washed and ironed this _____.
12. I will hang your _____ in the hall.
13. The nurse called the _____ immediately.
14. Please answer the _____ for me.

114

Expository Writing

Spelling and the Writing Process

You may wish to use this writing assignment to help students master the writing process. For other writing ideas, see pages 258–259 in the Student Edition.

Explain that students will write instructions for making some useful object. The audience might include classmates, teachers, and parents.

Prewriting Hint: You may wish to help students plan their writing by recommending the chart on this page. Have them replicate the chart, filling in the columns with specific details that they remember.

Supplies Needed:	brown paper bag
Begin by–	cutting the bottom out of the bag
Then–	
Finally–	

Revising Hint: Remind students that when they revise what they have written, they should make sure that they have included every step. Encourage them to use active verbs, such as **cut, move,** and **place**.

WORKSHOP

 Proofreading Strategy

Box It Up!

Good writers always proofread their work for spelling errors. Here's a strategy that you can use to proofread your papers.

Cut a small hole or box in a piece of paper. Slide it over your work so that one or two words appear inside the box. You won't be able to see a whole sentence at one time. Instead of reading **The rider jumped onto the horse and galloped away!** you might see **rider jumped** or **and galloped**.

This may sound like a strange thing to do, but this strategy helps you focus on word spelling, not meaning. Try it!

Electronic Spelling

Spell Checkers

Computers have many programs and tools that help you proofread. Many have spell checkers that signal misspelled words. But even the best spell checker won't find every mistake, so you must be alert for problems.

Sometimes the misspelling of one word will spell a different word. For example, you might mean to write the word **dessert** and write **desert** instead. Since both words are spelled correctly, a spell checker would not catch the mistake.

A spell checker was used to correct the misspelled words in these sentences. Find the words it missed and write them correctly.

1. Hang the pitcher on the wall.
2. You will need allot of wrapping paper.
3. At the party well see many of our friends.
4. I one first prize in the writing contest!
5. Dry your hands before you doe that.
6. Their were many people in the room.

Electronic Spelling

1. picture
2. a lot
3. we'll
4. won
5. do
6. There

115

Objectives

Spelling and Writing

Students will
- **learn** a proofreading strategy.
- **understand** the importance of correct spelling when using a computer spell checker.
- **proofread** for misspellings that spell unintended words.

Optional Enrichment

Using Proofreading Strategies

Students are often unaware that there are a variety of techniques they can use to proofread their own writing. Building a repertory of strategies is important to improving students' writing and editing skills.

Spelling and Technology

The advent of word processing, computer protocols, and the Internet has actually increased, not lessened, the pressure on users to be better, more aware spellers. Spell checkers, for example, create circumstances in which the ability to discriminate between an acceptable and unacceptable spelling is a critical skill. A homophone substitution, a correct spelling of the wrong word, an inadvertent word omission—these are examples of situations in computer usage that require a deeper understanding of spelling principles and a more adroit proofreading capability. It may be worthwhile to underscore this increased need as a whole-class discussion after students finish this unit's **Electronic Spelling** activity.

Unit 19 Home Spelling Practice

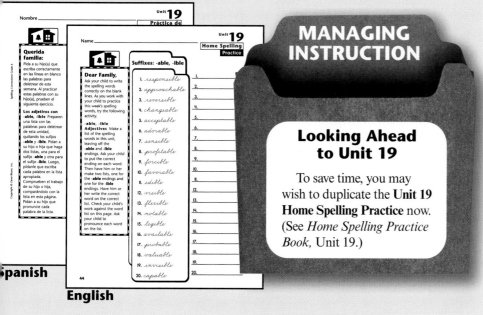

Spanish

English

MANAGING INSTRUCTION

Looking Ahead to Unit 19

To save time, you may wish to duplicate the **Unit 19 Home Spelling Practice** now. (See *Home Spelling Practice Book,* Unit 19.)

T115

Basic Spelling List

responsible	edible
approachable	visible
reversible	flexible
changeable	notable
acceptable	legible
adorable	available
sensible	probable
profitable	valuable
forcible	invisible
favorable	capable

Strategy Words

Review
divisible	inflate(able)
force(ible)	suit(able)
impossible	

Preview
admirable	noticeable
eligible	remarkable
incredible	

Content Words

Social Studies: Agriculture
agriculture	scarcity
irrigate	famine
arable	

Science: Digestion
digestive	saliva
pancreas	liver
enzyme	

Individual Needs

Challenge Words
breakable	deductible
perceptible	understandable
amiable	digestible

Alternate Word List ★
responsible	visible
changeable	flexible
acceptable	available
sensible	valuable
favorable	invisible

★ For students who need to study fewer Basic Spelling words

MATERIALS

Student Edition
Pages 116–121
Challenge Activities, p. 239

Teacher Edition
Pages T116A–T121
Challenge Activities, p. T239

Teacher Resource Book
Unit 19 Homework Master
Unit 19 Practice Masters
Flip Folder Practice Master
Unit 19 Test Master

Home Spelling Practice Book
Unit 19 Home Spelling Practice
(English or Spanish)

Other *Spelling Connections* Resources
- Audiotape, Grade 6
- Practice Book for Grammar, Usage, and Mechanics, Grade 6
- Spelling Support for Second Language Learners, Grade 6
- Support Software on CD-ROM
- Transparency Book, Grade 6
- Word Sort CD-ROM, Grade 6

OBJECTIVES

Spelling and Thinking
Students will
- **read** the spelling words in list form and in context.
- **sort** the spelling words according to spelling changes made to the base word or root word.
- **read** and remember this week's spelling strategy.

Spelling and Vocabulary
Students will
- **write** spelling words to match definitions.
- **replace** words in sentences with spelling words that have the same or nearly the same meaning.
- **identify** spelling words by their origin.

Spelling and Reading
Students will
- **solve** analogies using spelling words.
- **complete** sentences using spelling words.
- **complete** a paragraph using spelling words.

Spelling and Writing
Students will
- **proofread** a descriptive paragraph.
- **use** the writing process to persuade others to follow a fad.
- **proofread** their writing.

MEETING INDIVIDUAL NEEDS
Learning Styles

 Visual

Have the students write each spelling word on a 3" × 5" card. Have them write the words with the **-able** suffix in black and the words with the **-ible** suffix in red. As you write each spelling word on the chalkboard, ask a volunteer to pronounce the word and tell whether it is a black or a red word.

 Auditory

Write the suffix **-able** on eleven 3" × 5" cards and the suffix **-ible** on nine 3" × 5" cards, and place them in a container. Write each base word or root of the spelling words on a separate card and place these twenty cards in another container. Form the class into two teams: Team A draws suffix cards; Team B draws root and base cards. The first player on Team A pronounces the suffix he has drawn and spells it aloud. Each Team B player who has drawn a card that will form a word with the suffix steps forward. Each pronounces the spelling word formed and spells it aloud. The spelling word cards are returned to the container, and a Team B player selects a new card for the next round.

 Kinesthetic

Divide the class into two groups, the **-ibles** and the **-ables**. Tell the students you will pronounce the base words from which the spelling words were formed. As you say each base word, either the **-ibles** or the **-ables** should stand up, depending on which suffix is contained in the adjective formed from that base. If the students catch on quickly, start saying the words faster.

Hands-On Practice
All students will benefit from practicing with a **Flip Folder**. See page Z18.

Language and Cultural Differences

In Spanish, there are similar suffixes but there are no /ə/ and /əl/ sounds. Spanish-speaking students may, therefore, have difficulty hearing, pronouncing, and spelling these sounds.

Write **-able** and **-ible** as headings on the chalkboard. Have volunteers write words that have these suffixes under the appropriate headings. Have the students repeat each word as they write it in their spelling notebooks.

MANAGING INSTRUCTION

3–5 Day Plan		Average	Below Average	Above Average
Day 1	Day 1	Pretest Spelling Mini-Lesson, p. T116 Spelling and Thinking, p. 116	Pretest Spelling Mini-Lesson, p. T116 Spelling and Thinking, p. 116	Pretest Spelling and Thinking, p. 116
	Day 2	Spelling and Vocabulary, p. 117	Spelling and Vocabulary, p. 117 (or) Unit 19 Practice Master, A and B	Spelling and Vocabulary, p. 117 Spelling and Reading, p. 118
Day 2	Day 3	Spelling and Reading, p. 118	Spelling and Reading, p. 118 (or) Unit 19 Practice Master, C and D	Challenge Activities, p. 239
	Day 4	Spelling and Writing, p. 119 Unit 19 Homework Master	Spelling and Writing, p. 119	Spelling and Writing, p. 119 Unit 19 Homework Master
Day 3	Day 5	Weekly Test	Weekly Test	Weekly Test

Vocabulary Connections (pages 120 and 121) may be used anytime during this unit.

Objectives

Spelling and Thinking

Students will
- **read** the spelling words in list form and in context.
- **sort** the spelling words according to spelling changes made to the base word or root word.
- **read** and remember this week's spelling strategy.

UNIT PRETEST

Use **Pretest Sentences** below. Refer to the self-checking procedures on student page 256. You may wish to use the **Unit 19 Word List Overhead Transparency** as part of the checking procedure.

TEACHING THE STRATEGY

Spelling Mini-Lesson

All the words on this week's list end in the suffix **-able** or **-ible**. Explain that **-ible** is really a different form of **-able**.

Write the spelling words on the chalkboard. Ask volunteers to identify as many base words as they can. Write each identified base word next to its spelling word. (favorable, favor; profitable, profit; acceptable, accept; approachable, approach; available, avail; changeable, change; notable, note; adorable, adore; valuable, value; sensible, sense; flexible, flex; forcible, force; reversible, reverse; responsible, response)

Ask, "What conclusions can you draw about how the base word changes when suffixes are added?" Guide the students to these conclusions:
- The suffixes **-able** and **-ible** can be added without changing the spelling of the base word: **favorable, profitable, acceptable, approachable, available, changeable, flexible**.
- Final silent **e** is often dropped when these suffixes are added: **notable, adorable, valuable, sensible, forcible, reversible, responsible**. (Explain that changeable may be an exception because retaining final e keeps the pronunciation of g "soft.")

Explain that the suffix **-ible** is used more commonly with root words and that it often follows /s/ or soft **g** (/**j**/).

Read **Remember the Spelling Strategy** on page 116.

T116

Spelling and Thinking

Order of answers may vary.

no change in base word
1. approachable
2. changeable ★
3. acceptable ★
4. profitable
5. favorable ★
6. flexible ★
7. available ★

silent e dropped
8. responsible ★
9. reversible
10. adorable
11. sensible ★
12. forcible
13. notable
14. valuable ★

suffix added to root
15. edible
16. visible ★
17. legible
18. probable
19. invisible ★
20. capable

116

READ THE SPELLING WORDS

1. responsible	*responsible*	I am **responsible** for the accident.
2. approachable	*approachable*	My friendly boss is **approachable**.
3. reversible	*reversible*	Her new rain jacket is **reversible**.
4. changeable	*changeable*	Our weather is often **changeable**.
5. acceptable	*acceptable*	That silly answer is not **acceptable**.
6. adorable	*adorable*	The baby's teddy bear is **adorable**.
7. sensible	*sensible*	We all like your **sensible** ideas.
8. profitable	*profitable*	Her store had a **profitable** year.
9. forcible	*forcible*	Was entry into the house **forcible**?
10. favorable	*favorable*	He wrote a **favorable** play review.
11. edible	*edible*	Some wild mushrooms are **edible**.
12. visible	*visible*	Cars were not **visible** in the fog.
13. flexible	*flexible*	The doctor's schedule is **flexible**.
14. notable	*notable*	DaVinci was a **notable** painter.
15. legible	*legible*	I hope you find my writing **legible**.
16. available	*available*	It is **available** for your use.
17. probable	*probable*	I tried to find the **probable** cause.
18. valuable	*valuable*	Be careful with that **valuable** vase.
19. invisible	*invisible*	The star is **invisible** in the daylight.
20. capable	*capable*	You are a very **capable** writer.

SORT THE SPELLING WORDS

1.–7. Write the words in which the spelling of the base word does not change when **-able** or **-ible** is added.

8.–14. Write the spelling words in which the **silent e** is dropped from the base word when **-able** or **-ible** is added.

15.–20. Write the spelling words in which the suffix **-able** or **-ible** is added to a root word.

REMEMBER THE SPELLING STRATEGY

Remember that the suffixes **-able** and **-ible** can be added to base words and root words to form new words: **favorable** and **visible**.

Pretest Sentences (See procedures on pages Z10–Z11.)

★ 1. Each player is **responsible** for the team's success.
  2. A good manager demands discipline but is always **approachable**.
  3. Her **reversible** coat is red on one side and plaid on the other.
★ 4. The **changeable** weather at this time of year can ruin a picnic.
★ 5. We agreed that the plan was **acceptable** but not exciting.
  6. Did you see the **adorable** puppy in the pet shop?
★ 7. Please give me a **sensible** answer to the question.
  8. Are discount sales always **profitable**?
  9. The police made a **forcible** entry into the abandoned house.
★10. The performance received a **favorable** response.
  11. These mushrooms are not **edible**.
★12. The house was **visible** through the trees.
★13. Rubber is a **flexible** material.
  14. The scientist became famous after her **notable** discovery.
  15. It is important to strive for **legible** handwriting.
★16. Will you be **available** to attend our meeting tomorrow?
  17. An insect is the **probable** carrier of that disease.
★18. She wore a **valuable** necklace to the dinner party.
★19. The secret message became **invisible** after the fluid dried.
  20. A **capable** tennis player would win the game easily.

Spelling and Vocabulary

Word Meanings

Write a spelling word to match each definition.

1. able to be seen
2. able to be forced
3. worthy of notice
4. able to be approached
5. able to be reversed
6. able to be bent
7. likely to change
8. worthy of acceptance
9. likely to happen
10. of great value

Word Replacements

Write a spelling word that could replace each underlined word.

11. They have two <u>lovable</u> puppies.
12. The apartment is <u>obtainable</u> for rent.
13. The doctor gave the patient a very <u>encouraging</u> report about his health.
14. These berries are <u>safe for eating</u>.
15. Selling the land was <u>moneymaking</u> for the company.
16. Winslow Homer was a gifted and <u>skillful</u> artist.

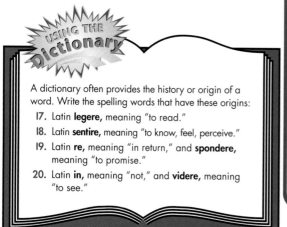

USING THE Dictionary

A dictionary often provides the history or origin of a word. Write the spelling words that have these origins:

17. Latin **legere,** meaning "to read."
18. Latin **sentire,** meaning "to know, feel, perceive."
19. Latin **re,** meaning "in return," and **spondere,** meaning "to promise."
20. Latin **in,** meaning "not," and **videre,** meaning "to see."

Word Meanings

1. visible
2. forcible
3. notable
4. approachable
5. reversible
6. flexible
7. changeable
8. acceptable
9. probable
10. valuable

Word Replacements

11. adorable
12. available
13. favorable
14. edible
15. profitable
16. capable

Using the Dictionary

17. legible
18. sensible
19. responsible
20. invisible

Objectives

Spelling and Vocabulary

Students will
• **write** spelling words to match definitions.
• **replace** words in sentences with spelling words that have the same or nearly the same meaning.
• **identify** spelling words by their origin.

Developing Oral Language Skills

Do a word sort by syllables. Write **three syllables** and **four syllables** on a chalkboard or overhead. Then ask volunteers to read the spelling word list. Ask students to place each word under one of the two headings according to the number of syllables it contains. When students have finished listing the words, ask them to consider the letters in each word that spell the suffix. Then have volunteers come to the board, say the word, and circle the letters that spell the sound.

MEETING INDIVIDUAL NEEDS

Providing More Help

To aid these students, write the following pairs of words on the chalkboard and have the students take turns underlining the words that are correctly spelled:

available, availible
changeable, changeible
invisable, **invisible**
forcible, forcable
responsable, **responsible**
capible, **capable**

★Students who need to study fewer words should use the **Alternate Word List**. This list is starred on page T116 in the Teacher Edition. The **Unit 19 Practice Masters** (*Teacher Resource Book*) provide additional practice with these words.

Unit 19 Practice Masters

Name _____   **Practice Master** 19

1. favorable   3. available   5. valuable   7. visible   9. flexible
2. acceptable   4. changeable   6. sensible   8. invisible   10. responsible

A. Write the spelling word that goes with each definition.

1. capable of being seen _____
2. capable of bending repeatedly _____
3. not capable of being seen _____
4. having great worth _____
5. capable of being satisfactory _____
6. capable of being obtained _____

B. These words are misspelled. Write the spelling words correctly.

1. responsable _____
2. flexable _____
3. sensable _____
4. favorible _____
5. availible _____

Practice Master 19

... ble   visible   flexible
... ble   invisible   responsible

... g words. Write the words.

Objectives

Spelling and Reading

Students will
- **solve** analogies using spelling words.
- **complete** sentences using spelling words.
- **complete** a paragraph using spelling words.

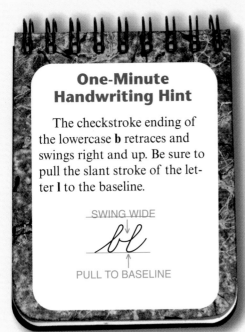

One-Minute Handwriting Hint

The checkstroke ending of the lowercase **b** retraces and swings right and up. Be sure to pull the slant stroke of the letter **l** to the baseline.

SWING WIDE

PULL TO BASELINE

Legible handwriting can boost spelling scores by as much as 20%.

Solve the Analogies
1. legible
2. edible
3. valuable
4. visible
5. adorable
6. responsible
7. changeable

Complete the Sentences
8. forcible
9. acceptable
10. approachable
11. reversible
12. sensible
13. probable
14. invisible
15. profitable

Complete the Paragraph
16. notable
17. flexible
18. capable
19. favorable
20. available

118

Spelling and Reading

responsible	approachable	reversible	changeable
acceptable	adorable	sensible	profitable
forcible	favorable	edible	visible
flexible	notable	legible	available
probable	valuable	invisible	capable

Solve the Analogies Write a spelling word to complete each analogy.

1. **Speech** is to **understandable** as **handwriting** is to ____.
2. **Water** is to **drinkable** as **food** is to ____.
3. **Seldom** is to **often** as **worthless** is to ____.
4. **Dull** is to **shiny** as **concealed** is to ____.
5. **Grateful** is to **appreciative** as **delightful** is to ____.
6. **Knowledgeable** is to **ignorant** as **unreliable** is to ____.
7. **Cautious** is to **careful** as **variable** is to ____.

Complete the Sentences Write a spelling word to complete each sentence.

8. Police officers made a ____ entry into the building.
9. Your test scores were not great, but they were ____.
10. The salesperson's smile made her seem ____.
11. Once the judge makes a decision, it is not ____.
12. The counselor offered a ____ solution to the problem.
13. I think a lightning strike was the ____ cause of the fire.
14. The lighthouse beam was nearly ____ in the fog.
15. The family is pleased with the ____ sale of the house.

Complete the Paragraph Write spelling words from the box to complete the paragraph.

One _16._ fad was the Slinky, which was invented in 1945. The Slinky consists of 87 feet of _17._ wire coiled into small circles. This toy is _18._ of "walking" down stairs. The Slinky made a _19._ impression on millions. It is still _20._ in stores today.

| capable |
| available |
| favorable |
| notable |
| flexible |

MEETING INDIVIDUAL NEEDS
Providing More Challenge

Challenge Words and **Challenge Activities** for Unit 19 appear on page 239. **Challenge Word Test Sentences** appear on page T239.

Unit 19 Challenge Activities

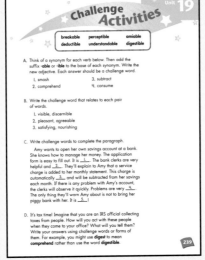

Weekly Test Options

Option 1:
One Spelling Word Per Sentence
(See procedures on pages Z10–Z11.)

★ 1. Were the plans we made **acceptable** to you?
2. Most babies are **adorable**.
★ 3. How soon will the book be **available**?
4. She is **capable** of doing many things.
★ 5. The weather is very **changeable** in March.
6. The senator seems very friendly and **approachable**.
7. Are these berries **edible**?
★ 8. The odds are **favorable** that we will win the game.
★ 9. Exercise helps keep your body **flexible**.
10. The thief made a **forcible** entry into the house.
★11. Air is composed of **invisible** gases.
12. Her handwriting is very **legible**.
13. His skill as an artist is **notable**.
14. It is **probable** that he will be later than usual.
15. His efforts were very **profitable** for the company.
★16. You are **responsible** for our triumph.

T118

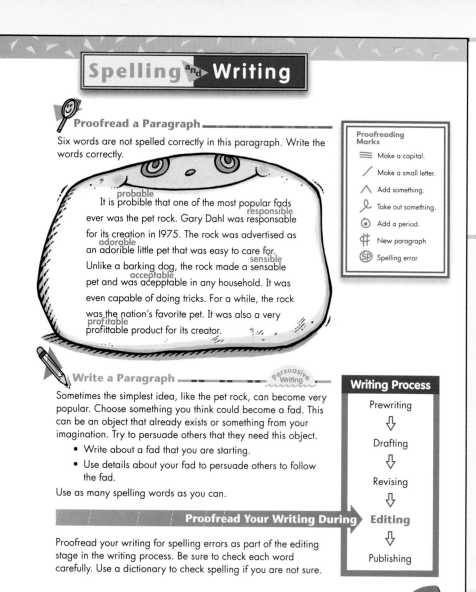

Spelling and Writing

Proofread a Paragraph

Six words are not spelled correctly in this paragraph. Write the words correctly.

probable
It is probible that one of the most popular fads
responsible
ever was the pet rock. Gary Dahl was responsable
for its creation in 1975. The rock was advertised as
adorable
an adorible little pet that was easy to care for.
sensible
Unlike a barking dog, the rock made a sensable
acceptable
pet and was aceptable in any household. It was
even capable of doing tricks. For a while, the rock
was the nation's favorite pet. It was also a very
profitable
profittable product for its creator.

Proofreading Marks

≡ Make a capital.
/ Make a small letter.
∧ Add something.
⌖ Take out something.
⊙ Add a period.
⌗ New paragraph
SP Spelling error

Write a Paragraph

Persuasive Writing

Sometimes the simplest idea, like the pet rock, can become very popular. Choose something you think could become a fad. This can be an object that already exists or something from your imagination. Try to persuade others that they need this object.

- Write about a fad that you are starting.
- Use details about your fad to persuade others to follow the fad.

Use as many spelling words as you can.

Writing Process

Prewriting
⇩
Drafting
⇩
Revising
⇩
Editing
⇩
Publishing

Proofread Your Writing During →

Proofread your writing for spelling errors as part of the editing stage in the writing process. Be sure to check each word carefully. Use a dictionary to check spelling if you are not sure.

119

Objectives

Spelling and Writing

Students will
- **proofread** a descriptive paragraph.
- **use** the writing process to persuade others to follow a fad.
- **proofread** their writing.

Using the Writing Process

Before assigning **Write a Paragraph,** see pages 258–259 in the Student Edition for a complete review of the writing assignments. You may also wish to refer to pages Z12–Z13 in the Teacher Edition.

Keeping a Spelling Journal

Encourage students to record the words they misspelled on the weekly test in a personal spelling journal. These words may be recycled for future study. Students may also wish to include words from their writing. See pages Z12–Z13 in the Teacher Edition for more information.

---

17. His **reversible** jacket could be white or green.
★18. She is a **sensible** girl who never does foolish things.
★19. He learned a **valuable** lesson from his error.
★20. The cars were scarcely **visible** in the fog.

Option 2:
Multiple Spelling Words Per Sentence
(See procedures on pages Z10–Z11.)

1. A **reversible** jacket is handy in **changeable** weather.
2. The **acceptable** plan also became **profitable**.
3. It is **probable** that the facts will soon be **available** to you.
4. Since this is an **edible** root, it is a **sensible** one to plant.
5. The artist's most **notable** work is also quite **valuable**.
6. Because he was **capable** of the deed, he was held **responsible** for it.
7. The sign was **visible** but only barely **legible**.
8. The **adorable** child often talked to an **invisible** "friend."
9. Since the woman was **flexible** in her views, most people found her to be **approachable**.
10. **Forcible** commands are not received in a **favorable** way.

Option 3:
Standardized Test
(See *Teacher Resource Book,* Unit 19.)

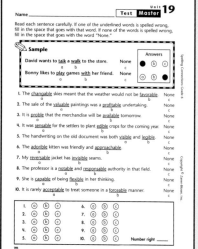

**Unit 19
Test Master**

T119

Objectives

Strategy Words

Students will

- **review** words studied previously that are related to the spelling strategy.
- **preview** unknown words that are related to the spelling strategy.

Strategy Words

Remind the students that the **Strategy Words** are related to the spelling patterns they have studied in this unit. The **Review Words** are below grade level, and the **Preview Words** are above grade level. You may wish to use the following sentences to introduce the words in context.

Review Words:
Words From Grade 5

1. The number nine is evenly **divisible** by three.
2. We should not **force** the locker open.
3. It is **impossible** to resist her friendliness.
4. Mother will **inflate** my bicycle tire.
5. My brother wore a **suit** to the wedding.

Preview Words:
Words From Grade 7

6. His skill in public speaking is **admirable**.
7. My sister is **eligible** for a discount at the department store.
8. A flight to the moon seemed **incredible** to my grandparents.
9. There was a **noticeable** difference in the quality of his work after a good night's sleep.
10. They told us that our food drive had **remarkable** results.

Review Words

1. inflate
2. impossible
3. divisible
4. suit
5. force

Preview Words

6. noticeable
7. remarkable
8. admirable
9. incredible
10. eligible

Unit 19 enrichment

VOCABULARY CONNECTIONS

Strategy Words

Review Words: Suffixes -able, -ible

Write words from the box to complete the sentences. Use the underlined words as clues.

divisible	force	impossible	inflate	suit

1. You can _____ this ball. It is <u>inflatable</u>.
2. Your idea is _____. It is <u>not possible</u>.
3. The project is _____. It is capable of being <u>divided</u> into separate tasks.
4. I think this dress will _____ you. You will find it <u>suitable</u> to your tastes.
5. He had to _____ the window open. The entry was <u>forcible</u>.

Preview Words: Suffixes -able, -ible

Write words from the box to replace the underlined words.

admirable	eligible	incredible
	noticeable	remarkable

6.–10. The makers of Smile announce a new toothpaste. You will see <u>observable</u> differences in the whiteness of your teeth. Enter a contest to describe your experience with our <u>memorable</u> new product. All <u>praiseworthy</u> contributions will be rewarded with a free tube of Smile. This is an <u>unbelievable</u> offer that you should not pass up. Anyone over the age of twelve is <u>qualified</u> to enter.

120

Unit 19 RECAP

You may wish to assign the **Unit 19 Homework Master** (*Teacher Resource Book*, Unit 19) as a fun way to recap the spelling words.

Unit 19 Homework Master

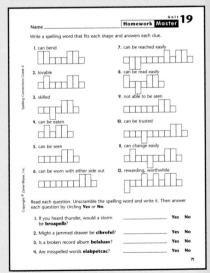

T120

Content Words

Social Studies: Agriculture

Write words from the box to complete the paragraph.

| agriculture | irrigate | arable | scarcity | famine |

As a nation's population increases, the availability of ___1.___ land decreases. The construction of new buildings and roadways also adds to a possible ___2.___ of land in the future. Today, efforts are being made in the field of ___3.___ to teach people how to ___4.___ their land and maintain rich soil. Such planning can help prevent a major ___5.___.

Science: Digestion

Write the words from the box that complete the paragraph.

| digestive | pancreas | enzyme | saliva | liver |

The ___6.___ juices play an important role in digestion. An ___7.___ such as ___8.___, which is produced in the mouth, helps break down food. The ___9.___, a gland behind the stomach, also secretes juices into the small intestine to aid in the process. The ___10.___ is a large organ near the stomach that transfers nutrients into the blood.

Apply the Spelling Strategy

Circle the suffixes **-able** and **-ive** in two of the Content Words you wrote.

Word Study

Multiple Meanings

Some words have more than one meaning. For example, you can **sign** your name on the paper or you can watch for the street **sign**. Write the one Strategy Word that fits each phrase:

- ____ of clothes
- bathing ____
- cards in a ____

121

Social Studies: Agriculture
1. ar(able)
2. scarcity
3. agriculture
4. irrigate
5. famine

Science: Digestion
6. digest(ive)
7. enzyme
8. saliva
9. pancreas
10. liver

Multiple Meanings
1. suit

Objectives

Content Words

Students will
- **expand** vocabulary with content-related words.
- **relate** the spelling strategy to words outside the basic spelling list.
- **understand** that the same word can have different meanings depending on context

Content Words

Social Studies: Agriculture

Use these sentences to introduce the words and their meanings.
1. Early in our country's history the economy was based on **agriculture**.
2. Farmers can increase production if they **irrigate** their fields.
3. This land was chosen for crops because it is **arable**.
4. There is not a **scarcity** of food in our country.
5. We are able to help when another country suffers a **famine**.

Science: Digestion

Use these sentences to introduce the words and their meanings.
6. The **digestive** tract of an earthworm is very simple.
7. The human **pancreas** aids in our absorption of food.
8. Scientists have learned how each **enzyme** aids in our digestion.
9. The process of absorbing food begins with the **saliva** in our mouth.
10. The **liver** of humans is located in the abdominal cavity.

Word Study

Multiple Meanings

Discuss the ways in which the same word can convey a variety of meanings depending on context. Encourage students to come up with yet another meaning for **suit**. (Possible response: "fits," as in "it suits you")

Unit 20 Home Spelling Practice

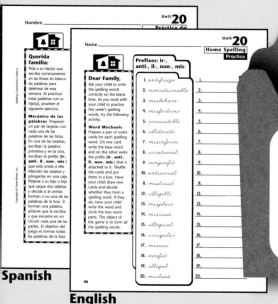

Spanish

English

MANAGING INSTRUCTION

Looking Ahead to Unit 20

To save time, you may wish to duplicate the **Unit 20 Home Spelling Practice** now. (See *Home Spelling Practice Book*, Unit 20.)

T121

Basic Spelling List

antifreeze	mistrust
nonreturnable	illegible
misbehave	misplace
misfortune	misread
irresistible	illogical
illiterate	irregular
misinform	misuse
irrational	nonfat
nonprofit	illegal
antisocial	mislead

Strategy Words

Review
antislavery   nonfiction
misjudge   nonviolent
(mis)calculate

Preview
(non)toxic
(non)consumable
inexpensive
mistaken
misunderstanding

Content Words

Social Studies: Insurance
collect   provision
policy   nonrenewal
insure

Language Arts: Usage
appositive   tense
modifier   linking verb
grammar

Individual Needs

Challenge Words
antidote   misunderstand
mispronounce   nonchalant
nondescript   nonproductive

Alternate Word List ★
antifreeze	illiterate
nonreturnable	irregular
misbehave	nonfat
misfortune	illegal
irresistible	mislead

★ For students who need to study
   fewer Basic Spelling words

MATERIALS

Student Edition
Pages 122–127
Challenge Activities, p. 240

Teacher Edition
Pages T122A–T127
Challenge Activities, p. T240

Teacher Resource Book
Unit 20 Homework Master
Unit 20 Practice Masters
Flip Folder Practice Master
Unit 20 Test Master

Home Spelling Practice Book
Unit 20 Home Spelling Practice
   (English or Spanish)

Other *Spelling Connections* Resources
- Audiotape, Grade 6
- Practice Book for Grammar, Usage, and Mechanics, Grade 6
- Spelling Support for Second Language Learners, Grade 6
- Support Software on CD-ROM
- Transparency Book, Grade 6
- Word Sort CD-ROM, Grade 6

OBJECTIVES

Spelling and Thinking
Students will
- **read** the spelling words in list form and in context.
- **sort** the spelling words according to their prefixes.
- **read** and remember this week's spelling strategy.

Spelling and Vocabulary
Students will
- **use** the definition of prefixes and base words to write spelling words.
- **replace** words in a sentence with spelling words that have the same or nearly the same meaning.
- **use** the **Spelling Dictionary** to determine the part of speech of spelling words.

Spelling and Reading
Students will
- **solve** analogies using spelling words.
- **complete** sentences using spelling words.
- **correct** a paragraph using spelling words.

Spelling and Writing
Students will
- **proofread** a paragraph.
- **use** the writing process to write a paragraph about a hobby.
- **proofread** their writing.

MEETING INDIVIDUAL NEEDS
Learning Styles

 Visual

Divide the class into two teams. Have each team write each prefix and each base word of the spelling words on 3" × 5" cards. Have them write the prefixes in green and the base words in red. Each team will have one stack of cards with the prefixes and another stack with the base words. When you say "Go," have the teams match the prefixes to the base words to form the spelling words. The first team to match them all correctly wins.

 Auditory

Have the students play "Word Box." Write each spelling word on a slip of paper and place the papers in a box. A student draws a word, pronounces the word in a tone indicative of the word's meaning, and spells the word aloud without looking at the paper. If the word is spelled correctly, that paper may be discarded. If the word is misspelled, the student keeps the slip of paper in order to study that word.

 Kinesthetic

Designate various areas of the room for the different prefixes. For example, you could label the center of the room **mis-** and the corners **ir-, anti-, il-,** and **non-**. Pronounce a spelling word and call on a student. The student must stand, identify the prefix in the word, walk to the appropriate part of the room, and spell the word. If correct, the student stays in that place. If incorrect, the student sits down and waits for another turn.

> **Hands-On Practice**
> All students will benefit from practicing with a **Flip Folder**. See page Z18.
>

Language and Cultural Differences

Give the students ample opportunity to hear and repeat the correct pronunciation of the spelling words in this unit, as they are words that are commonly mispronounced and misspelled.

Create on the chalkboard—and have the students copy on paper—five columns, each headed by a prefix (**ir-, il-,** **non-, mis-, anti-**). Pronounce each spelling word and ask a volunteer to identify the column in which the word belongs. Have the students write the word in the proper column of their papers as you write it on the board.

MANAGING INSTRUCTION

3–5 Day Plan		Average	Below Average	Above Average
Day 1	**Day 1**	Pretest Spelling Mini-Lesson, p. T122 Spelling and Thinking, p. 122	Pretest Spelling Mini-Lesson, p. T122 Spelling and Thinking, p. 122	Pretest Spelling and Thinking, p. 122
	Day 2	Spelling and Vocabulary, p. 123	Spelling and Vocabulary, p. 123 (or) Unit 20 Practice Master, A and B	Spelling and Vocabulary, p. 123 Spelling and Reading, p. 124
Day 2	**Day 3**	Spelling and Reading, p. 124	Spelling and Reading, p. 124 (or) Unit 20 Practice Master, C and D	Challenge Activities, p. 240
	Day 4	Spelling and Writing, p. 125 Unit 20 Homework Master	Spelling and Writing, p. 125	Spelling and Writing, p. 125 Unit 20 Homework Master
Day 3	**Day 5**	Weekly Test	Weekly Test	Weekly Test

Vocabulary Connections (pages 126 and 127) may be used anytime during this unit.

Objectives

Spelling and Thinking

Students will
- **read** the spelling words in list form and in context.
- **sort** the spelling words according to their prefixes.
- **read** and remember this week's spelling strategy.

UNIT PRETEST

Use **Pretest Sentences** below. Refer to the self-checking procedures on student page 256. You may wish to use the **Unit 20 Word List Overhead Transparency** as part of the checking procedure.

TEACHING THE STRATEGY

Spelling Mini-Lesson

Write these words on the chalkboard: **irregular, antisocial, illegal, nonprofit, misread.** Ask volunteers to identify the base word in each word. (regular, social, legal, profit, read)

Discuss the differences in meaning between each spelling word and its base word. (They are antonyms of each other.) Explain to the students that the prefixes **ir-, anti-, il-, non-,** and **mis-** are all added to base words to form a new word that has the opposite meaning of the base word. Explain that **ir-, anti-, il-, non-,** and **mis-** are termed "negative prefixes." You may also wish to point out that the prefixes **ir-** and **il-** are variant forms of the prefix **in-** (meaning "not").

Write the remaining spelling words on the board. Ask volunteers to identify the base word of each word. Discuss the ways in which the meaning of each base word changes when the negative prefix is added.

Read **Remember the Spelling Strategy** on page 122.

Order of answers may vary.

il-, ir-
1. irresistible ★
2. illiterate ★
3. irrational
4. illegible
5. illogical
6. irregular ★
7. illegal ★

mis-
8. misbehave ★
9. misfortune ★
10. misinform
11. mistrust
12. misplace
13. misread
14. misuse
15. mislead ★

non-
16. nonreturnable ★
17. nonprofit
18. nonfat ★

anti-
19. antifreeze ★
20. antisocial

122

Spelling and Thinking

READ THE SPELLING WORDS

1.	antifreeze	*antifreeze*	Does your car need **antifreeze**?
2.	nonreturnable	*nonreturnable*	We recycle **nonreturnable** cans.
3.	misbehave	*misbehave*	Try not to **misbehave** in class.
4.	misfortune	*misfortune*	I am sorry for your **misfortune**.
5.	irresistible	*irresistible*	I find these cookies **irresistible**.
6.	illiterate	*illiterate*	He teaches **illiterate** adults.
7.	misinform	*misinform*	Juan did not **misinform** you.
8.	irrational	*irrational*	Some fears are totally **irrational**.
9.	nonprofit	*nonprofit*	Charities are **nonprofit** groups.
10.	antisocial	*antisocial*	He is **antisocial**, so he sits alone.
11.	mistrust	*mistrust*	I **mistrust** his motives.
12.	illegible	*illegible*	She rewrote her **illegible** paper.
13.	misplace	*misplace*	Dad tends to **misplace** his keys.
14.	misread	*misread*	I **misread** the map and got lost.
15.	illogical	*illogical*	Your argument is **illogical**.
16.	irregular	*irregular*	The dog's heartbeat is **irregular**.
17.	misuse	*misuse*	The toy broke from **misuse**.
18.	nonfat	*nonfat*	I bought a gallon of **nonfat** milk.
19.	illegal	*illegal*	It is **illegal** to park here.
20.	mislead	*mislead*	False headlines **mislead** readers.

SORT THE SPELLING WORDS

1.–7. Write the spelling words with the prefixes **il-** or **ir-**.

8.–15. Write the spelling words with the prefix **mis-**.

16.–18. Write the spelling words with the prefix **non-**.

19.–20. Write the spelling words with the prefix **anti-**.

REMEMBER THE SPELLING STRATEGY

Remember that the prefixes **ir-, anti-, il-, non-,** and **mis-** can be added to base words to form new words. These new words mean the opposite of the base word.

Pretest Sentences (See procedures on pages Z10–Z11.)

★ 1. Dad replaced the **antifreeze** in our car for the coming winter.

★ 2. That swimsuit is a **nonreturnable** item.

★ 3. Students who **misbehave** are often kept after school.

★ 4. It was a **misfortune** that the gold ring had been lost.

★ 5. The sandwiches were so **irresistible** that we ate them all.

★ 6. A person who is **illiterate** cannot read and write.

7. I am not sure of the facts and do not wish to **misinform** you.

8. Bill's wild actions made him seem like an **irrational** person.

9. Most charitable institutions are **nonprofit** organizations.

10. Since the boy would not talk to us, we felt he was **antisocial**.

11. It is easy to **mistrust** someone who has lied to you.

12. Her handwriting is so **illegible** that I cannot read her notes.

13. Did you **misplace** my keys, or are they in their usual spot?

14. If you **misread** the recipe, this dish will be ruined.

15. Sheila's argument was **illogical** because the facts did not support her conclusion.

★16. A word with an **irregular** spelling pattern requires study.

17. Do not **misuse** the equipment if you want it to run smoothly.

★18. Some adults who are on diets drink **nonfat** milk.

★19. Any action that breaks the law is **illegal**.

★20. She is not certain of the way and might **mislead** others.

Spelling and Vocabulary

Word Structure

Replace the first word in each pair with a prefix and write the spelling word.

1. badly + lead
2. badly + inform
3. badly + read
4. not + legal
5. not + rational
6. not + profit
7. not + returnable
8. not + social

Word Replacement

Write a spelling word that could replace each underlined word.

9. His handwriting is nearly <u>unreadable</u>.
10. I am concerned about the dog's <u>unusual</u> behavior.
11. If you <u>mistreat</u> the violin strings, they might break.
12. He is <u>uneducated</u> in the subject of modern art.
13. If you <u>disobey</u> once more, you will have to leave.
14. I had an <u>overwhelming</u> urge to open the gift early.

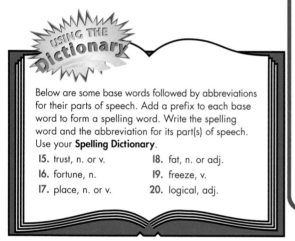

USING THE Dictionary

Below are some base words followed by abbreviations for their parts of speech. Add a prefix to each base word to form a spelling word. Write the spelling word and the abbreviation for its part(s) of speech. Use your **Spelling Dictionary**.

15. trust, n. or v.
16. fortune, n.
17. place, n. or v.
18. fat, n. or adj.
19. freeze, v.
20. logical, adj.

Word Structure
1. mislead
2. misinform
3. misread
4. illegal
5. irrational
6. nonprofit
7. nonreturnable
8. antisocial

Word Replacement
9. illegible
10. irregular
11. misuse
12. illiterate
13. misbehave
14. irresistible

Using the Dictionary
15. mistrust, n. or v.
16. misfortune, n.
17. misplace, v.
18. nonfat, adj.
19. antifreeze, n.
20. illogical, adj.

Objectives

Spelling and Vocabulary

Students will
- **use** the definition of prefixes and base words to write spelling words.
- **replace** words in a sentence with spelling words that have the same or nearly the same meaning.
- **use** the **Spelling Dictionary** to determine the part of speech of spelling words.

Developing Oral Language Skills

Write **irregular** on the chalkboard. Have students pronounce **irregular** and note whether they pronounce the word as four syllables or three syllables. If necessary, remind them that **irregular** is pronounced with four syllables. Remind students that words like **irregular** (/ĭ rĕg´ yə lər/) may cause spelling problems because the third syllable is weak or disappears entirely when the word is pronounced.

MEETING INDIVIDUAL NEEDS

Providing More Help

Write the five prefixes (**ir-, il-, non-, mis-,** and **anti-**) at the top of the chalkboard. Also write these words: **regular, social, literate, profit, behave, resistible**. Have the students take turns adding a prefix to a base word.

★Students who need to study fewer words should use the **Alternate Word List**. This list is starred on page T122 in the Teacher Edition. The **Unit 20 Practice Masters** (*Teacher Resource Book*) provide additional practice with these words.

Unit 20 Practice Masters

Objectives

Spelling and Reading

Students will
- **solve** analogies using spelling words.
- **complete** sentences using spelling words.
- **correct** a paragraph using spelling words.

One-Minute Handwriting Hint

Keep the loop open in the lowercase **l**. Begin the letter with a wide undercurve, and then loop back and pull the slant stroke to the baseline.

WIDE UNDERCURVE ↓ ℓ

Legible handwriting can boost spelling scores by as much as 20%.

Solve the Analogies

1. illiterate
2. nonreturnable
3. irrational
4. mistrust
5. misinform
6. nonfat
7. illegal
8. antifreeze

Complete the Sentences

9. misfortune
10. nonprofit
11. misbehave
12. misplace
13. misread
14. misuse
15. mislead

Correct the Paragraph

16. irresistible
17. antisocial
18. illogical
19. irregular
20. illegible

124

Spelling and Reading

antifreeze	nonreturnable	misbehave	misfortune
irresistible	illiterate	misinform	irrational
nonprofit	antisocial	mistrust	illegible
misplace	misread	illogical	irregular
misuse	nonfat	illegal	mislead

Solve the Analogies Write a spelling word to complete each analogy.

1. **High** is to **low** as **literate** is to _____.
2. **Accept** is to **unacceptable** as **return** is to _____.
3. **Reasonable** is to **unreasonable** as **rational** is to _____.
4. **Enjoyment** is to **misery** as **confidence** is to _____.
5. **Include** is to **exclude** as **inform** is to _____.
6. **Little** is to **none** as **low fat** is to _____.
7. **Strong** is to **powerful** as **unlawful** is to _____.
8. **Summer** is to **coolant** as **winter** is to _____.

Complete the Sentences Write a spelling word to complete each sentence.

9. It took him five years to recover from his _____.
10. Our _____ organization holds an annual fundraiser.
11. I hope you will not _____ while I am gone.
12. Try not to _____ your book. We do not have any extras.
13. I got lost when I _____ a sign on the highway.
14. Some people tend to _____ a word if they have never seen or heard it used properly.
15. The angry neighbors thought we had tried to _____ them.

Correct the Paragraph Correct the paragraph by adding prefixes to the underlined words. Write the spelling words.

16.–20. Julian finds coin collecting an <u>resistible</u> pursuit. Some people say coin collectors are <u>social</u>, but Julian claims that this is <u>logical</u>. He often meets with others to compare the <u>regular</u> markings on old coins. Because some of the lettering is <u>legible</u>, he frequently consults experts.

MEETING INDIVIDUAL NEEDS

Providing More Challenge

Challenge Words and **Challenge Activities** for Unit 20 appear on page 240. **Challenge Word Test Sentences** appear on page T240.

Unit 20 Challenge Activities

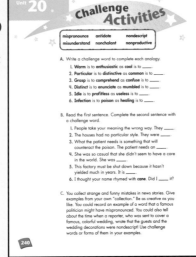

Weekly Test Options

Option 1:
One Spelling Word Per Sentence
(See procedures on pages Z10–Z11.)

★ 1. She thought her car might need **antifreeze**.
  2. He is very shy, but not **antisocial**.
★ 3. Keeping wild animals as pets is **illegal** in many states.
  4. The note he wrote was almost **illegible**.
★ 5. Many years ago most people were **illiterate**.
  6. His argument was quite **illogical**.
  7. That man has an **irrational** fear of cats.
★ 8. The shirt is marked **irregular** because it is damaged.
  9. The delicious food was **irresistible**.
★10. I will teach the new puppy not to **misbehave**.
★11. Her family has had much **misfortune** recently.
  12. He may **misinform** you about the assignment.
★13. A false clue was left to **mislead** the police.
  14. Sometimes a scientist must **mistrust** common sense.
  15. If you **misread** the directions, you won't get the answer

---

T124

Spelling and Writing

Proofread a Paragraph

Six words are not spelled correctly in this paragraph. Write the words correctly.

Proofreading Marks
- ≡ Make a capital.
- / Make a small letter.
- ∧ Add something.
- ℓ Take out something.
- ⊙ Add a period.
- ⌗ New paragraph
- SP Spelling error

> ‎   irregular
> Because stamps rarely come in irreguler shapes, they can be easily placed in special albums so collectors will not misplace them. Unused stamps are the most valuable, since the cancellation mark on a stamped envelope may
>   illegible
> make the stamp's words ilegible. If you buy old stamps in
>   nonreturnable   illegal
> a store, they are often nonreturnible. It is illegle to reuse
>   nonprofit
> a cancelled stamp; the U.S. Postal Service, a nonprofiit
> government-owned corporation, does not tolerate this
>   misuse
> missuse of stamps.

Write a Paragraph

Expository Writing

There are all kinds of hobbies. Some involve sports. Others, like stamp collecting, require research. Write a paragraph about a hobby.

- Describe a hobby that you have or would like to have. Tell why it is an interesting hobby.
- Follow the form used in the proofreading sample.

Use as many spelling words as you can.

Writing Process

Prewriting
⇩
Drafting
⇩
Revising
⇩
Editing
⇩
Publishing

Proofread Your Writing During Editing

Proofread your writing for spelling errors as part of the editing stage in the writing process. Be sure to check each word carefully. Use a dictionary to check spelling if you are not sure.

125

Objectives

Spelling and Writing
Students will
- **proofread** a paragraph.
- **use** the writing process to write a paragraph about a hobby.
- **proofread** their writing.

Using the Writing Process

Before assigning **Write a Paragraph,** see pages 258–259 in the Student Edition for a complete review of the writing process and additional writing assignments. You may also wish to refer to pages Z12–Z13 in the Teacher Edition.

Keeping a Spelling Journal

Encourage students to record the words they misspelled on the weekly test in a personal spelling journal. These words may be recycled for future study. Students may also wish to include words from their writing. See pages Z12–Z13 in the Teacher Edition for more information.

---

16. Did she **misplace** her books again?
17. If you **misuse** the tools, you may injure yourself.
★18. The doctor told him to drink only **nonfat** milk.
19. A church is a **nonprofit** organization.
★20. Anything you buy on sale is **nonreturnable**.

Option 2:
Multiple Spelling Words Per Sentence
(See procedures on pages Z10–Z11.)

1. It is **illogical** to remain **illiterate**.
2. If you **mislead** and **misinform** people, they will soon come to **mistrust** you.
3. This **antifreeze** is a **nonreturnable** item.
4. If you **misbehave**, it may lead you into **misfortune**.
5. It is easy to **misread** handwriting that is **illegible**.
6. This **irresistible** cake was made with **nonfat** milk.
7. The **nonprofit** group was accused of **illegal** activity.
8. Be careful not to **misuse** or **misplace** the tools.
9. The lawyer labeled him **antisocial** because he had acted in such an **irregular** and **irrational** way.

Option 3:
Standardized Test
(See *Teacher Resource Book,* Unit 20.)

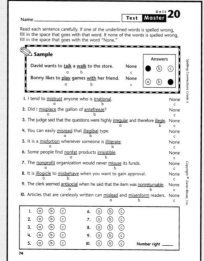

Unit 20 Test Master

T125

Objectives

Strategy Words

Students will
- **review** words studied previously that are related to the spelling strategy.
- **preview** unknown words that are related to the spelling strategy.

Optional Enrichment

VOCABULARY CONNECTIONS

► Strategy Words ◄

Remind the students that the **Strategy Words** are related to the spelling patterns they have studied in this unit. The **Review Words** are below grade level, and the **Preview Words** are above grade level. You may wish to use the following sentences to introduce the words in context.

Review Words:
Words From Grade 5

1. Before the Civil War, **antislavery** laws were passed in many northern states.
2. It is easy to **misjudge** others when we are not sure of all the facts.
3. The clerk was careful not to **miscalculate** the sales tax.
4. The book about Abraham Lincoln is **nonfiction**.
5. We believe that protests should be **nonviolent**.

Preview Words:
Words From Grade 7

6. These chemicals are **nontoxic** and therefore not dangerous.
7. China dishes are **nonconsumable**.
8. The jewelry seemed very **inexpensive**.
9. I was **mistaken** about his identity.
10. We solved our **misunderstanding**.

Review Words

1. (anti)slavery
2. (non)violent
3. (mis)calculate
4. (non)fiction
5. (mis)judge

Preview Words

6. misunderstanding
7. mistaken
8. nontoxic
9. nonconsumable
10. inexpensive

► Strategy Words ◄

Review Words: Prefixes ir-, anti-, il-, non-, mis-

Write the word from the box that completes each sentence. Circle the prefix in each word you write.

antislavery	misjudge	miscalculate
	nonfiction	nonviolent

1. Abolitionists were against slavery. They were ＿＿＿.
2. The protest must not be violent. It should be ＿＿＿.
3. We do not want to badly calculate this math problem. We do not want to ＿＿＿ it.
4. Biographies are not fiction. Because they are about real people, like Dr. Martin Luther King, Jr., they are ＿＿＿.
5. I do not want to judge him wrongly. Because he may be a nice person, I do not want to ＿＿＿ him.

Preview Words: Prefixes ir-, anti-, il-, non-, mis-

Add the correct prefix to each underlined word and write the new word. You will write words from the box.

nontoxic	nonconsumable	inexpensive
	mistaken	misunderstanding

6. I apologize for our <u>understanding</u>.
7. I had <u>taken</u> your meaning and was incorrect.
8. I thought the flowers were <u>toxic</u>.
9. You knew they were <u>consumable</u>.
10. We both knew, however, that they were <u>expensive</u>.

126

Unit 20 RECAP

You may wish to assign the **Unit 20 Homework Master** (*Teacher Resource Book,* Unit 20) as a fun way to recap the spelling words.

Unit 20 Homework Master

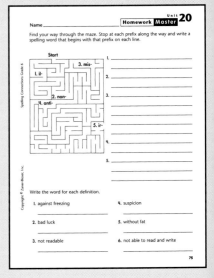

TI26

Objectives

Content Words

Students will
- **expand** vocabulary with content-related words.
- **relate** the spelling strategy to words outside the basic spelling list.
- **rearrange** some or all of the letters in a given word to spell other words.

Content Words

Social Studies: Insurance

Write words from the box to complete the paragraph.

| collect | policy | insure | provision | nonrenewal |

The job of an insurance agency is to __1.__ you in the event of accident or injury. The agency will __2.__ payments from you on a regular basis. This is a __3.__ of the written contract, or __4.__, that covers you against loss. Sometimes a __5.__ clause will be included to protect the insurance company against risk.

Language Arts: Usage

The underlined words in the sentences are examples of each term in the box. Write the words from the box that match the underlined words.

| appositive | modifier | grammar | tense | linking verb |

6. Jill, a sixth grader, will be twelve in April.
7. She laughed, laughs, will laugh all the way home.
8. He is feeling lighthearted today.
9. I only want advice. I want only advice.
10. all of the above

Apply the Spelling Strategy

Circle the prefix that means "not" in one of the Content Words you wrote.

Word Study

Find the Word

How many new words can you make from just one word? Quite a few! All of these words are made from letters in just one of the Content Words: **mode, dime, for, form, fire, dome, fried.** Write the Content Word.

Social Studies: Insurance
1. insure
2. collect
3. provision
4. policy
5. (non)renewal

Language Arts: Usage
6. appositive
7. tense
8. linking verb
9. modifier
10. grammar

Find the Word
1. modifier

127

Content Words

Social Studies: Insurance

Use these sentences to introduce the words and their meanings.

1. I was able to **collect** enough money from insurance to pay for the repairs on my car.
2. This **policy** is limited in the amount it will pay for an accident.
3. We will **insure** our home in case of wind damage.
4. A special **provision** was added to cover earthquakes.
5. I do not want health insurance that has a **nonrenewal** clause.

Language Arts: Usage

Use these sentences to introduce the words and their meanings.

6. An **appositive** renames something.
7. An adjective can be a **modifier** of a noun or pronoun.
8. We study **grammar** in order to communicate more effectively.
9. Use the past **tense** form of the verb to talk about the past.
10. A **linking verb** does not show action.

Word Study

Find the Word

Word games increase students' awareness of letters, syllables, and word parts within the words they are studying. Challenge students to rearrange letters in other words in the unit to see how many additional words they can find.

Unit 21 Home Spelling Practice

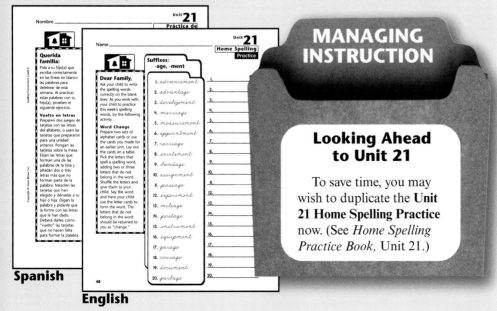

Spanish

English

MANAGING INSTRUCTION

Looking Ahead to Unit 21

To save time, you may wish to duplicate the **Unit 21 Home Spelling Practice** now. (See *Home Spelling Practice Book,* Unit 21.)

T127

Basic Spelling List

advancement	passage
advantage	experiment
development	mileage
marriage	postage
measurement	instrument
appointment	equipment
carriage	garage
excitement	courage
bandage	document
assignment	garbage

Strategy Words

Review

amusement	prepackage
employment	voyage
judgment	

Preview

acreage	encouragement
amazement	management
coverage	

Content Words

Math: Percentages

discount	portion
percentage	percent
interest rate	

Science: Atmosphere

nitrogen	environment
pollution	water vapor
carbon dioxide	

Individual Needs

Challenge Words

leverage	breakage
puzzlement	detriment
enrichment	compartment

Alternate Word List ★

development	equipment
marriage	garage
excitement	courage
experiment	document
mileage	garbage

★ For students who need to study fewer Basic Spelling words

MATERIALS

Student Edition
Pages 128–133
Challenge Activities, p. 241

Teacher Edition
Pages T128A–T133
Challenge Activities, p. T241

Teacher Resource Book
Unit 21 Homework Master
Unit 21 Practice Masters
Flip Folder Practice Master
Unit 21 Test Master

Home Spelling Practice Book
Unit 21 Home Spelling Practice
(English or Spanish)

Other *Spelling Connections* Resources
- Audiotape, Grade 6
- Practice Book for Grammar, Usage, and Mechanics, Grade 6
- Spelling Support for Second Language Learners, Grade 6
- Support Software on CD-ROM
- Transparency Book, Grade 6
- Word Sort CD-ROM, Grade 6

OBJECTIVES

Spelling and Thinking

Students will
- **read** the spelling words in list form and in context.
- **sort** the spelling words according to whether the suffix is added to a base word or a root word.
- **read** and remember this week's spelling strategy.

Spelling and Vocabulary

Students will
- **write** spelling words for clues.
- **write** spelling words that complete a series of meaning-related words.
- **use** guide words to locate spelling words in a dictionary.

Spelling and Reading

Students will
- **solve** analogies using spelling words.
- **complete** sentences using spelling words.
- **complete** a paragraph using spelling words.

Spelling and Writing

Students will
- **proofread** a paragraph.
- **use** the writing process to describe a job.
- **proofread** their writing.

MEETING INDIVIDUAL NEEDS
Learning Styles

 Visual

Write the suffixes of the spelling words on 3" × 5" cards (ten cards with **-age,** ten cards with **-ment**). Write each root and base word of the spelling words on separate 3" × 5" cards. Place the suffix cards on the chalk tray; place the remaining cards face-down on a desk. Ask each student in turn to choose a card with a root or base word and to place it beside a suffix card to form a spelling word. Have the student pronounce the word and write it on the chalkboard. Then have the rest of the students write the word at their desks.

 Auditory

Attach a spinner to a board that you have divided into two sections—one labeled **-age,** the other labeled **-ment**. Have the students take turns spinning. Give each student a spelling word that ends with a suffix identified by the spinner. Have that student pronounce the word, write it on the chalkboard, and spell it aloud. Have all the students write the word at their desks, saying it quietly to themselves. Continue until all of the students have had a turn with the spinner.

 Kinesthetic

Have the students play the game described in the auditory activity with this modification: As the student at the board spells the word aloud, have the other students trace each letter in the air with their fingertips.

> **Hands-On Practice**
> All students will benefit from practicing with a **Flip Folder**. See page Z18.

Language and Cultural Differences

Because the /ĭj/ sound combination does not exist in Spanish, Spanish-speaking students may have difficulty with words that end with this suffix. They may pronounce the suffix **-age** as /ch/ and therefore spell it **ch** as well. The /ĭ/ sound also does not exist in Spanish, which may make **experiment** difficult for some students to pronounce and spell. They may require extra help with the spelling words of this unit. Have them complete the activities for their dominant learning modalities.

MANAGING INSTRUCTION

3–5 Day Plan		Average	Below Average	Above Average
Day 1	**Day 1**	Pretest Spelling Mini-Lesson, p. T128 Spelling and Thinking, p. 128	Pretest Spelling Mini-Lesson, p. T128 Spelling and Thinking, p. 128	Pretest Spelling and Thinking, p. 128
	Day 2	Spelling and Vocabulary, p. 129	Spelling and Vocabulary, p. 129 (or) Unit 21 Practice Master, A and B	Spelling and Vocabulary, p. 129 Spelling and Reading, p. 130
Day 2	**Day 3**	Spelling and Reading, p. 130	Spelling and Reading, p. 130 (or) Unit 21 Practice Master, C and D	Challenge Activities, p. 241
	Day 4	Spelling and Writing, p. 131 Unit 21 Homework Master	Spelling and Writing, p. 131	Spelling and Writing, p. 131 Unit 21 Homework Master
Day 3	**Day 5**	Weekly Test	Weekly Test	Weekly Test
Vocabulary Connections (pages 132 and 133) may be used anytime during this unit.				

Objectives

Spelling and Thinking

Students will
- **read** the spelling words in list form and in context.
- **sort** the spelling words according to whether the suffix is added to a base word or a root word.
- **read** and remember this week's spelling strategy.

UNIT PRETEST

Use **Pretest Sentences** below. Refer to the self-checking procedures on student page 256. You may wish to use the **Unit 21 Word List Overhead Transparency** as part of the checking procedure.

TEACHING THE STRATEGY

Spelling Mini-Lesson

Write **bandage, mileage, advantage, advancement,** and **equipment** on the chalkboard. Ask volunteers to read the words and decide if each word is a noun, adjective, or verb. (**Each word is a noun.**)

Explain that the suffixes **-age** and **-ment** are added to base words and roots to form nouns. Read the rest of the words.

Explain the meaning of each suffix:
- **-age** means "collection," "relationship," or "condition";
- **-ment** adds the meaning "action" or "process" (or "the result of an action or process").

You may wish to discuss the ways in which the meanings of an individual suffix relate to the meanings of the words.

Review the difference between a base word and a root. A base word can stand alone as a word with its own meaning. A root does not stand alone in modern English; a root becomes an English word when a prefix or suffix is added. For example, **advantage** is derived from the Latin root **abante,** which means "from before." "To have an advantage" means "to be ahead" or "before" another.

Point out that **mileage** can be spelled either **mileage** or **milage**. The preferred spelling, **mileage,** is an exception to this spelling guideline: Drop final **e** before adding a suffix that begins with a vowel.

TI28

Order of answers may vary.

suffix added to base word

1. (advance)ment
2. (develop)ment ★
3. (measure)ment
4. (appoint)ment
5. (excite)ment ★
6. (band)age
7. (assign)ment
8. (pass)age
9. (mile)age ★
10. (post)age
11. (equip)ment ★

suffix added to root word

12. advantage
13. marriage ★
14. carriage
15. experiment ★
16. instrument
17. garage ★
18. courage ★
19. document ★
20. garbage ★

128

READ THE SPELLING WORDS

1. advancement	*advancement*	I hope to get a job **advancement**.
2. advantage	*advantage*	Studying is to your **advantage**.
3. development	*development*	What is the latest **development**?
4. marriage	*marriage*	Their **marriage** was a surprise.
5. measurement	*measurement*	His height **measurement** is six feet.
6. appointment	*appointment*	She has a doctor's **appointment**.
7. carriage	*carriage*	I pushed the baby's **carriage**.
8. excitement	*excitement*	Their victory caused **excitement**.
9. bandage	*bandage*	The **bandage** will protect that cut.
10. assignment	*assignment*	Your **assignment** is a book report.
11. passage	*passage*	A secret **passage** leads to the attic.
12. experiment	*experiment*	The **experiment** led to a discovery.
13. mileage	*mileage*	We kept track of the trip **mileage**.
14. postage	*postage*	Your package has enough **postage**.
15. instrument	*instrument*	He plays a musical **instrument**.
16. equipment	*equipment*	We set up our camera **equipment**.
17. garage	*garage*	The **garage** holds two cars.
18. courage	*courage*	That firefighter has great **courage**.
19. document	*document*	Ina's lawyer signed the **document**.
20. garbage	*garbage*	Please take out the **garbage**.

SORT THE SPELLING WORDS

1.–11. Write the spelling words that have the suffix **-age** or **-ment** added to a base word. Circle the base word.

12.–20. Write the spelling words that have the suffix **-age** or **-ment** added to a root word.

REMEMBER THE SPELLING STRATEGY

Remember that the suffixes **-age** and **-ment** can be added to root words and base words to form new words. These new words are nouns: **courage, equipment**.

Pretest Sentences (See procedures on pages Z10–Z11.)

1. The leader's goal was the **advancement** of liberty.
2. Kara's great speed gave her the **advantage** in the race.
★ 3. The **development** of ideas requires critical thinking skills.
★ 4. Their **marriage** certificate proves they are husband and wife.
5. Take the room's **measurement** before buying a rug.
6. Did you make an **appointment** to see the doctor?
7. Did you take the baby for a ride in the **carriage**?
★ 8. There is **excitement** about the upcoming basketball tournament.
9. When I accidentally cut my finger, I put a **bandage** on it.
10. The homework **assignment** was more difficult than we expected.
11. The workers built a tunnel-like **passage** through the mountain.
★12. What were the results of your science **experiment**?
★13. What is the **mileage** reading on Dad's car?
14. How much **postage** is required to mail this package?
15. Which **instrument** will you study, the piano or the violin?
★16. Our school's science lab contains expensive **equipment**.
★17. Our **garage** is large enough for two cars.
★18. The diver needed all of his **courage** to make the final dive.
★19. Your birth certificate is a very important **document**.
★20. I set the **garbage** out last night for pickup this morning.

Word Clues

Write a spelling word for each clue.

1. the collective term for **supplies**
2. the process of determining dimensions
3. the result of setting a time for a meeting
4. a means by which people are carried
5. the process of conducting a test
6. the collective term for **miles covered**
7. movement forward

Word Groups

Write a spelling word to complete each group of words.

8. letter, envelope, address, _____
9. bravery, valor, fearlessness, _____
10. certificate, license, diploma, _____
11. thrill, adventure, agitation, _____
12. peelings, trash, leftovers, _____
13. homework, chore, duty, _____
14. benefit, upper hand, asset, _____

USING THE Dictionary

Write the spelling words that you would find between these pairs of guide words.

15. industrious • interest rate
16. machinery • midway
17. output • patriotism
18. background • bleed
19. debug • development
20. flow chart • geologist

Word Clues
1. equipment
2. measurement
3. appointment
4. carriage
5. experiment
6. mileage
7. advancement

Word Groups
8. postage
9. courage
10. document
11. excitement
12. garbage
13. assignment
14. advantage

Using the Dictionary
15. instrument
16. marriage
17. passage
18. bandage
19. development
20. garage

129

Objectives

Spelling and Vocabulary

Students will
- **write** spelling words for clues.
- **write** spelling words that complete a series of meaning-related words.
- **use** guide words to locate spelling words in a dictionary.

Developing Oral Language Skills

Have students work in pairs. The first student asks a question that includes a spelling word with the **-age** suffix. For example, the student might ask, "Have you read this **passage** from our literature book?" The second student answers the question. The answer must also include a spelling word, but the spelling word must contain the **-ment** suffix. For example, the second student might answer, "I didn't know it was part of the **assignment**."

MEETING INDIVIDUAL NEEDS

Providing More Help

To aid students in understanding these suffixes, write **-age** and **-ment** as headings on the right side of the board and these roots and base words on the left side of the board: **post, develop, docu, measure, gar, assign, mile, excite, carry,** and **marry.** Have the students take turns writing each root or base word under the appropriate suffix heading. Then have them write the spelling word next to each root or base. Point out that in **marry** and **carry** the **y** is changed to **i** before the suffix is added.

★Students who need to study fewer words should use the **Alternate Word List**. This list is starred on page T128 in the Teacher Edition. The **Unit 21 Practice Masters** (*Teacher Resource Book*) provide additional practice with these words.

Unit 21 Practice Masters

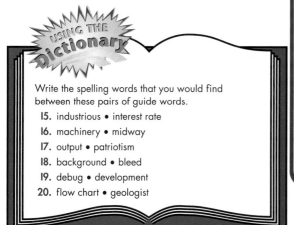

Objectives

Spelling and Reading

Students will
• **solve** analogies using spelling words.
• **complete** sentences using spelling words.
• **complete** a paragraph using spelling words.

One-Minute Handwriting Hint

The overcurve ending of the lowercase **g** crosses at the baseline, then quickly turns into a deep undercurve and loop to form the letter **e**.

CROSS AT BASELINE

Legible handwriting can boost spelling scores by as much as 20%.

Solve the Analogies

1. garage
2. experiment
3. instrument
4. advancement
5. postage

Complete the Sentences

6. carriage
7. passage
8. mileage
9. measurement
10. advantage
11. development
12. appointment
13. document

Complete the Paragraph

14. marriage
15. courage
16. garbage
17. equipment
18. assignment
19. bandage
20. excitement

Spelling and Reading

advancement	advantage	development	marriage
measurement	appointment	carriage	excitement
bandage	assignment	passage	experiment
mileage	postage	instrument	equipment
garage	courage	document	garbage

Solve the Analogies Write a spelling word to complete each analogy.

1. **Airplane** is to **hangar** as **car** is to _____.
2. **Surgeon** is to **operation** as **scientist** is to_____.
3. **Rake** is to **tool** as **violin** is to _____.
4. **Indecision** is to **certainty** as **retreat** is to _____.
5. **Supermarket** is to **groceries** as **post office** is to _____.

Complete the Sentences Write a spelling word to complete each sentence.

6. The young mother pushed the baby _____ down the street.
7. I would like to read you a _____ from this book.
8. We should check the car _____ before we start on our trip.
9. The tailor took a final _____ before hemming the skirt.
10. You should take _____ of the wonderful sale.
11. The parents were pleased with the baby's _____.
12. I am afraid I will be late for my dentist _____.
13. The lawyer asked me to sign the legal _____.

Complete the Paragraph Write spelling words from the box to complete the paragraph.

During their first year of __14.__, the Fischers bought an old horse farm. When Alex got up enough __15.__ to ask for a part-time job, they hired her. She cleaned all the __16.__ and broken __17.__ out of the old barn. Her major __18.__ was to groom the horses. She even had to change the __19.__ on a lame horse. Alex loved the __20.__ of being around horses.

excitement
garbage
assignment
marriage
courage
bandage
equipment

130

MEETING INDIVIDUAL NEEDS

Providing More Challenge

Challenge Words and **Challenge Activities** for Unit 21 appear on page 241. **Challenge Word Test Sentences** appear on page T241.

Unit 21 Challenge Activities

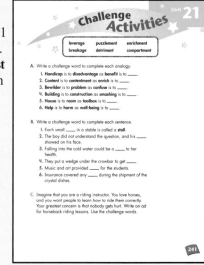

Weekly Test Options

Option 1:
One Spelling Word Per Sentence
(See procedures on pages Z10–Z11.)

1. Hard work helped in the **advancement** of her career.
2. What is the **advantage** of the choice you made?
3. My **appointment** with the dentist has been canceled.
4. This **assignment** will take a week to complete.
5. Put a **bandage** on that bad cut.
★ 6. The circus act required great **courage**.
★ 7. The scientist will study the **development** of tadpoles.
★ 8. Show the officer the **document**.
★ 9. Is this the correct **equipment** for the job?
★10. The crowd showed little **excitement** during the game.
★11. She likes to **experiment** when she cooks.
★12. Drive the car into the **garage**.
★13. Did you remember to put out the **garbage** today?
14. The piano is my favorite **instrument**.
★15. Their **marriage** has lasted more than fifty years.

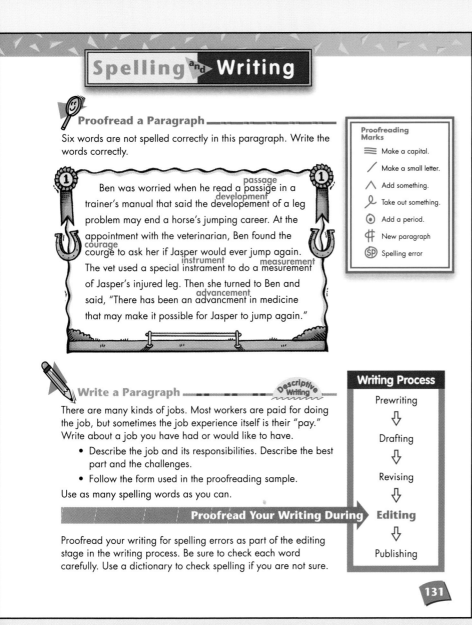

Spelling and Writing

Proofread a Paragraph

Six words are not spelled correctly in this paragraph. Write the words correctly.

> Ben was worried when he read a passige [passage] in a trainer's manual that said the developement [development] of a leg problem may end a horse's jumping career. At the appointment with the veterinarian, Ben found the courge [courage] to ask her if Jasper would ever jump again. The vet used a special instrament [instrument] to do a mesurement [measurement] of Jasper's injured leg. Then she turned to Ben and said, "There has been an advancment [advancement] in medicine that may make it possible for Jasper to jump again."

Proofreading Marks

- Make a capital.
- Make a small letter.
- Add something.
- Take out something.
- Add a period.
- New paragraph
- Spelling error

Write a Paragraph

Descriptive Writing

There are many kinds of jobs. Most workers are paid for doing the job, but sometimes the job experience itself is their "pay." Write about a job you have had or would like to have.

- Describe the job and its responsibilities. Describe the best part and the challenges.
- Follow the form used in the proofreading sample.

Use as many spelling words as you can.

Writing Process

Prewriting → Drafting → Revising → Editing → Publishing

Proofread Your Writing During Editing

Proofread your writing for spelling errors as part of the editing stage in the writing process. Be sure to check each word carefully. Use a dictionary to check spelling if you are not sure.

131

Objectives

Spelling and Writing

Students will
- **proofread** a paragraph.
- **use** the writing process to describe a job.
- **proofread** their writing.

Using the Writing Process

Before assigning **Write a Paragraph,** see pages 258–259 in the Student Edition for a complete review of the writing process and additional writing assignments. You may also wish to refer to pages Z12–Z13 in the Teacher Edition.

Keeping a Spelling Journal

Encourage students to record the words they misspelled on the weekly test in a personal spelling journal. These words may be recycled for future study. Students may also wish to include words from their writing. See pages Z12–Z13 in the Teacher Edition for more information.

16. What is the **measurement** of that picture frame?
17. The ancient **carriage** was drawn by two horses.
★18. What is the actual **mileage** of that car?
19. The calm water made our **passage** safe.
20. Put a **postage** stamp on the envelope, please.

Option 2:
Multiple Spelling Words Per Sentence

(See procedures on pages Z10–Z11.)

1. Dad keeps his **equipment** in the **garage**.
2. Is this enough **postage** to mail the **document**?
3. The **development** of **courage** is part of growing up.
4. The coming **marriage** created **excitement** in the family.
5. What is the **measurement** of the **carriage** wheels?
6. One **advantage** of this car is the great **mileage** it gets.
7. She cut her hand during the **experiment** and asked for a **bandage**.
8. Your **assignment** is to practice your musical **instrument**.
9. Mom made an **appointment** with the **garbage** company to pick up the old sofa.
10. This **passage** is about the **advancement** of science.

Option 3:
Standardized Test

(See *Teacher Resource Book,* Unit 21.)

Unit 21 Test Master

Name ____________ Test Master Unit 21

Read each sentence carefully. If one of the underlined words is spelled wrong, fill in the space that goes with that word. If none of the words is spelled wrong, fill in the space that goes with the word "None."

Sample
- David wants to taik (a) a walk (b) to the store. None (c) — Answers: ● ⓑ ⓒ
- Bonny likes to play (a) games with (b) her friend. None (c) — Answers: ⓐ ⓑ ●

1. A marrage (a) certificate is a legal document (b). None (c)
2. What is the advantage (a) of performing this experament (b)? None (c)
3. Throw that old bandage (a) in the garbige (b). None (c)
4. A ruler is an instrument (a) of measurement (b). None (c)
5. The baby's carrige (a) was stored in the garage (b). None (c)
6. Her appointment (a) to the new position is a major advancment (b). None (c)
7. The assignment (a) created a stir of excitement (b) in class. None (c)
8. The developement (a) of courage (b) is something we all admire. None (c)
9. Is there enough postage (a) on the package of equipment (b)? None (c)
10. What is the total milaege (a) of this narrow passage (b)? None (c)

1.	ⓐ	ⓑ	ⓒ	6.	ⓐ	ⓑ	ⓒ
2.	ⓐ	ⓑ	ⓒ	7.	ⓐ	ⓑ	ⓒ
3.	ⓐ	ⓑ	ⓒ	8.	ⓐ	ⓑ	ⓒ
4.	ⓐ	ⓑ	ⓒ	9.	ⓐ	ⓑ	ⓒ
5.	ⓐ	ⓑ	ⓒ	10.	ⓐ	ⓑ	ⓒ

Number right ____

78

Spelling Connections Grade 6

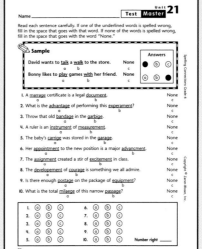

Objectives

Strategy Words

Students will
- **review** words studied previously that are related to the spelling strategy.
- **preview** unknown words that are related to the spelling strategy.

Optional Enrichment

Unit 21 enrichment

VOCABULARY CONNECTIONS

Strategy Words

Remind the students that the **Strategy Words** are related to the spelling patterns they have studied in this unit. The **Review Words** are below grade level, and the **Preview Words** are above grade level. You may wish to use the following sentences to introduce the words in context.

Review Words:
Words From Grade 5
1. The clown performed for our **amusement**.
2. We asked for **employment** at the grocery store.
3. It is my **judgment** that we need to proceed cautiously.
4. Will they **prepackage** the equipment before it is delivered?
5. The students asked about the **voyage** of Christopher Columbus.

Preview Words:
Words From Grade 7
6. We asked about the **acreage** of the park.
7. The children's eyes were wide in **amazement**.
8. This channel provides good news **coverage**.
9. Without my **encouragement** he never would have finished the job.
10. He was seeking a position in **management**.

Review Words
1. amusement
2. judgment
3. prepackage
4. voyage
5. employment

Preview Words
6. coverage
7. amazement
8. acreage
9. management
10. encouragement

Strategy Words

Review Words: Suffixes -age, -ment

Write words from the box to complete this advertisement.

amusement	employment	judgment
	prepackage	voyage

Looking for a vacation that offers a lot of excitement and __1.__? Come to Wendall Island. In our __2.__, this is the best vacation spot for the entire family. We will even __3.__ your entire trip so that your stay will be paid for before you arrive. Included in the package is a five-day __4.__ on a clipper ship. We have __5.__ opportunities available, too.

Preview Words: Suffixes -age, -ment

Write words from the box to complete the paragraph.

acreage	amazement	coverage
encouragement	management	

The governor watched the television __6.__ of the forest fire with shock and __7.__. He had no idea that the fire had destroyed so much __8.__. He was pleased to learn about the effective __9.__ of the fire so that it would not spread farther. He immediately placed a call to fire-fighting headquarters to add his words of __10.__.

132

Unit 21 RECAP

You may wish to assign the **Unit 21 Homework Master** (*Teacher Resource Book,* Unit 21) as a fun way to recap the spelling words.

Unit 21 Homework Master

Name _____   Homework **Master** Unit 21

Read each question. Unscramble the spelling words and write them. Then answer each question by circling **Yes** or **No.**

1. Does mail need **tospeag**? _____ Yes No
2. Do you sleep on **brageag**? _____ Yes No
3. Can a car be kept in the **ragage**? _____ Yes No
4. Do astronauts have **rugoace**? _____ Yes No
5. Would you use a dirty **degnaba**? _____ Yes No
6. Can a **sagsape** be called a trip? _____ Yes No

Add and subtract letters to form your spelling words. Write each word.

1. expert – t + immediate – mediate + ent = _____
2. add – d + dvan – d + t + age = _____
3. meant – nt + ls – l + pure – p + ment = _____
4. appear – ear + oi + nbt – b + ment = _____
5. expert – pert + cfit – f + em + ent = _____
6. assist – st + lgn – l + ment = _____

Circle the seven spelling words hidden around the track. In the center of the track, write the one spelling word that means "growth."

79

TI32

◢Content Words◣

Math: Percentages

Write words from the box to complete this advertisement.

discount	percentage	interest rate
	portion	percent

Adco Mortgage Company has just lowered its __1.__ from eight to seven __2.__. You will not find this low a __3.__ rate anywhere else. We will even pay a __4.__ of your closing costs. We also offer a __5.__ for first-time home buyers.

Science: Atmosphere

Write the words from the box that complete the paragraph.

nitrogen	pollution	carbon dioxide
	environment	water vapor

The effects of __6.__ can be seen in our __7.__. The automobile engine is a major cause of this problem in cities. Earth's atmosphere is made up of oxygen, __8.__, and __9.__. When car fumes mix with __10.__, the balance of these elements is upset, producing acid rain.

Apply the Spelling Strategy

Circle the suffixes **-age** and **-ment** in two of the Content Words you wrote.

◢Word Study◣

Word History

This Strategy Word probably came from a very old word, **viage,** which meant "a traveling" or "a journey." Write the Strategy Word.

133

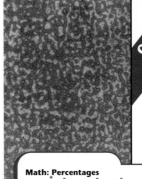

Math: Percentages
1. **interest rate**
2. **percent**
3. **percent(age)**
4. **portion**
5. **discount**

Science: Atmosphere
6. **pollution**
7. **environ(ment)**
8. **nitrogen** or
9. **carbon dioxide**
10. **water vapor**

Word History
1. **voyage**

Optional Enrichment

Objectives

Content Words

Students will
- **expand** vocabulary with content-related words.
- **relate** the spelling strategy to words outside the basic spelling list.
- **understand** the history of the word **voyage**.

◢Content Words◣

Math: Percentages

Use these sentences to introduce the words and their meanings.

1. The store will **discount** the merchandise because it is damaged.
2. We asked what **percentage** of the loan should be repaid now.
3. The **interest rate** can vary from month to month at banks.
4. What **portion** of the loan has he repaid?
5. She hopes to earn at least seven **percent** interest on her savings.

Science: Atmosphere

Use these sentences to introduce the words and their meanings.

6. Dad asked if **nitrogen** should be added to the soil in our garden.
7. **Pollution** is a major concern.
8. Plants need **carbon dioxide**.
9. Industry has not always worked to protect the **environment**.
10. **Water vapor** escaped from the pan on the stove.

◢Word Study◣

Word History

Remind students that a word history, or **etymology,** traces the origin of a word and the development of its meaning. Etymologies are shown after the entry word in most dictionaries.

Unit 22 Home Spelling Practice

Spanish

English

MANAGING INSTRUCTION

Looking Ahead to Unit 22

To save time, you may wish to duplicate the **Unit 22 Home Spelling Practice** now. (See *Home Spelling Practice Book,* Unit 22.)

Suffixes: -ful, -less, -some

1. successful
2. thoughtless
3. wholesome
4. wonderful
5. worthless
6. worrisome
7. delightful
8. lonesome
9. priceless
10. fanciful
11. eventful
12. fruitless
13. forgetful
14. senseless
15. doubtful
16. tiresome
17. tireless
18. dutiful
19. fearless
20. pitiful

Dear Family,
Ask your child to write the spelling words correctly on the blank lines. As you work with your child to practice this week's spelling words, try the following activity.

More Work for a Mechanic Prepare a pair of index cards for each spelling word. On one card write the base word and on the other write the suffix (**-ful, -less, -some**) that is attached to it. Shuffle the cards and put them in a box. Have your child draw two cards and decide whether they form a spelling word. If they do, have your child write the word and circle the two word parts. The object of the game is to form all the spelling words.

Querida familia:
Pida a su hijo(a) que escriba correctamente en las líneas en blanco las palabras para deletrear de esta semana. Al practicar estas palabras con su hijo(a), prueben el siguiente ejercicio.

Más trabajo para un mecánico Preparen un par de tarjetas con cada una de las palabras de las listas. En una de las tarjetas, escriban la palabra primitiva y en la otra, escriban el sufijo (**-ful, -less, -some**) que está unido a ella. Mezclen las tarjetas y póngalas en una caja. Pídanle a su hijo o hija que saque dos tarjetas y decida si al unirlas forman o no una palabra. Si forman una palabra, pídanle que la escriba y que encierre en un círculo cada una de las partes. El objetivo del juego es formar todas las palabras de la lista.

T133

Basic Spelling List

successful	eventful
thoughtless	fruitless
wholesome	forgetful
wonderful	senseless
worthless	doubtful
worrisome	tiresome
delightful	tireless
lonesome	dutiful
priceless	fearless
fanciful	pitiful

Strategy Words

Review

awful	handsome
beauty(ful)	homeless
delight(ful)	

Preview

distasteful	thoughtlessness
fearlessness	regardless
adventuresome	

Content Words

Fine Arts: Crafts

ceramics	glaze
kiln	pottery
pewter	

Science: Astronomy

astronomy	stellar
nebula	galaxy
constellation	

Individual Needs

Challenge Words

faithful	blameless
forceful	countless
troublesome	speechless

Alternate Word List ★

successful	delightful
thoughtless	lonesome
wholesome	doubtful
wonderful	fearless
worthless	pitiful

★ For students who need to study fewer Basic Spelling words

MATERIALS

Student Edition
Pages 134–139
Challenge Activities, p. 242

Teacher Edition
Pages T134A–T139
Challenge Activities, p. T242

Teacher Resource Book
Unit 22 Homework Master
Unit 22 Practice Masters
Flip Folder Practice Master
Unit 22 Test Master

Home Spelling Practice Book
Unit 22 Home Spelling Practice (English or Spanish)

Other *Spelling Connections* Resources
- Audiotape, Grade 6
- Practice Book for Grammar, Usage, and Mechanics, Grade 6
- Spelling Support for Second Language Learners, Grade 6
- Support Software on CD-ROM
- Transparency Book, Grade 6
- Word Sort CD-ROM, Grade 6

OBJECTIVES

Spelling and Thinking

Students will
- **read** the spelling words in list form and in context.
- **sort** the spelling words according to the suffixes **-ful, -less,** and **-some**.
- **read** and remember this week's spelling strategy.

Spelling and Vocabulary

Students will
- **add** suffixes to base words to form spelling words.
- **write** spelling words for given words with the same or nearly the same meaning.
- **use** the **Writing Thesaurus** to find synonyms for spelling words.

Spelling and Reading

Students will
- **solve** analogies using spelling words.
- **complete** sentences using spelling words.

Spelling and Writing

Students will
- **proofread** a paragraph.
- **use** the writing process to write a paragraph about owning a pet.
- **proofread** their writing.

MEETING INDIVIDUAL NEEDS
Learning Styles

 Visual

Create a word puzzle to be played individually or in groups. Write each spelling word on a 3" × 5" card. Cut each card between the base word and the suffix, using a different type of cut for each card (for example, zigzag, arc). Mix the word cards and place them facedown on a desk. Have the students match the cards to form each spelling word. Then have the students pronounce the word and write it.

 Auditory

Use the puzzle in the visual activity with these alterations: Have the students pronounce each word as they match the cards. Have them point to another student, who then spells the word aloud. After all the words have been matched, have the students look at each word, pronounce it, and write it as they spell the word softly to themselves.

 Kinesthetic

Use the puzzle cards described in the visual activity. Randomly distribute the cards to the students so that each student has a card that shows only half of a spelling word. Have the students open their books to page 134 to see which spelling words contain the word part on their cards. Have them write the spelling words. Then have them look at each other's cards and match them to form all of the spelling words.

Hands-On Practice
All students will benefit from practicing with a **Flip Folder**. See page Z18.

Language and Cultural Differences

Spanish-speaking students may have difficulty pronouncing and spelling the suffix **-ful,** since the /əl/ sound does not exist in the Spanish language. Explain to the students that nine of the spelling words listed end in the suffix **-ful**. Write the suffix on the chalkboard and have the students pronounce it after you write it. Ask the students to provide the base words that go with this suffix and write them on the chalkboard. Add the suffix to each base word and ask the students to pronounce the spelling word. Repeat this activity with all of the spelling words that end in the suffix **-ful**.

MANAGING INSTRUCTION

3–5 Day Plan		Average	Below Average	Above Average
Day 1	**Day 1**	Pretest Spelling Mini-Lesson, p. T134 Spelling and Thinking, p. 134	Pretest Spelling Mini-Lesson, p. T134 Spelling and Thinking, p. 134	Pretest Spelling and Thinking, p. 134
	Day 2	Spelling and Vocabulary, p. 135	Spelling and Vocabulary, p. 135 (or) Unit 22 Practice Master, A and B	Spelling and Vocabulary, p. 135 Spelling and Reading, p. 136
Day 2	**Day 3**	Spelling and Reading, p. 136	Spelling and Reading, p. 136 (or) Unit 22 Practice Master, C and D	Challenge Activities, p. 242
	Day 4	Spelling and Writing, p. 137 Unit 22 Homework Master	Spelling and Writing, p. 137	Spelling and Writing, p. 137 Unit 22 Homework Master
Day 3	**Day 5**	Weekly Test	Weekly Test	Weekly Test
Vocabulary Connections (pages 138 and 139) may be used anytime during this unit.				

Objectives

Spelling and Thinking

Students will
- **read** the spelling words in list form and in context.
- **sort** the spelling words according to the suffixes **-ful, -less,** and **-some**.
- **read** and remember this week's spelling strategy.

UNIT PRETEST

Use **Pretest Sentences** below. Refer to the self-checking procedures on student page 256. You may wish to use the **Unit 22 Word List Overhead Transparency** as part of the checking procedure.

TEACHING THE STRATEGY

Spelling Mini-Lesson

Write these sentences on the board:

- We had a **delightful** time!
- The **fearless** dog rescued the child.
- The **tiresome** TV show tired me out.

Draw students' attention to **delightful, fearless,** and **tiresome**. Ask them to read the sentences and decide which part of speech each underlined word is in that sentence. (adjective) Ask them to identify the base word in each underlined word. (delight, fear, tire) Explain that when one of these suffixes— **-ful, -less,** and **-some**—is added to a base word, the new word is not the same part of speech as the original word. The original words are usually nouns or verbs.

Ask them if the spelling of these base words changed when the suffix was added. (no) Write **priceless, tireless, senseless, lonesome,** and **wholesome** on the board. Ask them if the spelling of these base words changed when the suffix was added. (no) Ask the students why final **e** was retained. (Each suffix begins with a consonant.)

Write **dutiful, pitiful, fanciful,** and **worrisome** on the board. Ask volunteers to read these words and to identify the base word in each of these spelling words. (duty, pity, fancy, worry) Ask them how the spelling of the base word changed when each suffix was added. (Final y was changed to i before the suffix was added.)

TI34

Unit 22
Suffixes: -ful, -less, -some

Spelling and Thinking

Order of answers may vary.

-ful
1. successful ★
2. wonderful ★
3. delightful ★
4. fanciful
5. eventful
6. forgetful
7. doubtful ★
8. dutiful
9. pitiful ★

-less
10. thoughtless ★
11. worthless ★
12. priceless
13. fruitless
14. senseless
15. tireless
16. fearless ★

-some
17. wholesome ★
18. worrisome
19. lonesome ★
20. tiresome

READ THE SPELLING WORDS

1. successful	successful	She is a **successful** and skilled artist.
2. thoughtless	thoughtless	I apologized for being **thoughtless**.
3. wholesome	wholesome	Eat a **wholesome** breakfast daily.
4. wonderful	wonderful	We had a **wonderful** vacation.
5. worthless	worthless	Throw out this **worthless** item.
6. worrisome	worrisome	It is **worrisome** that he is so late.
7. delightful	delightful	The warm weather was **delightful**.
8. lonesome	lonesome	He was **lonesome** without his family.
9. priceless	priceless	Your friendship is **priceless** to me.
10. fanciful	fanciful	The child made **fanciful** drawings.
11. eventful	eventful	The weekend was busy and **eventful**.
12. fruitless	fruitless	Our search for the ring was **fruitless**.
13. forgetful	forgetful	Were you always so **forgetful**?
14. senseless	senseless	That joke was cruel and **senseless**.
15. doubtful	doubtful	It is **doubtful** that I will be there.
16. tiresome	tiresome	To recopy his work was **tiresome**.
17. tireless	tireless	She is a **tireless** worker.
18. dutiful	dutiful	He is a **dutiful** parent.
19. fearless	fearless	She performed a **fearless** rescue.
20. pitiful	pitiful	The injured bird was a **pitiful** sight.

SORT THE SPELLING WORDS

1.–9. Write the spelling words that have the suffix **-ful**.
10.–16. Write the spelling words that have the suffix **-less**.
17.–20. Write the spelling words that have the suffix **-some**.

REMEMBER THE SPELLING STRATEGY

Remember that the suffixes **-ful, -less,** and **-some** can be added to base words to form adjectives such as **wonderful, priceless,** and **worrisome**.

Pretest Sentences (See procedures on pages Z10–Z11.)

★ 1. Be confident and work hard if you wish to be **successful**.
★ 2. Although he is usually considerate, his recent actions have been **thoughtless**.
★ 3. Some **wholesome** foods are really delicious.
★ 4. The party was so **wonderful** that everyone raved about it.
★ 5. Years ago, people thought that paper money was **worthless**.
6. The patient's condition was **worrisome** to his family.
★ 7. The fireworks made the celebration especially **delightful**.
★ 8. He is **lonesome** when his friends are away.
9. A **priceless** painting was given to the museum.
10. Many of the costumes at the party were very **fanciful**.
11. We had an **eventful** vacation, but it is nice to be home.
12. Noriko's efforts to solve the problem were **fruitless**.
13. He is **forgetful** and often cannot remember where he put his keys.
14. Television comedy shows sometimes seem **senseless**.
★15. It is **doubtful** that she will arrive on time since she is often late.
16. One senator spoke for so long that his remarks became **tiresome**.
17. Her **tireless** efforts helped to make the party a success.
18. The **dutiful** nurse took very good care of his patients.
★19. The sergeant was **fearless** as he led his troops into battle.
★20. The dog looked so **pitiful** with its paw bandaged.

Spelling and Vocabulary

Word Clues

Use the clues to write spelling words by adding a suffix to the underlined words. You may have to change the spelling of the base word before adding the suffix.

1. full of pity
2. without worth
3. full of fancy
4. full of success
5. inclined to worry
6. full of delight
7. full of doubt
8. inclined to forget
9. full of duty

Word Meanings

Write the spelling word that could best replace the underlined word or words.

10. He prepared a delicious and healthy meal.
11. She thanked them for their never-ending efforts.
12. They showed their guests their invaluable art collection.
13. The day was filled with important happenings.
14. Several people fell asleep during the boring speech.
15. Our search for the missing papers was unsuccessful.

USING THE Thesaurus

Write a spelling word that is a synonym for each series of words.

16. meaningless, pointless, foolish
17. spectacular, superb, fabulous
18. lonely, forlorn, desolate
19. courageous, brave, bold
20. tactless, unthinking, careless

Word Clues
1. pitiful
2. worthless
3. fanciful
4. successful
5. worrisome
6. delightful
7. doubtful
8. forgetful
9. dutiful

Word Meanings
10. wholesome
11. tireless
12. priceless
13. eventful
14. tiresome
15. fruitless

Using the Thesaurus
16. senseless
17. wonderful
18. lonesome
19. fearless
20. thoughtless

135

Developing Oral Language Skills

Do a word sort by sound. Write the suffixes **-ful, -less,** and **-some** on the chalkboard or overhead. Then have a student read the spelling word list aloud, asking students to place each word under one of the headings according to the suffix they hear. When they have finished listing the words, ask students to consider the letters in each word that spells the suffix. Then have volunteers come to the board, say the words, and circle the suffixes.

MEETING INDIVIDUAL NEEDS

Providing More Help

To aid the students in understanding the suffixes **-ful, -less,** and **-some,** play the following game. Divide the class into three groups, giving each group a suffix. Have the students in each group identify and write all of the spelling words that contain their suffix. Tell the students within a group to exchange papers and check each other's spelling. Have the groups switch suffixes twice until all of the students have written all of the spelling words.

★Students who need to study fewer words should use the **Alternate Word List**. This list is starred on page T134 in the Teacher Edition. The **Unit 22 Practice Masters** (*Teacher Resource Book*) provide additional practice with these words.

Unit 22 Practice Masters

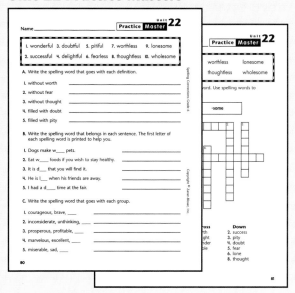

Spelling and Reading

Students will
- **solve** analogies using spelling words.
- **complete** sentences using spelling words.

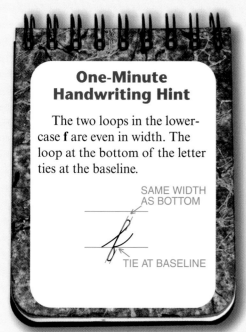

One-Minute Handwriting Hint

The two loops in the lower-case **f** are even in width. The loop at the bottom of the letter ties at the baseline.

SAME WIDTH AS BOTTOM

TIE AT BASELINE

Legible handwriting can boost spelling scores by as much as 20%.

Solve the Analogies

1. fanciful
2. priceless
3. wonderful
4. fruitless
5. doubtful
6. tireless
7. senseless
8. thoughtless
9. dutiful
10. delightful

Complete the Sentences

11. worthless
12. successful
13. tiresome
14. forgetful
15. eventful
16. pitiful
17. worrisome
18. fearless
19. lonesome
20. wholesome

Spelling and Reading

successful	thoughtless	wholesome	wonderful
worthless	worrisome	delightful	lonesome
priceless	fanciful	eventful	fruitless
forgetful	senseless	doubtful	tiresome
tireless	dutiful	fearless	pitiful

Solve the Analogies Write a spelling word to complete each analogy.

1. **Agreeable** is to **pleasant** as **imaginative** is to _____.
2. **Lively** is to **inactive** as **worthless** is to _____.
3. **Hope** is to **hopeful** as **wonder** is to _____.
4. **Careful** is to **careless** as **fruitful** is to _____.
5. **Generous** is to **greedy** as **certain** is to _____.
6. **Inaccurate** is to **incorrect** as **industrious** is to _____.
7. **Meaningful** is to **meaningless** as **sensible** is to _____.
8. **Awkward** is to **graceful** as **considerate** is to _____.
9. **Lazy** is to **energetic** as **disobedient** is to _____.
10. **Beauty** is to **beautiful** as **delight** is to _____.

Complete the Sentences Write the spelling word to complete each sentence.

11. I am sorry to say that your broken clock is now _____.
12. Frank Lloyd Wright was a _____ architect.
13. Answering the phone all day was boring and _____.
14. If I were not so _____, I would not have misplaced my lunch.
15. We will keep busy during this very _____ weekend.
16. How _____ our garden looked after the storm.
17. Her illness made for a _____ situation.
18. The lion tamer seemed _____ as he entered the cage.
19. With everyone gone, she spent the _____ evening reading.
20. Everyone benefits from a _____ diet.

136

MEETING INDIVIDUAL NEEDS

Providing More Challenge

Challenge Words and **Challenge Activities** for Unit 22 appear on page 242. **Challenge Word Test Sentences** appear on page T242.

Unit 22 Challenge Activities

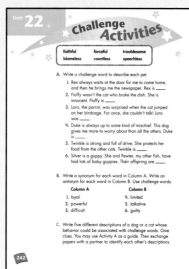

Weekly Test Options

Option 1:
One Spelling Word Per Sentence
(See procedures on pages Z12–Z13.)

★ 1. I had a **delightful** time at the festival.
★ 2. It is **doubtful** that we will arrive on time.
  3. The **dutiful** soldier obeyed his orders.
  4. The speaker planned an **eventful** program for the audience.
  5. Many children enjoy **fanciful** tales and legends.
★ 6. The **fearless** tiger stalked the larger animal.
  7. He is so **forgetful** that he often loses things.
  8. Our efforts to help were **fruitless.**
★ 9. The sad song was about a **lonesome** cowboy.
★10. The tired dog was a **pitiful** sight.
  11. The thief planned to steal the **priceless** jewels.
  12. It is **senseless** to worry about events that may never happen.
★13. The pilot made a **successful** landing in terrible weather.
★14. It was **thoughtless** of you to hurt her feelings.
  15. He was **tireless** in his effort to achieve his goal.
  16. Waiting for my brother to finish shopping is **tiresome.**

T136

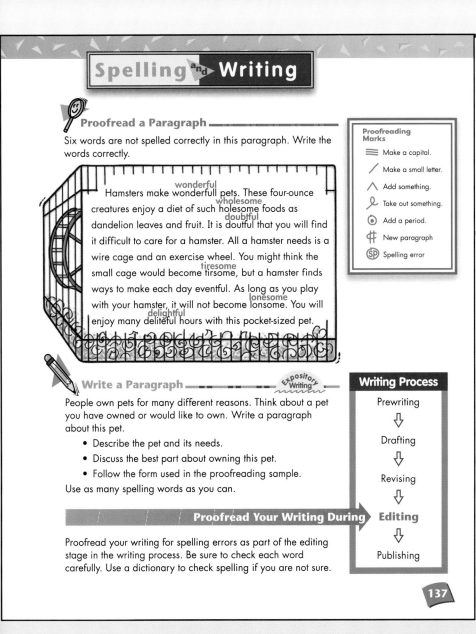

Spelling and Writing

Proofread a Paragraph

Six words are not spelled correctly in this paragraph. Write the words correctly.

wonderful

Hamsters make wonderfull pets. These four-ounce creatures enjoy a diet of such holesome foods as dandelion leaves and fruit. It is doutful that you will find it difficult to care for a hamster. All a hamster needs is a wire cage and an exercise wheel. You might think the small cage would become tirsome, but a hamster finds ways to make each day eventful. As long as you play with your hamster, it will not become lonsome. You will enjoy many deliteful hours with this pocket-sized pet.

wholesome
doubtful
tiresome
lonesome
delightful

Proofreading Marks

≡ Make a capital.
/ Make a small letter.
∧ Add something.
ℰ Take out something.
⊙ Add a period.
⌗ New paragraph.
(SP) Spelling error

Write a Paragraph

Expository Writing

People own pets for many different reasons. Think about a pet you have owned or would like to own. Write a paragraph about this pet.

- Describe the pet and its needs.
- Discuss the best part about owning this pet.
- Follow the form used in the proofreading sample.

Use as many spelling words as you can.

Writing Process

Prewriting
⇩
Drafting
⇩
Revising
⇩
Editing
⇩
Publishing

Proofread Your Writing During → Editing

Proofread your writing for spelling errors as part of the editing stage in the writing process. Be sure to check each word carefully. Use a dictionary to check spelling if you are not sure.

137

Objectives

Spelling and Writing

Students will
- **proofread** a paragraph.
- **use** the writing process to write a paragraph about owning a pet.
- **proofread** their writing.

Using the Writing Process

Before assigning **Write a Paragraph,** see pages 258–259 in the Student Edition for a complete review of the writing process and additional writing assignments. You may also wish to refer to pages Z12–Z13 in the Teacher Edition.

Keeping a Spelling Journal

Encourage students to record the words they misspelled on the weekly test in a personal spelling journal. These words may be recycled for future study. Students may also wish to include words from their writing. See pages Z12–Z13 in the Teacher Edition for more information.

★17. Eat **wholesome** foods if you wish to stay healthy.
★18. The story told of a **wonderful** adventure.
19. The mean dog was **worrisome** to the neighbors.
★20. This document is **worthless** without your signature.

Option 2:
Multiple Spelling Words Per Sentence

(See procedures on pages Z10–Z11.)

1. She was so **lonesome** that it was **pitiful** to see.
2. This item is **fanciful** and **delightful** but **worthless** in terms of money.
3. He is often **forgetful** and at times even **thoughtless**.
4. It is **doubtful** that anyone eats a more **wholesome** diet than you do.
5. Her **tireless** efforts made the day **eventful** and **successful**.
6. Her parents find it **worrisome** that she is not more **dutiful**.
7. This **wonderful** jewel is **priceless**.
8. He is **fearless,** and never does **senseless** things.
9. Time spent in **fruitless** activity is **tiresome**.

Option 3:
Standardized Test

(See *Teacher Resource Book,* Unit 22.)

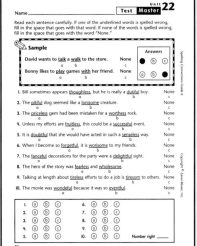

**Unit 22
Test Master**

T137

Objectives

Strategy Words

Students will

- **review** words studied previously that are related to the spelling strategy.
- **preview** unknown words that are related to the spelling strategy.

Strategy Words

Remind the students that the **Strategy Words** relate to the spelling patterns they have studied in this unit. The **Review Words** are below grade level, and the **Preview Words** are above grade level. You may wish to use the following sentences to introduce the words in context.

Review Words:
Words From Grade 5

1. The accident seemed so **awful** we hid our eyes.
2. **Beauty** can be seen in nature.
3. The child was a **delight** to her grandparents.
4. A **handsome** prince will fight the dragon.
5. Our community set up a shelter for people who were **homeless**.

You may wish to ask students to add one of the targeted suffixes to form new words and to discuss how the meaning of each word changes when the suffix is added.

Preview Words:
Words From Grade 7

6. The whole experience was very **distasteful**.
7. We were amazed at the **fearlessness** of the astronauts as they began their adventure.
8. The **adventuresome** child was rescued from the dangerous situation.
9. Were her actions because of **thoughtlessness**?
10. **Regardless** of the outcome, we will still be friends.

Review Words
1. handsome
2. homeless
3. awful
4. beauty
5. delight

Preview Words
6. regardless
7. adventuresome
8. distasteful
9. thoughtlessness
10. fearlessness

Strategy Words

Review Words: Suffixes -ful, -less, -some

Replace the underlined word or words in this poster with words from the box.

| awful | beauty | delight | handsome | homeless |

Give a Hoot About the Owls

1.–5. Some of these <u>attractive</u> birds, including the spotted owl, are <u>without a home</u>. Help them escape their <u>dreadful</u> situation. They prefer a home in a huge old tree in the evergreen forest of the Pacific Northwest. The <u>loveliness</u> of their surroundings is important to them. They work nights and keep to themselves, so they would be a <u>pleasure</u> to have as neighbors.

Preview Words: Suffixes -ful, -less, -some

Write a word from the box to complete each sentence.

| distasteful | fearlessness | adventuresome |
| thoughtlessness | regardless | |

6. Max does what he wants, _____ of the rules.
7. He is always seeking adventure. He is _____.
8. Don't you think those green scrambled eggs are _____?
9. His _____ caused us great disappointment.
10. The movie hero's _____ helps him conquer the villain.

138

Unit 22 RECAP

You may wish to assign the **Unit 22 Homework Master** (*Teacher Resource Book,* Unit 22) as a fun way to recap the spelling words.

Unit 22 Homework Master

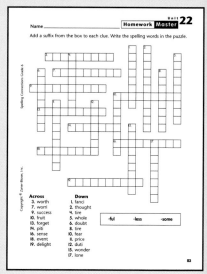

Content Words

Fine Arts: Crafts

Write words from the box to complete the paragraph.

ceramics	kiln	pewter	glaze	pottery

The art of making __1.__ is called __2.__. Porcelain is a very fine clay to which a __3.__ is applied before the object is fired in a __4.__. Porcelain dishes and __5.__ candlesticks can make a simple meal a festive occasion.

Science: Astronomy

Write the word from the box that fits each definition.

astronomy	nebula	constellation	stellar	galaxy

6. a hazy patch of light visible in the sky
7. the science that deals with the universe beyond Earth
8. an easily recognized group of stars that appear close together in the sky, like Ursa Minor
9. a large, self-contained mass of stars, like the Milky Way
10. an adjective that means "having to do with a star"

Apply the Spelling Strategy

Circle the two Content Words you wrote with the **short a** sound. Underline the two Content Words you wrote with the **long a** sound.

Word Study

Related Words

If something is **nebulous**, it is "confused, cloudlike, vague, or hazy." Write the Content Word that is related to this word.

Fine Arts: Crafts
1. pottery
2. (ceramics)
3. glaze
4. kiln
5. pewter

Science: Astronomy
6. nebula
7. astronomy
8. constellation
9. (galaxy)
10. stellar

Related Words
1. nebula

139

Objectives

Content Words

Students will
- **expand** vocabulary with content-related words.
- **relate** the spelling strategy to words outside the basic spelling list.
- **understand** the ways in which words from the same root are related.

Content Words

Fine Arts: Crafts

Use these sentences to introduce the words and their meanings.

1. Father enrolled in a **ceramics** class at our community college.
2. The clay puppy was fired in a **kiln**.
3. **Pewter** bowls full of dried flowers were used as decorations.
4. Does the **glaze** contain lead?
5. This **pottery** was made by Aztecs.

Science: Astronomy

Use these sentences to introduce the words and their meanings.

6. Ancient people learned **astronomy** by studying the moon and stars.
7. Scientists are studying the **nebula** that is closest to the sun.
8. The Big Dipper is found in the **constellation** Ursa Major.
9. The study was done to see if there is a **stellar** effect on animals.
10. The size of our **galaxy** can be measured in light years.

Word Study

Related Words

Discuss the ways in which something that is "vague" is "cloudlike." Encourage students to suggest other examples of related words; e.g., **constellation** and **stellar**.

Unit 23 Home Spelling Practice

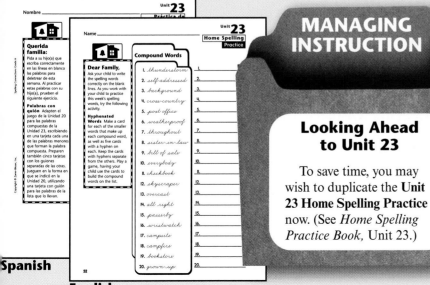

Spanish

English

MANAGING INSTRUCTION

Looking Ahead to Unit 23

To save time, you may wish to duplicate the **Unit 23 Home Spelling Practice** now. (See *Home Spelling Practice Book*, Unit 23.)

Basic Spelling List

thunderstorm	checkbook
self-addressed	skyscraper
background	overcast
cross-country	all right
post office	passerby
weatherproof	wristwatch
throughout	campsite
sister-in-law	campfire
bill of sale	bookstore
everybody	grown-up

Strategy Words

Review
home run	sweatshirt
make-believe	waterproof
peanut butter	

Preview
briefcase	well-known
classmate	word processing
newsstand	

Content Words

Science: Machines
automation	mechanize
machinery	hydraulic
horsepower	

Science: Light
medium	wavelength
spectrum	refract
reflect	

Individual Needs

Challenge Words
videotape	bookmobile
volleyball	public school
hindsight	weather-beaten

Alternate Word List★
thunderstorm	all right
background	campfire
throughout	bookstore
everybody	grown-up
skyscraper	
self-addressed	

★ For students who need to study fewer Basic Spelling words

MATERIALS

Student Edition
Pages 140–145
Challenge Activities, p. 243

Teacher Edition
Pages T140A–T145
Challenge Activities, p. T243

Teacher Resource Book
Unit 23 Homework Master
Unit 23 Practice Masters
Flip Folder Practice Master
Unit 23 Test Master

Home Spelling Practice Book
Unit 23 Home Spelling Practice
(English or Spanish)

Other *Spelling Connections* Resources
- Audiotape, Grade 6
- Practice Book for Grammar, Usage, and Mechanics, Grade 6
- Spelling Support for Second Language Learners, Grade 6
- Support Software on CD-ROM
- Transparency Book, Grade 6
- Word Sort CD-ROM, Grade 6

OBJECTIVES

Spelling and Thinking
Students will
- **read** the spelling words in list form and in context.
- **sort** the spelling words according to closed, hyphenated, and open compounds.
- **read** and remember this week's spelling strategy.

Spelling and Vocabulary
Students will
- **write** spelling words for given words with the same or nearly the same meaning.
- **substitute** word parts to form spelling words.
- **use** guide words to find spelling words in the **Spelling Dictionary**.

Spelling and Reading
Students will
- **solve** analogies using spelling words.
- **complete** sentences using spelling words.
- **complete** a paragraph using spelling words.

Spelling and Writing
Students will
- **proofread** a paragraph.
- **use** the writing process to write a paragraph about an outdoor adventure.
- **proofread** their writing.

MEETING INDIVIDUAL NEEDS
Learning Styles

Visual

Write each of the main words that makes up each compound word on a separate card. Make five smaller cards with a hyphen on each, plus cards for **in** and **of**. Place these last seven cards on your desk. Place the other cards in a receptacle. Have each student select a card without looking at it. Tell students, "You will have three minutes to find the person or persons with the other part or parts of your word. You may not say anything during this time. If you need a hyphen or the words **in** or **of** get them from my desk. As soon as your word is formed, sit down and raise your hand." The winners are the students who first form their words correctly.

Auditory

Use the word cards described in the visual activity. Tell the students they can talk to each other as they search for the cards to complete their words.

Kinesthetic

Give each student a small ball. Pronounce each spelling word. As each word is pronounced, have the students spell the word aloud, bouncing the ball twice between each word of an open compound, once between each word of a hyphenated compound, and not at all for a closed compound. Then have the students pronounce each spelling word softly to themselves and write the word.

Hands-On Practice
All students will benefit from practicing with a **Flip Folder**. See page Z18.

Language and Cultural Differences

The students should have few problems with these compound words, other than problems associated with the original words from which the compounds were formed.

Separate the words that make up the spelling words and write them on the chalkboard. Then have volunteers match them and write each compound word correctly, using one color of chalk for closed compounds, another color for hyphenated compounds, and a third color for open compounds.

MANAGING INSTRUCTION

3–5 Day Plan		Average	Below Average	Above Average
Day 1	**Day 1**	Pretest Spelling Mini-Lesson, p. T140 Spelling and Thinking, p. 140	Pretest Spelling Mini-Lesson, p. T140 Spelling and Thinking, p. 140	Pretest Spelling and Thinking, p. 140
	Day 2	Spelling and Vocabulary, p. 141	Spelling and Vocabulary, p. 141 (or) Unit 23 Practice Master, A and B	Spelling and Vocabulary, p. 141 Spelling and Reading, p. 142
Day 2	**Day 3**	Spelling and Reading, p. 142	Spelling and Reading, p. 142 (or) Unit 23 Practice Master, C and D	Challenge Activities, p. 243
	Day 4	Spelling and Writing, p. 143 Unit 23 Homework Master	Spelling and Writing, p. 143	Spelling and Writing, p. 143 Unit 23 Homework Master
Day 3	**Day 5**	Weekly Test	Weekly Test	Weekly Test
Vocabulary Connections (pages 144 and 145) may be used anytime during this unit.				

Objectives

Spelling and Thinking

Students will
- **read** the spelling words in list form and in context.
- **sort** the spelling words according to closed, hyphenated, and open compounds.
- **read** and remember this week's spelling strategy.

UNIT PRETEST

Use **Pretest Sentences** below. Refer to the self-checking procedures on student page 256. You may wish to use the **Unit 23 Word List Overhead Transparency** as part of the checking procedure.

TEACHING THE STRATEGY

Spelling Mini-Lesson

Remind the students that compound words combine two or more words to make a new word or word group. Write the terms **closed compound, hyphenated compound,** and **open compound** on the chalkboard. Also write these spelling words on the board: **bookstore, cross-country, post office.**

Explain that there are different types of compound words.

- When two words, like **book** and **store,** are united into one word (**bookstore**), the new word is called a **closed compound**.
- When two words, like **cross** and **country,** are joined by a hyphen (**cross-country**), the new word is called a **hyphenated compound**.
- When two words, like **post** and **office,** are not actually joined but are placed together in a word group and have a special meaning (**post office**), the new word is called an **open compound**.

Ask volunteers to read the rest of the spelling words. Discuss the ways in which the meanings of the words within each compound word relate to the meaning of the compound.

Read **Remember the Spelling Strategy** on page 140.

Spelling and Thinking

Order of answers may vary.
closed compound
1. thunderstorm ★
2. background ★
3. weatherproof
4. throughout ★
5. everybody ★
6. checkbook
7. skyscraper ★
8. overcast
9. passerby
10. wristwatch
11. campsite
12. campfire ★
13. bookstore ★
hyphenated compound ★
14. self-addressed
15. cross-country
16. sister-in-law
17. grown-up ★
open compound
18. post office
19. bill of sale
20. all right ★

READ THE SPELLING WORDS

1.	thunderstorm	*thunderstorm*	The **thunderstorm** was loud.
2.	self-addressed	*self-addressed*	Send a **self-addressed** card.
3.	background	*background*	She stood in the **background**.
4.	cross-country	*cross-country*	We drove **cross-country**.
5.	post office	*post office*	The **post office** sells stamps.
6.	weatherproof	*weatherproof*	My coat is **weatherproof**.
7.	throughout	*throughout*	Listen **throughout** the day.
8.	sister-in-law	*sister-in-law*	Ollie is my **sister-in-law**.
9.	bill of sale	*bill of sale*	Here is your **bill of sale**.
10.	everybody	*everybody*	He told **everybody** the news.
11.	checkbook	*checkbook*	She balanced her **checkbook**.
12.	skyscraper	*skyscraper*	How tall is that **skyscraper**?
13.	overcast	*overcast*	It is **overcast**, not sunny.
14.	all right	*all right*	It is **all right** to call.
15.	passerby	*passerby*	A **passerby** stopped to help.
16.	wristwatch	*wristwatch*	I like my new **wristwatch**.
17.	campsite	*campsite*	The **campsite** is near a river.
18.	campfire	*campfire*	We sat around the **campfire**.
19.	bookstore	*bookstore*	Arno works at a **bookstore**.
20.	grown-up	*grown-up*	Ask a **grown-up** to help.

SORT THE SPELLING WORDS

1.–13. Write the spelling words that are closed compounds (written as a single word).

14.–17. Write the spelling words that are hyphenated compounds.

18.–20. Write the spelling words that are open compounds (made up of two or more words).

REMEMBER THE SPELLING STRATEGY

Remember that a compound word is formed from two or more words that make a new word or group of words, such as **bookstore, all right,** and **grown-up**.

140

Pretest Sentences (See procedures on pages Z10–Z11.)

★ 1. The **thunderstorm** frightened the dog.
★ 2. Give me a **self-addressed** envelope, and I will send your documents back to you.
★ 3. The garden will make a lovely **background** for your portrait.
4. On our **cross-country** trip, we visited twenty states.
5. I have to mail this package from the **post office**.
6. Wear your **weatherproof** boots when it rains.
★ 7. The telephone rang constantly **throughout** the day.
8. My brother's wife is my **sister-in-law**.
9. We must have your **bill of sale** to exchange the merchandise.
★10. The comedian's jokes made **everybody** in the audience laugh.
11. She could not pay the bill because she forgot her **checkbook**.
★12. The **skyscraper** is so tall that it seems to touch the clouds.
13. The skies were **overcast,** so we were sure that it would rain.
★14. The doctor told us that our sister would be **all right**.
15. The **passerby** witnessed the accident.
16. Please look at your **wristwatch** and tell me what time it is.
17. This place near the lake will make a good **campsite**.
★18. When we camped, we often sat around the **campfire** and talked.
★19. The book for this course is on sale in the **bookstore**.
★20. My older sister is a **grown-up** with a family of her own.

Spelling and Vocabulary

Word Meanings

Write a spelling word that could replace the underlined words.

1. A person who walked by helped untangle the dog from its leash.
2. Trees protected the site where we chose to set up camp.
3. I bought a novel at a store that sells books.
4. We went inside during the storm that raged with thunder.
5. The fire at our camp went out during the night.
6. Enclose an envelope that is addressed to yourself.
7. She went shopping with her husband's sister.
8. He checked his clock he wears on his wrist.
9. They planned a trip across the country.

Word Structure

Change the underlined parts of these compound words to write spelling words.

10. backpack
11. without
12. outcast
13. skylight
14. bill of fare
15. fireproof
16. everyone

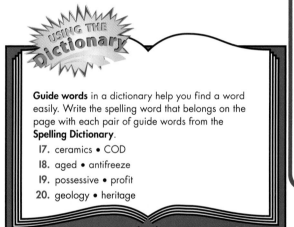

USING THE Dictionary

Guide words in a dictionary help you find a word easily. Write the spelling word that belongs on the page with each pair of guide words from the **Spelling Dictionary**.

17. ceramics • COD
18. aged • antifreeze
19. possessive • profit
20. geology • heritage

Word Meanings
1. passerby
2. campsite
3. bookstore
4. thunderstorm
5. campfire
6. self-addressed
7. sister-in-law
8. wristwatch
9. cross-country

Word Structure
10. background
11. throughout
12. overcast
13. skyscraper
14. bill of sale
15. weatherproof
16. everybody

Using the Dictionary
17. checkbook
18. all right
19. post office
20. grown-up

141

Developing Oral Language Skills

Do a word sort by syllable. Write the following on the chalkboard: **two-syllables, three syllables, more than three syllables**. Have a student think of a sentence using a spelling word and state the sentence to the class. Have that student call on a classmate to say the spelling word used in the sentence and to write that word under the proper heading. When the students are finished listing the words, ask volunteers to say each word aloud again and to draw a line between the syllables. Finally, ask the students to note the spelling of each syllable and to circle those syllables that form a word.

MEETING INDIVIDUAL NEEDS

Providing More Help

Write the following sets of words on the chalkboard. Have a volunteer circle the correctly spelled word in each set.

1. back-ground   **background**   back ground
2. **grown-up**   grown up   grownup
3. allright   **all right**   all-right
4. **campsite**   camp site   camp-site
5. postoffice   **post office**   post-office
6. over-cast   over cast   **overcast**

★Students who need to study fewer words should use the **Alternate Word List**. This list is starred on page T140 in the Teacher Edition. The **Unit 23 Practice Masters** (*Teacher Resource Book*) provide additional practice with these words.

Unit 23 Practice Masters

Name _____

Practice Master **23**

1. bookstore 3. throughout 5. skyscraper 7. thunderstorm 9. grown-up
2. campfire 4. background 6. everybody 8. self-addressed 10. all right

A. The underlined part of each compound word below is also part of a spelling word. Write each spelling word.

1. backfire _____
2. outside _____
3. right-hand _____
4. skyline _____
5. bookmark _____
6. anybody _____
7. firefly _____
8. self-serve _____

B. Match a word from Column A with a word in Column B to make a spelling word. Write the spelling word.

Column A	Column B
1. grown •	• storm
2. thunder •	• store
3. self •	• up
4. book •	• body
5. back •	• addressed
6. every •	• ground

84

Practice Master **23**

thunderstorm   grown-up
self-addressed   all right

the spelling word.

letters circled will form another

addressed to oneself
satisfactory
every person
store for books

85

T141

Objectives

Spelling and Reading

Students will
- **solve** analogies using spelling words.
- **complete** sentences using spelling words.
- **complete** a paragraph using spelling words.

One-Minute Handwriting Hint

The spacing between letters should look even. The joining stroke controls the spacing between letters. Swing wide as you join letters. There should be enough space between letters to insert a small oval.

imagine

Legible handwriting can boost spelling scores by as much as 20%.

Solve the Analogies
1. wristwatch
2. checkbook
3. overcast
4. grown-up
5. post office
6. everybody
7. self-addressed

Complete the Sentences
8. passerby
9. all right
10. skyscraper
11. sister-in-law
12. bill of sale
13. campfire
14. throughout

Complete the Paragraph
15. cross-country
16. bookstore
17. campsite
18. weatherproof
19. thunderstorm
20. background

142

Spelling and Reading

thunderstorm	self-addressed	background	cross-country
post office	weatherproof	throughout	sister-in-law
bill of sale	everybody	checkbook	skyscraper
overcast	all right	passerby	wristwatch
campsite	campfire	bookstore	grown-up

Solve the Analogies Write a spelling word to complete each analogy.

1. **Neck** is to **necklace** as **wrist** is to _____.
2. **Recipe** is to **cookbook** as **check** is to _____.
3. **Permanent** is to **unstable** as **clear** is to _____.
4. **Child** is to **young** as **adult** is to _____.
5. **Book** is to **bookstore** as **stamp** is to _____.
6. **None** is to **all** as **no one** is to _____.
7. **Tour** is to **self-guided** as **envelope** is to _____.

Complete the Sentences Write a spelling word to complete each sentence.

8. The _____ stopped to help the man with the flat tire.
9. I hope it will be _____ if we park here.
10. The invention of the elevator made it realistic to build a _____.
11. When my brother got married, his wife became my _____.
12. When we sold our house, we were given a _____.
13. We gathered wood and kindling to build a _____.
14. The lonely dog howled _____ the night.

Complete the Paragraph Write the spelling words from the box to complete the paragraph.

The photographers planned their __15.__ trip well. They bought guidebooks in a __16.__, rented equipment, and arranged to stay at a different __17.__ each night. Their __18.__ clothing would protect them from a __19.__. They planned to photograph animals against the __20.__ of national parks.

> campsite
> cross-country
> weatherproof
> background
> bookstore
> thunderstorm

MEETING INDIVIDUAL NEEDS

Providing More Challenge

Challenge Words and **Challenge Activities** for Unit 23 appear on page 243. **Challenge Word Test Sentences** appear on page T243.

Unit 23 Challenge Activities

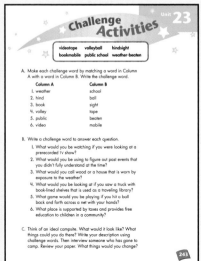

Weekly Test Options

Option 1:
One Spelling Word Per Sentence
(See procedures on pages Z10–Z11.)

★ 1. Are you feeling **all right** today?
★ 2. If you stand in the **background,** no one will see you.
   3. Did the clerk give you a **bill of sale** for the purchase?
★ 4. I bought this notebook in the **bookstore**.
★ 5. The group leader taught us how to make a **campfire**.
   6. Is this a good place for a **campsite**?
   7. He always takes his **checkbook** when he goes to that store.
   8. That route is a **cross-country** highway.
★ 9. **Everybody** wanted to ride in the new car.
★10. The children liked to dress in **grown-up** clothes.
  11. Suddenly, the sun broke through the **overcast** sky.
  12. The innocent **passerby** was injured in the crash.
  13. The **post office** has a flag over the door.
★14. The directions said to enclose a **self-addressed** envelope.
  15. Her husband's sister is her **sister-in-law**.
★16. The view from the top of the **skyscraper** is beautiful.

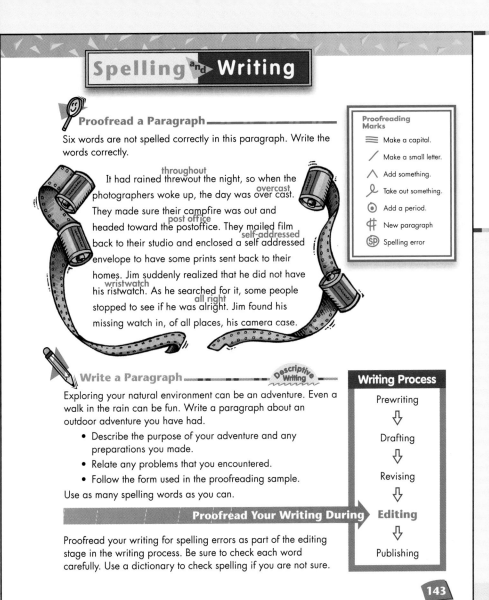

Spelling and Writing

Proofread a Paragraph

Six words are not spelled correctly in this paragraph. Write the words correctly.

throughout
It had rained threwout the night, so when the
overcast
photographers woke up, the day was over cast.
They made sure their campfire was out and
post office
headed toward the postoffice. They mailed film
self-addressed
back to their studio and enclosed a self addressed
envelope to have some prints sent back to their
homes. Jim suddenly realized that he did not have
wristwatch
his ristwatch. As he searched for it, some people
all right
stopped to see if he was alright. Jim found his
missing watch in, of all places, his camera case.

Proofreading Marks

☰ Make a capital.

／ Make a small letter.

∧ Add something.

ℒ Take out something.

⊙ Add a period.

⌗ New paragraph

ⓈⓅ Spelling error

Write a Paragraph

Descriptive Writing

Exploring your natural environment can be an adventure. Even a walk in the rain can be fun. Write a paragraph about an outdoor adventure you have had.

- Describe the purpose of your adventure and any preparations you made.
- Relate any problems that you encountered.
- Follow the form used in the proofreading sample.

Use as many spelling words as you can.

Writing Process

Prewriting
⇩
Drafting
⇩
Revising
⇩
Editing
⇩
Publishing

Proofread Your Writing During ➤

Proofread your writing for spelling errors as part of the editing stage in the writing process. Be sure to check each word carefully. Use a dictionary to check spelling if you are not sure.

143

Objectives

Spelling and Writing

Students will
- **proofread** a paragraph.
- **use** the writing process to write a paragraph about an outdoor adventure.
- **proofread** their writing.

Using the Writing Process

Before assigning **Write a Paragraph,** see pages 258–259 in the Student Edition for a complete review of the writing process and additional writing assignments. You may also refer to pages Z12–Z13 in the Teacher Edition.

Keeping a Spelling Journal

Encourage students to record the words they misspelled on the weekly test in a personal spelling journal. These words may be recycled for future study. Students may also wish to include words from their writing. See pages Z12–Z13 in the Teacher Edition for more information.

★**17.** The ship makes many voyages **throughout** the year.
★**18.** The children were not frightened during the **thunderstorm.**
19. My **weatherproof** boots are bright red and shiny.
20. Her parents gave her a **wristwatch** for her birthday.

Option 2:
Multiple Spelling Words Per Sentence
(See procedures on pages Z10–Z11.)

1. Did you bring your **checkbook** with you to the **bookstore**?
2. A **passerby** asked me to check the time on my **wristwatch**.
3. The **bill of sale** said he paid $70 for the **weatherproof** boots.
4. **Everybody** was expecting a **thunderstorm** since the sky was **overcast**.
5. Take this **self-addressed** envelope to the **post office**.
6. On her **cross-country** trip, she went to see her **sister-in-law**.
7. Everyone at the **campsite** wanted to help build the **campfire**.
8. The dark sky was a beautiful **background** for the **skyscraper**.
9. A **grown-up** may be busy **throughout** the day making sure that everything is going **all right**.

Option 3:
Standardized Test
(See *Teacher Resource Book,* Unit 23.)

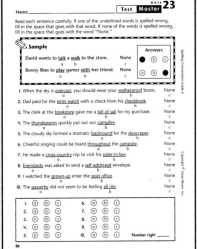

**Unit 23
Test Master**

T143

Objectives

Strategy Words

Students will
- **review** words studied previously that are related to the spelling strategy.
- **preview** unknown words that are related to the spelling strategy.

VOCABULARY CONNECTIONS

Strategy Words

Remind the students that the **Strategy Words** relate to the spelling patterns they have studied in this unit. The **Review Words** are below grade level, and the **Preview Words** are above grade level. You may wish to use the following sentences to introduce the words in context.

Review Words:
Words From Grade 5

1. Mark McGwire is the **home run** champion.
2. My little brother likes to play **make-believe**.
3. A **peanut butter** sandwich makes a great snack.
4. The grass stain came out of my **sweatshirt** when it was laundered.
5. I thought the coat was **waterproof**, but I got wet in the hard rain.

Preview Words:
Words From Grade 7

6. The attorney carried his **briefcase** into the courtroom.
7. Is Sherika your **classmate**?
8. Today's paper just arrived at the **newsstand**.
9. John is **well-known** for his terrific singing voice.
10. I practiced my **word processing** skills.

Review Words
1. peanut butter
2. make-believe
3. home run
4. waterproof
5. sweatshirt

Preview Words
6. newsstand
7. word processing
8. briefcase
9. classmate
10. well-known

144

Strategy Words

Review Words: Compound Words

Write a word from the box to match each clue.

home run	make-believe	peanut butter
	sweatshirt	waterproof

1. a spread that was created by a scientist as a health food
2. the opposite of factual
3. what most baseball batters strive for
4. capable of keeping water from coming through
5. a heavy, long-sleeved jersey worn especially by athletes

Preview Words: Compound Words

Write words from the box to complete the paragraph.

briefcase	classmate	newsstand
	well-known	word processing

As Tai stood at the ___6.___ looking for a magazine on ___7.___, she noticed a man nearby holding a leather ___8.___. Although she had not seen him since high school, Tai recognized her old ___9.___. She knew that he was now a ___10.___ writer of children's books.

Unit 23 RECAP

You may wish to assign the **Unit 23 Homework Master** (*Teacher Resource Book*, Unit 23) as a fun way to recap the spelling words.

Unit 23 Homework Master

Name _____   Homework Master Unit 23

Use the clues to write spelling words. The letters circled will form two words that tell what the spelling words have in common.

1. covered over
2. receipt, document
3. place for camping
4. outdoor fire
5. faraway scene
6. in every part of
7. adult
8. every person
9. arm clock
10. store for books
11. satisfactory
12. thunder and lightning storm
13. person going by

Unscramble and write each spelling word.

1. k a p r e s s y c r
2. h e b o c o k c k
3. s s o r c - t r y o n u c
4. t o p s   f o c i e f
5. t h e a w o o r p f e r
6. f l i s e - r e e s s d d d a
7. i s t e r s - n i - w l a

87

Content Words

Science: Machines

Write the words from the box to complete the paragraph.

automation	machinery	horsepower
mechanize	hydraulic	

Before automatic __1.__ was invented, it would take a farmer weeks to plow several acres. The __2.__ of farm work brought tremendous changes in agriculture. Oxen and horses were replaced by machines with engines whose strength is measured in __3.__. Today's plows use __4.__ power to raise and lower the blades. Efforts are continuing to be made to __5.__ farming techniques.

Science: Light

Write the words from the box that complete the paragraph.

medium	spectrum	reflect	wavelength	refract

Light waves __6.__, or bend, as they pass through mist. Fine raindrops can create the __7.__ through which all the sun's colors can be seen. The water separates the light into a __8.__ of colors. The colors that the sky will __9.__ are different because they each have a different __10.__.

Apply the Spelling Strategy

Circle the two compound Content Words you wrote.

Word Study

Coined Words

A **coined word** is made up to name something new. **Horseless carriage** meant "automobile." Write the Content Word that means "machine power equivalent to the power of one horse."

145

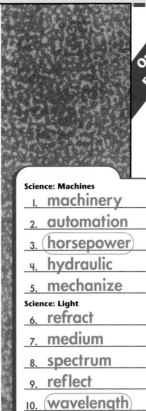

Science: Machines
1. machinery
2. automation
3. (horsepower)
4. hydraulic
5. mechanize

Science: Light
6. refract
7. medium
8. spectrum
9. reflect
10. (wavelength)

Coined Words
1. horsepower

Objectives

Content Words

Students will
- **expand** vocabulary with content-related words.
- **relate** the spelling strategy to words outside the basic spelling list.
- **recognize** that a coined word is made up to name something new.

Content Words

Science: Machines

Use these sentences to introduce the words and their meanings.

1. The **automation** of factories greatly increased the quantity of goods.
2. **Machinery** must be kept in good repair to run efficiently.
3. The power of a car's engine is measured in **horsepower**.
4. The hospital will **mechanize** its diagnostic equipment.
5. An **hydraulic** lift was used to lift the car at the garage.

Science: Light

Use these sentences to introduce the words and their meanings.

6. We are able to watch the nightly news through the **medium** of television.
7. A rainbow shows the colors of the **spectrum**.
8. I took the picture when I could see the water **reflect** the mountains.
9. Sound is a vibration transmitted to our ears by **wavelength**.
10. The prism will **refract** the light.

Word Study

Coined Words

Explain that when something new is discovered or invented, a word has to be coined to identify it. Encourage students to suggest other words they think might be coined words, and have them tell how the name may have originated (e.g., **milkshake, liftoff, firefighter**).

Unit 24 Home Spelling Practice

Spanish

English

MANAGING INSTRUCTION

Looking Ahead to Unit 24

To save time, you may wish to duplicate the **Unit 24 Home Spelling Practice** now. (See *Home Spelling Practice Book,* Unit 24.)

T145

Assessment Words

indivisible	imaginable
attachment	nonverbal
misprint	usage
motionless	plentiful
contact lens	birthstone
worn-out	typewriter
bothersome	fearful
ailment	wreckage
misspell	antibody
audible	enjoyable

Review Words

Unit 19
acceptable*	available
changeable*	sensible
valuable*	visible
responsible*	invisible
favorable	flexible

Unit 20
irresistible*	antifreeze
illiterate*	illegal
nonreturnable*	nonfat
misbehave*	mislead
irregular	misfortune

Unit 21
mileage*	development
marriage*	garbage
equipment*	excitement
document*	courage
garage	experiment

Unit 22
successful*	doubtful
pitiful*	delightful
thoughtless*	fearless
wholesome*	worthless
wonderful	lonesome

Unit 23
all right*	background
self-addressed*	campfire
everybody*	skyscraper
throughout*	thunderstorm
bookstore	grown-up

* Posttest sentences and the **Unit 24 Test Master** test these words. Students review all words listed.

MATERIALS

Student Edition
Pages 146–151

Teacher Edition
Pages T146A–T151

Teacher Resource Book
Flip Folder Practice Master
Unit 24 Test Master

Home Spelling Practice Book
Unit 24 Home Spelling Practice
(English or Spanish)

Other *Spelling Connections* Resources
• Transparency Book, Grade 6

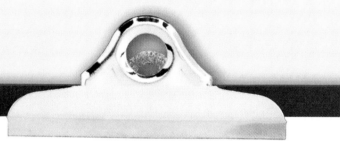

OBJECTIVES

Spelling and Assessment
Students will
• **assess** their spelling success by matching new words to the spelling strategies presented in Units 19–23.
• **connect** new words to the spelling strategies in Units 19–23.
• **write** new words that relate to the spelling strategies taught in Units 19–23.

Spelling and Review
• **review** and practice the spelling strategies and words in Units 19–23.
• **learn** an alternative spelling study strategy.

Spelling and Writing
Students will
• **review** action verbs and linking verbs.
• **compose** a persuasive letter to an editor.
• **learn** a proofreading strategy.
• **understand** the importance of technical language when using a computer.
• **proofread** for misspellings of technical terms.

MEETING INDIVIDUAL NEEDS
Learning Styles

 ### Visual

Have students form two teams. Have each team write each prefix and each base word of the spelling words on 3" × 5" cards. Have them write the prefixes in green and the base words in red. Each team will have one stack of cards with the prefixes and another stack with the base words. Tell each team to shuffle each stack of cards before starting the game. When you say "Go," have the teams match the prefixes to the base words to form the spelling words. The first team to match them all correctly wins.

Repeat the activity using suffixes and base words.

 ### Auditory

Have students play "Word Box." Write each spelling word on a slip of paper and place the papers in a box. A student draws a word, pronounces the word in a tone indicative of the word's meaning, and spells the word aloud without looking at the paper. If the word is spelled correctly, that paper may be discarded. If the word is misspelled, the student keeps the slip of paper in order to study that word.

 ### Kinesthetic

Designate various areas of the room for different prefixes and suffixes. Pronounce a spelling word and call on a student. The student must stand, identify the prefix or suffix in the word, walk to the appropriate part of the room, and spell the word. If correct, the student stays in that place. If incorrect, the student sits down and waits for another turn.

> **Hands-On Practice**
> All students will benefit from practicing with a **Flip Folder**. See page Z18.

Language and Cultural Differences

Give the students ample opportunity to hear and repeat the correct pronunciation of the spelling words in Units 19–23. Many of these words are commonly mispronounced and misspelled.

Because the sounds /ĭj/ and /əl/ do not exist in Spanish, Spanish-speaking students may have trouble with words that have these sounds. Students may need extra help pronouncing and spelling the words.

MANAGING INSTRUCTION

3–5 Day Plan		Average	Below Average	Above Average
Day 1	**Day 1**	Assessment: Units 19–23, p. 146 (Option 1 or 2, p. T146)	Assessment: Units 19–23, p. 146 (Option 1 or 2, p. T146)	Assessment: Units 19–23, p. 146 (Option 1 or 2, p. T146)
	Day 2	Review: Units 19 and 20, p. 147	Review: Units 19 and 20, p. 147	Review: Units 19 and 20, p. 147 Review: Units 21 and 22, p. 148
Day 2	**Day 3**	Review: Units 21 and 22, p. 148	Review: Units 21 and 22, p. 148	Review: Unit 23, p. 149 Spelling Study Strategy, p. 149
	Day 4	Review: Unit 23, p. 149 Spelling Study Strategy, p. 149	Review: Unit 23, p. 149 Spelling Study Strategy, p. 149	Writer's Workshop, pages 150–151
Day 3	**Day 5**	Weekly Test, Option 1 or 2, p. T149	Weekly Test, Option 1 or 2, p. T149	Weekly Test, Option 1 or 2, p. T149

Writer's Workshop (pages 150 and 151) may be used anytime during this unit.

Spelling and Assessment

Students will
- **assess** their spelling success by matching new words to the spelling strategies presented in Units 19–23.
- **connect** new words to the spelling strategies in Units 19–23.
- **write** new words that relate to the spelling strategies taught in Units 19–23.

Unit 24
Review Units 19–23

Assessment and Review

Assessment Units 19–23

Unit 19
1. indivisible
2. audible
3. imaginable
4. enjoyable

Unit 20
5. misprint
6. misspell
7. nonverbal
8. antibody

Unit 21
9. attachment
10. ailment
11. usage
12. wreckage

Unit 22
13. motionless
14. bothersome
15. plentiful
16. fearful

Unit 23
17. contact lens
18. worn-out
19. birthstone
20. typewriter

146

Each Assessment Word in the box fits one of the spelling strategies you have studied over the past five weeks. Read the spelling strategies. Then write each Assessment Word under the unit number it fits.

Unit 19 _____
1.–4. The suffixes **-able** and **-ible** can be added to base words and root words to form new words: **favorable, visible**.

Unit 20 _____
5.–8. The prefixes **ir-, anti-, il-, non-,** and **mis-** can be added to base words to form new words. These new words mean the opposite of the base word.

Unit 21 _____
9.–12. The suffixes **-age** and **-ment** can be added to root words and base words to form new words. These new words are nouns: **courage, equipment**.

Unit 22 _____
13.–16. The suffixes **-ful, -less,** and **-some** can be added to base words to form adjectives such as **wonderful, priceless,** and **worrisome**.

Unit 23 _____
17.–20. A compound word is formed from two or more words that make a new word or group of words, such as **bookstore, all right,** and **grown-up**.

indivisible
attachment
misprint
motionless
contact lens
worn-out
bothersome
ailment
misspell
audible
imaginable
nonverbal
usage
plentiful
birthstone
typewriter
fearful
wreckage
antibody
enjoyable

ASSESSMENT: UNITS 19–23

Option 1

   Assessment Option 1 is the test that appears in the Student Edition on page 146. You may wish to have students take this test to determine their ability to recognize the spelling strategy in each unit and to match words not previously taught to that strategy. **Assessment Option 1** also serves as additional review and practice.

   ▲ Words designated with this symbol include more than one of the targeted spelling strategies. The answer key has placed them according to the most obvious spelling emphasis. However, if a student places a word in another category, and the word fits that generalization, accept that response. Remember, the objective is to place each word with any appropriate spelling generalization.

Option 2

   Assessment Option 2 is a dictation test using the sentences on page T147. This test assesses students' ability to spell words not previously taught but that are exemplars of a spelling strategy. This test more specifically assesses students' ability to apply the spelling knowledge they have learned.

   In either assessment test option, the words are identified by unit in the Teacher Edition. You may wish to index those misspelled words to the review exercises that follow in this unit. Determine which units students need to review and use the additional unit exercises found in this **Assessment and Review Unit** for reteaching the skill in a more focused way.

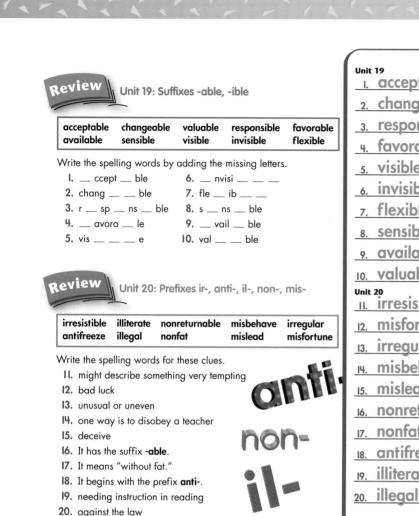

Review Unit 19: Suffixes -able, -ible

acceptable	changeable	valuable	responsible	favorable
available	sensible	visible	invisible	flexible

Write the spelling words by adding the missing letters.

1. __ ccept __ ble
2. chang __ __ ble
3. r __ sp __ ns __ ble
4. __ avora __ le
5. vis __ __ __ e
6. __ nvisi __ __ __
7. fle __ ib __ __
8. s __ ns __ ble
9. __ vail __ ble
10. val __ __ ble

Review Unit 20: Prefixes ir-, anti-, il-, non-, mis-

irresistible	illiterate	nonreturnable	misbehave	irregular
antifreeze	illegal	nonfat	mislead	misfortune

Write the spelling words for these clues.

11. might describe something very tempting
12. bad luck
13. unusual or uneven
14. one way is to disobey a teacher
15. deceive
16. It has the suffix **-able**.
17. It means "without fat."
18. It begins with the prefix **anti-**.
19. needing instruction in reading
20. against the law

Unit 19
1. acceptable
2. changeable
3. responsible
4. favorable
5. visible
6. invisible
7. flexible
8. sensible
9. available
10. valuable

Unit 20
11. irresistible
12. misfortune
13. irregular
14. misbehave
15. mislead
16. nonreturnable
17. nonfat
18. antifreeze
19. illiterate
20. illegal

147

Objectives

Spelling and Review

Students will
- **review** and practice the spelling strategy and words taught in Unit 19.
- **review** and practice the spelling strategy and words taught in Unit 20.

Assessing Progress: The Spelling Journal

If your students have been keeping a personal spelling journal, a periodical review of these journals can be a rich assessment tool. Students should include the words they have misspelled from each unit spelling test. They should also be encouraged to write the words they consistently misspell in their own writing and content-area words that present a challenge. Being able to discriminate the words in their everyday writing whose spelling they need to master is a powerful spelling skill.

Pretest Sentences: Assessment Words

(See procedures on pages Z10–Z11.)

1. Part of the Pledge of Allegiance includes the words "one nation **indivisible**."
2. I think this **attachment** goes on the end of the pole.
3. The newsletter contained a noticeable **misprint**.
4. The sails were **motionless** without any wind.
5. She lost one **contact lens** and had to wear her glasses.
6. We're throwing away the old, **worn-out** chair.
7. Hearing so much noise is **bothersome**.
8. For which **ailment** is he going to the doctor?
9. Don't **misspell** any words in your letter.
10. Is the clicking of the machine still **audible**?
11. I've tried every way **imaginable** to open this box.
12. The coach gave a **nonverbal** signal from the bench.
13. Rough **usage** is not recommended for this equipment.
14. The tomato crop was **plentiful** this year.
15. My birthday is in May, and my **birthstone** is the emerald.
16. Grandma uses a **typewriter** to write letters, but I use a computer.
17. Aren't you **fearful** of running out of supplies?
18. The divers found the **wreckage** of the old ship.
19. This vaccine has an **antibody** that will prevent the disease.
20. The vacation in Rome was an **enjoyable** experience.

Spelling and Review

Students will
- **review** and practice the spelling strategy and words taught in Unit 21.
- **review** and practic the spelling strategy and words taught in Unit 22.

Unit 21
1. mileage
2. marriage
3. equipment
4. garage
5. development
6. excitement
7. courage
8. experiment
9. document
10. garbage

Unit 22
11. pitiful
12. successful
13. wholesome
14. wonderful
15. thoughtless
16. delightful
17. doubtful
18. fearless
19. worthless
20. lonesome

 Review Unit 21: Suffixes -age, -ment

mileage	marriage	equipment	document	garage
development	garbage	excitement	courage	experiment

Write the spelling word that completes the sentence.
1. Our old car has a lot of (mileage, marriage).
2. Ken and Barb's (mileage, marriage) was in June.
3. The lab has expensive computer (courage, equipment).
4. Park the car in the (garbage, garage).
5. There's been an interesting (development, equipment) in the case.
6. The child squealed with (experiment, excitement).
7. It takes (garage, courage) to face your mistakes.
8. Today we'll do a science (experiment, excitement).
9. Take this important (excitement, document) to the office.
10. The cafeteria throws out many cans of (courage, garbage) every day.

 Review Unit 22: Suffixes -ful, -less, -some

successful	pitiful	thoughtless	wholesome	wonderful
doubtful	delightful	fearless	worthless	lonesome

Write the spelling word for each meaning.
11. full of pity
12. full of success
13. healthy
14. full of wonder
15. inconsiderate
16. full of delight
17. full of doubt
18. without fear
19. without worth
20. lonely

148

Bulletin Board Idea

Rainbow Poetry

Print the poem on this page on a piece of construction paper. Place it on the bulletin board under the title **Rainbow Poetry**. The letters of that title should be cut out of construction paper in the seven colors of the rainbow. Have the students draw or paint pictures of rainbows and write poems about rainbows to go with their art work. If any students are having trouble deciding what poetry form to use, encourage them to write haiku. Mount the students' work around the original poem. Underline the compound words in the poem.

RAINBOW POETRY

Resting briefly in the watery sky
you turn the cloud's teary
raindrops into shades of sunlight.

Each wavelength standing out
in perfect harmony with the arc
above and the arc below.

As the overcast sky dries, the light
waves silently align, like the closing
of a fan. You return as mysteriously
as you came to a place only
thunderstorms can find.

Review Unit 23: Compound Words

all right	self-addressed	everybody	throughout
bookstore	background	campfire	skyscraper
	thunderstorm	grown-up	

The underlined part of each compound word below is also part of a spelling word. Write each spelling word.

1. every<u>one</u>
2. <u>sky</u>writing
3. <u>book</u>end
4. <u>back</u>bone
5. <u>bon</u>fire
6. <u>through</u>way

Write the spelling words for these clues.

7.–8. They have hyphens.
9. It means "satisfactory" or "yes."
10. It involves rain and lightning.

Unit 23

1. everybody
2. skyscraper
3. bookstore
4. background
5. campfire
6. throughout
7. self-addressed
8. grown-up
9. all right
10. thunderstorm

 Spelling Study Strategy

Sorting by Prefixes and Suffixes

One good way to practice spelling is to place words into groups according to some spelling pattern. Here is a way to practice some of the words you studied in the past few weeks.

1. Make two columns on a large piece of paper or on the chalkboard.

2. At the top of one column write **Prefixes: ir-, anti-, il-, non-, mis-**. At the top of the other column write **Suffixes: -able, -ible, -age, -ment, -ful, -less, -some**.

3. Have a partner choose a spelling word from Units 19 through 22 and say it aloud.

4. Write the spelling word under the prefix or suffix column.

149

Objectives

Spelling and Review

Students will
- **review** and practice the spelling strategy and words taught in Unit 23.
- **learn** an alternative spelling study strategy.

Learning an Alternative Spelling Study Strategy

Students should always have a number of study strategies to draw from when it comes to learning their spelling words. **Sorting by Prefixes and Suffixes** is a fun way of differentiating between words based on their affixes. Encourage students to remember this spelling study strategy and to consider using it with any appropriate list they need to study and learn.

Weekly Test Options

Option 1:
One Spelling Word Per Sentence
(See procedures on pages Z10–Z11.)

1. Are the plans we made **acceptable** to you?
2. The weather is very **changeable** in March.
3. He learned a **valuable** lesson from his error.
4. You are **responsible** for our triumph.
5. Five hundred years ago most people were **illiterate**.
6. The delicious food was **irresistible**.
7. Teach the puppy not to **misbehave**.
8. Since this is a final sale, anything you buy is **nonreturnable**.
9. Is this the right **equipment** for the job?
10. Their **marriage** has lasted fifty years.
11. What is the **mileage** for that car?
12. Show the officer the **document**.
13. She was a **pitiful** sight in her torn clothes.
14. The pilot made a **successful** landing in spite of the terrible weather.
15. It was **thoughtless** of you to be late.
16. Eat **wholesome** foods to stay healthy.
17. Are you feeling **all right** today?
18. **Everybody** wanted to ride in the car.
19. We enclosed a **self-addressed** envelope.
20. I play baseball **throughout** the year.

Option 2:
Standardized Test

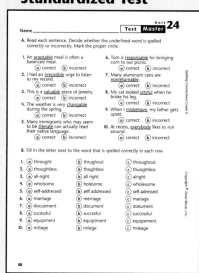

Unit 24 Test Master

(See *Teacher Resource Book*, Unit 24.)

Objectives

Spelling and Writing

Optional Enrichment

Students will
- **review** action verbs and linking verbs.
- **compose** a persuasive letter to an editor. (See **Spelling and the Writing Process** below.)

A
1. smiled
2. explained
3. will be
4. appear
5. looks
6. fly
7. practiced

B
Answers may vary.
Possible answers:
8. irresistible
9. responsible
10. nonreturnable
11. fearless
12. valuable
13. illegal
14. worthless

Grammar, Usage, and Mechanics

Action Verbs and Linking Verb

An action verb shows action. A linking verb does not show action. Instead, it connects the subject of a sentence to one or more words that describe or rename the subject. Common linking verbs include **am, is, are, was, were,** and **will be.** The verbs **become, seem, appear,** and **look** can also be used as linking verbs.

Action Verb: The men **painted** the barn.
Linking Verb: I **am** hungry, but you **seem** thirsty.

Practice Activity

A. Write the verb in each sentence below. Circle all the action verbs you write.
  1. Martin smiled at the photographer.
  2. The teacher explained the problem.
  3. After the game, we will be tired.
  4. Both kittens appear healthy.
  5. That vegetable soup looks delicious!
  6. Those butterflies fly to Mexico.
  7. The team practiced for one hour.

B. Follow each linking verb with a word from a spelling list in Units 19–23.
  8. The aroma of the cookies is ____.
  9. The father was ____ for the toddler's behavior.
  10. Those bottles are ____, so throw them out.
  11. Those early explorers seem ____!
  12. That gold watch looks ____.
  13. Parking next to the fire hydrant is ____.
  14. The broken vase is now ____.

150

Spelling and the Writing Process

Persuasive Writing

You may wish to use this writing assignment to help students master the writing process. For other writing ideas, see pages 258–259 in the Student Edition.

Explain that students will write a letter to the editor of a local or school paper about a problem. The student will try to persuade readers to take some action.

Prewriting Hint: You may wish to help students plan their writing by recommending the graphic organizer on this page. Have them replicate the organizer, filling in the blank circles with possible solutions.

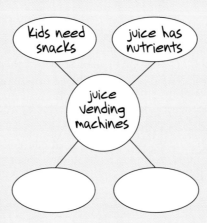

Kids need snacks

juice has nutrients

juice vending machines

Revising Hint: Remind students that when they revise their letters, they should arrange their reasons in some sort of order, such as from least important to most important. They should use transitions, such as **first** and **most important,** to signal the order.

WORKSHOP

 Proofreading Strategy

First and Last

Good writers always proofread their work for spelling errors. Here's a strategy you can use to proofread your papers.

Instead of reading in the regular way, look at one sentence at a time. Pay close attention to the first and last word. Make sure that the first word starts with a capital letter. Then make sure that the last word is followed by a punctuation mark.

This way of looking at a paper helps you focus on details, such as capital letters and punctuation, instead of ideas. It may sound funny, but it works. Try it!

Electronic Spelling

Technical Language

Computers have created a whole new language. We often see words like **diskettes** and **icons**.

Much of this technical language is not found by spell checkers, so you need to learn the spelling yourself. You can do this by making a personal dictionary of such words and their meanings. How many of these terms do you know?

byte: a unit of memory on a computer

cache: a type of computer memory

digitize: to put into a form that a computer can read

hypertext: text that is connected to other text

morph: to change from one form to another

FAQ: frequently asked questions

Which of the following are misspelled? Write the misspelled words correctly. Write **OK** if a term is correct.

1. cashe
2. morf
3. digitize
4. bite
5. hypertext
6. FAQ

Electronic Spelling

1. cache
2. morph
3. OK
4. byte
5. OK
6. OK

151

Unit 25 Home Spelling Practice

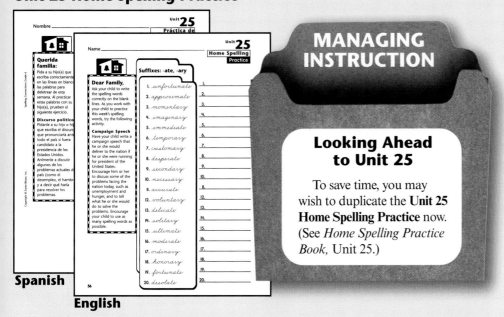

Spanish

English

MANAGING INSTRUCTION

Looking Ahead to Unit 25

To save time, you may wish to duplicate the **Unit 25 Home Spelling Practice** now. (See *Home Spelling Practice Book,* Unit 25.)

Objectives

Spelling and Writing

Students will
- **learn** a proofreading strategy.
- **understand** the importance of technical language when using a computer.
- **proofread** for misspellings of technical terms.

Using Proofreading Strategies

Students are often unaware that there are a variety of techniques they can use to proofread their own writing. Building a repertory of strategies is important to improving students' writing and editing skills.

Spelling and Technology

The advent of word processing, computer protocols, and the Internet has actually increased, not lessened, the pressure on users to be better, more aware spellers. Spell checkers, for example, create circumstances in which the ability to discriminate between an acceptable and unacceptable spelling is a critical skill. A homophone substitution, a correct spelling of the wrong word, an inadvertent word omission—these are examples of situations in computer usage that require a deeper understanding of spelling principles and a more adroit proofreading capability. It may be worthwhile to underscore this increased need as a whole-class discussion after students finish this unit's **Electronic Spelling** activity.

Basic Spelling List

unfortunate	accurate
approximate	voluntary
momentary	delicate
imaginary	solitary
immediate	ultimate
temporary	moderate
customary	ordinary
desperate	honorary
secondary	fortunate
necessary	desolate

Strategy Words

Review

circulate	operate
cooperate	populate
legislate	

Preview

anniversary	initiate
contemplate	precautionary
frustrate	

Content Words

Language Arts: The Media

broadcast	literate
journalist	expert
columnist	

Social Studies: Cultures

heritage	tribe
taboo	mores
kinsman	

Individual Needs

Challenge Words

extemporary	culinary
dietary	intricate
immaculate	considerate

Alternate Word List ★

unfortunate	necessary
imaginary	accurate
immediate	delicate
temporary	ordinary
desperate	fortunate

★ For students who need to study fewer Basic Spelling words

MATERIALS

Student Edition
Pages 152–157
Challenge Activities, p. 244

Teacher Edition
Pages T152A–T157
Challenge Activities, p. T244

Teacher Resource Book
Unit 25 Homework Master
Unit 25 Practice Masters
Flip Folder Practice Master
Unit 25 Test Master

Home Spelling Practice Book
Unit 25 Home Spelling Practice
(English or Spanish)

Other *Spelling Connections* Resources
- Audiotape, Grade 6
- Practice Book for Grammar, Usage, and Mechanics, Grade 6
- Spelling Support for Second Language Learners, Grade 6
- Support Software on CD-ROM
- Transparency Book, Grade 6
- Word Sort CD-ROM, Grade 6

OBJECTIVES

Spelling and Thinking

Students will
- **read** the spelling words in list form and in context.
- **sort** the spelling words according to their suffixes.
- **read** and remember this week's spelling strategy.

Spelling and Vocabulary

Students will
- **replace** underlined words in sentences with spelling words that have the same or nearly the same meaning.
- **write** spelling words that are synonyms or antonyms for given words.
- **write** spelling words from dictionary respellings.
- **use** the **Spelling Dictionary** respellings to identify the primary and secondary accents in spelling words.

Spelling and Reading

Students will
- **solve** analogies using spelling words.
- **complete** sentences using spelling words.
- **complete** a paragraph using spelling words.

Spelling and Writing

Students will
- **proofread** a paragraph.
- **use** the writing process to write a paragraph about an invention.
- **proofread** their writing.

MEETING INDIVIDUAL NEEDS
Learning Styles

 Visual

Divide the class into an **-ate** team and an **-ary** team. Each team assigns each member a spelling word that contains that team's suffix. At the word "Go," the students begin to play "Spelling Tag." The first player of each team writes his or her spelling word on the chalkboard and then runs back to tap the next player, who writes his or her spelling word, and so on. When a team's players have written all their words, they raise their hands to indicate they are finished. Each team checks the other team's spelling. If a word is misspelled, the other team wins by spelling the word correctly.

 Auditory

Have the students create two columns on their papers—one with the heading **Yes,** the other with the heading **No**. Pronounce a spelling word and then spell it aloud, either correctly or incorrectly. If you have spelled the word correctly, the students are to write the word in the **Yes** column. If you have misspelled it, they are to write the word, correctly spelled, in the **No** column.

 Kinesthetic

Write each letter of each spelling word on a separate 3" × 5" card and place all of the cards for each word in an envelope. Divide the class into teams and give each team an envelope. At "Go," each team opens its envelope, identifies the spelling word within, and distributes the letter cards among the members, who then align themselves in such a way that the individual cards they are holding spell the word. The first team to spell its word correctly scores a point. Continue until all the words have been used.

Hands-On Practice
All students will benefit from practicing with a **Flip Folder**. See page Z18.

Language and Cultural Differences

Those students whose first language is not English may need special help with the pronunciation and spelling of words in this unit. Create two columns on the chalkboard and have the students copy them on paper. Head one column **-ate,** the other **-ary**. Have volunteers write the spelling words in the proper column on the board while the other students write them on paper. Pronounce the words, and then have the students pronounce them.

MANAGING INSTRUCTION

3–5 Day Plan		Average	Below Average	Above Average
Day 1	Day 1	Pretest Spelling Mini-Lesson, p. T152 Spelling and Thinking, p. 152	Pretest Spelling Mini-Lesson, p. T152 Spelling and Thinking, p. 152	Pretest Spelling and Thinking, p. 152
	Day 2	Spelling and Vocabulary, p. 153	Spelling and Vocabulary, p. 153 (or) Unit 25 Practice Master, A and B	Spelling and Vocabulary, p. 153 Spelling and Reading, p. 154
Day 2	Day 3	Spelling and Reading, p. 154	Spelling and Reading, p. 154 (or) Unit 25 Practice Master, C and D	Challenge Activities, p. 244
	Day 4	Spelling and Writing, p. 155 Unit 25 Homework Master	Spelling and Writing, p. 155	Spelling and Writing, p. 155 Unit 25 Homework Master
Day 3	Day 5	Weekly Test	Weekly Test	Weekly Test
Vocabulary Connections (pages 156 and 157) may be used anytime during this unit.				

Objectives

Spelling and Thinking

Students will

• **read** the spelling words in list form and in context.
• **sort** the spelling words according to their suffixes.
• **read** and remember this week's spelling strategy.

UNIT PRETEST

Use **Pretest Sentences** below. Refer to the self-checking procedures on student page 256. You may wish to use the **Unit 25 Word List Overhead Transparency** as part of the checking procedure.

TEACHING THE STRATEGY

Spelling Mini-Lesson

Write **fortunate** and **honorary** on the board. Ask volunteers to read the words and identify the base word and suffix in each word. (fortune + ate, honor + ary)

Review with the students that a suffix is a word ending that can change both the meaning and the part of speech of the original word. Write each suffix and its meanings on the chalkboard as you explain the meanings of each suffix:

• The suffix **-ate** means "having" or "characterized by."
• The suffix **-ary** means "of," "relating to," "connected with," or "place of."

Discuss how the meanings of each base word and suffix combine to convey a new meaning in the new word. (For example, **fortunate** means "having good fortune"; **honorary** means "of or relating to honor.")

Explain that both **honorary** and **fortunate** are words that describe nouns, i.e., they are adjectives. Explain that the suffixes **-ate** and **-ary** can be used to form adjectives.

Ask volunteers to read the rest of the spelling words and to discuss the ways in which the meaning of each suffix affects the meaning of each spelling word.

Ask a volunteer to read **Remember the Strategy** on page 152.

Order of answers may vary.

-ate

1. unfortunate ★
2. (approximate)
3. (immediate) ★
4. desperate ★
5. (accurate) ★
6. delicate ★
7. ultimate
8. moderate
9. fortunate ★
10. desolate

-ary

11. (momentary)
12. (imaginary) ★
13. temporary ★
14. (customary)
15. (secondary)
16. necessary ★
17. voluntary
18. solitary
19. ordinary ★
20. (honorary)

152

READ THE SPELLING WORDS

1.	unfortunate	*unfortunate*	It is **unfortunate** that he is sick.
2.	approximate	*approximate*	What is your **approximate** height?
3.	momentary	*momentary*	The game delay was **momentary**.
4.	imaginary	*imaginary*	The child has an **imaginary** friend.
5.	immediate	*immediate*	She wants an **immediate** response.
6.	temporary	*temporary*	The power outage was **temporary**.
7.	customary	*customary*	It is **customary** to tip a cab driver.
8.	desperate	*desperate*	He was **desperate** to find his dad.
9.	secondary	*secondary*	For her, fun is **secondary** to work.
10.	necessary	*necessary*	It is **necessary** that I leave soon.
11.	accurate	*accurate*	She drew an **accurate** map.
12.	voluntary	*voluntary*	My decision to quit was **voluntary**.
13.	delicate	*delicate*	Be careful with the **delicate** plate.
14.	solitary	*solitary*	One **solitary** car was in the lot.
15.	ultimate	*ultimate*	His **ultimate** goal is to succeed.
16.	moderate	*moderate*	Drive at a **moderate** rate of speed.
17.	ordinary	*ordinary*	My dress is plain and **ordinary**.
18.	honorary	*honorary*	He is an **honorary** club member.
19.	fortunate	*fortunate*	I am **fortunate** to have friends.
20.	desolate	*desolate*	The street was dark and **desolate**.

SORT THE SPELLING WORDS

1.–10. Write the spelling words with the **-ate** suffix. Circle the words with a double consonant in their spelling.

11.–20. Write the spelling words with the **-ary** suffix. Circle the words in which the suffix has been added to a base word.

REMEMBER THE SPELLING STRATEGY

Remember that the suffixes **-ate** and **-ary** can be added to root words and base words to form adjectives such as **delicate** and **honorary**.

Pretest Sentences (See procedures on pages Z10–Z11.)

★ **1.** The tragedy produced many **unfortunate** results.
 2. I did not know the exact number, so my guess was **approximate**.
 3. There was a **momentary** delay in the broadcast.
★ **4.** Some stories are about **imaginary** characters.
★ **5.** The police officer's **immediate** action prevented a tragedy.
★ **6.** The substitute was a **temporary** replacement for our teacher.
 7. It is **customary** to celebrate the Fourth of July with fireworks.
★ **8.** The situation was so **desperate** that nothing seemed to help.
 9. The ninth grade is usually the beginning of **secondary** school.
★**10.** Is it **necessary** to read this chapter carefully?
★**11.** If most of your answers are **accurate,** you will pass the test.
 12. We were asked to work for the cause on a **voluntary** basis.
★**13.** The bride's gown was trimmed with **delicate** lace.
 14. She is a **solitary** person who likes to be alone.
 15. The last, or **ultimate,** phase of the operation begins today.
 16. Since her views are not extreme, she takes a **moderate** position.
★**17.** The meal was not special but **ordinary**.
 18. She was given an **honorary** degree, even though she had never attended that school.
★**19.** It was very **fortunate** that Alan came along to assist me.
 20. The ghost town is a very **desolate** place.

Spelling and Vocabulary

Word Replacement

Write spelling words to replace the underlined words.

1. She made a <u>frantic</u> attempt to score a goal in the final moments of the game.
2. Your decision to join the club should be <u>by choice</u>.
3. The <u>final</u> cost of the job is one hundred dollars.
4. His degree from the university is <u>a token of honor</u>.
5. It was a <u>favorable</u> day when we moved here.
6. It is <u>traditional</u> to take off your hat at the door.

Synonyms and Antonyms

Write the spelling words that are synonyms or antonyms for these words.

Synonyms
7. uninhabited
8. required
9. brief; taking only a moment
10. without delay
11. correct

Antonyms
12. excessive
13. exact
14. tough
15. permanent
16. lucky

Write the spelling words for these respellings.

17. /ôr′ dn ĕr′ē/
18. /sĕk′ ən dĕr′ē/
19. /sŏl′ ĭ tĕr′ē/
20. /ĭ măj′ ə nĕr′ē/

In the words you wrote:
- Circle the syllable with the primary stress, shown in boldface and followed by an accent mark.
- Underline the syllable with the secondary stress, shown in regular type and followed by an accent mark.

Word Replacement
1. desperate
2. voluntary
3. ultimate
4. honorary
5. fortunate
6. customary

Synonyms and Antonyms
7. desolate
8. necessary
9. momentary
10. immediate
11. accurate
12. moderate
13. approximate
14. delicate
15. temporary
16. unfortunate

Using the Dictionary
17. (or)dinary
18. (sec)ondary
19. (sol)itary
20. i(mag)inary

153

Developing Oral Language Skills

Ask students to work in pairs. The first student asks a question that includes one of the spelling words from the list. For example, the student might say, "Did something unfortunate happen to you?" The second student answers the question. The answer must also include a spelling word, but the spelling word must have a different suffix. For example, the second student might respond, "Nothing out of the ordinary has happened to me lately." Have each pair of students continue until they have used as many spelling words as possible.

MEETING INDIVIDUAL NEEDS

Providing More Help

Read the following pairs of words aloud. Tell the students that only one word in each pair is correct and that they are to write that word.

immediate, immediary
accurary, **accurate**
desperary, **desperate**
desolate, desolary
fortunary, **fortunate**
secondate, **secondary**
honorary, honorate
necessary, necessate
solitate, **solitary**
voluntary, voluntate

★Students who need to study fewer words should use the **Alternate Word List**. This list is starred on page T152 in the Teacher Edition. The **Unit 25 Practice Masters** (*Teacher Resource Book*) provide additional practice with these words.

Unit 25 Practice Masters

Name _____

Practice Master 25

1. immediate 3. delicate 5. fortunate 7. necessary 9. ordinary
2. accurate 4. desperate 6. unfortunate 8. temporary 10. imaginary

A. These words are misspelled. Write the spelling words correctly.

1. desparate _____
2. temperary _____
3. fortuneate _____
4. immaginary _____
5. neccesary _____
6. imediate _____
7. unfortuneate _____
8. acurate _____

B. A **thesaurus** is used to find synonyms and antonyms. Write the spelling words that are synonyms or antonyms for these words.

Synonyms
1. make-believe _____
2. direct _____
3. short-lived _____

Antonyms
4. tough _____
5. unusual _____
6. fortunate _____

C. Write the spelling word that answers each question.

1. Which word means "mild" or "soft"? _____
2. Which word means "usual"? _____
3. Which word means "needed"? _____
4. Which word means "without mistakes"? _____

89

Practice Master 25

necessary   ordinary
temporary   imaginary

hidden in the puzzle. Circle

a	t	e	r	p	s	i
p	e	r	a	t	e	n
c	f	j	w	h	y	m
t	b	w	s	h	n	x
s	s	a	r	y	b	a
s	u	a	l	c	f	x
o	g	k	m	e	h	d
g	d	r	w	e	z	r
r	t	u	n	a	t	e
q	e	i	k	q	n	l

90

Objectives

Spelling and Reading

Students will
- **solve** analogies using spelling words.
- **complete** sentences using spelling words.
- **complete** a paragraph using spelling words.

One-Minute Handwriting Hint

The two slant strokes in the lowercase **y** should be parallel. Do not loop the undercurve-slant stroke.

PARALLEL

Legible handwriting can boost spelling scores by as much as 20%.

Solve the Analogies

1. secondary
2. delicate
3. solitary
4. voluntary
5. approximate
6. ordinary
7. momentary

Complete the Sentences

8. unfortunate
9. honorary
10. customary
11. desolate
12. accurate
13. moderate
14. desperate

Complete the Paragraph

15. fortunate
16. imaginary
17. necessary
18. immediate
19. temporary
20. ultimate

---

unfortunate	approximate	momentary	imaginary
immediate	temporary	customary	desperate
secondary	necessary	accurate	voluntary
delicate	solitary	ultimate	moderate
ordinary	honorary	fortunate	desolate

Solve the Analogies Write a spelling word to complete each analogy.

1. **First** is to **second** as **primary** is to ____.
2. **Reckless** is to **careless** as **fragile** is to ____.
3. **Loyal** is to **faithful** as **single** is to ____.
4. **Tragic** is to **comic** as **forced** is to ____.
5. **Definite** is to **vague** as **exact** is to ____.
6. **Difficult** is to **troublesome** as **common** is to ____.
7. **Caution** is to **cautionary** as **moment** is to ____.

Complete the Sentences Write a spelling word to complete each sentence.

8. It was ____ that you could not see the wonderful play.
9. The politician was given an ____ position on the board.
10. It is ____ in Chan's home to eat with chopsticks.
11. The landscape was ____ after the tornado swept through.
12. Every detail of the plan must be ____ before I begin to build.
13. Her ____ approach to the crisis kept everyone calm.
14. The survivors of the hurricane were ____ for food and water.

Complete the Paragraph Write spelling words from the box to complete the paragraph.

Ice skaters were __15.__ in 1817 when Joseph Merlin, a Belgian, dreamed up skates that could move on dry land. To make his __16.__ skates into real ones, it was __17.__ to replace ice-skate blades with wheels. Merlin's roller skates became an __18.__ success and not just a __19.__ fad. Roller-skating became the __20.__ summer sport for ice skaters.

necessary
ultimate
immediate
temporary
fortunate
imaginary

154

MEETING INDIVIDUAL NEEDS

Providing More Challenge

Challenge Words and **Challenge Activities** for Unit 25 appear on page 244. **Challenge Word Test Sentences** appear on page T244.

Unit 25 Challenge Activities

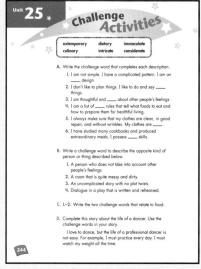

Weekly Test Options

Option 1:
One Spelling Word Per Sentence
(See procedures on pages Z10–Z11.)

★ 1. The student checked her answer to be sure it was **accurate**.
2. What is the **approximate** time of the meeting?
3. In some countries it is **customary** for men to wear hats indoors.
★ 4. An egg has a very **delicate** shell.
5. The land was **desolate** after the fire.
★ 6. The hungry animal was **desperate** for food.
★ 7. He is **fortunate** to have his own horse.
8. They were made **honorary** members of the club.
★ 9. She told the class a tale about an **imaginary** kingdom.
★10. He gave an **immediate** answer to the question.
11. He holds **moderate** beliefs on most subjects.
12. She had a **momentary** angry spell.
★13. Do you have the **necessary** tools for the experiment?
★14. In June the lake regained its **ordinary** water level.

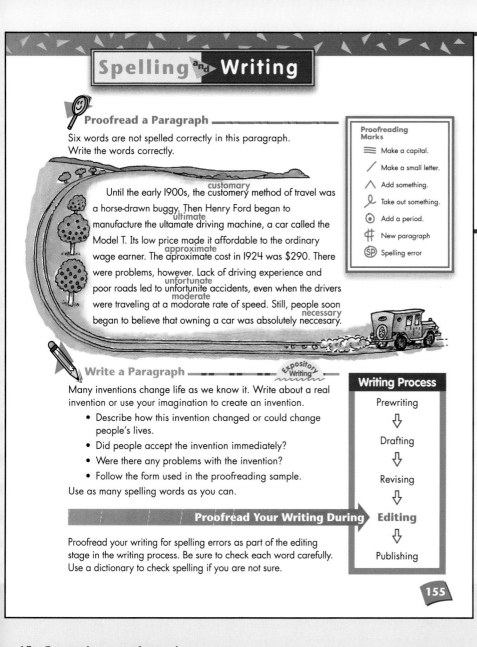

Spelling and Writing

Proofread a Paragraph

Six words are not spelled correctly in this paragraph. Write the words correctly.

> customary
> Until the early 1900s, the customery method of travel was
> a horse-drawn buggy. Then Henry Ford began to
> ultimate
> manufacture the ultamate driving machine, a car called the
> Model T. Its low price made it affordable to the ordinary
> approximate
> wage earner. The aproximate cost in 1924 was $290. There
> were problems, however. Lack of driving experience and
> unfortunate
> poor roads led to unfortunite accidents, even when the drivers
> moderate
> were traveling at a modorate rate of speed. Still, people soon
> necessary
> began to believe that owning a car was absolutely neccesary.

Proofreading Marks

≡ Make a capital.
/ Make a small letter.
∧ Add something.
ℓ Take out something.
⊙ Add a period.
¶ New paragraph.
SP Spelling error

Write a Paragraph

Expository Writing

Many inventions change life as we know it. Write about a real invention or use your imagination to create an invention.

- Describe how this invention changed or could change people's lives.
- Did people accept the invention immediately?
- Were there any problems with the invention?
- Follow the form used in the proofreading sample.

Use as many spelling words as you can.

Proofread Your Writing During → Editing

Proofread your writing for spelling errors as part of the editing stage in the writing process. Be sure to check each word carefully. Use a dictionary to check spelling if you are not sure.

Writing Process

Prewriting
⇩
Drafting
⇩
Revising
⇩
Editing
⇩
Publishing

155

---

15. Orange is a **secondary** color.
16. She spent a **solitary** day with little to do.
★17. I had a **temporary** job during the summer.
18. His **ultimate** goal is success.
★19. The **unfortunate** remark hurt the boy's feelings.
20. He made a **voluntary** choice about his career.

Option 2:
Multiple Spelling Words Per Sentence
(See procedures on pages Z10–Z11.)

1. Please take **immediate** steps to solve this **delicate** problem.
2. It is not **necessary** to have a perfectly **accurate** answer, only an **approximate** one.
3. He is an **unfortunate** and **desperate** person.
4. She received an **honorary** degree for her **voluntary** work.
5. It is **customary** to wear **ordinary** clothes to the movies.
6. We were **fortunate** to find a **temporary** baby sitter.
7. Her **momentary** distraction did not affect the **ultimate** success of her **secondary** goals.
8. A **solitary** child will often invent **imaginary** friends.
9. There was **moderate** flood damage in the **desolate** area.

Option 3:
Standardized Test
(See *Teacher Resource Book,* Unit 25.)

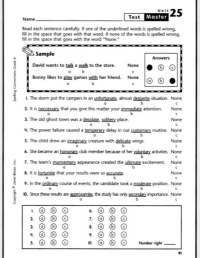

**Unit 25
Test Master**

TI55

Objectives

Strategy Words

Students will
- **review** words studied previously that are related to the spelling strategy.
- **preview** unknown words that are related to the spelling strategy.

Optional Enrichment

VOCABULARY CONNECTIONS

Strategy Words

Remind the students that the **Strategy Words** relate to the spelling patterns they have studied in this unit. The **Review Words** are below grade level, and the **Preview Words** are above grade level. You may wish to use the following sentences to introduce the words in context.

Review Words:
Words From Grade 5
1. They will **circulate** this bulletin among the workers.
2. Please **cooperate** with the leader of the group.
3. They will **legislate** laws that prevent the abuse of animals.
4. We must **operate** the machinery very carefully.
5. Europeans wanted to **populate** the colonies to gain wealth.

Preview Words:
Words From Grade 7
6. My birthday is the **anniversary** of my birth.
7. Did you **contemplate** the consequences of your action?
8. It will **frustrate** the puppy if you are not consistent in his training.
9. I will **initiate** the proceedings now.
10. The **precautionary** measures he had taken were extremely important.

Review Words
1. cooperate
2. legislate
3. operate
4. populate
5. circulate

Preview Words
6. anniversary
7. frustrate
8. precautionary
9. contemplate
10. initiate

Strategy Words

Review Words: Suffixes -ate, -ary

Write words from the box to complete this news article.

| circulate | cooperate | legislate | operate | populate |

Conservationists are working hard to persuade Congress to **1.** ____ with their efforts to save the fish in southern waters. They are urging their representatives to **2.** ____ restrictions for oil and gas companies that **3.** ____ offshore drilling equipment. It also may be necessary to **4.** ____ the waters with more shrimp and fish. The conservationists will soon begin to **5.** ____ a flier promoting their efforts.

Preview Words: Suffixes -ate, -ary

Write a word from the box to complete each sentence.

| anniversary | contemplate | frustrate |
| initiate | precautionary | |

6. It was the first ____ of the opening of their bookstore.
7. The difficult homework assignment seemed to ____ him.
8. Before the storm, she gathered supplies as a ____ measure.
9. I need to ____ your request before I respond.
10. We will soon ____ a different way of resolving disagreements.

156

Unit 25 RECAP

You may wish to assign the **Unit 25 Homework Master** (*Teacher Resource Book*, Unit 25) as a fun way to recap the spelling words.

Unit 25 Homework Master

Name _____ Homework Master Unit 25

Twenty spelling words are hidden in the puzzle. Read down, backwards, and across. Circle the words. (Note: The letters of one word will form a square when you circle them.)

c	a	e	t	a	m	i	x	o	r	p	p	a	c	u	s
s	t	a	t	i	o	n	s	h	o	u	y	v	t	o	m
y	r	a	r	o	p	m	e	t	r	a	r	o	a	r	y
e	e	t	a	r	u	c	c	a	d	e	a	l	i	f	m
t	e	a	l	m	e	e	o	w	i	u	s	u	y	o	o
a	y	d	m	o	u	n	n	t	n	l	s	n	r	r	d
r	r	e	i	m	m	e	d	i	a	t	e	t	a	t	e
e	a	s	i	n	n	n	a	m	r	i	c	a	n	u	r
p	r	o	e	e	d	u	r	e	y	m	e	r	i	n	a
s	o	l	i	t	a	r	y	a	m	a	n	y	g	a	t
e	n	a	t	r	u	n	f	o	r	t	u	n	a	t	e
d	o	t	o	a	y	r	a	t	n	e	m	o	m	e	s
s	h	e	p	d	e	l	i	c	a	t	e	c	i	n	o

Write a spelling word to answer each question.

1. Which word means "mild" or "soft"? _____
2. Which word means "alone"? _____
3. Which word means "not extreme"? _____
4. Which word means "of one's own choice"? _____
5. Which word means "usual"? _____

Write three similar questions of your own. Answer them with a spelling word.

1. _____
2. _____
3. _____

92

Spelling Connections Grade 6

Copyright © Zaner-Bloser, Inc.

Content Words

Language Arts: The Media

Write a word from the box to complete each sentence.

broadcast	journalist	columnist	literate	expert

1. If you can read and write, you are ____.
2. If you write and publish the news, you are a ____.
3. If you are knowledgeable about a certain subject, you are an ____.
4. If you write a magazine column, you are a ____.
5. The transmission of a television program is a ____.

Social Studies: Cultures

Write each scrambled word from the box correctly.

heritage	taboo	kinsman	tribe	mores

6. A male relative is a <u>maskinn</u>.
7. When several villages share a common ancestry, language, culture, and name, the result is a <u>brite</u>.
8. The customs accepted by a particular social group are considered this group's <u>romes</u>.
9. When a society forbids the use or even the mention of something, that subject or object is <u>tooba</u>.
10. Our <u>gearithe</u> is passed on through the generations.

Apply the Spelling Strategy

Circle the suffix **-ate** in one of the Content Words you wrote.

Word Study

Synonyms

Synonyms are words with meanings that are the same or almost the same. **Baffle, irk, thwart,** and **disappoint** are synonyms for **frustrate**. Write the one Strategy Word that is a synonym for these words: **start, introduce, inaugurate.**

Language Arts: The Media
1. liter(ate)
2. journalist
3. expert
4. columnist
5. broadcast

Social Studies: Cultures
6. kinsman
7. tribe
8. mores
9. taboo
10. heritage

Synonyms
1. initiate

157

Unit 26 Home Spelling Practice

Spanish

English

MANAGING INSTRUCTION

Looking Ahead to Unit 26

To save time, you may wish to duplicate the **Unit 26 Home Spelling Practice** now. (See *Home Spelling Practice Book,* Unit 26.)

Objectives

Content Words

Students will
- **expand** vocabulary with content-related words.
- **relate** the spelling strategy to words outside the basic spelling list.
- **understand** and identify synonyms.

Content Words

Language Arts: The Media

Use these sentences to introduce the words and their meanings.

1. We heard the **broadcast** of the World Series on the radio.
2. It takes hard work to succeed as a **journalist**.
3. My favorite **columnist** is on vacation.
4. It is absolutely necessary that we become **literate** to live independently.
5. She is an **expert** in science.

Social Studies: Cultures

Use these sentences to introduce the words and their meanings.

6. The ideas and beliefs our families instill in us are part of our **heritage**.
7. In some cultures it is **taboo** to use modern conveniences.
8. My uncle is a **kinsman**.
9. We studied how each **tribe** of Native Americans grew food.
10. The **mores** of most nations developed slowly through the years.

Word Study

Synonyms

Review the use of a thesaurus, and challenge students to use it to identify synonyms for overused words in their writing. Ask students to identify synonyms for other words in the unit, such as **expert** and **contemplate**.

Basic Spelling List

underground	interact
interchange	midway
intramural	underpass
submarine	superstar
underneath	subway
midsummer	intersect
interstate	supervise
supersonic	interface
undercover	subtotal
intrastate	interview

Strategy Words

Review
midnight	internal
underline	midafternoon
subhead	

Preview
intermission	superficial
midpoint	underestimate
subterranean	

Content Words

Language Arts: Sentences
declarative	fragment
imperative	exclamatory
interrogative	

Social Studies: Maps
boundary	settlement
local	subdivide
real estate	

Individual Needs

Challenge Words
midyear	interfere
interject	superpower
substandard	underlying

Alternate Word List ★
underground	midsummer
interchange	interstate
intramural	subway
submarine	supervise
underneath	interview

★ For students who need to study fewer Basic Spelling words

MATERIALS

Student Edition
Pages 158–163
Challenge Activities, p. 245

Teacher Edition
Pages T158A–T163
Challenge Activities, p. T245

Teacher Resource Book
Unit 26 Homework Master
Unit 26 Practice Masters
Flip Folder Practice Master
Unit 26 Test Master

Home Spelling Practice Book
Unit 26 Home Spelling Practice
(English or Spanish)

Other *Spelling Connections* Resources
- Audiotape, Grade 6
- Practice Book for Grammar, Usage, and Mechanics, Grade 6
- Spelling Support for Second Language Learners, Grade 6
- Support Software on CD-ROM
- Transparency Book, Grade 6
- Word Sort CD-ROM, Grade 6

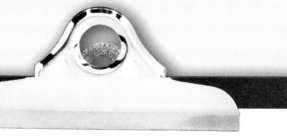

OBJECTIVES

Spelling and Thinking
Students will
- **read** the spelling words in list form and in context.
- **sort** the spelling words according to the meanings of their prefixes.
- **read** and remember this week's spelling strategy.

Spelling and Vocabulary
Students will
- **replace** underlined words in sentences with spelling words that have the same or nearly the same meaning.
- **write** spelling words for clues.
- **alphabetize** spelling words beyond their first letter.

Spelling and Reading
Students will
- **solve** analogies using spelling words.
- **complete** sentences using spelling words.
- **complete** a paragraph using spelling words.

Spelling and Writing
Students will
- **proofread** a paragraph.
- **use** the writing process to write a paragraph about a construction project.
- **proofread** their writing.

MEETING INDIVIDUAL NEEDS
Learning Styles

 Visual

Divide the class into two teams. Print each spelling word on a piece of construction paper. Cut each word apart into individual letters. Give the letters for half of the spelling words to one team and the letters for the rest of the spelling words to the other team. Tell each team that—when you say "Begin!"—they are to put their letters together to form ten spelling words. The team that is first to form their spelling words correctly wins.

 Auditory

Assign each player one spelling word. Have the player scramble the letters. Each player in turn writes the scrambled word on the chalkboard, pronounces the letters in scrambled order, and calls on a volunteer to identify the word, pronounce it again, and spell it aloud correctly.

 Kinesthetic

Have the students make up grids similar to Bingo grids, each with twenty squares. Each student writes a spelling word of his or her choice in each square. Play "Spelling Bingo" by saying a spelling word and having each student cover the square on the grid that contains that word when it is called. The first student to cover all of his or her squares wins the game.

> **Hands-On Practice**
> All students will benefit from practicing with a **Flip Folder**. See page Z18.

Language and Cultural Differences

Spanish-speaking students may have difficulty pronouncing and spelling the words that have the **short i** sound, since this sound does not exist in Spanish. You may wish to write the words **international, midnight,** and **intrapersonal** on the chalkboard. Identify the prefixes and have the students pronounce each prefix as you circle it. Then have volunteers identify the spelling words that begin with the prefixes **mid-, intro-,** and **intra-**. Have them then write the words on the chalkboard and pronounce them.

MANAGING INSTRUCTION

3–5 Day Plan		Average	Below Average	Above Average
Day 1	**Day 1**	Pretest Spelling Mini-Lesson, p. T158 Spelling and Thinking, p. 158	Pretest Spelling Mini-Lesson, p. T158 Spelling and Thinking, p. 158	Pretest Spelling and Thinking, p. 158
	Day 2	Spelling and Vocabulary, p. 159	Spelling and Vocabulary, p. 159 (or) Unit 26 Practice Master, A and B	Spelling and Vocabulary, p. 159 Spelling and Reading, p. 160
Day 2	**Day 3**	Spelling and Reading, p. 160	Spelling and Reading, p. 160 (or) Unit 26 Practice Master, C and D	Challenge Activities, p. 245
	Day 4	Spelling and Writing, p. 161 Unit 26 Homework Master	Spelling and Writing, p. 161	Spelling and Writing, p. 161 Unit 26 Homework Master
Day 3	**Day 5**	Weekly Test	Weekly Test	Weekly Test

Vocabulary Connections (pages 162 and 163) may be used anytime during this unit.

Objectives

Spelling and Thinking

Students will
- **read** the spelling words in list form and in context.
- **sort** the spelling words according to the meanings of their prefixes.
- **read** and remember this week's spelling strategy.

UNIT PRETEST

Use **Pretest Sentences** below. Refer to the self-checking procedures on student page 256. You may wish to use the **Unit 26 Word List Overhead Transparency** as part of the checking procedure.

TEACHING THE STRATEGY

Spelling Mini-Lesson

Write these words on the chalkboard: **subway, midsummer, underpass, superstar, interact, intrastate.** Ask volunteers to read the words and identify the base word and prefix that were combined to form each word. (sub- + way; mid- + summer; under- + pass; super- + star; inter- + act; intra- + state)

Review the fact that a prefix can change both the meaning and part of speech of the original word. Explain that these prefixes indicate position. Write each prefix and its meaning on the board as you explain the meaning of each prefix:
- **under-** and **sub-** mean "under" or "beneath";
- **mid-** means "middle";
- **super-** means "above";
- **inter-** means "between";
- **intra-** means "within."

Discuss the ways in which the meaning of each base word and the meaning of each prefix combine to convey a new meaning in the new word.

Ask volunteers to read the rest of the spelling words and to discuss the ways in which the meaning of each prefix affects the meaning of each spelling word.

Read **Remember the Spelling Strategy** on page 158.

Unit 26
Prefixes: under-, sub-, super-, inter-, intra-, mid-

Spelling and Thinking

Order of answers may vary.

middle
1. midsummer ★
2. midway

under or beneath
3. underground ★
4. submarine ★
5. underneath ★
6. undercover
7. underpass
8. subway ★
9. subtotal

above
10. supersonic
11. superstar
12. supervise ★

between
13. interchange ★
14. interstate ★
15. interact
16. intersect
17. interface
18. interview ★

within
19. intramural ★
20. intrastate

158

READ THE SPELLING WORDS

1. underground	*underground*	A mole lives **underground**.
2. interchange	*interchange*	It was an **interchange** of ideas.
3. intramural	*intramural*	He plays **intramural** soccer.
4. submarine	*submarine*	The **submarine** is underwater.
5. underneath	*underneath*	Dust is **underneath** the bed.
6. midsummer	*midsummer*	Our picnic is in **midsummer**.
7. interstate	*interstate*	Is this an **interstate** highway?
8. supersonic	*supersonic*	He pilots a **supersonic** aircraft.
9. undercover	*undercover*	She is an **undercover** officer.
10. intrastate	*intrastate*	Our **intrastate** taxes rose.
11. interact	*interact*	Some toddlers **interact** well.
12. midway	*midway*	We plan to meet **midway**.
13. underpass	*underpass*	A car stalled in the **underpass**.
14. superstar	*superstar*	He is a baseball **superstar**.
15. subway	*subway*	Did you travel by **subway**?
16. intersect	*intersect*	Those two streets **intersect**.
17. supervise	*supervise*	She will **supervise** the project.
18. interface	*interface*	Will all the software **interface**?
19. subtotal	*subtotal*	Add tax to the bill's **subtotal**.
20. interview	*interview*	A reporter will **interview** you.

SORT THE SPELLING WORDS

Write the word with the prefix that means:

1.–2. "middle."   13.–18. "between."
3.–9. "under" or "beneath."   19.–20. "within."
10.–12. "above."

REMEMBER THE SPELLING STRATEGY

Remember that the prefix **mid-** means "middle," **under-** and **sub-** mean "under" or "beneath," **super-** means "above," **inter-** means "between," and **intra-** means "within."

Pretest Sentences (See procedures on pages Z10–Z11.)

★ 1. Earth's water table is an **underground** water supply.
★ 2. Our conversation was a lively **interchange** of ideas.
★ 3. Our school's **intramural** athletic program is popular.
★ 4. Have you ever watched a **submarine** descend into the water?
★ 5. The grass felt cool **underneath** our bare feet.
★ 6. His garden is beautiful in **midsummer**.
★ 7. My father drove to New York on a large **interstate** highway.
  8. The **supersonic** transport travels faster than the speed of sound.
  9. The detectives used an **undercover** operation to catch them.
 10. Players from each county entered the **intrastate** competition.
 11. A psychologist studies how people **interact** in certain situations.
 12. The runner was tagged out **midway** between second and third base.
 13. That truck is too high to get through the **underpass**.
 14. She is a **superstar** whose movies are known all over the world.
★15. A **subway** is a train that runs below the ground.
 16. The street I live on does not **intersect** a major avenue.
★17. Who will **supervise** the activities of the youngest children?
 18. The computer **interface** helps us use the computer.
 19. The **subtotal** of the bill did not include the tax or tip.
★20. After the job **interview**, she was hired immediately.

Spelling and Vocabulary

Word Meanings

Write the spelling word that could best replace each underlined word or phrase.

1. The puppies did not cooperate well with each other.
2. The heat in the middle of the summer can be unbearable.
3. Parts of an electrical system must connect at a common point smoothly.
4. We are supposed to meet them where the two roads cross.
5. The mutual exchange of ideas at the meeting helped us all.
6. He asked us to oversee the building project.
7. Add the tip to the partial total of our dinner check.

Word Clues

Write the spelling words that match these definitions.

8. middle distance
9. below ground
10. beneath cover
11. below sea
12. above the speed of sound
13. road beneath a railroad
14. train beneath the ground
15. between one state and another

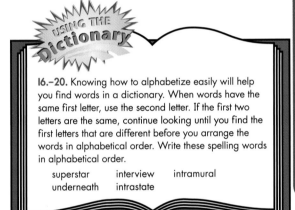

16.–20. Knowing how to alphabetize easily will help you find words in a dictionary. When words have the same first letter, use the second letter. If the first two letters are the same, continue looking until you find the first letters that are different before you arrange the words in alphabetical order. Write these spelling words in alphabetical order.

superstar   interview   intramural
underneath   intrastate

Word Meanings	
1.	interact
2.	midsummer
3.	interface
4.	intersect
5.	interchange
6.	supervise
7.	subtotal

Word Clues	
8.	midway
9.	underground
10.	undercover
11.	submarine
12.	supersonic
13.	underpass
14.	subway
15.	interstate

Using the Dictionary	
16.	interview
17.	intramural
18.	intrastate
19.	superstar
20.	underneath

159

Spelling and Vocabulary

Students will
- **replace** underlined words in sentences with spelling words that have the same or nearly the same meaning.
- **write** spelling words for clues.
- **alphabetize** spelling words beyond their first letter.

Developing Oral Language Skills

Have students work with a partner. Ask them to imagine that they are driving across the country. They should role play a dialogue that might take place as they travel, using as many spelling words as possible. After practicing a few times, have volunteers perform their role play for the entire class. Have the class keep a list of all the spelling word used.

MEETING INDIVIDUAL NEEDS

Providing More Help

To aid the students in understanding these prefixes that indicate position, write the six prefixes as headings for columns on the chalkboard. Write a one-word meaning for the prefix under each heading, as follows: **mid- (middle); under- (below); super-(above); sub- (beneath); inter- (among); intra- (within)**. Have volunteers write the spelling words under the appropriate columns.

★Students who need to study fewer words should use the **Alternate Word List**. This list is starred on page T158 in the Teacher Edition. The **Unit 26 Practice Masters** (*Teacher Resource Book*) provide additional practice with these words.

Unit 26 Practice Masters

Spelling and Reading

Students will
- **solve** analogies using spelling words.
- **complete** sentences using spelling words.
- **complete** a paragraph using spelling words.

One-Minute Handwriting Hint

Be sure to close the oval in the lowercase **d**. Pause at the top of the first undercurve, and then pull the slant stroke to the baseline. Do not loop the letter.

d
↑
PULL TO BASELINE

Legible handwriting can boost spelling scores by as much as 20%.

Solve the Analogies
1. undercover
2. underneath
3. superstar
4. underpass
5. submarine

Complete the Sentences
6. intrastate
7. interface
8. intersect
9. supersonic
10. intramural
11. interview
12. subtotal
13. interstate
14. interchange

Complete the Paragraph
15. subway
16. midsummer
17. underground
18. midway
19. interact
20. supervise

160

Spelling and Reading

underground	interchange	intramural	submarine
underneath	midsummer	interstate	supersonic
undercover	intrastate	interact	midway
underpass	superstar	subway	intersect
supervise	interface	subtotal	interview

Solve the Analogies Write a word to complete each analogy.

1. **Alert** is to **attentive** as **secret** is to _____.
2. **Over** is to **above** as **below** is to _____.
3. **Author** is to **writer** as **celebrity** is to _____.
4. **Bridge** is to **tunnel** as **overpass** is to _____.
5. **Above** is to **ocean liner** as **below** is to _____.

Complete the Sentences Write a spelling word that completes each sentence.

6. The rates for both out-of-state and _____ calls will rise.
7. I must get these two software programs to _____.
8. There is a disabled car where the roads _____.
9. The first _____ flight occurred in 1947.
10. He is organizing an _____ basketball league after school.
11. The senator answered many questions during the _____.
12. Because he was low on cash, he asked the cashier for a _____ before she rang up all of his groceries.
13. One _____ highway extends from California to Florida.
14. You can _____ the parts of these two machines.

Complete the Paragraph Write spelling words from the box to complete the paragraph.

Work is going forward on the city's new ___15.___ The ___16.___ heat made the work difficult for those working in small ___17.___ spaces. "Thanks to your hard work," the foreman told his workers, "we are at the ___18.___ point in the project. You have shown that you can ___19.___ well together. It is a pleasure to ___20.___ you."

| midsummer |
| midway |
| interact |
| underground |
| supervise |
| subway |

MEETING INDIVIDUAL NEEDS
Providing More Challenge

Challenge Words and **Challenge Activities** for Unit 26 appear on page 245. **Challenge Word Test Sentences** appear on page T245.

Unit 26 Challenge Activities

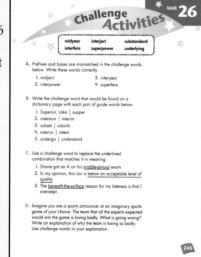

Weekly Test Options

Option 1:
One Spelling Word Per Sentence
(See procedures on pages Z10–Z11.)

1. When chemicals **interact,** the result can be dangerous.
★ 2. Free **interchange** of ideas is an important American liberty.
3. When oil floats on water, the two substances **interface**.
4. The two roads **intersect** in the middle of town.
★ 5. The three governors signed the **interstate** agreement.
★ 6. I will **interview** the school principal for my newspaper article.
★ 7. Our school has a large **intramural** sports program.
8. She is the Texas **intrastate** high scorer in basketball.
★ 9. Our camp runs a **midsummer** swimming contest.
10. We decided to meet **midway** between her house and mine.
★11. A **submarine** operates under the water.
12. What is the **subtotal** before tax?
★13. Do you ride the **subway** to work?
14. A rocket moves at **supersonic** speed.
15. A **superstar** may have only passing fame.

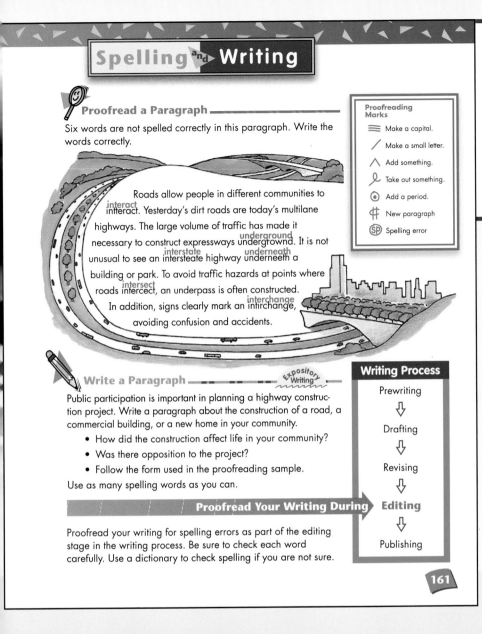

Spelling and Writing

😊 **Proofread a Paragraph**

Six words are not spelled correctly in this paragraph. Write the words correctly.

Roads allow people in different communities to
interact
interract. Yesterday's dirt roads are today's multilane
highways. The large volume of traffic has made it
underground
necessary to construct expressways undergrownd. It is not
interstate   *underneath*
unusual to see an intersteate highway underneeth a
building or park. To avoid traffic hazards at points where
intersect
roads intercect, an underpass is often constructed.
interchange
In addition, signs clearly mark an intirchange,
avoiding confusion and accidents.

Proofreading Marks
≡ Make a capital.
/ Make a small letter.
∧ Add something.
ℰ Take out something.
⊙ Add a period.
⌗ New paragraph
(SP) Spelling error

✏️ **Write a Paragraph** — *Expository Writing*

Public participation is important in planning a highway construction project. Write a paragraph about the construction of a road, a commercial building, or a new home in your community.
- How did the construction affect life in your community?
- Was there opposition to the project?
- Follow the form used in the proofreading sample.

Use as many spelling words as you can.

Writing Process
Prewriting
⇩
Drafting
⇩
Revising
⇩
Editing
⇩
Publishing

Proofread Your Writing During ➤

Proofread your writing for spelling errors as part of the editing stage in the writing process. Be sure to check each word carefully. Use a dictionary to check spelling if you are not sure.

161

Using the Writing Process

Before assigning **Write a Paragraph,** see pages 258–259 in the Student Edition for a complete review of the writing process and additional writing assignments. You may also wish to refer to pages Z12–Z13 in the Teacher Edition.

Keeping a Spelling Journal

Encourage students to record the words they misspelled on the weekly test in a personal spelling journal. These words may be recycled for future study. Students may also wish to include words from their writing. See pages Z12–Z13 in the Teacher Edition for more information.

★16. I agreed to **supervise** the project.
17. The police went **undercover** to surprise the thief.
★18. Many animals make their homes **underground**.
★19. He stayed **underneath** the covers to keep warm.
20. The exit is just beyond the **underpass**.

Option 2:
Multiple Spelling Words Per Sentence

(See procedures on pages Z10–Z11.)

1. In **midsummer** our **intramural** teams do not play any games.
2. Who will **supervise** the **intrastate** games?
3. That **superstar** took a **supersonic** jet across the ocean.
4. The **submarine** quietly moved **underneath** the water.
5. A **subway** runs **underground**.
6. **Midway** through the **interview** she asked me to define **interface**.
7. An **undercover** officer must **interact** with many people.
8. The **subtotal** will be correct if you **interchange** these numbers.
9. Just beyond the **underpass,** this road will **intersect** the **interstate** highway.

Option 3:
Standardized Test

(See *Teacher Resource Book,* Unit 26.)

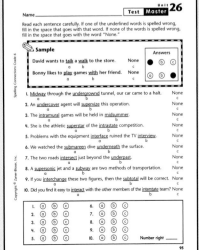

**Unit 26
Test Master**

Strategy Words

Students will
• **review** words studied previously that are related to the spelling strategy.
• **preview** unknown words that are related to the spelling strategy.

Optional Enrichment

Unit 26 enrichment

VOCABULARY CONNECTIONS

Strategy Words

Remind the students that the **Strategy Words** relate to the spelling patterns they have studied in this unit. The **Review Words** are below grade level, and the **Preview Words** are above grade level. You may wish to use the following sentences to introduce the words in context.

Review Words:
Words From Grade 5

1. We stayed awake until **midnight** to see the comet.
2. We should **underline** this part of our letter.
3. What did you use for a **subhead** in your report?
4. The company asked for an **internal** audit.
5. My friend did not arrive until **midafternoon**.

Preview Words:
Words From Grade 7

6. We bought popcorn during the **intermission**.
7. We rested at the **midpoint** of our job.
8. The scientist considered building a **subterranean** colony in Antarctica.
9. I am not happy when my friend behaves in a **superficial** way.
10. The company did not want to **underestimate** the cost of the project.

Review Words
1. internal
2. midnight
3. midafternoon
4. subhead
5. underline

Preview Words
6. intermission
7. superficial
8. underestimate
9. midpoint
10. subterranean

Strategy Words

Review Words: Prefixes

Write words from the box to complete the paragraph.

midnight	underline	subhead
internal	midafternoon	

The reporter had asked for a two-hour extension on his 10 p.m. deadline. His article on __1.__ politics was now due at __2.__ . It was already __3.__ , and he had not even stopped for lunch. Thus far he had written an introduction and a __4.__ , which he decided to __5.__ for emphasis. It was going to be a long day.

Preview Words: Prefixes

Write the word from the box that could best replace the underlined word or words.

intermission	midpoint	subterranean
superficial	underestimate	

6. The play will have a ten-minute <u>break</u>.
7. Fortunately, she sustained only <u>surface</u> cuts in the accident.
8. Do not <u>undervalue</u> his potential as a hard worker.
9. The bus stops for a break near the <u>halfway mark</u> of the trip.
10. A long <u>underground</u> passage led from one castle to another.

162

Unit 26 RECAP

You may wish to assign the **Unit 26 Homework Master** (*Teacher Resource Book*, Unit 26) as a fun way to recap the spelling words.

Unit 26 Homework Master

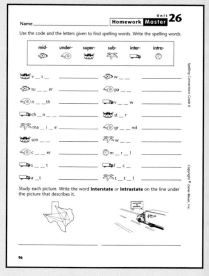

Objectives

Content Words

Students will
- **expand** vocabulary with content-related words.
- **relate** the spelling strategy to words outside the basic spelling list.
- **understand** a word root and find it in a word.

Content Words

Language Arts: Sentences

Write a word to identify each sentence or phrase.

declarative	imperative	interrogative
fragment	exclamatory	

1. Proper manners are easy to learn.
2. Watch out for that car!
3. The bright blue sky
4. Why is your dog chewing the TV remote?
5. Call home by six o'clock.

Social Studies: Maps

Write words from the box to complete the paragraph.

boundary	local	real estate	settlement	subdivide

The neighbors had been feuding for years. A __6.__ broker was encouraging them to sell their land to a developer, who would __7.__ it and build several homes. But the neighbors disagreed over the __8.__ between their two parcels of land. Finally, they hired a __9.__ attorney whom they all knew from neighborhood get-togethers. A __10.__ was reached that was agreeable to all parties.

Apply the Spelling Strategy

One of the Content Words you wrote has a prefix that indicates position. Circle that word.

Word Study

Word Roots

The Latin root **terra** means "land" or "earth." Someone who protects land is **territorial**. **Terrain** means "land." Write the Strategy Word that means "under the ground."

163

Language Arts: Sentences
1. declarative
2. exclamatory
3. fragment
4. interrogative
5. imperative

Social Studies: Maps
6. real estate
7. (subdivide)
8. boundary
9. local
10. settlement

Word Roots
1. subterranean

Content Words

Language Arts: Sentences

Use these sentences to introduce the words and their meanings.
1. A **declarative** sentence makes a statement and ends with a period.
2. An **imperative** sentence is a command.
3. An **interrogative** sentence is a question and ends with a question mark.
4. A sentence **fragment** does not express a complete thought.
5. An **exclamatory** sentence shows excitement.

Note: The **inter** in interrogative indicates "in the presence of," not "position."

Social Studies: Maps

Use these sentences to introduce the words and their meanings.
1. It was easy to mark the **boundary** of our state on this map.
2. We found the **local** restaurants to be outstanding.
3. Did you believe the **real estate** investment was a wise one?
4. The **settlement** was finalized.
5. The builder will **subdivide** this land and build more homes.

Word Study

Word Roots

Point out that a **word root** is a word or word part from which other words are made. Word roots for English words often come from Latin or Greek. Understanding word roots can help students build their vocabulary.

Unit 27 Home Spelling Practice

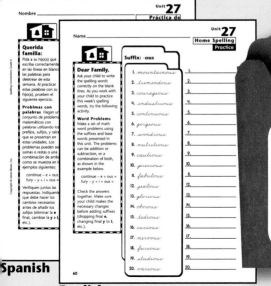

Spanish

English

MANAGING INSTRUCTION

Looking Ahead to Unit 27

To save time, you may wish to duplicate the **Unit 27 Home Spelling Practice** now. (See *Home Spelling Practice Book,* Unit 27.)

TI63

Basic Spelling List

mountainous	fabulous
tremendous	jealous
courageous	glorious
industrious	obvious
continuous	tedious
gorgeous	curious
wondrous	nervous
nutritious	furious
cautious	studious
precious	various

Strategy Words

Review

dangerous	joyous
generous	mysterious
humorous	

Preview

ambitious	superfluous
copious	vivacious
spacious	

Content Words

Science: Geology

avalanche	shale
sediment	delta
debris	

Social Studies: The Desert

caravan	traveler
sultan	turban
oasis	

Individual Needs

Challenge Words

hideous	monstrous
anxious	contagious
harmonious	treacherous

Alternate Word List ★

tremendous	precious
courageous	glorious
industrious	curious
continuous	nervous
cautious	various

★ For students who need to study fewer Basic Spelling words

MATERIALS

Student Edition
Pages 164–169
Challenge Activities, p. 246

Teacher Edition
Pages T164A–T169
Challenge Activities, p. T246

Teacher Resource Book
Unit 27 Homework Master
Unit 27 Practice Masters
Flip Folder Practice Master
Unit 27 Test Master

Home Spelling Practice Book
Unit 27 Home Spelling Practice (English or Spanish)

Other *Spelling Connections* Resources
- Audiotape, Grade 6
- Practice Book for Grammar, Usage, and Mechanics, Grade 6
- Spelling Support for Second Language Learners, Grade 6
- Support Software on CD-ROM
- Transparency Book, Grade 6
- Word Sort CD-ROM, Grade 6

OBJECTIVES

Spelling and Thinking
Students will
- **read** the spelling words in list form and in context.
- **sort** the spelling words according to whether **-ous** is added to base words or root words.
- **read** and remember this week's spelling strategy.

Spelling and Vocabulary
Students will
- **replace** underlined words in sentences with spelling words that have the same or nearly the same meaning.
- **write** spelling words for clues.
- **write** spelling words to match word histories.

Spelling and Reading
Students will
- **solve** analogies using spelling words.
- **complete** sentences using spelling words.
- **complete** a paragraph using spelling words.

Spelling and Writing
Students will
- **proofread** a paragraph.
- **use** the writing process to write a persuasive paragraph.
- **proofread** their writing.

MEETING INDIVIDUAL NEEDS
Learning Styles

Visual

Write some of the spelling words on the chalkboard, but omit some letters of each, leaving blanks for the missing letters. For example:

va _ _ ous
_ o_ dr _ _ _
f _ _ ul _ _ _
m _ _ _ t _ _ _ ous
_ bv _ _ _ s

Ask the students to take turns filling in the missing letters within a five- to ten-second time limit. Have the other students write the words at their desks.

Auditory

Write the spelling words on the chalkboard in syllables. Have the students take turns sounding out the syllables, as follows: Have the first student choose a spelling word and sound out the first syllable; the next student sounds out the second syllable; and so on, until the word is pronounced. Another student then pronounces the entire word, and still another student spells it. Erase that word from the chalkboard. Continue until all the spelling words have been used.

Kinesthetic

Bring a ball to class to play "Hot Potato." Give the ball to a student. The student who has the ball spells a word and then tosses the ball to another student. The student who catches the ball says the word, spells another word, and throws the ball to a third student. The game continues in this fashion.

> **Hands-On Practice**
> All students will benefit from practicing with a **Flip Folder**. See page Z18.

Language and Cultural Differences

There is no schwa sound in Spanish. Therefore, the **-ous** ending, pronounced /əs/, may be difficult for some Spanish-speaking students to pronounce and spell. To help them make the sound/symbol connection, write the spelling words on the chalkboard and leave a blank for the **-ous** suffix. Have the students say each word, emphasizing the **-ous** suffix as you add it.

MANAGING INSTRUCTION

3–5 Day Plan		Average	Below Average	Above Average
Day 1	Day 1	Pretest Spelling Mini-Lesson, p. T164 Spelling and Thinking, p. 164	Pretest Spelling Mini-Lesson, P. T164 Spelling and Thinking, p. 164	Pretest Spelling and Thinking, p. 164
	Day 2	Spelling and Vocabulary, p. 165	Spelling and Vocabulary, p. 165 (or) Unit 27 Practice Master, A and B	Spelling and Vocabulary, p. 165 Spelling and Reading, p. 166
Day 2	Day 3	Spelling and Reading, p. 166	Spelling and Reading, p. 166 (or) Unit 27 Practice Master, C and D	Challenge Activities, p. 246
	Day 4	Spelling and Writing, p. 167 Unit 27 Homework Master	Spelling and Writing, p. 167	Spelling and Writing, p. 167 Unit 27 Homework Master
Day 3	Day 5	Weekly Test	Weekly Test	Weekly Test
Vocabulary Connections (pages 168 and 169) may be used anytime during this unit.				

Objectives

Spelling and Thinking

Students will
- **read** the spelling words in list form and in context.
- **sort** the spelling words according to whether **-ous** is added to base words or root words.
- **read** and remember this week's spelling strategy.

UNIT PRETEST

Use **Pretest Sentences** below. Refer to the self-checking procedures on student page 256. You may wish to use the **Unit 27 Word List Overhead Transparency** as part of the checking procedure.

TEACHING THE STRATEGY

Spelling Mini-Lesson

Write **mountainous, glorious,** and **nervous** on the board. Ask students to identify the suffix (-ous) and base word (mountain, glory, nerve) in each word.

Discuss how each base word was affected when the suffix was added.

- When **-ous** is added to a base word ending in a consonant (**mountain**), the suffix is added without changing the base word (**mountainous**).
- When **-ous** is added to a base word that ends in **y** (**glory**), the **y** is changed to **i** before the suffix is added (**glorious**).
- When a base word ends in **e** (**nerve**), the **e** is dropped before the suffix is added (**nervous**).

Ask the students to find the exception to the last guideline. (courageous) Explain that final **e** is retained to keep the pronunciation of the **g** "soft."

Point out that the base word **wonder** changes spelling when **-ous** is added to form **wondrous**.

Write the remaining spelling words on the board. Ask the students if they can identify a base word for each. (no)

Explain that some of the words on the list were formed by adding **-ous** to a root, i.e., a word part that becomes a word when an affix is attached.

Ask if the spelling words are nouns or adjectives. (adjectives)

T164

Unit 27
Suffix: -ous

Spelling and Thinking

Order of answers may vary.

no change to base word
1. mountainous
2. courageous ★

-ous added to base word
3. industrious ★
4. continuous ★
5. wondrous
6. nutritious
7. cautious ★
8. glorious ★
9. tedious
10. nervous ★
11. furious
12. studious
13. various ★

-ous added to root word
14. tremendous ★
15. gorgeous
16. precious ★
17. fabulous
18. jealous
19. obvious
20. curious ★

164

READ THE SPELLING WORDS

1.	mountainous	*mountainous*	The terrain was **mountainous**.
2.	tremendous	*tremendous*	She has a **tremendous** workload.
3.	courageous	*courageous*	What a **courageous** girl she is!
4.	industrious	*industrious*	Ants are **industrious** creatures.
5.	continuous	*continuous*	A **continuous** rain caused floods.
6.	gorgeous	*gorgeous*	The view from here is **gorgeous**.
7.	wondrous	*wondrous*	Sunsets at sea are **wondrous**!
8.	nutritious	*nutritious*	Eat a **nutritious** breakfast daily.
9.	cautious	*cautious*	Be **cautious** on the icy roads.
10.	precious	*precious*	Rubies are **precious** gems.
11.	fabulous	*fabulous*	He accumulated **fabulous** wealth.
12.	jealous	*jealous*	The dog is **jealous** of the baby.
13.	glorious	*glorious*	We spent a **glorious** day at sea.
14.	obvious	*obvious*	His embarrassment was **obvious**.
15.	tedious	*tedious*	The **tedious** chores tired me out.
16.	curious	*curious*	Ask questions if you are **curious**.
17.	nervous	*nervous*	I get **nervous** in front of a crowd.
18.	furious	*furious*	He gets **furious** when we are late.
19.	studious	*studious*	The **studious** girl got good grades.
20.	various	*various*	We sell **various** types of boots.

SORT THE SPELLING WORDS

1.–2. Write the spelling words in which the spelling of the base word does not change when **-ous** is added.

Write the other spelling words in which

3.–13. **-ous** was added to a base word whose spelling changed.

14.–20. **-ous** was added to a root word.

REMEMBER THE SPELLING STRATEGY

Remember that the suffix **-ous** can be added to base words or root words to form adjectives such as **mountainous, nervous,** and **obvious**.

Pretest Sentences (See procedures on pages Z10–Z11.)

1. The **mountainous** regions of the American West are beautiful.
★ 2. The explosion made a **tremendous** crashing noise.
★ 3. That **courageous** firefighter saved the child's life.
★ 4. The **industrious** ant carried a crumb larger than itself.
★ 5. The **continuous** blare of the siren caused me to cover my ears.
6. That necklace is a **gorgeous** piece of jewelry.
7. The Milky Way is a **wondrous** sight in the nighttime sky.
8. A **nutritious** meal is one that is well-balanced.
★ 9. He was taught to be **cautious** when crossing the street.
★10. This old photograph is very **precious** to me.
11. We all agreed that the fireworks made a **fabulous** display.
12. She is **jealous** of her sister's mathematical ability.
★13. The **glorious** sunset was a perfect ending to the day.
14. David's expression made it **obvious** that he dislikes frogs.
15. Doing the same chore over and over again can become **tedious**.
★16. The **curious** boy searched for the hidden birthday presents.
★17. Do you get **nervous** before taking an exam?
18. The thoughtless driver made the pedestrians **furious**.
19. The **studious** girl always does extra assignments.
★20. There are **various** causes of the common cold.

Spelling and Vocabulary

Word Meanings

Write the spelling word that could best replace each underlined word.

1. One <u>unbroken</u> chalk line marked mid-field.
2. Even the steam shovel seemed to struggle as it moved the <u>enormous</u> boulder.
3. The answer was <u>clear</u> to all of us.
4. She is getting <u>anxious</u> about giving her speech.
5. I am <u>envious</u> of people who finish their homework early.
6. I am <u>interested</u> to know how you made those pancakes.

Word Clues

Write the spelling word that matches each clue.

7. of high elevation
8. full of intense anger
9. full of diligence
10. devoted to study
11. full of bravery
12. full of glory
13. of diverse kinds
14. full of wonder
15. full of nutrition

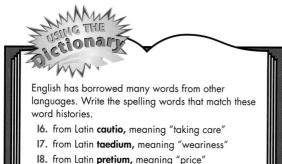

USING THE Dictionary

English has borrowed many words from other languages. Write the spelling words that match these word histories.

16. from Latin **cautio,** meaning "taking care"
17. from Latin **taedium,** meaning "weariness"
18. from Latin **pretium,** meaning "price"
19. from Middle English **gorgayse,** meaning "elegant"
20. from Latin **fabula,** meaning "fable"

165

Word Meanings
1. continuous
2. tremendous
3. obvious
4. nervous
5. jealous
6. curious

Word Clues
7. mountainous
8. furious
9. industrious
10. studious
11. courageous
12. glorious
13. various
14. wondrous
15. nutritious

Using the Dictionary
16. cautious
17. tedious
18. precious
19. gorgeous
20. fabulous

Objectives

Spelling and Vocabulary

Students will
- **replace** underlined words in sentences with spelling words that have the same or nearly the same meaning.
- **write** spelling words for clues.
- **write** spelling words to match word histories.

Developing Oral Language Skills

Write each spelling word on an index card and have one student draw a card and say the word. This student then points to a second student who must use the word in a sentence. The second student then draws a different word and chooses another student to create a sentence. Continue until all the words have been used.

MEETING INDIVIDUAL NEEDS

Providing More Help

Write the following groups of words on the chalkboard, and have each student write the correctly spelled word from each group:

nervis, **nervous,** nervus
gorgeous, gorgoius, gorgious
caushus, **cautious,** cautous
furous, **furious,** furyous
obvous, obveous, **obvious**

★Students who need to study fewer words should use the **Alternate Word List.** This list is starred on page T164 in the Teacher Edition. The **Unit 27 Practice Masters** (*Teacher Resource Book*) provide additional practice with these words.

Unit 27 Practice Masters

Name _____

Practice Master Unit **27**

1. continuous 3. nervous 5. glorious 7. curious 9. cautious
2. tremendous 4. various 6. industrious 8. precious 10. courageous

A. Add and subtract letters to form spelling words. Write the words.

1. vary – y + i + ous = _____ _____
2. industry – y + i + ous = _____ _____
3. glory – y + i + ous = _____ _____
4. continue – e + ous = _____ _____
5. nerve – e + ous = _____

B. Write the spelling word that goes with each definition. Then circle the base word. Finally, write each base word. Notice how the spelling of the base word changed when the suffix was added.

1. full of diligence

2. full of bravery

3. of the nerves

4. of diverse kinds

5. goes on without stopping

97

Practice Master Unit **27**

curious   cautious
precious   courageous

98

Objectives

Spelling and Reading

Students will
- **solve** analogies using spelling words.
- **complete** sentences using spelling words.
- **complete** a paragraph using spelling words.

One-Minute Handwriting Hint

The checkstroke ending of the lowercase **o** swings right and up; a pause is followed by the first slant stroke of the letter **u**.

↓ PAUSE
ou
SLANT

Legible handwriting can boost spelling scores by as much as 20%.

Solve the Analogies

1. gorgeous
2. industrious
3. nutritious
4. glorious
5. wondrous
6. precious

Complete the Sentences

7. continuous
8. furious
9. studious
10. various
11. curious
12. jealous
13. mountainous

Complete the Paragraph

14. courageous
15. cautious
16. tremendous
17. nervous
18. obvious
19. tedious
20. fabulous

mountainous	tremendous	courageous	industrious
continuous	gorgeous	wondrous	nutritious
cautious	precious	fabulous	jealous
glorious	obvious	tedious	curious
nervous	furious	studious	various

Solve the Analogies Write a spelling word to complete each analogy.

1. **Simple** is to **elaborate** as **unattractive** is to ____.
2. **Indifferent** is to **enthusiastic** as **lazy** is to ____.
3. **Miserable** is to **wretched** as **wholesome** is to ____.
4. **Virtue** is to **virtuous** as **glory** is to ____.
5. **Grace** is to **gracious** as **wonder** is to ____.
6. **Miniature** is to **tiny** as **valuable** is to ____.

Complete the Sentences Write the spelling word that completes each sentence.

7. A ____ line of cars stretched as far as the eye could see.
8. He was ____ at me for forgetting to pick him up on time.
9. She does not study on weekends, yet she is very ____.
10. I enjoy ____ types of movies, but I prefer action films.
11. I am ____ to know where you bought that heavy sweater.
12. Sherman is ____ when we pay attention to another dog.
13. Near the sea the land was flat, but inland it was ____.

Complete the Paragraph Write spelling words from the box to complete the paragraph.

Most ski resorts rely on the __14.__ efforts of their brave ski patrol to keep skiers safe. Ski patrol members are trained to be __15.__ when moving injured skiers. They are a __16.__ help to __17.__ skiers who need encouragement. Ski patrol members show an __18.__ enthusiasm for their job. They say that their job never becomes __19.__, and they tell some __20.__ tales of daring rescue missions.

nervous
cautious
courageous
tedious
tremendous
fabulous
obvious

166

MEETING INDIVIDUAL NEEDS

Providing More Challenge

Challenge Words and **Challenge Activities** for Unit 27 appear on page 246. **Challenge Word Test Sentences** appear on page T246.

Unit 27 Challenge Activities

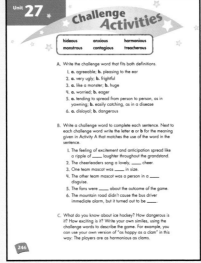

Weekly Test Options

Option 1:
One Spelling Word Per Sentence
(See procedures on pages Z10–Z11.)

⭐ 1. She was **cautious** about taking part in the adventure.
⭐ 2. The water flowed in a **continuous** stream.
⭐ 3. That singer has a **glorious** voice.
⭐ 4. The soldiers performed many **courageous** acts.
⭐ 5. An **industrious** student is usually successful.
6. They were excited about their **fabulous** vacation.
7. What did he do to make you so **furious**?
8. The famous actor had **gorgeous** blue eyes.
9. Try not to be **jealous** of others.
10. I live in a **mountainous** area near a lake.
⭐ 11. He is **nervous** about the results of the test.
12. Did you eat a **nutritious** breakfast?
13. They look so much alike that it is **obvious** they are sisters.
⭐ 14. She wore a necklace of **precious** jewels.
15. His **studious** habits help him achieve good grades.

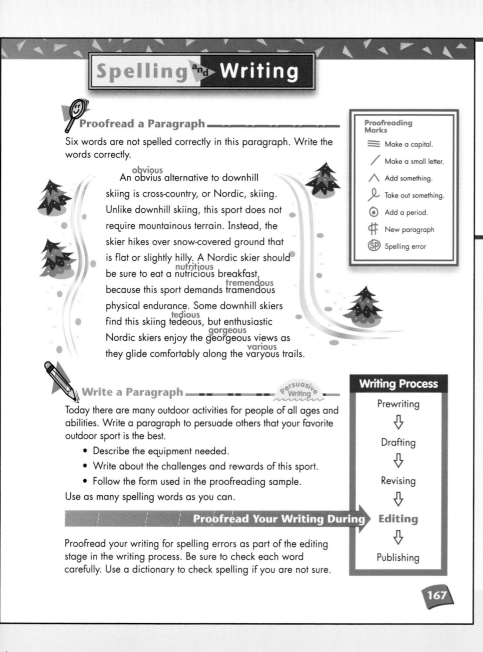

Spelling *and* Writing

Proofread a Paragraph

Six words are not spelled correctly in this paragraph. Write the words correctly.

obvious
An obvius alternative to downhill skiing is cross-country, or Nordic, skiing. Unlike downhill skiing, this sport does not require mountainous terrain. Instead, the skier hikes over snow-covered ground that is flat or slightly hilly. A Nordic skier should be sure to eat a *nutritious* nutricious breakfast, because this sport demands *tremendous* tramendous physical endurance. Some downhill skiers find this skiing *tedious* tedeous, but enthusiastic Nordic skiers enjoy the *gorgeous* georgeous views as they glide comfortably along the *various* varyous trails.

Proofreading Marks

≡ Make a capital.
/ Make a small letter.
∧ Add something.
ℒ Take out something.
⊙ Add a period.
⌗ New paragraph.
(SP) Spelling error.

Write a Paragraph

Persuasive Writing

Today there are many outdoor activities for people of all ages and abilities. Write a paragraph to persuade others that your favorite outdoor sport is the best.

- Describe the equipment needed.
- Write about the challenges and rewards of this sport.
- Follow the form used in the proofreading sample.

Use as many spelling words as you can.

Proofread Your Writing During → **Editing**

Proofread your writing for spelling errors as part of the editing stage in the writing process. Be sure to check each word carefully. Use a dictionary to check spelling if you are not sure.

Writing Process

Prewriting
⇩
Drafting
⇩
Revising
⇩
Editing
⇩
Publishing

167

Objectives

Spelling and Writing

Students will
- **proofread** a paragraph.
- **use** the writing process to write a persuasive paragraph.
- **proofread** their writing.

Using the Writing Process

Before assigning **Write a Paragraph,** see pages 258–259 in the Student Edition for a complete review of the writing process and additional writing assignments. You may also wish to refer to pages Z12–Z13 in the Teacher Edition.

Keeping a Spelling Journal

Encourage students to record the words they misspelled on the weekly test in a personal spelling journal. These words may be recycled for future study. Students may also wish to include words from their writing. See pages Z12–Z13 in the Teacher Edition for more information.

★**16.** A cat is a **curious** animal.
17. His job becomes more **tedious** every day.
★**18.** The carnival was a **tremendous** success.
★**19.** Each child had **various** chores to complete.
20. The view from our window was a **wondrous** sight.

Option 2:
Multiple Spelling Words Per Sentence

(See procedures on pages Z10–Z11.)

1. She was **jealous** of her **gorgeous** friend.
2. He was **furious** that the **glorious** flowers had been torn off the bush.
3. There are **wondrous** views along the **mountainous** road.
4. He is so **cautious** that he makes others **nervous**.
5. This **precious** jewel has **tremendous** value.
6. He is **industrious** to the point of being **tedious**.
7. A **nutritious** meal includes food from **various** food groups.
8. She is **studious** because she is **curious** about so many things.
9. His **courageous** deeds have made him a **fabulous** hero.
10. It is **obvious** that the sidewalk should be **continuous**.

Option 3:
Standardized Test

(See *Teacher Resource Book,* Unit 27.)

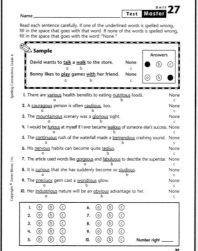

Unit 27 Test Master

T167

Strategy Words

Students will

- **review** words studied previously that are related to the spelling strategy.
- **preview** unknown words that are related to the spelling strategy.

Optional Enrichment

Strategy Words

Remind the students that the **Strategy Words** relate to the spelling patterns they have studied in this unit. The **Review Words** are below grade level, and the **Preview Words** are above grade level. You may wish to use the following sentences to introduce the words in context.

Review Words:
Words From Grade 5

1. A stop sign was placed at the **dangerous** intersection.
2. My sister is a **generous** person.
3. The speaker told a **humorous** story.
4. The birth of a baby is a **joyous** occasion.
5. Although my family had been acting in a **mysterious** way, I was still surprised by the party.

Preview Words:
Words From Grade 7

6. The teacher told us it was an **ambitious** project, but he was sure we would be able to complete it.
7. **Copious** amounts of paper were required to complete the report.
8. My bedroom is **spacious** enough to have friends stay overnight.
9. His writing seemed **superfluous** because of the many adjectives used to describe the scenery.
10. I enjoy the fact that my friend is **vivacious** because I am rather quiet and shy.

Review Words
1. humorous
2. dangerous
3. generous
4. mysterious
5. joyous

Preview Words
6. ambitious
7. vivacious
8. spacious
9. superfluous
10. copious

Unit 27 enrichment

VOCABULARY CONNECTIONS

Strategy Words

Review Words: Suffix -ous

1.–5. Write words from the box that could replace the underlined words in this book review.

dangerous generous humorous joyous mysterious

The Incredible Cat Tale describes the <u>funny</u> adventures of two sisters who smuggle a cat named Simon into their parents' apartment, where pets are restricted. The girls' escapades are more silly than they are <u>risky</u>. The landlord discovers Simon but, in a <u>charitable</u> mood, allows the girls to keep their cat. In fact, he is even responsible for the <u>puzzling</u> appearance of another cat who keeps Simon company. This book will make you feel <u>happy</u>.

Preview Words: Suffix -ous

Write the adjective from the box that best completes each description.

ambitious copious spacious superfluous vivacious

6. Eli's goal is to become a famous doctor. Eli is _____.
7. Lucy is lively and very animated. Lucy is _____.
8. The rooms in the old house were large, and the ceilings were high. The house was _____.
9. He has many art books. Another one will be _____.
10. The secretary recorded every word that was said during the meeting. She took _____ notes.

168

Unit 27 RECAP

You may wish to assign the **Unit 27 Homework Master** (*Teacher Resource Book,* Unit 27) as a fun way to recap the spelling words.

Unit 27 Homework Master

Name _____ Homework **Master** Unit 27

Complete each spelling word in the letter.

Dear Friend,

I hope you're not f _ ◯ _ _ _ _ that I haven't written sooner, but I find letter writing a bit t _ _ ◯ _ _ _. So far I've seen many w _ _ _ _ _ _ _ sights and I'm having a f _ _ _ _ _ _ _ time. Does that make you c _ _ _ _ ◯ _?

We drove up the mountain and the view from the top was g _ _ _ _ _ _ _ _; however, I was very n _ _ _ _ ◯ as we wound around the m _ _ ◯◯ _ _ _ roads on the way up. All the drivers had to be extremely c _ _ ◯ _ _ _.

The sunset was g _ r _ _ _ _ _ as it cast shadows upon the v _ _ _ _ _ _ sights in the valley. Mile after mile of t _ _ _ _ _ _ _ evergreen trees filled the forests lining the roads.

I guess it's ◯ _ _ _ _ _ _ that I'm having a good time. One thing is certain, I've begun to appreciate the many p _ _ _ _ _ _ ◯ natural resources in our country!

See you soon,
Your secret pal

The letters circled in the words above form a spelling word. Unscramble it and write the word here. _ _ _ _ _ _ _ _ _ _

Now write a short reply on the post card. Use the words **continuous, jealous, studious, industrious,** and **courageous.**

100

Content Words

Science: Geology

Write the words from the box that will complete the sentences.

avalanche	sediment	debris	shale	delta

1.–2. After an ____, there is a lot of ____ to clean up.

3.–4. At the ____ of a river, ____ collects.

5. A rock composed of fine-grained sediments is ____.

Social Studies: The Desert

Write words from the box to complete the paragraph.

caravan	sultan	oasis	traveler	turban

In days gone by, a __6.__ from Persia sent a small __7.__ of nomads in search of a new, temporary home. Loading their belongings onto their camels, they set off. Each __8.__ wore a __9.__ for protection from the desert's scorching sun. By midday, they had settled at a fertile __10.__ where they found a welcoming water supply. Caravans continue even today.

Apply the Spelling Strategy

A word inventor made up two words: **middeltaous** and **antiturbaneous**. Circle their base words in two of the Content Words you wrote.

Word Study

Words From Other Languages

Sometimes English words that came from other languages have unusual spellings. For example, **bureau** came from the French language, and the **eau** is pronounced /**oh**/. Write the Content Word that also came from French and has an unexpected silent letter. The word means "litter" or "rubble."

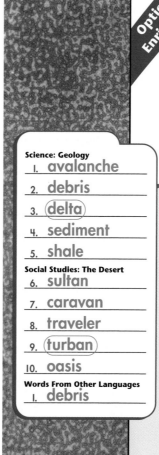

Science: Geology
1. avalanche
2. debris
3. (delta)
4. sediment
5. shale

Social Studies: The Desert
6. sultan
7. caravan
8. traveler
9. (turban)
10. oasis

Words From Other Languages
1. debris

169

Objectives

Content Words

Students will

- **expand** vocabulary with content-related words.
- **relate** the spelling strategy to words outside the basic spelling list.
- **understand** that some words are borrowed from other languages.

Content Words

Science: Geology

Use these sentences to introduce the words and their meanings.

1. The skiers were warned about the **avalanche**.
2. We could see the **sediment** at the bottom of the mountain stream.
3. **Debris** was scattered throughout our neighborhood after the hurricane.
4. This rock is **shale**.
5. The Mississippi **delta** has rich soil.

Social Studies: The Desert

Use these sentences to introduce the words and their meanings.

6. Long ago it took a camel **caravan** to carry supplies across the desert.
7. He was named the **sultan**.
8. The weary men reached an **oasis** after their long trip across the desert.
9. A **traveler** today expects better accommodations.
10. In my friend's country a **turban** is a popular head covering.

Word Study

Words From Other Languages

As people have moved to America from other countries, the English language has grown by absorbing new words from the different languages of the newcomers. Challenge students to suggest other words derived from French. Possible responses include **beret, restaurant,** and **cafe**.

Unit 28 Home Spelling Practice

Spanish

English

MANAGING INSTRUCTION

Looking Ahead to Unit 28

To save time, you may wish to duplicate the **Unit 28 Home Spelling Practice** now. (See *Home Spelling Practice Book,* Unit 28.)

Basic Spelling List

restaurant	sauce
appreciate	jewelry
probably	captain
different	pigeon
bargain	athlete
victory	amateur
bureau	license
surely	muscle
perspire	villain
rhythm	similar

Strategy Words

Review

business	polite
career	remember
delicious	

Preview

cafeteria	sufficient
potatoes	schedule
privilege	

Content Words

Language Arts: Research

encyclopedia	almanac
guidebook	atlas
thesaurus	

Science: Computers

floppy disk	terminal
printer	hardware
diskette	

Individual Needs

Challenge Words

sherbet	guidance
banquet	naive
luncheon	jeopardize

Alternate Word List ★

probably	pigeon
different	athlete
surely	license
sauce	muscle
captain	similar

★ For students who need to study fewer Basic Spelling words

MATERIALS

Student Edition
Pages 170–175
Challenge Activities, p. 247

Teacher Edition
Pages T170A–T175
Challenge Activities, p. T247

Teacher Resource Book
Unit 28 Homework Master
Unit 28 Practice Masters
Flip Folder Practice Master
Unit 28 Test Master

Home Spelling Practice Book
Unit 28 Home Spelling Practice
(English or Spanish)

Other *Spelling Connections* Resources
- Audiotape, Grade 6
- Practice Book for Grammar, Usage, and Mechanics, Grade 6
- Spelling Support for Second Language Learners, Grade 6
- Support Software on CD-ROM
- Transparency Book, Grade 6
- Word Sort CD-ROM, Grade 6

OBJECTIVES

Spelling and Thinking
Students will
- **read** the spelling words in list form and in context.
- **sort** the spelling words according to number of syllables.
- **read** and remember this week's spelling strategy.

Spelling and Vocabulary
Students will
- **write** spelling words to complete a series of meaning-related words.
- **replace** underlined words in sentences with spelling words that have the same or nearly the same meaning.
- **write** spelling words for dictionary respellings.

Spelling and Reading
Students will
- **solve** analogies using spelling words.
- **complete** sentences using context clues.
- **complete** a paragraph using spelling words.

Spelling and Writing
Students will
- **proofread** a paragraph.
- **use** the writing process to write an expository paragraph about a sports-related topic.
- **proofread** their writing.

MEETING INDIVIDUAL NEEDS
Learning Styles

 Visual

Ask each student to create a "Word Search" puzzle using some of the spelling words. Have each student make a grid in which each square can hold one letter. The grid should contain some spelling words running vertically, some horizontally and some diagonally, plus random letters to fill the empty spaces. Have the students exchange puzzles and circle the spelling words they find.

 Auditory

Have the students play a memory game. The first student begins by saying, "My grandmother has a trunk, and in the trunk she has jewelry, j-e-w-e-l-r-y." (Substitute any appropriate spelling word.) The second student adds another spelling word to the narrative, for example, "My grandmother has a trunk, and in the trunk she has jewelry and different, d-i-f-f-e-r-e-n-t, things," and so on. If a student misspells a word, or omits part of the story, he or she must drop out. The story continues until no student can repeat all of it, or until all the spelling words have been used.

 Kinesthetic

Invent a paragraph using the spelling words and read it to the class. As you read it, have a student walk slowly around the room. When you read a spelling word in the paragraph, the student must stop, spell the word, and then tap the nearest student on the shoulder. That student then begins walking until he or she hears a spelling word. If you say a spelling word and the student who is walking doesn't realize it, the other students should raise their hands. Recognize one of these students. If that student spells the word correctly, she or he takes the place of the walker.

Hands-On Practice
All students will benefit from practicing with a **Flip Folder**. See page Z18.

Language and Cultural Differences

Students from different language backgrounds may have problems making the correct sound-symbol associations for these words. Special attention should be given to the short vowel sounds, to words with double letters, and—in the case of Spanish-speaking students—to spelling patterns that do not exist in Spanish.

Have each student make a set of 3" × 5" spelling word cards. Have the students write the dictionary respelling under each spelling word. Encourage them to use these cards to memorize the spellings and pronunciations.

MANAGING INSTRUCTION

3–5 Day Plan		Average	Below Average	Above Average
Day 1	**Day 1**	Pretest Spelling Mini-Lesson, p. T170 Spelling and Thinking, p. 170	Pretest Spelling Mini-Lesson, p. T170 Spelling and Thinking, p. 170	Pretest Spelling and Thinking, p. 170
	Day 2	Spelling and Vocabulary, p. 171	Spelling and Vocabulary, p. 171 (or) Unit 28 Practice Master, A and B	Spelling and Vocabulary, p. 171 Spelling and Reading, p. 172
Day 2	**Day 3**	Spelling and Reading, p. 172	Spelling and Reading, p. 172 (or) Unit 28 Practice Master, C and D	Challenge Activities, p. 247
	Day 4	Spelling and Writing, p. 173 Unit 28 Homework Master	Spelling and Writing, p. 173	Spelling and Writing, p. 173 Unit 28 Homework Master
Day 3	**Day 5**	Weekly Test	Weekly Test	Weekly Test

Vocabulary Connections (pages 174 and 175) may be used anytime during this unit.

Spelling and Thinking

Students will
• **read** the spelling words in list form and in context.
• **sort** the spelling words according to number of syllables.
• **read** and remember this week's spelling strategy.

UNIT PRETEST

Use **Pretest Sentences** below. Refer to the self-checking procedures on student page 256. You may wish to use the **Unit 28 Word List Overhead Transparency** as part of the checking procedure.

TEACHING THE STRATEGY

Spelling Mini-Lesson

Read **Remember the Spelling Strategy** on page 170. Share a word whose spelling is difficult for you to remember; share the strategy you use to remember it. Encourage the students to share words that challenge them and the strategies they use to spell those words.

Explain that the words in this unit are often misspelled by writers. Ask volunteers to read the spelling list and discuss reasons why these words are challenging. Guide the students to these conclusions about why words may be misspelled:

• The word is mispronounced and a syllable is dropped or added when the word is written. (probably, athlete)
• The spelling included silent letters that are omitted when the word is written. (pigeon)
• The spelling includes letters that have the same sound as other letters. For example, in **license** and **sauce**, c and s in each word have the same pronunciation.

Discuss different mnemonics, or sayings, the students could create to remember these words. For example, "You can gain with a **bargain**" can help students remember how to spell **bargain**.

Note: Explain to students that even though **rhythm** has only one vowel, it has two syllables.

Order of answers may vary.
one syllable
1. sauce ★
two syllables
2. bar/gain
3. bu/reau
4. sure/ly ★
5. rhy/thm
6. per/spire
7. cap/tain ★
8. pi/geon ★
9. ath/lete ★
10. li/cense ★
11. mus/cle ★
12. vil/lain
three or more syllables
13. res/tau/rant
14. ap/pre/ci/ate
15. prob/a/bly ★
16. dif/fer/ent ★
17. vic/to/ry
18. jew/el/ry
19. am/a/teur
20. sim/i/lar ★

170

READ THE SPELLING WORDS

1. restaurant	*restaurant*	He dined at a fine **restaurant**.
2. appreciate	*appreciate*	I **appreciate** your help with the chores.
3. probably	*probably*	We will **probably** be home by noon.
4. different	*different*	Each room had **different** wallpaper.
5. bargain	*bargain*	Those shoes are a **bargain** at that price.
6. victory	*victory*	The team celebrated after the **victory**.
7. bureau	*bureau*	The top drawer in my **bureau** is stuck.
8. surely	*surely*	I thought that **surely** he would be here.
9. perspire	*perspire*	I am beginning to **perspire** in this heat.
10. rhythm	*rhythm*	We enjoyed the **rhythm** of the music.
11. sauce	*sauce*	She makes a special **sauce** for pasta.
12. jewelry	*jewelry*	I bought a watch at the **jewelry** store.
13. captain	*captain*	Team members chose a new **captain**.
14. pigeon	*pigeon*	A **pigeon** flew over to the park bench.
15. athlete	*athlete*	The talented **athlete** plays four sports.
16. amateur	*amateur*	The **amateur** artist shows great talent.
17. license	*license*	She just received her driver's **license**.
18. muscle	*muscle*	The tennis player pulled a leg **muscle**.
19. villain	*villain*	The **villain** stole the money and ran.
20. similar	*similar*	We have **similar** taste in clothes.

SORT THE SPELLING WORDS

1. Write the spelling word that has one syllable.
2.–12. Write the spelling words that have two syllables. Draw a line between the syllables.
13.–20. Write the spelling words that have three or more syllables. Draw a line between the syllables.

REMEMBER THE SPELLING STRATEGY

Remember that it is important to learn the spellings of words that writers often misspell.

Pretest Sentences (See procedures on pages Z10–Z11.)

1. My family has dinner in a **restaurant** on special occasions.
2. I really **appreciate** the favor you did for me.
★ 3. Although he thinks he failed, he will **probably** pass the test.
★ 4. The clown wore a **different** colored sock on each foot.
5. Gina considered her purchase to be a real **bargain**.
6. The team's last **victory** clinched the championship.
7. Where can I find the **bureau** that issues passports?
★ 8. She will **surely** win the race if she continues at that pace.
9. It is normal for a person to **perspire** while exercising.
10. Parade music has a **rhythm** suitable for marching.
★11. A cream **sauce** tastes delicious on fresh strawberries.
12. We looked in the **jewelry** store for a ring to buy for our mother.
★13. Each **captain** will choose his team members.
★14. My friend's parents are training a carrier **pigeon**.
★15. The injured **athlete** was on the bench for three weeks.
16. One must be an **amateur** to compete in college football.
★17. Driving a car without a **license** is a violation of the law.
★18. Not a **muscle** in the dog's body moved as he stood pointing at the squirrel.
19. Everyone in the theater booed when the **villain** appeared.
★20. These two buildings are very **similar** in appearance.

Spelling and Vocabulary

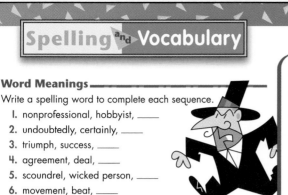

Word Meanings

Write a spelling word to complete each sequence.

1. nonprofessional, hobbyist, _____
2. undoubtedly, certainly, _____
3. triumph, success, _____
4. agreement, deal, _____
5. scoundrel, wicked person, _____
6. movement, beat, _____

Word Replacement

Write the spelling word that could best replace the underlined word or words.

7. I am thankful for your efforts in organizing the party.
8. We will likely go to a lake for our vacation.
9. It is so hot in here, I am beginning to sweat.
10. Our tastes in music are not alike.
11. She went to the passport office to fill out a form.
12. He got his driver's document of permission last week.
13. The women's dresses were nearly alike.

USING THE Dictionary

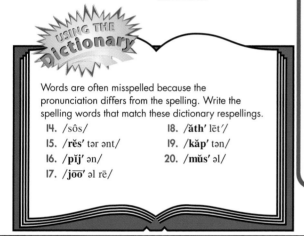

Words are often misspelled because the pronunciation differs from the spelling. Write the spelling words that match these dictionary respellings.

14. /sôs/
15. /rĕs' tər ənt/
16. /pĭj' ən/
17. /jōō' əl rē/
18. /ăth' lēt/
19. /kăp' tən/
20. /mŭs' əl/

Word Meanings
1. amateur
2. surely
3. victory
4. bargain
5. villain
6. rhythm

Word Replacement
7. appreciate
8. probably
9. perspire
10. different
11. bureau
12. license
13. similar

Using the Dictionary
14. sauce
15. restaurant
16. pigeon
17. jewelry
18. athlete
19. captain
20. muscle

171

Objectives

Spelling and Vocabulary

Students will
- **write** spelling words to complete a series of meaning-related words.
- **replace** underlined words in sentences with spelling words that have the same or nearly the same meaning.
- **write** spelling words for dictionary respellings.

Developing Oral Language Skills

Have students pronounce **athlete** and note whether they pronounce the word as two syllables or three syllables. If they pronounce it as a three-syllable word, remind them that there are only two syllables in **athlete**. Write **athlete** on the chalkboard. Underline the two syllables, and point to each syllable as students pronounce the word aloud. Remind students that words like athlete (/**ăth' lēt**/) may cause spelling problems because an additional syllable is inserted when **athlete** is pronounced.

MEETING INDIVIDUAL NEEDS

Providing More Help

Write the following groups of words on the chalkboard, and have the students write the one word in each group that is correctly spelled:

probably, pidgeon, buraeu
villan, **amateur,** prespire
sause, **license,** captian
restaurant, victery, athelete
rhythm, shurely, apreciate
jewelery, **similar,** musle

Tell the students that many people have trouble spelling these words.

★Students who need to study fewer words should use the **Alternate Word List**. This list is starred on page T170 in the Teacher Edition. The **Unit 28 Practice Masters** (*Teacher Resource Book*) provide additional practice with these words.

Unit 28 Practice Masters

Name _____

Practice Master Unit **28**

| 1. different | 3. athlete | 5. pigeon | 7. surely | 9. license |
| 2. probably | 4. similar | 6. captain | 8. muscle | 10. sauce |

A. Write the spelling words in alphabetical order.

1. _____ 6. _____
2. _____ 7. _____
3. _____ 8. _____
4. _____ 9. _____
5. _____ 10. _____

B. These words are misspelled. Write the spelling words correctly.

1. diffrent _____
2. sause _____
3. probly _____
4. athalete _____
5. musle _____
6. shurly _____
7. pigin _____
8. similar _____
9. captin _____
10. lisence _____

101

Practice Master Unit **28**

| surely | license |
| muscle | sauce |

102

T171

Objectives

Spelling and Reading

Students will
- **solve** analogies using spelling words.
- **complete** sentences using context clues.
- **complete** a paragraph using spelling words.

One-Minute Handwriting Hint

A smooth and even line is maintained by relaxing the hand and using the proper writing instrument. Do not press too hard on the pen or pencil or you will get a heavy or uneven line.

fixed
TOO HEAVY

Legible handwriting can boost spelling scores by as much as 20%.

Solve the Analogies
1. surely
2. sauce
3. pigeon
4. restaurant
5. captain
6. jewelry
7. bargain

Complete the Sentences
8. bureau
9. villain
10. perspire
11. victory
12. similar
13. amateur
14. license

Complete the Paragraph
15. probably
16. appreciate
17. athlete
18. rhythm
19. different
20. muscle

172

Spelling and Reading

restaurant	appreciate	probably	different
bargain	victory	bureau	surely
perspire	rhythm	sauce	jewelry
captain	pigeon	athlete	amateur
license	muscle	villain	similar

Solve the Analogies   Write a spelling word to complete each analogy.
1. **Carefully** is to **cautiously** as **definitely** is to _____.
2. **Flour** is to **bread** as **tomato** is to _____.
3. **Fish** is to **trout** as **bird** is to _____.
4. **Movie** is to **theater** as **meal** is to _____.
5. **Airplane** is to **pilot** as **ship** is to _____.
6. **Hammer** is to **tool** as **necklace** is to _____.
7. **Markdown** is to **discount** as **sale** is to _____.

Complete the Sentences   Write the spelling word that completes each sentence.
8. She carefully folded her sweaters and put them in the _____.
9. The story ends when the nasty _____ surrenders to the hero.
10. All this exercise is making me _____.
11. The game ended in a _____ for our team.
12. The two windows are not identical in size, but they are _____.
13. Although he is an _____, he is a very good golfer.
14. The police officer asked to see her driver's _____.

Complete the Paragraph   Write spelling words from the box to complete the paragraph.

If you have ever seen gymnasts perform, then you _15._ can _16._ what a beautiful sport gymnastics is to watch. One particularly artful form of gymnastics is a routine that an _17._ performs to the _18._ of music. Rhythmic gymnasts perform with _19._ pieces of equipment, such as hoops, ribbons, and jump ropes. Over time, gymnasts develop _20._ strength, a sense of balance, and flexibility.

muscle
appreciate
probably
rhythm
different
athlete

MEETING INDIVIDUAL NEEDS

Providing More Challenge

Challenge Words and **Challenge Activities** for Unit 28 appear on page 247. **Challenge Word Test Sentences** appear on page T247.

Unit 28 Challenge Activities

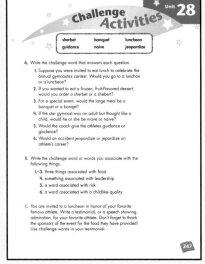

Weekly Test Options

Option 1:
One Spelling Word Per Sentence
(See procedures on pages Z10–Z11.)

1. He is an **amateur** painter.
2. I **appreciate** all your help.
★ 3. She is training to become an **athlete**.
4. Did you **bargain** with the man for the best price?
★ 5. She was elected **captain** of the basketball team.
6. Please put your clean clothes in your **bureau**.
★ 7. In what ways are the twins **different**?
8. She likes to wear fine **jewelry**.
★ 9. My parents keep their marriage **license** in a safe.
★10. The body is made of fat, bone, and **muscle**.
★11. We watched the **pigeon** fly skyward.
12. You **perspire** when your body is working hard.
★13. I will **probably** be late again today.
14. I enjoy having dinner at that **restaurant**.
15. Can you feel the **rhythm** of the music?
★16. May I have some cranberry **sauce** with my turkey?

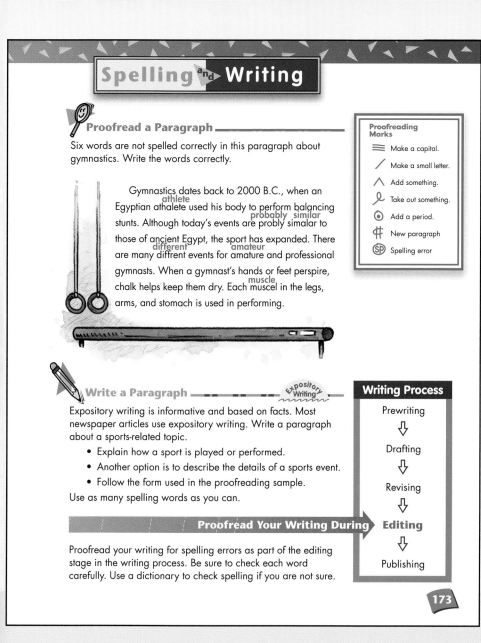

Spelling and Writing

Proofread a Paragraph

Six words are not spelled correctly in this paragraph about gymnastics. Write the words correctly.

Gymnastics dates back to 2000 B.C., when an Egyptian athlete used his body to perform balancing stunts. Although today's events are probly simalar to those of ancient Egypt, the sport has expanded. There are many diffrent events for amature and professional gymnasts. When a gymnast's hands or feet perspire, chalk helps keep them dry. Each muscel in the legs, arms, and stomach is used in performing.

Proofreading Marks

≡ Make a capital.
/ Make a small letter.
∧ Add something.
⌒ Take out something.
⊙ Add a period.
⌗ New paragraph
🆂🅿 Spelling error

Write a Paragraph

Expository Writing

Expository writing is informative and based on facts. Most newspaper articles use expository writing. Write a paragraph about a sports-related topic.

- Explain how a sport is played or performed.
- Another option is to describe the details of a sports event.
- Follow the form used in the proofreading sample.

Use as many spelling words as you can.

Writing Process

Prewriting
⇩
Drafting
⇩
Revising
⇩
Editing
⇩
Publishing

➤ **Proofread Your Writing During Editing**

Proofread your writing for spelling errors as part of the editing stage in the writing process. Be sure to check each word carefully. Use a dictionary to check spelling if you are not sure.

173

Objectives

Spelling and Writing

Students will
- **proofread** a paragraph.
- **use** the writing process to write an expository paragraph about a sports-related topic.
- **proofread** their writing.

Using the Writing Process

Before assigning **Write a Paragraph,** see pages 258–259 in the Student Edition for a complete review of the writing process and additional writing assignments. You may also wish to refer to pages Z12–Z13 in the Teacher Edition.

Keeping a Spelling Journal

Encourage students to record the words they misspelled on the weekly test in a personal spelling journal. These words may be recycled for future study. Students may also wish to include words from their writing. See pages Z12–Z13 in the Teacher Edition for more information.

★17. Your hat and mine are **similar** in style.
★18. The club will **surely** accept her as a member.
19. Our team won a **victory** over our rivals.
20. The wolf is a **villain** in many folk tales.

Option 2:
Multiple Spelling Words Per Sentence
(See procedures on pages Z10–Z11.)

1. The **athlete** won a **victory** in the games.
2. The **pigeon** is **surely** a city bird.
3. She paid a **bargain** price for the **jewelry**.
4. The **captain** is the officer in charge of this **license bureau**.
5. The audience did not **appreciate** the way the **villain** behaved.
6. The cook will **probably perspire** all the time in this hot **restaurant** kitchen.
7. This **sauce** tastes **different** because of the salt.
8. He is an **amateur muscle** builder.
9. The **rhythm** of the music is very **similar** to the sound of falling rain.

Option 3:
Standardized Test
(See *Teacher Resource Book,* Unit 28.)

**Unit 28
Test Master**

T173

Objectives

Strategy Words

Students will
- **review** words studied previously that are related to the spelling strategy.
- **preview** unknown words that are related to the spelling strategy.

Optional Enrichment

VOCABULARY CONNECTIONS

Remind the students that the **Strategy Words** relate to the spelling patterns they have studied in this unit. The **Review Words** are below grade level, and the **Preview Words** are above grade level. You may wish to use the following sentences to introduce the words in context.

Review Words:
Words From Grade 5

1. My uncle has his own **business**.
2. The counselor spoke about the **career** choices which are available to us.
3. My mother prepared a **delicious** lunch.
4. It is always a good idea to be **polite**.
5. Can you **remember** how to spell the words from the last unit?

Preview Words:
Words From Grade 7

6. The school **cafeteria** is very busy during lunch hour.
7. On St. Patrick's Day we ate green mashed **potatoes**.
8. Education is a **privilege** that we sometimes take for granted.
9. Did you get **sufficient** rest?
10. If we keep to the **schedule,** we will finish tomorrow.

Review Words
1. business
2. polite
3. delicious
4. career
5. remember

Preview Words
6. privilege
7. cafeteria
8. schedule
9. potatoes
10. sufficient

Strategy Words

Review Words: Words Writers Use

Write the word from the box that best completes each sentence.

business	career	delicious	polite	remember

1. She has started her own computer _____.
2. It is _____ to give up your bus seat to a senior citizen.
3. She prepared a _____ meal of meatballs and spaghetti.
4. He retired from a thirty-year _____ as an electrician.
5. I will always _____ the day I learned how to ride a bike.

Preview Words: Words Writers Use

Write words from the box to complete this sign posted in a storefront window.

cafeteria	potatoes	privilege	sufficient	schedule

Annie's Place

It is our __6.__ to announce the opening of our new __7.__ on the first day of May. The __8.__ of hours will be posted soon. Annie's Place will feature home-cooked dishes, such as roast chicken and mashed __9.__. Our menu choices will be __10.__ for every appetite!

174

Unit 28 RECAP

You may wish to assign the **Unit 28 Homework Master** (*Teacher Resource Book,* Unit 28) as a fun way to recap the spelling words.

Unit 28 Homework Master

Name _____   Homework **Master** **28**

Each of the spelling words is misspelled. First, write the words correctly. Then write the words in alphabetical order on the lines at the bottom of this page.

1. restrant _____
2. victry _____
3. diffrent _____
4. jewlry _____
5. probly _____
6. simlar _____
7. athalete _____
8. captin _____
9. amatur _____
10. musle _____

11. apreciat _____
12. lisence _____
13. purspire _____
14. pigin _____
15. bargin _____
16. villin _____
17. burau _____
18. shurly _____
19. rythm _____
20. sause _____

1. ___   11. ___
2. ___   12. ___
3. ___   13. ___
4. ___   14. ___
5. ___   15. ___
6. ___   16. ___
7. ___   17. ___
8. ___   18. ___
9. ___   19. ___
10. ___   20. ___

104

Content Words

Language Arts: Research

Which reference book would you use to find the answer to each of the following questions? Write a word from the box.

| encyclopedia guidebook thesaurus almanac atlas |

1. What is the history of the Olympic games?
2. Which country won the most medals in the Olympics?
3. Where can you find a map of Finland?
4. What is a synonym for **athletic**?
5. Where do you find out about sights to see in Tokyo?

Science: Computers

Write words from the box to complete the paragraph.

| floppy disk   printer   diskette   terminal   hardware |

In some businesses, several people share a single computer system by means of a piece of ___6.___ called a ___7.___ . Users store their files on a ___8.___, or ___9.___ . When they finish a document, they signal the ___10.___ to print it.

Apply the Spelling Strategy

Circle the following three Content Words you wrote: the one with the **y** pronounced **long i,** the one with the double consonant in the second syllable, and the one with the /ô/ sound spelled **au**.

Word Study

Word History

When Christopher Columbus met the Taino people in the West Indies, they had a food they called **batata**. The Spanish word for this food was **papa**. Over many years, these two words combined to form this Strategy Word. Write the word.

Language Arts: Research
1. (encyclopedia)
2. almanac
3. atlas
4. (thesaurus)
5. guidebook

Science: Computers
6. hardware
7. terminal
8. floppy disk
9. (diskette)
10. printer

Word History
1. potatoes

175

Unit 29 Home Spelling Practice

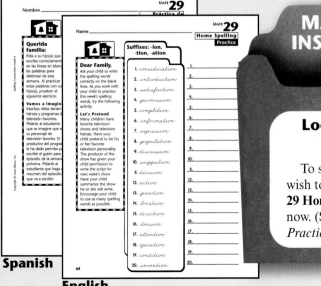

Spanish

English

MANAGING INSTRUCTION

Looking Ahead to Unit 29

To save time, you may wish to duplicate the **Unit 29 Home Spelling Practice** now. (See *Home Spelling Practice Book,* Unit 29.)

Objectives

Content Words

Students will
- **expand** vocabulary with content-related words.
- **relate** the spelling strategy to words outside the basic spelling list.
- **understand** the history of the word **potatoes**.

Content Words

Language Arts: Research

Use these sentences to introduce the words and their meanings.

1. The **encyclopedia** is one source of information.
2. This **guidebook** identifies all the trees in the park.
3. I used the **thesaurus** to find a synonym for a word in my report.
4. I found a list of all the no-hit pitchers in the **almanac**.
5. Please check the **atlas** to see how many states border our state.

Science: Computers

Use these sentences to introduce the words and their meanings.

6. I saved the information on the **floppy disk**.
7. I used the **printer** to make invitations to her birthday party.
8. This **diskette** has the information.
9. Use this **terminal** to search the library's catalog.
10. The defective **hardware** slowed my computer.

Word Study

Word History

Remind students that a word history, or **etymology,** traces the origin of a word and the development of its meaning. Some etymologies, such as this one, reflect interesting stories of the ways language grows and changes.

T175

Basic Spelling List

consideration	decision
introduction	action
satisfaction	position
permission	location
completion	direction
information	tension
expression	attention
population	operation
discussion	condition
suggestion	invention

Strategy Words

Review

companion	mention
composition	onion
fiction	

Preview

compassion	omission
condensation	recognition
hesitation	

Content Words

Language Arts: Mechanics

abbreviation	quotation
punctuation	capitalization
apostrophe	

Math: Estimating

computation	trillion
estimation	rounding
difference	

Individual Needs

Challenge Words

connection	contribution
collection	recession
donation	explanation

Alternate Word List ★

completion	decision
information	action
expression	position
population	direction
suggestion	attention

★ For students who need to study fewer Basic Spelling words

MATERIALS

Student Edition
Pages 176–181
Challenge Activities, p. 248

Teacher Edition
Pages T176A–T181
Challenge Activities, p. T248

Teacher Resource Book
Unit 29 Homework Master
Unit 29 Practice Masters
Flip Folder Practice Master
Unit 29 Test Master

Home Spelling Practice Book
Unit 29 Home Spelling Practice
(English or Spanish)

Other *Spelling Connections* Resources
• Audiotape, Grade 6
• Practice Book for Grammar, Usage, and Mechanics, Grade 6
• Spelling Support for Second Language Learners, Grade 6
• Support Software on CD-ROM
• Transparency Book, Grade 6
• Word Sort CD-ROM, Grade 6

OBJECTIVES

Spelling and Thinking
Students will
• **read** the spelling words in list form and in context.
• **sort** the spelling words according to base words and spelling patterns.
• **read** and remember this week's spelling strategy.

Spelling and Vocabulary
Students will
• **replace** underlined words in sentences with spelling words that have the same or nearly the same meaning.
• **drop** and add letters and suffixes to write spelling words.
• **write** spelling words by adding and subtracting prefixes and suffixes from given words.

Spelling and Reading
Students will
• **solve** analogies using spelling words.
• **complete** sentences using spelling words.
• **complete** a paragraph using spelling words.

Spelling and Writing
Students will
• **proofread** an advertisement.
• **use** the writing process to write an advertisement.
• **proofread** their writing.

MEETING INDIVIDUAL NEEDS
Learning Styles

 Visual

Divide the class into pairs to play the spelling game called "Daisy." Student A secretly chooses a spelling word and draws a dotted line on paper, with each segment of the line representing one letter of the word. Student B must guess the letters of the word, one by one. Each time Student B guesses a letter of the word, Student A writes that letter in the proper place on the dotted line. If Student B guesses a letter that is not in the word, Student A draws a petal on a daisy "stem." For every missed letter, another petal is added. The object of the game is to guess the mystery word before the drawing of the flower (which has five petals) is complete.

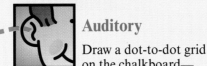 **Auditory**

Draw a dot-to-dot grid on the chalkboard— five dots across and four dots down. Divide the class into two teams and give the teams names. The teams alternate turns. Pronounce a spelling word for the first member of Team A to spell aloud. If the word is spelled correctly, the student goes to the chalkboard and connects two dots on the grid. Then it is Team B's turn. When four dots are connected to form a square, the team that completed the square places its name inside the square.

Hands-On Practice

All students will benefit from practicing with a **Flip Folder**. See page Z18.

 Kinesthetic

For a game of "Spelling Baseball," divide the class into two teams. Designate parts of the classroom as home plate, first base, second base, and third base. Pronounce a spelling word for the member of one team to spell aloud, while the others on that team write the word on paper. If the word is spelled aloud correctly, the student advances one base, and the next team member comes to bat. Four correctly spelled words earn a run. Each additional word spelled correctly earns another run, as another student crosses home plate. Every misspelled word is an out. After three outs, the other team takes a turn at bat.

Language and Cultural Differences

Write each spelling word on the chalkboard. Pronounce the spelling words and point out the suffixes. Underline the **-tion** and the **-sion** in each word to help students remember the correct spelling pattern.

MANAGING INSTRUCTION

3–5 Day Plan		Average	Below Average	Above Average
Day 1	**Day 1**	Pretest Spelling Mini-Lesson, p. T176 Spelling and Thinking, p. 176	Pretest Spelling Mini-Lesson, p. T176 Spelling and Thinking, p. 176	Pretest Spelling and Thinking, p. 176
	Day 2	Spelling and Vocabulary, p. 177	Spelling and Vocabulary, p. 177 (or) Unit 29 Practice Master, A and B	Spelling and Vocabulary, p. 177 Spelling and Reading, p. 178
Day 2	**Day 3**	Spelling and Reading, p. 178	Spelling and Reading, p. 178 (or) Unit 29 Practice Master, C and D	Challenge Activities, p. 248
	Day 4	Spelling and Writing, p. 179 Unit 29 Homework Master	Spelling and Writing, p. 179	Spelling and Writing, p. 179 Unit 29 Homework Master
Day 3	**Day 5**	Weekly Test	Weekly Test	Weekly Test

Vocabulary Connections (pages 180 and 181) may be used anytime during this unit.

Objectives

Spelling and Thinking
Students will
- **read** the spelling words in list form and in context.
- **sort** the spelling words according to base words and spelling patterns.
- **read** and remember this week's spelling strategy.

UNIT PRETEST

Use **Pretest Sentences** below. Refer to the self-checking procedures on student page 256. You may wish to use the **Unit 29 Word List Overhead Transparency** as part of the checking procedure.

TEACHING THE STRATEGY

Spelling Mini-Lesson

Write **action, election, information, migration, population, decision,** and **permission** on the chalkboard. Ask volunteers to identify the base word in each word. (act, elect, inform, migrate, populate, decide, permit) Ask the students to explain the ways in which the spelling of each base word changes, or does not change, when the suffix is added. (no change: action, election, information; drop final e: migration, population; final letter changed to s or ss: decision, permission)

Tell the students that the words on this week's list have one of three suffixes: **-ion, -tion, -ation.** Explain that **-tion** is a variant of **-ion.** Write **attention** and **attend** on the board. Use these words to explain that sometimes final **d** changes to **t** before a suffix is added: **attend + ion = attention.**

Ask volunteers to read the spelling list. Explain that the final syllable of each word ending in **ion** is pronounced /shən/. The pronunciation does not vary no matter which letter(s) precedes **ion.** Remind them that they should pay special attention to the spelling of these final syllables because, although they are pronounced the same, they are **not** spelled the same.

Read **Remember the Spelling Strategy** on page 176.

Order of answers may vary.

no change to base word
1. consideration
2. information ★
3. expression ★
4. discussion
5. suggestion ★
6. action ★
7. direction ★
8. invention

change to base word
9. introduction
10. satisfaction
11. permission
12. completion ★
13. population ★
14. decision ★
15. location
16. tension
17. attention ★
18. operation

no base words
19. position ★
20. condition

READ THE SPELLING WORDS

1.	consideration	*consideration*	I appreciate your **consideration**.
2.	introduction	*introduction*	The book's **introduction** was brief.
3.	satisfaction	*satisfaction*	My work gives me **satisfaction**.
4.	permission	*permission*	I have **permission** to leave early.
5.	completion	*completion*	He carried his plan to **completion**.
6.	information	*information*	We will mail you the **information**.
7.	expression	*expression*	His **expression** was sad and lonely.
8.	population	*population*	Our city has a growing **population**.
9.	discussion	*discussion*	We had a lively class **discussion**.
10.	suggestion	*suggestion*	Your **suggestion** was excellent.
11.	decision	*decision*	It was his **decision** to stay home.
12.	action	*action*	The firefighter sprang into **action**.
13.	position	*position*	Get into a comfortable **position**.
14.	location	*location*	The store moved to a new **location**.
15.	direction	*direction*	He is going in the wrong **direction**.
16.	tension	*tension*	I sense **tension** between the rivals.
17.	attention	*attention*	Pay **attention** to the instructions.
18.	operation	*operation*	He needs an **operation** on his foot.
19.	condition	*condition*	My old car is in great **condition**.
20.	invention	*invention*	Describe your latest **invention**.

SORT THE SPELLING WORDS

1.–8. Write the words that add **-ion** or **-ation** to a base word.

9.–18. Write the words in which the spelling of the base word changes before the suffix **-ion** or **-tion** is added.

19.–20. Write the words that are not formed from base words.

REMEMBER THE SPELLING STRATEGY

Remember that the suffixes **-ion, -tion,** and **-ation** can be added to a base word or root to form a noun, such as **action, introduction,** and **information.**

176

Pretest Sentences (See procedures on pages Z10–Z11.)

1. He took traffic into **consideration** when he planned his route.
2. Some people did not hear the brief **introduction** of the speaker.
3. I think I solved the problem to everyone's **satisfaction**.
4. You will need **permission** to go on the class outing.
★ 5. Upon **completion** of this lesson, you can do your homework.
★ 6. Will I be able to locate the **information** I need in this book?
★ 7. Her **expression** revealed what she was thinking.
★ 8. The **population** of our town is 40,000.
9. We had a **discussion** about the pros and cons of space travel.
★ 10. Will you make a **suggestion** about how to complete the project?
★ 11. The jury was unable to come to a **decision** in the case.
★ 12. The mother's quick **action** saved the child from falling.
★ 13. Standing on one foot is a difficult **position** to hold.
14. Please look at your map and determine the **location** of Peru.
★ 15. His skillful **direction** helped to make the play a success.
16. There was much **tension** in the audience as the tightrope walker began her journey.
★ 17. The teacher demanded the students' complete **attention**.
18. The surgeon assured us that the **operation** was a success.
19. The doctor said that the patient's **condition** was stable.
20. The **invention** of the airplane was a major achievement.

Spelling and Vocabulary

Word Replacement

Write spelling words that best replace the underlined words.

1. The windsurfer is a recent <u>creation</u>.
2. It is important to keep your windsurfer in good <u>shape</u>.
3. Be sure to get accurate weather <u>data</u>.
4. Your hand and body <u>stance</u> on the windsurfer is important.
5. Check the <u>path</u> of the wind.
6. Pay <u>heed</u> to safety rules for water sports.
7. The <u>beginning</u> of windsurfing added a new sport for surfers.
8. It takes practice to master the <u>working</u> of a windsurfer.

Word Structure

When the suffix **-ion** is added to a verb root or base word, a noun is formed. Follow the directions and write the spelling words.

9. locate – e + ion = _____
10. populate – e + ion = _____
11. permit – t + ss + ion = _____
12. express + ion = _____
13. tense – e + ion = _____
14. discuss + ion = _____

USING THE Dictionary

A dictionary often provides other forms of an entry word. By changing prefixes and suffixes, several words can be formed from one stem. Add and subtract prefixes and suffixes to the words below to write spelling words.

15. inactivity
16. indecisive
17. suggestible
18. inconsiderate
19. incomplete
20. unsatisfactory

Word Replacement
1. invention
2. condition
3. information
4. position
5. direction
6. attention
7. introduction
8. operation

Word Structure
9. location
10. population
11. permission
12. expression
13. tension
14. discussion

Using the Dictionary
15. action
16. decision
17. suggestion
18. consideration
19. completion
20. satisfaction

177

Objectives

Spelling and Vocabulary
Students will
- **replace** underlined words in sentences with spelling words that have the same or nearly the same meaning.
- **drop** and add letters and suffixes to write spelling words.
- **write** spelling words by adding and subtracting prefixes and suffixes from given words.

Developing Oral Language Skills

Have students work in pairs. The first student asks a question that includes the base word of one of the spelling words. For example, the student might ask, "Did you **inform** the team of the new schedule?" The second student answers the question using the spelling word formed from the base word. For example, the student might answer, "Yes, I gave them the **information**."

MEETING INDIVIDUAL NEEDS

Providing More Help

Write these words on the chalkboard: **act, inform, populate, tense, consider,** and **direct.** Have volunteers go to the chalkboard to add the suffix to each word that forms a spelling word. (In two cases, the students must delete the final **e** before adding the suffix.)

★Students who need to study fewer words should use the **Alternate Word List.** This list is starred on page T176 in the Teacher Edition. The **Unit 29 Practice Masters** (*Teacher Resource Book*) provide additional practice with these words.

Unit 29 Practice Masters

Name _____

Practice Master 29

1. action   3. suggestion   5. population   7. position   9. expression
2. direction   4. information   6. completion   8. attention   10. decision

A. When the suffix **-ion** is added to verb roots or bases, nouns are formed. Add and subtract letters to form spelling words. Write the words.

1. act + ion = _____   _____
2. populate – e + ion = _____   _____
3. express + ion = _____   _____
4. attend – d + t + ion = _____   _____
5. complete – e + ion = _____   _____
6. suggest + ion = _____   _____

B. Write the spelling words that stem from these Latin word origins.

1. **dirigere,** meaning "to give direction to" _____
2. **suggerere,** meaning "to carry up" _____
3. **informare,** meaning "to inform" _____
4. **populus,** meaning "the people" _____
5. **complere,** meaning "to fill out" _____
6. **decidere,** meaning "to decide" _____

105

106

Spelling and Reading

Students will
- **solve** analogies using spelling words.
- **complete** sentences using spelling words.
- **complete** a paragraph using spelling words.

One-Minute Handwriting Hint

The checkstroke joining of the lowercase **o** swings right and curves up, then overcurves quickly into the first slant stroke of the letter **n**.

OVERCURVE

SLANT

Legible handwriting can boost spelling scores by as much as 20%.

Solve the Analogies

1. consideration
2. operation
3. invention
4. completion
5. permission

Complete the Sentences

6. expression
7. location
8. condition
9. tension
10. information
11. population
12. action
13. attention

Complete the Paragraph

14. introduction
15. discussion
16. suggestion
17. position
18. decision
19. satisfaction
20. direction

Spelling and Reading

consideration	introduction	satisfaction	permission
completion	information	expression	population
discussion	suggestion	decision	action
position	location	direction	tension
attention	operation	condition	invention

Solve the Analogies   Write a spelling word to complete each analogy.

1. **Approval** is to **acceptance** as **thoughtfulness** is to _____.
2. **Builder** is to **construction** as **surgeon** is to _____.
3. **Digest** is to **digestion** as **invent** is to _____.
4. **Narrate** is to **narration** as **complete** is to _____.
5. **Receive** is to **gift** as **obtain** is to _____.

Complete the Sentences   Write a spelling word to complete each sentence.

6. He had a relieved _____ on his face.
7. Look on the map for the exact _____ of Hill Road.
8. I will go to the picnic on the _____ that you will come, too.
9. There was _____ between the friends after their argument.
10. She asked the librarian for _____ on tornadoes.
11. China has the highest _____ of any other country.
12. The movie is full of adventure and _____.
13. We must devote more _____ to our new puppy.

Complete the Paragraph   Write spelling words from the box to complete the paragraph.

Lee Kravitz, a surfboarding instructor, gives a basic __14.__ to surfing while beginner students are still on shore. First, he holds a __15.__ about surfing safety. Then he gives a __16.__ about selecting a surfboard. This lesson includes learning the correct foot __17.__ for standing and balancing. The __18.__ to ride a wave is up to the surfer. There is great __19.__ in catching a wave in the right __20.__ and riding all the way to shore.

satisfaction
introduction
decision
direction
suggestion
discussion
position

178

MEETING INDIVIDUAL NEEDS

Providing More Challenge

Challenge Words and **Challenge Activities** for Unit 29 appear on page 248. **Challenge Word Test Sentences** appear on page T248.

Unit 29 Challenge Activities

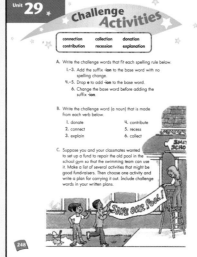

Weekly Test Options

Option 1:
One Spelling Word Per Sentence
(See procedures on pages Z10–Z11.)

★ 1. The captain was a man of **action**.
★ 2. May I have your **attention,** please?
★ 3. The **completion** of her homework meant that Sally could join her friends Saturday afternoon.
4. The doctor reported that his **condition** had improved.
5. Always try to show **consideration** for others.
★ 6. What is your **decision** about going to the movies?
★ 7. In what **direction** is the park?
8. Since no one could agree, our **discussion** was fruitless.
★ 9. The **expression** on her face told us she won.
★10. You need more **information** to solve the puzzle.
11. The **introduction** of the speaker was brief but clever.
12. Her **invention** could bring her great fame.
13. What is the exact **location** of the hospital?
14. Correct **operation** of this equipment takes great skill.
15. Ask your parent to sign the **permission** form.

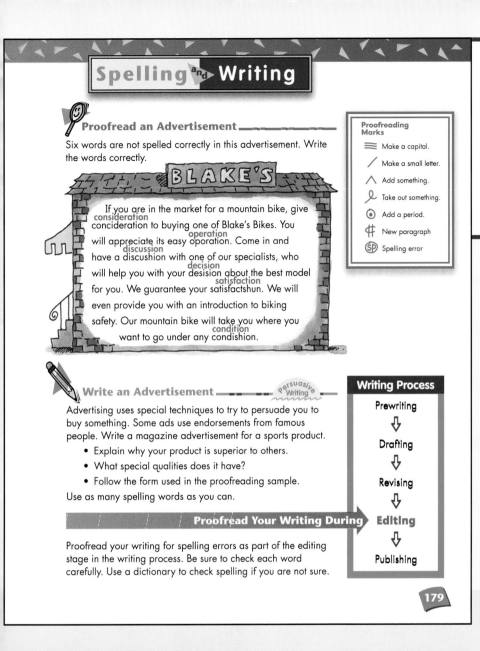

Spelling and Writing

Proofread an Advertisement

Six words are not spelled correctly in this advertisement. Write the words correctly.

BLAKE'S

If you are in the market for a mountain bike, give
consideration
concideration to buying one of Blake's Bikes. You
operation
will appreciate its easy oporation. Come in and
discussion
have a discushion with one of our specialists, who
decision
will help you with your desision about the best model
satisfaction
for you. We guarantee your satisfactshun. We will
even provide you with an introduction to biking
safety. Our mountain bike will take you where you
condition
want to go under any condishion.

Proofreading Marks

≡ Make a capital.
／ Make a small letter.
∧ Add something.
℣ Take out something.
⊙ Add a period.
⌗ New paragraph
⑤Ⓟ Spelling error

Write an Advertisement

Persuasive Writing

Advertising uses special techniques to try to persuade you to buy something. Some ads use endorsements from famous people. Write a magazine advertisement for a sports product.

• Explain why your product is superior to others.
• What special qualities does it have?
• Follow the form used in the proofreading sample.

Use as many spelling words as you can.

Proofread Your Writing During

Proofread your writing for spelling errors as part of the editing stage in the writing process. Be sure to check each word carefully. Use a dictionary to check spelling if you are not sure.

Writing Process

Prewriting
⇩
Drafting
⇩
Revising
⇩
Editing
⇩
Publishing

179

★16. What is the **population** of this state?
★17. He holds an important **position** in that company.
  18. The applause gave the actor great **satisfaction**.
★19. My **suggestion** was praised by the teacher.
  20. The **tension** between the rivals was obvious to all.

Option 2:
Multiple Spelling Words Per Sentence
(See procedures on pages Z10–Z11.)

  1. Please pay **attention** to the **discussion**.
  2. Your **suggestion** is under **consideration**.
  3. This **information** will take the study in a new **direction**.
  4. This **invention** makes the **operation** possible.
  5. Does the **decision** meet with your **satisfaction**?
  6. State your **position** in the **introduction** to the essay.
  7. **Permission** will be given on the **condition** that you act in a responsible way.
  8. This **action** marks the **completion** of the program.
  9. Which **location** has the largest **population**?
 10. His **expression** showed the **tension** he was feeling.

Option 3:
Standardized Test
(See *Teacher Resource Book,* Unit 29.)

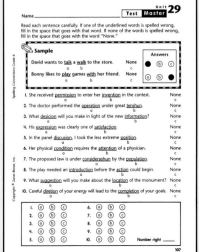

**Unit 29
Test Master**

TI79

Objectives

Strategy Words

Students will
- **review** words studied previously that are related to the spelling strategy.
- **preview** unknown words that are related to the spelling strategy.

VOCABULARY CONNECTIONS

►Strategy Words◄

Remind the students that the **Strategy Words** relate to the spelling patterns they have studied in this unit. The **Review Words** are below grade level, and the **Preview Words** are above grade level. You may wish to use the following sentences to introduce the words in context.

Review Words:
Words From Grade 5
1. My **companion** for the trip was my cousin.
2. Did you finish your English **composition**?
3. I enjoy reading **fiction** books.
4. Will you **mention** the meeting to your friend?
5. An **onion** was listed as one of the ingredients for the soup.

Preview Words:
Words From Grade 7
6. Their **compassion** for our feelings helped us through the crisis.
7. Even though it had not rained, the grass was wet because of **condensation**.
8. His **hesitation** gave the other team a chance to score.
9. The **omission** of the directions was the cause of our problems when we tried to put the toy together.
10. My friend was given **recognition** at the assembly for his good grades.

Review Words
1. fiction
2. onion
3. companion
4. composition
5. mention

Preview Words
6. condensation
7. compassion
8. recognition
9. omission
10. hesitation

►Strategy Words◄

Review Words: Suffixes -ion, -tion, -ation

Write a word from the box to complete each sentence.

companion composition fiction mention onion

1. Although the book is ____, it is based on a true story.
2. Peeling an ____ always makes me cry.
3. My little sister has an imaginary ____.
4. Our teacher asked us to write a ____ about a heroic person in our family.
5. Please ____ my name if you call the plumber.

Preview Words: Suffixes -ion, -tion, -ation

Write words from the box to complete this review for a television show.

compassion   condensation   hesitation
omission   recognition

Do not miss tonight's one-hour __6.__ of the key events of the most recent summer Olympics. The events are told with __7.__ and humor. The producer gives proper __8.__ to those athletes who did not win a medal but revealed their talents in other ways. The only flaw that I noticed was the __9.__ of coverage of the diving event, which I always enjoy. In spite of this, I would recommend this show without __10.__ .

180

Unit
29
RECAP

You may wish to assign the **Unit 29 Homework Master** (*Teacher Resource Book*, Unit 29) as a fun way to recap the spelling words.

Unit 29 Homework Master

Name _____   Homework **Master** Unit **29**

Use the code to write the spelling words.

△ = o	□ = a	◇ = u	☆ = i	♡ = e	✱ = tion

d☆♡c✱   1. _____
p△s☆✱   2. _____
s□t☆sf□c✱   3. _____
t♡ns☆△n   4. _____
□c✱   5. _____
l△c□✱   6. _____
□tt♡n✱   7. _____
☆nv♡n✱   8. _____
d♡c☆s☆△n   9. _____
p♡m☆ts☆☆△n   10. _____

The letters in the boxes above form another spelling word. Unscramble and write it here.   ___ ___ ___ ___ ___ ___ ___ ___

Study the structure of the first two words. Complete the analogy following the same structural pattern.

1. direct : direction :: suggest : _____
2. operate : operation :: complete : _____
3. discuss : discussion :: express : _____
4. inform : information :: consider : _____
5. reduce : reduction :: introduce : _____
6. celebrate : celebration :: populate : _____
7. donate : donation :: operate : _____

108

Spelling Connections Grade 6

Copyright © Zaner-Bloser, Inc.

Objectives

Content Words

Students will
- **expand** vocabulary with content-related words.
- **relate** the spelling strategy to words outside the basic spelling list.
- **understand** the history of the word **apostrophe**.

▾Content Words▾

Language Arts: Mechanics

Write a word from the box to complete each sentence.

| abbreviation | punctuation | apostrophe |
| quotation | capitalization | |

1. Use _____ at the beginning of every sentence.
2. Periods and commas are examples of _____.
3. **Dr.** is the _____ for **doctor**.
4. In a contraction, put an _____ where letters have been omitted.
5. Use _____ marks to show someone's exact words.

Math: Estimating

Write the words from the box that complete the paragraph.

| computation | trillion | estimation | rounding | difference |

When engineers bid on a project, they give an __6.__ of the cost. There should not be a large __7.__ between the estimate and the actual costs. Engineers usually use a computer to do the __8.__ of expenses. It is common to give an estimate by __9.__ off to the nearest hundred. No single project has yet cost one __10.__ dollars.

Apply the Spelling Strategy

Circle the six Content Words you wrote with the suffix **-ation**.

▾Word Study▾

Word History

This Content Word came from an old Greek word, **apostrophos,** which meant "omission." Write the Content Word.

Language Arts: Mechanics
1. capitalization
2. punctuation
3. abbreviation
4. apostrophe
5. quotation

Math: Estimating
6. estimation
7. difference
8. computation
9. rounding
10. trillion

Word History
1. apostrophe

181

▾Content Words▾

Language Arts: Mechanics

Use these sentences to introduce the words and their meanings.

1. The **abbreviation** Dr. is standard for doctor.
2. He often forgets the **punctuation** at the end of a sentence.
3. We can show possession with an **apostrophe**.
4. That **quotation** originally came from the wise Benjamin Franklin.
5. We studied all of the rules of **capitalization** in fifth grade.

Math: Estimating

Use these sentences to introduce the words and their meanings.

6. Deandre practiced her math **computation** skills every day.
7. A **trillion** is a single number with twelve zeros behind it.
8. We can use **estimation** in math.
9. When I am **rounding** the cost of something, I usually round up.
10. The **difference** between the two answers was not noticed.

▾Word Study▾

Word History

Remind students that a word history, or **etymology,** traces the origin of a word and the development of its meaning. Some etymologies, such as this one, reflect interesting stories of the ways language grows and changes.

Unit 30 Home Spelling Practice

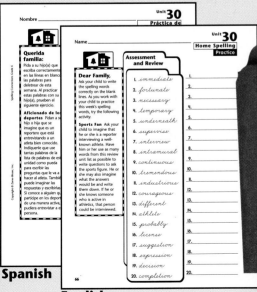

Spanish

English

MANAGING INSTRUCTION

Looking Ahead to Unit 30

To save time, you may wish to duplicate the **Unit 30 Home Spelling Practice** now. (See *Home Spelling Practice Book,* Unit 30.)

T181

Assessment Words

veterinary	nonpoisonous
understanding	exception
hilarious	instruction
transfusion	poisonous
exclamation	subtitle
glamorous	inaccurate
intermediate	intercept
sanitary	affectionate
inadequate	outrageous
midweek	appreciation

Review Words

Unit 25

immediate*	delicate
fortunate*	unfortunate
necessary*	ordinary
temporary*	desperate
accurate	imaginary

Unit 26

underneath*	underground
supervise*	subway
interview*	submarine
intramural*	interstate
midsummer	interchange

Unit 27

continuous*	various
tremendous*	glorious
industrious*	curious
courageous*	precious
nervous	cautious

Unit 28

different*	pigeon
athlete*	captain
probably*	surely
license*	muscle
similar	sauce

Unit 29

suggestion*	direction
expression*	information
decision*	population
completion*	position
action	attention

* Posttest sentences and the **Unit 30 Test Master** test these words. Students review all words listed.

MATERIALS

Student Edition
Pages 182–187

Teacher Edition
Pages T182A–T187

Teacher Resource Book
Flip Folder Practice Master
Unit 30 Test Master

Home Spelling Practice Book
Unit 30 Home Spelling Practice (English or Spanish)

Other *Spelling Connections* Resources
• Transparency Book, Grade 6

OBJECTIVES

Spelling and Assessment

Students will
• **assess** their spelling success by matching new words to the spelling strategies presented in Units 25–27, 29.
• **connect** new words to the spelling strategies in Units 25–27, 29.
• **write** new words that relate to the spelling strategies taught in Units 25–27, 29.

Spelling and Review

Students will
• **review** and practice the spelling strategies and words in Units 25–29.
• **learn** an alternative spelling study strategy.

Spelling and Writing

Students will
• **review** coordinating and subordinating conjunctions.
• **compose** a historical narrative.
• **learn** a proofreading strategy.
• **understand** that they may encounter foreign spellings on the Internet.
• **proofread** for British spelling.

MEETING INDIVIDUAL NEEDS
Learning Styles

 Visual

Divide the class into two teams. Print spelling words on pieces of construction paper and cut the words apart into individual letters. Give the letters for half of the spelling words to one team and the letters for the rest of the spelling words to the other team. Tell each team that—when you say "Begin!"—they are to put their letters together to form ten spelling words. The team that is first to form their spelling words correctly wins.

 Auditory

Assign each player one spelling word. Have the player scramble the letters. Each player in turn writes the scrambled word on the chalkboard, pronounces the letters in scrambled order, and calls on a volunteer to identify the word, pronounce it again, and spell it aloud correctly.

 Kinesthetic

Bring a ball to class for playing "Hot Potato." The student who has the ball spells a word and then passes the ball to another student. The student who catches the ball says the word, spells another word, and hands the ball to a third student. The game continues in this fashion until all of the targeted words are reviewed.

Hands-On Practice
All students will benefit from practicing with a **Flip Folder**. See page Z18.

Language and Cultural Differences

Spanish-speaking students may have difficulty pronouncing and spelling the words that have the **short i** sound because this sound does not exist in Spanish. Also, there is no schwa sound in Spanish, which could cause difficulty for pronouncing and spelling some words in Units 25–29.

To help students with the spelling task, have them make a set of 3" × 5" spelling word cards. Have the students write the dictionary respelling under each spelling word. Encourage them to use these cards to memorize the spellings and pronunciations.

MANAGING INSTRUCTION

3–5 Day Plan		Average	Below Average	Above Average
Day 1	Day 1	Assessment: Units 25–29, p. 182 (Option 1 or 2, p. T182)	Assessment: Units 25–29, p. 182 (Option 1 or 2, p. T182)	Assessment: Units 25–29, p. 182 (Option 1 or 2, p. T182)
	Day 2	Review: Units 25 and 26, p. 183	Review: Units 25 and 26, p. 183	Review: Units 25 and 26, p. 183 Review: Units 27 and 28, p. 184
Day 2	Day 3	Review: Units 27 and 28, p. 184	Review: Units 27 and 28, p. 184	Review: Unit 29, p. 185 Spelling Study Strategy, p. 185
	Day 4	Review: Unit 29, p. 185 Spelling Study Strategy, p. 185	Review: Unit 29, p. 185 Spelling Study Strategy, p. 185	Writer's Workshop, pages 186–187
Day 3	Day 5	Weekly Test, Option 1 or 2, p. T185	Weekly Test, Option 1 or 2, p. T185	Weekly Test, Option 1 or 2, p. T185

Writer's Workshop (pages 186 and 187) may be used anytime during this unit.

Objectives

Spelling and Assessment

Students will
- **assess** their spelling success by matching new words to the spelling strategies presented in Units 25–27, 29.
- **connect** new words to the spelling strategies in Units 25–27, 29.
- **write** new words that relate to the spelling strategies taught in Units 25–27, 29.

Note: Because the spelling strategy in Unit 28 does not reflect regular spelling patterns, there are no **Assessment Words** relating to this unit.

Unit 25
1. veterinary
2. intermediate ▲
3. sanitary
4. inadequate
5. inaccurate
6. affectionate

Unit 26
7. understanding
8. midweek
9. subtitle
10. intercept

Unit 27
11. hilarious
12. glamorous
13. nonpoisonous
14. poisonous
15. outrageous

Unit 29
16. transfusion
17. exclamation
18. exception
19. instruction
20. appreciation

Assessment Units 25–29

Each Assessment Word in the box fits one of the spelling strategies you have studied over the past five weeks. Read the spelling strategies. Then write each Assessment Word under the unit number it fits. You will not write any words from Unit 28.

Unit 25 _____

1.–6. The suffixes **-ate** and **-ary** can be added to root words and base words to form adjectives such as **delicate** and **honorary**.

Unit 26 _____

7.–10. The prefix **mid-** means "middle," **under-** and **sub-** mean "under" or "beneath," **super-** means "above," **inter-** means "between," and **intra-** means "within."

Unit 27 _____

11.–15. The suffix **-ous** can be added to base words or root words to form adjectives such as **mountainous**, **nervous**, and **obvious**.

Unit 28 _____

It is important to learn the spellings of words that writers often misspell.

Unit 29 _____

16.–20. The suffixes **-ion, -tion,** and **-ation** can be added to a base word or root to form a noun, such as **action, introduction,** and **information**.

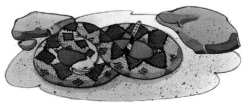

veterinary
understanding
hilarious
transfusion
exclamation
glamorous
intermediate
sanitary
inadequate
midweek
nonpoisonous
exception
instruction
poisonous
subtitle
inaccurate
intercept
affectionate
outrageous
appreciation

182

ASSESSMENT: UNITS 25–29

Option 1

Assessment Option 1 is the test that appears in the Student Edition on page 182. You may wish to have students take this test to determine their ability to recognize the spelling strategy in each unit and to match words not previously taught to that strategy. **Assessment Option 1** also serves as additional review and practice.

▲ Words designated with this symbol include more than one of the targeted spelling strategies. The answer key has placed them according to the most obvious spelling emphasis. However, if a student places a word in another category, and the word fits that generalization, accept that response. Remember, the objective is to place each word with any appropriate spelling generalization.

Option 2

Assessment Option 2 is a dictation test using the sentences on page T183. This test assesses students' ability to spell words not previously taught but that are exemplars of a spelling strategy. This test more specifically assesses students' ability to apply the spelling knowledge they have learned.

In either assessment test option, the words are identified by unit in the Teacher Edition. You may wish to index those misspelled words to the review exercises that follow in this unit. Determine which units students need to review and use the additional unit exercises found in this **Assessment and Review Unit** for reteaching the skill in a more focused way.

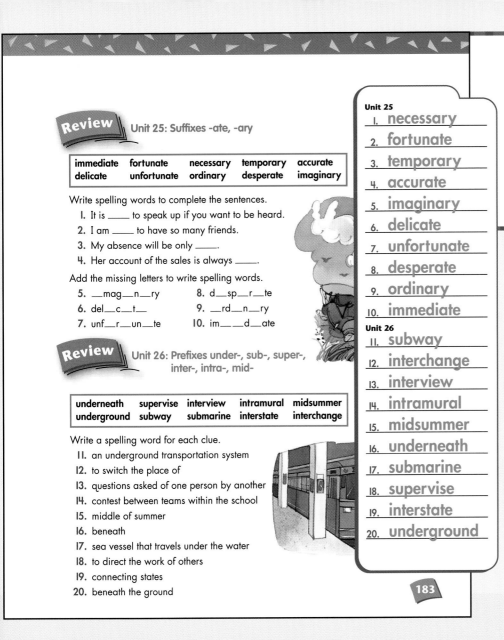

Review
Unit 25: Suffixes -ate, -ary

immediate	fortunate	necessary	temporary	accurate
delicate	unfortunate	ordinary	desperate	imaginary

Write spelling words to complete the sentences.

1. It is ＿＿ to speak up if you want to be heard.
2. I am ＿＿ to have so many friends.
3. My absence will be only ＿＿.
4. Her account of the sales is always ＿＿.

Add the missing letters to write spelling words.

5. ＿mag＿n＿ry
6. del＿c＿t＿
7. unf＿r＿un＿te
8. d＿sp＿r＿te
9. ＿rd＿n＿ry
10. im＿＿d＿ate

Review
Unit 26: Prefixes under-, sub-, super-, inter-, intra-, mid-

underneath	supervise	interview	intramural	midsummer
underground	subway	submarine	interstate	interchange

Write a spelling word for each clue.

11. an underground transportation system
12. to switch the place of
13. questions asked of one person by another
14. contest between teams within the school
15. middle of summer
16. beneath
17. sea vessel that travels under the water
18. to direct the work of others
19. connecting states
20. beneath the ground

Unit 25
1. necessary
2. fortunate
3. temporary
4. accurate
5. imaginary
6. delicate
7. unfortunate
8. desperate
9. ordinary
10. immediate

Unit 26
11. subway
12. interchange
13. interview
14. intramural
15. midsummer
16. underneath
17. submarine
18. supervise
19. interstate
20. underground

183

Objectives

Spelling and Review
Students will
• **review** and practice the spelling strategy and words taught in Unit 25.
• **review** and practice the spelling strategy and words taught in Unit 26.

Assessing Progress: The Spelling Journal

If your students have been keeping a personal spelling journal, a periodical review of these journals can be a rich assessment tool. Students should include the words they have misspelled from each unit spelling test. They should also be encouraged to write the words they consistently misspell in their own writing and content-area words that present a challenge. Being able to discriminate the words in their everyday writing whose spelling they need to master is a powerful spelling skill.

Pretest Sentences: Assessment Words
(See procedures on pages Z10–Z11.)

1. Our pets have always had excellent **veterinary** care.
2. Caring for a child takes a great deal of **understanding**.
3. We thought her joke was **hilarious**.
4. Grandma needed a blood **transfusion** after her surgery.
5. His shout was an **exclamation** of joy.
6. The **glamorous** model strolled down the aisle.
7. This is an **intermediate** step on the way to success.
8. The nurse makes sure that the hospital room is **sanitary**.
9. Our savings account for the new computers is still **inadequate**.
10. We have a test **midweek** and another on Friday.
11. All the snakes in this region are **nonpoisonous**.
12. There is one big **exception** to the rule.
13. Listen carefully to this fire drill **instruction**.
14. Some spiders are **poisonous**.
15. Under the title is the **subtitle**.
16. I'm afraid that these figures are **inaccurate**.
17. The defender was able to **intercept** the pass.
18. Our kitten has become very **affectionate**.
19. That store charges **outrageous** prices for milk.
20. We gave our teacher a card to show our **appreciation** for her help.

Objectives

Spelling and Review

Students will

- **review** and practice the spelling strategy and words taught in Unit 27.
- **review** and practice the spelling strategy and words taught in Unit 28.

Unit 27

1. glorious
2. courageous
3. industrious
4. various
5. nervous
6. continuous
7. tremendous
8. precious
9. cautious
10. curious

Unit 28

11. muscle
12. license
13. probably
14. similar
15. surely
16. different
17. athlete
18. sauce
19. pigeon
20. captain

 Review Unit 27: Suffix -ous

| continuous | tremendous | industrious | courageous | nervous |
| various | glorious | curious | precious | cautious |

Complete the sentence by adding the suffix **-ous** to the underlined word.

1. The victory was filled with <u>glory</u>. It was a _____ day.
2. Her actions took great <u>courage</u>. She is a _____ person.
3. Our city has much <u>industry</u>. We live in an _____ city.
4. The weather will <u>vary</u>. I enjoy the _____ types of weather.

Write the spelling word for these meanings.

5. excited
6. ongoing
7. huge; great
8. dear
9. careful
10. interested

 Review Unit 28: Words Writers Use

| different | athlete | probably | license | similar |
| pigeon | captain | surely | muscle | sauce |

Find the misspelled word in each sentence and write it correctly.

11. It takes strong mussle to lift this box.
12. David just got his driver's lisense.
13. We probly won't go early to the game.
14. Our new jackets are simmilar, aren't they?
15. You surley will learn the music piece by Monday.
16. Saira has a diffrent outfit for each role in the play.
17. She showed great talent as an athelete.
18. Do you know how he makes that lemon sause?
19. We saw the same pijon at the park every day.
20. The captin of the ship spoke to the crew.

184

Bulletin Board Idea

Word Games and Puzzles

Design a bulletin board entitled "Word Games and Puzzles." Place that title at the top of the bulletin board. Cut five sheets of construction paper—each a different color—into various geometric shapes. Place these, too, on the board. Put one of these headings at the top of each sheet: **Mixed-up Sentences, Scrambled Syllables, Word Search, Secret Code,** and **Create the Compound**. Ask students to invent puzzles to go on these sheets. The students who solve the puzzles then place their answers beside the game.

To create a mixed-up sentence, for example, a student writes a sentence, scrambles the words, and then writes all the letters together without spaces or capitalization. For scrambled syllables, a student breaks a word into syllables and then mixes them up. For a word search, a student follows the standard format for this type of puzzle. To create the compound, a student identifies five or more actual compound words and then writes the small words that make up the compounds in random order. To make a secret code, a student encodes a message following the code of three—every third letter is part of the message.

Review Unit 29: Suffixes -ion, -tion, -ation

suggestion	expression	decision	completion	action
direction	information	population	position	attention

Write a spelling word that ends with the same letters as the underlined part of the words below.

1. inten**tion**
2. excla**mation**
3. circu**lation**
4. que**stion**
5. de**letion**
6. compre**ssion**
7. in**cision**
8. subtra**ction**
9. impo**sition**
10. ele**ction**

Unit 29

1. attention
2. information
3. population
4. suggestion
5. completion
6. expression
7. decision
8. action
9. position
10. direction

GAME Spelling Study Strategy

Spelling Questions

Practicing spelling can be fun if you make it into a game. Here's an idea you can try with a friend.

1. Swap spelling lists with your friend. Be sure you can each read the other's list.

2. Your friend should pick one of the words on your list but not say it.

3. You may ask your friend three questions about the word. For example, you could ask, "Does it end with **ion**?" If you guess the word with your three questions, you get two points. Write the word.

4. Ask your friend to check the spelling. If you have the word spelled correctly, you get two points. If not, ask one question. If you get the spelling right this time, you get one point. If not, your friend will tell you the spelling, but you don't get any points.

5. If you don't guess the word, ask your friend to tell you the word. You don't get any points just now.

6. Now it's your friend's turn to guess a word and write it.

7. Keep going until you have both practiced all the words.

185

Objectives

Spelling and Review

Students will
- **review** and practice the spelling strategy and words taught in Unit 29.
- **learn** an alternative spelling study strategy.

Learning an Alternative Spelling Study Strategy

Students should always have a number of study strategies to draw from when it comes to learning their spelling words. **Spelling Questions** is a partner game that makes practicing spelling fun to do. Encourage students to remember this spelling study strategy and to consider using it with any list they need to study and learn.

Weekly Test Options

Option 1:
One Spelling Word Per Sentence
(See procedures on pages Z10–Z11.)

1. He is **fortunate** to have his own horse.
2. She gave an **immediate** answer.
3. Do you have the **necessary** tools?
4. I was given **temporary** charge of the team.
5. He will **interview** the school principal.
6. Our school has a large **intramural** sports program.
7. I agreed to **supervise** the experiment.
8. Stay **underneath** the covers to keep warm.
9. The water flowed in a **continuous** stream.
10. The soldier performed a **courageous** act.
11. Ants are **industrious** insects.
12. The carnival was a **tremendous** success.
13. In what ways are the twins **different**?
14. Keep your driver's **license** in a safe place.
15. She is training to become a better **athlete**.

16. I will **probably** be late again today.
17. The **completion** of her homework meant that Sally could join us.
18. What is your **decision** about dinner?
19. He used a clever **expression** from a foreign language.
20. Her **suggestion** was quickly accepted.

Option 2:
Standardized Test

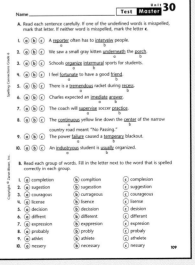

Unit 30 Test Master

(See *Teacher Resource Book*, Unit 30.)

Objectives

Spelling and Writing

Students will
- **review** coordinating and subordinating conjunctions.
- **compose** a historical narrative. (See **Spelling and the Writing Process** below.)

Optional Enrichment

 Unit 30 enrichment

 **WRITER'S**

Grammar, Usage, and Mechanics

Conjunctions

Coordinating conjunctions, such as **and, but,** and **or,** connect words or groups of words (including independent clauses) that are similar.

> Jenny **and** I wanted to go, **but** we were too late.

Subordinating conjunctions, such as **although, because, since, so, if,** and **before,** show how one clause is related to another. Subordinating conjunctions are often used at the beginning of dependent clauses.

> **Since** Jamal was on time, he caught the bus.

 Practice Activity

A. Write the conjunction in each sentence below. Circle it if it is a subordinating conjunction.

1. We can call ahead, or we can just arrive.
2. This trail is easy, but it is long.
3. Although I speak Spanish, I do not speak it well.
4. If Lori comes, we will have eight people.
5. Because it's a school night, I can't go.

B. Complete each sentence with a conjunction from the box. Capitalize the conjunction if it begins a sentence.

but	or	because	if	before

6. You may come, _____ you may stay at home.
7. _____ it rained earlier, puddles were everywhere.
8. _____ Alexis left, she had walked the dog.
9. I see Dan's bike, _____ I don't see him.
10. _____ more snow falls, we can go sledding.

186

A

1. or
2. but
3. (Although)
4. (If)
5. (Because)

Answers may vary. Possible answers are given.

B

6. or
7. Because
8. Before
9. but
10. If

 Narrative Writing

Spelling and the Writing Process

You may wish to use this writing assignment to help students master the writing process. For other writing ideas, see pages 258–259 in the Student Edition.

Explain that students will write a historical narrative about some incident that interests them.

Prewriting Hint: You may wish to help students plan their writing by recommending that they list events and then number them to show their order. Display the following as an example.

> 3. Phoebe served George Washington peas.
> 2. The peas had been poisoned.
> 4. She warned Washington.
> 5. He threw out the peas.
> 1. Thomas Hickey had asked her to help him.

Revising Hint: Remind students that when they revise their narratives, they should make sure that they have included transitions such as **first, then,** and **while** to show when things happen. They should also use such cause-and-effect transitions as **because** and **so** to show why things happened.

Proofreading Strategy

Read it Backwards!

Good writers always proofread their writing for spelling errors. Here's a strategy that you can use to proofread your papers.

Usually, you read a paper from the first word to the last. This time, try reading it backwards. In other words, read it from the last word to the first. You would read the sentence **I finished my homework.** like this: **homework. my finished I**

It sounds like a funny way to proofread, but reading backwards helps you think about the spelling of each word instead of the meaning of the sentence. Try it!

Electronic Spelling
1. honor
2. theater
3. organization
4. realize
5. color
6. labor

Electronic Spelling

Foreign Spellings

Although the people of England and the United States both speak and write English, they do not always speak and write it the same way. They also do not spell everything the same way.

When you visit British sites on the Internet, you may notice spelling differences. Unless you are quoting, you should use the American spelling rather than the British.

Try doing that now. Below are six words that you might see on a British site. Write the American spelling of each word.

1. honour
2. theatre
3. organisation
4. realise
5. colour
6. labour

187

Objectives

Writer's Workshop

Students will
- **learn** a proofreading strategy.
- **understand** that they may encounter foreign spellings on the Internet.
- **proofread** for British spelling.

Optional Enrichment

Using Proofreading Strategies

Students are often unaware that there are a variety of techniques they can use to proofread their own writing. Building a repertory of strategies is important to improving students' writing and editing skills.

Spelling and Technology

The advent of word processing, computer protocols, and the Internet has actually increased, not lessened, the pressure on users to be better, more aware spellers. Spell checkers, for example, create circumstances in which the ability to discriminate between an acceptable and an unacceptable spelling is a critical skill. A homophone substitution, a correct spelling of the wrong word, an inadvertent word omission—these are examples of situations in computer usage that require a deeper understanding of spelling principles and a more adroit proofreading capability. It may be worthwhile to underscore this increased need as a whole-class discussion after students finish this unit's **Electronic Spelling** activity.

Unit 31 Home Spelling Practice

Spanish

English

MANAGING INSTRUCTION

Looking Ahead to Unit 31

To save time, you may wish to duplicate the **Unit 31 Home Spelling Practice** now. (See *Home Spelling Practice Book*, Unit 31.)

Basic Spelling List

lieutenant	engineer
superintendent	custodian
merchant	assistant
volunteer	resident
participant	servant
electrician	agent
comedian	guardian
opponent	musician
applicant	tenant
attendant	librarian

Strategy Words

Review

amphibian	rodent
impatient	sergeant
patient	

Preview

consistent	proficient
descendant	vegetarian
detergent	

Content Words

Social Studies: The Military

civilian	protection
military	endanger
defense	

Fine Arts: Music

cellist	pianist
flutist	composer
violinist	

Individual Needs

Challenge Words

auctioneer	historian
pediatrician	vice president
defendant	contestant

Alternate Word List ★

lieutenant	engineer
merchant	assistant
volunteer	servant
opponent	musician
applicant	librarian

★ For students who need to study fewer Basic Spelling words

MATERIALS

Student Edition
Pages 188–193
Challenge Activities, p. 249

Teacher Edition
Pages T188A–T193
Challenge Activities, p. T249

Teacher Resource Book
Unit 31 Homework Master
Unit 31 Practice Masters
Flip Folder Practice Master
Unit 31 Test Master

Home Spelling Practice Book
Unit 31 Home Spelling Practice
(English or Spanish)

Other *Spelling Connections* Resources
• Audiotape, Grade 6
• Practice Book for Grammar, Usage, and Mechanics, Grade 6
• Spelling Support for Second Language Learners, Grade 6
• Support Software on CD-ROM
• Transparency Book, Grade 6
• Word Sort CD-ROM, Grade 6

OBJECTIVES

Spelling and Thinking

Students will
• **read** the spelling words in list form and in context.
• **sort** the spelling words according to the suffixes **-eer, -ian, -ant,** and **-ent**.
• **read** and remember this week's spelling strategy.

Spelling and Vocabulary

Students will
• **write** spelling words that are related in meaning to other words.
• **write** spelling words based on clues.
• **use** dictionary etymologies to write spelling words.

Spelling and Reading

Students will
• **solve** analogies using spelling words.
• **complete** job descriptions using spelling words.
• **complete** a paragraph using spelling words.

Spelling and Writing

Students will
• **proofread** a paragraph.
• **use** the writing process to write a job description.
• **proofread** their writing.

MEETING INDIVIDUAL NEEDS
Learning Styles

 Visual

Write each spelling word on a 3" × 5" card. Write the word's suffix on the back of the card. Spread the cards facedown on a desk. One student names and writes a spelling word. The student then turns over a card, using the suffix as a clue that the card may be the one on which the word is written. If the choice is correct (and the word is spelled correctly), the student keeps the card. If the choice is incorrect (or the word is misspelled), the card is again placed facedown. In either case, the next player has a turn.

 Auditory

Divide the class into groups of four. Then divide each foursome into two-person teams. The players on Team A take turns pronouncing the first part of each spelling word, omitting the suffix. The players on Team B take turns guessing the suffix and then pronouncing and spelling the word aloud. After half of the spelling words have been used, the teams trade places.

 Kinesthetic

Use the word cards described in the visual activity. Place the cards on the chalk tray with the spelling words facedown so that the suffixes can be seen. Divide the class into two teams. Pronounce a spelling word. One member of each team walks to the chalkboard and attempts to find the word. The first player to find the proper word card scores a point for the team. Both players must then spell the word aloud and write it on the chalkboard.

Hands-On Practice
All students will benefit from practicing with a **Flip Folder**. See page Z18.

Language and Cultural Differences

Some students may have difficulty with the spelling words because of regional pronunciations. In many regions of the United States, dialects and localisms in oral language result in pronunciation differences.

Spanish-speaking students may have difficulty with the short vowel sounds and schwa sound in these words. In addition, the final **t** (present in several of the words) is a sound that does not occur in Spanish. Write the spelling words on the chalkboard. Point at each word as you pronounce it slowly and carefully, and have the students pronounce it after you. Discuss the meaning of each word.

MANAGING INSTRUCTION

3–5 Day Plan		Average	Below Average	Above Average
Day 1	**Day 1**	Pretest Spelling Mini-Lesson, p. T188 Spelling and Thinking, p. 188	Pretest Spelling Mini-Lesson, p. T188 Spelling and Thinking, p. 188	Pretest Spelling and Thinking, p. 188
	Day 2	Spelling and Vocabulary, p. 189	Spelling and Vocabulary, p. 189 (or) Unit 31 Practice Master, A and B	Spelling and Vocabulary, p. 189 Spelling and Reading, p. 190
Day 2	**Day 3**	Spelling and Reading, p. 190	Spelling and Reading, p. 190 (or) Unit 31 Practice Master, C and D	Challenge Activities, p. 249
	Day 4	Spelling and Writing, p. 191 Unit 31 Homework Master	Spelling and Writing, p. 191	Spelling and Writing, p. 191 Unit 31 Homework Master
Day 3	**Day 5**	Weekly Test	Weekly Test	Weekly Test
Vocabulary Connections (pages 192 and 193) may be used anytime during this unit.				

Objectives

Spelling and Thinking

Students will
- **read** the spelling words in list form and in context.
- **sort** the spelling words according to the suffixes **-eer, -ian, -ant,** and **-ent**.
- **read** and remember this week's spelling strategy.

UNIT PRETEST

Use **Pretest Sentences** below. Refer to the self-checking procedures on student page 256. You may wish to use the **Unit 31 Word List Overhead Transparency** as part of the checking procedure.

TEACHING THE STRATEGY

Spelling Mini-Lesson

Explain that the suffix **-eer** means "one associated with." Write **mountaineer** on the chalkboard. Ask students to identify the base word. (mountain) Explain that a **mountaineer** is "one who is associated with mountains."

Explain that the suffix **-ian** means "one relating to." Write **comedian** on the board. Ask students to identify the base word. (comedy) Guide them to combine the meaning of the suffix and the meaning of the base word to conclude that a **comedian** is "one who is related to comedy."

Explain that the suffixes **-ant** and **-ent** mean "one who performs." Write **servant** on the board. Ask students to identify the base word. (serve) Guide them to combine the meaning of the suffix and the meaning of the base word to conclude that a **servant** is "one who serves or performs a service."

To help the students distinguish between words spelled with **-ant** or **-ent,** divide the class into pairs. Ask each pair to make a set of flash cards using the spelling words that end in **-ant** and **-ent.** Ask them to cut each card into two pieces at the point where the suffix begins. Each team must shuffle their cards and then put them back together correctly, matching the suffixes with the base words or roots. The team to finish first is the winner.

Read **Remember the Spelling Strategy** on page 188.

Order of answers may vary.

-eer
1. volunteer ★
2. engineer ★

-ian
3. electrician
4. comedian
5. custodian
6. guardian
7. musician ★
8. librarian ★

-ant
9. lieutenant ★
10. merchant ★
11. participant
12. applicant ★
13. attendant
14. assistant ★
15. servant ★
16. tenant

-ent
17. superintendent
18. opponent ★
19. resident
20. agent

188

READ THE SPELLING WORDS

1. lieutenant	lieutenant	The **lieutenant** saluted.
2. superintendent	superintendent	She is our **superintendent**.
3. merchant	merchant	This **merchant** sells jewelry.
4. volunteer	volunteer	He is a hospital **volunteer**.
5. participant	participant	Each **participant** had a turn.
6. electrician	electrician	The **electrician** fixed the bell.
7. comedian	comedian	We laughed at the **comedian**.
8. opponent	opponent	She debated her **opponent**.
9. applicant	applicant	He is a college **applicant**.
10. attendant	attendant	An **attendant** moved her car.
11. engineer	engineer	He is chief project **engineer**.
12. custodian	custodian	A **custodian** cleans the office.
13. assistant	assistant	Dr. Ito hired an **assistant**.
14. resident	resident	He is a **resident** of our town.
15. servant	servant	A mayor is a public **servant**.
16. agent	agent	The singer fired her **agent**.
17. guardian	guardian	Who is the child's **guardian**?
18. musician	musician	The **musician** plays piano.
19. tenant	tenant	A new **tenant** just moved in.
20. librarian	librarian	The **librarian** has the book.

SORT THE SPELLING WORDS

1.–2. Write the spelling words that end in the suffix **-eer**.

3.–8. Write the spelling words that end in the suffix **-ian**.

9.–16. Write the spelling words that end in the suffix **-ant**.

17.–20. Write the spelling words that end in the suffix **-ent**.

REMEMBER THE SPELLING STRATEGY

Remember that the suffixes **-eer, -ian, -ant,** and **-ent** can be used to form nouns. These nouns often name people: **engineer, librarian, assistant,** and **resident.**

Pretest Sentences (See procedures on pages Z10–Z11.)

★ 1. The **lieutenant** ordered his troops to stand at attention.
2. The principal of our school reports to the **superintendent**.
★ 3. The **merchant** sells different kinds of fabric.
★ 4. My sister does **volunteer** work at the hospital after school.
5. He enjoys watching sports but is rarely a **participant**.
6. Dad called an **electrician** to install the new light fixture.
7. The **comedian** told such bad jokes that no one laughed.
★ 8. I will fight hard to beat my **opponent** in the chess match.
★ 9. The job **applicant** was called in for an interview.
10. The parking **attendant** asked Dad if the keys were in the car.
★11. Becoming an **engineer** requires many years of schooling.
12. The building **custodian** has come to repair the leaky faucet.
★13. The **assistant** reminded her boss of the day's appointments.
14. He is the newest **resident** of our building.
★15. The butler had been the wealthy man's **servant** for years.
16. Our school hired an **agent** to publicize our charity drive.
17. A child's legal **guardian** is responsible for the child's well-being.
★18. Ladonna hopes to be an accomplished **musician** when she grows up.
19. The **tenant** was upset because the landlord raised the rent.
★20. The **librarian** suggested that I look in the computerized catalogue.

Spelling and Vocabulary

Related Meanings

Write a spelling word that is related in meaning to each word.

1. apply
2. voluntary
3. agency
4. reside
5. library
6. engine

Word Clues

Write the spelling word that matches each clue.

7. the person in charge
8. installs electrical equipment
9. composes or performs music
10. makes people laugh
11. takes care of a building
12. a rival or competitor
13. a military officer
14. a renter or boarder

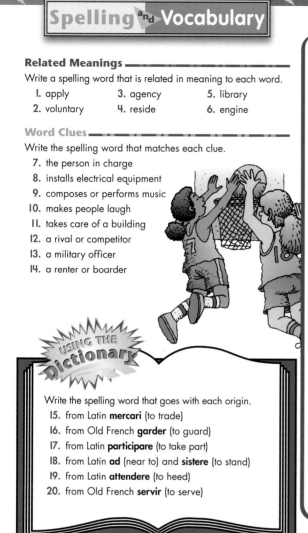

USING THE Dictionary

Write the spelling word that goes with each origin.

15. from Latin **mercari** (to trade)
16. from Old French **garder** (to guard)
17. from Latin **participare** (to take part)
18. from Latin **ad** (near to) and **sistere** (to stand)
19. from Latin **attendere** (to heed)
20. from Old French **servir** (to serve)

Related Meanings
1. applicant
2. volunteer
3. agent
4. resident
5. librarian
6. engineeer

Word Clues
7. superintendent
8. electrician
9. musician
10. comedian
11. custodian
12. opponent
13. lieutenant
14. tenant

Using the Dictionary
15. merchant
16. guardian
17. participant
18. assistant
19. attendant
20. servant

189

Objectives

Spelling and Vocabulary
Students will
- **write** spelling words that are related in meaning to other words.
- **write** spelling words based on clues.
- **use** dictionary etymologies to write spelling words.

Developing Oral Language Skills

Have students work in pairs. The first student asks a question about an occupation that is one of the words from the spelling list. For example, the student might say, "What does a **guardian** do?" The second student uses that word's base word in a sentence to answer the question. For example, the second student might say, "The **guardian** will **guard** the children."

MEETING INDIVIDUAL NEEDS

Providing More Help

Assign each student a suffix. Pronounce each spelling word. Have the students raise their hands when they hear their suffix pronounced. They then write the word on paper while you write it on the chalkboard. Then switch the students' suffixes and continue the game until they have written all of the words.

★Students who need to study fewer words should use the **Alternate Word List**. This list is starred on page T188 in the Teacher Edition. The **Unit 31 Practice Masters** (*Teacher Resource Book*) provide additional practice with these words.

Unit 31 Practice Masters

Name _____

Practice Master 31

1. engineer 3. librarian 5. merchant 7. applicant 9. lieutenant
2. volunteer 4. musician 6. servant 8. assistant 10. opponent

A. Write the spelling word that is made from each base word.

1. library _____
2. serve _____
3. apply _____
4. music _____
5. assist _____

B. The suffixes **-eer**, **-ian**, **-ant**, and **-ent** all convey the meaning of "one who." The origins of the roots of the spelling words are given below, along with their literal definitions. Write each of these spelling words.

1. from Latin **opponere** (to oppose): one who opposes _____
2. from Latin **mercari** (to trade): one who trades _____
3. from Latin **ad** (near to) and **sistere** (to stand): one who stands near to _____
4. from Old French **servir** (to serve): one who serves _____
5. from Old French **lieu** (place) and **tenir** (to hold): one who holds the place of or acts in place of _____

C. Unscramble the letters to form and write the spelling words.

1. nenigere _____
2. tenorluve _____
3. nasimuci _____
4. hernamct _____

110

Practice Master 31

applicant   lieutenant
assistant   opponent

Objectives

Spelling and Reading

Students will
- **solve** analogies using spelling words.
- **complete** job descriptions using spelling words.
- **complete** a paragraph using spelling words.

One-Minute Handwriting Hint

The lowercase **n** contains two overcurves. Be sure to pause after the first overcurve-slant motion. The two slant strokes should be parallel.

OVERCURVES

Legible handwriting can boost spelling scores by as much as 20%.

Solve the Analogies

1. opponent
2. guardian
3. servant
4. resident
5. assistant
6. attendant
7. lieutenant
8. tenant

Complete the Descriptions

9. comedian
10. librarian
11. musician
12. volunteer
13. electrician
14. superintendent

Complete the Paragraph

15. participant
16. agent
17. engineer
18. custodian
19. merchant
20. applicant

190

Spelling and Reading

lieutenant	superintendent	merchant	volunteer
participant	electrician	comedian	opponent
applicant	attendant	engineer	custodian
assistant	resident	servant	agent
guardian	musician	tenant	librarian

Solve the Analogies Write a word to complete each analogy.

1. **Friend** is to **foe** as **teammate** is to _____.
2. **Head** is to **chief** as **parent** is to _____.
3. **Help** is to **helper** as **serve** is to _____.
4. **Occupy** is to **occupant** as **reside** is to _____.
5. **Teacher** is to **instructor** as **aide** is to _____.
6. **Immigrate** is to **immigrant** as **attend** is to _____.
7. **General** is to **colonel** as **captain** is to _____.
8. **Hotel** is to **guest** as **apartment** is to _____.

Complete the Descriptions Write a spelling word to match each job description.

9. Wanted: a _____ to make people laugh.
10. Book lover needed to assist a _____.
11. Band will hold auditions for a _____.
12. Hospital seeks a _____ to visit patients.
13. An _____ needed to rewire building.
14. New school system looking for school _____.

Complete the Paragraph Write spelling words from the box to complete the paragraph.

As a _15._ in the job search process, Mr. Arnold needed assistance. So he talked to an _16._ at an employment office. He described his goal to be an _17._ of bridges. Then, Mr. Arnold described his work as head _18._ in a school and his work with a local _19._ who owned a computer store. Mr. Arnold feels that he is a qualified _20._ for a better job.

engineer
merchant
applicant
participant
agent
custodian

MEETING INDIVIDUAL NEEDS

Providing More Challenge

Challenge Words and **Challenge Activities** for Unit 31 appear on page 249. **Challenge Word Test Sentences** appear on page T249.

Unit 31 Challenge Activities

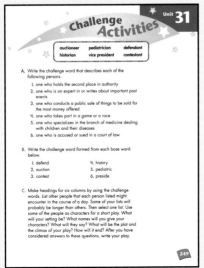

Weekly Test Options

Option 1:
One Spelling Word Per Sentence
(See procedures on pages Z10–Z11.)

⭐ 1. My brother is studying to be an **engineer**.
  2. Our school **custodian** works from 3 P.M. until 11 P.M.
  3. We have a new **resident** in our neighborhood.
⭐ 4. Only one **applicant** will be chosen for the position.
⭐ 5. I need a **volunteer** to write this sentence on the board.
⭐ 6. An **assistant** can be a valuable employee.
  7. His **guardian** shows much concern for his well-being.
⭐ 8. It takes practice to become a skilled **musician**.
⭐ 9. My sister's husband is an army **lieutenant**.
 10. The **electrician** impressed me with his knowledge.
 11. The **tenant** learned about his rent increase.
 12. The **attendant** will park our car.
 13. Will you be a **participant** in the game?
⭐14. The **merchant** profited little from the sale.
 15. Our school **superintendent** is very popular.

T190

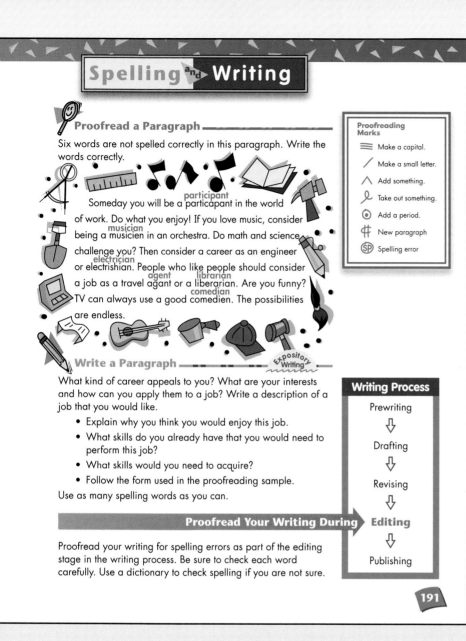

Spelling and Writing

Proofread a Paragraph

Six words are not spelled correctly in this paragraph. Write the words correctly.

participant
Someday you will be a participant in the world of work. Do what you enjoy! If you love music, consider being a **musician** in an orchestra. Do math and science challenge you? Then consider a career as an engineer or **electrician**. People who like people should consider a job as a travel **agent** or a **librarian**. Are you funny? TV can always use a good **comedian**. The possibilities are endless.

Proofreading Marks

≡ Make a capital.
/ Make a small letter.
∧ Add something.
ℒ Take out something.
⊙ Add a period.
⌗ New paragraph.
(SP) Spelling error

Write a Paragraph

Expository Writing

What kind of career appeals to you? What are your interests and how can you apply them to a job? Write a description of a job that you would like.

- Explain why you think you would enjoy this job.
- What skills do you already have that you would need to perform this job?
- What skills would you need to acquire?
- Follow the form used in the proofreading sample.

Use as many spelling words as you can.

Writing Process

Prewriting
⇩
Drafting
⇩
Revising
⇩
Editing
⇩
Publishing

Proofread Your Writing During

Proofread your writing for spelling errors as part of the editing stage in the writing process. Be sure to check each word carefully. Use a dictionary to check spelling if you are not sure.

191

Objectives

Spelling and Writing
Students will
- **proofread** a paragraph.
- **use** the writing process to write a job description.
- **proofread** their writing.

Using the Writing Process

Before assigning **Write a Paragraph**, see pages 258–259 in the Student Edition for a complete review of the writing process and additional writing assignments. You may wish to refer to pages Z12–Z13 in the Teacher Edition.

Keeping a Spelling Journal

Encourage students to record the words they misspelled on the weekly test in a personal spelling journal. These words may be recycled for future study. Students may also wish to include words from their writing. See pages Z12–Z13 in the Teacher Edition for more information.

★16. He is a loyal **servant**.
★17. The **librarian** may ask you to leave if you disturb others.
18. The board hired a **comedian** for the annual affair.
19. I will contact a travel **agent** to make my vacation plans.
★20. You have a worthy **opponent** in this game.

Option 2:
Multiple Spelling Words Per Sentence
(See procedures on pages Z10–Z11.)

1. The **applicant** wanted the job of **custodian**.
2. He is an **assistant** to the **engineer** on the **merchant** ship.
3. The **lieutenant** asked for a **volunteer**.
4. The **comedian** had really wanted to become a **musician**.
5. The **librarian** asked whether I am a **resident** of the city.
6. His **agent** got him the part of the **servant** in the new play.
7. The **tenant** asked the **superintendent** of the building to call an **electrician**.
8. The **attendant** was a **participant** in the wedding.
9. She felt that she was a **guardian** of truth and an **opponent** of illogical thinking.

Option 3:
Standardized Test
(See *Teacher Resource Book*, Unit 31.)

Unit 31 Test Master

T191

Objectives

Strategy Words

Students will
• **review** words studied previously that are related to the spelling strategy.
• **preview** unknown words that are related to the spelling strategy.

Optional Enrichment

►Strategy Words◄

Remind the students that the **Strategy Words** relate to the spelling patterns they have studied in this unit. The **Review Words** are below grade level, and the **Preview Words** are above grade level. You may wish to use the following sentences to introduce the words in context.

Review Words:
Words From Grade 5

1. An **amphibian** can live on land or water.
2. Try not to be **impatient** while waiting for lunch.
3. The doctor treated the **patient** with great skill.
4. My sister does not like my pet **rodent**.
5. She is a **sergeant** in the police force.

Preview Words:
Words From Grade 7

6. Because he is **consistent** in his study habits, he usually gets good grades.
7. I am a **descendant** of William Seward.
8. This **detergent** was advertised on television.
9. Mary is **proficient** on the word processor.
10. Someone who does not eat meat is a **vegetarian**.

Review Words
1. impatient
2. sergeant
3. patient
4. rodent
5. amphibian

Preview Words
6. descendant
7. vegetarian
8. detergent
9. consistent
10. proficient

►Strategy Words◄

Review Words: Suffixes -eer, -ian, -ant, -ent

Write a word from the box to match each clue.

amphibian	impatient	patient	rodent	sergeant

1. not willing to put up with delay or trouble
2. a soldier's rank
3. willing to put up with delay or trouble; also, someone being treated by a doctor
4. an animal characterized by large front teeth for gnawing
5. an animal that breathes water when it is young

Preview Words: Suffixes -eer, -ian, -ant, -ent

Write words from the box to complete this book review.

consistent	descendant	detergent
proficient		vegetarian

Chef Claude is a direct __6.__ of the famous cook, Paul Plouffe. A strict __7.__, Chef Claude presents his vegetable dishes with delightful originality. One lesson this writer learned in reading the book was to wash all vegetables well before cooking. There is no need to use __8.__; plain water will do. Chef Claude's book is __9.__ with his previous books in its creativity and beautiful pictures. The chef is as __10.__ in writing as he is in cooking.

192

Unit **31** RECAP

You may wish to assign the **Unit 31 Homework Master** (*Teacher Resource Book*, Unit 31) as a fun way to recap the spelling words.

Unit 31 Homework Master

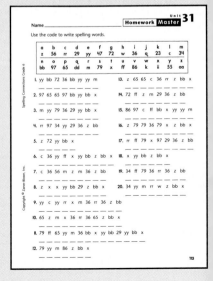

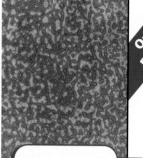

Content Words

Social Studies: The Military

Write words from the box to complete the paragraph.

civilian	military	defense	protection	endanger

The armed forces include all of the groups that might fight in __1.__ of our country. Every United States citizen helps to support the armed forces through taxes. When threats of foreign invasion __2.__ our freedom, the armed forces prepare to provide __3.__ for us. A citizen not serving in the __4.__ is referred to as a __5.__.

Fine Arts: Music

Write words from the box to complete the sentences.

cellist	flutist	violinist	pianist	composer

6. George Gershwin was a _____ of both popular and classical music.
7. Gershwin began his career as a _____, playing the piano for musicals and shows.
8. A _____ must control her breathing to play well.
9.–10. Before the performance, both the _____ and _____ repaired the broken strings on their instruments.

Apply the Spelling Strategy

Circle the Content Word you wrote that ends in the suffix **-ian**.

Word Study

Related Words

The Latin word **civilis** meant "of or proper to a citizen." **Civilization, civil,** and **civil rights** are words related to this word. Write the Content Word that shares this relationship.

193

Social Studies: The Military
1. defense
2. endanger
3. protection
4. military
5. (civilian)

Fine Arts: Music
6. composer
7. pianist
8. flutist

Order of answers for 9 and 10 may vary.
9. cellist or
10. violinist

Related Words
1. civilian

Objectives

Content Words

Students will
- **expand** vocabulary with content-related words.
- **relate** the spelling strategy to words outside the basic spelling list.
- **understand** that many words are related by meaning and spelling.

Content Words

Social Studies: The Military

Use these sentences to introduce the words and their meanings.

1. Since I am not in the military, I am a **civilian**.
2. The **military** offers opportunities.
3. Our country's **defense** is a major responsibility of government.
4. The police provide **protection**.
5. Care will be taken so that we will not **endanger** the animals.

Fine Arts: Music

Use these sentences to introduce the words and their meanings.

6. He is a **cellist** in the orchestra.
7. It takes many years of practice to become an accomplished **flutist**.
8. The **violinist** rehearsed many times.
9. We watched the **pianist** perform.
10. George Gershwin was a **composer**.

Word Study

Related Words

Encourage students to use another common root, such as **circ**, to generate a list of related words. Possible responses for words related to **circ** include **circle, circuitry, circular, circumference, circumstance**. Challenge students to generate other lists of related words.

Unit 32 Home Spelling Practice

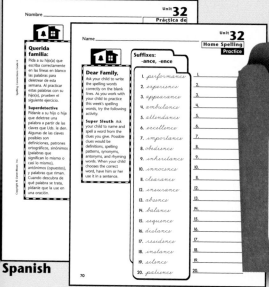

Spanish

English

Looking Ahead to Unit 32

To save time, you may wish to duplicate the **Unit 32 Home Spelling Practice** now. (See *Home Spelling Practice Book,* Unit 32.)

MANAGING INSTRUCTION

T193

Basic Spelling List

performance	clearance
experience	insurance
appearance	absence
ambulance	balance
attendance	sequence
excellence	distance
importance	residence
obedience	instance
inheritance	silence
innocence	patience

Strategy Words

Review

allowance	nuisance
audience	ordinance
entrance	

Preview

conscience	insistence
endurance	maintenance
ignorance	

Content Words

Math: Measurement

arc	radius
pi	circumference
chord	

Social Studies: Banking

finance	stockbroker
invest	partnership
fiscal	

Individual Needs

Challenge Words

admittance	reluctance
annoyance	existence
diligence	indifference

Alternate Word List ★

performance	balance
experience	distance
appearance	instance
attendance	silence
importance	patience

★ For students who need to study
  fewer Basic Spelling words

MATERIALS

Student Edition
Pages 194–199
Challenge Activities, p. 250

Teacher Edition
Pages T194A–T199
Challenge Activities, p. T250

Teacher Resource Book
Unit 32 Homework Master
Unit 32 Practice Masters
Flip Folder Practice Master
Unit 32 Test Master

Home Spelling Practice Book
Unit 32 Home Spelling Practice
  (English or Spanish)

Other *Spelling Connections* Resources
- Audiotape, Grade 6
- Practice Book for Grammar, Usage, and Mechanics, Grade 6
- Spelling Support for Second Language Learners, Grade 6
- Support Software on CD-ROM
- Transparency Book, Grade 6
- Word Sort CD-ROM, Grade 6

OBJECTIVES

Spelling and Thinking
Students will
- **read** the spelling words in list form and in context.
- **sort** the spelling words according to whether the suffix **-ance** or **-ence** is added to a base word or to a root.
- **read** and remember this week's spelling strategy.

Spelling and Vocabulary
Students will
- **complete** sentences with spelling words that are related to underlined words.
- **write** spelling words that are homophones for given words.
- **use** a thesaurus to find synonyms for underlined words in sentences.

Spelling and Reading
Students will
- **solve** analogies using spelling words.
- **complete** sentences using spelling words.
- **complete** a paragraph using spelling words.

Spelling and Writing
Students will
- **proofread** a letter.
- **use** the writing process to write a persuasive letter.
- **proofread** their writing.

MEETING INDIVIDUAL NEEDS
Learning Styles

 Visual

Have the students create a set of word cards together, writing each spelling word on a 3" × 5" card. Then ask them to trace the suffixes. Have them write over the **-ance** suffix in one color and the **-ence** suffix in another color. Display these cards on the bulletin board.

 Auditory

Pronounce each spelling word, and have the students spell the word aloud together. Then have a volunteer spell out just the letters of the suffix. If the students have difficulty, allow them to look at the spelling words in their books.

 Kinesthetic

Use the word cards created for the visual activity. Write the suffixes **-ance** and **-ence** on lengths of masking tape, and apply the tape to two separate receptacles that can hold the cards. Stack the cards facedown. Have the students take turns choosing a word card. The student reads aloud the spelling word on the card, spells the letters of the suffix in the word, and then spells the complete word. If the word is spelled correctly, the student drops the card into the proper receptacle. If the word is spelled incorrectly, the student returns the card to the stack. Continue until all the cards are in the proper receptacles.

Hands-On Practice
All students will benefit from practicing with a **Flip Folder**. See page Z18.

Language and Cultural Differences

The spelling words in this unit may be difficult for some students because of regional pronunciations. Spanish-speaking students may have difficulty with some of the short vowel sounds and the schwa sound in these words, since these sounds do not exist in Spanish.

On the chalkboard, label two columns **-ance** and **-ence**. Have the students copy them on their papers. Pronounce each spelling word and have a volunteer tell in which column the word belongs. Write the words on the chalkboard as the students write them on paper.

MANAGING INSTRUCTION

3–5 Day Plan		Average	Below Average	Above Average
Day 1	**Day 1**	Pretest Spelling Mini-Lesson, p. T194 Spelling and Thinking, p. 194	Pretest Spelling Mini-Lesson, p. T194 Spelling and Thinking, p. 194	Pretest Spelling and Thinking, p. 194
	Day 2	Spelling and Vocabulary, p. 195	Spelling and Vocabulary, p. 195 (or) Unit 32 Practice Master, A and B	Spelling and Vocabulary, p. 195 Spelling and Reading, p. 196
Day 2	**Day 3**	Spelling and Reading, p. 196	Spelling and Reading, p. 196 (or) Unit 32 Practice Master, C and D	Challenge Activities, p. 250
	Day 4	Spelling and Writing, p. 197 Unit 32 Homework Master	Spelling and Writing, p. 197	Spelling and Writing, p. 197 Unit 32 Homework Master
Day 3	**Day 5**	Weekly Test	Weekly Test	Weekly Test

Vocabulary Connections (pages 198 and 199) may be used anytime during this unit.

Objectives

Spelling and Thinking

Students will
- **read** the spelling words in list form and in context.
- **sort** the spelling words according to whether the suffix **-ance** or **-ence** is added to a base word or to a root.
- **read** and remember this week's spelling strategy.

UNIT PRETEST

Use **Pretest Sentences** below. Refer to the self-checking procedures on student page 256. You may wish to use the **Unit 32 Word List Overhead Transparency** as part of the checking procedure.

TEACHING THE STRATEGY

Spelling Mini-Lesson

Tell the students that the suffixes **-ance** and **-ence** are used to form many nouns. (Four of the spelling words—**balance, silence, distance** and **sequence**—can also be used as verbs.) Explain that these words are formed in a variety of ways. The word **clearance,** for example, is formed from the word **clear,** but the word **experience** is formed from a root, **experi,** which in turn comes from the Latin verb **experiri,** "to try."

Review the definitions of base words (words that can stand alone), roots (parts of words that require prefixes or suffixes to become words), and suffixes (letters added to the ends of words or roots to form new words).

Explain that the suffixes **-ance** and **-ence** are both pronounced /əns/. Because the pronunciation is the same for each suffix, thorough study and memorization are essential for learning to spell these words.

Read **Remember the Spelling Strategy** on page 194.

Spelling and Thinking

Order of answers may vary.
-ance added to base word
1. (perform)ance ★
2. (appear)ance ★
3. (attend)ance ★
4. (import)ance ★
5. (inherit)ance
6. (clear)ance
final consonant in base word doubled
7. excellence
-ance or -ence added to root
8. experience ★
9. ambulance
10. obedience
11. innocence
12. insurance
13. absence
14. balance ★
15. sequence
16. distance ★
17. residence
18. instance ★
19. silence ★
20. patience ★

194

READ THE SPELLING WORDS

1. performance	*performance*	Did you like our **performance**?
2. experience	*experience*	I had a frightening **experience**.
3. appearance	*appearance*	He disguised his **appearance**.
4. ambulance	*ambulance*	Call an **ambulance** at once!
5. attendance	*attendance*	He recorded class **attendance**.
6. excellence	*excellence*	She performed with **excellence**.
7. importance	*importance*	This clue has great **importance**.
8. obedience	*obedience*	Our parents expect **obedience**.
9. inheritance	*inheritance*	The house was his **inheritance**.
10. innocence	*innocence*	I will prove my **innocence**.
11. clearance	*clearance*	The bridge has a low **clearance**.
12. insurance	*insurance*	Car **insurance** is expensive.
13. absence	*absence*	I am in charge in her **absence**.
14. balance	*balance*	He lost his **balance** on the stairs.
15. sequence	*sequence*	Follow the steps in **sequence**.
16. distance	*distance*	She ran the **distance** in an hour.
17. residence	*residence*	Her legal **residence** is in Utah.
18. instance	*instance*	He is excused in this **instance**.
19. silence	*silence*	The audience sat in **silence**.
20. patience	*patience*	Have **patience** while you wait.

SORT THE SPELLING WORDS

Write the spelling words in which
1.–6. the suffix **-ance** is added to a base word that does not change spelling. Circle the base words.
7. the final consonant of the base word is doubled.
8.–20. the suffixes **-ance** or **-ence** were added to a root.

REMEMBER THE SPELLING STRATEGY

Remember that the suffixes **-ance** and **-ence** can be used to form nouns: **clearance, experience**.

Pretest Sentences (See procedures on pages Z10–Z11.)

★ 1. Everyone in the audience seemed to enjoy the **performance**.
★ 2. He had little **experience** in handling animals.
★ 3. The **appearance** of the crocus is a sure sign of spring.
4. A siren alerted us to the approach of the **ambulance**.
★ 5. She received a certificate for perfect school **attendance**.
6. This award honors your achievement of **excellence** in English.
★ 7. The lawyer advised his client about a matter of great **importance**.
8. They are sending their dog to **obedience** school.
9. They used the **inheritance** to buy a new home.
10. The child's parents wanted to protect her **innocence** so they monitored the television shows she watched.
11. The store is running a **clearance** sale on old merchandise.
12. Do you have **insurance** to protect your home in case of fire?
13. In our teacher's **absence**, a substitute took over the class.
★14. You must have good **balance** to ride a bicycle.
15. Please list the exact **sequence** in which these events occurred.
★16. What is the **distance** in miles from Cleveland to Chicago?
17. The family is moving to their new **residence** next week.
★18. Give me one **instance** that proves your statement.
★19. We walked down the road in **silence**.
★20. Some tasks are difficult and require **patience**.

Spelling and Vocabulary

Word Meanings

Write spelling words to complete the sentences. Use the underlined words as clues.

1. I am sending my <u>disobedient</u> dog to ____ school.
2. Let's <u>clear</u> out the shelves with a ____ sale.
3. When stars <u>appear</u> in the sky, I welcome their ____.
4. If you are <u>absent</u>, bring a note explaining your ____.
5. Any <u>imbalance</u> will be corrected when you ____ the wheels.
6. The <u>distant</u> city was only a short ____ from the border.
7. A <u>sequential</u> set of directions make the ____ easy to follow.
8. If the injured are not <u>ambulatory</u>, they may need an ____.
9. If you <u>inherit</u> money, taxes will take part of that ____.
10. The goal of ____ is to <u>insure</u> you against major losses.

Word Structure

Write the spelling words that are homophones for these words.

11. patients
12. residents
13. attendants
14. innocents
15. instants
16. excellents

USING THE Thesaurus

Replace the underlined words in the sentences below with synonyms from the spelling list.

17. A paper route provides valuable <u>training</u>.
18. There was complete <u>quiet</u> when Mom spoke.
19. The captain praised the soldier's <u>accomplishment</u>.
20. We all understand the <u>significance</u> of getting to school on time.

Word Meanings
1. obedience
2. clearance
3. appearance
4. absence
5. balance
6. distance
7. sequence
8. ambulance
9. inheritance
10. insurance

Word Structure
11. patience
12. residence
13. attendance
14. innocence
15. instance
16. excellence

Using the Thesaurus
17. experience
18. silence
19. performance
20. importance

195

Objectives

Spelling and Vocabulary

Students will
- **complete** sentences with spelling words that are related to underlined words.
- **write** spelling words that are homophones for given words.
- **use** a thesaurus to find synonyms for underlined words in sentences.

Developing Oral Language Skills

Have students pronounce **excellence**. Note whether they pronounce the second syllable clearly. If necessary, remind them that the second syllable should be clearly pronounced. Practice saying **excellence** several times. Write **excellence** on the chalkboard. Remind students that the word **excellence** (/ĕk′ sə ləns/) may cause spelling problems because the second syllable is weak or disappears entirely when it is pronounced.

MEETING INDIVIDUAL NEEDS

Providing More Help

Write **-ance** and **-ence** as headings on the chalkboard. Have the students take turns writing spelling words under the headings. Then, as you read the spelling words in random order, have the students raise their left hands for words that end in **-ence** and their right hands for words that end in **-ance**. Read the spelling words again, this time more quickly, and have the students again raise their hands to match the suffixes.

★Students who need to study fewer words should use the **Alternate Word List**. This list is starred on page T194 in the Teacher Edition. The **Unit 32 Practice Masters** (*Teacher Resource Book*) provide additional practice with these words.

Unit 32 Practice Masters

Name ____

Practice Master 32

1. appearance 3. performance 5. balance 7. distance 9. patience
2. attendance 4. importance 6. instance 8. silence 10. experience

A. Write the spelling words in alphabetical order.

1. ____ 6. ____
2. ____ 7. ____
3. ____ 8. ____
4. ____ 9. ____
5. ____ 10. ____

B. Write the spelling word that goes with each group.

1. equalize, weigh, ____ ____
2. looks, sight, ____ ____
3. stillness, quiet, ____ ____
4. background, practice, ____ ____
5. value, significance, ____ ____

C. Fill in the missing letters to form spelling words. Write the words.

1. ____ ten ____ ____
2. ____ pear ____ ____ ____
3. ____ port ____ ____ ____
4. ____ form ____ ____
5. ____ tie ____ ____

114

Practice Master 32

____ce   distance   patience
____ce   silence   experience

____rds hidden in the puzzle. Circle

```
n c e f j b k
f a n c e a z
e a d g k l p
y c m v d a e
l e n c e n f
e r i e n c e
u c q i s e x
s t a n c e j
o r m a n c e
```

115

Objectives

Spelling and Reading

Students will

- **solve** analogies using spelling words.
- **complete** sentences using spelling words.
- **complete** a paragraph using spelling words.

One-Minute Handwriting Hint

The undercurve ending of the lowercase **c** swings wide to allow room for the loop in the letter **e**.

LOOP
SWING WIDE

Legible handwriting can boost spelling scores by as much as 20%.

Solve the Analogies
1. balance
2. innocence
3. silence
4. appearance
5. clearance
6. obedience

Complete the Sentences
7. experience
8. sequence
9. absence
10. residence
11. ambulance
12. distance
13. instance

Complete the Paragraph
14. inheritance
15. insurance
16. importance
17. attendance
18. patience
19. performance
20. excellence

Spelling and Reading

performance	experience	appearance	ambulance
attendance	excellence	importance	obedience
inheritance	innocence	clearance	insurance
absence	balance	sequence	distance
residence	instance	silence	patience

Solve the Analogies   Write a spelling word to complete each analogy.

1. **Sincerity** is to **honesty** as **stability** is to _____.
2. **Cowardice** is to **courage** as **guilt** is to _____.
3. **Loud** is to **noise** as **quiet** is to _____.
4. **Confidence** is to **certainty** as **image** is to _____.
5. **Perform** is to **performance** as **clear** is to _____.
6. **Disturb** is to **disturbance** as **obey** is to _____.

Complete the Sentences   Write spelling words to complete these interview questions. The first letter of each word is provided.

7. What past e_____ qualifies you for this job?
8. Tell me about your previous employment in s_____, starting with your first job.
9. Can you explain your a_____ from your last job?
10. How far is your current r_____ from R and B Vehicle Services?
11. Have you ever driven an a_____?
12. Are you comfortable driving a long d_____?
13. Describe an i_____ that shows you can think quickly.

SSHHHH!

Complete the Paragraph   Write spelling words from the box to complete the paragraph.

Jack Kramer's __14.__ of the family __15.__ business is a great opportunity. He realizes the __16.__ of customer service, so he insists on faithful __17.__. In turn, Jack's staff appreciates his __18.__ with their questions and his fairness in evaluating their daily __19.__. Kramer Insurance is known for its excellent record, and Jack plans to continue this __20.__.

attendance
patience
insurance
performance
inheritance
importance
excellence

196

MEETING INDIVIDUAL NEEDS

Providing More Challenge

Challenge Words and **Challenge Activities** for Unit 32 appear on page 250. **Challenge Word Test Sentences** appear on page T250.

Unit 32 Challenge Activities

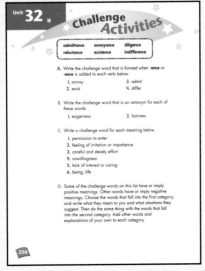

Weekly Test Options

Option 1:
One Spelling Word Per Sentence
(See procedures on pages Z10–Z11.)

1. His **absence** was noticed at once.
2. I was taken to the hospital in an **ambulance**.
★ 3. She has a pleasant **appearance**.
★ 4. His **attendance** record has been perfect this year.
★ 5. Do these items **balance** each other on the scale?
6. There is not enough **clearance** for tall trucks to pass under this bridge.
7. The jury believed in his **innocence**.
★ 8. He lives a great **distance** from his family.
9. This teacher expects **excellence** from all students.
★10. How much **experience** will I need for this job?
★11. What is the **importance** of this message?
12. Property is sometimes gained by **inheritance**.
★13. The act was one more **instance** of the boy's courage.
14. It is advisable to have **insurance** on your car.
15. The class was rewarded for its **obedience**.

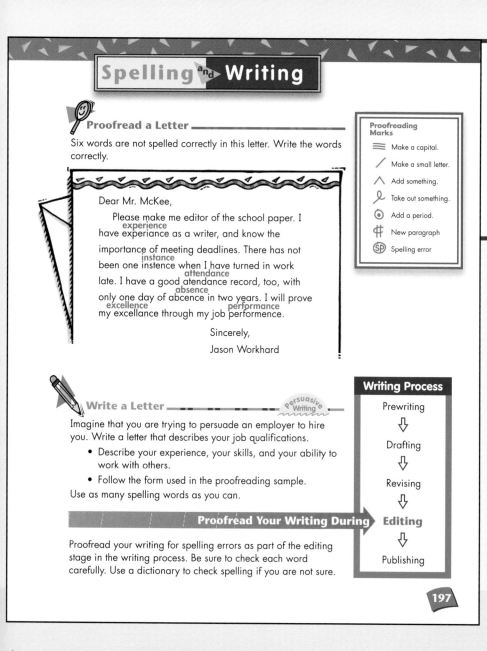

Spelling and Writing

Proofread a Letter

Six words are not spelled correctly in this letter. Write the words correctly.

Dear Mr. McKee,

Please make me editor of the school paper. I
experience
have experance as a writer, and know the
importance of meeting deadlines. There has not
instance
been one instence when I have turned in work
attendance
late. I have a good atendance record, too, with
absence
only one day of abcence in two years. I will prove
excellence   performance
my excellance through my job performence.

Sincerely,

Jason Workhard

Proofreading Marks

≡ Make a capital.
/ Make a small letter.
∧ Add something.
ℓ Take out something.
⊙ Add a period.
New paragraph
SP Spelling error

Write a Letter — *Persuasive Writing*

Imagine that you are trying to persuade an employer to hire you. Write a letter that describes your job qualifications.

- Describe your experience, your skills, and your ability to work with others.
- Follow the form used in the proofreading sample.

Use as many spelling words as you can.

Proofread Your Writing During → **Editing**

Proofread your writing for spelling errors as part of the editing stage in the writing process. Be sure to check each word carefully. Use a dictionary to check spelling if you are not sure.

Writing Process

Prewriting
⇩
Drafting
⇩
Revising
⇩
Editing
⇩
Publishing

197

Objectives

Spelling and Writing

Students will
- **proofread** a letter.
- **use** the writing process to write a persuasive letter.
- **proofread** their writing.

Using the Writing Process

Before assigning **Write a Letter,** see pages 258–259 in the Student Edition for a complete review of the writing process and additional writing assignments. You may wish to refer to pages Z12–Z13 in the Teacher Edition.

Keeping a Spelling Journal

Encourage students to record the words they misspelled on the weekly test in a personal spelling journal. These words may be recycled for future study. Students may also wish to include words from their writing. See pages Z12–Z13 in the Teacher Edition for more information.

★16. You must have **patience** when playing with small children.
★17. The singer was pleased with his **performance**.
18. How long have you lived at your current **residence**?
★19. We sat in **silence** without speaking.
20. List these events in correct **sequence**.

Option 2:
Multiple Spelling Words Per Sentence
(See procedures on pages Z10–Z11.)

1. **Attendance** at the **performance** broke all house records.
2. Her **patience** and **obedience** make her a delightful child.
3. My **inheritance** includes the old family **residence**.
4. Does your **insurance** cover **ambulance** costs?
5. In the **sequence** of events, when did her **absence** take place?
6. During the **clearance** sale, the store had a messy **appearance**.
7. Her **experience** in covering a long **distance** gave her the edge in the race.
8. The **innocence** of the child was obvious from his **silence**.
9. In this **instance, excellence** is necessary for success.
10. Can you explain the **importance** of **balance** in walking?

Option 3:
Standardized Test
(See *Teacher Resource Book,* Unit 32.)

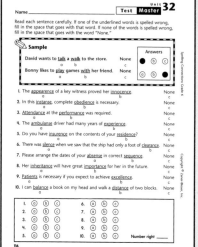

**Unit 32
Test Master**

T197

Objectives

Strategy Words

Students will
- **review** words studied previously that are related to the spelling strategy.
- **preview** unknown words that are related to the spelling strategy.

Optional Enrichment

Unit 32 enrichment

VOCABULARY CONNECTIONS

►Strategy Words◄

Remind the students that the **Strategy Words** relate to the spelling patterns they have studied in this unit. The **Review Words** are below grade level, and the **Preview Words** are above grade level. You may wish to use the following sentences to introduce the words in context.

Review Words:
Words From Grade 5
1. Each week I save half of my **allowance**.
2. The **audience** applauded as the cast made a curtain call.
3. The **entrance** to the cave is marked with a sign saying "Danger."
4. Sometimes my little sister is a **nuisance**.
5. The city passed an **ordinance** against jaywalking.

Preview Words:
Words From Grade 7
6. My **conscience** tells me when I have done something wrong.
7. She has great **endurance** because of many hours of training.
8. **Ignorance** does not always excuse bad behavior.
9. We agreed to go because of my parents' **insistence**.
10. The **maintenance** of the school's buses is a full-time job.

Review Words
1. allowance
2. entrance
3. ordinance
4. nuisance
5. audience

Preview Words
6. maintenance
7. insistence
8. endurance
9. ignorance
10. conscience

►Strategy Words◄

Review Words: Suffixes -ance, -ence

Write words from the box to complete the paragraph.

allowance	audience	entrance
	nuisance	ordinance

Ernest decided to spend part of his weekly __1.__ on a movie ticket. Not wanting to leave his new puppy home alone, however, he brought Shadow with him. At the theater __2.__, he was told that an __3.__ prohibits dogs. "I promise that Shadow will not be a __4.__," Ernest pleaded. "The __5.__ will not even know that she is there."

Preview Words: Suffixes -ance, -ence

Write a word from the box to complete each sentence.

conscience	endurance	ignorance
	insistence	maintenance

6. Quality control standards at the factory ensure that your new washing machine will need little ____.
7. At our mother's ____, we wrote a note of apology.
8. Running a marathon requires great ____.
9. She did not intentionally break the rules. Her ____ of the restrictions caused the problem.
10. His ____ told him that what he was about to do was not right.

198

Unit 32 RECAP

You may wish to assign the **Unit 32 Homework Master** (*Teacher Resource Book,* Unit 32) as a fun way to recap the spelling words.

Unit 32 Homework Master

Name_____

Homework Master Unit 32

Read up, down, across, backwards, and diagonally to find 14 spelling words hidden in the puzzle. Circle each spelling word.

```
o n l y f o u r t e e n r d s
t b a l a n c e c n e s b a t
p i e a r m e c n a t s n i e
d a n d y a b o u t e n o e x
s i t o i n s u r a n c e c p
p o s i l e n t l e a r n n e
t e n t e x n t o a n o w e r
z e l s a n d c o i n t o d i
s e q u e n c e o n c g i e
a s i l e n c e t s o m e s n
b a l a e c n e c o n n i e c
l n e c n e l l e c x e x r e
```

Put in the missing letters to form spelling words. Then write the words on the lines.

1. ___ ___ ten ___ ___ ___ ___ ___ ___   _____
2. ___ ___ her ___ ___ ___ ___ ___   _____
3. ___ ___ pear ___ ___ ___ ___   _____
4. ___ ___ ear ___ ___ ___ ___   _____
5. ___ ___ port ___ ___ ___ ___ ___   _____
6. ___ ___ ___ form ___ ___ ___   _____

Spelling Connections Grade 6

Copyright © Zaner-Bloser, Inc.

117

Content Words

Math: Measurement

Write words from the box to complete the paragraph.

arc	pi	chord	radius	circumference

The distance around a circle is called its __1.__ . This can be determined by multiplying __2.__ , or 3.14, times the __3.__ times 2. An __4.__ is a part of a circle. A __5.__ is a line segment joining two points on a circle.

Social Studies: Banking

Write a word from the box to complete each sentence.

finance	invest	fiscal	stockbroker	partnership

6. The study of money management is the study of _____.
7. A business of two or more individuals is a _____.
8. A _____ buys and sells stocks for a living.
9. A _____ matter pertains to the subject of money.
10. When you put money into something to make a profit, you _____ it.

Apply the Spelling Strategy

Circle the suffix **-ance** or **-ence** in two of the Content Words you wrote.

Word Study

Word Roots

The Latin root **audiere** meant "to hear." Write the Strategy Word that comes from this root and means "a group who hears" or "listeners."

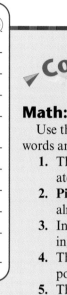

Math: Measurement
1. circumfer(ence)
2. pi
3. radius
4. arc
5. chord

Social Studies: Banking
6. fin(ance)
7. partnership
8. stockbroker
9. fiscal
10. invest

Word Roots
1. audience

199

Objectives

Content Words

Students will
- **expand** vocabulary with content-related words.
- **relate** the spelling strategy to words outside the basic spelling list.
- **understand** a word root and find it in a word.

Content Words

Math: Measurement

Use these sentences to introduce the words and their meanings.
1. The **arc** within the circle was created when we drew a right angle.
2. **Pi** is a mathematical ratio that is almost equal to 3.14.
3. In math, a **chord** is a line connecting two points on a curve.
4. The **radius** is a line from the center point to the outer edge of the circle.
5. The **circumference** is the distance around a circle.

Social Studies: Banking

Use these sentences to introduce the words and their meanings.
6. I can buy the house if I plan carefully to **finance** it.
7. I want to **invest** my money to help pay for college when I am older.
8. The **fiscal** year of his business begins on July 1.
9. The **stockbroker** has worked for several companies in our city.
10. My mother and my aunt formed a **partnership** and opened a business.

Word Study

Word Roots

Point out that a **word root** is a word or word part from which other words are made. Word roots for English words often come from Latin or Greek. Understanding word roots can help students build their vocabulary.

Unit 33 Home Spelling Practice

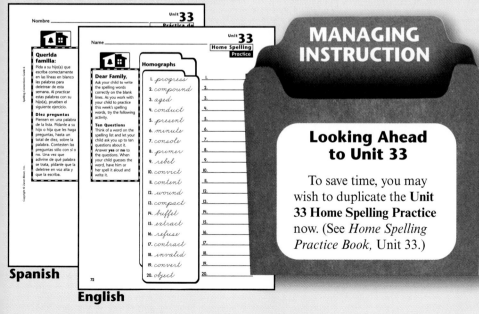

Spanish

English

MANAGING INSTRUCTION

Looking Ahead to Unit 33

To save time, you may wish to duplicate the **Unit 33 Home Spelling Practice** now. (See *Home Spelling Practice Book*, Unit 33.)

T199

Basic Spelling List

progress	content
compound	wound
aged	compact
conduct	buffet
present	extract
minute	refuse
console	contract
primer	invalid
rebel	convert
convict	object

Strategy Words

Review

alternate	contest
estimate	subject
separate	

Preview

annex	excuse
combine	suspect
complex	

Content Words

Social Studies: Government

bilingual	province
premier	parliament
cabinet	

Social Studies: Russia

czar	tyrant
steppes	serf
peasant	

Individual Needs

Challenge Words

verses	versus
cession	session
palate	pallet

Alternate Word List ★

progress	minute
compound	content
aged	wound
conduct	refuse
present	object

★ For students who need to study fewer Basic Spelling words

MATERIALS

Student Edition
Pages 200–205
Challenge Activities, p. 251

Teacher Edition
Pages T200A–T205
Challenge Activities, p. T251

Teacher Resource Book
Unit 33 Homework Master
Unit 33 Practice Masters
Flip Folder Practice Master
Unit 33 Test Master

Home Spelling Practice Book
Unit 33 Home Spelling Practice (English or Spanish)

Other *Spelling Connections* Resources
- Audiotape, Grade 6
- Practice Book for Grammar, Usage, and Mechanics, Grade 6
- Spelling Support for Second Language Learners, Grade 6
- Support Software on CD-ROM
- Transparency Book, Grade 6
- Word Sort CD-ROM, Grade 6

OBJECTIVES

Spelling and Thinking
Students will
- **read** the spelling words in list form and in context.
- **sort** the spelling words according to the number of syllables in each word.
- **read** and remember this week's spelling strategy.

Spelling and Vocabulary
Students will
- **match** homographs to their definitions.
- **replace** underlined words in sentences with spelling words that are homographs.
- **use** their **Spelling Dictionary** to write spelling words for synonyms and to determine accented syllables.

Spelling and Reading
Students will
- **solve** analogies using spelling words.
- **complete** sentences using spelling words.
- **complete** a paragraph using spelling words.

Spelling and Writing
Students will
- **proofread** a paragraph.
- **use** the writing process to write a paragraph about a problem and solution.
- **proofread** their writing.

MEETING INDIVIDUAL NEEDS
Learning Styles

 Visual

Hold a spelling bee. Tell the students that you will pronounce each spelling word and that they will go, one by one, to the chalkboard to spell the word. If the first student spells the word correctly, the next student goes to the chalkboard and spells the next word. If the word is misspelled, the next student tries to spell the same word. Play the game until all the words are spelled correctly.

 Auditory

Hold a spelling bee, as described in the visual activity, but have the students spell the words aloud rather than write them.

 Kinesthetic

Divide each spelling word (except **wound,** which is only one syllable) into syllables, and write each syllable on a card. Then mix up the cards. Tape one syllable of a word to each student's back, showing the card to the student before taping it. Make sure all the syllables are distributed. Then have the students walk around, forming pairs when they find the other part of their word. If the students enjoy the exercise, do it again, giving each student a different card. To make it more difficult, use both pronunciations of two-syllable homographs: **pres′** ent, pre **sent′**; re **bel′, reb′** el; re **fuse′, ref′** use; **prog′** ress, pro **gress′; min′** ute, mi **nute′; in′** va lid, in **val′** id.

> **Hands-On Practice**
> All students will benefit from practicing with a **Flip Folder**. See page Z18.

Language and Cultural Differences

Due to the evolution of the English language and its multicultural inheritance, homographs occur more frequently in English than in most other languages. Therefore, it may be difficult for students whose primary language is not English to understand what a homograph is.

Write a few of the spelling words on the chalkboard, and then write the dictionary respellings for each pronunciation, highlighting the accented syllables in colored chalk. Have the students pronounce each respelling and use each word in a sentence.

MANAGING INSTRUCTION

3–5 Day Plan		Average	Below Average	Above Average
Day 1	**Day 1**	Pretest Spelling Mini-Lesson, p. T200 Spelling and Thinking, p. 200	Pretest Spelling Mini-Lesson, p. T200 Spelling and Thinking, p. 200	Pretest Spelling and Thinking, p. 200
	Day 2	Spelling and Vocabulary, p. 201	Spelling and Vocabulary, p. 201 (or) Unit 33 Practice Master, A and B	Spelling and Vocabulary, p. 201 Spelling and Reading, p. 202
Day 2	**Day 3**	Spelling and Reading, p. 202	Spelling and Reading, p. 202 (or) Unit 33 Practice Master, C and D	Challenge Activities, p. 251
	Day 4	Spelling and Writing, p. 203 Unit 33 Homework Master	Spelling and Writing, p. 203	Spelling and Writing, p. 203 Unit 33 Homework Master
Day 3	**Day 5**	Weekly Test	Weekly Test	Weekly Test
Vocabulary Connections (pages 204 and 205) may be used anytime during this unit.				

Spelling and Thinking

Spelling and Thinking

Students will
- **read** the spelling words in list form and in context.
- **sort** the spelling words according to the number of syllables in each word.
- **read** and remember this week's spelling strategy.

UNIT PRETEST

Use **Pretest Sentences** below. Refer to the self-checking procedures on student page 256. You may wish to use the **Unit 33 Word List Overhead Transparency** as part of the checking procedure.

TEACHING THE STRATEGY

Spelling Mini-Lesson

Tell the students that the spelling words in this lesson are called **homographs,** i.e., words that are spelled the same, but have different meanings, origins, and sometimes pronunciations. Write **homograph** and **homophone** on the board. Explain the differences in meaning.

Write **wound** on the board. Explain that this spelling, w-o-u-n-d, may be one of two entirely different words; it can mean the past tense of **wind,** as in "I **wound** the clock," or it can mean an injury, as in "Please bandage this **wound**."

With some other words, the placement of the accent when the word is pronounced reveals whether the word is a noun or a verb. For example, when the stress is placed on the first syllable, **progress** is a noun that means "movement" or "improvement." When the stress is on the second syllable, **progress** is a verb that means "to advance."

Write these sentences on the board:
- I **object** to having an **object** blocking my view when I drive.
- I **refuse** to put this **refuse** in a garbage can that has holes in it.

Read the sentences and contrast the meanings and pronunciations of the words in each homograph pair. Encourage students to generate similar sentences for the remaining words on this week's list.

Read **Remember the Spelling Strategy** on page 200.

Spelling Words List

one or two syllables depending on meaning
1. **aged** ★

one-syllable word
2. **wound** ★

two-syllable words
3. **progress** ★
4. **compound** ★
5. **conduct** ★
6. **present** ★
7. **minute** ★
8. **console**
9. **primer**
10. **rebel**
11. **convict**
12. **content** ★
13. **compact**
14. **buffet**
15. **extract**
16. **refuse** ★
17. **contract**
18. **convert**
19. **object** ★

three-syllable word
20. **invalid**

200

READ THE SPELLING WORDS

1. progress	*progress*	He has made **progress** in school.
2. compound	*compound*	Try not to **compound** the problem.
3. aged	*aged*	The toy is for babies **aged** one.
4. conduct	*conduct*	Try to **conduct** yourselves properly.
5. present	*present*	She bought a small **present**.
6. minute	*minute*	We will be ready in one **minute**.
7. console	*console*	She tried to **console** the sad child.
8. primer	*primer*	I read a **primer** on how to play golf.
9. rebel	*rebel*	She will **rebel** if she has to work late.
10. convict	*convict*	The **convict** sat in a jail cell.
11. content	*content*	We were **content** to just sit and read.
12. wound	*wound*	Your **wound** will heal in a few days.
13. compact	*compact*	A **compact** car will fit in that space.
14. buffet	*buffet*	We enjoyed the **buffet** dinner.
15. extract	*extract*	My dentist had to **extract** my tooth.
16. refuse	*refuse*	Please do not **refuse** this gift.
17. contract	*contract*	The writer signed a book **contract**.
18. invalid	*invalid*	Her driver's license is **invalid**.
19. convert	*convert*	I will **convert** dollars to pesos.
20. object	*object*	Do you **object** to wearing uniforms?

SORT THE SPELLING WORDS

1. Write the spelling word that has either one or two syllables depending on its meaning.
2. Write the spelling word that has only one syllable.
3.–19. Write the spelling words that have two syllables.
20. Write the spelling word that has three syllables.

REMEMBER THE SPELLING STRATEGY

Remember that **homographs** are words that are spelled the same but have different meanings, origins, or pronunciations.

Pretest Sentences (See procedures on pages Z10–Z11.)

★ 1. Our boss insists we will **progress** by working on Saturdays.
★ 2. Try to keep matters simple and don't **compound** the problem.
★ 3. That **aged** couple used to walk two miles every day.
★ 4. People should **conduct** themselves properly in public.
★ 5. Let me **present** all the facts before you decide.
★ 6. There is only a **minute** amount of glue left in the tube.
7. Our television set and radio are combined in a **console**.
8. It is best to use **primer** on a house before painting it.
9. The small nation is likely to **rebel** against its occupiers.
10. If the man is found guilty, the jury will **convict** him.
★11. Surprisingly, the kitten was **content** lying next to the dog.
★12. The doctor **wound** the bandage around my swollen arm.
13. Our car is **compact,** yet four adults can fit into it.
14. One local restaurant offers a **buffet** lunch every day.
15. My dentist will only **extract** a tooth if it is absolutely necessary.
★16. Place the **refuse** in the trash can.
17. Most materials **contract** in cold temperatures.
18. It is a serious offense to drive a car with an **invalid** operator's license.
19. Will we ever **convert** to the metric system?
★20. I will not be pleased if you **object** to my plan.

Spelling and Vocabulary

Word Meanings

Write the spelling word that matches both definitions.

1. thing inside; satisfied
2. textbook; paint
3. pull out; flavoring
4. reduce; agreement
5. type of meal; knock about
6. reject; garbage
7. combine; enclosed area
8. advance; improvement

Word Replacements

Write a spelling word that could be used twice in each sentence to replace the underlined words.

9. He <u>wrapped</u> the bandage around the <u>injury</u>.
10. The prosecutor will <u>prove the guilt of</u> the <u>prisoner</u>.
11. I tried to <u>comfort</u> him when his TV <u>cabinet</u> broke.
12. The <u>sick, weak person</u> has a will that is <u>not legally enforceable</u>.
13. This machine will <u>compress</u> your trash into a <u>tightly packed</u> bundle.

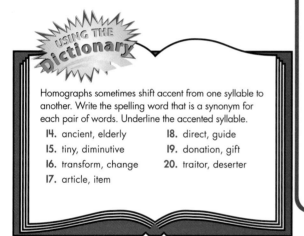

USING THE Dictionary

Homographs sometimes shift accent from one syllable to another. Write the spelling word that is a synonym for each pair of words. Underline the accented syllable.

14. ancient, elderly
15. tiny, diminutive
16. transform, change
17. article, item
18. direct, guide
19. donation, gift
20. traitor, deserter

Word Meanings

1. content
2. primer
3. extract
4. contract
5. buffet
6. refuse
7. compound
8. progress

Word Replacements

9. wound
10. convict
11. console
12. invalid
13. compact

Using the Dictionary

14. aged
15. minute
16. convert
17. object
18. conduct
19. present
20. rebel

201

Objectives

Spelling and Vocabulary

Students will
- **match** homographs to their definitions.
- **replace** underlined words in sentences with spelling words that are homographs.
- **use** their **Spelling Dictionary** to write spelling words for synonyms and to determine accented syllables.

Developing Oral Language Skills

Have students work in pairs. The first student makes a statement or asks a question that includes one of the words from the spelling list. For example, the student might say, "What is that **object** over there?" The second student makes another statement or asks a question. The second student must use the homograph of the spelling word. For example, the second student might say, "I **object** to that question."

MEETING INDIVIDUAL NEEDS

Providing More Help

Write the following homographs on the chalkboard: **wound, compound, contract, convert, conduct, object, present, rebel**. Have the students take turns explaining the two meanings of each spelling word.

★Students who need to study fewer words should use the **Alternate Word List**. This list is starred on page T200 in the Teacher Edition. The **Unit 33 Practice Masters** (*Teacher Resource Book*) provide additional practice with these words.

Unit 33 Practice Masters

Name _____

Practice Master Unit **33**

| 1. aged | 3. compound | 5. content | 7. refuse | 9. progress |
| 2. wound | 4. conduct | 6. object | 8. present | 10. minute |

A. Write the spelling word that goes with each group.

1. conductive, conductor, _____
2. contentment, contented, _____
3. progression, progressive, _____
4. presentation, presented, _____
5. objective, objection, _____

B. Write the missing spelling words with spaces between the syllables. Add accent marks to show proper stress.

1. The _____ senior citizen walked with a child _____ six years.
2. They'll _____ the problems if they move prisoners from that _____.
3. When it was her turn to _____ a school tour, the student's _____ was commendable.
4. I will _____ to dispose of their _____.
5. Will you _____ the medal and the _____?
6. A _____ speck of dust settled on the table only a _____ after it was cleaned.

118

Practice Master Unit **33**

| refuse | progress |
| present | minute |

...lling words correctly.

...objekt
...ajed
...woond
...kompound
...minit

...y respelling.

119

Spelling and Reading
Students will
- **solve** analogies using spelling words.
- **complete** sentences using spelling words.
- **complete** a paragraph using spelling words.

One-Minute Handwriting Hint

Be sure to pause after the first undercurve in the lower-case **t**. Pull the slant stroke to the baseline, and cross the letter carefully. Do not loop the letter.

PAUSE
t
PULL TO BASELINE

Legible handwriting can boost spelling scores by as much as 20%.

Solve the Analogies
1. wound
2. convict
3. contract
4. compact
5. extract
6. object

Complete the Sentences
7. content
8. aged
9. compound
10. conduct
11. refuse
12. present
13. primer
14. buffet

Complete the Paragraph
15. rebel
16. invalid
17. console
18. minute
19. progress
20. convert

202

Spelling and Reading

progress	compound	aged	conduct	present
minute	console	primer	rebel	convict
content	wound	compact	buffet	extract
refuse	contract	invalid	convert	object

Solve the Analogies Write the spelling word that completes each analogy.
1. **Grind** is to **ground** as **wind** is to _____.
2. **Traveler** is to **wanderer** as **prisoner** is to _____.
3. **Big** is to **expand** as **small** is to _____.
4. **Wide** is to **narrow** as **spacious** is to _____.
5. **In** is to **inject** as **out** is to _____.
6. **Agree** is to **endorse** as **oppose** is to _____.

Complete the Sentences For each sentence, write one spelling word that would make the sentence complete.
7. I am not _____ with the _____ of the package.
8. The _____ senior citizen walked with a child _____ six.
9. They will _____ the problem if they move inmates from the prison _____.
10. I expect good _____ from you as I _____ the tour.
11. I _____ to dispose of their _____.
12. The child will _____ the birthday _____ to the mayor.
13. This _____ on painting suggests using a _____ coat.
14. While waves _____ the boat, we serve a _____ lunch.

Complete the Paragraph Write spelling words from the box to complete the paragraph.

Why be a __15.__ when it is time to visit the dentist? Any excuses are __16.__. A receptionist sits at a computer __17.__ and keeps track of each patient's checkup date. The dentist scolds me if I am even a __18.__ late. I have made __19.__ in taking care of my teeth and have become a __20.__ to proper dental care.

| minute |
| invalid |
| convert |
| rebel |
| console |
| progress |

MEETING INDIVIDUAL NEEDS
Providing More Challenge

Challenge Words and **Challenge Activities** for Unit 33 appear on page 251. **Challenge Word Test Sentences** appear on page T251.

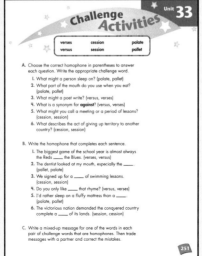

Unit 33 Challenge Activities

Weekly Test Options

Option 1:
One Spelling Word Per Sentence
(See procedures on pages Z10–Z11.)

1. My older brother bought a **compact** car.
★ 2. The officer entered the **compound** to speak to the soldiers.
3. The child tried to **console** her baby brother.
4. You must sign the **contract** to complete the agreement.
★ 5. Last week he won the school's good **conduct** award.
★ 6. He seems to have **aged** since I last saw him.
★ 7. This plane will leave in about one **minute**.
★ 8. Please place this **object** on the shelf to your right.
★ 9. He gave me a **present** on my birthday.
10. She is the **rebel** of the family.
★11. I hope you will not **refuse** their offer.
12. The woman was a recent **convert** to their cause.
13. The **convict** was denied an early release.
14. Can you come to my house for a **buffet** supper?
★15. The nurse carefully cleansed his **wound**.
16. If you don't sign a check, it is **invalid**.

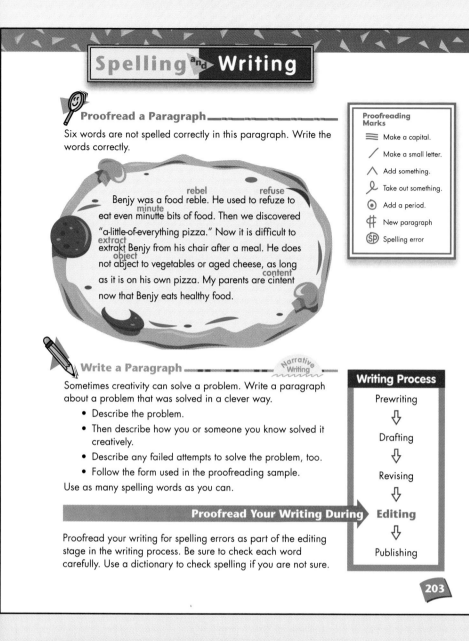

Spelling and Writing

Proofread a Paragraph

Six words are not spelled correctly in this paragraph. Write the words correctly.

> rebel · refuse
> Benjy was a food reble. He used to refuze to
> minute
> eat even minutte bits of food. Then we discovered
> "a-little-of-everything pizza." Now it is difficult to
> extract
> extrakt Benjy from his chair after a meal. He does
> object
> not abject to vegetables or aged cheese, as long
> content
> as it is on his own pizza. My parents are cintent
> now that Benjy eats healthy food.

Proofreading Marks

≡ Make a capital.
/ Make a small letter.
∧ Add something.
℘ Take out something.
⊙ Add a period.
New paragraph
SP Spelling error

Write a Paragraph

Narrative Writing

Sometimes creativity can solve a problem. Write a paragraph about a problem that was solved in a clever way.

- Describe the problem.
- Then describe how you or someone you know solved it creatively.
- Describe any failed attempts to solve the problem, too.
- Follow the form used in the proofreading sample.

Use as many spelling words as you can.

Proofread Your Writing During

Proofread your writing for spelling errors as part of the editing stage in the writing process. Be sure to check each word carefully. Use a dictionary to check spelling if you are not sure.

Writing Process

Prewriting
⇩
Drafting
⇩
Revising
⇩
Editing
⇩
Publishing

203

Objectives

Spelling and Writing

Students will
- **proofread** a paragraph.
- **use** the writing process to write a paragraph about a problem and solution.
- **proofread** their writing.

Using the Writing Process

Before assigning **Write a Paragraph,** see pages 258–259 in the Student Edition for a complete review of the writing process and additional writing assignments. You may wish to refer to pages Z12–Z13 in the Teacher Edition.

Keeping a Spelling Journal

Encourage students to record the words they misspelled on the weekly test in a personal spelling journal. These words may be recycled for future study. Students may also wish to include words from their writing. See pages Z12–Z13 in the Teacher Edition for more information.

---

17. The dentist will have to **extract** your tooth.
★18. You are making great **progress** in spelling.
19. A coat of **primer** will help the paint to cover evenly.
★20. I am **content** to let my cat sleep on my bed.

Option 2:
Multiple Spelling Words Per Sentence
(See procedures on pages Z10–Z11.)

1. What is the **content** of the **progress** report?
2. The **convict** had been a **rebel** in his youth.
3. Do you **refuse** to be **present** for the meeting?
4. The doctor will **extract** the glass from the **wound**.
5. The walls of the **compound** were coated with **primer** before painting.
6. The judge decided that the **contract** was **invalid**.
7. Older people might **object** to being called **aged**.
8. How did he **conduct** himself at the **buffet**?
9. From the **minute** her parents left, no one could **console** her.
10. I can **convert** this **compact** bag into a small suitcase.

Option 3:
Standardized Test
(See *Teacher Resource Book,* Unit 33.)

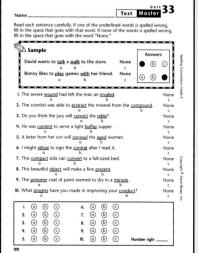

Unit 33 Test Master

T203

Objectives

Strategy Words

Students will

- **review** words studied previously that are related to the spelling strategy.
- **preview** unknown words that are related to the spelling strategy.

Optional Enrichment

►Strategy Words◄

Remind the students that the **Strategy Words** relate to the spelling patterns they have studied in this unit. The **Review Words** are below grade level, and the **Preview Words** are above grade level. You may wish to use the following sentences to introduce the words in context.

Review Words:
Words From Grade 5

1. Tom will act as **alternate** in case Tanner cannot attend the meeting.
2. Can you **estimate** your time of arrival?
3. We drove in **separate** cars but arrived within fifteen minutes of each other.
4. The rules of the **contest** are posted in the school library.
5. Shawn's favorite **subject** in school is spelling.

Preview Words:
Words From Grade 7

6. The city planned to **annex** the land where a new subdivision was being built.
7. If we **combine** these chemicals, we may create a dangerous situation.
8. Because of the many steps involved in solving the problem, we felt it was too **complex** for the students.
9. Please **excuse** me while I finish my homework.
10. We **suspect** that the birthday party will not be a surprise.

Review Words

1. contest
2. subject
3. alternate
4. separate
5. estimate

Preview Words

6. suspect
7. complex
8. excuse
9. annex
10. combine

Unit 33 enrichment

VOCABULARY CONNECTIONS

►Strategy Words◄

Review Words: Homographs

Write words from the box to complete the paragraph.

| alternate | estimate | separate | contest | subject |

We have decided to enter the essay __1.__. We can write about any __2.__ that has to do with an endangered animal, such as the bald eagle. An __3.__ topic is to write about endangered plants. If we write more than one essay, we are to mail each one in a __4.__ envelope. The officials __5.__ that it will take about a month to process all the entries.

Preview Words: Homographs

Write one word from the box to complete each sentence. The same word should fit in both blanks.

| annex | combine | complex | excuse | suspect |

6. I ____ that the robbery ____ is hiding somewhere.
7. You are going to give me a ____ about my math ability if you continue to give me such ____ problems to solve.
8. Please ____ me, but I have an ____ for being late.
9. The university is planning to ____ the library ____ to its main building.
10. The farmer will drive the ____ through the field and then ____ the grain he cuts with the rest of the grain in the barn.

204

Unit 33 RECAP

You may wish to assign the **Unit 33 Homework Master** (*Teacher Resource Book*, Unit 33) as a fun way to recap the spelling words.

Unit 33 Homework Master

Name _____   **Homework Master Unit 33**

Write the spelling word for each dictionary respelling.

1. I /wound/ the string into a ball. _____
2. The people will /rĭ **bôl**′/ against strict laws. _____
3. I /rĭ **fyōōz**′/ to wear a skirt on cold days. _____
4. The television /**kŏn**′sōl/ is made of oak. _____
5. We agreed to all terms of the /**kŏn**′trăkt/. _____
6. This bread with mold is /ā′ **j**ĭld/. _____
7. A /**kŏm**′pound/ is made from two or more words. _____
8. The chairperson will /prĭ **zĕnt**′/ the award. _____
9. Will you /kan **dŭkt**′/ the orchestra? _____
10. The snow in this snowball is /kam **păkt**′/. _____
11. Sixty seconds equal one /**mĭn**′ĭt/. _____
12. What is the /**kŏn**′tĕnt/ of the package? _____
13. Our /**prŏg**′rĕs/ through the traffic was slow. _____
14. A freezer can /kan **vŭrt**′/ water into ice. _____
15. The /**kŏn**′vĭkt/ has been found guilty. _____
16. My little brother is reading a /**prĭm**′ər/. _____
17. The dentist has to /ĭk **străkt**′/ her tooth. _____
18. I /ab **jĕkt**′/ to being called silly. _____
19. The unsigned check was /ĭn **văl**′ĭd/. _____
20. The /ba **fā**′/ table was loaded with food. _____

Spelling Connections Grade 6

Copyright © Zaner-Bloser, Inc.

121

Content Words

Social Studies: Government

Write words from the box to complete the paragraph.

| bilingual | premier | cabinet | province | parliament |

Quebec is Canada's largest __1.__. Many people here are __2.__, speaking both French and English. The __3.__ of Quebec is the head of the provincial government. However, the chief executive for all of Canada is the prime minister. A __4.__ of about forty ministers helps govern. Canada's legislative body is a __5.__, which is divided into two sections.

Social Studies: Russia

Write words from the box to complete the paragraph.

| czar | steppes | peasant | tyrant | serf |

For hundreds of years, Russia was ruled by a king called a __6.__. One was Ivan IV, known as Ivan the Terrible because he was a __7.__. During his reign, a hired farm worker, or __8.__, was often bound to the landlord as a __9.__, or slave. Farm workers planted grain on the __10.__, the flat, treeless plains in southern Russia.

Apply the Spelling Strategy

Circle the one Content Word you wrote that is a homograph.

Word Study

Multiple Meanings

Originally, this Content Word meant "a closed space." Now it can mean "a storage area in the kitchen" or "a council or group of advisors." Write the Content Word.

205

Social Studies: Government
1. **province**
2. **bilingual**
3. (**premier**)
4. **cabinet**
5. **parliament**

Social Studies: Russia
6. **czar**
7. **tyrant**
8. **peasant**
9. **serf**
10. **steppes**

Multiple Meanings
1. **cabinet**

Objectives

Content Words

Students will
- **expand** vocabulary with content-related words.
- **relate** the spelling strategy to words outside the basic spelling list.
- **understand** that the same word can have different meanings depending on context.

Content Words

Social Studies: Government

Use these sentences to introduce the words and their meanings.

1. Andrew, who was born in Portugal, is **bilingual**.
2. Do you know who is the **premier** of Ontario?
3. Each president may appoint his own **cabinet**.
4. We named each Canadian **province**.
5. **Parliament** is the lawmaking body of Great Britain.

Social Studies: Russia

Use these sentences to introduce the words and their meanings.

6. The **czar** of Russia was overthrown.
7. Few people live on the **steppes** of Siberia.
8. The life of a **peasant** was hard.
9. The leader was a **tyrant** who refused basic freedoms.
10. A **serf** was owned by the lord of the manor.

Word Study

Multiple Meanings

Discuss the ways in which the same word can convey different meanings depending on context. Encourage students to brainstorm meanings for other words such as **bureau** ("a chest" or "an office") and **chair** ("a seat" or "the head of something").

Unit 34 Home Spelling Practice

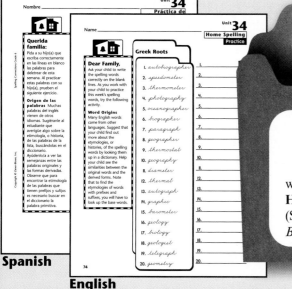

Spanish

English

MANAGING INSTRUCTION

Looking Ahead to Unit 34

To save time, you may wish to duplicate the **Unit 34 Home Spelling Practice** now. (See *Home Spelling Practice Book,* Unit 34.)

T205

Basic Spelling List

autobiographer	diameter
speedometer	thermal
thermometer	autograph
photography	graphic
oceanographer	barometer
biographer	geology
paragraph	biology
geographer	geologist
thermostat	telegraph
geography	geometry

Strategy Words

Review

biography	perimeter
homograph	telecast
kilowatt	

Preview

autobiographical	
diagram	telephone
physiology	topography

Content Words

Science: Matter

atom	proton
nucleus	neutron
electron	

Science: Weather

cirrus	nimbostratus
stratus	cumulonimbus
cumulus	

Individual Needs

Challenge Words

bibliography	lexicographer
altimeter	telephoto
biologist	antibiotic

Alternate Word List ★

thermometer	diameter
photography	biology
biographer	geologist
paragraph	telegraph
geography	geometry

★ For students who need to study fewer Basic Spelling words

MATERIALS

Student Edition
Pages 206–211
Challenge Activities, p. 252

Teacher Edition
Pages T206A–T211
Challenge Activities, p. T252

Teacher Resource Book
Unit 34 Homework Master
Unit 34 Practice Masters
Flip Folder Practice Master
Unit 34 Test Master

Home Spelling Practice Book
Unit 34 Home Spelling Practice
(English or Spanish)

Other *Spelling Connections* Resources
• Audiotape, Grade 6
• Practice Book for Grammar, Usage, and Mechanics, Grade 6
• Spelling Support for Second Language Learners, Grade 6
• Support Software on CD-ROM
• Transparency Book, Grade 6
• Word Sort CD-ROM, Grade 6

OBJECTIVES

Spelling and Thinking
Students will
• **read** the spelling words in list form and in context.
• **sort** the spelling words according to their roots, suffixes, and endings.
• **read** and remember this week's spelling strategy.

Spelling and Vocabulary
Students will
• **use** definition and word part clues to write spelling words.
• **combine** word parts to form spelling words.
• **write** spelling words from their Greek roots.

Spelling and Reading
Students will
• **solve** analogies using spelling words.
• **complete** sentences using spelling words.
• **complete** a paragraph using spelling words.

Spelling and Writing
Students will
• **proofread** a paragraph.
• **use** the writing process to write a paragraph about a scientist.
• **proofread** their writing.

MEETING INDIVIDUAL NEEDS
Learning Styles

 Visual

Divide the class into pairs. Give each student of the pair a different colored pen or pencil. Each pair works together on a single piece of paper. First, the students write all of the words that contain the Greek root **graph**. Student A of each pair writes the part of the word with the root (**graphy, grapher**); Student B writes the rest of the word. In the same way, they write all of the words stemming from **geo,** from **meter,** and from **therm**. You may end the game here or have the students continue writing words with other Greek roots.

 Auditory

To play "What's My Word?," each student in turn chooses a spelling word to describe. Then the student gives the class a clue about the chosen word. The clue can concern either the meaning of the word or its spelling pattern. The teacher calls on students to guess the word. After the word is guessed, the person who identified it spells the word aloud and all of the students write the word.

Kinesthetic

Have the students memorize these activities: touch the nose for **graph;** tug the ear for **bio;** touch the top of the head for **therm;** place hand on waist for **geo;** and raise the hand for **meter**. Tell the students to listen for these word parts as you pronounce the spelling words. Pronounce each word, and have the students make the appropriate movement or movements.

> **Hands-On Practice**
> All students will benefit from practicing with a **Flip Folder**. See page Z18.

Language and Cultural Differences

The /r/ in these words may be difficult for many students because **r** sounds are altered in several regional dialects.

Spanish-speaking students may have problems with the short vowel sounds and the schwa sound in these words, as well as with the **t** and **er** endings, since none of these exist in Spanish. Furthermore, several of the words have the digraph **ph** pronounced /f/; in Spanish the /f/ is represented by its corresponding letter.

Write the spelling words on the chalkboard. Circle the **t, gy, al, at, er, ry, ph,** and **phy** in the words. Stress the pronunciation of the words, particularly the sounds made by the circled letters.

MANAGING INSTRUCTION

3–5 Day Plan		Average	Below Average	Above Average
Day 1	**Day 1**	Pretest Spelling Mini-Lesson, p. T206 Spelling and Thinking, p. 206	Pretest Spelling Mini-Lesson, p. T206 Spelling and Thinking, p. 206	Pretest Spelling and Thinking, p. 206
	Day 2	Spelling and Vocabulary, p. 207	Spelling and Vocabulary, p. 207 (or) Unit 34 Practice Master, A and B	Spelling and Vocabulary, p. 207 Spelling and Reading, p. 208
Day 2	**Day 3**	Spelling and Reading, p. 208	Spelling and Reading, p. 208 (or) Unit 34 Practice Master, C and D	Challenge Activities, p. 252
	Day 4	Spelling and Writing, p. 209 Unit 34 Homework Master	Spelling and Writing, p. 209	Spelling and Writing, p. 209 Unit 34 Homework Master
Day 3	**Day 5**	Weekly Test	Weekly Test	Weekly Test

Vocabulary Connections (pages 210 and 211) may be used anytime during this unit.

Objectives

Spelling and Thinking

Students will
- **read** the spelling words in list form and in context.
- **sort** the spelling words according to their roots, suffixes, and endings.
- **read** and remember this week's spelling strategy.

UNIT PRETEST

Use **Pretest Sentences** below. Refer to the self-checking procedures on student page 256. You may wish to use the **Unit 34 Word List Overhead Transparency** as part of the checking procedure.

TEACHING THE STRATEGY

Spelling Mini-Lesson

Read **Remember the Spelling Strategy** on page 206. Tell the students that the words on this week's list have all been formed by combining Greek word parts. Write **meter** and **to measure** on the chalkboard with these other Greek roots and their meanings: **graph** (writing), **photo** (light), **tele** (far), **para** (beside), **auto** (self), **bio** (life), **thermo** (heat), **stat** (stabilizer), **dia** (through or across), **baro** (weight or pressure), **geo** (earth), **logy** (study), **okeanos** (great river encircling the earth). Explain that while the spellings of words built from these Greek roots are not phonetic (e.g., **ph** spells **/f/**), they are logical because they represent the Greek roots.

Show the students how the definitions of the word parts can help them with the definitions of all the spelling words. For example, the word **geography** can be broken down into these Greek word parts: **geo** ("earth") and **graph** ("writing"). So, **geography** is "writing about the earth." Ask volunteers to generate other words that stem from this Greek root (e.g., **geology, geographer, geometry, oceanography**).

Encourage them to break each spelling word down into its various parts on the board and to generate a definition for each word based on its Greek parts.

Conclude by working with the students to generate lists of other words that include some of the Greek roots that helped build the words on this week's list.

T206

Order of answers may vary.
-meter or -metry
1. **speedometer**
2. **thermometer** ★
3. **diameter** ★
4. **barometer**
5. **geometry** ★
graph
6. **autobiographer**
7. **photography** ★
8. **oceanographer**
9. **biographer** ★
10. **paragraph** ★
11. **geographer**
12. **geography** ★
13. **autograph**
14. **graphic**
15. **telegraph** ★
-ology or -ologist
16. **geology**
17. **biology** ★
18. **geologist** ★
-al or -stat
19. **thermostat**
20. **thermal**

206

Spelling and **Thinking**

READ THE SPELLING WORDS

1.	autobiographer	*autobiographer*	I am an **autobiographer**.
2.	speedometer	*speedometer*	Check the **speedometer**.
3.	thermometer	*thermometer*	The **thermometer** says zero.
4.	photography	*photography*	I took a **photography** class.
5.	oceanographer	*oceanographer*	She is an **oceanographer**.
6.	biographer	*biographer*	His **biographer** was truthful.
7.	paragraph	*paragraph*	Write a brief **paragraph**.
8.	geographer	*geographer*	A **geographer** read the map.
9.	thermostat	*thermostat*	A **thermostat** regulates heat.
10.	geography	*geography*	The land's **geography** is hilly.
11.	diameter	*diameter*	What is the circle's **diameter**?
12.	thermal	*thermal*	The skier's socks are **thermal**.
13.	autograph	*autograph*	The star signed an **autograph**.
14.	graphic	*graphic*	Sue is a **graphic** designer.
15.	barometer	*barometer*	Check the **barometer**.
16.	geology	*geology*	Jim studied Alaska's **geology**.
17.	biology	*biology*	We studied insects in **biology**.
18.	geologist	*geologist*	A **geologist** studied the rocks.
19.	telegraph	*telegraph*	He sent a **telegraph** message.
20.	geometry	*geometry*	I study shapes in **geometry**.

SORT THE SPELLING WORDS

1.–5. Write the spelling words that end in **-meter** or **-metry**.

6.–15. Write the spelling words that have the root **graph** in them.

16.–18. Write the spelling words that end in **-ology** or **-ologist**.

19.–20. Write the spelling words that end with **-al** or **-stat**.

REMEMBER THE SPELLING STRATEGY

Remember that many English words have Greek roots. For example, the words **thermometer, barometer,** and **speedometer** all share the root **meter,** meaning "measure."

Pretest Sentences (See procedures on pages Z10–Z11.)

1. An **autobiographer** must decide what to tell about his or her life.
2. The **speedometer** told us how fast the car was going.
★ 3. According to the **thermometer,** she had a high temperature.
★ 4. **Photography** is my favorite hobby.
5. The **oceanographer** made a study of marine life.
★ 6. The **biographer** vividly recaptured the life story of the famous athlete.
★ 7. What is the main idea of this **paragraph**?
8. The **geographer** studied the coastline of Maine on the map.
9. The **thermostat** was set at a temperature of 75 degrees.
★10. We studied facts about the Rocky Mountains in **geography** class.
★11. The **diameter** of a circle divides it perfectly in half.
12. In cold climates, people wear **thermal** clothing to keep warm.
13. We waited to ask the actor for his **autograph**.
14. The diagram was a **graphic** representation of the study.
15. A **barometer** measures air pressure.
16. **Geology** is the scientific study of the earth.
★17. In **biology** class, we learned how blood circulates.
★18. The **geologist** analyzed the structure of the mineral.
★19. We will have to go to the **telegraph** office to send the wire.
★20. My teacher prefers **geometry** to all other kinds of math.

Spelling and Vocabulary

Word Meanings

Write spelling words to match these clues.

1. one who studies the earth, its features, and inhabitants
2. the study of the composition of the earth's structure
3. an instrument that measures air pressure
4. the study of solid and plain figures
5. an instrument that measures speed
6. one who writes the story of someone else's life
7. the process of taking pictures
8. one who studies the composition of the earth's structure
9. the study of the earth, its features, and inhabitants

Word Structure

Match a word part from Group A with one from Group B to write spelling words.

10.–14.
| A. | para | bio | dia | therm | ocean |
| B. | meter | al | graph | logy | ographer |

USING THE Dictionary

Write the spelling words that can be formed from the Greek roots.

15. **graphein** (to write)
16. **therme** (heat) + **states** (one that causes to stand)
17. **tele** (at a distance) + **graphein** (to write)
18. **therme** (heat) + **metron** (measure)
19. **autos** (self) + **graphein** (to write)
20. **autos** (self) + **bios** (life) + **graphein** (to write)

Order of answers may vary.

Word Meanings

1. geographer
2. geology
3. barometer
4. geometry
5. speedometer
6. biographer
7. photography
8. geologist
9. geography

Word Structure

10. paragraph
11. biology
12. diameter
13. thermal
14. oceanographer

Using the Dictionary

15. graphic
16. thermostat
17. telegraph
18. thermometer
19. autograph
20. autobiographer

207

Objectives

Spelling and Vocabulary

Students will
- **use** definition and word part clues to write spelling words.
- **combine** word parts to form spelling words.
- **write** spelling words from their Greek roots.

Developing Oral Language Skills

Ask students to work in pairs. The first student uses a spelling word in a sentence, and the second student responds with another sentence in which the word is defined. For example, the first student might say, "I love **biology**." The second student responds, "Yes, the **study of life** is interesting."

MEETING INDIVIDUAL NEEDS

Providing More Help

Write the following groups of words on the chalkboard. Have the students take turns circling the correct word in each group.

diathermo, **diameter,** autodia
geospeed, **geometry,** geotele
autopara, **autograph,** autodia
meterbar, **barometer,** paratherm
thermometer, photology, photoin

★Students who need to study fewer words should use the **Alternate Word List**. This list is starred on page T206 in the Teacher Edition. The **Unit 34 Practice Masters** (*Teacher Resource Book*) provide additional practice with these words.

Unit 34 Practice Masters

Name _____
Practice Master Unit **34**

1. photography 3. paragraph 5. biology 7. diameter 9. geometry
2. thermometer 4. biographer 6. telegraph 8. geologist 10. geography

A. Write spelling words by combining roots. Draw lines to match a root from Column A with a root from Column B. Use all of the roots.

Column A	Column B
tele •	• meter
bio •	• graph
dia •	• logy
thermo •	

1. _____
2. _____
3. _____
4. _____

B. Write the spelling words that match the clues. You may use the spelling dictionary to look up the definitions of the spelling words.

1. measuring through a circle _____
2. earth measuring _____
3. someone who tells a life history in writing _____
4. written description of the earth _____
5. measuring heat _____

122

Practice Master Unit **34**

diameter   geometry
___ph   geologist   geography

___der.

_____
_____
_____

= graph   □ = geo
___d symbols spell.

123

T207

Objectives

Spelling and Reading

Students will
- **solve** analogies using spelling words.
- **complete** sentences using spelling words.
- **complete** a paragraph using spelling words.

One-Minute Handwriting Hint

The checkstroke joining of the lowercase **o** retraces and then swings wide to form the top of the letter **g**.

SWING WIDE

og

Legible handwriting can boost spelling scores by as much as 20%.

Solve the Analogies

1. thermostat
2. geologist
3. paragraph
4. speedometer
5. diameter
6. autograph
7. photography

Complete the Sentences

8. graphic
9. biographer
10. geology
11. geometry
12. barometer
13. telegraph
14. autobiographer
15. biology

Complete the Paragraph

16. oceanographer
17. thermal
18. thermometer
19. geography
20. geographer

---

autobiographer	speedometer	thermometer	photography
oceanographer	biographer	paragraph	geographer
thermostat	geography	diameter	thermal
autograph	graphic	barometer	geology
biology	geologist	telegraph	geometry

Solve the Analogies Write a spelling word to complete each analogy.

1. **Water** is to **faucet** as **heat** is to ____.
2. **Animal** is to **zoologist** as **rock** is to ____.
3. **Letter** is to **word** as **sentence** is to ____.
4. **Time** is to **watch** as **speed** is to ____.
5. **Around** is to **circumference** as **through** is to ____.
6. **Picture** is to **photograph** as **signature** is to ____.
7. **Stove** is to **cookery** as **camera** is to ____.

Complete the Sentences Write a spelling word to complete each sentence.

8. The company hired a ____ design artist to illustrate the book.
9. The ____ wrote Martin Luther King, Jr.'s life story.
10. The scientists studied the ____ of the earthquake site.
11. You can use ____ to determine the area of that field.
12. The ____ dropped rapidly, indicating an approaching storm.
13. In 1866, the first successful ____ cable was laid.
14. Frederick Douglass, an ____, wrote about his own life.
15. They are studying the ____ of pond life.

Complete the Paragraph Write spelling words from the box to complete the paragraph.

To explore the ocean, an __16.__ must wear a __17.__ suit for protection from the cold. The diver uses a special __18.__ to record water temperature. The diver explores the __19.__ of the ocean floor. A __20.__ uses this information to learn about the earth.

thermometer
thermal
oceanographer
geographer
geography

208

MEETING INDIVIDUAL NEEDS

Providing More Challenge

Challenge Words and **Challenge Activities** for Unit 34 appear on page 252. **Challenge Word Test Sentences** appear on page T252.

Unit 34 Challenge Activities

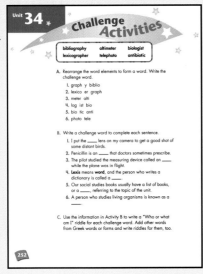

Weekly Test Options

Option 1:
One Spelling Word Per Sentence
(See procedures on pages Z10–Z11.)

1. The violinist is also an able **autobiographer**.
2. She asked the baseball player for his **autograph**.
3. The **barometer** reading signaled the possibility of rain.
★ 4. What is the **diameter** of that round table?
5. The **geographer** spoke to the class about erosion.
★ 6. Today we will study the **geography** of Montana.
7. We study different kinds of rocks in **geology** class.
★ 8. The **geologist** said our rocks are rare.
★ 9. We learned to measure angles in **geometry** class today.
10. I appreciate the **graphic** design of that poster.
11. An **oceanographer** came to our class to teach us about coastal environments.
★12. Read the third **paragraph** to find the answer.
★13. Anyone interested in **photography** can join our club.
14. Has Dad had the **speedometer** on the car fixed?
★15. The **telegraph** was used often in the Civil War.

Spelling and Writing

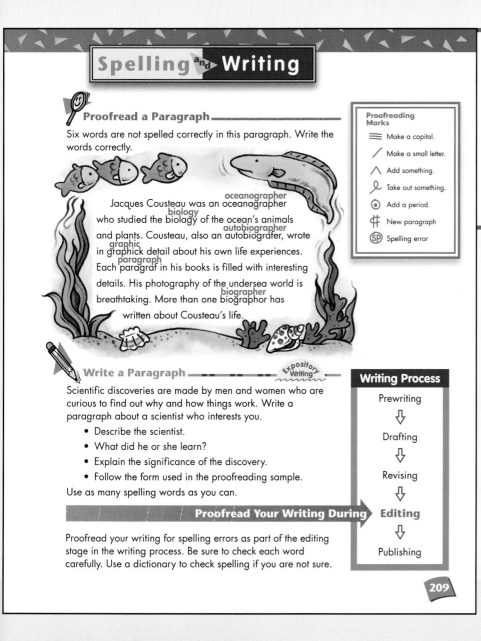

Proofread a Paragraph

Six words are not spelled correctly in this paragraph. Write the words correctly.

oceanographer

Jacques Cousteau was an oceanagrapher
biology
who studied the biology of the ocean's animals
autobiographer
and plants. Cousteau, also an autobiografer, wrote
graphic
in graphick detail about his own life experiences.
paragraph
Each paragraf in his books is filled with interesting
details. His photography of the undersea world is
biographer
breathtaking. More than one biographor has
written about Cousteau's life.

Proofreading Marks

≡ Make a capital.
／ Make a small letter.
∧ Add something.
⌐ Take out something.
⊙ Add a period.
¶ New paragraph.
(SP) Spelling error

Write a Paragraph

Expository Writing

Scientific discoveries are made by men and women who are curious to find out why and how things work. Write a paragraph about a scientist who interests you.

- Describe the scientist.
- What did he or she learn?
- Explain the significance of the discovery.
- Follow the form used in the proofreading sample.

Use as many spelling words as you can.

Proofread Your Writing During → **Editing**

Proofread your writing for spelling errors as part of the editing stage in the writing process. Be sure to check each word carefully. Use a dictionary to check spelling if you are not sure.

Writing Process

Prewriting
⇩
Drafting
⇩
Revising
⇩
Editing
⇩
Publishing

209

---

16. A **thermal** blanket is a comfort in winter.
★17. What is the temperature reading on your **thermometer**?
18. The **thermostat** in our house is automatic.
★19. **Biology** is the study of living things.
★20. A famous author agreed to be her **biographer**.

Option 2:
Multiple Spelling Words Per Sentence
(See procedures on pages Z10–Z11.)

1. The **biographer** will **autograph** his book.
2. **Biology** and **geology** are difficult subjects for some.
3. A **geologist** may use **photography** in his work.
4. A **barometer,** a **thermometer,** and a **speedometer** are all tools of measurement.
5. In **geometry** class I studied the **diameter** of a circle.
6. A **geographer** and an **oceanographer** both study the natural world.
7. Did you write the **paragraph** for **geography** class?
8. The **autobiographer** related **graphic** adventures of the early days of **telegraph** service.
9. Lower the **thermostat** and wear **thermal** clothes.

Option 3:
Standardized Test
(See *Teacher Resource Book,* Unit 34.)

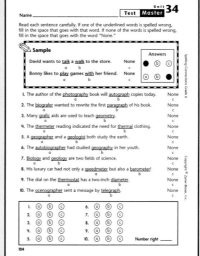

**Unit 34
Test Master**

T209

Objectives

Strategy Words

Students will
- **review** words studied previously that are related to the spelling strategy.
- **preview** unknown words that are related to the spelling strategy.

Optional Enrichment

Unit 34 enrichment

VOCABULARY CONNECTIONS

►Strategy Words◄

Remind the students that the **Strategy Words** relate to the spelling patterns they have studied in this unit. The **Review Words** are below grade level, and the **Preview Words** are above grade level. You may wish to use the following sentences to introduce the words in context.

Review Words:
Words From Grade 5

1. We read the **biography** of Harry Truman.
2. "Content" is a **homograph** that has two pronunciations.
3. Electricity is measured in **kilowatt** hours.
4. We measured the **perimeter** of our yard before buying materials for a fence.
5. The **telecast** came live from Cape Canaveral.

Preview Words:
Words From Grade 7

6. This **autobiographical** account of Thomas Jefferson's life was found among his papers.
7. We can **diagram** this sentence after we learn the parts of speech.
8. **Physiology** is the study of the human body.
9. A **telephone** which was once considered a convenience is today a necessity.
10. This map indicates the **topography** of the area, and we can learn how many hills we will climb if we hike there.

Review Words
1. perimeter
2. telecast
3. homograph
4. biography
5. kilowatt

Preview Words
6. topography
7. diagram
8. autobiographical
9. physiology
10. telephone

►Strategy Words◄

Review Words: Greek Roots

Write a word from the box that matches each clue.

biography	homograph	kilowatt
	perimeter	telecast

1. the measurement of distance around an area
2. a television broadcast
3. a word that has the same spelling as another word but differs in meaning, origin, and sometimes pronunciation
4. a written account of a person's life
5. a unit of electric power

Preview Words: Greek Roots

Write a word from the box to complete each sentence.

autobiographical	diagram	physiology
	telephone	topography

6. The hikers used a map to study the _____ of the region.
7. He drew a _____ showing how bicycle gears work.
8. *Anne Frank: The Diary of a Young Girl* is an _____ book.
9. Joan went to South America to study the _____ of rain forest plants.
10. Alexander Graham Bell patented the first successful _____ in 1876.

210

Unit 34 RECAP

You may wish to assign the **Unit 34 Homework Master** (*Teacher Resource Book,* Unit 34) as a fun way to recap the spelling words.

Unit 34 Homework Master

Name_____

Homework Master Unit **34**

Read the definitions. Then fill in the missing letters to complete the spelling words.

something that writes, records, or draws; something written, recorded, or drawn _____ graph

1. person's signature _ _ _ _ graph
2. way of sending a written message or telegram _ _ _ _ graph
3. written group of sentences about the same idea _ _ _ _ graph
4. practice of making photographs _ _ _ _ graph
5. shown by a graph graph _ _
6. study of the earth and all its features graph _ _
7. someone who writes a book about a person _ _ _ _ graph _ _
8. specialist who studies the earth and its surface _ _ _ graph _ _
9. scientist who studies and explores the ocean _ _ _ _ _ graph _ _
10. person who writes about himself or herself _ _ _ _ _ graph _ _ _

Write the missing word parts that can be combined with the parts given to form spelling words.

1. _____ stat 4. _____ metry 7. baro _____
2. _____ logy 5. _____ logist 8. speedo _____
3. _____ al 6. _____ logy 9. dia _____

Write the word that has not been used as yet. Combine two word parts used above to form the word. _____

125

T210

Content Words

Science: Matter

Write words from the box to complete the paragraph.

atom	nucleus	electron	proton	neutron

An __1.__ is the building block of matter. As tiny as it is, it is made up of even tinier parts. At the center is a core called a __2.__ . A __3.__ carries one unit of positive electricity. An atomic particle that carries no electric charge is a __4.__ . A tiny particle carrying one unit of negative electricity is an __5.__ . Together these particles make up atomic matter.

Science: Weather

Write a word from the box to match each definition.

cirrus	nimbostratus	stratus	cumulus	cumulonimbus

6. a low-altitude cloud, often resembling fog
7. a high-altitude cloud composed of narrow bands
8. a dense, white, fluffy cloud
9. an extremely dense, vertical cloud with a hazy outline
10. a low gray cloud that may cause snow or sleet

Apply the Spelling Strategy

These words are all from Greek roots and may be hard to pronounce. Listening for syllables can help. Circle the Content Words you wrote that have two syllables.

Word Study

Clipped Words

A **clipped word** is a short, familiar form of a longer word. For example, **lunch** is short for **luncheon**. Write the Strategy Word whose clipped form is **bio**.

211

Science: Matter
1. atom
2. nucleus
3. proton
4. neutron
5. electron

Science: Weather
6. stratus
7. cirrus
8. cumulus
9. cumulonimbus
10. nimbostratus

Clipped Words
1. biography

Optional Enrichment

Objectives

Content Words

Students will

- **expand** vocabulary with content-related words.
- **relate** the spelling strategy to words outside the basic spelling list.
- **recognize** that a clipped word is a shortened form of a longer word.

Content Words

Science: Matter

Use these sentences to introduce the words and their meanings.

1. The **atom** is the smallest building block of matter.
2. An atom's center is its **nucleus**.
3. An **electron** is the part of an atom with a negative charge.
4. A **proton** is the part of an atom with a positive charge.
5. An atom's **neutron** has neither a negative nor positive charge.

Science: Weather

Use these sentences to introduce the words and their meanings.

6. The airplane flew through a layer of high clouds called **cirrus**.
7. Low gray clouds known as **stratus** made the day seem dreary.
8. These clouds are **cumulus** and showers are a possibility.
9. Clouds called **nimbostratus** often bring rain.
10. **Cumulonimbus** clouds often bring severe thunderstorms.

Note: The Greek roots in the Content Words are not included in this unit. A common spelling strategy (syllabification) is targeted.

Word Study

Clipped Words

Explain that when a long word is used frequently, people often "clip" the word, making it more convenient to use. In many cases, the clipped form almost entirely replaces the original word. Ask students to name other clipped words.

T211

Unit 35 Home Spelling Practice

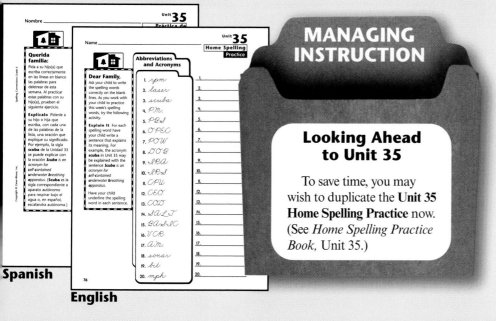

MANAGING INSTRUCTION

Looking Ahead to Unit 35

To save time, you may wish to duplicate the **Unit 35 Home Spelling Practice** now. (See *Home Spelling Practice Book,* Unit 35.)

Spanish

English

Basic Spelling List

rpm	CPU
laser	CEO
scuba	COD
P.M.	SALT
PBS	BASIC
OPEC	VCR
POW	A.M.
DOB	sonar
IRA	bit
IRS	mph

Strategy Words

Review

etc.	wt.
modem	yd.
TX	

Preview

acre	laboratory
edition	organization
facsimile	

Content Words

Health: Nutrition

calorie	nutrition
nourish	metabolism
dietitian	

Science: Experiments

Celsius	squared
Fahrenheit	exponent
scientific notation	

Individual Needs

Challenge Words

emcee	R.S.V.P.
Fortran	COBOL
NASA	NATO

Alternate Word List ★

rpm	DOB
laser	IRS
scuba	BASIC
P.M.	VCR
PBS	A.M.

★ For students who need to study fewer Basic Spelling words

MATERIALS

Student Edition
Pages 212–217
Challenge Activities, p. 253

Teacher Edition
Pages T212A–T217
Challenge Activities, p. T253

Teacher Resource Book
Unit 35 Homework Master
Unit 35 Practice Masters
Flip Folder Practice Master
Unit 35 Test Master

Home Spelling Practice Book
Unit 35 Home Spelling Practice
(English or Spanish)

Other *Spelling Connections* Resources
- Audiotape, Grade 6
- Practice Book for Grammar, Usage, and Mechanics, Grade 6
- Spelling Support for Second Language Learners, Grade 6
- Support Software on CD-ROM
- Transparency Book, Grade 6
- Word Sort CD-ROM, Grade 6

OBJECTIVES

Spelling and Thinking

Students will
- **read** the spelling words in list form and in context.
- **sort** the spelling words according to whether they are written in lowercase or uppercase.
- **read** and remember this week's spelling strategy.

Spelling and Vocabulary

Students will
- **write** spelling words that are abbreviations or acronyms for given phrases.
- **replace** underlined phrases in sentences with spelling words.
- **use** the **Spelling Dictionary** to write abbreviations and acronyms correctly.

Spelling and Reading

Students will
- **answer** questions with spelling words.
- **complete** sentences using spelling words.
- **complete** a paragraph using spelling words.

Spelling and Writing

Students will
- **proofread** a paragraph.
- **use** the writing process to write a descriptive paragraph about a modern invention.
- **proofread** their writing.

MEETING INDIVIDUAL NEEDS
Learning Styles

 Visual

Give the definition of a spelling word or abbreviation, and point to a student. That student must write the acronym or abbreviation on the chalkboard, while the other students write it at their desks. The student then gives the definition of another spelling word and points to another student. Continue until you are satisfied that the class understands the spelling words.

 Auditory

Follow the directions for the visual activity, but have the student you point to also pronounce the word and spell it aloud after she or he writes it on the chalkboard. If the student makes an error, call on another student to correct it.

 Kinesthetic

Have the students stand in line. Give a definition for an abbreviation or acronym and have the first student spell it. The student must point out any periods or capital letters. For **A.M.**, for example, the student would say, "Capital **A** period capital **M** period." If the student is correct, he or she moves to the end of the line and the next student takes a turn. If the student is incorrect, he or she gets one more try before going to the back of the line. If the student is incorrect the second time, the next student in line gets a chance to spell the word.

> **Hands-On Practice**
> All students will benefit from practicing with a **Flip Folder**. See page Z18.

Language and Cultural Differences

Spanish-speaking students may need extra assistance with acronyms, which are less common in Spanish than in English. Also, some of the abbreviations may be particularly difficult for all students to learn because of inconsistencies in the way they are written. When the abbreviations can be written two ways, this unit gives the preferred form, but the other form is also correct. The **Spelling Dictionary** includes the various forms in which these abbreviations can appear: **mph** or **m.p.h.**, **rpm** or **r.p.m.**, **A.M.** or **a.m.**, **POW** or **P.O.W.**

MANAGING INSTRUCTION

3–5 Day Plan		Average	Below Average	Above Average
Day 1	**Day 1**	Pretest Spelling Mini-Lesson, p. T212 Spelling and Thinking, p. 212	Pretest Spelling Mini-Lesson, p. T212 Spelling and Thinking, p. 212	Pretest Spelling and Thinking, p. 212
	Day 2	Spelling and Vocabulary, p. 213	Spelling and Vocabulary, p. 213 (or) Unit 35 Practice Master, A and B	Spelling and Vocabulary, p. 213 Spelling and Reading, p. 214
Day 2	**Day 3**	Spelling and Reading, p. 214	Spelling and Reading, p. 214 (or) Unit 35 Practice Master, C and D	Challenge Activities, p. 253
	Day 4	Spelling and Writing, p. 215 Unit 35 Homework Master	Spelling and Writing, p. 215	Spelling and Writing, p. 215 Unit 35 Homework Master
Day 3	**Day 5**	Weekly Test	Weekly Test	Weekly Test

Vocabulary Connections (pages 216 and 217) may be used anytime during this unit.

Objectives

Spelling and Thinking

Students will
- **read** the spelling words in list form and in context.
- **sort** the spelling words according to whether they are written in lowercase or uppercase.
- **read** and remember this week's spelling strategy.

UNIT PRETEST

Use **Pretest Sentences** below. Refer to the self-checking procedures on student page 256. You may wish to use the **Unit 35 Word List Overhead Transparency** as part of the checking procedure.

TEACHING THE STRATEGY

Spelling Mini-Lesson

Write **NASA** on the chalkboard. Ask what **NASA** stands for. (National Aeronautics and Space Administration) Explain that **NASA** is an **acronym**, i.e., a word formed from the initial or beginning letters or parts of words in a series of words. Discuss the advantages of using acronyms. Explain that acronyms appear as entries in the dictionary.

Explain that abbreviations are another shortened form of words. Abbreviations are formed from the first letters of a word or from various letters within a word. For example, **Mr.** is formed from the first and last letters of **mister**.

Point out that abbreviations are also listed in the dictionary. In most dictionaries, they appear in a special section.

Explain that there is more than one correct way to spell some of the abbreviations on this week's word list but that the preferred spelling appears on the list. (See **Language and Cultural Differences** on page T212B.)

Point out that acronyms and abbreviations are often used in newspaper stories. Bring in several newspapers, and ask the students to circle as many acronyms and abbreviations as they can find.

Read the word list aloud. Clarify meanings as necessary.

Read **Remember the Spelling Strategy** on page 212.

Order of answers may vary.
lowercase
1. rpm ★
2. laser ★
3. scuba ★
4. sonar
5. bit
6. mph

uppercase
7. P.M. ★
8. PBS ★
9. OPEC
10. POW
11. DOB ★
12. IRA
13. IRS ★
14. CPU
15. CEO
16. COD
17. SALT
18. BASIC ★
19. VCR ★
20. A.M. ★

212

READ THE SPELLING WORDS

1.	rpm	*rpm*	The car shifted gears at 40,000 **rpm**.
2.	laser	*laser*	A powerful **laser** beam cut the steel.
3.	scuba	*scuba*	The **scuba** divers took pictures of the fish.
4.	P.M.	*P.M.*	Herb's play will begin at 7 **P.M.** sharp.
5.	PBS	*PBS*	We watched a science special on **PBS**.
6.	OPEC	*OPEC*	Many **OPEC** nations are in the Middle East.
7.	POW	*POW*	The **POW** spent a year in prison.
8.	DOB	*DOB*	The form asks for **DOB** and place of birth.
9.	IRA	*IRA*	He adds some money every year to his **IRA**.
10.	IRS	*IRS*	The **IRS** collects federal taxes.
11.	CPU	*CPU*	Every digital machine contains a **CPU**.
12.	CEO	*CEO*	The bank **CEO** approved the new plan.
13.	COD	*COD*	Pay for the package when it arrives **COD**.
14.	SALT	*SALT*	The **SALT** meetings started in 1969.
15.	BASIC	*BASIC*	She knows how to program in **BASIC**.
16.	VCR	*VCR*	We taped the TV special on the **VCR**.
17.	A.M.	*A.M.*	His alarm went off at 7 **A.M.**
18.	sonar	*sonar*	Submarines rely on their **sonar** devices.
19.	bit	*bit*	A **bit** is information stored on a computer.
20.	mph	*mph*	The speed limit in this area is 30 **mph**.

SORT THE SPELLING WORDS

1.–6. Write the spelling words that are written with all lowercase letters.

7.–20. Write the spelling words that are written with all uppercase letters.

REMEMBER THE SPELLING STRATEGY

Remember that an **abbreviation** is a shortened form of a word or phrase. For example, **mph** is the abbreviation for "miles per hour." An **acronym** is a word formed by combining the first letters or parts of a series of words. The acronym **bit** stands for "binary digit."

Pretest Sentences (See procedures on pages Z10–Z11.)

★ 1. All 45 **rpm** records turn at a speed of forty-five revolutions per minute.
★ 2. **Laser** means "light amplification by stimulated emission of radiation."
★ 3. **Scuba** means "self-contained underwater breathing apparatus."
★ 4. Post meridiem, or **P.M.**, is Latin for "after midday."
★ 5. **PBS**, the Public Broadcasting System, offers varied programs.
6. **OPEC** is the Organization of Petroleum Exporting Countries.
7. A **POW** is a prisoner of war.
★ 8. I wrote my **DOB**, or date of birth, on the application.
9. They save money in an **IRA**, or Individual Retirement Account.
★10. The Internal Revenue Service, or **IRS**, collects taxes.
11. A computer's central processing unit is called the **CPU** for short.
12. A chief executive officer is also known as a **CEO**.
13. I paid for the merchandise **COD**, that is, cash on delivery.
14. The Strategic Arms Limitations Talks are also known as **SALT**.
★15. **BASIC** means "beginner's all-purpose symbolic instruction code."
★16. Our school has a **VCR**, or videocassette recorder, in the lab.
★17. Ante meridiem, or **A.M.**, is Latin for "before midday."
18. "Sound navigation ranging" is known as **sonar** for short.
19. A **bit**, or binary digit, is either of the numerals 0 or 1.
20. The posted speed limit was 55 **mph**, which means "miles per hour."

Spelling and Vocabulary

Word Meanings

Write the spelling word that is an abbreviation or acronym for each phrase.

1. self-contained underwater breathing apparatus
2. in the afternoon or evening
3. Organization of Petroleum Exporting Countries
4. cash on delivery
5. sound navigation ranging

Word Replacements

Write the spelling words that are abbreviations or acronyms for the underlined phrases.

6.–10. Computer technology has added its own vocabulary to the American language. Shortened forms of computer terms make them easier to say and remember. The smallest unit that a central processing unit can store is a binary digit. Using Beginner's All-purpose Symbolic Instruction Code, a programmer can record information in the computer. You probably know that light amplification by stimulated emission of radiation printing is one means of getting computer information on paper. One byproduct of the computer age is the videocassette recorder.

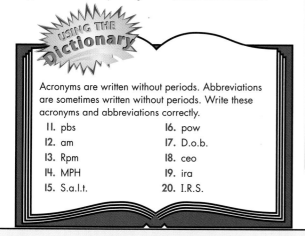

Acronyms are written without periods. Abbreviations are sometimes written without periods. Write these acronyms and abbreviations correctly.

11. pbs	16. pow
12. am	17. D.o.b.
13. Rpm	18. ceo
14. MPH	19. ira
15. S.a.l.t.	20. I.R.S.

Word Meanings

1. scuba
2. P.M.
3. OPEC
4. COD
5. sonar

Word Replacements

6. CPU
7. bit
8. BASIC
9. laser
10. VCR

Using the Dictionary

11. PBS
12. A.M.
13. rpm
14. mph
15. SALT
16. POW
17. DOB
18. CEO
19. IRA
20. IRS

213

Objectives

Spelling and Vocabulary

Students will
- **write** spelling words that are abbreviations or acronyms for given phrases.
- **replace** underlined phrases in sentences with spelling words.
- **use** the **Spelling Dictionary** to write abbreviations and acronyms correctly.

Developing Oral Language Skills

Have students work in pairs. The first student asks a question that includes one of the abbreviations or acronyms in the spelling list. For example, the student might ask, "Do you know how to use a **VCR**?" The second student answers the question. The answer must include another abbreviation or acronym from the spelling list. For example, the second student might say, "Meet me at 6 **P.M.** and I will show you how to use a VCR." Have each pair of students see how many words from the spelling list they can use this way.

MEETING INDIVIDUAL NEEDS

Providing More Help

Write the abbreviations and acronyms on the chalkboard. Have volunteers write next to them the words for which they stand. Then erase the abbreviations and acronyms, and have the students take turns writing them.

★Students who need to study fewer words should use the **Alternate Word List**. This list is starred on page T212 in the Teacher Edition. The **Unit 35 Practice Masters** (*Teacher Resource Book*) provide additional practice with these words.

Unit 35 Practice Masters

Name	Practice **Master** Unit **35**

1. rpm	3. scuba	5. P.M.	7. PBS	9. DOB
2. laser	4. A.M.	6. VCR	8. BASIC	10. IRS

A. Write the abbreviations correctly.

1. pbs _____ 6. Laser _____
2. am _____ 7. basic _____
3. Rpm _____ 8. Vcr _____
4. D.o.b _____ 9. P.m. _____
5. I.r.S. _____ 10. Scuba _____

B. Write the missing words. Use the spelling dictionary. Write each abbreviation.

1. revolutions per _____
2. ____ of birth _____
3. Internal Revenue _____
4. videocassette _____
5. ____ Broadcasting System _____
6. ante ____ _____

C. Write the acronyms or abbreviations specifically related to each subject.

1. computers 3. U.S. taxes
2. television 4. oceanographic equipment

126

Practice **Master** Unit **35**

PBS DOB
BASIC IRS

...ed by the picture. Use spelling words.

127

Spelling and Reading

Students will
- **answer** questions with spelling words.
- **complete** sentences using spelling words.
- **complete** a paragraph using spelling words.

One-Minute Handwriting Hint

All letters of the same size should be even in height.

align
INCORRECT

align
CORRECT

Legible handwriting can boost spelling scores by as much as 20%.

Answer the Questions

1. DOB
2. POW
3. CEO
4. IRA
5. SALT
6. OPEC
7. bit

Complete the Sentences

8. BASIC
9. CPU
10. PBS
11. IRS
12. mph
13. VCR
14. laser
15. rpm

Complete the Paragraph

16. COD
17. scuba
18. P.M.
19. sonar
20. A.M.

Spelling and Reading

rpm	laser	scuba	P.M.	PBS
OPEC	POW	DOB	IRA	IRS
CPU	CEO	COD	SALT	BASIC
VCR	A.M.	sonar	bit	mph

Answer the Questions Write spelling words to answer these questions.

1. What piece of information is on a driver's license?
2. What is someone held captive during a war called?
3. Who is at the head of a company?
4. What helps people save for their retirement?
5. What meetings were held to limit nuclear weapons?
6. What organization was formed by nations dependent on oil exports for their income?
7. What is the smallest unit of storage in a computer?

Complete the Sentences Write a spelling word to complete each sentence.

8. There are many versions of the _____ programming language.
9. A _____ frequently scans the computer for new instructions from the keyboard or from a program.
10. _____ is a network of public television stations.
11. He filed his income tax form with the _____ late this year.
12. The radar detector shows he is driving 60 _____.
13. They rented a video to play on their new _____.
14. The doctor used a _____ to perform the delicate surgery.
15. The new engine gives off less heat at a high _____.

Complete the Paragraph Write spelling words from the box to complete the paragraph.

A package arrived _16._, so Erin paid the mail carrier. The package contained her new _17._ gear. When the sun set at 8 _18._, she and a friend boarded the research vessel. At sea, they used a _19._ device to find their exact diving location. They waited until 7 _20._ the next day to begin their dive.

P.M.
COD
sonar
A.M.
scuba

214

MEETING INDIVIDUAL NEEDS

Providing More Challenge

Challenge Words and **Challenge Activities** for Unit 35 appear on page 253. **Challenge Word Test Sentences** appear on page T253.

Unit 35 Challenge Activities

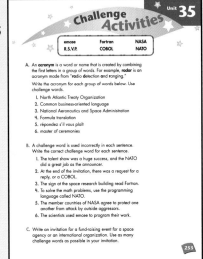

Weekly Test Options

Option 1:
One Spelling Word Per Sentence
(See procedures on pages Z10–Z11.)

★ 1. You must arrive at school by 8 **A.M.**
★ 2. One language used in programming is **BASIC**.
 3. A **bit** is a single unit of information.
 4. Who is the **CEO** of that corporation?
 5. You may pay for the item **COD**.
 6. These computers are connected to a single **CPU**.
★ 7. The space marked **DOB** is for your date of birth.
 8. The worker saved money in an **IRA**.
★ 9. The **IRS** collects taxes for the United States government.
★10. Some operations can be performed by **laser**.
 11. She drove the car at a speed of 55 **mph**.
 12. The **OPEC** nations meet to discuss oil prices and production.
★13. Our school day ends at 2 **P.M.**
★14. Many educational programs appear on **PBS**.
 15. That man was a **POW** in World War II.

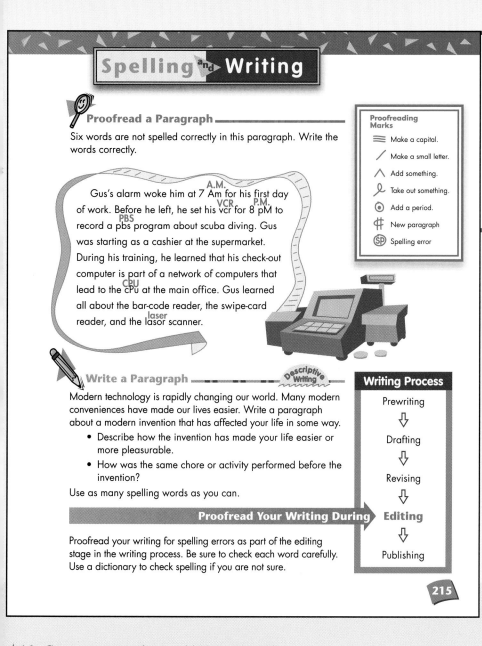

Spelling and Writing

Proofread a Paragraph

Six words are not spelled correctly in this paragraph. Write the words correctly.

> Gus's alarm woke him at 7 ~~Am~~ **A.M.** for his first day of work. Before he left, he set his ~~vcr~~ **VCR** for 8 ~~pM~~ **P.M.** to record a ~~pbs~~ **PBS** program about scuba diving. Gus was starting as a cashier at the supermarket. During his training, he learned that his check-out computer is part of a network of computers that lead to the ~~cpu~~ **CPU** at the main office. Gus learned all about the bar-code reader, the swipe-card reader, and the ~~lasor~~ **laser** scanner.

Proofreading Marks
- ☰ Make a capital.
- / Make a small letter.
- ∧ Add something.
- ℘ Take out something.
- ⊙ Add a period.
- ⌗ New paragraph
- (SP) Spelling error

Write a Paragraph

Descriptive Writing

Modern technology is rapidly changing our world. Many modern conveniences have made our lives easier. Write a paragraph about a modern invention that has affected your life in some way.

- Describe how the invention has made your life easier or more pleasurable.
- How was the same chore or activity performed before the invention?

Use as many spelling words as you can.

Writing Process
Prewriting
⇩
Drafting
⇩
Revising
⇩
Editing
⇩
Publishing

Proofread Your Writing During → **Editing**

Proofread your writing for spelling errors as part of the editing stage in the writing process. Be sure to check each word carefully. Use a dictionary to check spelling if you are not sure.

215

Objectives

Spelling and Writing
Students will
- **proofread** a paragraph.
- **use** the writing process to write a descriptive paragraph about a modern invention.
- **proofread** their writing.

Using the Writing Process

Before assigning **Write a Paragraph,** see pages 258–259 in the Student Edition for a complete review of the writing process and additional writing assignments. You may wish to refer to pages Z12–Z13 in the Teacher Edition.

Keeping a Spelling Journal

Encourage students to record the words they misspelled on the weekly test in a personal spelling journal. These words may be recycled for future study. Students may also wish to include words from their writing. See pages Z12–Z13 in the Teacher Edition for more information.

★**16.** Can your stereo play an old 78-**rpm** record?
17. Where did the last **SALT** meeting take place?
★**18.** You need the right equipment to go **scuba** diving.
19. **Sonar** is used to locate objects on the ocean floor.
★**20.** We watched a movie that we had taped on our **VCR**.

Option 2:
Multiple Spelling Words Per Sentence
(See procedures on pages Z10–Z11.)

1. Speed can be measured in **rpm** or **mph**.
2. The computer manual explained **BASIC** and **bit**.
3. Did you telephone at 9 **A.M.** or **P.M.**?
4. Use your **VCR** to tape the program on **PBS** about the **SALT** talks and **OPEC** meetings.
5. The **POW** was asked his **DOB**.
6. My **IRA** decreased my payment to the **IRS**.
7. He paid for the **scuba** equipment **COD**.
8. Two modern developments are **laser** and **sonar**.
9. The **CEO** was informed that the computer problem was in the **CPU**.

Option 3:
Standardized Test
(See *Teacher Resource Book,* Unit 35.)

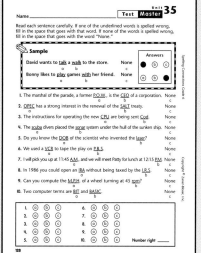

Unit 35 Test Master

Read each sentence carefully. If one of the underlined words is spelled wrong, fill in the space that goes with that word. If none of the words is spelled wrong, fill in the space that goes with the word "None."

Sample

		Answers
David wants to talk a walk to the store. None		● ⓑ ⓒ
Bonny likes to play games with her friend. None		ⓐ ⓑ ⓒ

1. The marshal of the parade, a former P.O.W., is the CEO of a corporation. None
2. OPEC has a strong interest in the renewal of the SALT treaty. None
3. The instructions for operating the new CPU are being sent Cod. None
4. The scuba divers placed the sonar system under the hull of the sunken ship. None
5. Do you know the DOB of the scientist who invented the laser? None
6. We used a VCR to tape the play on P.B.S. None
7. I will pick you up at 11:45 A.M., and we will meet Patty for lunch at 12:15 P.M. None
8. In 1986 you could open an IRA without being taxed by the I.R.S. None
9. Can you compute the M.P.H. of a wheel turning at 45 rpm? None
10. Two computer terms are BIT and BASIC. None

1. ⓐ ⓑ ⓒ		6. ⓐ ⓑ ⓒ		
2. ⓐ ⓑ ⓒ		7. ⓐ ⓑ ⓒ		
3. ⓐ ⓑ ⓒ		8. ⓐ ⓑ ⓒ		
4. ⓐ ⓑ ⓒ		9. ⓐ ⓑ ⓒ		
5. ⓐ ⓑ ⓒ		10. ⓐ ⓑ ⓒ		Number right ____

128

VOCABULARY CONNECTIONS

Objectives

Strategy Words

Students will
- **review** words studied previously that are related to the spelling strategy.
- **preview** unknown words that are related to the spelling strategy.

►Strategy Words◄

Remind the students that the **Strategy Words** relate to the spelling patterns they have studied in this unit. The **Review Words** are below grade level, and the **Preview Words** are above grade level. You may wish to use the following sentences to introduce the words in context.

Review Words:
Words From Grade 5

1. An abbreviation meaning "and others of a similar class" is **etc.**
2. I wish that the **modem** on my computer was faster when it converts data.
3. **TX** is the abbreviation for Texas.
4. When we refer to weight, it is sometimes proper to use the abbreviation **wt.**
5. On the bill of sale, the word "yard" was written as **yd.**

Preview Words:
Words From Grade 7

6. A football field covers over an **acre.**
7. This is a very early **edition** of the book I wanted.
8. We sent a **facsimile** of the document to the lawyer.
9. The experiment was performed in the medical **laboratory.**
10. I belong to an **organization** that sponsors programs for young people.

Review Words
1. modem
2. etc.
3. wt.
4. yd.
5. TX

Preview Words
6. A; a.; A.; ac.
7. lab
8. fax
9. org.
10. ed. or edit.

►Strategy Words◄

Review Words: Abbreviations and Acronyms

Write the word from the box that fits each clue.

etc.	modem	TX	wt.	yd.

1. a device that converts data from one form to another; acronym from **modulator** and **demodulator**
2. abbreviation for **et cetera,** meaning "and other things"
3. abbreviation for **weight**
4. abbreviation for **yard**
5. abbreviation for **Texas;** used in addresses

Preview Words: Abbreviations and Acronyms

Each sentence can be completed by a word in the box. Write the abbreviation or shortened version of the word. Consult a dictionary if you are not sure.

acre	edition	facsimile
laboratory	organization	

6. The farmer agreed to sell one _____ of his land.
7. The biologist went to the _____ to study the cells.
8. She sent me a _____ about the construction of the new library.
9. The _____ is working to protect civil rights.
10. This is only the second _____ of the dictionary.

216

Unit **35** RECAP

You may wish to assign the **Unit 35 Homework Master** (*Teacher Resource Book,* Unit 35) as a fun way to recap the spelling words.

Unit 35 Homework Master

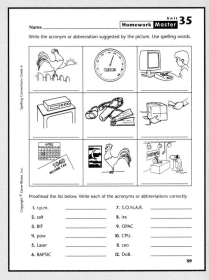

T216

Content Words

Health: Nutrition

Write words from the box to complete the paragraph.

calorie	nourish	dietitian	nutrition	metabolism

A __1.__ studies foods to learn what will best __2.__ the human body. She determines an individual's rate of __3.__ to see how fast the energy from one __4.__ is burned. Then, she can provide patients with a plan for good __5.__.

Science: Experiments

Write words from the box to complete these sentences.

Celsius	Fahrenheit	exponent
squared	scientific notation	

6.–7. The temperature scale that registers the freezing point of water at 0° is called ____; the one that registers freezing at 32° is called ____.

8. The ____ of a number shows how many times the base number is to be multiplied by itself.

9. Writing numbers in powers of ten is called ____.

10. When a number is ____, it is multiplied by itself.

Apply the Spelling Strategy

Circle the Content Words you wrote that have the following abbreviations: **cal., C, F**.

Word Study

Eponyms

An **eponym** is a word that comes from someone's name. For example, the **Celsius** temperature scale was named after its inventor, Anders Celsius. Write the Content Word that came from a German physicist who developed another scale.

217

Health: Nutrition
1. dietitian
2. nourish
3. metabolism
4. (calorie)
5. nutrition

Science: Experiments
6. (Celsius)
7. (Fahrenheit)
8. exponent
9. scientific notation
10. squared

Eponyms
1. Fahrenheit

Unit 36 Home Spelling Practice

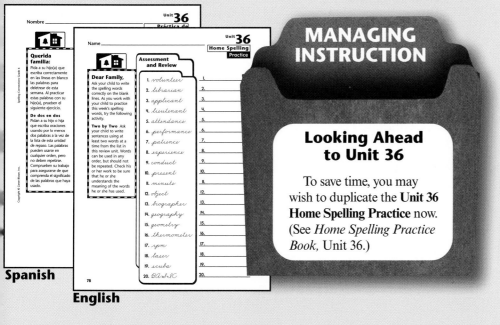

Spanish

English

MANAGING INSTRUCTION

Looking Ahead to Unit 36

To save time, you may wish to duplicate the **Unit 36 Home Spelling Practice** now. (See *Home Spelling Practice Book,* Unit 36.)

Objectives

Content Words

Students will
- **expand** vocabulary with content-related words.
- **relate** the spelling strategy to words outside the basic spelling list.
- **understand** and identify an eponym.

Content Words

Health: Nutrition

Use these sentences to introduce the words and their meanings.

1. A **calorie** is actually a unit of heat.
2. We should eat the foods that will **nourish** our bodies.
3. A **dietitian** planned the meals.
4. Scientists have studied the effect of poor **nutrition** on health.
5. A slow rate of **metabolism** can be controlled with medication.

Science: Experiments

Use these sentences to introduce the words and their meanings.

6. On a **Celsius** thermometer, water boils at 100 degrees.
7. On a **Fahrenheit** thermometer, water freezes at 32 degrees.
8. In math an **exponent** means that a number is to be multiplied by itself that many times.
9. If we have **squared** a number, we have multiplied the number by itself.
10. To use **scientific notation,** we must state numbers in decimal form between 1 and 10 and multiplied by a power of 10.

Word Study

Eponyms

Challenge students to name other eponyms they know (e.g., the **teddy bear** was named for President Theodore Roosevelt, the **Morse code** after Samuel Morse, and the **braille** system of writing for Louis Braille). Point out that if they do something to become famous, a word could be named after them!

T217

Assessment Words

beautician	telemeter
interference	photographer
autopilot	radiance
PTA	migrant
odometer	Y2K
presence	accountant
mountaineer	sow
EPA	resistance
magician	photosynthesis
conference	P.S.

Review Words

Unit 31
volunteer*	musician
librarian*	merchant
applicant*	servant
lieutenant*	assistant
engineer	opponent

Unit 32
attendance*	silence
performance*	importance
patience*	balance
experience*	instance
appearance	distance

Unit 33
conduct*	wound
present*	compound
minute*	content
object*	refuse
aged	progress

Unit 34
biographer*	telegraph
geography*	paragraph
geometry*	biology
thermometer*	diameter
photography	geologist

Unit 35
rpm*	P.M.
laser*	VCR
scuba*	PBS
BASIC*	DOB
A.M.	IRS

* Posttest sentences and the **Unit 36 Test Master** test these words. Students review all words listed.

MATERIALS

Student Edition
Pages 218–223

Teacher Edition
Pages T218A–T223

Teacher Resource Book
Flip Folder Practice Master
Unit 36 Test Master

Home Spelling Practice Book
Unit 36 Home Spelling Practice
(English or Spanish)

Other *Spelling Connections* Resources
• Transparency Book, Grade 6

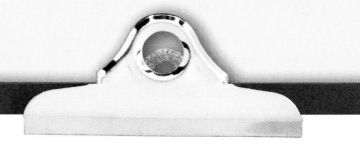

OBJECTIVES

Spelling and Assessment
Students will
• **assess** their spelling success by matching new words to the spelling strategies presented in Units 31–35.
• **connect** new words to the spelling strategies in Units 31–35.
• **write** new words that relate to the spelling strategies taught in Units 31–35.

Spelling and Review
Students will
• **review** and practice the spelling strategies and words taught in Units 31–35.
• **learn** an alternative spelling study strategy.

Spelling and Writing
Students will
• **review** interjections.
• **compose** an expository piece of writing that describes a natural process.
• **learn** a proofreading strategy.
• **understand** that computer language has created many new words.
• **proofread** for misspelled technical words containing the prefix **multi-** and the suffix **-tion**.

MEETING INDIVIDUAL NEEDS

Learning Styles

Visual

Hold a spelling bee. Tell the students that you will pronounce each spelling word and that they will go, one by one, to the chalkboard to spell the word. If the first student spells the word correctly, the next student goes to the chalkboard and spells the next word. If the word is misspelled, the next student tries to spell the same word. Play the game until all the words are spelled correctly.

Auditory

Hold a spelling bee as described in the visual activity, but have the students spell the words aloud rather than write them.

Kinesthetic

Divide the words into syllables and write each syllable on a card. Then mix up the cards. Tape one syllable of a word to each student's back after showing the card to the student. Make sure all the syllables are distributed. Then have the students walk around, forming pairs when they find another part that will join theirs to make a word. Have the pairs write their words. Some students may find that there is more than one student with whom they can join. Ask them to explain why that is so.

Hands-On Practice
All students will benefit from practicing with a **Flip Folder**. See page Z18.

Language and Cultural Differences

The spelling words may be difficult for some students because of regional pronunciations and differing language backgrounds. Spanish-speaking students may have difficulty with some of the short vowel sounds and the schwa sound. It may be difficult for students whose primary language is not English to understand the concept of homographs.

Write a few of the spelling words on the chalkboard, and then write the dictionary respellings for each pronunciation. Highlight the accented syllables in colored chalk. Have the students pronounce each respelling and use each word in a sentence.

MANAGING INSTRUCTION

3–5 Day Plan		Average	Below Average	Above Average
Day 1	**Day 1**	Assessment: Units 31–35, p. 218 (Option 1 or 2, p. T218)	Assessment: Units 31–35, p. 218 (Option 1 or 2, p. T218)	Assessment: Units 31–35, p. 218 (Option 1 or 2, p. T218)
	Day 2	Review: Units 31 and 32, p. 219	Review: Units 31 and 32, p. 219	Review: Units 31 and 32, p. 219 Review: Units 33 and 34, p. 220
Day 2	**Day 3**	Review: Units 33 and 34, p. 220	Review: Units 33 and 34, p. 220	Review: Unit 35, p. 221 Spelling Study Strategy, p. 221
	Day 4	Review: Unit 35, p. 221 Spelling Study Strategy, p. 221	Review: Unit 35, p. 221 Spelling Study Strategy, p. 221	Writer's Workshop, pages 222–223
Day 3	**Day 5**	Weekly Test, Option 1 or 2, p. T221	Weekly Test, Option 1 or 2, p. T221	Weekly Test, Option 1 or 2, p. T221

Writer's Workshop (pages 222 and 223) may be used anytime during this unit.

Objectives

Spelling and Assessment

Students will

- **assess** their spelling success by matching new words to the spelling strategies presented in Units 31–35.
- **connect** new words to the spelling strategies in Units 31–35.
- **write** new words that relate to the spelling strategies taught in Units 31–35.

Unit 36
Review Units 31–35

Assessment and Review

Unit 31
1. beautician
2. mountaineer
3. magician
4. migrant
5. accountant

Unit 32
6. interference
7. presence
8. conference
9. radiance
10. resistance

Unit 33
11. sow

Unit 34
12. autopilot
13. odometer
14. telemeter
15. photographer
16. photosynthesis

Unit 35
17. PTA
18. EPA
19. Y2K
20. P.S.

218

Assessment Units 31–35

Each Assessment Word in the box fits one of the spelling strategies you have studied over the past five weeks. Read the spelling strategies. Then write each Assessment Word under the unit number it fits.

Unit 31
1.–5. The suffixes **-eer, -ian, -ant,** and **-ent** can be used to form nouns. These nouns often name people: **engineer, librarian, assistant,** and **resident**.

Unit 32
6.–10. The suffixes **-ance** and **-ence** can be used to form nouns: **clearance, experience**.

Unit 33
11. **Homographs** are words that are spelled the same but have different meanings, origins, or pronunciations.

Unit 34
12.–16. Many English words have Greek roots. For example, the words **thermometer, barometer,** and **speedometer** all share the root **meter,** meaning "measure."

Unit 35
17.–20. An **abbreviation** is a shortened form of a word or phrase. For example, **mph** is the abbreviation for "miles per hour." An **acronym** is a word formed by combining the first letters or parts of a series of words. The acronym **bit** stands for "binary digit."

beautician
interference
autopilot
PTA
odometer
presence
mountaineer
EPA
magician
conference
telemeter
photographer
radiance
migrant
Y2K
accountant
sow
resistance
photosynthesis
P.S.

ASSESSMENT: UNITS 31–35

Option 1

Assessment Option 1 is the test that appears in the Student Edition on page 218. You may wish to have students take this test to determine their ability to recognize the spelling strategy in each unit and to match words not previously taught to that strategy. **Assessment Option 1** also serves as additional review and practice.

Option 2

Assessment Option 2 is a dictation test using the sentences on page T219. This test assesses students' ability to spell words not previously taught but that are exemplars of a spelling strategy. This test more specifically assesses students' ability to apply the spelling knowledge they have learned.

In either assessment test option, the words are identified by unit in the Teacher Edition. You may wish to index those misspelled words to the review exercises that follow in this unit. Determine which units students need to review and use the additional unit exercises found in this **Assessment and Review Unit** for reteaching the skill in a more focused way.

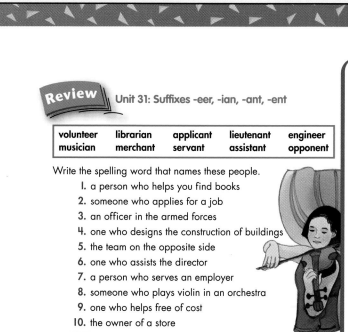

Review Unit 31: Suffixes -eer, -ian, -ant, -ent

volunteer	librarian	applicant	lieutenant	engineer
musician	merchant	servant	assistant	opponent

Write the spelling word that names these people.

1. a person who helps you find books
2. someone who applies for a job
3. an officer in the armed forces
4. one who designs the construction of buildings
5. the team on the opposite side
6. one who assists the director
7. a person who serves an employer
8. someone who plays violin in an orchestra
9. one who helps free of cost
10. the owner of a store

Review Unit 32: Suffixes -ance, -ence

attendance	performance	patience	experience	appearance
silence	importance	balance	instance	distance

Find the misspelled words. Write each word correctly.

11. We have learned much by experence.
12. Please maintain silance when you enter.
13. You need to have more pashunse with the new players.
14. How much distunce have the runners covered?
15. There is a balence of $3.50 in the treasury.
16. This is a matter of great importence.
17. The rule is just for this instanse.
18. She gives the apearance of being calm.
19.–20. The attendce at last night's performance was small.

Unit 31
1. librarian
2. applicant
3. lieutenant
4. engineer
5. opponent
6. assistant
7. servant
8. musician
9. volunteer
10. merchant

Unit 32
11. experience
12. silence
13. patience
14. distance
15. balance
16. importance
17. instance
18. appearance
19. attendance
20. performance

219

Objectives

Spelling and Review

Students will
- **review** and practice the spelling strategy and words taught in Unit 31.
- **review** and practice the spelling strategy and words taught in Unit 32.

Assessing Progress: The Spelling Journal

If your students have been keeping a personal spelling journal, a periodical review of these journals can be a rich assessment tool. Students should include the words they have misspelled from each unit spelling test. They should also be encouraged to write the words they consistently misspell in their own writing and content-area words that present a challenge. Being able to discriminate the words in their everyday writing whose spelling they need to master is a powerful spelling skill.

Pretest Sentences: Assessment Words

(See procedures on pages Z10–Z11.)

1. Latisha enjoys going to the **beautician**.
2. I'd like to finish my work without any more **interference**.
3. After a little while, the plane can fly by **autopilot**.
4. The president of the **PTA** spoke to our class.
5. The **odometer** shows that the car has gone only 2,000 miles.
6. The president requested our **presence** at the ceremony.
7. This shop features equipment for a **mountaineer**.
8. All new homes near the lake must be approved by the **EPA**.
9. The guest **magician** fooled everyone with her tricks.
10. All the teachers went to a special **conference**.
11. The **telemeter** in the spacecraft sent data automatically.
12. How many cameras does the **photographer** use?
13. We could tell she had won by the **radiance** of her expression.
14. The **migrant** workers work long hours in the fields.
15. A team of experts fixed the **Y2K** problem with our computers.
16. We have an **accountant** to keep track of our costs and sales.
17. It is important to **sow** the seeds at the right time of year.
18. There was much **resistance** to the plan to enlarge the parking lot.
19. In biology we studied the process of **photosynthesis**.
20. Sales letters always seem to include a **P. S.**

Spelling and Review

Students will

- **review** and practice the spelling strategy and words taught in Unit 33.
- **review** and practice the spelling strategy and words taught in Unit 34.

Unit 33

1. wound
2. present
3. minute
4. object
5. aged
6. content
7. compound
8. refuse
9. progress
10. conduct

Unit 34
Order of answers may vary.

11. biographer
12. geography
13. geometry
14. thermometer
15. telegraph
16. photography
17. diameter
18. biology
19. paragraph
20. geologist

Review Unit 33: Homographs

conduct	present	minute	object	aged
wound	compound	content	refuse	progress

Write the spelling word that fits both places in each sentence.

1. She _____ the bandage around the _____ on her knee.
2. I'd like to _____ you this _____ for your birthday.
3. One _____ will make only a _____ difference.
4. Do you _____ to looking for the lost _____?
5. Her _____ grandparents are _____ 88 and 90.
6. We're quite _____ with the _____ of the lecture.
7. Be careful not to _____ the problem by adding the wrong chemical _____.
8. I _____ to take out smelly _____ I didn't create.
9. At last, we _____ slowly toward making successful _____.
10. The judge will _____ an investigation into the _____ of the group.

Review Unit 34: Greek Roots

biographer	geography	geometry	thermometer	photography
telegraph	paragraph	biology	diameter	geologist

Write a spelling word by combining a word part from each column.

11.	bio	metry	16.	photo	logist
12.	geo	mometer	17.	dia	graphy
13.	geo	graph	18.	bio	logy
14.	ther	grapher	19.	para	graph
15.	tele	graphy	20.	geo	meter

220

Bulletin Board Idea

The World of Work

Have the students bring in photographs of themselves to display on the bulletin board. Ask each student to write a short paragraph in which she or he describes herself or himself working at a job that the student hopes to hold some day. For example, a student might write: "Talisha Brannen. Photographer for the local newspaper. I take pictures of people, places, and events to illustrate newspaper articles. I like my job because I stay active and get to work with people." Tell the students to include all of these elements in their paragraphs: name, job title, a sentence describing what they do, and a sentence explaining why they like the work.

Put each description on the bulletin board beside or beneath the student's photo. On small banners cut out of construction paper, carefully print the job titles and place them just below the photos.

Review Unit 35: Abbreviations and Acronyms

rpm	laser	scuba	BASIC	A.M.
P.M.	VCR	PBS	DOB	IRS

Write the abbreviation or acronym that fits the clue.

1. hours of the morning
2. hours of the evening
3. public television
4. needed for many applications
5. the place taxes are sent
6. referring to underwater diving
7. for showing movies on television sets
8. is used in some surgeries
9. refers to how fast something goes around
10. a computer programming language

Unit 35

1. A.M.
2. P.M.
3. PBS
4. DOB
5. IRS
6. scuba
7. VCR
8. laser
9. rpm
10. BASIC

WORD SORT Spelling Study Strategy

Sorting by Endings

One good way to practice spelling words is to place words into groups according to some spelling pattern. Here is a way to practice some of the spelling words you have been studying in the past few weeks.

1. Make six columns across a large piece of paper or on the chalkboard.

2. Write one of these words at the top of each column: **volunteer, librarian, assistant, opponent, attendance,** and **experience.** Include the underlines.

3. Have a partner choose a spelling word from Units 31 and 32 and say it aloud.

4. Write the spelling word in the column under the word with the same ending.

221

Objectives

Spelling and Review

Students will
• **review** and practice the spelling strategy and words taught in Unit 35.
• **learn** an alternative spelling study strategy.

Learning an Alternative Spelling Study Strategy

Students should always have a number of study strategies to draw from when it comes to learning their spelling words. **Sorting by Endings** is a fun way of differentiating sound and letter patterns. Encourage students to remember this spelling study strategy and to consider using it with any appropriate list they need to study and learn.

Weekly Test Options

Option 1:
One Spelling Word Per Sentence
(See procedures on pages Z10–Z11.)

1. Is she the job **applicant**?
2. The **librarian** found the book.
3. The **lieutenant** commanded his troops to stand at attention.
4. I do **volunteer** work at the hospital.
5. His **attendance** has improved lately.
6. Is **experience** needed for this job?
7. You must have **patience** with children.
8. The singer gave a great **performance**.
9. Last week he won the school's good **conduct** award.
10. This plane will leave in about one **minute**.
11. Please place this **object** on the shelf.
12. He gave me a **present** on my birthday.
13. We studied the **geography** of Asia.
14. We learned about angles in **geometry** class.
15. What is the reading on your **thermometer**?
16. A famous author will be her **biographer**.
17. The programming language is **BASIC**.
18. Some operations can be done with a **laser**.
19. Can your stereo play a 78 **rpm** record?
20. You need proper training to go **scuba** diving.

Option 2:
Standardized Test

Unit 36 Test Master

(See *Teacher Resource Book,* Unit 36.)

Objectives

Spelling and Writing

Students will
- **review** interjections.
- **compose** an expository piece of writing that describes a natural process. (See **Spelling and the Writing Process** below.)

Unit 36 enrichment

WRITER'S

Sentences and Their Parts

An interjection expresses emotion. **Oh, ouch, hey, hurray,** and **wow** are common interjections.

Wow, that is a big dog!

Practice Activity

A. Write the interjection in each sentence below.

1. Hey, we're going to be late if you don't hurry.
2. Paula said, "Gee, I'd like to see that movie, too."
3. When I showed Dad my report, he said, "Wow! That's good!"
4. Ouch, that railing gave me a splinter.
5. Take your lunch; oh, don't forget your thermos.
6. Hurray, your poster won first prize!
7. Gee, I really liked that show.

B. Complete each sentence with a word from the spelling lists in Units 31–35.

8. Oh, can we attend the next ____?
9. Well, a ____ will show you the temperature.
10. Hey, I'm better at ____ than I was at algebra.
11. Gee, you are the first ____ for this job.
12. Wow, that portrait shows you have a future in ____.
13. The ____ began, "Hurray, you're now a cousin!"
14. Ouch, I just learned the ____ of well-fitting shoes.

222

A
1. Hey
2. Gee
3. Wow
4. Ouch
5. oh
6. Hurray
7. Gee

Answers may vary. Possible answers are given.

B
8. performance
9. thermometer
10. geometry
11. applicant
12. photography
13. paragraph
14. importance

Spelling and the Writing Process

Expository Writing

You may wish to use this writing assignment to help students master the writing process. For other writing ideas, see pages 258–259 in the Student Edition.

Explain that students will write an explanation of some natural process such as erosion.

Prewriting Hint: You may wish to help students plan their writing by recommending the graphic organizer on this page. Have them replicate the graphic, filling in the blank circles with topics they might wish to explain.

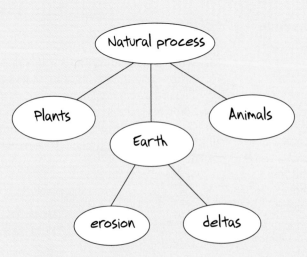

Revising Hint: Encourage students to exchange papers with a partner during revision. The partners can identify places where a cause or effect is unclear, or a section that requires more details or transitions.

WORKSHOP

Proofreading Strategy

Pair Up With a Partner!

Good writers always proofread their papers for spelling errors. Here's a strategy that you can use to proofread your writing.

Instead of proofreading all by yourself, pair up with a partner. Ask your partner to read your work aloud slowly. While your partner reads, you look at each word. Is it spelled correctly?

Hearing each word read aloud helps you focus on the word and its spelling instead of on the sentence. A second benefit is that a partner can help you fix misspellings. This strategy works. Try it!

Electronic Spelling

Electronic Spelling
1. multimedia
2. resolution
3. multitask
4. OK
5. OK
6. OK

Electronic Spelling

Computer Language

Technology is changing language and bringing new words into common use. Some of these words are so new that they may not appear in older dictionaries or spell checkers.

A knowledge of prefixes and suffixes can help you spell such words. Several, for instance, begin with the prefix **multi-** or end with the suffix **-tion**. Knowing these word parts can help you spell words correctly.

Look at these words. Which are misspelled? Write those words correctly. Write **OK** if a word is correct.

1. multemedia
2. resolutoin
3. mutitask

4. protection
5. introduction
6. multilevel

223

Objectives

Spelling and Writing

Students will
- **learn** a proofreading strategy.
- **understand** that computer language has created many new words.
- **proofread** for misspelled technical words containing the prefix **multi-** and the suffix **-tion**.

Using Proofreading Strategies

Students are often unaware that there are a variety of techniques they can use to proofread their own writing. Building a repertory of strategies is important to improving students' writing and editing skills.

Spelling and Technology

The advent of word processing, computer protocols, and the Internet has actually increased, not lessened, the pressure on users to be better, more aware spellers. Spell checkers, for example, create circumstances in which the ability to discriminate between an acceptable and an unacceptable spelling is a critical skill. A homophone substitution, a correct spelling of the wrong word, an inadvertent word omission—these are examples of situations in computer usage that require a deeper understanding of spelling principles and a more adroit proofreading capability. It may be worthwhile to underscore this increased need as a whole-class discussion after students finish this unit's **Electronic Spelling** activity.

Challenge Activities

| adequate | elastic | container |
| ancestor | exclaim | complaint |

The **Challenge Words, Challenge Activities,** and **Challenge Word Test Sentences** (provided in the Teacher Edition) were developed for students who have mastered the spelling list in the Student Edition. The **Challenge Words** are high-frequency words one to two grade levels above the level of the basic spelling list.

Challenge Words do not appear in the **Spelling Dictionary** so students will have the additional challenge of researching word meanings, as needed, in other reference materials.

A
1. elastic
2. adequate
3. complaint
4. ancestor
5. container
6. exclaim

B
1. ancestor
2. adequate
3. elastic
4. complaint
5. exclaim
6. container

C
Answers will vary.

A. Write the challenge word that fits each "Who or What Am I" statement.

1. I return to my normal shape after I'm stretched.
2. I may be enough or suitable, but I'm not of the best quality.
3. I am a statement expressing annoyance or unhappiness. Sign me "Gripe."
4. I am family. I was born before your grandparents.
5. I am used to hold something. Call me a box or a barrel.
6. I am a verb that tells how you might speak.

B. Write challenge words to complete this "vacation album" story.

A great-grandfather, one __1.__ of mine, enjoyed spending his summer vacation at home. But he hated to live in his home in the winter. His landlord never provided __2.__ heat for the house. He said it was cold enough to freeze __3.__! My great-grandfather did not write the landlord a letter of __4.__. He did not knock on the landlord's door to __5.__ about how cold it was. He put one piece of coal into a __6.__ and sent it to the landlord as a hint!

C. Pretend that you are the landlord mentioned in Activity B. Write a letter in response to the man who sent you a piece of coal. Tell what you think he should have done. Tell him how you plan to correct the situation. Use as many challenge words as possible.

224

Challenge Word Test Sentences

1. There was **adequate** interest from the class for a trip to the museum.
2. Pat has an **ancestor** who came from Europe.
3. Pulling on your sock will weaken the **elastic**.
4. The acid **container** must be airtight.
5. The teacher's major **complaint** was that he had too much paperwork.
6. The winner will **exclaim** his happiness after the race.

Challenge Activities

definite	velvet	appeal
prevent	cheetah	charity

A. Write the challenge word that completes each analogy.

   1. **Unclear** is to **exact** as **uncertain** is to _____.

   2. **Wild pig** is to **boar** as **wild cat** is to _____.

   3. **Stingy** is to **selfishness** as **generous** is to _____.

   4. **Metal** is to **steel** as **fabric** is to _____.

   5. **Answer** is to **ask** as **help** is to _____.

   6. **Work for** is to **encourage** as **hold off** is to _____.

B. Write the challenge word that belongs in each group.

   1. stop, halt, check

   2. ask, request, plea

   3. good will, sympathy, brotherly love

   4. precise, exact, certain

   5. tiger, leopard, lion

   6. cotton, silk, corduroy

C. Write a story about a musical event given at a zoo to raise money for your favorite charity. Use some of the challenge words in your story.

A
1. definite
2. cheetah
3. charity
4. velvet
5. appeal
6. prevent

B
1. prevent
2. appeal
3. charity
4. definite
5. cheetah
6. velvet

C
Answers will vary.

225

Challenge Word Test Sentences

   1. The adventure began when the **cheetah** got out of its cage.

   2. My sister wore a **velvet** dress to the school dance.

   3. The plans for the museum trip were not **definite**.

   4. My mother helps at fairs to raise money for **charity**.

   5. The science program has a lot of **appeal** for many students.

   6. Brushing your teeth daily can help **prevent** decay.

Challenge Activities

categorize	hibernate	logic
glimpse	citrus	inhabit

A
1. categorize
2. logic
3. hibernate
4. glimpse
5. inhabit

B
1. citrus
2. categorize
3. logic
4. hibernate
5. inhabit
6. glimpse

C
Answers will vary.

A. Write the challenge word that would be part of the answer to each question. Tell what you could do in the situation given.

1. You see a stack of books that is not arranged in any kind of order. What could you do with these books?
2. You are Sherlock Holmes explaining how you solved a mystery. What do you claim helped you to solve the mystery?
3. You are a bear who doesn't want to be active in the winter. What could you do?
4. You are in a crowded store. You think you see a friend of yours walk by, but you do not get a good look. What kind of a look were you able to get?
5. Your family has bought a new house. What will you do there?

B. Write the challenge word that would be found on a dictionary page with each pair of guide words below.
1. cause | city
2. catchy | citizen
3. log | logrolling
4. glisten | hiccup
5. hibiscus | inhale
6. glimmer | hibachi

C. Write what the main character, Blob, might do in a science fiction story that takes place on a strange planet covered with fruit trees. Use as many challenge words as possible.

226

Challenge Word Test Sentences
1. The black bear can **hibernate** through the winter.
2. It will be hard to **categorize** that rare fossil.
3. The frost did a lot of damage to the **citrus** crop.
4. He waited to catch a **glimpse** of the President.
5. Sometimes **logic** cannot solve a problem.
6. Snakes do not **inhabit** the polar regions.

Challenge Activities

focus	melodious	devote
commotion	Congress	monument

A. Write challenge words to complete the news story. One of these words should be capitalized.

A concert was held on the steps of the Lincoln Memorial. It was in honor of the brave men and women who ___1.___ their lives in service to their country. People from across the country, as well as members of ___2.___, crowded around this historic ___3.___. Police were standing by in case there was any ___4.___, but the crowd was orderly. The band struck up a ___5.___ tune. Then the speeches began. The ___6.___ of the speeches was on national pride.

B. Write a challenge word that relates to each group.

1. Statue of Liberty, Jefferson Memorial, Mount Rushmore
2. camera, eye, attention
3. lawmakers, legislators, representatives
4. voice, violin, bird
5. pledge, vow, dedicate
6. riot, mutiny, disorder

C. Write a short report telling about an event that you would organize if you were the President of the United States. What would be the focus of the event? Who would be invited? Where would the event be held? Use some of the challenge words in your report.

A
1. devote
2. Congress
3. monument
4. commotion
5. melodious
6. focus

B
1. monument
2. focus
3. Congress
4. melodious
5. devote
6. commotion

C
Answers will vary.

227

Challenge Word Test Sentences

1. Be sure the camera is in **focus** before you snap the picture.
2. The strong steel base held up the heavy **monument**.
3. The stray animal caused a lot of **commotion** in the classroom.
4. She will **devote** one hour each night to piano practice.
5. The robin chirped a **melodious** tune.
6. The bill in **Congress** needed sixteen votes to pass.

Challenge Activities

confusion	strenuous	substance
continual	punishment	sculpture

A

1. strenuous
2. continual
3. confusion
4. punishment
5. sculpture
6. substance

B
1. punishment
2. sculpture
3. confusion
4. continual

C
1. strenuous
2. substance

D
Answers will vary.

A. Complete this short story about a tour guide's first day on the job at the Statue of Liberty.

   "This is __1.__ work!" I thought to myself. All day long there is a __2.__ flow of sightseers. Surprisingly, things run quite smoothly. There is very little __3.__ . But standing on my feet all day is torture. My shoes take a lot of __4.__ . It's all worth it, however. The Lady is a marvelous piece of __5.__ , and she stands for important ideas with great __6.__ .

B. Look at each base word in parentheses. To complete each sentence, write a challenge word that is the same part of speech as the abbreviation shown beside the base word. Then underline the suffix in each challenge word.

  1. Should the (punish, *n.*) fit the crime?

  2. What is the name of this huge (sculpt, *n.*)?

  3. I lost my keys in all this (confuse, *n.*).

  4. This month, it seemed as though I was on a (continue, *adj.*) diet of fresh fruit.

C. Write the challenge word that is related to each word.

  1. strain   **2.** substantial

D. Write two tongue twisters. In the first, use words beginning with the letter **c,** and include two challenge words. Your tongue twister could be, for example, "Cam's cousin created continual confusion." In the second, use words beginning with the letter **s**. Include three challenge words.

228

Challenge Word Test Sentences

  1. The artist put the modern **sculpture** in the flower garden.
  2. We did an acid test on the unknown **substance**.
  3. We had a **strenuous** workout during football practice.
  4. The machines in the factory made a **continual** noise.
  5. There was some **confusion** as the band marched onto the field.
  6. Missing practice may result in **punishment**.

Challenge Activities

renewal	juvenile	supermarket
distribute	supreme	bulldozer

A. Write an antonym for each word in Column A. Write a synonym for each word in Column B. Use challenge words.

Column A

1. adult
2. collect
3. cancellation

Column B

4. highest
5. tractor
6. self-service store

B. Read the sentences. Write a challenge word to replace the underlined word(s) in each sentence.

1. Mr. Moyer's lease was up last year. He went to the landlord to ask for <u>an extension</u>.
2. Miss Andrews was new in the neighborhood. She was looking for a <u>store where she could buy groceries</u>.
3. Steve loved his younger brother Eddie, but sometimes Eddie was too <u>young</u> to be included in Steve's activities.
4. There was a farm auction last week. The best <u>tractor for moving earth</u> was sold right away.
5. Divide the stacks of newspapers and <u>give</u> them <u>out</u>.
6. The case went before the <u>highest Court in the country</u>.

C. What could you say or do to show good manners in each of the following situations?

1. You accidentally bump your shopping cart into someone at the store.
2. You are walking past a construction site. You recognize one of the workers.
3. You forgot to renew your library card.
4. A neighbor asks you to watch her child for an hour.

A
1. juvenile
2. distribute
3. renewal
4. supreme
5. bulldozer
6. supermarket

B
1. renewal
2. supermarket
3. juvenile
4. bulldozer
5. distribute
6. Supreme

C
Answers will vary.

229

Challenge Word Test Sentences

1. The lesson we learned was of **supreme** value.
2. I paid the young boy ten dollars to **distribute** the papers.
3. It is important for adults to be good examples for a **juvenile**.
4. The radio station planned a **renewal** of the old show.
5. A giant **bulldozer** can level a large area of land.
6. My family does all their shopping at that **supermarket**.

Challenge Activities

overview	fiendish	chiefly
surveillance	deceit	piercing

A. Write the challenge word that would be part of the answer to each question.

1. What kind of noise or cry could penetrate the air?
2. What kind of wicked act could you expect in a mystery movie?
3. What do you call the practice of telling a falsehood in order to trick someone?
4. What might a speaker give in his or her speech to let the audience know the broad picture of a topic?
5. What do you call the close observation of a person under suspicion by the police?
6. Which challenge word is an adverb?

B. Use challenge words to complete this list started by Detective R3.

__1.__ **of Contents of Detective Kit**

- One whistle with __2.__ tone to use __3.__ in emergencies
- A pair of binoculars to use for __4.__
- A scary face disguise with __5.__ grin
- A shiny badge that is for show, not __6.__

C. Complete this science fiction story. Include as many challenge words as you can.

Detective R3 heard a chilling sound near the secret lab station. He quickly boarded his rocket car that had special equipment.

A
1. piercing
2. fiendish
3. deceit
4. overview
5. surveillance
6. chiefly

B
1. Overview
2. piercing
3. chiefly
4. surveillance
5. fiendish
6. deceit

C
Answers will vary.

Challenge Word Test Sentences

1. The detective set up **surveillance** in the apartment across the street.
2. The coastal town counted **chiefly** on the tourist industry for income.
3. The teacher gave the class an **overview** of the problem.
4. The lead wolf let out a **piercing** cry.
5. Do you believe that some people get money through **deceit**?
6. The thief had a **fiendish** plot to steal the jewel.

Challenge Activities

nursery	garment	dormitory
departure	porcelain	formation

A. Write the challenge word that relates to each group.

  1. room, babies, cribs
  2. rooms, school, beds
  3. dress, shirt, sweater
  4. good-bye, takeoff, liftoff
  5. china, earthenware, teacups
  6. arrangement, order, organization

B. Read each job description. Then write the challenge word that would be in the answer to each question.

  1. I work in a college. My job is to supply fresh laundry to the rooms where the students sleep. Where do I spend my working hours?
  2. I work in a factory. My job is to sew clothes that will be sold in stores. In which type of industry do I work?
  3. I work outdoors where young trees and plants are raised for transplanting. Where do I work?
  4. I work in a studio. I make fine cups and dishes out of clay. What is the material I often use in my work?

C. Write the challenge word that is formed from each of these base words.

  1. depart   2. form

D. Write a job description of a job you would like to have. Use challenge words when you can.

A
1. nursery
2. dormitory
3. garment
4. departure
5. porcelain
6. formation

B
1. dormitory
2. garment
3. nursery
4. procelain

C
1. departure
2. formation

D
Answers will vary.

231

Challenge Word Test Sentences

1. The **departure** time for our flight is nine o'clock.
2. The young parents will prepare the **nursery** for their new child.
3. The girl was assigned a room in the new **dormitory**.
4. The vase at the exhibit was made of fine **porcelain**.
5. This beautiful blue **garment** is made of cotton.
6. The earthquake caused the **formation** of that mountain.

Challenge Activities

hysterical	interval	jovial
cordial	frequent	inhabitant

A
1. jovial
2. hysterical
3. inhabitant
4. cordial
5. interval
6. frequent

B
1. interval, N
2. inhabitant, N
3. cordial, A
4. jovial, A
5. hysterical, A
6. frequent, A

C
Answers will vary.

A. Answer each "What would you be?" question with a challenge word.

1. What would you be if you were good-hearted and full of fun?
2. What would you be if you were unusually emotional or showing a lack of self-control?
3. What would you be if you lived in a certain town?
4. What would you be if you had a warm and friendly nature?
5. What would you be if you were a period of time between now and then?
6. What would you be if you were something that happened often?

B. Write challenge words to complete each sentence. After each word, write **N** if it was used as a noun and **A** if it was used as an adjective.

At each __1.__ in the road was an __2.__ of the town who was helping people evacuate the area during the emergency. This police officer tried to be __3.__, even __4.__, to drivers who became __5.__ when they got stuck in __6.__ traffic jams in the Midtown Tunnel.

C. Imagine that you are a smart and friendly mole. You like to have many guests over to your tunnel home. Write a fanciful story about one of the "down-to-earth" parties you gave. Use some of the challenge words in your story. If you'd prefer to be a rat or a chipmunk or some other animal, go right ahead and change the main character.

232

Challenge Word Test Sentences

1. The young girl became **hysterical** when she heard the strange noise.
2. A large black bear was the **inhabitant** of that cave.
3. We extended a **cordial** greeting to our new neighbor.
4. My grandfather was very **jovial** after winning the prize.
5. I felt that the **interval** between each act was too long.
6. When Father got a new automobile we made **frequent** visits to my aunt.

Challenge Activities

frontward	politely	actively
practically	perfectly	vigorously

A. Write a challenge word to complete each analogy.

1. **Back** is to **front** as **backward** is to _____.
2. **Nearly** is to **closely** as **almost** is to _____.
3. **Faultily** is to **imperfectly** as **ideally** is to _____.
4. **Noisily** is to **quietly** as **rudely** is to _____.
5. **Powerfully** is to **forcefully** as **strenuously** is to _____.
6. **Tamely** is to **wildly** as **passively** is to _____.

B. Write a challenge word to complete each sentence.

1. Shake the bottle _____ so the two liquids blend.
2. Move the chess piece _____ to advance two spaces.
3. Ask the operator _____ for the phone number of the nearest library.
4. Check the content, grammar, and punctuation to make sure you wrote your report _____.
5. Your heart rate increases when you _____ play sports.
6. When you turn left at the barn, you'll know you are _____ at the farmhouse.

C. Answer each question with a complete sentence that includes a challenge word.

1. If you wanted a favor from your parents, how would you ask them?
2. If you went to a parade and you wanted to get a good view, which way would you move?
3. If someone offered you a free ticket to see a famous rock star, how would you answer?

A
1. frontward
2. practically
3. perfectly
4. politely
5. vigorously
6. actively

B
1. vigorously
2. frontward
3. politely
4. perfectly
5. actively
6. practically

C
Answers will vary.

233

Challenge Word Test Sentences

1. We will exercise **vigorously** before the game next week.
2. The sweater she received for her birthday fit **perfectly**.
3. The runner **actively** tried to win the contest.
4. We **politely** thanked the driver for the ride to school.
5. The desk at the office faced **frontward**.
6. **Practically** everyone in town went to the country fair.

Challenge *Activities*

finalist	tariff	offense
fantastic	sheriff	phobia

A. Write the challenge word that fits each definition.

1. a breaking of the law
2. a system of taxes on imports or exports
3. a person who takes part in a final competition
4. a deep, unreasonable fear of something
5. the chief law-enforcement official of a county
6. fanciful or imaginary

B. Write a challenge word to complete each sentence.

1. If you get into trouble in this county, call the _____.
2. Jay took part in the event as a _____.
3. You can be fined or imprisoned for an _____.
4. Their fear of riding on escalators may be a _____.
5. Sandy's dream was strange and _____.
6. On imported cars there is a high _____.

C. A person could have several different feelings about a dream, a fear, or an incident. Write a sentence about more than one feeling someone might have in each situation below. Use the underlined challenge word in the sentence.

1. Someone becomes a <u>finalist</u> in a talent contest for the very first time.
2. The <u>sheriff</u> gives someone a ticket for a speeding <u>offense</u>.
3. Someone dreams that he or she has to pay a high <u>tariff</u> for the imported watch he or she bought.
4. The shapes someone sees in clouds are <u>fantastic</u>.
5. Someone has a <u>phobia</u> of heights but had to climb a ladder one day.

234

A
1. offense
2. tariff
3. finalist
4. phobia
5. sheriff
6. fantastic

B
1. sheriff
2. finalist
3. offense
4. phobia
5. fantastic
6. tariff

C
Answers will vary.

Challenge Word Test Sentences

1. The football team will practice their new **offense** all week.
2. The **sheriff** must patrol a large region in the north.
3. Our family trip out West this summer was **fantastic**.
4. My sister is a **finalist** in the state skating contest.
5. Fear of heights is a common **phobia**.
6. A **tariff** was added to the cost of the gasoline.

Challenge Activities

drizzle	disaster	excursion
amusing	mayonnaise	pleasurable

A. Complete this silly poem with a challenge word that rhymes with the underlined word above it.

Yesterday was quite <u>confusing</u>,
Though I found it rather __1.__.
The sun was so hot, it began to <u>sizzle</u>.
Then from the clouds it began to __2.__.
It poured and poured, faster and <u>faster</u>
Until there was almost a major __3.__ !
Then it happened. What a sight!
Everyone running to get a bite.
They ran for the jar they all thought so <u>treasurable</u>.
In it was something smooth and __4.__.
Could it be? Could that explain their <u>ways</u>?
Surely they weren't eating all the __5.__ !
No, it was just a <u>diversion</u>,
Surely it was a very strange __6.__ !

A
1. amusing
2. drizzle
3. disaster
4. pleasurable
5. mayonnaise
6. excursion

B
1. amusing
2. mayonnaise
3. excursion
4. disaster
5. drizzle
6. pleasurable

B. Write the challenge word associated with each set of words.

1. joke, silly song, comics
2. salad dressing, sandwich spread, egg salad
3. ferryboat ride, field day, family hike
4. earthquake, forest fire, plane crash
5. cloud, sleet, light rain
6. fun, enjoyable, pleasing

235

Challenge Word Test Sentences

1. He put **mayonnaise** on the bread before he made a sandwich.
2. The baseball game was played through a slight **drizzle**.
3. In fact, the entire game was a complete **disaster**.
4. The baseball team didn't find that a bit **amusing**.
5. My class at school took an **excursion** to the mountains.
6. The trip was **pleasurable** as well as interesting.

| discovered | satisfied | overlapped |
| discovering | satisfying | overlapping |

A. Write the challenge word or words that were formed by following these rules.

1. + **ed** only
2. change **y** to **i** + **ed**
3. double final consonant + **ed**
4.–5. + **ing** only
6. double final consonant + **ing**

B. Write the challenge word that can be used as a synonym for the group of words given below.

1. fulfilling, convincing, gratifying
2. found, came upon, learned
3. coincided partly, extended over, shingled

C. Use the correct ending for each word in parentheses to complete the sentences. Write the challenge words.

1. He is (overlap) the wallpaper as he hangs it.
2. The teacher is not (satisfy) with our test results.
3. Scientists are (discover) new things every day.

D. Write a short report about the things a group of friends can do or share together. Mention the satisfactions or rewards that come from sharing experiences as a group. Use some of the challenge words.

A
Order of answers 4 and 5 may vary.
1. discovered
2. satisfied
3. overlapped
4. discovering
5. satisfying
6. overlapping

B
1. satisfying
2. discovered
3. overlapped

C
1. overlapping
2. satisfied
3. discovering

D
Answers will vary.

236

Challenge Word Test Sentences

1. **Discovering** fire was important to the caveman.
2. The fossil of the rare fish was **discovered** in a cave.
3. My books and papers **overlapped** the edge of my desk.
4. It was very **satisfying** to receive a good grade on my paper.
5. My teacher was quite **satisfied** with my book report.
6. The boards on the house are **overlapping** each other.

Challenge Activities

| rhinoceros | symptom | naphtha |
| rhubarb | subpoena | condemn |

A. What do you associate with certain occupations? Answer each question below with a challenge word.

1. What might a pie baker use?
2. What might a lawyer send someone?
3. What might a dry cleaner use to get out stains?
4. What might a doctor check a patient for?
5. What might a zookeeper show off?
6. What might a building inspector do to a dilapidated building?

B. Decide what the challenge word is for each clue. Write the challenge word.

1. I am a liquid made from coal. I am used as fuel or as a spot remover.
2. I am a written summons to appear in a court of law.
3. I am a plant used for making sauces or pies.
4. I am what you do to someone or something you disapprove of strongly.
5. I am a change in the normal working of the body that shows sickness.
6. I am a large thick-skinned mammal with horns.

C. You are a newspaper reporter who wants to know everything and find out who is the busiest person in town. Use the cast of characters given in Activity A. Write your findings and your final decision. Give reasons for your decision. Use challenge words where you can.

A
1. rhubarb
2. subpoena
3. naphtha
4. symptom
5. rhinoceros
6. condemn

B
1. naphtha
2. subpoena
3. rhubarb
4. condemn
5. symptom
6. rhinoceros

C
Answers will vary.

237

Challenge Word Test Sentences

1. The giant **rhinoceros** lives in the grasslands.
2. You should not **condemn** anyone until you know the whole story.
3. The **subpoena** said to appear before the judge on Monday.
4. A fever may be a **symptom** of the common cold.
5. Mom will make a pie from the **rhubarb** growing in our garden.
6. Dad got a pint of **naphtha** to clean his paintbrush.

Challenge Activities

quizzical	irritate	plummeted
rapport	possession	propeller

A
1. plummeted
2. propeller
3. quizzical
4. irritate
5. rapport
6. possession

B
1. rapport
2. irritate
3. propeller
4. quizzical
5. plummeted
6. possession

C
Answers will vary.

A. Choose a challenge word that is more descriptive than the underlined word in each sentence. Write the word.

1. The two kites collided and <u>fell</u> to the ground.
2. A mechanic repaired the <u>fanlike device</u> on the boat.
3. The student had a <u>perplexed</u> expression on his face because he didn't understand the question.
4. Some soaps <u>bother</u> my skin.
5. My friend and I have a good <u>relationship</u> because we agree on many things.
6. Ellen has many books in her <u>holding</u>.

B. Write the challenge word that is suggested by each situation. Look for hidden clues in each statement.

1. "You and I get along," said one musician to another.
2. "You rub me the wrong way," said the dog to the flea.
3. "You can't move without oars," said the plane forcefully to the boat.
4. "How does this thing work?" the customer asked the salesperson.
5. "I hope this parachute opens!" said the skydiver.
6. "Everything here is mine!" said the spoiled child.

C. Choose a living being from the animal kingdom that you might like to be for a day. Then write a short story as if you were that animal. Mention the things you might value. For example, if you were a bird you might value nature, freedom, and communicating with other birds. Use some of the challenge words in your story.

238

Challenge Word Test Sentences

1. There was a **propeller** on each wing of the airplane.
2. The hawk **plummeted** from the sky and tried to catch a fish in the brook.
3. A small speck of dirt can **irritate** your eye.
4. The teacher had excellent **rapport** with his students.
5. As the pianist read the review, a **quizzical** look crossed her face.
6. Her stuffed brown bear was her favorite **possession**.

| breakable | perceptible | amiable |
| deductible | understandable | digestible |

A. Think of a synonym for each verb below. Then add the suffix **-able** or **-ible** to the base of each synonym. Write the new adjective. Each answer should be a challenge word.

1. smash
2. comprehend
3. subtract
4. consume

B. Write the challenge word that relates to each pair of words.

1. visible, discernible
2. pleasant, agreeable
3. satisfying, nourishing

C. Write challenge words to complete the paragraph.

  Amy wants to open her own savings account at a bank. She knows how to manage her money. The application form is easy to fill out. It is __1.__. The bank clerks are very helpful and __2.__. They'll explain to Amy that a service charge is added to her monthly statement. This charge is automatically __3.__ and will be subtracted from her savings each month. If there is any problem with Amy's account, the clerks will observe it quickly. Problems are very __4.__. The only thing they'll warn Amy about is not to bring her piggy bank with her. It is __5.__!

D. It's tax time! Imagine that you are an IRS official collecting taxes from people. How will you act with these people when they come to your office? What will you tell them? Write your answers using challenge words or forms of them. For example, you might use **digest** to mean **comprehend** rather than use the word **digestible**.

A
1. breakable
2. understandable
3. deductible
4. digestible

B
1. perceptible
2. amiable
3. digestible

C
1. understandable
2. amiable
3. deductible
4. perceptible
5. breakable

D
Answers will vary.

Challenge Word Test Sentences

1. The circus clown was **amiable** toward his young audience.
2. Be careful with that vase, because porcelain is **breakable**.
3. The more you chew your food, the more **digestible** it is.
4. The difference between black and white is very **perceptible**.
5. We will list the **deductible** items on our tax form.
6. His success at football was **understandable** because of his great speed.

Challenge Activities

mispronounce	antidote	nondescript
misunderstand	nonchalant	nonproductive

A
1. nonchalant
2. nondescript
3. misunderstand
4. mispronounce
5. nonproductive
6. antidote

B
1. misunderstand
2. nondescript
3. antidote
4. nonchalant
5. nonproductive
6. mispronounce

C
Answers will vary.

A. Write a challenge word to complete each analogy.

1. **Warm** is to **enthusiastic** as **cool** is to _____.
2. **Particular** is to **distinctive** as **common** is to _____.
3. **Grasp** is to **comprehend** as **confuse** is to _____.
4. **Distinct** is to **enunciate** as **mumbled** is to _____.
5. **Idle** is to **profitless** as **useless** is to _____.
6. **Infection** is to **poison** as **healing** is to _____.

B. Read the first sentence. Complete the second sentence with a challenge word.

1. People take your meaning the wrong way. They _____.
2. The houses had no particular style. They were _____.
3. What the patient needs is something that will counteract the poison. The patient needs an _____.
4. She was so casual that she didn't seem to have a care in the world. She was _____.
5. This factory must be shut down because it hasn't yielded much in years. It is _____.
6. I thought your name rhymed with **cane**. Did I _____ it?

C. You collect strange and funny mistakes in news stories. Give examples from your own "collection." Be as creative as you like. You could record an example of a word that a famous politician might have mispronounced. You could also tell about the time when a reporter, who was sent to cover a famous, colorful wedding, wrote that the guests and the wedding decorations were nondescript! Use challenge words or forms of them in your examples.

240

Challenge Word Test Sentences

1. The runner was very **nonchalant** about his win in the hundred-yard dash.
2. It is easy to see how a student could **mispronounce** that difficult word.
3. The doctor used a common **antidote** for the snakebite.
4. The factory was **nonproductive** because it lacked raw materials.
5. The little puppy was a plain, **nondescript** animal.
6. Did the new student **misunderstand** the teacher's directions?

Challenge Activities

| leverage | puzzlement | enrichment |
| breakage | detriment | compartment |

A. Write a challenge word to complete each analogy.

1. **Handicap** is to **disadvantage** as **benefit** is to _____.
2. **Content** is to **contentment** as **enrich** is to _____.
3. **Bewilder** is to **problem** as **confuse** is to _____.
4. **Building** is to **construction** as **smashing** is to _____.
5. **House** is to **room** as **toolbox** is to _____.
6. **Help** is to **harm** as **well-being** is to _____.

B. Write a challenge word to complete each sentence.

1. Each small _____ in a stable is called a **stall**.
2. The boy did not understand the question, and his _____ showed on his face.
3. Falling into the cold water could be a _____ to her health.
4. They put a wedge under the crowbar to get _____.
5. Music and art provided _____ for the students.
6. Insurance covered any _____ during the shipment of the crystal dishes.

C. Imagine that you are a riding instructor. You love horses, and you want people to learn how to ride them correctly. Your greatest concern is that nobody gets hurt. Write an ad for horseback riding lessons. Use the challenge words.

A
1. leverage
2. enrichment
3. puzzlement
4. breakage
5. compartment
6. detriment

B
1. compartment
2. puzzlement
3. detriment
4. leverage
5. enrichment
6. breakage

C
Answers will vary.

241

Challenge Word Test Sentences

1. They packed the box with cotton to help prevent **breakage**.
2. We used a long pole to get **leverage** on the heavy load.
3. The trip to the museum was a great **enrichment** to the young boy's life.
4. Smoke and smog can be a **detriment** to one's health.
5. His face showed his **puzzlement** at the question.
6. The clue to the mystery was found in the hidden **compartment**.

Challenge Activities

faithful	forceful	troublesome
blameless	countless	speechless

A
1. faithful
2. blameless
3. speechless
4. troublesome
5. forceful
6. countless

B
1. faithful
2. forceful
3. troublesome
4. countless
5. speechless
6. blameless

C
Answers will vary.

A. Write a challenge word to describe each pet.

1. Rex always waits at the door for me to come home, and then he brings me the newspaper. Rex is _____.

2. Fluffy wasn't the cat who broke the dish. She is innocent. Fluffy is _____.

3. Lora, the parrot, was surprised when the cat jumped on her birdcage. For once, she couldn't talk! Lora was _____.

4. Duke is always up to some kind of mischief. This dog gives me more to worry about than all the others. Duke is _____.

5. Twinkle is strong and full of drive. She protects her food from the other cats. Twinkle is _____.

6. Silver is a guppy. She and Pewter, my other fish, have had lots of baby guppies. Their offspring are _____.

B. Write a synonym for each word in Column A. Write an antonym for each word in Column B. Use challenge words.

Column A
1. loyal
2. powerful
3. difficult

Column B
4. limited
5. talkative
6. guilty

C. Write five different descriptions of a dog or a cat whose behavior could be associated with challenge words. Give clues. You may use Activity A as a guide. Then exchange papers with a partner to identify each other's descriptions.

242

Challenge Word Test Sentences

1. The factory workers were very **forceful** in their effort to get more pay.
2. The bus made **countless** stops on the way to the city.
3. The little puppy was **faithful** to its kind owner.
4. The driver was found to be **blameless** for the accident.
5. The division problem in math was quite **troublesome** for the young student.
6. The soprano's beautiful solo left the audience **speechless**.

Challenge Activities

videotape	volleyball	hindsight
bookmobile	public school	weather-beaten

A. Make each challenge word by matching a word in Column A with a word in Column B. Write the challenge word.

Column A	Column B
1. weather	school
2. hind	ball
3. book	sight
4. volley	tape
5. public	beaten
6. video	mobile

B. Write a challenge word to answer each question.

1. What would you be watching if you were looking at a prerecorded TV show?

2. What would you be using to figure out past events that you didn't fully understand at the time?

3. What would you call wood or a house that is worn by exposure to the weather?

4. What would you be looking at if you saw a truck with book-lined shelves that is used as a traveling library?

5. What game would you be playing if you hit a ball back and forth across a net with your hands?

6. What place is supported by taxes and provides free education to children in a community?

C. Think of an ideal campsite. What would it look like? What things could you do there? Write your description using challenge words. Then interview someone who has gone to camp. Review your paper. What things would you change?

A
1. weather-beaten
2. hindsight
3. bookmobile
4. volleyball
5. public school
6. videotape

B
1. videotape
2. hindsight
3. weather-beaten
4. bookmobile
5. volleyball
6. public school

C
Answers will vary.

Challenge Word Test Sentences

1. **Hindsight** is understanding an event after it has happened.
2. The **bookmobile** stops at our school every Thursday.
3. Our team viewed the **videotape** of the game last Saturday.
4. My **volleyball** team lost three players due to injury.
5. There was a **weather-beaten** barn on the farm.
6. There is an adult night class at the local **public school**.

Unit 25 — Challenge Activities

extemporary	dietary	immaculate
culinary	intricate	considerate

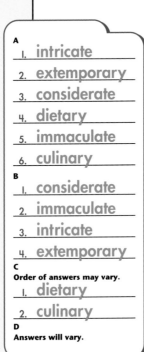

A
1. intricate
2. extemporary
3. considerate
4. dietary
5. immaculate
6. culinary

B
1. considerate
2. immaculate
3. intricate
4. extemporary

C
Order of answers may vary.
1. dietary
2. culinary

D

Answers will vary.

A. Write the challenge word that completes each description.

1. I am not simple. I have a complicated pattern. I am an ____ design.
2. I don't like to plan things. I like to do and say ____ things.
3. I am thoughtful and ____ about other people's feelings.
4. I am a list of ____ rules that tell what foods to eat and how to prepare them for healthful living.
5. I always make sure that my clothes are clean, in good repair, and without wrinkles. My clothes are ____.
6. I have studied many cookbooks and produced extraordinary meals. I possess ____ skills.

B. Write a challenge word to describe the opposite kind of person or thing described below.

1. A person who does not take into account other people's feelings.
2. A room that is quite messy and dirty.
3. An uncomplicated story with no plot twists.
4. Dialogue in a play that is written and rehearsed.

C. 1.–2. Write the two challenge words that relate to food.

D. Complete this story about the life of a dancer. Use the challenge words in your story.

I love to dance, but the life of a professional dancer is not easy. For example, I must practice every day. I must watch my weight all the time.

244

Challenge Word Test Sentences

1. His **extemporary** movements caused much concern to the defense.
2. The mayor and council were very **considerate** of all the people in their town.
3. The machine cut a pattern that was very **intricate**.
4. My doctor gave me a list of **dietary** restrictions.
5. The cook's **culinary** ability was known throughout the kingdom.
6. The woman who cleans the church keeps everything **immaculate**.

Challenge Activities

midyear	interject	substandard
interfere	superpower	underlying

A. Prefixes and bases are mismatched in the challenge words below. Write these words correctly.

1. midject
2. interpower
3. interyear
4. superfere

B. Write the challenge word that would be found on a dictionary page with each pair of guide words below.

1. Superior, Lake | supper
2. intention | interim
3. subset | suburb
4. interior | intern
5. undergo | understand

C. Use a challenge word to replace the underlined combination that matches it in meaning.

1. Shane got an A on his <u>middle-annual</u> exam.
2. In my opinion, this car is <u>below an acceptable level of quality</u>.
3. The <u>beneath-the-surface</u> reason for my lateness is that I overslept.

D. Imagine you are a sports announcer at an imaginary sports game of your choice. The team that all the experts expected would win the game is losing badly. What is going wrong? Write an explanation of why the team is losing so badly. Use challenge words in your explanation.

A
Order of answers 2 and 3 may vary.
1. midyear
2. interfere
3. interject
4. superpower

B
1. superpower
2. interfere
3. substandard
4. interject
5. underlying

C
1. midyear
2. substandard
3. underlying

D
Answers will vary.

245

Challenge Word Test Sentences

1. The **underlying** reason for our victory was constant practice.
2. The **substandard** product was produced from poor material.
3. My teacher wants us to **interject** our ideas into each class discussion.
4. I asked my baby sister not to **interfere** with my piano practice.
5. The new students all knew the routine by **midyear**.
6. One **superpower** is the United States.

Challenge Activities

hideous	anxious	harmonious
monstrous	contagious	treacherous

A. Write the challenge word that fits both definitions.

1. **a.** agreeable; **b.** pleasing to the ear
2. **a.** very ugly; **b.** frightful
3. **a.** like a monster; **b.** huge
4. **a.** worried; **b.** eager
5. **a.** tending to spread from person to person, as in yawning; **b.** easily catching, as in a disease
6. **a.** disloyal; **b.** dangerous

B. Write a challenge word to complete each sentence. Next to each challenge word write the letter **a** or **b** for the meaning given in Activity A that matches the use of the word in the sentence.

1. The feeling of excitement and anticipation spread like a ripple of _____ laughter throughout the grandstand.
2. The cheerleaders sang a lovely, _____ cheer.
3. One team mascot was _____ in size.
4. The other team mascot was a person in a _____ disguise.
5. The fans were _____ about the outcome of the game.
6. The mountain road didn't cause the bus driver immediate alarm, but it turned out to be _____.

C. What do you know about ice hockey? How dangerous is it? How exciting is it? Write your own similes, using the challenge words to describe the game. For example, you can use your own version of "as happy as a clam" in this way: The players are as harmonious as clams.

246

Answer key (margin)

A
1. harmonious
2. hideous
3. monstrous
4. anxious
5. contagious
6. treacherous

B
1. contagious, a
2. harmonious, b
3. monstrous, b
4. hideous, a
5. anxious, a
6. treacherous, b

C
Answers will vary.

Challenge Word Test Sentences

1. A tenor and a soprano sang a **harmonious** duet.
2. Many students missed school because of a **contagious** disease.
3. The **monstrous** bird flew down from the tree.
4. The five-headed creature in the movie had **hideous** purple hair.
5. The rocks in the stream were **treacherous** for small boats.
6. We were very **anxious** to see our aunt again.

Challenge Activities

sherbet	banquet	luncheon
guidance	naive	jeopardize

A. Write the challenge word that answers each question.

1. Suppose you were invited to eat lunch to celebrate the annual gymnastics contest. Would you go to a lunchon or a luncheon?

2. If you wanted to eat a frozen, fruit-flavored dessert, would you order a sherbet or a shebert?

3. For a special event, would the large meal be a banquet or a banqet?

4. If the star gymnast was an adult but thought like a child, would he or she be niave or naive?

5. Would the coach give the athletes guidance or giudance?

6. Would an accident jeopardize or jepardize an athlete's career?

B. Write the challenge word or words you associate with the following things.

1.–3. three things associated with food

4. something associated with leadership

5. a word associated with risk

6. a word associated with a childlike quality

C. You are invited to a luncheon in honor of your favorite famous athlete. Write a testimonial, or a speech showing admiration, for your favorite athlete. Don't forget to thank the sponsors of the event for the food they have provided! Use challenge words in your testimonial.

A
1. luncheon
2. sherbet
3. banquet
4. naive
5. guidance
6. jeopardize

B
Order of answers 1, 2, and 3 may vary.
1. sherbet
2. banquet
3. luncheon
4. guidance
5. jeopordize
6. naive

C
Answers will vary.

247

Challenge Word Test Sentences

1. Young children need a lot of **guidance** from their parents.
2. A **luncheon** was planned for the former town mayor.
3. My favorite late-night snack is orange **sherbet**.
4. If you eat too much, you can **jeopardize** your health.
5. The **naive** bunny went for a walk with a fox.
6. The prize was given at a special **banquet**.

Challenge Activities

connection	collection	donation
contribution	recession	explanation

A Order of answers may vary.

1. connection
2. collection
3. recession
4. donation
5. contribution
6. explanation

B

1. donation
2. connection
3. explanation
4. contribution
5. recession
6. collection

C Answers will vary.

A. Write the challenge words that fit each spelling rule below.

    1.–3. Add the suffix **-ion** to the base word with no spelling change.

    4.–5. Drop **e** to add **-ion** to the base word.

      6. Change the base word before adding the suffix **-ion**.

B. Write the challenge word (a noun) that is made from each verb below.

    1. donate   **4.** contribute

    2. connect   **5.** recess

    3. explain   **6.** collect

C. Suppose you and your classmates wanted to set up a fund to repair the old pool in the school gym so that the swimming team can use it. Make a list of several activities that might be good fund-raisers. Then choose one activity and write a plan for carrying it out. Include challenge words in your written plans.

Challenge Word Test Sentences

    1. My mom has a large **collection** of milk glass.

    2. It is hard to hear when the phone **connection** is poor.

    3. The governor said the **recession** would be over soon.

    4. Our **contribution** to the museum helped raise money to build the new wing.

    5. Our family always gives a big **donation** to the fire department.

    6. His **explanation** for why he was late was a fib.

Challenge Activities

auctioneer	pediatrician	defendant
historian	vice president	contestant

A. Write the challenge word that describes each of the following persons.

1. one who holds the second place in authority
2. one who is an expert in or writes about important past events
3. one who conducts a public sale of things to be sold for the most money offered
4. one who takes part in a game or a race
5. one who specializes in the branch of medicine dealing with children and their diseases
6. one who is accused or sued in a court of law

B. Write the challenge word formed from each base word below.

1. defend
2. auction
3. contest
4. history
5. pediatric
6. preside

C. Make headings for six columns by using the challenge words. List other people that each person listed might encounter in the course of a day. Some of your lists will probably be longer than others. Then select one list. Use some of the people as characters for a short play. What will your setting be? What names will you give your characters? What will they say? What will be the plot and the climax of your play? How will it end? After you have considered answers to these questions, write your play.

A
1. vice president
2. historian
3. auctioneer
4. contestant
5. pediatrician
6. defendant

B
1. defendant
2. auctioneer
3. contestant
4. historian
5. pediatrician
6. vice president

C
Answers will vary.

249

Challenge Word Test Sentences

1. The artist asked the **auctioneer** to sell his artwork.
2. That **contestant** will be difficult to defeat in the spelling bee.
3. The **vice president** represented the company at the meeting.
4. Father took my baby sister to the **pediatrician** for her monthly checkup.
5. We found the **historian** reading books in the library.
6. The judge said the **defendant** was innocent of all charges.

Challenge Activities

admittance	annoyance	diligence
reluctance	existence	indifference

A
1. annoyance
2. existence
3. admittance
4. indifference

B
1. reluctance
2. diligence

C
1. admittance
2. annoyance
3. diligence
4. reluctance
5. indifference
6. existence

D
Answers will vary.

A. Write the challenge word that is formed when **-ance** or **-ence** is added to each verb below.

1. annoy
2. exist
3. admit
4. differ

B. Write the challenge word that is an antonym for each of these words.

1. eagerness
2. laziness

C. Write a challenge word for each meaning below.

1. permission to enter
2. feeling of irritation or impatience
3. careful and steady effort
4. unwillingness
5. lack of interest or caring
6. being; life

D. Some of the challenge words on this list have or imply positive meanings. Other words have or imply negative meanings. Choose the words that fall into the first category, and write what they mean to you and what situations they suggest. Then do the same thing with the words that fall into the second category. Add other words and explanations of your own to each category.

250

Challenge Word Test Sentences

1. The **indifference** of the cyclist almost caused an accident.
2. The **diligence** of the basketball player during practice paid off in the game.
3. Many insects are a major **annoyance** to local farmers.
4. The horse and pony entered the barn with **reluctance**.
5. **Admittance** to the theme park was only ten dollars for a family.
6. Scientists believe in the **existence** of life on other planets.

Challenge Activities

verses	cession	palate
versus	session	pallet

A. Choose the correct homophone in parentheses to answer each question. Write the appropriate challenge word.

1. What might a person sleep on? (palate, pallet)
2. What part of the mouth do you use when you eat? (palate, pallet)
3. What might a poet write? (versus, verses)
4. What is a synonym for **against**? (versus, verses)
5. What might you call a meeting or a period of lessons? (cession, session)
6. What describes the act of giving up territory to another country? (cession, session)

B. Write the homophone that completes each sentence.

1. The biggest game of the school year is almost always the Reds _____ the Blues. (verses, versus)
2. The dentist looked at my mouth, especially the _____. (pallet, palate)
3. We signed up for a _____ of swimming lessons. (cession, session)
4. Do you only like _____ that rhyme? (versus, verses)
5. I'd rather sleep on a fluffy mattress than a _____. (palate, pallet)
6. The victorious nation demanded the conquered country complete a _____ of its lands. (session, cession)

C. Write a mixed-up message for one of the words in each pair of challenge words that are homophones. Then trade messages with a partner and correct the mistakes.

A
1. pallet
2. palate
3. verses
4. versus
5. session
6. cession

B
1. versus
2. palate
3. session
4. verses
5. pallet
6. cession

C
Answers will vary.

251

Challenge Word Test Sentences
1. The roof of the mouth is called the hard **palate**.
2. The town council holds a special **session** to decide on a curfew.
3. It is the farmer **versus** the elements in many rural areas.
4. A poet may write several **verses** in a short time.
5. The stock boy used a lift to put the heavy boxes on the **pallet**.
6. The **cession** of the western lands was considered a major loss to that country.

Challenge Activities

bibliography	altimeter	biologist
lexicographer	telephoto	antibiotic

A
1. bibliography
2. lexicographer
3. altimeter
4. biologist
5. antibiotic
6. telephoto

B
1. telephoto
2. antibiotic
3. altimeter
4. lexicographer
5. bibliography
6. biologist

C
Answers will vary.

A. Rearrange the word elements to form a word. Write the challenge word.

   1. graph y biblio
   2. lexico er graph
   3. meter alti
   4. log ist bio
   5. bio tic anti
   6. photo tele

B. Write a challenge word to complete each sentence.

   1. I put the _____ lens on my camera to get a good shot of some distant birds.
   2. Penicillin is an _____ that doctors sometimes prescribe.
   3. The pilot studied the measuring device called an _____ while the plane was in flight.
   4. **Lexis** means **word**, and the person who writes a dictionary is called a _____.
   5. Our social studies books usually have a list of books, or a _____, referring to the topic of the unit.
   6. A person who studies living organisms is known as a _____.

C. Use the information in Activity B to write a "Who or what am I" riddle for each challenge word. Add other words from Greek words or forms and write riddles for them, too.

252

Challenge Word Test Sentences
1. The photographer used a **telephoto** lens to take the picture of the plane in the sky.
2. The **altimeter** of the airplane showed that we were flying at twenty thousand feet.
3. The **bibliography** in the back of the book gave us much information.
4. The juice from a rare plant was the base for the new **antibiotic**.
5. The **biologist** worked to discover the life cycle of that rare plant.
6. A **lexicographer** is a person who puts together or writes a dictionary.

Challenge Activities

emcee	Fortran	NASA
R.S.V.P.	COBOL	NATO

A. An **acronym** is a word or name that is created by combining the first letters in a group of words. For example, **radar** is an acronym made from "**ra**dio **d**etection **a**nd **r**anging."

Write the acronym for each group of words below. Use challenge words.

1. North Atlantic Treaty Organization
2. Common business-oriented language
3. National Aeronautics and Space Administration
4. Formula translation
5. répondez s'il vous plaît
6. master of ceremonies

B. A challenge word is used incorrectly in each sentence. Write the correct challenge word for each sentence.

1. The talent show was a huge success, and the NATO did a great job as the announcer.
2. At the end of the invitation, there was a request for a reply, or a COBOL.
3. The sign at the space research building read Fortran.
4. To solve the math problems, use the programming language called NATO.
5. The member countries of NASA agree to protect one another from attack by outside aggressors.
6. The scientists used emcee to program their work.

C. Write an invitation for a fund-raising event for a space agency or an international organization. Use as many challenge words as possible in your invitation.

A
1. NATO
2. COBOL
3. NASA
4. Fortran
5. R.S.V.P.
6. emcee

B
1. emcee
2. R.S.V.P.
3. NASA
4. Fortran
5. NATO
6. COBOL

C
Answers will vary.

253

Challenge Word Test Sentences

1. You should send an **R.S.V.P.** whether you go to the party or not.
2. The famous **emcee** gave a short speech before the luncheon.
3. **NASA** has plans to build a space station.
4. **COBOL** is a language that is used in many computer programs.
5. Another language used by computers is **Fortran**.
6. For safety reasons, **NATO** put guards at each door.

WRITER'S HANDBOOK
Contents

The list of high frequency writing words on pages 262–266 was taken from *Teaching Kids to Spell* by J. Richard Gentry and Jean Gillet (Heinemann, 1993).

254

T254

255

Spelling Strategy
When You Take a Test

1 **Get** ready for the test. Make sure your paper and pencil are ready.

2 **Listen** carefully as your teacher says each word and uses it in a sentence. Don't write before you hear the word **and** the sentence.

3 **Write** the word carefully. Make sure your handwriting is easy to read. If you want to print your words, ask your teacher.

4 **Use** a pen to correct your test. Look at the word as your teacher says it.

5 **Say** the word aloud. Listen carefully as your teacher spells the word. Say each letter aloud. Check the word one letter at a time.

6 **Circle** any misspelled parts of the word.

7 **Look** at the correctly written word. Spell the word again. Say each letter out loud.

8 **Write** any misspelled word correctly.

Spelling Strategy
When You Write a Paper

1 **Think** of the exact word you want to use.

2 **Write** the word, if you know how to spell it.

3 **Say** the word to yourself, if you are not sure how to spell it.

4 **Picture** what the word looks like when you see it written.

5 **Write** the word.

6 **Ask** yourself whether the word looks right.

7 **Check** the word in a dictionary if you are not sure.

SPELLING AND THE Writing Process

Writing anything—a friendly letter, a paper for school—usually follows a process. The writing process has five steps. It might look like this if you tried to draw a picture of it:

Notice that part of the writing process forms a loop. That is because not every writing task is the same. It is also because writers often jump back and forth between the steps as they change their minds and think of new ideas.

Here is a description of each step:

Prewriting This is thinking and planning ahead to help you write.

Drafting This means writing your paper for the first time. You usually just try to get your ideas down on paper. You can fix them later.

Revising This means fixing your final draft. Here is where you rewrite, change, and add words.

Editing This is where you feel you have said all you want to say. Now you proofread your paper for spelling errors and errors in grammar and punctuation.

Publishing This is making a copy of your writing and sharing it with your readers. Put your writing in a form that your readers will enjoy.

Confident spellers are better writers. Confident writers understand better their own writing process. Know the five steps. Know how they best fit the way you write.

258

SPELLING AND Writing Ideas

Being a good speller can help make you a more confident writer. Writing more can make you a better writer. Here are some ideas to get you started.

Ideas for Descriptive Writing

You might…

- describe something very, very small and something very, very big.
- describe something from the point of view of an insect.
- describe your most prized possession.

Ideas for Narrative Writing

You might…

- write a story about your first visit to someplace new.
- write a story about an event that helped you "grow up."
- write a story about a bad day or a best day playing your favorite sport.

Ideas for Persuasive Writing

You might…

- try to persuade your classmates to read a book you like.
- try to persuade your parents to let you have a pet.
- try to persuade your teacher to change a class rule.

Ideas for Expository Writing

You might…

- write how to prepare your favorite dish.
- inform your classmates how to create a craft object.
- write instructions on how to care for a lawn mower or carpentry tool.

More Ideas for Expository Writing

You might…

- find out how your local government works and write a report.
- interview an animal caregiver and write a report about the job.
- choose a career you might like and write a report about it.

259

Manuscript Handwriting Models

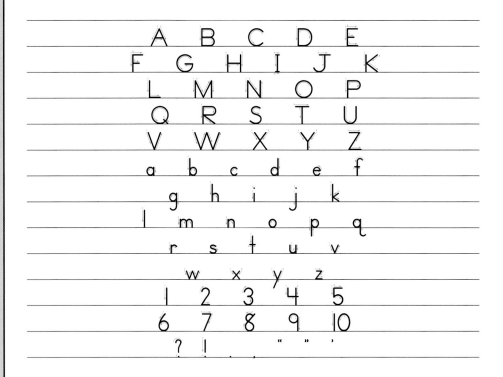

A B C D E
F G H I J K
L M N O P
Q R S T U
V W X Y Z
a b c d e f
g h i j k
l m n o p q
r s t u v
w x y z
1 2 3 4 5
6 7 8 9 10
? ! . , " " '

Cursive Handwriting Models

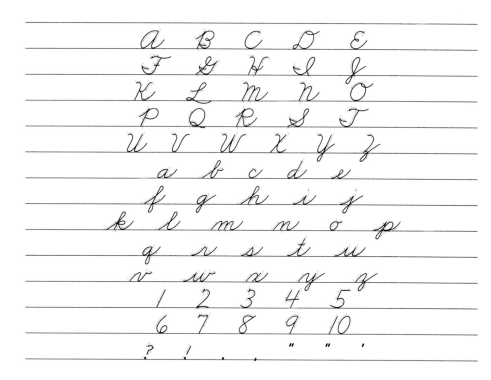

A B C D E
F G H I J
K L M N O
P Q R S T
U V W X Y Z
a b c d e
f g h i j
k l m n o p
q r s t u
v w x y z
1 2 3 4 5
6 7 8 9 10
? ! . , " " .

261

High Frequency Writing Words

A

a
about
afraid
after
again
air
all
almost
also
always
am
America
an
and
animal
animals
another
any
anything
are
around
as
ask
asked
at
ate

away

B

baby
back
bad
ball
balloons
baseball
basketball
be
bear
beautiful
because
become
bed
been
before
being
believe
best
better
big
bike
black
boat
book

books
both
boy
boys
bring
broke
brother
build
bus
but
buy
by

C

call
called
came
can
candy
can't
car
care
cars
cat
catch
caught
change

charge
children
Christmas
circus
city
class
clean
clothes
come
comes
coming
could
couldn't
country
cut

D

Dad
day
days
decided
did
didn't
died
different
dinner
do

does
doesn't
dog
dogs
doing
don't
done
door
down
dream

E

each
earth
eat
eighth
else
end
enough
even
every
everybody
everyone
everything
except
eyes

F

family
fast
father
favorite
feel
feet
fell
few
field
fight
finally
find
fire
first
fish
five
fix
food
football
for
found
four
free
Friday
friend
friends
from

front
fun
funny
future

G

game
games
gas
gave
get
gets
getting
girl
girls
give
go
God
goes
going
good
got
grade
grader
great
ground
grow

H

had
hair
half
happened
happy
hard
has
have
having
he
head
heard
help
her
here
he's
high
hill
him
his
hit
home
homework
hope
horse
horses
hot

263

High Frequency Writing Words (continued)

hour
house
how
hurt

I

I
I'd
if
I'm
important
in
into
is
it
its
it's

J

job
jump
just

K

keep
kept
kids

killed
kind
knew
know

L

lady
land
last
later
learn
leave
left
let
let's
life
like
liked
likes
little
live
lived
lives
long
look
looked
looking
lost

lot
lots
love
lunch

M

mad
made
make
making
man
many
math
may
maybe
me
mean
men
might
miss
Mom
money
more
morning
most
mother
mouse
move

Mr.
Mrs.
much
music
must
my
myself

N

name
named
need
never
new
next
nice
night
no
not
nothing
now

O

of
off
oh
OK
old

on
once
one
only
or
other
our
out
outside
over
own

P

parents
park
party
people
person
pick
place
planet
play
played
playing
police
president
pretty
probably

problem
put

R

ran
read
ready
real
really
reason
red
responsibilities
rest
ride
riding
right
room
rules
run
running

S

said
same
saw
say
scared
school

schools
sea
second
see
seen
set
seventh
she
ship
shot
should
show
sick
since
sister
sit
sleep
small
snow
so
some
someone
something
sometimes
soon
space
sport
sports

start
started
states
stay
still
stop
stopped
store
story
street
stuff
such
sudden
suddenly
summer
sure
swimming

T

take
talk
talking
teach
teacher
teachers
team
tell
than

265

Thanksgiving
that
that's
the
their
them
then
there
these
they
they're
thing
things
think
this
thought
three
through
throw
time
times
to
today
together
told
too
took

top
tree
trees
tried
trip
trouble
try
trying
turn
turned
TV
two

U

united
until
up
upon
us
use
used

V

very

W

walk
walked
walking
want
wanted
war
was
wasn't
watch
water
way
we
week
weeks
well
went
were
what
when
where
which
while
white
who
whole
why

will
win
winter
wish
with
without
woke
won
won't
work
world
would
wouldn't

Y

yard
year
years
yes
you
your
you're

266

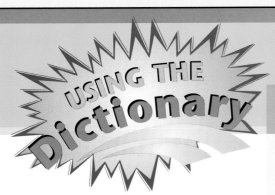
USING THE Dictionary

Guide Words

The **guide words** at the top of each dictionary page can help you find the word you want quickly. The first guide word tells you the first word on that page. The second guide word tells you the last word on that page. The entries on the page fall in alphabetical order between these two guide words.

Entries

Words you want to check in the dictionary are called **entries**. Entries provide a lot of information besides the correct spelling. Look at the sample entry below.

Tips for Finding a Word in a Dictionary

- Practice using guide words in a dictionary. Think of words to spell. Then use the guide words to find each word's entry. Do this again and again until you can use guide words easily.

- Some spellings are listed with the base word. To find **easiest,** you would look up **easy**. To find **remaining,** you would look up **remain**. To find **histories,** you would look up **history**.

- If you do not know how to spell a word, guess the spelling before looking it up. Try to find the first three letters of the word. (If you just use the first letter, you will probably take too long.)

- If you can't find a word, think of how else it might be spelled. For example, if a word starts with the **/k/ sound,** the spelling might begin with **k, c,** or even **ch**.

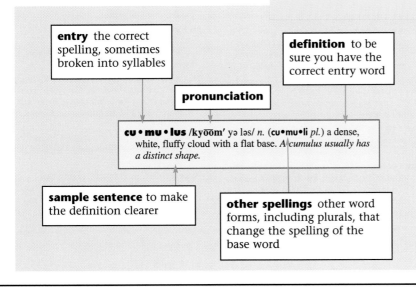

entry the correct spelling, sometimes broken into syllables

pronunciation

definition to be sure you have the correct entry word

cu • mu • lus /kyōōm′ yə ləs/ *n.* (**cu•mu•li** *pl.*) a dense, white, fluffy cloud with a flat base. *A cumulus usually has a distinct shape.*

sample sentence to make the definition clearer

other spellings other word forms, including plurals, that change the spelling of the base word

Using the Spelling Dictionary

You may wish to use these mini-lessons to help your students better utilize the **Spelling Dictionary**.

Dictionary Mini-Lesson: Pronunciation Key

Tell the students that a **Pronunciation Key** appears on every second page in the **Spelling Dictionary**. Ask the students to find a **Pronunciation Key**. (It first appears on page 269.)

Explain that each symbol in the **Pronunciation Key** represents a sound in the English language. The word(s) that follow each symbol include that sound. The letters that spell the sound in each word are printed in bold type. Tell the students that these symbols are used in the dictionary respellings that appear in the **Spelling Dictionary**.

Remind the students that, in a dictionary respelling, a syllable that receives primary stress, or accent, is printed in bold type and is followed by an accent mark. A syllable that receives secondary stress is printed in regular type and is followed by an accent mark.

---

ab • bre • vi • a • tion /ə brē′ vē ā′ shən/ *n.* a shortened form of a word; a syllable, a letter, or letters standing for a word or words. *"Dr." is an abbreviation for "Doctor."*

-able a suffix, used to form adjectives, that means: **a.** capable of: *understandable.* **b.** worthy of: *lovable.*

ab • sence /ăb′ səns/ *n.* **a.** being away. *Ryan brought a note to excuse his absence.* **b.** not having; a lack: *an absence of interest.*

ab • sent /ăb′ sənt/ *adj.* away; not here. *Kate was absent on Monday but present on Tuesday.*

ac • cent¹ /ăk′ sĕnt/ *n.* **a.** a mark (′) used to show stress. *A syllable with an accent is pronounced more strongly.* **b.** a distinctive way of speaking: *a British accent.*

ac • cent² /ăk′ sĕnt/ *v.* **a.** to stress; to emphasize. *Accent the first syllable.* **b.** to add to; to enhance. *Beth's pink scarf accents her white dress.*

ac • cept • a • ble /ăk sĕp′ tə bəl/ *adj.* (**ac•cept•a•bly,** *adv.*) agreeable; satisfactory. *Everyone at the meeting found the plan acceptable.*

ac • ci • dent /ăk′ sĭ dənt/ *n.* **a.** a harmful or unexpected event. *Ali had an accident on his bike.* **b.** something that occurs without being planned for. *The cure for the disease was discovered by accident.*

ac • cord /ə kôrd′/ *n.* agreement; harmony. *The nations were in accord on the issue of world hunger.*

ac • cu • rate /ăk′ yər ĭt/ *adj.* correct; without mistakes. *The witness's testimony was accurate and consistent with the evidence.*

ac • cuse /ə kyōōz′/ *v.* (**ac•cus•es, ac•cused, ac•cus•ing**) to blame for wrongdoing. *The police accused him of speeding and reckless driving.*

a • chieve /ə chēv′/ *v.* (**a•chieves, a•chieved, a•chiev•ing**) to reach; to accomplish. *If you wish to achieve success you must work hard.*

ac • tion /ăk′ shən/ *n.* **a.** a thing done; a deed. *The firefighter was praised for her brave action.* **b.** motion; movement. *Debbie likes action, but David prefers peace and quiet.*

a • cute /ə kyōōt′/ *adj.* **a.** severe or sharp; intense: *acute pain.* **b.** having fewer than 90 degrees. *A triangle must have at least two acute angles.*

ad • di • tion • al • ly /ə dĭsh′ ə nə lē/ *adv.* also; moreover; in addition. *Additionally, the movie has won international awards.*

ad • mit /ăd′ mĭt′/ *v.* (**ad•mits, ad•mit•ted, ad•mit•ting**) **a.** to let in. *If you don't have a ticket they can't admit you to the show.* **b.** to acknowledge; to confess. *The mayor admitted that she had not been aware of the problem.* [Latin *admittere,* from *ad-,* to + *mittere,* to send.]

a • dor • a • ble /ə dôr′ ə bəl/ or /ə dōr′-/ *adj.* lovable; charming. *The stuffed animals were cuddly and adorable.*

a • dore /ə dôr′/ or /-dōr′/ *v.* (**a•dores, a•dored, a•dor•ing**) to feel deep love and respect for. *Gandhi was adored by millions of Indians.*

ad • vance¹ /ăd văns′/ *v.* to go forward. *Please advance to the front of the line.*

ad • vance² /ăd văns′/ *n.* any forward movement; progress. *Medical research has made great advances.*

ad • vance • ment /ăd văns′ mənt/ *n.* improvement; progress; promotion. *They dedicated their new club to the advancement of poetry.*

ad • van • tage /ăd văn′ tĭj/ *n.* **a.** anything that helps bring about success. *That basketball player has the advantage of being tall.* **b.** help; benefit; gain. *Studying is to your advantage.*

af • ter • ward /ăf′ tər wərd/ *adv.* later. *We'll do some shopping and have lunch afterward.*

-age a suffix, used to form nouns, that means: **a.** a collective or a general group: *baggage.* **b.** a state or condition of: *marriage.* **c.** an act of: *breakage.*

268

Ask volunteers to read the sample words in the **Pronunciation Key** and to name the letters in dark type that spell the sounds. Encourage the class to name other words that have these sounds. Remind the students that two or more letters may spell a single sound. (For example, **ai** spells /ā/ and **dge** spells /j/.)

Pronounce several spelling words and write them on the chalkboard. Ask the students to use the **Pronunciation Key** to write a dictionary respelling for each word. Then ask them to check their answers in the **Spelling Dictionary**.

ag•ed /ā′ jĭd/ *adj.* **a.** old; having lived long. *The aged man was having difficulty walking.* **b.** /ājd/ having a certain age: *aged three.*

a•gent /ā′ jənt/ *n.* **a.** a person or company whose business is to represent another: *an insurance agent.* **b.** a substance that causes a certain action to begin. *Yeast is the agent that causes bread to rise.* [Latin *agēns,* doing, from *agere,* to do.]

ag•ri•cul•ture /ăg′ rĭ kŭl′ chər/ *n.* farming; raising food and farm animals. *We all depend on agriculture for food.*

aisle /īl/ *n.* a passage between rows of seats. *The usher stood in the aisle.*

▶ Aisle sounds like **isle.**

al•bum /ăl′ bəm/ *n.* **a.** a book with blank pages on which photographs, stamps, etc., may be kept. *Will you sign my autograph album?* **b.** a recording of several different pieces of music. *I like the title song on that album.*

all right¹ /ôl′ rīt′/ *adj.* satisfactory. *Your answer looks all right to me.*

all right² /ôl′ rīt′/ *adv.* **a.** yes; very well. *All right, I'll come home early.* **b.** in a satisfactory way. *Is everything going all right?*

al•ly /ăl′ ī/ *n.* (**al•lies** *pl.*) a person or country united with others for a specific purpose. *During World War II the United States and Great Britain were allies.*

al•ma•nac /ôl′ mə năk′/ *n.* a reference book published yearly. *A farmer may read an almanac to find out when to plant crops.*

al•mond /ä′ mənd/ *n.* the nut of the almond tree. *Toasted almonds make a good snack.*

A.M. or **a.m.** an abbreviation meaning in the morning. *My appointment is Tuesday at 10 A.M.* [Latin *ante meridiem,* before noon.]

am•a•teur /ăm′ ə tûr′/ or /-chŏor′/ *n.* a person who participates in an activity for fun, not money. *Even an amateur can become skillful with regular practice.*

a•maze /ə māz′/ *v.* (**a•maz•es, a•mazed, a•maz•ing**) to surprise or astonish. *We were amazed at the acrobat's ability to do high jumps.*

am•bu•lance /ăm′ byə ləns/ *n.* a vehicle for taking people who are hurt or sick to the hospital. *An ambulance is equipped with special lights and a siren.*

ambulance

a•mend•ment /ə mĕnd′ mənt/ *n.* a formal change in a law or a bill. *An amendment to the Constitution gave women the right to vote.*

am•pli•tude /ăm′ plĭ tōōd′/ or /-tyōōd′/ *n.* the distance between the highest and the lowest point of a wave. *As the amplitude of a sound wave increases, so does the loudness of the sound.*

-ance a suffix, used to form nouns, that means: **a.** state or quality of: *resemblance.* **b.** act of: *resistance.* **c.** thing that: *conveyance.*

an•nounce /ə nouns′/ *v.* (**an•nounc•es, an•nounced, an•nounc•ing**) **a.** to tell; to make known; to give notice. *Would the principal announce that school will be closing early?* **b.** to provide commentary and deliver announcements on radio or TV. *The sportscaster announces the tennis match.*

-ant a suffix used with verbs: **a.** to form adjectives that mean "having the quality of": *resistant.* **b.** to form nouns that mean "person or thing that": *assistant.*

anti- a prefix that means "against": *antiseptic.*

an•ti•freeze /ăn′ tĭ frēz′/ *n.* a liquid mixed with another liquid to keep it from freezing. *Cars need antifreeze during the winter.*

Using the Spelling Dictionary

You may wish to use these mini-lessons to help your students better utilize the **Spelling Dictionary**.

Objective

Students will
• **become** familiar with and use the **Spelling Dictionary**.

Dictionary Mini-Lesson: Dictionary Features

Ask the students to name some of the uses of a dictionary. (Dictionaries are used to look up the meanings, spellings, and pronunciations of words. Many dictionaries also give the histories, or etymologies, of words.)

Tell the students that their **Spelling Dictionaries** give them information about their spelling words. As the students look through the **Spelling Dictionary,** point out the following:

• Entry words are listed in alphabetical order, and each word is followed by its respelling, its part of speech, and its definition.

• Each definition is followed by a sentence or phrase that shows how the word is used.

Read the information on the **Using the Dictionary** page in the Student Edition with the students. Use the sample entry and the following additional information to discuss the **Spelling Dictionary:**

an • ti • so • cial /ăn´ tē sō´ shəl/ *adj.* avoiding the company of others. *It is a mistake to assume that a shy person is deliberately antisocial.*

a • pos • tro • phe /ə pŏs´ trə fē/ *n.* a mark (´) used: **a.** to show that a letter or letters have been purposely left out of a word: *it'll, you've.* **b.** to show possession: *Jim's, girls'.*

ap • pear • ance /ə pîr´ əns/ *n.* **a.** being seen by the public. *The TV star made a personal appearance at the shopping mall.* **b.** the looks of a place or person. *New paint really improved the room's appearance.*

ap • pli • cant /ăp´ lĭ kənt/ *n.* a person applying for a job or position. *There were many applicants for the after-school job.*

ap • ply /ə plī´/ *v.* (ap•plies, ap•plied, ap•ply•ing) **a.** to put on: *apply paint.* **b.** to put to use. *We did an experiment to apply what we learned in science.* **c.** to make a request. *She applied to join the Girl Scouts.*

ap • point • ment /ə point´ mənt/ *n.* an arrangement to meet someone at a certain time. *I have a two o'clock appointment.*

ap • pos • i • tive /ə pŏz´ ə tĭv/ *n.* a noun or noun phrase placed next to another noun for further explanation or description. *In the sentence "Brian, Dan's brother, also came," the appositive is "Dan's brother."*

ap • pre • ci • ate /ə prē´ shē āt´/ *v.* (ap•pre•ci•ates, ap•pre•ci•at•ed, ap•pre•ci•at•ing) **a.** to see the value of something. *The recital made us appreciate my brother's hours of piano practice.*

ap • proach /ə prōch´/ *v.* to come near. *The deer ran away as we approached.*

ap • proach • a • ble /ə prō´ chə bəl/ *adj.* friendly; easy to approach. *The librarian's smile made her seem approachable.*

ap • prove /ə prōōv´/ *v.* (ap•proves, ap•proved, ap•prov•ing) **a.** to give official consent to. *The board approved the plans for the new gym.* **b.** to have a good opinion of. *Do you approve of his choice of colors?*

ap • prox • i • mate /ə prŏks´ ə mĭt/ *adj.* nearly right; almost correct. *The architect gave them an approximate cost of the new house.*

ap • ti • tude /ăp´ tĭ tōōd´/ or /-tyōōd´/ *n.* a talent or ability for learning. *She has an aptitude for languages; she speaks French, German, and Italian.*

ar • a • ble /ăr´ ə bəl/ *adj.* able to be farmed or cultivated. *Rocky land is not arable.*

arc /ärk/ *n.* a curved line; a line that is part of a circle. *A famous landmark in St. Louis is an arc.*

arc

a • rise /ə rīz´/ *v.* (a•ris•es, a•rose, a•ris•en, a•ris•ing) **a.** to get up. *On school days we arise early.* **b.** to appear; to begin. *If any problems should arise, phone us at this number.*

ar • ter • y /är´ tə rē/ *n.* (ar•ter•ies *pl.*) any of the body's vessels that carry blood from the heart to all parts of the body. *Which artery carries blood to the brain?*

-ary a suffix that means "of" or "relating to," used to form adjectives: *honorary.*

as • sign /ə sīn´/ *v.* **a.** to give out; to distribute. *Our teacher assigns us homework every evening.* **b.** to appoint to a position. *The teacher assigned him to be hall monitor this month.*

as • sign • ment /ə sīn´ mənt/ *n.* a thing assigned. *It took me three hours to complete my homework assignments.*

as • sist /ə sĭst´/ *v.* to help; to aid. *I assisted Mother in preparing dinner.*

as • sis • tant /ə sĭs´ tənt/ *n.* a person who assists another; a helper. *We need an assistant to help with the project.* [Latin *assistere,* to assist, from *ad-,* near to + *sistere,* to stand.]

as • so • ci • ate¹ /ə sō´ shē āt´/ *v.* **a.** to think of as related. *Most people associate tears with sadness, but many people cry when they are happy.* **b.** to join as a friend. *Joy associates with her softball teammates regularly.*

as • so • ci • ate² /ə so´ shē ĭt/ *n.* a friend or fellow worker. *Mr. Ortiz is an associate of my father's.*

as • sume /ə sōōm´/ *v.* (as•sumes, as•sumed, as•sum•ing) **a.** to accept as true; to take for granted. *People once assumed the earth was flat.* **b.** to accept; to take upon oneself. *Megan assumed the job of decorating the room.*

Spelling Dictionary

• **Guide Words:** The guide words at the top of each dictionary page show the first and last entries on that page. A word that comes between the guide words alphabetically will appear on that page.

• **Entry:** The entry is made up of the entry word and the information about it (i.e., the phonetic spelling, part(s) of speech, definition(s), sample sentence(s), inflected forms, and homophones and etymology, if any).

as • tron • o • my /ə strŏn′ ə mē/ *n.* the study of planets, stars, and other bodies in outer space. *Telescopes are used in astronomy.*

-ate a suffix used: **a.** to form adjectives that mean "having" or "characterized by": *fortunate.* **b.** to form verbs that mean "to act upon": *renovate.*

ath • lete /ăth′ lēt′/ *n.* a person who performs in competitive sports. *An athlete trains daily.*

athlete

-ation a suffix, used to form nouns, that means: **a.** an action or process: *consideration.* **b.** the result of an action or process: *inflammation.*

at • las /ăt′ ləs/ *n.* (**at•las•es** *pl.*) a book of maps. *Our atlas has maps of all the major highways.*

at • om /ăt′ əm/ *n.* the smallest particle into which a chemical element can be divided. *Everything around us is made up of atoms.*

at • tend /ə tĕnd′/ *v.* to go to; to be present at. *Did you attend the last meeting?*

at • ten • dance /ə tĕn′ dəns/ *n.* **a.** the act of being present. *His attendance at school has been perfect all year.* **b.** the number of persons present. *During a losing streak attendance drops at baseball games.*

at • ten • dant /ə tĕn′ dənt/ *n.* a person who serves or waits on others. *There are always four attendants working at this gas station.*

at • ten • tion /ə tĕn′ shən/ *n.* **a.** staying alert to what is happening. *Always pay attention in class.* **b.** thoughtfulness; consideration. *Rhonda gave a lot of attention to her grandparents during their visit.*

at • tic /ăt′ ĭk/ *n.* a room just below the roof of a house. *We found a big box up in our attic.*

au • thor • i • ty /ə thôr′ ĭ tē/ or /-thŏr′-/ or /ō-/ *n.* (**au•thor•i•ties** *pl.*) **a.** the right or power to control, command, or enforce. *Police officers have the authority to enforce laws.* **b.** any source of correct information. *The encyclopedia is an authority on many different subjects.*

Pronunciation Key

ă	pat	ŏ	pot	th	thin
ā	pay	ō	toe	*th*	this
âr	care	ô	paw, for	hw	which
ä	father	oi	noise	zh	vision
ĕ	pet	ou	out	ə	about,
ē	be	ŏŏ	took		item,
ĭ	pit	ōō	boot		pencil,
ī	pie	ŭ	cut		gallop,
îr	pier	ûr	urge		circus

---

au • to • bi • og • ra • pher /ô′ tō bī ŏg′ rə fər/ *n.* a person who writes the story of his or her own life. *A good autobiographer is honest and descriptive.*

au • to • bi • og • ra • phy /ô′ tō bī ŏg′ rə fē/ *n.* (**au•to•bi•og•ra•phies** *pl.*) a person's life story told or written by himself or herself. *Helen Keller wrote an autobiography.* [Greek *autos,* self + *bios,* life + *graphein,* to write.]

au • to • graph¹ /ô′ tō grăf′/ *n.* anything written in a person's own handwriting, especially his or her name. *I collected the autographs of all the students in my class.*

au • to • graph² /ô′ tō grăf′/ *v.* to sign one's name. *She asked the pitcher to autograph her ball.* [Greek *autos,* self + *graphein,* to write.]

au • to • ma • tion /ô′ tə mā′ shən/ *n.* the automatic operation of a system, a process, or equipment. *Most factories rely heavily on automation.*

au • tumn /ô′ təm/ *n.* the season that comes after summer and before winter; fall. *In autumn, many leaves turn beautiful colors.*

a • vail • a • ble /ə vā′ lə bəl/ *adj.* able to be used or obtained. *The firefighters used all the available equipment.*

av • a • lanche /ăv′ ə lănch′/ *n.* **a.** a large mass of snow sliding swiftly down a mountain. *The avalanche buried several trees.* **b.** anything that comes on suddenly: *an avalanche of orders.*

Spelling Dictionary

- **Part of Speech:** The **Spelling Dictionary** gives the entry word's most frequently used part of speech. If a word is commonly used as more than one part of speech, a separate entry is provided for each usage.

- **Definitions/Sample Sentences:** Each definition is followed by a sentence that shows how the word is used. The form of the word in the sentence may vary from the entry word to provide additional information about the word's usage.

- **Homophones:** Common homophones are identified.

- **Inflected Forms:** The students should look for inflected forms of the spelling words under the base words. Inflected forms are shown only if the spelling of the base word changes when the ending is added.

- **Etymologies:** Etymologies, or word histories, are sometimes included. The etymology shows the words from which the entry word was derived. The earliest source is shown last. For more information on the histories of the spelling words, the students should refer to a standard dictionary.

- **Entry Word:** The entry word is usually a base word—that is, a word to which an inflected ending has not been added. The entry word is divided into syllables to show how it should be hyphenated.

- **Phonetic Spelling:** The phonetic spelling uses the symbols shown in the **Pronunciation Key** to show how the word is pronounced. Sometimes phonetic spellings showing alternative pronunciations of a word are also provided.

back•ground /băk′ ground′/ *n.* the distant part of a picture or scene. *Mountains are painted in the background.*

baf•fle /băf′ əl/ *v.* (baf•fles, baf•fled, baf•fling) to puzzle; to bewilder. *The riddles baffled the students.*

bal•ance¹ /băl′ əns/ *n.* **a.** equality in weight or number. *Our teacher keeps a good balance between praise and criticism.* **b.** a steady position. *I tripped and lost my balance.*

bal•ance² /băl′ əns/ *v.* **a.** to weigh or measure in or as in a balance. *Amy added one more weight to balance the scales.* **b.** to bring into a condition of balance. *Antoine balanced the basketball on his fingertip.*

bal•lad /băl′ əd/ *n.* a poem, often sung, that tells a simple story. *Many country and western songs are ballads.*

ban•dage /băn′ dĭj/ *n.* a strip of cloth used to cover a wound. *He put a bandage over the cut.* [French *bande*, band, strip.]

ban•ner¹ /băn′ ər/ *n.* **a.** a flag. *"The Star-Spangled Banner" is a song about the American flag.* **b.** a piece of cloth with a picture, design, or writing on it. *The owners hung a banner for the grand opening.*

banner

ban•ner² /băn′ ər/ *adj.* very good: *a banner season.*

bar•be•cue /băr′ bĭ kyo͞o′/ *n.* a meal cooked over an open fire, especially outdoors. *They served hamburgers at the barbecue.*

bare•ly /bâr′ lē/ *adv.* hardly; scarcely. *We could barely see the cars because of the fog.*

bar•gain¹ /băr′ gĭn/ *n.* **a.** an agreement. *I made a bargain with Molly to rake the leaves if she would bag them.* **b.** something with a low price. *He found a bargain at the sale.*

bar•gain² /băr′ gĭn/ *v.* to try to agree on the terms of a deal. *The employer and employees bargained over the new labor contract.*

ba•rom•e•ter /bə rŏm′ ĭ tər/ *n.* an instrument that measures air pressure. *A falling reading on a barometer can indicate worse weather to come.* [Greek *baros*, weight + *metron*, measure.]

BA•SIC /bā′ sĭk/ *n.* an acronym for a common computer programming language. *We wrote a math program in BASIC.* [**B**eginner's **A**ll-purpose **S**ymbolic **I**nstruction **C**ode.]

be•have /bĭ hāv′/ *v.* (be•haves, be•haved, be•hav•ing) **a.** to act properly; to do the right things. *If you don't behave, you won't be invited again.* **b.** to act; to conduct oneself. *How did the toddler behave at the movies?*

be•yond /bē ŏnd′/ or /bĭ ŏnd′/ *prep.* in a place farther away than; past. *The grocery store is just beyond the park.*

bi•lin•gual /bī lĭng′ gwəl/ *adj.* able to speak two languages equally well. *Manuel is bilingual; he speaks Spanish and English.*

bill of sale /bĭl′ əv sāl′/ *n.* a document stating that personal property has been transferred to a new owner. *The lawyers drew up a bill of sale for our old house.*

bi•og•ra•pher /bī ŏg′ rə fər/ *n.* a person who writes a life history of another person. *A good biographer does careful research.* [Greek *bios*, life + *graphein*, to write.]

bi•ol•o•gy /bī ŏl′ ə jē/ *n.* the scientific study of living things. *Botany and zoology are two branches of biology.* [Greek *bios*, life + *logos*, word, speech.]

bit /bĭt/ *n.* an acronym for the smallest unit of storage in a computer; a tiny memory space that can contain one of two choices. *A byte is made up of eight bits.* [**B**inary dig**it**.]

bleed /blēd/ *v.* (bleeds, bled, bleed•ing) to lose blood. *Her knee began to bleed when she scraped it.*

272

block • ade /blŏ **kād′**/ *n.* the closing off of an area. *During the Civil War, blockades were formed to prevent supplies from reaching the other army.*

book • store /bŏŏk′ stôr′/ or /-stōr′/ *n.* a store where books are sold. *That bookstore has a good selection of books for children.*

bound • a • ry /**boun′** də rē/ or /-drē/ *n.* (**bound•a•ries** *pl.*) the ending line or edge of one thing and the beginning edge or line of another. *The fence marks the boundary of our property.*

broad • cast¹ /**brŏd′** kăst′/ *v.* (**broad•cast** or **broad•cast•ed, broad•cast•ing**) to send through the air by radio or TV. *The President's speech was broadcast last evening.*

broad • cast² /**brŏd′** kăst′/ *n.* a radio or television program. *Many viewers watch the six o'clock news broadcast.*

bro • chure /brŏ **shŏŏr′**/ *n.* a small booklet or pamphlet. *Zachary sent for a brochure on soccer camps.*

bronze /brŏnz / *n.* an alloy of copper and tin or certain other metals. *The Olympic teams may win medals of gold, silver, or bronze.*

browse /brouz/ *v.* (**brows•es, browsed, brows•ing**) **a.** to look at in a leisurely way; to skim through. *Sam browsed through the magazines in the dentist's office.* **b.** to feed on leaves. *Giraffes browse on tall trees.*

budge /bŭj/ *v.* (**budg•es, budged, budg•ing**) to move slightly. *The car wheels were stuck in the mud and did not budge.*

buf • fet¹ /bə **fā′**/ or /bŏŏ-/ *n.* a meal at which guests may serve themselves from food laid out on a table or sideboard. *After the meeting, we served a salad buffet.*

buf • fet² /**bŭf′** ĭt/ *v.* to strike; to knock about with force. *The wind buffeted the fragile flowers.*

bu • gle /**byōō′** gəl/ *n.* a brass instrument similar to a trumpet, used for military signals. *The soldiers woke up to a bugle call.*

bugle

Pronunciation Key

ă	pat	ŏ	pot	th	thin	
ā	pay	ō	toe	*th*	this	
âr	care	ô	paw, for	hw	which	
ä	father	oi	noise	zh	vision	
ě	pet	ou	out	ə	about,	
ē	be	ŏŏ	took		item,	
ĭ	pit	ōō	boot		pencil,	
ī	pie	ŭ	cut		gallop,	
îr	pier	ûr	urge		circus	

bul • le • tin /**bŏŏl′** ĭ tn/ *n.* **a.** a short news report. *The television program was interrupted for a bulletin about the storm.* **b.** a small magazine or newspaper. *The club puts out a bulletin twice a month.*

bu • reau /**byŏŏr′** ō/ *n.* **a.** a chest of drawers for holding clothing. *My socks are in the top drawer of the bureau.* **b.** an office for a special kind of business. *We visited the passport bureau.*

cab • i • net /**kăb′** ə nĭt/ *n.* **a.** a piece of furniture in which things are stored on shelves: *a medicine cabinet.* **b.** a group of persons chosen by the head of state to help run the government. *Members of the cabinet are often heads of government departments.*

cal • o • rie /**kăl′** ə rē/ *n.* a unit of heat used to measure the energy-producing value of food. *Exercise burns up calories.*

camp • fire /**kămp′** fīr′/ *n.* a fire in a camp, for keeping warm or for cooking. *It is fun to sit around a campfire at night and sing songs.*

camp • site /**kămp′** sīt′/ *n.* a place to camp. *We chose a beautiful campsite near a waterfall.*

can • cel /**kăn′** səl/ *v.* **a.** to cross out; to mark with lines. *The post office cancels stamps.* **b.** to do away with; to call off. *The game was canceled due to rain.*

can • di • date /kăn′ dĭ dāt′/ or /-dĭt/ *n.* a person seeking an office or an honor. *She is a candidate for governor.*

ca • pa • ble /kā′ pə bəl/ *adj.* (**ca•pa•bly,** *adv.*) having the skill to; able to. *She is capable of fixing almost any machine.*

ca • pac • i • ty /kə păs′ ĭ tē/ *n.* **a.** the amount that can be held. *The capacity of that bottle is one quart.* **b.** ability; capability. *Sarah has a capacity for solving math problems quickly.*

cap • i • tal • i • za • tion /kăp′ ĭ tl ĭ zā′ shən/ *n.* the process of writing or printing in capital letters. *Do you know the rules of punctuation and capitalization?*

cap • tain /kăp′ tən/ *n.* a person who commands, as a ship, army, or team. *The captain is responsible for the safety of all those on board the ship.*

car • a • van /kăr′ ə văn′/ *n.* a band of people, pack animals, or vehicles traveling together. *The caravan of merchants and camels stretched across the Sahara.*

car • bon /kär′ bən/ *n.* a common chemical element found in all organic substances. *Diamonds are pure carbon, but carbon is also present in coal, graphite, and charcoal.*

car • bon di • ox • ide /kär′ bən dī ŏk′ sīd′/ *n.* a colorless, odorless gas composed of carbon and oxygen and present in Earth's atmosphere. *The carbon dioxide exhaled by animals is absorbed by green plants.*

care • ful • ly /kâr′ fə lē/ *adv.* with care; cautiously or thoroughly. *Peter dusted the tiny figurines carefully.*

Car • ib • be • an /kăr′ ə bē′ ən/ or /kə rĭb′ ē ən/ *adj.* relating to the Caribbean Sea and its islands. *The Caribbean islands attract tourists from all over the world.*

car • pen • ter /kär′ pən tər/ *n.* a person who can make things from wood or repair them. *We hired a carpenter to make the new cabinets.*

car • riage /kăr′ ĭj/ *n.* a four-wheeled vehicle pulled by horses and used for carrying people. *Carriages were popular until the car was invented.* [Norman French *carier,* to carry.]

car • ti • lage /kär′ tl ĭj/ *n.* the tough white connective tissue that is attached to the surfaces of bones near joints. *Cartilage helps protect the bones from injury.*

car • ton /kär′ tn/ *n.* a container made of cardboard or plastic. *We looked for a big enough carton to hold all the gifts.*

carton

cas • ta • nets /kăs′ tə nĕts′/ *n. pl.* a rhythm instrument consisting of hollow shells of wood or ivory that are clicked together with the fingers. *Spanish flamenco dancers often perform with castanets.*

ca • su • al /kăzh′ o͞o əl/ *adj.* **a.** without plan; happening by chance. *He paid a casual visit to his old friends.* **b.** everyday; informal. *We wore casual clothes to the party.*

cat • a • log or **cat • a • logue** /kăt′ l ôg′/ or /-ŏg′/ *n.* a list of things arranged in alphabetical order with descriptions. *A library has a catalog of all the books in it.*

cau • tious /kô′ shəs/ *adj.* careful; keeping away from danger. *The bus driver was cautious in the storm.* [Latin *cautiō,* from *cavēre,* to take care.]

ceil • ing /sē′ lĭng/ *n.* the top of a room. *In most rooms there is a light attached to the ceiling.*

cel • list /chĕl′ ĭst/ *n.* a person who plays the stringed instrument called the cello. *Cellists sit on chairs and hold their cellos between their knees.*

Cel • si • us /sĕl′ sē əs/ or /-shəs/ *adj.* relating to the Celsius temperature scale, which registers the freezing point of water as 0° and the boiling point as 100°. *Normal body temperature is about 37° Celsius.*

cen • tral /sĕn′ trəl/ *adj.* **a.** in or at the middle; near the center. *The biggest stores are in the central part of the city.* **b.** main; leading; chief. *What is the central idea that the author wants us to understand?*

CEO an abbreviation for "chief executive officer." *The CEO of the bank approves all loans.*

ce • ram • ics /sə răm′ ĭks/ *n.* the art or technique of making objects from clay and firing them at high temperatures. *In our class in ceramics, we made both soup mugs and figurines.*

cer • e • mo • ny /sĕr′ ə mō′ nē/ *n.* (**cer•e•mon•ies** *pl.*) a special set of acts done in a certain way. *The wedding ceremony was held outdoors.*

cer • tain • ly /sûr′ tn lē/ *adv.* definitely; surely. *Your grades will certainly improve if you study hard.*

change • a • ble /chān′ jə bəl/ *adj.* subject to change; variable: *changeable weather.*

chan • nel /chăn′ əl/ *n.* **a.** a body of water connecting two larger bodies of water. *The English Channel lies between the Atlantic Ocean and the North Sea.* **b.** any passage through which a liquid can flow. *The workers dug a channel to remove water.* **c.** a frequency used for radio or TV. *The community channel is asking viewers for money.*

chap • ter /chăp′ tər/ *n.* a part or main section of a book. *Each chapter is narrated by a different character.*

char • coal /chär′ kōl/ *n.* a black substance made by partly burning wood in a closed container. *Many people cook outdoors in the summer using charcoal as fuel.*

check • book /chĕk′ boŏk′/ *n.* a book of blank bank checks. *The monthly bank statement also tells how to balance a checkbook.*

chimes /chīmz/ *n. pl.* an instrument used to make bell-like sounds. *One of the percussionists in an orchestra plays the chimes.*

chis • el¹ /chĭz′ əl/ *n.* a tool with a strong, sharp blade. *A chisel is used for carving wood or stone.*

chis • el² /chĭz′ əl/ *v.* to cut or shape with a chisel. *The sculptor chiseled a statue out of marble.*

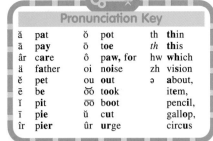
chisel

chord /kôrd/ *n.* three or more musical tones sounding together to produce harmony. *At our first lesson, the guitar instructor went over some basic chords.*

Pronunciation Key

ă	pat	ŏ	pot	th	thin
ā	pay	ō	toe	*th*	this
âr	care	ô	paw, for	hw	which
ä	father	oi	noise	zh	vision
ĕ	pet	ou	out	ə	about,
ē	be	ŏŏ	took		item,
ĭ	pit	ōō	boot		pencil,
ī	pie	ŭ	cut		gallop,
îr	pier	ûr	urge		circus

cir • cu • lar /sûr′ kyə lər/ *adj.* round; having the shape of a circle. *A lighthouse is usually a circular building.*

cir • cum • fer • ence /sər kŭm′ fər əns/ *n.* the distance around a circle. *You can measure the circumference of a tree trunk by putting a tape measure around it.*

cir • rus /sîr′ əs/ *n.* a high-altitude cloud consisting of narrow bands or white, fleecy patches. *A cirrus indicates fair weather, not rainfall.*

cit • i • zen • ship /sĭt′ ĭ zən shĭp′/ *n.* the rights, duties, and privileges that come with being a citizen. *Immigrants who apply for United States citizenship promise to uphold the principles of the Constitution.*

ci • vil • ian /sĭ vĭl′ yən/ *n.* a person not serving in the military. *Most civilians do not wear uniforms.*

clas • si • fy /klăs′ ə fī′/ *v.* to sort; to arrange according to category or class. *Librarians do not classify fairy tales with other fiction.*

cleanse /klĕnz/ *v.* to make clean; to remove dirt from. *Always cleanse a cut or scrape before bandaging it.*

clear • ance /klîr′ əns/ *n.* **a.** space; clearing. *There was only a foot of clearance between the branch and the roof.* **b.** a sale at which items are reduced in price for quick sale. *After a clearance, a store has room to display new merchandise.*

COD an abbreviation for "cash on delivery." *Catalog orders can sometimes be sent COD.*

Spelling Dictionary

275

col•lect /kə lĕkt'/ *v.* **a.** to gather; to bring or come together. *Jane collected the test papers.* **b.** to gather and keep as a hobby. *Bob collects stamps.* **c.** to get money that is owed. *The landlord collected the rent.*

col•lec•tive /kə lĕk' tĭv/ *adj.* **a.** of a number of persons acting as one: *the collective decision of the community.* **b.** having a singular form but a plural meaning. *The word "committee" is a collective noun.*

col•umn /kŏl' əm/ *n.* **a.** a support or pillar for a building. *The ivy twines around the porch columns.* **b.** a straight row that goes up and down. *Many books have two columns of print on each page.* **c.** articles appearing regularly and written by one author. *Mr. Vronski writes a column for the paper.*

col•um•nist /kŏl' əm nĭst/ *n.* a person who writes a regular series of articles for a newspaper or magazine. *Teresa is the advice columnist for the school newspaper.*

co•me•di•an /kə mē' dē ən/ *n.* a professional entertainer who tells jokes and does things to make people laugh. *Some comedians have become stars of situation comedies.*

com•mu•ni•ty /kə myōō' nĭ tē/ *n.* (com•mu•ni•ties *pl.*) all the people who live in one area; the residents of a town. *The park is for the entire community.* [Latin *commūnis,* common.]

com•pact¹ /kəm păkt'/ or /kŏm' păkt'/ *adj.* arranged within a small space. *Most portable appliances are compact.*

com•pact² /kəm păkt'/ *v.* to pack together tightly. *That machine compacts garbage.*

com•pact³ /kŏm' păkt'/ *n.* a small cosmetic case. *May I borrow the mirror in your compact?*

com•plain /kəm plān'/ *v.* **a.** to find fault. *Don't complain about a problem unless you're willing to help remedy it.* **b.** to report something bad. *The neighbors complained to the police about the noisy motocycle.* [Latin *com-* (intensive) + *plangere,* to lament.]

com•plete•ly /kəm plēt' lē/ *adv.* entirely; totally. *By the end of the party, the food was completely gone.*

276

com•ple•tion /kəm plē' shən/ *n.* a making or being completed; finishing. *The completion of a job gives one a feeling of accomplishment.* [Latin *complet-,* perfect stem of *complēre,* to fill out, from *com-* (intensive) + *plēre,* to fill.]

com•plex•ion /kəm plĕks' shən/ *n.* the appearance of the face with regard to color and texture. *Limiting your exposure to the sun will keep your complexion healthier.*

com•pos•er /kəm pō' zər/ *n.* a person who composes or creates music. *Leonard Bernstein, who wrote the music for* West Side Story, *earned fame as both conductor and composer.*

com•pound¹ /kŏm' pound'/ *n.* a chemical substance formed of two or more elements. *Water is a compound of hydrogen and oxygen.*

com•pound² /kŏm' pound'/ *adj.* formed of two or more parts: *a compound sentence.*

com•pound³ /kŏm' pound'/ *v.* to add to. *The sunshine compounded our happiness.*

com•pound⁴ /kŏm' pound'/ *n.* a group of buildings enclosed by barriers. *The security was tight around the compound.*

com•pu•ta•tion /kŏm' pyōō tā' shən/ *n.* the process of computing; a mathematical calculation. *The accountant used a calculator to make tax computations.*

com•pu•ter /kəm pyōō' tər/ *n.* an electronic device that stores and analyzes data or performs calculations at high speeds. *Some schools have computers in every classroom.*

computer

con•ceit /kən sēt'/ *n.* an exaggerated opinion of one's worth; vanity. *Conceit is an unattractive quality.*

con•cern /kən sûrn'/ *v.* **a.** to relate to; to have an effect on. *The problem of pollution concerns all of us.* **b.** to make anxious; to worry. *His illness concerned his parents.*

con•clude /kən klōōd'/ *v.* (con•cludes, con•clud•ed, con•clud•ing) to end; to finish. *She concluded her speech and sat down.*

Spelling Dictionary

con•clu•sion /kən klōō′ zhən/ *n.* **a.** the end. *We left in a hurry at the conclusion of the dinner.* **b.** an opinion arrived at by thinking carefully. *The judge's conclusion was that Mr. Benson was innocent.* [Latin *conclūsiō,* from *conclūdere,* to end, from *com-* (intensive) + *claudere,* to close.]

con•di•tion /kən dĭsh′ ən/ *n.* **a.** something that is needed before something else can be obtained. *Hard work is a condition of success.* **b.** the state in which a person or thing is. *The weather conditions were good.*

con•duct¹ /kŏn′ dŭkt′/ *n.* behavior; way of acting. *Nancy's conduct in class was good.*

con•duct² /kən dŭkt′/ *v.* **a.** to guide; to lead. *The student conducted the visitor through the new building.* **b.** to carry; to be a path for. *Copper conducts electricity.*

con•fide /kən fīd′/ *v.* (**con•fides, con•fid•ed, con•fid•ing**) to trust one's secrets to another. *Pedro confided his plan to his friend.*

con•firm /kən fûrm′/ *v.* to make certain or sure. *The experiment confirmed her theory.*

con•fuse /kən fyōōz′/ *v.* (**con•fus•es, con•fused, con•fus•ing**) to mix up in the mind; to throw into disorder. *The loud noises confused the wild animals.*

con•gru•ent /kŏng′ grōō ənt/ or /kən grōō′-/ *adj.* having exactly the same size and shape as another figure. *Two polygons are congruent if they match exactly.*

con•nect /kə nĕkt′/ *v.* **a.** to join; to link. *Before you turn on the water, connect the hose to the faucet.* **b.** to join two ideas, events, etc., in the mind. *I connect clowns with the circus.* [Latin *com-,* together + *nectere,* to bind.]

con•ser•va•tion /kŏn′ sûr vā′ shən/ *n.* the protection of natural resources from loss, harm, or waste. *The community's efforts toward conservation resulted in a wildlife sanctuary to protect animals.*

con•sid•er /kən sĭd′ ər/ *v.* **a.** to think carefully before doing something. *Have you considered the pros and cons?* **b.** to think of someone or something as; to regard as. *I consider that a compliment.*

con•sid•er•a•tion /kən sĭd′ ə rā′ shən/ *n.* **a.** careful thinking. *They gave our plan serious consideration.* **b.** regard for the feelings of others; thoughtfulness. *Selfish people have little consideration for others.*

con•sole¹ /kən sōl′/ *v.* to comfort in time of trouble or sorrow. *The mother tried to console the screaming toddler.*

con•sole² /kŏn′ sōl/ *n.* a cabinet or panel that houses the controls for mechanical or electrical equipment such as a TV, stereo, or computer. *Technicians operate all the theater lights from a central console.*

con•so•nant /kŏn′ sə nənt/ *n.* a speech sound made by partially or completely stopping the flow of air through the mouth; the letter or letters that stand for such a sound. *A is a vowel, but B and C are consonants.*

con•stant /kŏn′ stənt/ *adj.* never changing or stopping; happening again and again. *The constant beat of the rain put us to sleep.*

con•stel•la•tion /kŏn′ stə lā′ shən/ *n.* a group of stars with a name. *Many constellations were named after the animals they seemed to form in the sky.*

constellation

con•tact¹ /kŏn′ tăkt/ *n.* **a.** a coming together of objects; a touching. *My fingers came into contact with a cold, soft material.* **b.** a connection, especially of people: *a business contact.*

con•tact² /kŏn′ tăkt/ *v.* to communicate with. *The pilot contacted the control tower for landing instructions.*

con•tent¹ /kŏn′ tĕnt/ *n.* **a.** often **contents,** what is contained; what a thing holds or encloses. *The contents of the package are listed on the label.* **b.** the ideas expressed; the topic; the substance. *The teacher liked the content of my essay but said its grammar and punctuation needed work.*

con•tent² /kən tĕnt′/ *adj.* satisfied; pleased. *We were content with our one-point victory.*

con•tin•u•ous /kən tĭn′ yoō əs/ *adj.* going on without stopping; unbroken; connected. *A continuous line of people passed the window.*

con•tract¹ /kŏn′ trăkt/ *n.* a legal agreement. *The striking workers finally accepted the new contract.*

con•tract² /kon′ trăkt/ or /kən trăkt′/ *v.* **a.** to make a legal agreement. *We contracted to mow their lawn every two weeks.* **b.** to become smaller by shrinking. *Most things expand in warm weather and contract in cold weather.*

con•trib•ute /kən trĭb′ yoōt/ *v.* (**con•trib•utes, con•trib•ut•ed, con•trib•ut•ing**) to give; to donate. *Each student contributed two hours of work for the bake sale.*

con•vert¹ /kən vûrt/ *v.* to change into another form, substance, or condition. *Jim's dad converted their unfinished basement into a playroom.*

con•vert² /kŏn′ vûrt/ *n.* a person who has accepted a new belief. *There are few converts to the new tax proposal.*

con•vict¹ /kən vĭkt/ *v.* to find guilty. *The defendant was convicted of a felony.*

con•vict² /kŏn′ vĭkt/ *n.* **a.** a person found guilty of a crime. *The convict was led from the court.* **b.** a person serving a prison sentence. *Some convicts work in the prison garden.*

cor•al¹ /kôr′ əl/ or /kŏr′-/ *n.* a hard substance formed from the skeletons of tiny sea animals. *The island's gleaming beach consists of grains of coral.*

cor•al² /kôr′ əl/ or /kŏr′-/ *adj.* made of coral: *coral reefs.*

cor•rupt /kə rŭpt′/ *adj.* dishonest; influenced by bribery. *There was a citizens' campaign to remove corrupt officials from public office.*

could•'ve could have.

cour•age /kûr′ ĭj/ or /kŭr′-/ *n.* the quality of facing danger or a difficult task without giving in to fear. *It takes courage to admit your mistakes.* [French *corage,* from Latin *cor,* heart.]

cou•ra•geous /kə rā′ jəs/ *adj.* being brave; having courage. *The courageous skater attempted a triple jump.*

CPU an abbreviation for "central processing unit," the part of every computer that controls the most basic operations. *The CPU of older computers was found in the main frame.*

cra•ter /krā′ tər/ *n.* a hollow, bowl-shaped surface, such as that formed by a volcano or caused by the impact of a meteorite. *The astronauts photographed the moon's craters.*

crater

crease¹ /krēs/ *v.* (**creas•es, creased, creas•ing**) to fold, pleat, or wrinkle. *How do you crease paper to make an airplane?*

crease² /krēs/ *n.* a line made by pressing, folding, or wrinkling. *Jan ironed out the creases in her skirt.*

cross-coun•try /krôs′ kŭn′ trē/ or /krŏs′-/ *adj.* **a.** moving across open country instead of following paths or roads: *cross-country skiing.* **b.** from one side of the country to the other: *a cross-country trip.*

cru•el /kroō′ əl/ *adj.* wanting to make others suffer or causing them pain. *The cruel children threw stones at the birds.*

Spelling Dictionary

cruise[1] /krōoz/ *v.* (**cruis•es, cruised, cruis•ing**) **a.** to travel leisurely or aimlessly about. *The pleasure boat cruised the bay.* **b.** to travel at a constant, efficient speed. *The jet cruised high above the clouds.*

cruise[2] /krōoz/ *n.* a sea voyage taken for pleasure: *a Caribbean cruise.*

crumb /krŭm/ *n.* a small piece or fragment, especially of bread or cake. *We fed crumbs to the birds during the winter.*

cu•mu•lo•nim•bus /kyōōm′ yə lō nĭm′ bəs/ *n.* a very dense, vertically shaped cloud that may cause heavy rain or thunderstorms. *A cumulonimbus may bring hail.*

cu•mu•lus /kyōōm′ yə ləs/ *n.* (**cu•mu•li** *pl.*) a dense, white, fluffy cloud with a flat base. *A cumulus usually has a distinct shape.*

cumulus

cup•board /kŭb′ ərd/ *n.* a cabinet with shelves, used for storing food, dishes, etc. *We keep spices in the corner cupboard.*

cur•few /kûr′ fyōō/ *n.* an order requiring persons to remain indoors during set hours, especially at night. *The soldiers had a midnight curfew.*

cu•ri•ous /kyōōr′ ē əs/ *adj.* eager to learn or find out; interested. *I was curious about how the computer program worked.*

cur•tain /kûr′ tn/ *n.* a hanging piece of cloth used to decorate a door or window or to separate the audience from the stage in a theater. *We closed the curtains to darken the room.*

cush•ion /kōōsh′ ən/ *n.* a soft pad or a pillow. *Their poodle sleeps on a cushion in a basket.*

cus•to•di•an /kŭs stō′ dē ən/ *n.* a caretaker; a janitor. *The custodian of the building keeps the sidewalks free of snow during the winter.*

cus•to•dy /kŭs′ tə dē/ *n.* **a.** care; safekeeping; guardianship. *The judge granted the parents joint custody of the children.* **b.** detention. *The police have a suspect in custody.*

cus•tom•ar•y /kŭs′ tə měr′ ē/ *adj.* based on custom; usual; routine. *A tuna sandwich and an apple are my customary lunch.*

Pronunciation Key

ă	pat	ŏ	pot	th	thin
ā	pay	ō	toe	*th*	this
âr	care	ô	paw, for	hw	which
ä	father	oi	noise	zh	vision
ĕ	pet	ou	out	ə	about,
ē	be	ŏŏ	took		item,
ĭ	pit	ōō	boot		pencil,
ī	pie	ŭ	cut		gallop,
îr	pier	ûr	urge		circus

cus•tom•er /kŭs′ tə mər/ *n.* any person who buys something. *The store held a sale to attract new customers.*

czar /zär/ *n.* an emperor of Russia. *Czars had absolute power over their subjects.*

day•dream[1] /dā′ drēm′/ *n.* a pleasant, dreamy thought. *She has daydreams about being a famous poet.*

day•dream[2] /dā′ drēm′/ *v.* to have pleasant, dreamy thoughts. *Try not to daydream in class.*

deal /dēl/ *v.* (**deals, dealt, deal•ing**) **a.** to have to do with; to be concerned with. *The book deals with the history of America.* **b.** to hand out; to distribute. *Whose turn is it to deal the cards?*

dealt /dĕlt/ *v.* past tense and past participle of **deal**.

de•bate[1] /dĭ bāt′/ *n.* a discussion or argument on a particular subject. *We heard a debate on methods of teaching last night.*

de•bate[2] /dĭ bāt′/ *v.* to discuss or consider the pros and cons of a subject. *The students debated whether to have a dance or a field trip.*

de•bris /də brē′/ or /dā-/ *n.* remains of something broken, destroyed, or discarded. *The hurricane left much debris on the beach.*

debt /dĕt/ *n.* something owed to another person, usually money. *It is polite to repay a debt as soon as possible.*

Spelling Dictionary

de • bug /dē bŭg′/ *v.* (**de•bugs, de•bugged, de•bug•ging**) to locate and correct errors in a computer program. *If your procedure doesn't work, you'll have to debug it.*

dec • a • gon /děk′ ə gŏn′/ *n.* a geometric figure having ten sides and ten angles. *The sides of a regular decagon are all equal.*

decagon

dec • i • bel /děs′ ə bəl/ or /-běl′/ *n.* a unit used for measuring the relative intensity of sounds. *Ordinary conversation reaches a level of about 60 decibels.*

de • ci • sion /dǐ sǐzh′ ən/ *n.* **a.** a conclusion; a verdict. *Has the committee reached a decision?* **b.** firmness; decisiveness. *The defense lawyer is noted for her courage and decision.*

de • clar • a • tive /dǐ klăr′ ə tǐv/ *adj.* that which announces or states: *a declarative sentence.*

de • clare /dǐ klâr′/ *v.* (**de•clares, de•clared, de•clar•ing**) **a.** to announce publicly and formally; to make known. *The governor declared his opposition to the new bill.* **b.** to say positively and surely. *"I don't believe a word of it," she declared.*

de • fend /dǐ fěnd′/ *v.* **a.** to protect from harm or attack; to guard. *The soldiers continued to defend the fort.* **b.** to act or speak in defense of something; to justify: *defend a decision.* **c.** to represent the defendant in court. *The judge assigned a lawyer to defend him.*

de • fense /dǐ fěns′/ *n.* **a.** something that defends. *Washing your hands frequently is a good defense against colds.* **b.** the defending team or side. *Our team's defense was outstanding.*

del • i • cate /děl′ ǐ kǐt/ *adj.* **a.** light and pleasing to the senses: *a delicate perfume.* **b.** carefully and expertly done; requiring careful workmanship: *delicate repairs.* **c.** fragile; easily broken or hurt: *a delicate vase.*

de • light • ful /dǐ līt′ fəl/ *adj.* greatly pleasing; causing joy or delight. *We saw a delightful movie last night.*

del • ta /děl′ tə/ *n.* a deposit of mud and sand at the mouth of a river. *Deltas are formed when a river slows down and drops the materials that are carried by the current.*

dem • on • strate /děm′ ən strāt′/ *v.* **a.** to show; to make clear. *You must demonstrate a willingness to learn in school.* **b.** to prove through an experiment or by using logical thinking. *The teacher demonstrated the force of gravity by dropping objects to the floor.*

de • ple • tion /dǐ plē′ shən/ *n.* exhaustion; a state of being used up. *Many dry areas of Africa have experienced erosion and depletion of soil.*

der • ma • tol • o • gist /dûr′ mə tŏl′ ə jǐst/ *n.* a doctor who specializes in skin problems. *A dermatologist can tell you about the best treatments for your complexion.*

der • mis /dûr′ mǐs/ *n.* the layer of skin beneath the surface layer. *The dermis lies beneath the epidermis.*

der • rick /děr′ ǐk/ *n.* the structure above an oil well to which drilling and pumping equipment is attached. *When the gusher was drilled, the entire derrick was hidden by a spouting stream of oil.*

des • o • late /děs′ ə lǐt/ or /děz′-/ *adj.* **a.** barren; without vegetation: *desolate terrain.* **b.** uninhabited; deserted: *a desolate island.* **c.** lonely; dejected. *Julie was desolate when her best friend moved away.*

des • per • ate /děs′ pər ǐt/ *adj.* **a.** almost despairing; frantic. *I made a desperate attempt to catch the teetering vase.* **b.** very bad; critical; extreme. *The driver was in a desperate situation when the brakes failed.*

de • tain /dǐ tān′/ *v.* **a.** to delay; to hold back. *The flight was detained two hours due to heavy fog.* **b.** to keep in custody. *A suspect was detained for questioning.*

de • vel • op /dǐ věl′ əp/ *v.* **a.** to grow; to come into being. *The bud developed into a blossom.* **b.** to build up; to put to use. *Reading helps develop your mind.*

de • vel • op • ment /dǐ věl′ əp mənt/ *n.* **a.** the act of developing; growth. *The children enjoyed watching the kittens' development.* **b.** results; news. *What are the latest developments in the plans for a picnic?*

Spelling Dictionary

di•am•e•ter /dī ăm′ ĭ tər/ *n.* a straight line that passes through the center of a circle or other figure, dividing it into two equal parts. *The radius of a circle is half its diameter.* [Greek *dia*, through + *metron*, measure.]

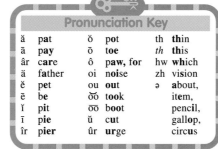
diameter

di•e•ti•tian /dī′ ĭ tĭsh′ ən/ *n.* a person who specializes in creating healthful diets. *Our school dietitian plans nutritious meals.*

dif•fer /dĭf′ ər/ *v.* **a.** to be unlike. *The two nations differ in their languages and customs.* **b.** to disagree; to have unlike ideas or opinions. *We couldn't resolve our argument, so we agreed to differ.*

dif•fer•ence /dĭf′ ər əns/ *n.* **a.** a way in which people or things are not alike. *There is a big difference in size between a mouse and an elephant.* **b.** the amount by which one number is greater than another. *The difference between 10 and 12 is 2.*

dif•fer•ent /dĭf′ ər ənt/ or /dĭf′ rənt/ *adj.* **a.** not alike. *Summer is different from winter.* **b.** not the same; separate. *My cousin and I go to different schools.*

dif•fi•cult /dĭf′ ĭ kŭlt′/ or /-kəlt/ *adj.* **a.** hard; not easy to do or understand. *Learning to play chess is difficult.* **b.** hard to get along with. *He has a reputation for being difficult.*

di•ges•tive /dī jĕs′ tĭv/ or /dĭ-/ *adj.* relating to or serving the process by which food is changed so the body can absorb it. *The digestive system breaks down the food we eat into nutrients.*

di•men•sion /dĭ mĕn′ shən/ or /dī-/ *n.* a measurement of the length, width, or height of something. *The dimensions of the package are three feet in length, two feet in width, and one foot in height.*

dip•lo•mat /dĭp′ lə măt′/ *n.* a person skilled in dealing with other persons or governments. *The diplomats tried to lessen the tension between their countries.*

di•rect¹ /dĭ rĕkt′/ or /dī-/ *v.* **a.** to point out the way. *The road map directed us to the town.* **b.** to be in charge of; to manage. *A police officer directed traffic.* **c.** to order; to command. *The doctor directed Will to eat more fresh fruit.* [Latin *dīrĕct-*, perfect stem of *dīregere*, to give direction to, from *dis-*, apart + *regere*, to guide.]

ă	pat	ŏ	pot	th	**thin**
ā	pay	ō	toe	*th*	**this**
âr	care	ô	paw, for	hw	**which**
ä	father	oi	noise	zh	vision
ĕ	pet	ou	out	ə	about,
ē	be	ŏŏ	took		item,
ĭ	pit	ōō	boot		pencil,
ī	pie	ŭ	cut		gallop,
îr	pier	ûr	urge		circus

di•rect² /dĭ rĕkt′/ or /dī-/ *adj.* **a.** straight; not roundabout: *a direct route.* **b.** honest; frank: *a direct answer.*

di•rec•tion /dĭ rĕk′ shən/ or /dī-/ *n.* **a.** managing; control. *The orchestra was under the direction of a famous conductor.* **b.** a point toward which one can face. *We walked in the direction of the bank.* **c. directions** an explanation of how to do something. *The directions were hard to follow.*

di•rect•ly /dĭ rĕkt′ lē/ *adv.* **a.** in a direct line; straight. *The city is directly north of us.* **b.** right away. *I'll be there directly.*

dir•ty /dûr′ tē/ *adj.* not clean; containing dirt. *Put all the dirty clothes into the washing machine.*

dis•a•gree•ment /dĭs ə grē′ mənt/ *n.* a dispute; a difference of opinion. *We had a disagreement over whose turn it was.*

dis•count /dĭs′ kount/ *n.* a reduction; an amount taken off a price. *Mary got a discount on the hat because it was on sale.*

dis•cus•sion /dĭ skŭsh′ ən/ *n.* a serious or thorough conversation. *Sandy and I had a long discussion about how to clean up our neighborhood.* [Latin *discuss-*, perfect stem of *discutere*, to discuss, from *dis-*, apart + *quatere*, to shake.]

dis•guise¹ /dĭs gīz′/ *v.* (**dis•guis•es, dis•guised, dis•guis•ing**) **a.** to change one's real appearance so that one will not be recognized. *In the play, the thief was disguised as a detective.* **b.** to hide; to mask; to cover up. *He disguised his anger by smiling.*

dis•guise² /dĭs gīz′/ *n.* a costume used to hide one's real identity: *a clown disguise.*

disk•ette /dĭ skĕt′/ *n.* a floppy disk on which computer data can be stored. *Dave stored his program on a high-density diskette.*

dis•pute[1] /dĭ spyōōt′/ *v.* (**dis•putes, dis•put•ed, dis•put•ing**) to argue; to debate; to have a different opinion about. *Our class disputed over the best date for the picnic.*

dis•pute[2] /dĭ spyōōt′/ *n.* argument; debate; quarrel. *Diplomats try to settle disputes between countries.*

dis•tance /dĭs′ təns/ *n.* the space between two points or places. *I live a short distance away.*

dis•tant /dĭs′ tənt/ *adj.* **a.** far away or long ago. *The speaker had traveled in distant lands.* **b.** not easy to talk with; keeping to oneself. *Shy persons can seem distant until you get to know them.*

dis•trict /dĭs′ trĭkt/ *n.* a part of a country, state, or county that has certain duties or functions. *We have school districts and voting districts.*

di•vis•i•bil•i•ty /dĭ vĭz′ ə bĭl′ ĭ tē/ *n.* the state of being able to divide without a remainder. *Factoring can show the divisibility of a number.*

DOB an abbreviation for "date of birth." *Write the date you were born in the space marked "DOB."*

doc•u•ment /dŏk′ yə mənt/ *n.* an official paper; any written record used as evidence for some fact. *Your birth certificate is an important document.* [Latin *documentum*, lesson, from *docēre*, to teach.]

do•nate /dō′ nāt′/ *v.* (**do•nates, do•nat•ed, do•nat•ing**) to give or contribute to a fund or a cause. *The class decided to donate the money from their bake sale to the animal shelter.*

doubt•ful /dout′ fəl/ *adj.* not sure; uncertain. *I am doubtful that we can finish the game in this rain.*

down•ward[1] /doun′ wərd/ *adv.* toward a lower place. *The car at the top of the hill rolled downward.*

down•ward[2] /doun′ wərd/ *adj.* going toward a lower place. *This downward path leads to the house.*

drought /drout/ *n.* a long period of time during which there is no rain. *The crops were ruined last summer by a two-month drought.*

du•ti•ful /dōō′ tĭ fəl/ or /dyōō′-/ *adj.* careful about performing one's duty; obedient; respectful. *Darrell is a dutiful son who helps care for his bedridden mother.*

east•ward[1] /ēst′ wərd/ *adv.* toward the east. *The river runs eastward.*

east•ward[2] /ēst′ wərd/ *adj.* in or toward the east. *The pilot set an eastward course.*

ed•i•ble /ĕd′ ə bəl/ *adj.* capable of being eaten. *Many wild berries are not edible.*

-eer a suffix that means "someone who works in or is involved with": *engineer.*

ef•fort /ĕf′ ərt/ *n.* **a.** the use of one's strength or power; exertion. *Riding a bicycle uphill requires effort.* **b.** an attempt; a try. *Make an effort to finish by three.* [Latin *ex-*, out + *fortis*, strong.]

e•lec•tri•cian /ĭ lĕk trĭsh′ ən/ or /ē lĕk-/ *n.* a person who installs and repairs electrical equipment. *The electrician rewired the old house.*

electrician

e•lec•tron /ĭ lĕk′ trŏn/ *n.* one of the tiny particles of negative matter that travel around the nucleus of an atom. *Electrons have a negative charge.*

e•mer•gen•cy /ĭ mûr′ jən sē/ *n.* (**e•mer•gen•cies** *pl.*) a serious situation that requires something to be done right away. *The police are trained to respond quickly in an emergency.*

e•mo•tion /ĭ mō′ shən/ *n.* a strong reaction or feeling. *Anger is a common emotion.*

em•pire /ĕm′ pīr/ *n.* a number of countries led by a single, powerful ruler or emperor. *Years ago, the Roman Empire included most of the world then known in the West.*

em•ploy•ee /ĕm ploi′ ē/ *n.* a person who works for another person or for a business. *The bank had a picnic for all its employees.*

282

-ence a suffix, used to form nouns, that means: **a.** an act or a result of acting: *dependence.* **b.** a state or a quality: *absence.*

en•cy•clo•pe•di•a /ĕn sī klə **pē′** dē ə/ *n.* a book or group of books that gives general information on many different subjects. *Topics in an encyclopedia are usually in alphabetical order.*

en•dan•ger /ĕn **dān′** jər/ *v.* to put in danger; to harm. *Pollution endangers wildlife.*

en•gi•neer /ĕn jə **nîr′**/ *n.* **a.** a person trained to use science and math for practical purposes such as designing and building systems or equipment. *My big sister is an electrical engineer.* **b.** a person who operates an engine: *a train engineer.*

en•grave /ĕn **grāv′**/ *v.* (en•graves, en•graved, en•grav•ing) to carve designs or letters into a surface. *The jeweler engraved my initials on my watch.*

en•list /ĕn **lĭst′**/ *v.* **a.** to join a branch of the armed forces voluntarily. *Lydia wants to enlist in the Navy when she finishes high school.* **b.** to gain the support of. *The principal enlisted us all to help clean up the school yard.*

-ent a suffix used: **a.** to form adjectives that means "causing" or "being": *absorbent.* **b.** to form nouns that means "one who": *president.*

en•vi•ron•ment /ĕn **vī′** rən mənt/ *n.* **a.** the total surroundings that allow a living organism to grow and develop. *Congress has passed bills to protect our environment from pollution.* **b.** surroundings. *The library is a quiet environment for study.*

en•zyme /**ĕn′** zīm/ *n.* a protein substance produced by living organisms. *Enzymes help our bodies break down food.*

ep•i•der•mis /ĕp ĭ **dûr′** mĭs/ *n.* the outer layer of the skin. *Humans and plants both have an epidermis.*

-er a suffix, used to form nouns, that means: **a.** one who: *teacher.* **b.** thing that: *toaster.*

e•quip•ment /ĭ **kwĭp′** mənt/ *n.* the things needed for a special purpose; supplies. *Paper, desks, and chairs are all office equipment.*

e•quiv•a•lent[1] /ĭ **kwĭv′** ə lənt/ *adj.* identical; equal. *Twelve inches are equivalent to one foot.*

Pronunciation Key

ă	pat	ŏ	pot	th	thin
ā	pay	ō	toe	th	this
âr	care	ô	paw, for	hw	which
ä	father	oi	noise	zh	vision
ĕ	pet	ou	out	ə	about,
ē	be	ŏŏ	took		item,
ĭ	pit	ōō	boot		pencil,
ī	pie	ŭ	cut		gallop,
îr	pier	ûr	urge		circus

e•quiv•a•lent[2] /ĭ **kwĭv′** ə lənt/ *n.* something equal or identical. *The equivalent of 12 x 12 is 144.*

e•ro•sion /ĭ **rō′** zhən/ *n.* the wearing or washing away of the earth's surface. *Soil conservation can help control erosion from wind or water.*

erosion

er•ror /**ĕr′** ər/ *n.* a mistake. *I was happy because my spelling test had no errors.*

es•pe•cial•ly /ĭ **spĕsh′** ə lē/ *adv.* mainly; in particular; unusually. *My brother likes all sports, but he especially enjoys soccer.*

es•ti•ma•tion /ĕs′ tə **mā′** shən/ *n.* **a.** a rough calculation. *The engineer gave an estimation of the costs for the building project.* **b.** judgment; opinion. *It was the engineer's estimation that the project could be finished on time.*

etch•ing /**ĕch′** ĭng/ *n.* a design cut into a plate by the action of acid or the print made from such a plate. *The artist printed the etching from a metal plate.*

e•vent•ful /ĭ **vĕnt′** fəl/ *adj.* filled with many events or an important happening. *Our most eventful month was May, when we moved.*

eve•ry•bod•y /**ĕv′** rē bŏd′ ē/ or /-bŭd′ē/ *pron.* all people; each person. *Everybody in our class went to see the parade.*

ex- a prefix that means: **a.** out of; away from: *expose.* **b.** former: *ex-senator.*

Spelling Dictionary

ex • act • ly /ĭg zăkt′ lē/ *adv.* **a.** precisely; without any change. *Do exactly as the teacher says.* **b.** true; quite so. *"Exactly!" exclaimed George in agreement.*

ex • am • ine /ĭg zăm′ ĭn/ *v.* (**ex•am•ines, ex•am•ined, ex•am•in•ing**) to look at closely to find out the condition of; to inspect. *Examine the apples before you buy them.*

ex • cel /ĭk sĕl′/ *v.* (**ex•cels, ex•celled, ex•cell•ing**) to do better than others; to perform at a high level. *Colleen excels in mathematics.*

ex • cel • lence /ĕk′ sə ləns/ *n.* something in which a person surpasses others. *The school offered an award for excellence in spelling.*

ex • cel • lent /ĕk′ sə lənt/ *adj.* very good. *Their excellent singing received loud applause.*

ex • cite • ment /ĭk sīt′ mənt/ *n.* an excited condition; the state of being stirred up. *The entrance of the tigers created great excitement among the circus crowd.*

ex • clam • a • to • ry /ĭk sklăm′ ə tôr′ ē/ or /-tōr′ ē/ *adj.* expressing a forceful statement or sudden cry. *An exclamatory sentence ends with an exclamation point.*

ex • hale /ĕks hāl′/ *v.* (**ex•hales, ex•haled, ex•hal•ing**) to breathe out. *Swimmers exhale with their faces in the water.*

ex • hib • it¹ /ĭg zĭb′ ĭt/ *v.* to display; to reveal publicly. *His paintings were exhibited at the art fair.*

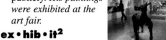

ex • hib • it² /ĭg zĭb′ ĭt/ *n.* a public show or display. *The school's trophies are on exhibit in the front lobby.*

exhibit

ex • per • i • ence /ĭk spîr′ ē əns/ *n.* **a.** a living through an event or series of events; a doing or feeling something. *Watching the baby birds hatch was a special experience.* **b.** what one learns from doing things. *I gained business experience from my paper route.*

ex • per • i • ment¹ /ĭk spĕr′ ə mənt/ *n.* a trial or test to learn, discover, or prove something. *An experiment with litmus paper will show whether a substance is an acid or a base.*

ex • per • i • ment² /ĭk spĕr′ ə mənt/ *v.* to test something to learn, discover, or prove something about it. *The artist experimented with several shades of paint.* [Latin *experīmentum,* from *experīrī,* to try.]

ex • pert¹ /ĕk′ spûrt/ *n.* a highly skilled or knowledgeable person. *Police detectives often consult a fingerprint expert.*

ex • pert² /ĕk′ spûrt/ *adj.* having a great deal of skill or knowledge: *an expert carpenter.*

ex • po • nent /ĭk spō′ nənt/ or /ĕk′ spō′ nənt/ *n.* a mathematical term that shows how many times the base number is to be multiplied by itself. *In the expression y^3, the 3 is an exponent.*

ex • press¹ /ĭk sprĕs′/ *v.* to tell; to make known. *Think for a moment before you try to express your idea.*

ex • press² /ĭk sprĕs′/ *adj.* quick and direct: *express mail.*

ex • pres • sion /ĭk sprĕsh′ ən/ *n.* **a.** a particular word or phrase. *"Hit the sack" is a slang expression for "go to bed."* **b.** a means of expressing something; an indication. *A sigh can be an expression of contentment.*

ex • tract¹ /ĭk străkt′/ *v.* **a.** to draw out or pull out by force: *extract a tooth.* **b.** to obtain a substance by a chemical process: *extract aluminum from bauxite.*

ex • tract² /ĕk′ străkt′/ *n.* **a.** a concentrated substance prepared from natural food or flavoring: *vanilla extract.* **b.** a passage from a literary work. *Our drama club presented extracts from Shakespeare's plays.*

fa • ble /fā′ bəl/ *n.* a brief tale or story, often with animal characters that speak and act like human beings, that teaches a useful lesson about human nature. *Her favorite fable is "The Tortoise and the Hare."*

284

fab • u • lous /făb′ yə ləs/ *adj.* **a.** belonging to legend or myth. *Elves are fabulous creatures.* **b.** amazing; wonderful. *It was a fabulous party.* [Latin *fābula*, fable.]

fac • tor[1] /făk′ tər/ *n.* **a.** any of the things that cause a certain result. *Time is an important factor to consider in cooking.* **b.** any of the numbers multiplied to obtain a product. *Factors of 21 are 3 and 7.*

fac • tor[2] /făk′ tər/ *v.* to separate into factors. *If you factor 21, you get 3 and 7.*

Fahr • en • heit /făr′ ən hīt′/ *adj.* of or according to the Fahrenheit scale, where the freezing point of water is 32° and the boiling point is 212°: *the Fahrenheit scale.*

faint[1] /fānt/ *adj.* **a.** lacking strength; weak and dizzy. *If you feel faint, sit or lie down.* **b.** unclear; dim. *A faint light came from a window in the house.*

faint[2] /fānt/ *v.* to lose consciousness and lie as if asleep because of illness, weakness, etc. *He fainted because he was very tired and hungry.*

fam • ine /făm′ ĭn/ *n.* an extreme shortage of food, causing widespread hunger. *The Red Cross shipped food and medicine to the areas of Africa hit by the famine.*

fan • ci • ful /făn′ sĭ fəl/ *adj.* imaginative; unreal. *Science fiction writers create fanciful worlds.*

fash • ion[1] /făsh′ ən/ *n.* **a.** a style of dressing or behaving. *Fashions change yearly.* **b.** way or manner. *She smiled in an odd fashion.*

fash • ion[2] /făsh′ ən/ *v.* to shape; to form. *Birds fashion nests of grass and twigs.*

fa • vor • a • ble /fā′ vər ə bəl/ or /fāv′ rə-/ *adj.* (**fa•vor•a•bly,** *adv.*) **a.** encouraging: *a favorable answer.* **b.** helpful: *favorable winds.*

fa • vor • ite[1] /fā′ vər ĭt/ or /fāv′ rĭt/ *adj.* most liked; preferred. *Broccoli is my favorite vegetable.*

fa • vor • ite[2] /fā′ vər ĭt/ or /fāv′ rĭt/ *n.* the one most liked or preferred. *Which is your favorite team in the World Series?*

fear • less /fîr′ lĭs/ *adj.* not afraid; brave. *The fearless kitten confronted the big dog.*

fee • ble /fē′ bəl/ *adj.* without much strength; weak. *Newborn animals are often feeble.*

fer • ti • liz • er /fûr′ tl ī′ zər/ *n.* something added to soil to make it more productive. *Compost makes a good garden fertilizer.*

fierce /fîrs/ *adj.* **a.** savage; wild. *The fierce lion growled and paced inside the cage.* **b.** violent. *The fierce wind blew down trees.*

film /fĭlm/ *n.* **a.** a thin, flat material coated with a chemical and used for taking photographs. *I put a new roll of film in my camera.* **b.** a motion picture. *Many old films are shown.* **c.** a thin coating: *a film of ice.*

fi • nal • ly /fī′ nə lē/ *adv.* at last. *I finally got the job done.*

fi • nance /fə năns′/ or /fī′ năns′/ *n.* the management of large amounts of money. *Bankers must be skilled in finance.*

fis • cal /fĭs′ kəl/ *adj.* relating to money matters. *A government's fiscal policy determines how much money it spends.*

flex • i • ble /flĕk′ sə bəl/ *adj.* **a.** capable of being bent. *The clay figures were still flexible enough to shape.* **b.** adjustable, changeable: *a flexible schedule.*

flop • py disk /flŏp′ ē dĭsk′/ *n.* a flexible plastic disk used to store computer data. *The information is stored on a floppy disk.*

floppy disk

flow • chart /flō′ chärt′/ *n.* a diagram showing the sequence of operations. *A flow chart is helpful in writing computer programs.*

flu • id /floo′ ĭd/ *n.* any substance, such as water or air, that flows easily. *"Drink plenty of fluids," the doctor advised.*

flut • ist /floo′ tĭst/ *n.* a person who plays a woodwind instrument called the flute. *The flutist and the oboist played a haunting duet.*

forc • i • ble /fôr′ sə bəl/ or /fōr′-/ *adj.* using or applying physical force: *a forcible entry.*

fore • man /fôr′ mən/ or /fōr′-/ *n.* a person in charge of a group of workers: *the construction foreman.*

for • get • ful /fər gĕt′ fəl/ or /fôr′-/ *adj.* tending to forget; unable to recall. *Because Sandra is often forgetful, she writes notes to remind herself to do things.*

for • mer¹ /fôr′ mər/ *adj.* coming earlier in time or before in position. *The former owner of this house painted the walls blue.*

for • mer² /fôr′ mər/ *n.* the first of two things talked about. *When Tom was given the choice of visiting Los Angeles or New York, he chose the former because he had never been to California.*

for • tu • nate /fôr′ chə nĭt/ *adj.* lucky. *You were fortunate to find the lost bracelet.*

frag • ment /frăg′ mənt/ *n.* **a.** a piece broken off. *The vase broke into fragments when it fell to the floor.* **b.** something incomplete. *An incomplete sentence is called a sentence fragment.*

freeze /frēz/ *v.* (**freez•es, froze, fro•zen, freez•ing**) **a.** to become ice; to turn to ice. *The lake froze during the night.* **b.** to chill something until it becomes cold and hard as ice. *We freeze the vegetables from our garden so they will last through the winter.*

fruit • less /froot′ lĭs/ *adj.* **a.** not producing any fruit. *The fig tree was fruitless.* **b.** unsuccessful; unproductive. *They conducted a fruitless search for the missing papers.*

-ful a suffix that means "full of" or "having," used to form adjectives: *joyful.*

ful • fill /fool fĭl′/ *v.* **a.** to bring into effect; to make real. *The team fulfilled their goal of having a winning season.* **b.** to finish; to complete. *Scouts must fulfill requirements to earn badges.*

fu • ri • ous /fyoor′ ē əs/ *adj.* **a.** very angry. *I was furious with myself for forgetting my homework.* **b.** strong; violent. *The furious storm raged for hours.*

fur • nace /fûr′ nĭs/ *n.* an enclosed structure in which to make a fire. *Furnaces are used to heat buildings, melt metal, and fire pottery.*

gal • ax • y /găl′ ək sē/ *n.* (**gal•ax•ies** *pl.*) a large group of stars. *Our solar system is part of the Milky Way galaxy.*

ga • rage /gə räzh′/ or /-räj′/ *n.* **a.** a building in which cars are kept. *She backed the car out of the garage.* **b.** a place where vehicles are repaired or stored. *The workers at the garage will install new brakes.* [French *garer,* to shelter.]

garage

gar • bage /gär′ bĭj/ *n.* spoiled food or waste matter that is thrown away. *We put our garbage in cans in the alley.*

ge • og • ra • pher /jē ŏg′ rə fər/ *n.* a person who specializes in the study of geography. *The geographer studied the terrain using maps.*

ge • og • ra • phy /jē ŏg′ rə fē/ *n.* **a.** the study of Earth and its features and inhabitants. *In geography we learn that trade and commerce depend upon rivers, mountains, and other natural features.* **b.** the landscape of a place. *The geography of Colorado is rugged.* [Greek *geō-,* from *gē,* earth + *graphein,* to write.]

ge • ol • o • gist /jē ŏl′ ə jĭst/ *n.* a person who specializes in the study of geology. *The geologist explained volcanic action.*

ge·ol·o·gy /jē ŏl′ ə jē/ *n.* the scientific study of the composition and history of the earth's structure. *Scientists use geology when they try to locate water or minerals underground.*

ge·om·e·try /jē ŏm′ ĭ trē/ *n.* the mathematical study of the measurements and relationships of solid and plane figures. *In geometry we learned that a circle has 360 degrees.* [Greek *geō-*, from *gē*, earth + *metron*, measure.]

glaze /glāz/ *n.* a coating applied to ceramics before firing. *After the pot was fired the glaze gave it a smooth, shiny surface.*

glo·ri·ous /glôr′ ē əs/ or /glōr′-/ *adj.* **a.** producing honor and glory; deserving praise. *The discovery of a way to prevent polio was a glorious triumph of medicine.* **b.** beautiful; brilliant. *This is a glorious day.* [Latin *glōria*, glory.]

golf /gŏlf/ or /gôlf/ *n.* a game played with a small hard ball and a set of clubs. *The object of golf is to hit the ball into certain holes using the fewest possible strokes.*

golf

good·ness /gŏŏd′ nĭs/ *n.* the condition of being good. *He determines the goodness of an apple by its taste.*

gor·geous /gôr′ jəs/ *adj.* very beautiful; stunning; magnificent. *From an airplane the view of the Grand Canyon is gorgeous.* [Old French *gorgias*, elegant.]

gram·mar /grăm′ ər/ *n.* the study of how words are arranged in sentences. *A knowledge of grammar helps us write effectively.*

graph·ic /grăf′ ĭk/ *adj.* **a.** vivid; strong; clear. *Your graphic description of the painting made it easier to find in the museum.* **b.** relating to art, printing, or engraving: *graphic arts.* [Greek *graphein*, to write.]

grav·i·ty /grăv′ ĭ tē/ *n.* the force that draws all objects toward the center of Earth. *A ball that is thrown into the air returns to the ground because of gravity.*

graze /grāz/ *v.* (**graz•es, grazed, graz•ing**) to eat grass in a field or pasture. *The cattle grazed by the river.*

Pronunciation Key

ă	pat	ŏ	pot	th	thin
ā	pay	ō	toe	th	this
âr	care	ô	paw, for	hw	which
ä	father	oi	noise	zh	vision
ĕ	pet	ou	out	ə	about,
ē	be	ŏŏ	took		item,
ĭ	pit	ōō	boot		pencil,
ī	pie	ŭ	cut		gallop,
îr	pier	ûr	urge		circus

grief /grēf/ *n.* great sorrow or sadness. *Eveyone felt grief when the great leader became ill.*

grown-up /grōn′ ŭp′/ *adj.* not childish; mature; adult. *Jason asked for a grown-up bike for his birthday.*

guard·i·an /gär′ dē ən/ *n.* **a.** a person or thing that takes care of or protects. *Every citizen must act as a guardian of democracy.* **b.** a person appointed by a court to care for another person. *The form has a blank for the name of your parent or guardian.* [Old French *garder*, to guard.]

guide·book /gīd′ bŏŏk′/ *n.* a handbook of information for tourists. *The city guidebook lists museums, restaurants, and parks.*

hand·ker·chief /hăng′ kər chĭf/ *n.* a small square of cloth used for wiping the nose or worn as decoration. *Mr. Weiss wore a maroon handerkerchief that matched his tie.*

hard·ware /härd′ wâr′/ *n.* **a.** articles made from metal. *Nails, bolts, and wire are hardware.* **b.** machines or other physical equipment needed to perform a particular task: *computer hardware.*

her·i·tage /hĕr′ ĭ tĭj/ *n.* that which is passed down from preceding generations; tradition. *The book* Roots *deals with the heritage of African Americans.*

Spelling Dictionary

287

home•ward[1] /hōm′ wərd/ *adv.* at or toward home. *The ship sailed homeward.*

home•ward[2] /hōm′ wərd/ *adj.* toward home: *the homeward journey.*

hon•or•ar•y /ŏn′ ə rĕr′ ē/ *adj.* given as a token of honor: *an honorary key to the city.*

hor•ri•ble /hôr′ ə bəl/ or /hŏr′-/ *adj.* **a.** causing horror; shocking; dreadful: *a horrible disease.* **b.** very unpleasant: *a horrible grating noise.*

horse•pow•er /hôrs′ pou′ ər/ *n.* a unit of power equal to the amount needed to raise a weight of 550 pounds one inch in one second. *An engine's strength is measured in horsepower.*

hue /hyōō/ *n.* a color or a shade or tint of a color. *The bright fabric contained some lovely red and purple hues.*

hus•band /hŭz′ bənd/ *n.* the man a woman is married to. *When they were married, her husband gave her a ring.*

hy•drau•lic /hī drô′ lĭk/ *adj.* powered by a liquid under pressure: *a hydraulic drill.*

hy•giene /hī′ jēn/ *n.* the science of keeping well; the study of rules of health. *We learn about hygiene in our health class.*

hymn /hĭm/ *n.* a song of praise. *The poet wrote a hymn in praise of nature.*

-ian a suffix, used to form nouns, that means "one who": *custodian.*

-ible a suffix, used to form adjectives, that means: **a.** capable of: *flexible.* **b.** tending toward: *sensible.*

i•de•al[1] /ī dē′ əl/ or /ī dēl′/ *n.* a perfect type; an idea of something that is perfect. *Our nation was founded on the ideal that citizens can govern themselves.*

i•de•al[2] /ī dē′ əl/ or /ī dēl′/ *adj.* perfect; exactly as one would wish. *A warm day and a clear sky are ideal conditions for a picnic.*

ig•no•rant /ĭg′ nər ənt/ *adj.* not having education or knowledge. *A person ignorant of history might think Brazilians speak Spanish.*

ig•nore /ĭg nôr′/ or /-nōr′/ *v.* (**ig•nores, ig•nored, ig•nor•ing**) to pay no attention to; to refuse to notice. *Anita ignored their silly remarks.*

il- a prefix that means "not": *illicit.* **Il-** replaces **in-** before words that begin with **l**.

il•le•gal /ĭ lē′ gəl/ *adj.* not legal; against the law. *In many states it is illegal to litter.*

il•leg•i•ble /ĭ lĕj′ ə bəl/ *adj.* (**il•leg•i•bly,** *adv.*) not able to be read; blurred or poorly written. *The handwriting on the old letter was nearly illegible.*

il•lit•er•ate /ĭ lĭt′ ər ĭt/ *adj.* unable to read or write. *Teaching illiterate persons to read will help them vote wisely and find new jobs.*

il•log•i•cal /ĭ lŏj′ ĭ kəl/ *adj.* senseless; not according to the principles of logic. *In* Alice's Adventures in Wonderland, *Alice finds herself in an illogical world.*

i•mag•i•nar•y /ĭ măj′ ə nĕr′ ē/ *adj.* not real; happening only in the mind. *Unicorns are imaginary animals.*

im•me•di•ate /ĭ mē′ dē ĭt/ *adj.* happening right away; without delay. *The immediate effect of the medicine was to stop his coughing.*

im•per•a•tive /ĭm pĕr′ ə tĭv/ *adj.* **a.** expressing a command. *An imperative sentence gives an order.* **b.** urgent; necessary. *It is imperative that you come at once.*

im•por•tance /ĭm pôr′ tns/ *n.* significance; value. *Never underestimate the importance of correct spelling.*

im•press /ĭm prĕs′/ *v.* **a.** to affect strongly or favorably. *Her fluent French impressed all of us.* **b.** to fix firmly in the mind. *He impressed upon us the need to remain quiet.*

in- a prefix that means "not": *inattentive.*

in•deed /ĭn dēd′/ *adv.* in fact; really. *This meal is indeed delicious.*

in•dict /ĭn dīt′/ *v.* to formally charge with a crime. *The grand jury indicted a suspect in the murder case.*

Spelling Dictionary

in • dus • tri • ous /ĭn dŭs′ trē əs/ *adj.*
hard-working; diligent. *Industrious students
usually enjoy school.*

in • for • ma • tion /ĭn′ fər mā′ shən/ *n.*
knowledge; facts; something that is told. *They
searched in the library for information about
the history of Alaska.* [Latin *īnfōrmāre,* to
inform, from *in-,* in + *fōrma,* form.]

in • hale /ĭn hāl′/ *v.* (in•hales, in•haled,
in•hal•ing) to breathe in; to take air into the
lungs. *The doctor told me to inhale deeply.*

in • her • it /ĭn hĕr′ ĭt/ *v.* **a.** to receive something from a person who has died. *Lisa
inherited her aunt's ring.* **b.** to receive from
a parent as a genetic trait. *Stuart inherited
his father's blue eyes.*

in • her • i • tance /ĭn hĕr′ ĭ təns/ *n.* heritage; something inherited. *Our instinct for
survival is an inheritance from many previous generations.*

in • no • cence /ĭn′ ə səns/ *n.* the state of
being innocent; the absence of guilt or
wrongdoing. *The suspect's alibi proved his
innocence.*

in • no • cent /ĭn′ ə sənt/ *adj.* **a.** not guilty.
She claimed she was innocent of the crime.
b. harmless; having no bad effect: *an innocent trick.* **c.** unaware of evil. *An innocent
child trusts everyone.*

in • put /ĭn′ po͝ot′/ *n.* anything put into a system to produce a result, or output. *For the
computer program to work, your input must
contain all the necessary data.*

in • sert /ĭn sûrt′/ *v.* **a.** to put into. *Insert a
coin into the slot.* **b.** to add. *Insert an example in this paragraph to strengthen it.*

in • stance /ĭn′ stəns/ *n.* an example; a case.
*In most instances students adjust quickly to
new schools.*

in • stant¹ /ĭn′ stənt/ *n.* a short time; a
moment. *The runner paused for an instant
to catch his breath.*

in • stant² /ĭn′ stənt/ *adj.* immediate; taking
place quickly. *She demanded an instant reply.*

in • stru • ment /ĭn′ strə mənt/ *n.* **a.** a tool.
A pen is a writing instrument. **b.** a device
for making music. *A piano is a musical
instrument.* [Latin *īnstrūmentum,* tool, from
īnstruere, to prepare.]

Pronunciation Key

ă	pat	ŏ	pot	th	thin
ā	pay	ō	toe	*th*	this
âr	care	ô	paw, for	hw	which
ä	father	oi	noise	zh	vision
ĕ	pet	ou	out	ə	about,
ē	be	o͝o	took		item,
ĭ	pit	o͞o	boot		pencil,
ī	pie	ŭ	cut		gallop,
îr	pier	ûr	urge		circus

in • sult¹ /ĭn sŭlt′/ *v.* to treat with rudeness;
to hurt feelings on purpose. *It is not polite
to insult someone.*

in • sult² /ĭn′ sŭlt′/ *n.* a rude or hurtful
remark or act. *I meant that as a compliment, not an insult.*

in • sur • ance /ĭn sho͝or′ əns/ *n.* the business of guaranteeing to cover specified
losses in the future, as in the case of accident, illness, theft, or death, in return for the
continuing payment of regular sums of
money. *Drivers in many states must maintain accident insurance.*

in • sure /ĭn sho͝or′/ *v.* (in•sures, in•sured,
in•sur•ing) to arrange for a payment of
money in case of loss or illness by paying
regularly to an insurance company. *My parents insured our house against fire.*

inter- a prefix that means "between" or
"among": *interlocking.*

in • ter • act /ĭn′ tər ăkt′/ *v.* to act on or
influence each other. *After-school activities
allow students to interact with each other.*

in • ter • change¹ /ĭn′ tər chānj′/ *v.*
(in•ter•chang•es, in•ter•changed,
in•ter•chang•ing) to switch the places of.
*The parts of a jigsaw puzzle cannot be
interchanged.*

in • ter • change²
/ĭn′ tər chānj′/ *n.* **a.** a mutual exchange: *an interchange
of ideas.* **b.** an intersection:
a highway interchange.

in • ter • est rate
/ĭn′ trĭst rāt′/ *n.* the rate
charged for borrowing money. *Low interest
rates encourage people to borrow money.*

interchange

in • ter • face /ĭn' tər fās'/ *v.* (in•ter•fac•es, in•ter•faced, in•ter•fac•ing) to join or connect at a common point or surface. *The parts of an electrical system must interface smoothly.* [Latin *inter,* between + *faciēs,* face.]

in • ter • rog • a • tive /ĭn' tə rŏg' ə tĭv/ *adj.* asking a question. *An interrogative sentence ends with a question mark.*

in • ter • sect /ĭn' tər sĕkt'/ *v.* to cross; to meet at a common point. *I'll meet you where Eighth Street intersects Main.* [Latin *inter,* between + *sect-,* perfect stem of *sēcare,* to cut.]

in • ter • state /ĭn' tər stāt'/ *adj.* connecting two or more states: *an interstate highway.*

in • ter • view[1] /ĭn' tər vyōō'/ *n.* a meeting of two people to discuss something. *The graduate had a job interview with an employer.*

in • ter • view[2] /ĭn' tər vyōō'/ *v.* to meet and talk with in the hope of getting information. *The reporter interviewed the committee members.*

intra- a prefix that means "within": *intravenous.*

in • tra • mu • ral /ĭn' trə myōōr' əl/ *adj.* consisting of participants from the same school: *intramural sports.* [Latin *intrā,* within + *mūrus,* wall.]

in • tra • state /ĭn' trə stāt'/ *adj.* existing within the boundaries of a state. *Intrastate telephone rates may be higher than those for out-of-state calls.*

in • tro • duce /ĭn' trə dōōs'/ or /-dyōōs'/ *v.* (in•tro•duc•es, in•tro•duced, in•tro•duc•ing) **a.** to present; to bring into contact with. *Mrs. Rogers, may I introduce my mother?* **b.** to bring in. *New inventions introduce different ways of doing things.* [Latin *intrōdūcere,* from *intro,* within + *dūcere,* to lead.]

in • tro • duc • tion /ĭn' trə dŭk' shən/ *n.* **a.** being brought in or acquainted with. *Visiting the school board meeting was an introduction to politics.* **b.** the first part, as of a book. *Read the chapter introduction carefully.* **c.** a basic explanation: *an introduction to first aid.* [Latin *intrōduct-,* perfect stem of *intrōdūcere,* to bring in, to introduce.]

in • trude /ĭn trōōd'/ *v.* (in•trudes, in•trud•ed, in•trud•ing) to interrupt; to break in without being asked. *It's not polite to intrude on a private conversation.*

in • va • lid[1] /ĭn' və lĭd/ *n.* an ill or injured person who needs care. *After he recovered from his injury, he was no longer an invalid.*

in • val • id[2] /ĭn văl' ĭd/ *adj.* not authentic; questionable. *If your pass isn't signed by the teacher or the principal, it is invalid.*

in • ven • tion /ĭn vĕn' shən/ *n.* a device, method, or process that is developed or created. *The electric light bulb and the phonograph are two inventions of Thomas A. Edison.*

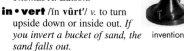
invention

in • vert /ĭn vûrt'/ *v.* to turn upside down or inside out. *If you invert a bucket of sand, the sand falls out.*

in • vest /ĭn vĕst'/ *v.* to put money into something to make a profit. *Many Americans invest in savings bonds.*

in • vis • i • ble /ĭn vĭz' ə bəl/ *adj.* not capable of being seen. *Her hearing aid is so tiny it is almost invisible.*

in • ward[1] /ĭn' wərd/ *adv.* toward the inside or center. *The door opened inward.*

in • ward[2] /ĭn' wərd/ *adj.* inside a thing or a person; inner: *inward doubts.*

-ion a suffix, used to form nouns, that means "the result of an action or process": *introduction.*

ir- a prefix that means "not": *irreversible.* **Ir-** replaces **in-** before words that begin with **r.**

IRA an abbreviation for "Individual Retirement Account." *I put the money from my summer job into an IRA.*

ir • ra • tion • al /ĭ răsh' ə nəl/ *adj.* without reason or clear thought. *Many fears are irrational.*

ir•reg•u•lar /ĭ rĕg′ yə lər/ *adj.* not conforming to the usual rule or practice; different. *The coin is valuable because of its irregular markings.*

ir•re•sis•ti•ble /ĭr′ ĭ zĭs′ tə bəl/ *adj.* too strong to be resisted; compelling. *Although he was on a diet, his desire for the food was irresistible.*

ir•ri•gate /ĭr′ i gāt′/ *v.* (**ir•ri•gates, ir•ri•gat•ed, ir•ri•gat•ing**) to supply water to by a system of ditches or pipes. *Farmers irrigate land that does not get enough rain.*

IRS an abbreviation for "Internal Revenue Service." *Most adults file income tax reports with the IRS each year.*

isle /īl/ *n.* an island, especially a small one. *The Isle of Wight is located off the coast of England.*

▶ **Isle** sounds like **aisle**.

is•sue /ĭsh′ ōō/ *v.* (**is•sues, is•sued, is•su•ing**) to circulate or distribute in an official capacity; to send out. *The principal issued a memo explaining the new fire drill procedure.*

i•tem /ī′ təm/ *n.* **a.** a separate article. *Which item shall we buy first?* **b.** a piece of news: *an item in a newspaper.*

jeal•ous /jĕl′ əs/ *adj.* worried about losing someone's affection to another person; resentful of another person's good fortune. *The toddler is jealous of the attention his new brother is getting.*

jew•el•ry /jōō′ əl rē/ *n.* jewels; ornaments of gold, silver, gems, etc. *The children enjoy dressing up in their grandmother's costume jewelry.*

jour•nal /jûr′ nəl/ *n.* a personal record of activities and feelings, kept on a regular basis. *Ramon kept a journal of his summer experiences.*

jour•nal•ist /jûr′ nə lĭst/ *n.* a person whose career is in writing, editing, or publishing news stories. *My mother is a journalist who covers courthouse news for the local paper.*

Pronunciation Key

ă	pat	ŏ	pot	th	thin
ā	pay	ō	toe	*th*	this
âr	care	ô	paw, for	hw	which
ä	father	oi	noise	zh	vision
ĕ	pet	ou	out	ə	about,
ē	be	ŏŏ	took		item,
ĭ	pit	ōō	boot		pencil,
ī	pie	ŭ	cut		gallop,
îr	pier	ûr	urge		circus

kiln /kĭln/ or /kĭl/ *n.* an oven used to bake or fire ceramics. *The kiln must be very hot for the pottery to harden.*

kins•man /kĭnz′ mən/ *n.* a male relative. *A kinsman is a male relative, and a kinswoman is a female relative.*

kiln

knack /năk/ *n.* a special talent for doing something. *Philip has a knack for writing short stories.*

kneel /nēl/ *v.* (**kneels, knelt** or **kneeled, kneel•ing**) to rest on bent knees. *Be careful not to kneel in the dirt.*

knob /nŏb/ *n.* a rounded handle on a door, TV set, drawer, etc. *The knob on the right of the radio controls the sound.*

knowl•edge /nŏl′ ĭj/ *n.* everything that one knows or understands about something. *Her knowledge of baseball statistics is impressive.*

la•bel /lā′ bəl/ *n.* a small piece of paper used for identification or instructions. *When you buy canned or packaged food, you can read the label to find out the contents.*

la•bor /lā′ bər/ *n.* physical work. *Moving these stones is hard labor.*

la•goon /lə gōōn′/ *n.* a shallow body of water near or connected with a larger body of water. *A lagoon may be separated from the sea by sandbars.*

la•ser /lā′ zər/ *n.* an acronym for a device that strengthens light to produce a thin, powerful beam. *Lasers are used in industry, medicine, and communications.* [**L**ight **a**mplification by **s**timulated **e**mission of **r**adiation.]

leath•er /lĕth′ ər/ *n.* the dressed or tanned hide of an animal. *Gloves and jackets made of leather are soft, warm, and durable.*

le•gal /lē′ gəl/ *adj.* permitted by law. *A left turn at this corner is not legal.*

leg•end /lĕj′ ənd/ *n.* a popular story handed down from earlier times. *The story of King Arthur and his knights is an English legend.*

leg•i•ble /lĕj′ ə bəl/ *adj.* (**leg•i•bly,** *adv.*) able to be read. *Check to be sure that your handwriting is legible.*

lei•sure /lē′ zhər/ *adj.* free; not busy. *Our leisure time was spent reading and listening to music.* [Latin *licēre,* to be permitted.]

lens /lĕnz/ *n.* (**lens•es** *pl.*) a piece of clear, curved glass or plastic used to bend light rays. *Lenses are used in eyeglasses, cameras, telescopes, and microscopes.*

lens

-less a suffix, used to form adjectives, that means "without": *endless.*

li•brar•i•an /lī′ brâr′ ē ən/ *n.* a person who specializes in library work. *The librarian can help you find the materials you need for your report.*

li•cense /lī′ səns/ *n.* a document giving official permission; a permit. *Ms. Soto obtained a pilot's license after she learned how to fly a plane.*

lieu•ten•ant /lōō tĕn′ ənt/ *n.* an officer usually ranking next below a captain. *The army officer was promoted from second to first lieutenant.* [Old French *lieu,* in place of + *tenant,* past participle of *tenir,* to hold.]

lim•it /lĭm′ ĭt/ *n.* the greatest amount permitted. *The speed limit on this street is thirty miles an hour.*

lin•e•ar /lĭn′ ē ər/ *adj.* of or relating to a straight line. *A foot is a linear measurement.*

lin•guis•tics /lĭng gwĭs′ tĭks/ *n.* the science of language that deals with the nature and structure of speech. *Phonetics is a branch of linguistics that is especially useful in spelling.*

link•ing verb /lĭngk′ ĭng vûrb′/ *n.* a verb, such as a form of "be," that links the predicate of a sentence to the subject. *In the sentence "They seemed happy," "seemed" is a linking verb.*

lit•er•ate /lĭt′ ər ĭt/ *adj.* able to read and write. *In school we are taught to be literate.*

liv•er /lĭv′ ər/ *n.* a large organ of the body located near the stomach that produces digestive juices. *The work of the liver includes helping change food into fuel for the body.*

lo•cal /lō′ kəl/ *adj.* having to do with a certain place or a nearby area. *Our local news programs inform us about our own area.*

lo•ca•tion /lō kā′ shən/ *n.* a place; a position. *This quiet field is a good location for our campsite.* [Latin *locātiō,* a placing, from *locāre,* to place, from *locus,* place.]

log•i•cal /lŏj′ ĭ kəl/ *adj.* using logic; sensible. *When asked to make a decision, he made the logical choice.*

lone•some /lōn′ səm/ *adj.* lonely; sad from being alone. *My little sister kept my puppy from getting lonesome while I was at school.*

loose /lōōs/ *adj.* (**loos•er, loos•est; loose•ly,** *adv.*) not fastened tightly; slack. *I have a loose button on my coat.*

loud•ness /loud′ nĭs/ *n.* the state of being loud. *The loudness of a sound is measured in units called decibels.*

lu•nar /lōō′ nər/ *adj.* of or relating to the moon: *a lunar eclipse.*

-ly a suffix, used to form adverbs, that means "in a way that is" or "in the manner of": *quietly.*

ma•chin•er•y /mə shē′ nə rē/ *n.*
machines or machine parts. *Farm machinery has made it possible for farmers to
grow larger crops.*

mag•a•zine /măg′ ə zēn′/ or
/măg′ ə zēn′/ *n.* a periodical publication
that may contain articles, stories, or poems.
We receive two monthly magazines.

man•ner /măn′ ər/ *n.* way; fashion. *The
students left the bus in an orderly manner.*

mar•ble /mär′ bəl/ *n.* a kind of rock that
can be polished to a smooth, shiny finish.
Many statues are carved from marble.

ma•rim•ba
/mə rĭm′ bə/ *n.* an
instrument played by
striking wooden bars
arranged in a musical
scale; a large xylo-
phone. *The marimba is
of African origin.*

marimba

mar•riage /măr′ ĭj/ *n.* the state of being
married; life as husband and wife. *The couple celebrated fifty years of marriage.*

mass /măs/ *n.* the volume or bulk of a body
or object. *The mass of an object does not
change when it is broken, melted, or frozen.*

ma•te•ri•al /mə tîr′ ē əl/ *n.* the parts or
substances from which a thing is made. *The
material for the roof was delivered before
the workers arrived.*

mead•ow /mĕd′ ō/ *n.* a field in which
grass or hay grows naturally. *The cows
grazed in the meadow.*

meas•ure•ment /mĕzh′ ər mənt/ *n.*
a. the act of measuring or the process of
being measured. *A gallon is a unit of liquid
measurement.* **b.** the length, size, or amount
of something. *Her waist measurement is
twenty-five inches.*

mech•a•nize /mĕk′ ə nīz′/ *v.*
(mech•a•niz•es, mech•a•nized,
mech•a•niz•ing) to equip with machinery:
mechanize a factory.

Pronunciation Key

ă	pat	ŏ	pot	th	thin
ā	pay	ō	toe	*th*	this
âr	care	ô	paw, for	hw	which
ä	father	oi	noise	zh	vision
ĕ	pet	ou	out	ə	about,
ē	be	ŏŏ	took		item,
ĭ	pit	ōō	boot		pencil,
ī	pie	ŭ	cut		gallop,
îr	pier	ûr	urge		circus

me•di•um /mē′ dē əm/ *adj.* having,
being, or occupying a middle position;
moderate. *Warm the soup over medium
heat.*

mel•o•dy /mĕl′ ə dē/ *n.* (mel•o•dies *pl.*)
a series of musical tones making up a tune.
He whistled the melody of a popular song.

-ment a suffix, used to form nouns, that
means "the result of an action or process":
advancement.

mer•chant /mûr′ chənt/ *n.* a person who
buys and sells goods. *The three fabric
stores in this area are owned by the same
merchant.* [Latin *mercari,* to trade.]

me•tab•o•lism /mə tăb′ ə lĭz′ əm/ *n.*
the physical and chemical processes that
maintain life. *Doctors can check the rate of
your metabolism.*

me•te•or•ite /mē′ tē ə rīt′/ *n.* a piece of
a meteor that does not burn up completely
in Earth's atmosphere and lands on the surface of Earth. *This rock may have been part
of a meteorite.*

meth•od /mĕth′ əd/ *n.* a system; a way of
doing something. *Broiling is one method of
preparing fish.*

mid- a prefix that means "a middle part, time
or location": *midway.*

mid•sum•mer /mĭd′ sŭm′ ər/ *n.* the
middle of the summer. *We had our family
reunion at the beach in midsummer.*

mid•way¹ /mĭd′ wā′/ *adv.* in the middle of
the way or distance; halfway. *The equator
circles Earth midway between the poles.*

Spelling Dictionary

293

mid•way² /mĭd′ wā′/ *adj.* in the middle of a way, distance, period of time, or succession of events: *at the midway point in the baseball season.*

mile•age /mīl′ ĭj/ *n.* the number of miles covered. *What was the total mileage of the trip?*

mil•i•tar•y¹ /mĭl′ ĭ tĕr ē/ *n.* the armed forces. *Soldiers and sailors serve in the military.*

mil•i•tar•y² /mĭl′ ĭ tĕr ē/ *adj.* having to do with the armed forces: *a military parade.*

min•ute¹ /mĭn′ ĭt/ *n.* **a.** one of the sixty equal parts into which an hour is divided; sixty seconds. *We were given ten minutes to do each part of the test.* **b.** the exact moment. *I recognized him the minute I saw him.*

mi•nute² /mī nōōt′/ or /-nyōōt′/ *adj.* tiny; very small. *Minute bits of dust floated through the ray of sunlight.*

mir•ror¹ /mĭr′ ər/ *n.* **a.** a glass or other reflective surface. *We saw the reflection in the mirror.* **b.** anything that gives a true account or picture. *The book is a mirror of modern society.*

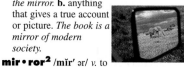

mir•ror² /mĭr′ ər/ *v.* to reflect. *The setting sun was mirrored on the surface of the lake.*

mirror

mis- a prefix that means: **a.** bad; badly; wrong; wrongly: *misconduct.* **b.** failure; lack: *misfire.*

mis•be•have /mĭs′ bĭ hāv′/ *v.* (mis•be•haves, mis•be•haved, mis•be•hav•ing) to act badly or improperly. *Puppies sometimes misbehave by chewing on shoes.*

mis•chief /mĭs′ chĭf/ *n.* **a.** conduct or actions that cause or could cause harm, injury, or damage. *Mother asked me to stay out of mischief.* **b.** harmless and merry teasing or pranks. *My kitten is full of mischief.* [Old French *meschief,* misfortune.]

mis•for•tune /mĭs fôr′ chən/ *n.* bad luck. *It was his misfortune to lose his wallet.*

mis•in•form /mĭs′ ĭn fôrm′/ *v.* to give wrong or false information. *We were misinformed about the day of the party; it was Thursday, not Tuesday.*

mis•lead /mĭs lēd′/ *v.* (mis•leads, mis•led, mis•lead•ing) to guide in the wrong direction; to confuse. *A misspelled word may mislead the reader.*

mis•place /mĭs plās′/ *v.* (mis•plac•es, mis•placed, mis•plac•ing) to put in a wrong place; to mislay. *Megan searched for the notebook she had misplaced.*

mis•read /mĭs rēd′/ *v.* (mis•reads, mis•read, mis•read•ing) to read or understand incorrectly. *Because he misread the instructions, he couldn't assemble the kite.*

mis•trust¹ /mĭs trŭst′/ *n.* lack of trust. *Her mistrust showed in her frowning expression.*

mis•trust² /mĭs trŭst′/ *v.* to view without confidence. *Don't mistrust your ability; I think you'll do a great job.*

mis•use¹ /mĭs yōōs′/ *n.* incorrect or improper use. *The misuse of a word can cause confusion.*

mis•use² /mĭs yōōz′/ *v.* (mis•us•es, mis•used, mis•us•ing) to use wrongly or incorrectly. *Don't misuse the piano by banging on the keys.*

mod•er•ate /mŏd′ ər ĭt/ *adj.* within reasonable limits; not extreme: *a moderate price.*

mod•i•fi•er /mŏd′ ə fī′ ər/ *n.* a word, phrase, or clause that limits or qualifies the meaning of another word or group of words. *Adjectives and adverbs are modifiers.*

mod•ule /mŏj′ ōōl/ *n.* a self-contained unit of a spacecraft; a unit with a specific function. *The engineers at NASA designed a new space module.*

mo•men•tar•y /mō′ mən tĕr′ ē/ *adj.* (mo•men•tar•i•ly, *adv.*) brief; lasting a short time. *There was a momentary lull in the storm.*

mo•res /môr′ āz/ or /mōr′-/ *n. pl.* the customs accepted by a particular social group. *We should respect the mores of other societies.*

mor • tar /môr′ tər/ *n.*
a. a mixture of cement or lime with sand and water. *The construction worker laid bricks with mortar.*
b. a bowl in which substances are crushed or ground. *The pharmacist uses a mortar and pestle to grind the medicines.*

mortar and pestle

moun • tain • ous /moun′ tə nəs/ *adj.* having mountains; filled with or covered by mountains. *The western part of the United States contains many mountainous areas.*

mph or **m.p.h.** an abbreviation for "miles per hour." *The speed limit in our town is 30 mph.*

mul • ti • ple¹ /mŭl′ tə pəl/ *adj.* having many parts. *His multiple interests include sports, music, and movies.*

mul • ti • ple² /mŭl′ tə pəl/ *n.* a quantity that can be evenly divided by another quantitiy. *Four is a multiple of two.*

mul • ti • pli • cand /mŭl′ tə plĭ kănd′/ *n.* a number multiplied by another. *In 2 x 7, 7 is the multiplicand.*

mul • ti • pli • er /mŭl′ tə plī′ ər/ *n.* a number by which another number is multiplied. *In 2 x 7, 2 is the multiplier.*

mu • ral /myŏor′ əl/ *n.* a picture painted directly on a wall. *The artist designed a mural for the lobby of the auditorium.*

mus • cle /mŭs′ əl/ *n.* body tissue composed of fibers that tighten or loosen to move parts of the body. *The athlete was careful to stretch his muscles before the race.*

mu • si • cian /myŏo zĭsh′ ən/ *n.* a person who composes or performs music. *The players in an orchestra are expert musicians.*

mut • ton /mŭt′ ən/ *n.* the meat of a full-grown sheep. *In England, roast mutton is a popular dish.*

myth /mĭth/ *n.* a story or legend that attempts to account for something in nature. *Some myths deal with the early history of a nation.*

Pronunciation Key

ă	pat	ŏ	pot	th	thin
ā	pay	ō	toe	*th*	this
âr	care	ô	paw, for	hw	which
ä	father	oi	noise	zh	vision
ĕ	pet	ou	out	ə	about,
ē	be	ŏŏ	took		item,
ĭ	pit	ōō	boot		pencil,
ī	pie	ŭ	cut		gallop,
îr	pier	ûr	urge		circus

na • tion • al /năsh′ ə nəl/ *adj.* belonging to a nation. *The national flag of the United States has stars and stripes.*

nat • u • ral /năch′ ər əl/ *adj.* **a.** produced by nature; not artificial. *Wood is a natural substance.* **b.** having a particular character by nature. *Eileen has a natural love for art.* **c.** normal; usual; to be expected. *It is natural for winters in Florida to be warm.*

neb • u • la /nĕb′ yə lə/ *n.* (**neb•u•las** or **neb•u•lae** *pl.*) a cloudy mass seen among the stars at night. *On a clear night, you may see a nebula in the sky.*

nec • es • sar • y /nĕs′ ĭ sĕr′ ē/ *adj.* (**nec•es•sar•i•ly,** *adv.*) needed; required. *A balanced diet is necessary for proper nutrition.*

neigh • bor • hood¹ /nā′ bər hŏŏd′/ *n.* a distinctive part of a town or city in which people live. *In a big city, some neighborhoods have apartment buildings and others have houses.*

neigh • bor • hood² /nā′ bər hŏŏd′/ *adj.* relating to the neighborhood: *a neighborhood park.*

ner • vous /nûr′ vəs/ *adj.* **a.** of the nerves. *All the nerves in the body make up the nervous system.* **b.** excited; not calm. *The kitten became nervous when everyone crowded around.*

Spelling Dictionary

295

neu • tral /nōō′ trəl/ or /nyōō′-/ *adj.* **a.** not favoring either side. *During two world wars, Switzerland remained a neutral country.* **b.** neither acidic nor alkaline: *a neutral solution.*

neu • tron /nōō′ trŏn′/ or /nyōō′-/ *n.* a part of an atomic nucleus that has no electrical charge. *Both neutrons and protons are subatomic particles.*

niece /nēs/ *n.* the daughter of one's brother or sister or of one's spouse's brother or sister. *Your parents' nieces are your cousins.*

nim • bo • stra • tus /nĭm′ bō strā′ təs/ or /-străt′ əs/ *n.* a low gray cloud that brings rain, snow, or sleet. *A nimbostratus sometimes indicates the arrival of snow.*

ni • tro • gen /nī′ trə jən/ *n.* a gas that forms about four-fifths of the air we breathe. *Nitrogen has no color, taste, or odor.*

nom • i • nate /nŏm′ ə nāt′/ *v.* (nom•i•nates, nom•i•nat•ed, nom•i•nat•ing) to choose a candidate for an office; to name. *Mary was nominated for president of her class.*

non- a prefix that means "not": *nonmetal.*

non • fat /nŏn′ făt′/ *adj.* lacking fat solids or having the fat content removed: *nonfat milk.*

non • prof • it /nŏn prŏf′ ĭt/ *adj.* not set up for the purpose of making a profit. *A charity is a nonprofit organization.*

non • re • new • al /nŏn′ rĭ nōō′ əl/ or /-nyōō′-/ *n.* a not granting of an extension. *The barber was upset by the nonrenewal of his lease.*

non • re • turn • a • ble /nŏn′ rĭ tûr′ nə bəl/ *adj.* not able to be returned: *nonreturnable bottles.*

no • ta • ble /nō′ tə bəl/ *adj.* **a.** worthy of notice; remarkable. *Writing a book is a notable accomplishment.* **b.** prominent; distinguished. *He is a notable physicist.*

no • tice[1] /nō′ tĭs/ *n.* an announcement. *The notice on the bulletin board gives the dates of the field hockey games.*

no • tice[2] /nō′ tĭs/ *v.* (no•tic•es, no•ticed, no•tic•ing) to pay attention to; to take notice of; to see. *Joan noticed Barbara's new dress right away.*

nour • ish /nûr′ ĭsh/ or /nŭr′-/ *v.* (nour•ish•es, nour•ished, nour•ish•ing) to feed; to cause to grow by giving enough of the right food. *Water and sunlight nourish the flowers.*

nov • el[1] /nŏv′ əl/ *n.* a book-length fictional story. *Mark Twain wrote several novels.*

nov • el[2] /nŏv′ əl/ *adj.* new or unusual: *a novel idea.*

nu • cle • us /nōō′ klē əs/ or /nyōō′-/ *n.* (nu•cle•i or nu•cle•us•es *pl.*) the central, positively charged core of an atom, composed of neutrons and protons. *A nucleus contains almost all the mass of an atom.*

numb /nŭm/ *adj.* without sensation or movement. *If you don't wear warm gloves, your fingers may become numb with cold.*

nu • tri • tion /nōō trĭsh′ ən/ or /nyōō-/ *n.* eating; nourishment. *Proper nutrition helps maintain good health.*

nu • tri • tious /nōō trĭsh′ əs/ or /nyōō-/ *adj.* providing nourishment. *Apples are a nutritious snack.* [Latin *nūtrīre*, to nourish.]

o • a • sis /ō ā′ sĭs/ *n.* (o•a•ses *pl.*) a place in the desert where there is water. *Trees, shrubs, or grass might grow in an oasis.*

oasis

ob- a prefix that means "toward" or "against": *objection, obstacle.*

o • be • di • ence /ō bē′ dē əns/ *n.* the act of obeying rules or laws. *Crossing the street safely requires obedience to traffic laws.*

ob • ject[1] /əb jĕkt′/ *v.* to make objection; to protest. *They objected that the weather was too cold to play outside.*

ob • ject[2] /ŏb′ jĭkt/ *n.* **a.** a thing that can be seen or touched. *The little shop had many objects made of china.* **b.** a purpose; a goal: *the object of the game.*

ob • tain /əb tān′/ *v.* to get. *He obtained a ticket to the play.*

ob•vi•ous /ŏb′ vē əs/ *adj.* easy to see or figure out; clear; plain. *It is obvious that the movie is popular, since the theater is so crowded.*

oc•ca•sion /ə kā′ zhən/ *n.* **a.** a particular happening or event. *Holidays are special occasions.* **b.** an opportunity; a good chance. *I hope you find an occasion to call us while you are traveling.*

o•cean•og•ra•pher /ō′ shə nŏg′ rə fər/ *n.* a scientist whose specialty is the study and exploration of the ocean. *The oceanographer told us about the Gulf Stream.* [Greek *Ōkeanos*, a great river encircling the earth + *graphein*, to write.]

of•fer /ô′ fər/ or /ŏf′ ər/ *v.* **a.** to say that one is willing. *We offered to help Mr. Patel start his car.* **b.** to present as a suggestion. *The President offered a plan for peace.*

of•fi•cer /ô′ fĭ sər/ *n.* **a.** a person in a position of authority: *a bank officer; an army officer.* **b.** a policeman or policewoman. *Officer, which way is Oak Street?*

officer

OPEC an acronym for "Organization of Petroleum Exporting Countries." *OPEC's decisions affect the price we pay for oil.*

op•er•a•tion /ŏp′ə rā′ shən/ *n.* **a.** the way in which something works. *Finally I understand the operation of an airplane.* **b.** a surgical treatment. *The patient recovered quickly after the operation.* [Latin *operātiōnem*, from *operāri*, to work.]

o•pin•ion /ə pĭn′ yən/ *n.* **a.** a belief or impression that cannot be proved. *Leon holds the opinion that soccer is more fun than football.* **b.** a judgment or verdict. *The judge handed down an opinion in favor of the plaintiff.*

op•po•nent /ə pō′ nənt/ *n.* a person or group that competes against another. *Our school's opponent for the game is Deerfield School.* [Latin *oppōnere*, to oppose.]

op•por•tu•ni•ty /ŏp′ ər tōō′ nĭ tē/ or /-tyōō′-/ *n.* (**op•por•tu•ni•ties** *pl.*) a time or chance that is right for doing something. *Let's find an opportunity to talk to Amy about the picnic.*

Pronunciation Key

ă	pat	ŏ	pot	th	thin
ā	pay	ō	toe	*th*	this
âr	care	ô	paw, for	hw	which
ä	father	oi	noise	zh	vision
ĕ	pet	ou	out	ə	about,
ē	be	ŏŏ	took		item,
ĭ	pit	ōō	boot		pencil,
ī	pie	ŭ	cut		gallop,
îr	pier	ûr	urge		circus

op•pose /ə pōz′/ *v.* (**op•pos•es, op•posed, op•pos•ing**) to be against; to act against. *The mayor opposed the building of a new highway.* [Latin *ob-*, against + *pos-*, perfect stem of *pōnere*, to put.]

op•po•site¹ /ŏp′ ə zĭt/ *adj.* contrary; completely different; exactly reverse: *opposite opinions.*

op•po•site² /ŏp′ ə zĭt/ *n.* the reverse of something else. *"Up" is the opposite of "down."*

op•po•site³ /ŏp′ ə zĭt/ *prep.* across from. *The library is opposite the school.* [Latin *ob-*, against + *pos-*, perfect stem of *pōnere*, to put.]

op•ti•mism /ŏp′ tə mĭz′ əm/ *n.* a hopeful disposition; the belief that our world is the best of all possible worlds. *Juanita's optimism and sunny outlook on life make her fun to be around.*

or•di•nar•y /ôr′ dn ĕr′ē/ *adj.* **a.** usual; normal. *The ordinary time it takes to drive downtown is twenty minutes.* **b.** not special; average: *an ordinary meal.*

-ous a suffix, used to form adjectives, that means "possessing" or "characterized by": *joyous.*

or•phan /ôr′ fən/ *n.* a child whose parents are absent or dead. *Oliver Twist is a story about an orphan.* [Greek *orphanos*, without parents.]

out•back /out′ băk′/ *n.* a rural, undeveloped part of a country, especially Australia and New Zealand. *Great distances separate the sheep stations of the Australian outback.*

out•put /out′ po͝ot′/ *n.* **a.** the amount of something produced or manufactured. *The supervisor praised her workers because their output had increased.* **b.** the information produced from a computer. *The output was inaccurate because some of the information input was wrong.*

out•ward¹ /out′ wərd/ *adv.* toward the outside. *Fire laws state that the doors of a public building must open outward.*

out•ward² /out′ wərd/ *adj.* of or toward the outside; exterior: *outward calm.*

o•ver•cast /ō′ vər kăst′/ *adj.* covered with clouds or mist. *The weather report called for an overcast day with a chance of rain.*

pad•dock /păd′ ək/ *n.* a fenced area used for grazing livestock. *The sheep were grazing in the paddock.*

palm¹ /päm/ *n.* the inside of a person's hand between the wrist and the fingers. *The child held her nickel tightly in her palm.*

palm² /päm/ *n.* a tree that grows in very warm places. *Coconuts grow on coconut palms.*

pam•phlet /păm′ flĭt/ *n.* a small book with a paper cover; a booklet. *A pamphlet of instructions came with the camera.*

pan•cre•as /păng′ krē əs/ or /păn′-/ *n.* a long, irregularly shaped gland located behind the stomach that secretes digestive juices. *The pancreas produces enzymes.*

pan•el•ist /păn′ ə lĭst/ *n.* a member of a panel. *One panelist was an expert on foreign affairs.*

par•a•graph /păr′ ə grăf′/ *n.* a clearly indicated part of a written work; a sentence or a group of sentences that develops one main idea or topic. *The first word of a paragraph is usually indented from the left margin.* [Greek *para-*, beside + *graphein*, to write.]

par•al•lel /păr′ ə lĕl/ *adj.* going in the same direction but not meeting; being always the same distance apart. *Railroad tracks are parallel.*

par•al•lel•o•gram /păr′ ə lĕl′ ə grăm′/ *n.* a four-sided plane figure with opposite sides parallel. *A rectangle is a parallelogram.*

parallelogram

par•lia•ment /pär′ lə mənt/ *n.* the legislative body of a country. *In England, the House of Commons and the House of Lords make up the British Parliament.*

par•tial /pär′ shəl/ *adj.* **a.** not complete. *We saw a partial eclipse of the moon.* **b.** inclined to favor one side. *An umpire should never be partial when he makes a decision.*

par•tic•i•pant /pär tĭs′ ə pənt/ *n.* a person who joins in and takes part in something. *The teachers agreed to be participants in a discussion with students.*

part•ner /pärt′ nər/ *n.* a person who shares something or joins with another. *The boys were partners on the camping trip.*

part•ner•ship /pärt′ nər shĭp′/ *n.* a business association of two or more individuals. *Their partnership was profitable.*

pas•sage /păs′ ĭj/ *n.* **a.** a way used for passing. *The passage leads to the back staircase.* **b.** part of a writing or a speech. *The passage about whales gives much interesting information.* [Old French *passer,* to pass.]

pas•ser-by /păs′ ər bī′/ *n.* (**pas•sers-by** *pl.*) a person who passes by. *The reporter interviewed passers-by about the upcoming election.*

pa•tience /pā′ shəns/ *n.* the calm endurance of a trying situation. *Our driver showed great patience during the traffic delay.*

pa•tri•ot /pā′ trē ət/ *n.* one who loves, supports, or defends his or her country. *George Washington was one of our greatest patriots.*

pa•tri•ot•ism /pā′ trē ə tĭz′ əm/ *n.* love of and loyalty to one's country. *Saluting the flag is a way of expressing patriotism.*

pat • tern /păt′ ərn/ *n.* a design or figure. *The vase has a flowered pattern.*

pause¹ /pôz/ *n.* a short stop or rest. *There was a dramatic pause in the music.*

pause² /pôz/ *v.* (**paus•es, paused, paus•ing**) to stop for a short time. *He paused to get a glass of water.*

PBS an abbreviation for "Public Broadcasting System." *We watched a science program on PBS.*

peas • ant /pĕz′ ənt/ *n.* a person who owns or rents a small farm or works for another landowner. *The peasants worked the farm for the wealthy landowner.*

per • cent or **per cent** /pər sĕnt′/ *adv.* out of each hundred. *Ten percent means ten out of one hundred.*

per • cent • age /pər sĕn′ tĭj/ *n.* a part in its relation to the whole. *A large percentage of the people voted in the election.*

per • cus • sion /pər kŭsh′ ən/ *n.* the section of an instrumental group consisting of the percussion instruments. *The band director asked percussion to play the drums and cymbals louder.*

per • form • ance /pər fôr′ məns/ *n.* **a.** the way in which someone or something functions. *Your performance on the test was very good.* **b.** the giving of a public show. *On Saturday there is a matinee performance.*

pe • ri • od • i • cal /pĭr′ ē ŏd′ ĭ kəl/ *n.* a publication that appears at regular intervals. *Many periodicals feature news stories.*

per • mis • sion /pər mĭsh′ ən/ *n.* consent, especially formal consent. *With the permission of the principal, our class visited the zoo.*

per • mit¹ /pər mĭt′/ *v.* (**per•mits, per•mit•ted, per•mit•ting**) to let; to allow; to give consent to. *Please permit me to read your magazine.*

per • mit² /pûr′ mĭt/ *n.* a written or printed statement that gives one permission; a license. *Most cities require permits for parades.*

per • pen • dic • u • lar /pûr′ pən dĭk′ yə lər/ *adj.* at right angles. *The walls are perpendicular to the floor.*

perpendicular

---

per • spire /pər spīr′/ *v.* (**per•spires, per•spired, per•spir•ing**) to sweat. *As she worked she began to perspire.*

pes • si • mism /pĕs′ ə mĭz′ əm/ *n.* a gloomy outlook; the belief that this is the worst of all possible worlds. *His pessimism made everyone unhappy.* [Latin *pessimus,* worst.]

pe • tro • le • um /pə trō′ lē əm/ *n.* a thick, liquid hydrocarbon mixture found beneath the earth's surface. *Gasoline, paraffin, and asphalt can be produced from petroleum.*

pew • ter /pyōō′ tər/ *n.* an alloy of tin used for making utensils and tableware. *The dark pewter in this exhibit is very old.*

phase /fāz/ *n.* **a.** a stage in development. *The first phase of our campaign to elect Andrew will be distributing posters.* **b.** a change in the shape of the moon when viewed from Earth. *The moon was in its crescent phase.*

phone¹ /fōn/ *n.* a telephone. *Please answer the phone.*

phone² /fōn/ *v.* (**phones, phoned, phon•ing**) to telephone. *Peggy's friends sometimes phone her just to chat.*

pho • to /fō′ tō/ *n.* a photograph. *Nancy brought in the photos of her summer vacation.*

pho • to • graph /fō′ tə grăf′/ *n.* a picture taken with a camera. *The photograph of the lake is in color.* [Greek *photo-*, light + *graphein*, to write.]

pho • tog • ra • phy /fə tŏg′ rə fē/ *n.* the art or process of taking and printing photographs. *In our class in photography, we learned how to develop our own film.*

phrase¹ /frāz/ *n.* **a.** a group of words that gives a single idea. *In "He swam during the summer," "during the summer" is a phrase.* **b.** a short expression: *a scientific phrase.*

phrase² /frāz/ *v.* (**phras•es, phrased, phras•ing**) to express in words. *Phrase your thoughts carefully.*

phy•si•cian /fĭ zĭsh′ ən/ *n.* a medical doctor. *When you are ill, you should see a physician.* [Old French *fisique,* medical science, from Greek *physis,* nature.]

pi /pī/ *n.* a Greek letter (π) used as a mathematical symbol to represent a specific number (about 3.14). *Pi is the ratio of a circle's circumference to its diameter.*

pi•an•ist /pē ăn′ ĭst/ or /pē′ ə nĭst/ *n.* one who plays the piano. *It takes years of training to become a concert pianist.*

pi•geon /pĭj′ ən/ *n.* a bird with a small head, stout body, and short legs. *Some pigeons are trained to carry messages.*

pigeon

pig•ment /pĭg′ mənt/ *n.* **a.** a substance used to give color to something. *There are yellow pigments in the green paint.* **b.** a substance that gives color to plant or animal tissue. *Chlorophyll is the pigment that makes plants green.*

pipe•line /pīp′ līn′/ *n.* a channel or pipe used to carry water, petroleum, or natural gas. *The Trans-Alaska Pipeline carries oil hundreds of miles.*

pit•i•ful /pĭt′ ĭ fəl/ *adj.* causing emotions of sorrow and compassion. *The injured dog was a pitiful sight.*

plat•form /plăt′ fôrm′/ *n.* any flat floor or surface raised above the area around it. *The train will be at the platform in five minutes.*

plumb•er /plŭm′ ər/ *n.* a person whose job is putting in and fixing sinks, pipes, and other plumbing fixtures. *We called a plumber when the basement pipes started leaking.*

plu•ral¹ /plŏŏr′ əl/ *n.* the form of a word that means more than one of something. *The plural of "leaf" is "leaves."*

plu•ral² /plŏŏr′ əl/ *adj.* showing that more than one is meant. *The plural form of most words is made by adding* **-s** *or* **-es.**

P.M. or **p.m.** an abbreviation that means "in the afternoon or evening." *She is usually asleep by 10 P.M.* [Latin *post meridiem,* after noon.]

pol•i•cy¹ /pŏl′ ĭ sē/ *n.* (**po•li•cies** *pl.*) a way of doing things. *The store's policy is to treat customers politely.*

pol•i•cy² /pŏl′ ĭ sē/ *n.* (**po•li•cies** *pl.*) a contract between an insurance company and those who are insured. *The school has a fire insurance policy.*

pol•lu•tion /pə lōō′ shən/ *n.* a harmful impurity. *Water pollution causes many fish to die.*

pop•u•la•tion /pŏp′ yə lā′ shən/ *n.* the number of people living in a country, state, town, or other area. *The town's population has greatly increased in the past five years.* [Latin *populus,* the people.]

por•tion /pôr′ shən/ or /pōr′-/ *n.* a part; a share. *A portion of the school day is spent in study hall.*

pose /pōz/ *v.* (**pos•es, posed, pos•ing**) **a.** to hold an expression or a position. *The parents posed with their children for a family portrait.* **b.** to present; to put forward: *pose a question.* [Latin *pausāre,* to rest, influenced by *pos-,* perfect stem of *pōnere,* to put, to place.]

po•si•tion /pə zĭsh′ ən/ *n.* **a.** place; location. *The navigator marked the ship's position on a chart.* **b.** a job; employment. *My brother has a new position with another company.*

pos•i•tive /pŏz′ ĭ tĭv/ *adj.* **a.** confident; certain; without doubt. *Gus is positive that his team will win.* **b.** approving; showing agreement: *a positive answer.* **c.** not negative: *a positive number.* [Latin *pos-* perfect stem of *pōnere,* to put, to place.]

pos•sess /pə zĕs′/ *v.* (**pos•sess•es, pos•sessed, pos•sess•ing**) to have; to own. *Heather's family possesses a sailboat.*

pos•ses•sive¹ /pə zĕs′ ĭv/ *adj.* showing ownership. *A possessive pronoun indicates to whom something belongs.*

T300

pos•ses•sive² /pə zĕs′ ĭv/ *n.* a word that shows possession. *Possessives such as "teacher's" and "its" are formed from nouns and pronouns.*

pos•si•bly /pŏs′ ə blē/ *adv.* perhaps; maybe. *Possibly we'll finish before noon.*

post•age /pō′ stĭj/ *n.* the cost of stamps needed to send a letter or package by mail. *The postage was forty cents.* [French *poste,* mail.]

post of•fice /pōst′ ô′ fĭs/ or /-ŏf′ ĭs/ *n.* **a.** an office or a building where people can buy stamps and mail letters or packages. *Mail these cards at the post office.* **b.** the public department in charge of mail. *The post office employs thousands of workers.*

pot•ter•y /pŏt′ ə rē/ *n.* pots, dishes, or ornaments made of clay that has been hardened by baking. *This shop sells beautiful pottery.*

pottery

POW or **P.O.W.** an abbreviation for "prisoner of war." *A great celebration awaited the POWs upon their return home.*

prac•ti•cal /prăk′ tĭ kəl/ *adj.* **a.** able to be done, used, or carried out. *Her practical solution took care of the problem.* **b.** dealing with facts rather than theory; concrete. *Her practical approach to children is a great help.*

pre•cious /prĕsh′ əs/ *adj.* **a.** having a high price; costing a great deal. *Diamonds are precious jewels.* **b.** much loved; dear. *Their precious child brought happiness to the parents.* [Latin *pretium,* price.]

pre•mi•er¹ /prĭ mîr′/ or /-myîr′/ or /prē′ mîr/ *adj.* first in importance; chief. *The economy was the premier concern of the voters.*

pre•mier² /prĭ mîr′/ *n.* the chief executive of a Canadian province. *Canadian premiers are leaders of their legislatures.*

pres•ent¹ /prĕz′ ənt/ *adj.* **a.** of the time between past and future; current: *the present moment.* **b.** at hand; not absent. *All the committee members were present for the final vote.*

Pronunciation Key

ă	pat	ŏ	pot	th	**th**in
ā	pay	ō	toe	*th*	**th**is
âr	care	ô	paw, for	hw	**wh**ich
ä	father	oi	noise	zh	vision
ĕ	pet	ou	out	ə	about,
ē	be	ŏŏ	took		item,
ĭ	pit	ōō	boot		pencil,
ī	pie	ŭ	cut		gallop,
îr	pier	ûr	urge		circus

pre•sent² /prĭ zĕnt′/ *v.* **a.** to give. *The prize was presented to the winner.* **b.** to offer; to bring up for consideration. *May I present a suggestion?*

pres•ent³ /prĕz′ ənt/ *n.* a gift. *The present was colorfully wrapped.*

pres•sure /prĕsh′ ər/ *n.* the act of pressing; use of force. *We applied pressure to the orange to squeeze out the juice.*

price•less /prīs′ lĭs/ *adj.* very worthy; invaluable. *The art collection is priceless.*

prim•er¹ /prĭm′ ər/ *n.* a textbook for early grades. *The children took out their primers and began the lesson.*

prim•er² /prī′ mər/ *n.* an undercoat of paint to prepare a surface for further painting. *The painter applied a primer first.*

print•er /prĭn′ tər/ *n.* the part of the computer that produces printed matter. *The printer was not working; it needed new toner.*

prob•a•ble /prŏb′ ə bəl/ *adj.* (**prob•a•bly,** *adv.*) likely to happen. *The dark clouds and lightning mean that rain is probable.*

proc•ess /prŏs′ ĕs′/ or /prō′ sĕs′/ *n.* (**proc•ess•es** *pl.*) **a.** a system of operations in the production of something: *the process of canning fresh fruit.* **b.** a series of actions with an expected end: *the growth process.*

prof•it¹ /prŏf′ ĭt/ *n.* **a.** the amount of money made after all expenses have been subtracted. *The profits in some businesses are small.* **b.** a benefit; an advantage. *Woo found both profit and enjoyment in his music lessons.*

prof•it² /prŏf′ ĭt/ *v.* to benefit. *I can profit from your experience.*

prof•it•a•ble /prŏf′ ĭ tə bəl/ *adj.* (prof•it•a•bly, *adv.*) bringing profit or benefit. *The store had a profitable year.*

pro•gram•ming /prō′ grăm′ ĭng/ or /-grəm-/ *n.* the designing or planning of a computer program. *Students interested in computer science should study programming.*

prog•ress[1] /prŏg′ rĕs′/ or /prō′ grĕs′/ *n.* **a.** a movement forward. *The train made steady progress.* **b.** development; improvement: *the progress of science.*

pro•gress[2] /prə grĕs′/ *v.* to advance; to improve. *Sarah will progress in her ability to spell.*

proj•ect[1] /prŏj′ ĕkt′/ *n.* a plan; a scheme. *The girls' next project is to build a radio.*

pro•ject[2] /prə jĕkt′/ *v.* **a.** to throw or shoot forward. *An arrow is projected from a bow.* **b.** to cause to fall on a surface. *Movies are projected on a white screen.*

proof /prŏof/ *n.* anything that shows that something is correct or true. *Do you have proof of your theory?*

prop•er /prŏp′ ər/ *adj.* **a.** correct; suitable. *A proper tool for smoothing wood is a plane.* **b.** indicating a particular person, place, or thing; belonging to one or to only a few. *Proper nouns, such as "Joan" and "Ohio," are always capitalized.*

pro•por•tion /prə pôr′ shən/ or /-pōr′-/ *n.* **a.** a part. *A large proportion of Earth is covered by water.* **b.** a proper relation. *This painting is in proportion to the size of the wall it hangs on.* **c.** a relation of equality between two ratios. *How do you find the missing element in a proportion?*

pro•tect /prə tĕkt′/ *v.* to guard; to defend; to keep from danger. *The police protect citizens from criminals.*

pro•tec•tion /prə tĕk′ shən/ *n.* watchful care; a keeping from danger. *The job of a gamekeeper is the protection of wildlife.*

pro•ton /prō′ tŏn′/ *n.* a positively charged subatomic particle. *Protons are found in the nucleus of an atom.*

prov•ince /prŏv′ ĭns/ *n.* **a.** a division of a country. *Canada is divided into ten provinces and two territories.* **b.** range of knowledge, activity, or authority. *The study of volcanoes falls within the province of geology.*

pro•vi•sion /prə vĭzh′ ən/ *n.* a condition. *One of the provisions for ordering tickets is that you must be a student.*

pub•li•ca•tion /pŭb′ lĭ kā′ shən/ *n.* **a.** the act or process of publishing printed matter. *The author was excited about the publication of her novel.* **b.** a book, magazine, or newspaper. *The library has more than twenty-five thousand publications.*

punc•tu•a•tion /pŭngk′ chōō ā′ shən/ *n.* the use of commas, periods, and other marks to make writing clearer. *In writing, correct punctuation is as important as correct usage.*

pun•ish /pŭn′ ĭsh/ *v.* to administer a penalty for a crime or misbehavior. *I will not punish you if you tell the truth.*

pur•chase[1] /pûr′ chĭs/ *v.* (pur•chas•es, pur•chased, pur•chas•ing) to buy. *We purchased folding chairs for the porch.*

pur•chase[2] /pûr′ chĭs/ *n.* a thing that is bought. *Mother's purchases will be delivered by the store.*

quad•ri•lat•er•al /kwŏd′ rə lăt′ ər əl/ *n.* a geometric figure with four sides and four angles. *The quadrilateral has four sides.*

quadrilateral

quo•ta /kwō′ tə/ *n.* **a.** due share; an allotment. *Not all the students used up their quota of free tickets.* **b.** a maximum number that may be admitted. *The club has a quota of ten new members each year.*

quo•ta•tion /kwō tā′ shən/ *n.* **a.** a passage that is quoted. *The speaker used quotations to illustrate his point.* **b.** a passage repeated from a well-known literary work. *"All the world's a stage" is a popular quotation from a play by Shakespeare.*

ra•di•us /rā′ dē əs/ *n.* (**ra•di•i** or **ra•di•us•es** *pl.*) a straight line from the center of a circle to its edge. *The radius of a circle is half its diameter.*

rap•id /răp′ ĭd/ *adj.* fast; quick. *The rapid current carried the canoe down the river.*

ra•tio /rā′ shō/ or /rā′ shē ō′/ *n.* **a.** the quotient that shows the comparison of two numbers. *The ratio of 1 to 4 is 1/4.* **b.** comparison in size or quantity between two things. *The recipe mixes flour and sugar in the ratio of two to one.*

ra•tion•al /răsh′ ən əl/ *adj.* based on reason; logical. *After thinking it over calmly, Jeff made a rational decision to sell his car.*

re- a prefix that means: **a.** again: *rebuild.* **b.** backwards; back: *react.*

re•al es•tate /rē′ əl ĭ stāt′/ or /rēl′-/ *n.* land and all buildings and properties on it. - *Matt's mother sells real estate.*

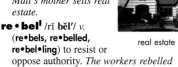

real estate

re•bel[1] /rĭ bĕl′/ *v.* (**re•bels, re•belled, re•bel•ing**) to resist or oppose authority. *The workers rebelled against the unfair demands of their employer.*

reb•el[2] /rĕb′ əl/ *n.* a person who reacts against authority. *Rebels challenge tradition.*

re•ceipt /rĭ sēt′/ *n.* **a.** a written statement showing that money or goods have been received. *I signed the receipt when the package was delivered.* **b.** the act of receiving. *On receipt of the good news, we felt happy.*

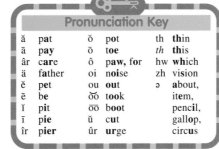

re•ceive /rĭ sēv′/ *v.* (**re•ceives, re•ceived, re•ceiv•ing**) to get. *You should receive the letter in two days.*

re•ceiv•er /rĭ sē′ vər/ *n.* **a.** a person or a thing that receives something. *The sender of a letter puts the address of the receiver on the envelope.* **b.** the part in a radio, telephone, or TV that picks up the signals. *I held the receiver to my ear.*

re•cess /rē′ sĕs′/ *n.* (**re•cess•es** *pl.*) a brief rest from work. *During the morning we have a fifteen-minute recess.*

re•cip•ro•cal[1] /rĭ sĭp′ rə kəl/ *n.* either of a pair of numbers whose product is 1. *The reciprocal of 3/4 is 4/3, since 3/4 x 4/3 = 1.*

re•cip•ro•cal[2] /rĭ sĭp′ rə kəl/ *adj.* mutual; felt by both sides: *reciprocal interest.*

re•flect /rĭ flĕkt′/ *v.* **a.** to throw back from a surface, as light or heat. *A mirror reflects light.* **b.** to give back an image of. *The trees were reflected in the clear lake.* **c.** to show; to make apparent. *His work reflects great effort.*

re•fract /rĭ frăkt′/ *v.* to cause the path of light to bend. *The lens of the human eye refracts light.*

re•fuse[1] /rĭ fyo͞oz′/ *v.* (**re•fus•es, re•fused, re•fus•ing**) **a.** to turn down; to reject. *She refused my offer of help.* **b.** to be unwilling; to decline. *I refuse to let them bother me.*

ref•use[2] /rĕf′ yo͞os/ *n.* useless matter; rubbish; garbage. *Please put your refuse in the wastebasket.*

re•gion•al /rē′ jə nəl/ *adj.* **a.** characteristic of a large geographic area. *In the sunbelt states, the growth of cities has been a regional asset.* **b.** characteristic of a particular area: *a regional accent.*

Spelling Dictionary

303

reg•u•lar /rĕg′ yə lər/ *adj.* **a.** usual; normal; ordinary. *Our regular practice on Sunday is to have dinner in the afternoon.* **b.** frequent: *regular customers.* **c.** occurring at fixed intervals. *We make regular visits to the dentist.*

reign[1] /rān/ *n.* the time during which a leader rules. *During the queen's reign, the people enjoyed many improvements.*

reign[2] /rān/ *v.* to rule. *The king reigned for thirty years.*

re•lease[1] /rĭ lēs′/ *v.* to let loose; to set free. *If you release the door, it will close by itself.*

re•lease[2] /rĭ lēs′/ *n.* **a.** the act of letting go or setting free. *The rangers planned the release of the bear cubs they had raised.* **b.** freedom; relief. *After the test was over, I felt a sense of release.*

re•lief /rĭ lēf′/ *n.* the removal or ease of worry, pain, etc. *Imagine my relief when I remembered the right answer.*

re•main /rĭ mān′/ *v.* **a.** to stay. *We remained at home because of the rain.* **b.** to continue; to last without changing. *The weather remained warm until the last week of October.* **c.** to be left. *All that remains of the old house is the foundation.*

re•quire /rĭ kwīr′/ *v.* (re•quires, re•quired, re•quir•ing) **a.** to need. *Humans require food and water to live.* **b.** to demand; to command. *Good manners require that you use a knife and a fork when you eat.*

res•i•dence /rĕz′ ĭ dəns/ *n.* **a.** the place where one lives; home. *His residence is on Spruce Street.* **b.** the act or fact of living in a place. *His family took up residence in Spain while he was working there.*

res•i•dent /rĕz′ ĭ dənt/ *n.* **a.** a person who lives in a particular area. *When our family moved to Idaho we became residents of that state.* **b.** a doctor who is doing clinical training. *Ms. Barin is a third-year resident at the hospital.* [Latin *residēre*, to reside, from *re-*, back + *sedēre*, to sit.]

res•pi•ra•to•ry /rĕs′ pər ə tôr′ē/ or /-tōr′ē/ *adj.* pertaining to the process of breathing. *Smoking is hazardous to the respiratory system.*

re•spond /rĭ spŏnd′/ *v.* **a.** to answer; to reply. *Susan did not respond when I asked her a question.* **b.** to react. *The patient responded well to the medicine.*

re•spon•si•ble /rĭ spŏn′ sə bəl/ *adj.* (re•spon•si•bly, *adv.*) **a.** trustworthy; reliable. *A responsible student was chosen to collect the money for the field trip.* **b.** required to answer for something. *Who is responsible for turning off the lights when we leave the room?* **c.** deserving credit or blame for something. *The cold weather was responsible for the small crowd at the picnic.*

res•tau•rant /rĕs′ tər ənt/ or /-tə ränt′/ *n.* a place where meals are sold and served. *We ate dinner in a restaurant downtown.*

re•sult[1] /rĭ zŭlt′/ *n.* outcome; effect. *He was late to work as a result of a delay in traffic.*

re•sult[2] /rĭ zŭlt′/ *v.* to happen as an effect. *The cold, damp weather resulted in icy roads.*

re•ver•ber•ate /rĭ vûr′ bə rāt′/ *v.* (re•ver•ber•ates, re•ver•ber•at•ed, re•ver•ber•at•ing) to sound again; to echo. *The thunder reverberated through the mountains.*

re•vers•i•ble /rĭ vûr′ sə bəl/ *adj.* capable of being turned backward or inside out; able to be reversed. *Jo wore her reversible coat.*

rhom•bus /rŏm′ bəs/ *n.* (rhom•bus•es or rhom•bi *pl.*) a parallelogram with equal sides. *Is every square a rhombus?*

rhombus

rhythm /rĭth′ əm/ *n.* a regular, repeated movement in which a beat or accent rises and falls or occurs steadily. *The rhythm in music is often provided by the drums.*

ri•val[1] /rī′ vəl/ *n.* one who is trying to do better than another; one who competes. *The two friends were rivals for the same part in the school play.*

ri•val[2] /rī′ vəl/ *adj.* competing; being rivals. *The rival stores lowered their prices to attract more customers.*

round /round/ *v.* to express as a whole number. *In math class we are learning to round off numbers to the nearest five or ten.*

rou•tine[1] /rōō tēn'/ *n.* a standard set of activities performed regularly. *Each morning Ann goes through her exercise routine.*

rou•tine[2] /rōō tēn'/ *adj.* ordinary; not special: *a routine day.*

rpm or **r.p.m.** an abbreviation for "revolutions per minute." *A long-playing record turns at 33⅓ rpm.*

ru•mor /rōō' mər/ *n.* uncertain information spread by word of mouth; hearsay. *We heard a rumor that our math quiz was cancelled.*

sa•li•va /sə lī' və/ *n.* the liquid that is secreted by glands in the mouth. *Saliva helps in the digestion of food.*

salm•on /săm' ən/ *n.* (**salm•on** or **salm•ons** *pl.*) a large fish with silver scales and pink flesh. *Salmon swim upstream from salt water to fresh water to lay their eggs.*

SALT an acronym for "Strategic Arms Limitation Talks." *The United States and the former Soviet Union originated the SALT treaty.*

sanc•tion /săngk' shən/ *n.* **a.** approval; support; encouragement. *The governor received public sanction for his views.* **b. sanc•tions** *n. pl.* a course of action several nations agree to take against a nation considered to have violated international law. *Governments may impose economic sanctions on another country for violations of human rights.*

sat•is•fac•tion /săt′ ĭs făk' shən/ *n.* a feeling of being satisfied or contented. *Dan gets satisfaction from doing his job well.*

sat•is•fy /săt' ĭs fī/ *v.* (**sat•is•fies, sat•is•fied, sat•is•fy•ing**) **a.** to please; to fill a need or desire. *You can satisfy the baby by giving her a toy.* **b.** to put an end to. *Water will satisfy my thirst.*

sauce /sôs/ *n.* a liquid that is served with food. *The chicken dish had a delicious ginger sauce.*

scarce•ly /skârs' lē/ *adv.* hardly; barely. *There are scarcely any people awake at five o'clock in the morning.*

scar•ci•ty /skâr' sĭ tē/ *n.* (**scar•ci•ties** *pl.*) a shortage in supply. *During a drought there is a scarcity of water.*

scheme /skēm/ *n.* **a.** a plan of action; a project. *We thought of a scheme for preventing graffiti.* **b.** a secret plot. *The scheme to give Mother a surprise party failed when she discovered the birthday cake.*

sci•en•tif•ic no•ta•tion /sī′ ən tĭf' ĭk nō tā' shən/ *n.* a method of writing numbers in terms of powers of ten. *In scientific notation the number 10,492 would be represented as 1.0492×10^4.*

scis•sors /sĭz' ərz/ *n. pl.* a cutting tool consisting of two handles and two sharp blades fastened together. *Scissors can cut through paper or fabric.*

scu•ba /skōō' bə/ or /skyōō'-/ *adj.* an acronym for a device with a mask, hose, and air tank used while swimming underwater.

scuba

Scuba divers often see schools of brightly colored tropical fish. [Self-contained **u**nder**w**ater **b**reathing **a**pparatus.]

sculp•tor /skŭlp' tər/ *n.* an artist who produces figures or designs that have depth. *Sculptors may choose to work in wood, stone, clay, or metal.*

sec•ond•ar•y /sĕk′ ən dĕr′ ē/ *adj.* **a.** not ranking first. *Her primary concern is content, and her secondary concern is style.* **b.** of or relating to the schooling one receives after elementary school: *secondary education.*

sed•i•ment /sĕd′ ə mənt/ *n.* the material that settles to the bottom of a liquid. *The river has a layer of sediment on the bottom.*

seize /sēz/ *v.* (**seiz•es, seized, seiz•ing**) to take hold of suddenly; to grasp; to grab. *He seized her hand and shook it eagerly.*

self-ad•dressed /sĕlf′ ə drĕst′/ *adj.* addressed to oneself. *If you would like a reply, please send a self-addressed envelope.*

sense•less /sĕns′ lĭs/ *adj.* without meaning; pointless: *a senseless waste of time.*

sen•si•ble /sĕn′ sə bəl/ *adj.* (**sen•si•bly,** *adv.*) full of good sense; reasonable; wise. *She is too sensible to accept a ride from strangers.*

se•quence /sē′ kwəns/ *n.* **a.** the coming of one thing after another; a succession. *Follow the sequence of steps to complete the model.* **b.** the order in which things follow one another. *The books are listed in alphabetical sequence.*

serf /sûrf/ *n.* in the Middle Ages, a laborer bound to a landlord. *Serfs worked the lord's land and gave crops to the lord as rent.*

se•ri•al /sîr′ ē əl/ *n.* a story or show produced in installments. *Many TV dramas are serials, with a story that continues from week to week.*

ser•vant /sûr′ vənt/ *n.* **a.** a person whose job is to work for another person. *Cooks, maids, and butlers are servants.* **b.** a person who works for a government or the public. *Firefighters are important public servants.* [Old French *servir,* to serve.]

set•tle•ment /sĕt′ l mənt/ *n.* **a.** a place where a number of people have gone to live; a colony. *There were many English settlements in this land.* **b.** a settling or resolution. *The settlement of the dispute satisfied both countries.*

shale /shāl/ *n.* a rock composed of layers of claylike, fine-grained sediments. *Shale is found throughout the world.*

shelf /shĕlf/ *n.* (**shelves** *pl.*) a flat piece of wood, glass, or metal that is used to hold things. *The clock is on a shelf in the kitchen.*

shield[1] /shēld/ *n.*
a. a piece of armor once carried on the arm by soldiers for protection in battle. *The knight's family emblem was on his shield.*
b. anything that protects. *Good nutrition is a shield against disease.*

shield

shield[2] /shēld/ *v.* to protect; to guard. *This umbrella will shield you from the rain.*

short sto•ry /shôrt′ stôr′ ē/ or /stōr′ ē/ *n.* a short piece of prose fiction. *Ernest Hemingway wrote some memorable short stories.*

should•'ve should have.

shriek[1] /shrēk/ *n.* a loud, sharp, high-pitched sound; a screech. *We heard the shrieks of the gulls before we saw the ocean.*

shriek[2] /shrēk/ *v.* to make a loud, sharp, high-pitched sound. *The children were shrieking with laughter.*

shut•ter•bug /shŭt′ ər bŭg′/ *n.* an amateur photographer. *Most shutterbugs start out by taking pictures of family members and pets.*

siege /sēj/ *n.* the surrounding of a place for a long time in order to capture it. *The city was under siege for three weeks.*

si•lence /sī′ ləns/ *n.* the absence of noise or sound; stillness. *There was silence while the principal spoke.*

sim•i•lar /sĭm′ ə lər/ *adj.* almost but not quite the same; alike but not identical. *The two girls wore similar clothes.*

sin•gu•lar /sĭng′ gyə lər/ *adj.* having to do with only one. *A singular noun names one person, place, or thing.*

sis•ter-in-law /sĭs′ tər ĭn lô′/ *n.* the sister of one's husband or wife or the wife of one's brother. *When my brother marries Donna, she'll be my sister-in-law.*

sky•scrap•er /skī′ skrā′ pər/ *n.* a very tall building. *The Empire State Building is one of New York's famous skyscrapers.*

sky•ward /skī′ wərd/ *adv.* in the direction of the sky. *As the plane ascended, its nose was facing skyward.*

sleet /slēt/ *n.* rain that freezes into drops of ice as it falls; a mixture of rain and snow or hail. *The sleet made the fields sparkle in the moonlight.*

sleigh /slā/ *n.* a carriage mounted on runners, used for traveling on ice or snow. *A sleigh is usually pulled by horses.*

sleigh

smudge¹ /smŭj/ *v.* (**smudg•es, smudged, smudg•ing**) to make dirty; to smear or to blotch. *Don't smudge the photographs with fingerprints!*

smudge² /smŭj/ *n.* a smear or blotch. *Maria got a smudge on her white shoes.*

sol•emn /sŏl′ əm/ *adj.* serious; earnest; grave: *a solemn promise.*

sol•i•tar•y /sŏl′ ĭ tĕr′ ē/ *adj.* **a.** existing, living, or going alone. *A solitary traveler was on the road that night.* **b.** remote, secluded: *a solitary place.*

-some a suffix, used to form adjectives, that means "having the quality, condition, or action of": *bothersome, troublesome.*

so•nar /sō′ när/ *n.* an acronym for a device that uses sound waves to locate objects underwater. *Submarines use sonar to judge their distance from the ocean floor.* [**S**ound **na**vigation **r**anging.]

soph•o•more /sŏf′ ə môr′/ or /-mōr′/ or /sŏf′ môr′/ or /-mōr′/ *n.* a person in the second year of high school or college. *The sophomores took the freshmen on a tour of the high school.* [Greek *sophos*, wise + *mōros*, foolish.]

spec•trum /spĕk′ trəm/ *n.* (**spec•tra** or **spec•trums** *pl.*) the group of colors formed by natural light when it is broken into its parts by being passed through a prism. *All the colors of the spectrum can be seen in a rainbow.*

speed•om•e•ter /spĭ dŏm′ ĭ tər/ or /spē-/ *n.* an instrument that indicates speed. *Every car has a speedometer.* [Speed + -meter, from Greek *metron*, measure.]

Pronunciation Key

ă	pat	ŏ	pot	th	thin
ā	pay	ō	toe	*th*	this
âr	care	ô	paw, for	hw	which
ä	father	oi	noise	zh	vision
ĕ	pet	ou	out	ə	about,
ē	be	ŏŏ	took		item,
ĭ	pit	ōō	boot		pencil,
ī	pie	ŭ	cut		gallop,
îr	pier	ûr	urge		circus

square /skwâr/ *v.* (**squares, squared, squar•ing**) to raise a number or an equation to the second power. *The number 4 squared is equal to 4 x 4 or 16.*

stel•lar /stĕl′ ər/ *adj.* **a.** of or relating to stars. *A stellar map shows the constellations.* **b.** excellent; of star quality: *a stellar cast of performers.*

steppe /stĕp/ *n.* a dry, grass-covered plain found in southeastern Europe and Siberia. *Vegetation is sparse in the steppes of Russia.*

ster•e•o /stĕr′ ē ō/ *adj.* using a sound system that has two or more separate channels. *Mick's dad got a state-of-the-art stereo system for the family room.* [From "stereophonic," from Greek *stereos*, solid + *phōnē*, sound.]

stock•bro•ker /stŏk′ brō′ kər/ *n.* a person who buys and sells stocks and other securities for a client. *The client trusted the stockbroker to invest his money wisely.*

stra•tus /strā′ təs/ or /străt′ əs/ *n.* a low-altitude cloud in horizontal layers. *Stratus often looks like dense fog.*

strike /strīk/ *v.* (**strikes, struck, strik•ing**) **a.** to hit. *A tennis player strikes the ball with a racket.* **b.** to sound. *The clock strikes every hour.* **c.** to stop work as a group. *The workers voted to strike for better working conditions.*

stub•born /stŭb′ ərn/ *adj.* not easily persuaded; having one's own definite idea. *Lee was stubborn and refused to follow my suggestions.*

Spelling Dictionary

307

stu • di • ous /stōō′ dē əs/ or /styōō′-/ *adj.* devoted to study; hardworking. *The class members usually become more studious as exam time nears.*

sub- a prefix that means: **a.** under or beneath: *submarine.* **b.** a subordinate or secondary part: *subdivision.* **c.** somewhat short of or less than: *subtropical.*

sub • di • vide /sŭb′ dĭ vīd′/ *v.* (sub•di•vides, sub•di•vid•ed, sub•di•vid•ing) to divide a part again into smaller parts. *The plot of land was subdivided into quarter-acre lots.*

sub • ma • rine¹ /sŭb′ mə rēn′/ or /sŭb′ mə rēn′/ *n.* a ship that can travel underwater. *Some submarines stay underwater for many weeks.*

submarine

sub • ma • rine² /sŭb′ mə rēn′/ or /sŭb′ mə rēn′/ *adj.* beneath the water surface; undersea. *Coral is a submarine organism.*

sub • to • tal /sŭb′ tōt′ l/ *n.* a partial or incomplete total. *The clerk added the amounts to get a subtotal, then added the tax to get the total.*

sub • way /sŭb′ wā′/ *n.* an electric railway beneath the ground. *In some large cities, subways are a vital part of the transportation system.*

suc • cess /sək sĕs′/ *n.* (suc•cess•es *pl.*) **a.** a favorable result or outcome; achievement. *Hard work often brings success.* **b.** a person or thing that succeeds. *The guest speaker was a huge success.*

suc • cess • ful /sək sĕs′ fəl/ *adj.* having success or a favorable outcome; turning out well. *Gwen is successful as both a student and an athlete.*

suf • fer /sŭf′ ər/ *v.* **a.** to feel pain or distress. *Our dog seems to suffer in the hot weather.* **b.** to endure; to put up with. *The pioneers suffered many hardships.*

suf • fix /sŭf′ ĭks/ *n.* (suf•fix•es *pl.*) a group of letters added to the end of a word to change its meaning. *The suffix "-ness" changes the adjective "sad" to the noun "sadness."* [Latin *suffīgere*, to affix, from *sub-*, secondary + *fīgere*, to fasten.]

suf • frage /sŭf′ rĭj′/ *n.* the right or privilege to vote. *Women won suffrage on August 18, 1920.*

sug • ges • tion /səg jĕs′ chən/ or /sə jĕs′-/ *n.* something suggested; a recommendation. *Her suggestion that we take an early plane was very sensible.* [Latin *suggest-*, perfect stem of *suggerere*, from *sub-*, up + *gerere*, to carry.]

sul • tan /sŭl′ tən/ *n.* a ruler of a Moslem country. *In ancient times, sultans had great wealth and power.*

sun • set /sŭn′ sĕt′/ *n.* the disappearance of the sun below the horizon. *A sunset can turn the sky pink and orange.*

super- a prefix that means: **a.** above; over: *superimpose.* **b.** excessive in degree: *supersaturate.*

su • per • in • tend • ent /sōō′ pər ĭn tĕn′ dənt/ *n.* a person with the authority to supervise or direct; the person in charge. *The superintendent of schools directs the activities of all the schools in a district.*

su • per • son • ic /sōō′ pər sŏn′ ĭk/ *adj.* caused by or related to a speed greater than sound. *Some jets can fly at supersonic speeds.* [Latin *super*, over, above + *sonus*, a sound.]

su • per • star /sōō′ pər stär′/ *n.* a performer who has great popular appeal. *Elvis Presley became a superstar at an early age.*

su • per • vise /sōō′ pər vīz′/ *v.* (su•per•vis•es, su•per•vised, su•per•vis•ing) to direct and inspect the work or performance of. *Mother supervised our cooking.* [Latin *supervīs-*, perfect stem of *supervīdere*, to look over, from *super-*, over + *vidēre*, to see.]

sure • ly /shŏŏr′ lē/ *adv.* **a.** undoubtedly; certainly. *Surely we will find a parking spot in this large lot!* **b.** with skill; in an expert way. *Slowly but surely, Bob carved a beautiful horse from the soft wood.*

sur • vey¹ /sər vā′/ or /sûr′ vā′/ *v.* **a.** to look over; to examine. *From a high tower, the ranger surveyed the forest for smoke.* **b.** to measure the exact size and shape of an area of land. *A team will survey the land before the new road is built.*

sur•vey² /sûr′ vā′/ *n.* **a.** a study or poll: *an opinion survey.* **b.** a measuring of land: *a geographical survey.*

sys•tem /sĭs′ təm/ *n.* **a.** a group of things or parts that work together. *The circulatory system consists of the heart, the blood vessels, and the blood.* **b.** an orderly way of doing things. *Use the system of keeping score that is easiest for you.* **c.** an arrangement; an order: *a system of government.*

ta•ble•spoon /tā′ bəl spoon′/ *n.* a large spoon used to serve food or to measure ingredients. *A tablespoon is equal to three teaspoons.*

ta•boo /tə boo′/ *adj.* forbidden; not approved: *a taboo topic.*

tal•ent /tăl′ ənt/ *n.* special ability; natural skill. *She has a great talent for writing.*

tank•er /tăng′ kər/ *n.* a ship, truck, or plane that transports oil or other liquids. *The tanker carries oil in the Gulf of Mexico.*

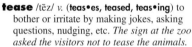

tanker

tap•es•try /tăp′ ĭ strē/ *n.* (**tap•es•tries** *pl.*) a heavy cloth with woven designs hung on walls for decoration. *The tapestry on the castle wall shows a hunting scene.*

tease /tēz/ *v.* (**teas•es, teased, teas•ing**) to bother or irritate by making jokes, asking questions, nudging, etc. *The sign at the zoo asked the visitors not to tease the animals.*

tea•spoon /tē′ spoon′/ *n.* the common small spoon used especially with beverages or for measuring. *In a table setting, the teaspoon goes to the right of the knife.*

te•di•ous /tē′ dē əs/ *adj.* tiresome; boring. *The politician's speech became so tedious that a few listeners got up to leave.* [Latin *taedium,* tedium.]

Pronunciation Key

ă	pat	ŏ	pot	th	thin
ā	pay	ō	toe	*th*	this
âr	care	ô	paw, for	hw	which
ä	father	oi	noise	zh	vision
ĕ	pet	ou	out	ə	about,
ē	be	o͝o	took		item,
ĭ	pit	o͞o	boot		pencil,
ī	pie	ŭ	cut		gallop,
îr	pier	ûr	urge		circus

tel•e•graph /tĕl′ ə grăf/ *n.* a device for sending and receiving signals over an electrical wire. *In the code used on a telegraph, dots and dashes represent letters of the alphabet.* [Greek *tēle,* far off + *graphein,* to write.]

tel•e•vi•sion /tĕl′ ə vĭzh′ ən/ *n.* a system of sending images and sound through the air by electricity or the set that receives and shows them; TV. *We watched a nature special on television.* [Greek *tēle,* far off + Latin *vis-,* perfect stem of *vidēre,* to see.]

tem•po•rar•y /tĕm′ pə rĕr′ ē/ *adj.* (**tem•po•rar•i•ly,** *adv.*) lasting for a brief time; not permanent. *While our teacher was ill, we had a temporary teacher.*

ten•ant /tĕn′ ənt/ *n.* a person who pays rent for the use of a house, apartment, or other property. *In that tall apartment building there are several hundred tenants.* [Old French *tenir,* to hold.]

tense¹ /tĕns/ *adj.* **a.** tightly stretched: *a tense wire.* **b.** nervous; uneasy: *a tense moment.*

tense² /tĕns/ *n.* any of the inflected forms of a verb that indicate time, continuance, or completion of an action or a state: *past, present, and future tenses.*

ten•sion /tĕn′ shən/ *n.* **a.** the process of stretching. *The heavy snow put tension on the electrical wires.* **b.** mental strain or stress. *There was a feeling of tension in the classroom before the test.*

ter•mi•nal /tûr′ mə nəl/ *n.* a computer device through which data can be entered. *A computer terminal consists of a video screen, a CPU, and a typewriter keyboard.*

Spelling Dictionary

309

ter•rain /tə rān′/ or /tĕ-/ *n.* a tract of land, especially with respect to its physical features. *From the airplane, we could see that the terrain below us was rugged.*

ter•ri•ble /tĕr′ ə bəl/ *adj.* (**ter•ri•bly,** *adv.*) **a.** causing terror or awe; alarming. *The monster in the movie was a terrible sight.* **b.** severe; intense; extreme. *The cold at the North Pole is terrible.*

ter•ri•to•ry /tĕr′ ĭ tôr′ē/ or /-tōr′ē/ *n.* (**ter•ri•to•ries** *pl.*) an area of land; a region. *Much of the territory in the central United States is used for farming.*

text /tĕkst/ *n.* **a.** written or printed words. *See the text under the map on page 73.* **b.** the words written by an author. *The novelist revised the text of the first chapter.*

theme /thēm/ *n.* **a.** a subject; a topic. *We selected school spirit as the theme of our discussion.* **b.** a short essay. *We write one theme a week in school.*

there•fore /thâr′ fôr′/ or /-fōr′/ *adv.* for that reason; consequently. *It turned the litmus paper blue; therefore, it must be a base.*

ther•mal /thûr′ məl/ *adj.* producing or caused by heat. *Skiers wear thermal clothing to protect themselves from the cold.* [Greek *thermē,* heat.]

ther•mom•e•ter /thər mŏm′ ĭ tər/ *n.* an instrument that measures and indicates temperatures. *The liquid in a thermometer expands and rises in the tube as the temperature rises.* [Greek *thermē,* heat + *metron,* measure.]

ther•mo•stat /thûr′ mə stăt′/ *n.* a device that automatically controls heating or cooling equipment. *The thermostat in our house keeps the temperature at 68 degrees.* [Greek *thermē,* heat + *-states,* one that causes to stand.]

the•sau•rus /thĭ sôr′ əs/ *n.* a book of synonyms and antonyms. *A thesaurus is a good place to find a more exact word.*

thief /thēf/ *n.* (**thieves** *pl.*) one who steals. *Our neighbor's dog was the thief that took our newspaper from the porch.*

thought•less /thôt′ lĭs/ *adj.* careless; inconsiderate. *It was thoughtless of you to invite only some of your friends.*

through /thrōō/ *prep.* **a.** in one side and out the opposite side. *Aleesha walked through the park to the library.* **b.** from the beginning to the end: *through the night.*

through•out /thrōō out′/ *prep.* **a.** during the entire time of. *Some states have warm weather throughout the year.* **b.** in every part of. *We looked for you throughout the building.*

thun•der•storm /thŭn′ dər stôrm′/ *n.* a heavy rainstorm with lightning and thunder. *That tree was struck by lightning during the thunderstorm.*

tim•pa•ni /tĭm′ pə nē/ *n. pl.* a set of kettledrums. *The timpani boomed out from the back of the orchestra.*

timpani

-tion a suffix, used to form nouns, that means "an action or process": *absorption.*

tire•less /tīr′ lĭs/ *adj.* not easily tired or fatigued. *Mother was tireless with her sewing project, spending hours on it until she finished.*

tire•some /tīr′ səm/ *adj.* tedious; boring. *Filing was the most tiresome part of the library job.*

tis•sue /tĭsh′ ōō/ *n.* **a.** a group of cells in a plant or animal that carry out a certain function: *skin tissue.* **b.** light, soft, thin paper or cloth. *I wiped my nose with a tissue.*

tomb /tōōm/ *n.* a burial place for the dead. *Egyptian pyramids are tombs.*

top•soil /tŏp′ soil′/ *n.* the surface layer of soil. *Flowers and shrubs grow best in rich topsoil.*

tour•ni•quet /tōōr′ nĭ kĭt/ or /tûr′-/ *n.* a cloth band used to temporarily stop the flow of blood through an artery. *A tourniquet should be applied only by someone well trained in first aid.*

tra•che•a /trā′ kē ə/ *n.* the passage that leads from the back of the mouth to the lungs. *The trachea carries air to the lungs.*

Spelling Dictionary

traf•fic /trăf′ ĭk/ *n.* the movement of people and vehicles. *There was very little
traffic on the turnpike.*

trait /trāt/ *n.* a feature or characteristic. *We
all inherit physical traits from our parents.*

trans•ver•sal /trăns vûr′ səl/ or /trănz-/
n. a line that intersects other lines. *When a
transversal crosses parallel lines it forms
sets of matching angles.*

trap•e•zoid /trăp′ ĭ zoid′/ *n.* a quadrilateral that has only one pair of parallel sides.
A trapezoid may have no equal sides.

trav•el•er /trăv′ əl ər/ or /trav′ lər/ *n.* a
person who travels. *Many travelers visit the
United States every year.*

tre•men•dous /trĭ mĕn′ dəs/ *adj.*
a. marvelous; wonderful. *She made a
tremendous catch.* **b.** terrible; dreadful. *The
new dam saved the town from tremendous
flood damage.* **c.** extremely large; enormous. *A tremendous wave rocked the boat.*

tribe /trīb/ *n.* a group of people who share a
common ancestry, common customs, and a
common leader. *The tribe moved west in
their search for food.*

tril•lion /trĭl′ yən/ *n.* the number equal to
one thousand billions. *The numeral for a
trillion has twelve zeros.*

tril•o•gy /trĭl′ ə jē/ *n.* a group of three literary works or dramas related by theme.
*The Lord of the Rings is a trilogy whose
three volumes tell the story of a ring with
mystical powers.* [Greek *trilogiă,* from *tri-,*
three + *logos,* word, speech.]

tri•pod /trī′ pŏd′/ *n.* a
three-legged stand for sup-
porting a camera or other
equipment. *A tripod can be
adjusted to different heights.*

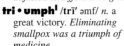
tripod

tri•umph¹ /trī′ əmf/ *n.* a
great victory. *Eliminating
smallpox was a triumph of
medicine.*

tri•umph² /trī′ əmf/ *v.* to win; to achieve a
victory; to succeed. *With practice, the boy
was able to triumph over his fear of the
water.*

trop•ics /trŏp′ ĭks/ *n. pl.* the region of Earth
on both sides of the equator. *The weather in
the tropics is usually hot and humid.*

tun•nel /tŭn′ əl/ *n.* a passage beneath the
ground. *The mole dug a tunnel under the
lawn.*

tur•ban /tûr′ bən/ *n.* a hat made of a scarf
wound around the head. *The first turbans
were worn as protection from the sun.*

tur•bu•lent /tûr′ byə lənt/ *adj.* disturbed
or violently agitated. *The ocean became
turbulent as the hurricane approached.*

typ•i•cal /tĭp′ ĭ kəl/ *adj.* being a certain
type; like others in its category. *Saturday
was a typical rainy day.*

ty•rant /tī′ rənt/ *n.* a person who rules very
harshly or unjustly. *The citizens rebelled
against the tyrant.*

ul•ti•mate /ŭl′ tə mĭt/ *adj.* **a.** farthest;
last; final. *Being an outstanding teacher is
my ultimate goal.* **b.** best; greatest. *Chess is
the ultimate game of logic.*

un- a prefix that means "not" or "the opposite of": *unable; untie.*

under- a prefix that means "beneath" or
"below in position": *underground.*

un•der•cov•er /ŭn′ dər kŭv′ ər/ *adj.*
done in secret: *an undercover police
investigation.*

un•der•ground /ŭn′ dər ground′/ *adv.*
below the surface of the earth. *The tunnel
led to an underground cavern.*

un•der•neath /ŭn′ dər nēth′/ *prep.*
beneath; below; under. *Sean found the note
that had been left underneath the doormat.*

Spelling Dictionary

311

un•der•pass /ŭn′ dər păs′/ *n.* a section of road that passes under another road or railroad. *The traffic noise echoed in the underpass.*

un•der•stand /ŭn′ dər stănd′/ *v.* (un•der•stands, un•der•stood, un•der•stand•ing) **a.** to know; to comprehend. *Do you understand how a vacuum cleaner works?* **b.** to learn; to hear. *I understand they are planning a trip.*

un•der•stood¹ /ŭn′ dər stŏŏd′/ *v.* past tense of **understand.**

un•der•stood² /ŭn′ dər stŏŏd′/ *adj.* assumed; implied. *It is understood that all sales are final.*

un•for•tu•nate /ŭn fôr′ chə nĭt/ *adj.* not fortunate; not lucky. *It is unfortunate that we missed the bus this morning.*

u•ni•form /yŏŏ′ nə fôrm′/ *n.* the special clothes worn by persons of a particular order or service when they are on duty. *Police and firefighters wear uniforms so they will be recognized.* [Latin *ūnus,* one + *forma,* shape.]

uniform

un•ion /yŏŏn′ yən/ *n.* **a.** a joining to make a single thing. *The nation called the United States was formed by the union of the original thirteen states.* **b.** a group of workers formed to protect their interests with respect to wages and working conditions. *The union of postal employees accepted the new contract.* [Latin *ūnus,* one.]

un•pleas•ant /ŭn plĕz′ ənt/ *adj.* not pleasant; disagreeable. *That medicine has an unpleasant taste.*

un•voiced /ŭn voist′/ *adj.* produced without vibration of the vocal cords. *The consonant s is unvoiced, but z is voiced.*

up•ward /ŭp′ wərd/ *adv.* toward a higher place, level, or position. *The balloons floated upward when they were let go.*

u•su•al /yŏŏ′ zhŏŏ əl/ *adj.* common; ordinary. *The usual tool for driving a nail is a hammer.*

va•ca•tion /vā kā′ shən/ *n.* a period of time during which one is free from work or school. *My father gets a two-week vacation every year.*

val•u•a•ble /văl′ yŏŏ ə bəl/ or /văl′ yə bəl/ *adj.* **a.** having great value or worth; important. *He is a valuable player on the team.* **b.** worth a great deal of money. *She keeps her valuable china on a high shelf.*

var•i•ous /vâr′ ē əs/ or /văr′-/ *adj.* of several different kinds; different. *I found shells of various sizes and shapes on the beach.*

VCR an abbreviation for "video cassette recorder." *We rented a VCR so we could tape the TV special.*

ve•loc•i•ty /və lŏs′ ĭ tē/ *n.* the rate at which an object moves in a specific direction; speed. *The coaches measured the velocity of the pitcher's fast ball.*

ver•dict /vûr′ dĭkt/ *n.* a decision reached by a jury or a judge at the end of a trial. *The jury handed down a verdict of "not guilty."*

vi•brate /vī′ brāt′/ *v.* (vi•brates, vi•brat•ed, vi•brat•ing) to move back and forth quickly. *The strings on a guitar vibrate when they are strummed.*

vic•to•ry /vĭk′ tə rē/ *n.* (vic•to•ries *pl.*) the act of winning; the defeat of the opposite side; triumph in a battle or contest. *The home team scored its first victory last night.*

vid•e•o¹ /vĭd′ ē ō/ *adj.* of or used in the transmitting and receiving of television images. *Our local record store will soon carry a line of video equipment.*

vid•e•o² /vĭd′ ē ō/ *n.* a videocassette tape; a recording on videotape. *Singers often create videos of their songs.* [Latin *vidēre,* to see.]

vil•lain /vĭl′ ən/ *n.* a wicked or evil character. *When the villain appeared onstage, the audience booed.*

vi•o•lin•ist
/vī′ ə **lĭn′** ĭst/ *n.* a person who plays the violin. *John hopes to become a great violinist.*

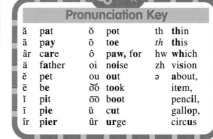

violinist

vis•i•ble /**vĭz′** ə bəl/ *adj.* able to be seen. *Because of the fog, the lights were no longer visible.*

vi•sion /**vĭzh′** ən/ *n.* **a.** something that is or has been seen. *Jan was a vision of beauty in her costume.* **b.** the sense of sight. *He has perfect vision in both eyes.* [Latin *vis-,* perfect stem of *vidēre,* to see.]

vis•i•tor /**vĭz′** ĭ tər/ *n.* a person who visits. *The visitor brought flowers.*

vis•u•al /**vĭzh′** yoo əl/ *adj.* capable of being seen; visible. *The laser light show was a visual treat for the audience.*

voiced /voist/ *adj.* sounded with the vibration of the vocal cords. *The **th** sound in "this" is a voiced consonant sound.*

vol•ume /**vŏl′** yoom/ *or* /-yəm/ *n.* **a.** the amount of space within an enclosed area. *Can you find the volume of this cube?* **b.** loudness. *Please turn down the volume of the radio.* **c.** one of a set of books: *a volume of the encyclopedia.*

vol•un•tar•y /**vŏl′** ən tĕr′ē/ *adj.* (**vol•un•tar•i•ly,** *adv.*) done by choice or on purpose. *He made a voluntary decision to stay home and study.*

vol•un•teer /vŏl′ ən **tîr′**/ *n.* one who offers to perform a service of his or her free will, usually without pay. *We need a volunteer to sell tickets to the school play.*

-ward a suffix, used to form adverbs or adjectives, that means "in a specified direction": *downward.*

wa•ter va•por /**wô′** tər vā′ pər/ *or* /**wŏt′** ər-/ *n.* water below the boiling point that is diffused as vapor in the atmosphere. *Water vapor forms in a steamy bathroom.*

wave•length /**wāv′** lĕngth′/ *n.* the distance between any point on a wave and the same point on the next wave. *Light has a shorter wavelength than sound.*

weath•er•proof /**wĕth′** ər proof′/ *adj.* able to be exposed to weather without damage. *Most houses are painted with weatherproof paint.*

weird /wîrd/ *adj.* strange; odd. *The group of people going to the costume party was a weird sight.*

whole•some /**hōl′** səm/ *adj.* healthful. *The doctor gave us advice on the importance of exercise and wholesome meals.*

wind /wīnd/ *v.* (**winds, wound, wind•ing**) **a.** to wrap or coil around. *Wind the thread around the spool.* **b.** to turn or crank. *Who will wind the clock?*

won•der•ful /**wŭn′** dər fəl/ *adj.* excellent; remarkable; marvelous. *What a wonderful sight the sunset is today!*

won•drous /**wŭn′** drəs/ *adj.* wonderful. *The Perseid meteor shower is a wondrous August event.*

wood•cut /**wood′** kŭt′/ *n.* a block of wood with a picture or design carved into it. *The artist carved the design into the block to form a woodcut.*

wor•ri•some /**wûr′** ē səm/ *or* /**wŭr′**-/ *adj.* causing concern or worry. *His jammed locker was a worrisome problem all day.*

worth•less /**wûrth′** lĭs/ *adj.* without worth or value. *The photographs were worthless to everyone but the family members.*

would • 've would have.

wound[1] /wōōnd/ *n.* an injury to the body. *The doctor put a bandage on the wound on my arm.*

wound[2] /wound/ *v.* past tense and past participle of **wind**.

wrist • watch /rĭst' wŏch'/ *n.* a watch worn on a band that fastens around the wrist. *The child was excited to get her first wristwatch.*

wristwatch

yield /yēld/ *v.* to surrender; to give up. *A traffic sign that says "yield" warns drivers to allow the other drivers to go first.*

USING THE Thesaurus

The **Writing Thesaurus** provides synonyms—words that mean the same or nearly the same—and antonyms—words that mean the opposite—for your spelling words. Use this sample to identify the various parts of each thesaurus entry.

- **Entry words** are listed in alphabetical order and are printed in boldface type.
- The abbreviation for the **part of speech** of each entry word follows the boldface entry word.
- The **definition** of the entry word matches the definition given of the word in your spelling dictionary. A **sample sentence** shows the correct use of the word in context.
- Each **synonym** for the entry word is listed under the entry word. Again, a sample sentence shows the correct use of the synonym in context.
- Where appropriate, **antonyms** for the entry word are listed at the end of the entry.

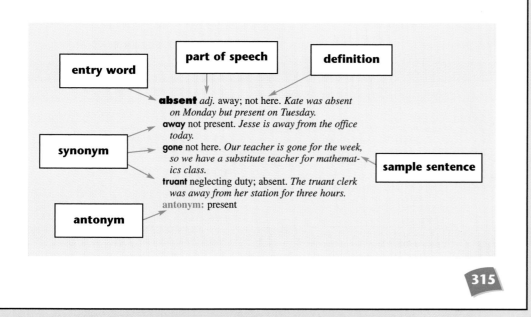

entry word

part of speech

definition

absent *adj.* away; not here. *Kate was absent on Monday but present on Tuesday.*

away not present. *Jesse is away from the office today.*

synonym

gone not here. *Our teacher is gone for the week, so we have a substitute teacher for mathematics class.*

sample sentence

truant neglecting duty; absent. *The truant clerk was away from her station for three hours.*

antonym: present

antonym

315

absent *adj.* away; not here. *Kate was absent on Monday but present on Tuesday.*
away not present. *Jesse is away from the office today.*
gone not here. *Our teacher is gone for the week, so we have a substitute teacher for mathematics class.*
truant neglecting duty; absent. *The truant clerk was away from her station for three hours.*
antonym: present

accurate *adj.* correct; without mistakes. *The witness's testimony was accurate and consistent with the evidence.*
definite clear or exact. *The flight attendant gave a definite time for the flight's departure from the airport.*
exact precise; correct. *She noted the exact location of the accident.*
factual concerned with facts; truthful. *Horace gave a factual account of the game's ending.*
precise correct; exact. *Because the kit had precise directions, we could build the birdhouse easily.*
unerring without mistakes. *Because of her unerring performance, she was sure to win the gold medal.*
antonyms: incorrect, wrong

accuse *v.* to blame for wrongdoing. *The police did accuse him of speeding and reckless driving.*
blame to hold responsible for. *No one would blame you for mistaking one twin for the other.*
censure to criticize. *For not having the proper data in his research report, the decision was made to censure him.*
criticize to find fault with. *Do not criticize him until you know all the facts.*
reproach to blame. *Be a person of good character so no one can reproach you.*

achieve *v.* to reach; accomplish. *If you wish to achieve success, you must work hard.*
accomplish to succeed in completing. *We will accomplish the task in record time.*

attain to arrive at; gain. *She will attain her goal through hard work.*
antonym: fail

admit *v.* to acknowledge; confess. *The mayor did admit that she had not been aware of the problem.*
acknowledge to admit to be true. *The accountant must acknowledge that the mistake on the books was her fault.*
concede to admit as true. *The actor had to concede that he had not learned his lines on time.*
confess to own up; admit. *Sami confessed that the floor was flooded because he had left the water running in the sink.*
reveal to make known. *The investigation might reveal that the mistake was due to computer error.*

adorable *adj.* lovable; charming. *The stuffed animals were cuddly and adorable.*
attractive pleasing. *My brother and his wife are an attractive couple.*
captivating charming; fascinating. *The story is a captivating tale of two best friends.*
charming delightful; adorable. *The children in the play were totally charming.*
cute good-looking and lovable. *That baby is so cute and sweet!*
darling dear and attractive. *Your new puppy is just darling.*

advance *v.* to go forward. *Please advance to the front of the line.*
forge ahead to move forward. *She needed to forge ahead to win the race by just a few steps.*
proceed to move forward. *The cars continued to proceed slowly through the dangerous intersection.*
progress to go ahead. *The work on the new bridge continued to progress on schedule.*
promote to advance; move upward. *I was promoted to seventh grade.*

aged *adj.* old; having lived long. *The aged man was having difficulty walking.*
ancient very old; of great age. *The Colosseum is one of Rome's ancient ruins.*
elderly old. *In this program, elderly men and women spend time teaching the young children in the day-care center.*
antonym: young

316

amateur *n.* a person who participates in activities for fun, not money. *Even an amateur can become skillful with regular practice.*

hobbyist amateur. *The hobbyist compared his paintings to those displayed by the professionals.*

nonprofessional not professional; amateur. *In this tournament, a nonprofessional played with the golf pros.*

amaze *v.* to surprise or astonish. *The acrobat's ability to do high jumps really did amaze us.*

astound to surprise greatly; astonish. *The cost of the project continues to astound us.*

dazzle to astonish; overwhelm with beauty. *The splendor of the mansion will dazzle the tourists.*

fascinate to strongly attract or charm. *Tonight's featured news stories fascinate me.*

stun to overwhelm; shock; surprise. *The damage caused by the storm has to stun even the weather bureau.*

antisocial *adj.* avoiding the company of others. *It is a mistake to assume that a shy person is deliberately antisocial.*

hostile unfriendly; not sociable. *He gave me such a hostile look that I knew he did not want to be disturbed.*

unfriendly not friendly; hostile. *The unfriendly dog frightened me.*

unsociable not friendly; antisocial. *The child's parents scolded her for displaying unsociable behavior at the restaurant.*

appreciate *v.* 1. to see the value of something. *The recital made us appreciate my brother's hours of piano practice.* 2. to be thankful for. *I appreciate your help.*

be grateful to be thankful. *Sandra should be grateful for the opportunity to visit Paris.*

prize to highly value. *The actor seems to prize his privacy.*

value to think highly of. *I truly value my right to vote.*

approve *v.* 1. to give official consent to. *The board needs to approve the plans for the new gym.* 2. to have a good opinion of. *Do you approve of his choice of colors?*

accept to consent to. *The park manager must accept the bid for repairing the tennis courts.*

commend to praise; approve. *My instructor stopped to commend me for my performance in the play.*

endorse to support; approve. *The political party will endorse the President's reelection campaign.*

ratify to confirm; approve. *Both houses of Congress must ratify the law.*

aptitude *n.* a talent or ability for learning. *She has an aptitude for languages; she speaks French, German, and Italian.*

ability capability; power to do. *The runner had the ability to run the marathon in record time.*

capability ability to learn to do. *He has the capability to learn how to operate the new computer system.*

faculty ability; power to do something. *Her faculty to understand difficult ideas is admired by the entire staff.*

flair talent. *The artist had a flair for combining color and light in his paintings.*

sense power to perceive. *The reporter had the good sense not to pursue that line of questioning.*

talent natural ability. *Because of her talent, Donna was a soloist in the school's chorus.*

assign *v.* 1. to give out; distribute. *Our teacher does assign us homework every evening.* 2. to appoint to a position. *The teacher will assign him to be hall monitor this month.*

appoint to name for an office; select. *They decided to appoint Henry chairperson of the special events committee.*

commission to appoint; give authority to. *The committee voted to commission this artist to paint the President's portrait.*

consign to give out; deliver. *Which airfreight company did you consign the shipment to?*

delegate to appoint or send. *We decided to delegate Mitch to represent us at the meeting.*

name to appoint; choose. *The president of the company will name Carole vice president of marketing.*

associate *v.* to think of as related. *Most people associate tears with sadness, but many people cry when they are happy.*

connect to link; think of in relation to. *Many people connect seeing a robin for the first time with the beginning of spring.*

correlate to relate to another. *Did you correlate your choice of classes with your career goals?*

baffle *v.* to puzzle; bewilder. *The riddles will baffle the students.*

bewilder to puzzle; confuse completely. *All the aisles of shelves in the library bewilder Trisha and remind her of a maze.*

confound to puzzle; confuse. *The lack of detail in the instructions did confound me.*

confuse to bewilder. *Driving on diagonal streets can confuse my sense of direction.*

perplex to bewilder; confuse; puzzle. *The results of the student's experiment did perplex the professor.*

puzzle to perplex; baffle. *Tom's solution to that math problem did puzzle me.*

balance *v.* to make both sides equal; to weigh or measure in or as in a balance. *The clown tried to balance a chair on his head.*

equalize to make even; balance. *Tara attempted to equalize her study time and the time for swimming practice.*

offset to balance or set off. *The trip to Mexico offset the long hours of work needed to complete the project.*

barely *adv.* hardly; scarcely. *We could barely see the cars because of the fog.*

hardly only just; barely. *The teacher had hardly any time to prepare the students for the contest.*

only just barely; hardly. *He had only just begun to sing when the sound system broke down.*

scarcely barely; not quite. *Scarcely anyone was in the theater when I arrived for the second show.*

beyond *prep.* in a place farther away than; past. *The grocery store is just beyond the park.*

after behind. *Turn left after the second light.*

past farther on than. *If you go past the school, you have driven too far and you should turn around.*

browse *v.* 1. to look at in a leisurely way; skim through. *Sam began to browse through the magazines in the dentist's office.* 2. to feed on leaves. *Giraffes browse on tall trees.*

graze to feed on grass or trees. *After we milked the cows, we sent them out to the field to graze.*

scan to glance at; skim. *Looking for store coupons, Rosa needed to scan the ads in the newspaper.*

thumb through to browse; look casually. *Jackie will thumb through the mystery books in the library to find one that interests her.*

cancel *v.* to do away with; to call off. *The official had to cancel the game because of rain.*

neutralize to make neutral; to stop something from taking effect. *The antidote will neutralize the effect of the poison.*

repeal to take back; do away with. *Congress will repeal the unpopular tax law during the current session.*

revoke to withdraw; cancel. *The city can revoke a building permit if building codes are violated.*

capable *adj.* having the skill to; able to. *She is capable of fixing almost any machine.*

able having skill; capable. *Norm is able to swim thirty laps at a time.*

competent able; qualified. *Rose is a competent news reporter who always checks the facts of a story.*

proficient skilled; expert. *Kathryn is a proficient reader and speller.*

qualified competent. *Marietta was one of the qualified job applicants.*

carefully *adv.* with care; cautiously or thoroughly. *Peter dusted the tiny figurines carefully.*

cautiously very carefully; not taking any chances. *Victor cautiously approached the intersection where the accident had occurred.*

conscientiously careful to do the right thing. *Anita conscientiously attended each lecture in the series.*

gingerly very cautiously. *Anton gingerly picked up the pieces of broken glass.*

painstakingly very carefully; scrupulously. *Tina painstakingly fitted together all the pieces of the 1000-piece jigsaw puzzle.*

thoroughly very carefully, completing an entire task. *The vet thoroughly examined the injured bird.*

cautious *adj.* careful; keeping away from danger. *The bus driver was cautious in the storm.*
careful showing care; watchful. *Carole was very careful while driving on the icy roads.*
discreet very careful in what is said or done; wisely cautious. *She gave a discreet response to the impolite question.*
unadventurous unwilling to take risks. *John is so unadventurous that he would not even think of going on the hiking trip through the park.*
wary on guard; cautious. *You should be wary when walking on unlit streets alone at night.*
antonym: careless

central *adj.* main; leading; chief. *What is the central idea that the author wants us to understand?*
cardinal foremost; chief. *The cardinal rule for getting along with your friends is to respect them.*
chief most important; main. *Corn is the chief crop raised by farmers in our state.*
main foremost; most important. *Who was the main character in the story?*
pivotal very important; central. *The President addressed the pivotal issues in his State of the Union Address.*
principal most important; main. *Name the principal rivers in the United States.*

certainly *adv.* definitely; surely. *Certainly your grades will improve if you study hard.*
absolutely certainly; without a doubt. *The star absolutely will attend the New York premiere of the movie.*
definitely certainly; surely. *Without glasses, he definitely could not see the third line of the eye chart.*
positively surely; absolutely. *This is positively the best restaurant in town.*
undoubtedly without doubt; certainly. *Undoubtedly the game will be delayed because of rain.*

classify *v.* to sort; arrange according to category or class. *Librarians do not classify fairy tales with other fiction.*
categorize to put into a category; classify. *For the lab test, we had to categorize items as PLANTS, ANIMALS, or MINERALS.*

grade to sort; place in classes. *We need to grade the peaches according to size.*
sort to arrange by class; put in order. *Ray will sort the sales figures by product.*

cleanse *v.* to make clean; remove dirt from. *Always cleanse a cut or scrape before bandaging it.*
clean to get rid of dirt; to make clean. *Be sure to clean behind your ears.*
rinse to wash lightly. *The dentist told me to rinse my mouth out with salt water.*
scour to make clean by rubbing; cleanse. *I will scour the tub until it shines.*
scrub to rub hard; wash by rubbing. *We needed to scrub and wax the floors.*
sponge to wipe clean. *Dad can sponge the dirt from Anna's scraped knee.*
wash to clean with soap and water. *We will wash our hands and faces before we sit down to eat.*
wipe to clean by rubbing. *Please wipe your feet before coming in the house.*

complain *v.* 1. to find fault. *Don't complain about a problem unless you're willing to help remedy it.* 2. to report something bad. *The neighbors called the police to complain about the noisy motorcycle.*
accuse to place blame on. *The sales representative tried to accuse the mail service of delaying my order.*
grumble to find fault; complain. *Jesse always seems to grumble about having too much homework to do.*
protest to object to; complain strongly. *The coach decided to protest the referee's decision.*
rail to complain bitterly. *The lawyer would rail against the injustice her client had experienced.*

conceit *n.* an exaggerated opinion of one's worth; vanity. *Conceit is an unattractive quality.*
egotism too much concern with oneself; conceit. *His egotism led him to believe he could never be wrong.*
self-esteem thinking well of oneself. *The success of her plan bolstered her self-esteem.*
vainglory extreme pride; vanity. *The vainglory of the senator was one reason he was not reelected.*
vanity too much pride; conceit. *The actor's vanity was greater than his talent.*

conclude *v.* to end; finish. *She concluded her speech and sat down.*

close to come together; to bring to an end. *The President closed his speech with a request for help from all the people.*

complete to make thorough; to get done. *Cheryl can complete her report before the deadline.*

end to stop; finish. *The story could end with the hero solving the mystery.*

finish to bring to an end; complete. *After I finish the book, I will lend it to my sister.*

terminate to put an end to. *When one partner left the company it was necessary to terminate the agreement.*

conduct *v.* to guide; lead. *The student will conduct the visitor through the new building.*

direct to manage; guide. *Matty tried to direct the actors in the movie.*

guide to show the way; lead. *The park ranger will guide us through the cave.*

lead to show the way; guide. *You can lead a horse to water, but you cannot make it drink.*

manage to guide; direct. *She continued to manage the account so well that its profits increased by fifty percent.*

usher to take to; escort. *The restaurant owner was pleased to usher us to our seats.*

confirm *v.* to make certain or sure. *The experiment will try to confirm her theory.*

authenticate to show to be valid; verify. *The scientific testing will authenticate the estimated age of the fossil.*

certify to confirm as true; guarantee. *This document does certify completion of the course.*

establish to prove; confirm. *The witness did establish the defendant's alibi.*

prove to show to be true or right. *The lawyer claimed she could prove her client's innocence.*

verify to confirm; prove the truth of. *Can scientific evidence be used to verify your conclusion?*

antonyms: contradict, disprove

connect *v.* 1. to join; link. *Before you turn on the water, connect the hose to the faucet.* 2. to join two ideas, events, etc., in the mind. *I connect clowns with the circus.*

bind to tie together; fasten. *We will bind the newspapers with twine before taking them to the recycling center.*

join to come together; connect. *Karen will join her friends at the theater.*

link to unite; connect. *The pieces of the puzzle link together perfectly.*

relate to connect ideas or events or things. *The increased attendance at home games is related to the team's long winning streak.*

unite to join together; combine. *The railroad does unite the two parts of the country.*

constant *adj.* never changing or stopping; happening again and again. *The constant beat of the rain put us to sleep.*

continual never stopping; over and over again. *The continual interruptions made it difficult for him to complete his work.*

persistent going on; continuing. *After most of my cold symptoms were gone, I still had a persistent cough.*

steady changing little; continuous. *The sun is finally shining after three days of steady rain.*

courage *n.* the quality of facing danger or a difficult task without giving in to fear. *It takes courage to admit your mistakes.*

bravery fearlessness. *The police officer won an award for bravery after saving the child from the fire.*

fortitude courage; firmness of convictions. *She has the fortitude to fight for what she believes is right.*

valor bravery; strength. *The valor of the colonists helped them win the American Revolution.*

cruel *adj.* wanting to make others suffer or causing them pain. *The cruel children threw stones at the birds.*

brutal extremely cruel. *The enemies waged a brutal battle against one another.*

insensitive slow to notice; uncaring. *The insensitive remark hurt her feelings.*

unkind harsh; cruel. *Children are sometimes unkind to one another.*

customary *adj.* based on custom; usual; routine. *A tuna sandwich and an apple are my customary lunch.*

everyday usual; not exciting. *This book details the everyday as well as the unusual events of the author's days living in the wilderness.*

habitual done by habit; regular. *We took our habitual evening walk along the beach.*

routine using routine; ordinary. *During one of our routine practices, the coach announced who would be the starting players in Saturday's game.*

traditional customary; handed down by tradition. *Turkey and cranberry sauce are two of the traditional foods for the Thanksgiving meal.*

usual common; ordinary; customary. *Although Lynne left for work at the usual time, she arrived fifteen minutes earlier than she expected.*

delicate *adj.* 1. light and pleasing to the senses. *This is a delicate perfume.* 2. carefully and expertly done; requiring careful workmanship. *Those are delicate repairs.* 3. fragile; easily broken or hurt. *Be careful with that delicate vase.*

dainty delicate in beauty; delicate in tastes. *The dainty spring flowers complemented the room's old-fashioned decor.*

exquisite very lovely; delicate. *This painting displayed by the museum is an exquisite example of impressionistic art.*

fine not coarse; delicate. *This fine cloth can be sewn into a beautiful summer suit.*

fragile easily broken; frail. *Because the package was marked fragile, I opened it very carefully.*

frail not very strong; easily broken. *My mother does not let anyone sit in the antique armchair because it is so frail.*

mild soft or lightly pleasing to the senses. *The mild aroma of the sauce made my mouth water.*

delightful *adj.* greatly pleasing; causing joy or delight. *We saw a delightful movie last night that made us remember our days as small children.*

charming delightful; very pleasing. *The child's retelling of "Goldilocks and the Three Bears" was charming.*

cheery pleasant; cheerful. *Sally sent me a cheery note when I was sick.*

enjoyable pleasant; able to be enjoyed. *We had an enjoyable time at the fair.*

lovely beautiful; pleasant. *It was a lovely evening at the concert.*

pleasurable agreeable; pleasant. *The cruise was a pleasurable way to spend a week.*

detain *v.* 1. to delay; hold back. *Heavy fog managed to detain their flight for two hours.* 2. to keep in custody. *They decided to detain the suspect for questioning.*

confine to restrict; limit. *At the meeting, we were asked to confine our comments to the topic being discussed.*

constrain to restrain; confine. *The restrictions placed on her project continued to constrain Natalie.*

delay to put off; hinder. *Because of switching problems, it was necessary to delay the train for an hour.*

hold up to stop; detain. *I knew the weather would hold up our departure.*

postpone to put off; delay. *It was decided to postpone the concert until a later date.*

retard to delay; hinder. *The lack of funds will retard the progress of the campaign.*

develop *v.* 1. to grow; come into being. *The bud will develop into a blossom.* 2. to build up; put to use. *Reading helps develop your mind.*

expand to enlarge; make or grow larger. *The class in geography will expand the student's knowledge of international relations.*

extend to stretch; increase. *Can you extend your answer to include the reasons for the American Revolution?*

grow to become bigger; develop. *Francesco is growing so quickly that he needs new shoes every three months.*

different *adj.* not alike. *Summer is different from winter.*

dissimilar unalike. *Our answers were so dissimilar that they could not be compared.*

diverse not alike; varied. *The candidates had diverse opinions on the issue.*

unlike not the same; different. *Although they are twins, they are very much unlike each other.*

varied having variety or choice. *The menu offered quite varied selections.*

antonyms: same, similar

difficult *adj.* hard; not easy to do or understand. *Learning to play chess is difficult.*

arduous hard to do; using much energy. *After her arduous workout, the gymnast wanted to do nothing but rest.*

hard difficult; troublesome. *At first, I had a hard time understanding what the toddler was trying to tell me.*

rigorous harsh; difficult. *Only after rigorous practice did I master the steps of the dance routine.*

tough hard. *Ed had a tough time trying to explain why he had not completed the project on time.*

antonym: easy

dirty *adj.* not clean; containing dirt. *Put all the dirty clothes into the washing machine.*

filthy very dirty; foul. *After playing in the mud, Johnny and Matthew were filthy from head to toe.*

foul very dirty; smelly. *The pollution released by the factory made the air foul.*

impure unclean; adulterated. *The addition of the incorrect chemical made the solution impure.*

antonym: clean

disguise *v.* 1. to change one's real appearance so that one will not be recognized. *In the play, the thief did disguise himself as a detective.* 2. to hide; mask; cover up. *He tried to disguise his anger by smiling.*

camouflage to conceal; disguise. *Chameleons camouflage themselves by changing their color.*

mask to cover or hide. *Al needed to mask his disappointment by cheerfully congratulating the winner.*

masquerade to disguise; falsely pretend. *To get the information he wanted, the private detective had to masquerade as a bartender.*

dispute *v.* to argue; debate; have a different opinion about. *Our class did dispute about the best date for the picnic.*

argue to discuss with someone who disagrees. *Abby would argue that her bedtime was much too early and that she should be allowed to stay up at least one hour longer.*

contend to argue. *Congress will contend that balancing the budget should be one of the country's highest priorities.*

contest to fight or dispute. *The defeated candidate did not contest the election returns, although the results were very close.*

debate to argue about; discuss pros and cons. *The city council will debate the need for additional taxes to pay for road repairs.*

disagree to quarrel; dispute. *If they disagree about who will be first, the friends will settle the argument by drawing lots.*

quarrel to argue; dispute. *I cannot quarrel with your account of the traffic accident.*

donate *v.* to give or contribute to a fund or cause. *The class decided to donate the money from the bake sale to the animal shelter.*

bestow to give as a gift. *France bestowed the Statue of Liberty on the United States for its centennial.*

confer to bestow. *The President will confer the Medal of Honor on three soldiers during the ceremony.*

contribute to give money or help. *Volunteers will contribute their time to the cleanup effort, since the storm left the city in a shambles.*

give to hand over. *We will give the clothes we collected for the poor to the local charity.*

grant to give what is asked. *The parent-teacher group voted to grant money to the school to build a new chemistry lab.*

effort *n.* 1. the use of one's strength or power; exertion. *Riding a bicycle uphill requires effort.* 2. an attempt; a try. *Make an effort to finish by three o'clock.*

attempt an effort or try. *The track star broke the record on his second attempt at the long jump.*

endeavor a strong attempt; effort. *The reporter's endeavor to gain an interview with the visiting official paid off when she agreed to speak with him.*

exertion effort. *The sheer exertion needed to complete the task on time was almost overwhelming.*

labor effort in doing. *The success of the summit made our labor to prepare for it worthwhile.*

error *n.* a mistake. *I was happy because my spelling test had no errors.*

blunder a foolish mistake. *Forgetting my mother's birthday was a real blunder.*

fault an error; a mistake. *A missing answer was the only fault I could find on my test paper.*

inaccuracy mistake. *It was an inaccuracy in the computer input that caused the program to fail.*

mistake error. *I corrected the mistake on my paper before I handed it in to the teacher.*

especially *adv.* mainly; in particular; unusually. *My brother likes all sports, but he especially enjoys soccer.*

notably in a notable manner; especially. *Karen is a good student in most subjects, but most notably in history and math.*

particularly especially; in particular. *The storm hit the eastern section of the city particularly hard.*

principally mainly. *Yvonne was the person principally responsible for the success of the school's fund-raising efforts.*

exactly *adv.* precisely; without any change. *Do exactly as the teacher says.*

accurately without errors. *The reporter accurately described the events leading to the tragedy.*

correctly without mistakes. *Andrew correctly named all the state capitals.*

definitely clearly; exactly. *It is definitely important to understand all the directions.*

literally precisely; actually. *Lynne followed the instructions for building the desk literally step by step.*

precisely exactly; in a precise manner. *What precisely is the total cost of the car when taxes are included?*

examine *v.* to look at closely to find out the condition of; inspect. *Examine the apples before you buy them.*

analyze to examine carefully. *The manager decided to analyze the reports to identify the trends in sales activity.*

audit to examine and check. *The state examiner will audit the bank's accounts once every two years.*

check to compare and examine. *The teacher will check the students' answers against the answer key.*

inspect to carefully examine. *Edna tried to examine the coat for flaws in the material.*

test to try out; examine. *The doctor used the chart to test my eyesight.*

excellence *n.* something in which a person surpasses others. *The school offered an award for excellence in spelling.*

merit something that deserves high praise; value. *The volunteer was honored for the merit of her work at our local children's hospital.*

quality excellence; merit. *The skill of the carpenter is reflected in the quality of the cabinet.*

superiority high in quality. *The superiority of this product makes it the best-selling stereo on the market.*

excitement *n.* an excited condition; the state of being stirred up. *The entrance of the tigers created great excitement among the circus crowd.*

ecstasy condition of great joy or delight. *The ecstasy of the occasion was evident on everyone's face.*

frenzy very great excitement. *The fans were in a frenzy when the home team won the World Series.*

thrill an exciting feeling. *I will always remember the thrill of my first summer vacation at the beach.*

exhibit *v.* to display; reveal publicly. *He decided to exhibit his paintings at the fair.*

display to put on view; show; exhibit. *The students will display their projects at the school's science fair.*

expose to show openly; make known; display. *The company's new product was first exposed to the public on national television.*

feature to draw special attention to. *The trade show will feature the latest technology.*

present to bring before the public. *The museum will present the works of the most noted realists.*

experience *n.* what one learns from doing things. *I gained business experience from my paper route.*

background past experience or knowledge. *My strong background in history helps me better understand today's political issues and events.*

knowledge what one knows and understands. *The new group had very limited knowledge of the music business.*

practice the condition of being skilled through repeated exercise. *The coach pointed out that sloppy practice doesn't make perfect.*

training practical education; experience. *Dan's training as a crime reporter helped him identify clues that could be used to solve the mystery.*

Writing Thesaurus

323

express *v.* to tell; make known. *Think for a moment before you try to express your idea.*

communicate to give information through writing or speaking, etc. *Her speech will communicate her viewpoint eloquently.*

convey to communicate. *Let me convey my best wishes for the success of your new business venture.*

delineate to describe in words. *Jeff will delineate the company's profit plan in his presentation to the board.*

phrase to express in a particular way. *Be sure to phrase your question so that only a "Yes" or "No" answer is needed.*

state to tell; say. *The mayor did clearly state his position on the property tax increase the council was proposing.*

verbalize to express in words. *I am going to verbalize my ideas to see if you think they will work.*

fabulous *adj.* amazing; wonderful. *It was a fabulous party.*

marvelous splendid; extraordinary. *We had a marvelous time at the annual charity ball sponsored by our organization.*

sensational outstanding; spectacular. *Both actors gave sensational performances on stage.*

spectacular marvelous; sensational. *The game ended with Sara's spectacular diving catch of the fly ball.*

splendid wonderful; excellent. *The restaurant offers a splendid choice of seafood as well as pasta dishes.*

striking very noticeable; fabulous. *Her striking rendition of the show's theme song brought the audience to its feet.*

wonderful causing wonder; remarkable. *We had a wonderful time vacationing in the Hawaiian Islands.*

fearless *adj.* not afraid; brave. *The fearless kitten confronted the big dog.*

bold without fear; daring. *Malcolm made a bold effort to outrun the older boys on the team.*

brave showing courage. *Jessie put on a brave smile as she entered the dentist's office for her appointment.*

courageous brave; fearless. *Saving the child was a courageous act by the firefighter, who received an award for his bravery.*

daring fearless; bold. *The daring high divers perform their spectacular acts every day.*

gallant brave; noble. *The gallant efforts of the volunteers helped protect the homes from being flooded.*

antonyms: afraid, frightened

feeble *adj.* without much strength; weak. *Newborn animals are often feeble.*

faint dizzy; weak. *Evelyn felt faint as she stood to give her speech in the school auditorium.*

flimsy slight; frail. *Anton gave a flimsy excuse for being late for his class.*

frail weak; feeble. *Although she appeared frail, Maxine was quite strong for her size.*

infirm lacking strength; feeble. *The patient was too infirm to walk without help.*

fierce *adj.* 1. savage; wild. *The fierce lion growled and paced inside the cage.* 2. violent. *The fierce wind blew down the trees.*

ferocious savage; very cruel. *The ferocious animal bared its teeth as it growled.*

furious violent; very fierce. *The furious storm tore roofs off houses and uprooted trees.*

raging violent. *The raging winds blew down power lines and tree branches.*

savage cruel; fierce. *The savage fight ended with both wild dogs bleeding and limping away.*

flexible *adj.* capable of being bent. *The clay figures were flexible and could be formed into any shape.*

pliable easily bent. *Because the vines were pliable, we could easily shape them into a wreath.*

pliant easily bent; flexible. *The sculptor heated the steel to make it pliant for forming the pieces of an enormous mobile.*

supple bending easily; flexible. *The supple dancer leaped and twirled throughout the ballet performance.*

former *adj.* coming earlier in time or before in position. *The former owner of this house painted the walls blue.*

earlier before; previous. *The author's earlier novel was better written that this one.*

previous earlier; coming before. *I did not see this exhibit on my previous visit to the museum.*

prior earlier than; before. *The coach gave a stirring speech prior to the start of the game.*

fortunate *adj.* lucky. *You were fortunate to find the lost bracelet.*

happy lucky; fortunate. *It was a happy co-incidence that my friend and I were in the same class.*

lucky having good luck. *We were lucky to get tickets for the playoff games from Pat's mother.*

furious *adj.* very angry. *I was furious with myself for forgetting my homework.*

angry feeling or showing anger. *Her angry tone of voice let me know she was not pleased.*

irate very angry. *The long delay made me irate because I knew I would miss my connecting flight.*

wrathful very angry. *With a wrathful roar, the tiger leaped to protect her cubs.*

garbage *n.* spoiled food or waste matter that is thrown away. *We put our garbage in cans in the alley.*

debris ruins; rubbish. *The stadium was filled with debris left by the fans.*

refuse waste; rubbish. *Keep the park clean by throwing your refuse in one of the trash containers.*

rubbish trash; waste. *It is illegal to burn rubbish in most communities.*

trash rubbish. *The students filled three bags with the trash picked up from the baseball field.*

waste refuse; unused materials. *It would be wrong to let so much food go to waste.*

glorious *adj.* beautiful; brilliant. *This is a glorious day.*

brilliant splendid; magnificent. *The actor's brilliant performance as Hamlet was given rave reviews in the newspaper.*

magnificent splendid; grand. *The magnificent work of the artist was displayed in the art museum.*

splendid glorious; brilliant. *We had a splendid time on the cruise through the canal.*

grief *n.* great sorrow or sadness. *Everyone felt grief when the great leader became ill.*

mourning expression of grief. *The flags were flown at half-mast in mourning for the victims of the disaster.*

sadness sorrow. *I was filled with sadness as I waved good-bye to my friend who was moving to a city on the west coast.*

sorrow sadness; grief. *She felt sorrow that her injury would cause her to give up the sport she loved so well.*

woe great grief; distress. *The young boy's woe over his lost puppy was replaced by his joy when the puppy was found.*

horrible *adj.* 1. causing horror; shocking; dreadful. *Jim let out a horrible scream.* 2. very unpleasant. *The old blender makes a horrible grating noise.*

awful terrible; very bad. *I went to the dentist so that he could look at the tooth that was causing the awful pain.*

frightful dreadful; terrible. *The monster rising out of the marsh was a frightful sight for the hunters.*

ghastly shocking; horrible. *The critic did not recommend the movie because it was filled with ghastly violence.*

grim frightful; horrible. *The storm was a grim reminder of our helplessness against nature's power.*

horrid terrible; very unpleasant. *The warm spring weather was a welcome relief from the horrid cold of last winter.*

shocking painfully surprising; horrible. *The damage caused by the forest fire was shocking even to firefighters who had battled other forest fires.*

ideal *adj.* perfect; exactly as one would wish. *A warm day and a clear sky are ideal conditions for a picnic.*

absolute free from imperfection; pure. *The quality of the diamond was absolute.*

perfect without defect; unspoiled. *The park's fall foliage made a perfect backdrop for the movie's opening and closing scenes.*

sublime grand; noble. *Her sublime contribution to American literature will long be remembered.*

superior best; high in quality. *The weather conditions were superior for the Mackinac sailing race.*

ignore *v.* to pay no attention to; to refuse to notice. *Anita tried to ignore their silly remarks.*

disdain to look down on; scorn. *The typist would disdain the use of a typewriter when a computer could be used.*

disregard to pay no attention to; neglect. *Fred was luckily not hurt when he decided to disregard the safety procedures.*

scorn look down upon; reject. *Traitors are scorned for betraying their countries.*

shrug off disregard. *Carrie tried to shrug off the pain and continued to run in the race.*

immediate *adj.* happening right away; without delay. *The immediate effect of the medicine was to stop his coughing.*

instantaneous coming at once; immediate. *The officer's response to the call for emergency assistance was instantaneous.*

quick sudden; swift. *When the bell rang, the students made a quick dash for the door.*

importance *n.* significance; value. *Never underestimate the importance of correct spelling.*

consequence importance. *Do you understand the consequence of this event to our history?*

gravity seriousness; importance. *The gravity of the situation was not lost on her.*

significance consequence; importance. *The significance of building the new factory is the creation of four hundred new jobs.*

value importance; worth. *The report had little value for the marketing department.*

impress *v.* to affect strongly or favorably. *Her fluent French did impress all of us.*

affect to stir the feelings. *The story of the young boy who saved his mother will affect you greatly.*

awe to fill with wonder. *The splendor of the painting always seems to awe the museum visitors.*

touch to affect with feeling. *Her quiet support always manages to touch me.*

insult *v.* to treat with rudeness; to hurt feelings on purpose. *It is not polite to insult someone.*

affront to offend; insult. *The dignitary was affronted by what he thought were inappropriate comments by the press.*

flout to treat with contempt. *Jim was suspended for three games for flouting team rules.*

offend to hurt the feelings of; unpleasantly affect. *The comedian's crude remarks managed to offend most of the audience.*

slur to insult; slight. *The rumors will slur the reputation of the governor.*

intrude *v.* to interrupt; to break in without being asked. *It's not polite to intrude on a private conversation.*

encroach to intrude; trespass. *The ranchers claimed that the farmers encroached on their grazing lands.*

interfere to get in the way of. *The unexpected meeting will interfere with my plans for the day.*

interrupt to break into. *Because constant phone calls interrupt my work, I will be late in submitting my report.*

irregular *adj.* not conforming to the usual rule or practice; different. *The coin was valuable because of its irregular markings.*

abnormal different from the ordinary; unusual. *Temperatures in the fifties are abnormal for this time of year.*

atypical not typical; irregular. *This is atypical behavior for a two-year-old.*

erratic irregular; uncertain. *The erratic schedule made it difficult for us to make plans ahead of time.*

fitful irregular; stopping and starting. *The class's attention during the lecture was fitful at best.*

uneven not uniform or regular. *The uneven performance of the leading tenor disappointed the theatergoers.*

antonyms: regular, normal, typical

jealous *adj.* worried about losing someone's affection to another person; resentful of another person's good fortune. *The toddler is jealous of the attention his new brother is getting.*

envious showing or feeling envy. *My sister is envious of my musical talent.*

grudging jealous. *He gave a grudging acknowledgment of my success in his field.*

knowledge *n.* everything that one knows or understands about something. *Her knowledge of baseball statistics is impressive.*

comprehension power or act of understanding. *The detective had total comprehension of the facts of the case.*

insight understanding and wisdom. *Her insight into the problem helped us immensely.*

understanding knowledge; comprehension. *Jake's understanding of math has helped him in science class.*

wisdom knowledge; judgment. *Wisdom was an important trait that contributed to his success as a ruler.*

labor *n.* physical work. *Moving these stones is hard labor.*

chore a difficult or disagreeable thing to do. *It is a real chore to clean out the barn.*

drudgery hard or disagreeable work. *The drudgery of working in the factory left the workers tired and bored.*

toil hard work. *The toil of years as a sales representative paid off when he was made a supervisor.*

work effort in doing something. *Some people say hard work is its own reward.*

legal *adj.* permitted by law. *A left turn at this corner is not legal.*

authorized granted permission; approved. *The biography was an authorized account of the President's days in the White House.*

lawful according to the law. *The lawful removal of the hazardous materials was monitored by state investigators.*

legitimate allowed by law. *She had a legitimate claim to the company's assets.*

limit *n.* the greatest amount permitted. *The speed limit on this street is thirty miles an hour.*

boundary limiting line; border; limit. *The Mississippi River forms the boundary between Illinois and Missouri.*

bounds boundaries; limits. *He kept his fears for her safety in bounds as he watched her perform the stunt.*

confines limits; boundaries. *He felt safe within the confines of his home.*

extent size, amount, or length. *What is the extent of your knowledge of the political process?*

location *n.* a place; position. *This quiet field is a good location for our campsite.*

place space or location. *We should set up our business in a place near the train station.*

position place; location. *The radio dispatcher asked the officer to describe her present position.*

site position or place. *This is the site of an ancient burial ground.*

spot a place. *What a lovely spot for a flower garden!*

lonesome *adj.* lonely; sad from being alone. *My little sister kept my puppy from being lonesome while I was at school.*

desolate forlorn. *The elderly woman felt desolate from the lack of company.*

forlorn miserable from being left alone. *The forlorn puppy brightened when the family returned from a day at the museum.*

lonely longing for company; lonesome. *You might be lonely when you first move to a new town.*

327

manner *n.* way; fashion. *The students left the bus in a quiet and orderly manner.*

fashion the way a thing is done; manner. *That conductor leads the orchestra in a fashion that inspires great performances.*

form way of doing something; method. *The judges rated the skater's form high but thought her routine was ordinary.*

mode manner; method. *His mode of operation was disliked by most employees.*

way manner of doing something. *She had a pleasant way of making everyone feel comfortable.*

material *n.* the parts or substances from which a thing is made. *The material for the roof was delivered before the workers arrived.*

element simple substance. *A question on the science test asked what elements are used to make steel.*

matter what things are made up of; material. *Water is a liquid matter that becomes solid when it freezes.*

substance material; matter. *Hydrogen and oxygen are the two substances that form water.*

meadow *n.* a field in which grass or hay grows naturally. *The cows grazed in the meadow.*

grassland land with grass often used as pasture. *The pampas are grasslands located in South America.*

lea grassy field; meadow. *The sheep graze on the lea during the day.*

pasture grassy field used for grazing. *In the evening, I help lead the cows home from the pasture.*

prairie large level or rolling grasslands. *The settlers left Pennsylvania to farm the Illinois prairie.*

melody *n.* a series of musical tones making up a tune. *He whistled the melody of a popular song.*

music arrangement of musical sounds. *I know the music for that song but I cannot remember the words.*

tune piece of music; melody. *What is the name of that lively tune the band just finished playing?*

merchant *n.* a person who buys and sells goods. *The three fabric stores in this area are owned by the same merchant.*

dealer a person who buys and sells for a living. *The car dealer was offering rebates on all new cars and selling all used cars at reduced prices.*

retailer a retail merchant or dealer. *The retailer promised to deliver the new appliances to my home before the end of the week.*

trader a person who buys and sells. *My older brother is a trader on the stock exchange.*

method *n.* a system; a way of doing something. *Broiling is one method of preparing fish.*

means the way something is done or brought about. *By what means do you plan to follow up on this account to ensure that we keep the customer happy?*

procedure way of doing something; method. *The doctor said that the ultrasound test is a simple procedure that would take very little time to complete.*

routine regular method. *She begins her morning routine by jogging two miles and then showering before she prepares breakfast.*

system way of getting things done; method. *Classifying plants by size is one system of rating them for pricing.*

tactics procedures; methods. *The parachutist changed her tactics when she realized that she could not open the chute by pulling the rip cord.*

minute *adj.* tiny; very small. *Minute bits of dust floated through the ray of sunlight.*

diminutive very small; minute. *She is so diminutive that she has trouble buying clothes.*

little small; not large. *I could not coax the baby into eating even a little bit of the vegetables.*

minuscule very small; minute. *You can see even the most minuscule cells through this microscope.*

tiny very small; wee. *The baby's fingers are so tiny!*

328

Writing Thesaurus

mischief *n.* harmless and merry teasing or pranks. *My kitten is full of mischief.*

antics odd acts; pranks. *The antics of the clowns amused the audience.*

caper prank; trick. *The teacher did not find our little caper in the classroom funny.*

prank playful mischief; trick. *I fell for their prank when I screamed at the sight of the plastic mouse.*

trick prank; mischief. *Every April Fool's Day Frank pulls the same trick on us and we always act as if we are fooled.*

misfortune *n.* bad luck. *It was his misfortune to lose his wallet.*

calamity great misfortune. *Many people were affected by the calamity caused by the flood.*

disaster great misfortune; events causing suffering. *The city set up temporary shelters for those who lost their homes in the hurricane disaster.*

ill fortune bad luck. *It was my ill fortune to be in the wrong place at the wrong time.*

misadventure unfortunate accident; bad luck. *Our trip started out with a misadventure when we had a flat tire just a mile from home.*

mishap unlucky accident. *Because of some mishap, we lost our electricity for three hours.*

tragedy great misfortune; terrible event. *The strain of reporting the tragedy was visible on the face of the news reporter.*

moderate *adj.* within reasonable limits; not extreme. *The price of the dress was moderate.*

gentle not harsh; moderate. *The beginners' slope has a gentle incline that new skiers can handle.*

mild not severe; temperate; moderate. *We were pleased that there was only a mild wind blowing across the lake.*

reasonable fair; inexpensive. *The rents for apartments in this city are reasonable.*

temperate moderate; using self-control. *She gave a temperate response to the rude question.*

momentary *adj.* brief; lasting a short time. *There was a momentary lull in the storm.*

brief lasting only a short time. *By a chance meeting, I had a brief visit with an old friend.*

instantaneous happening in an instant. *My reaction to the cold water in the pool was instantaneous.*

short not long. *She will be leaving for the airport in a short time.*

natural *adj.* 1. produced by nature; not artificial. *Wood is a natural substance.* 2. having a particular character by nature. *Eileen had a natural love of art.*

crude in a natural or raw state. *Thousands of barrels of crude oil are refined here every day.*

inbred instinctive; natural. *She has an inbred sense of humor that helps her handle almost any situation.*

instinctive not learned; natural. *Animals have an instinctive desire to take care of their young.*

native born into; natural. *Deer seem to have a native ability to sense danger.*

raw in a natural state. *Wood is one of the raw materials we use in our industry.*

unspoiled in a natural state. *The national forests have an unspoiled beauty that everyone can appreciate.*

necessary *adj.* needed; required. *A balanced diet is necessary for proper nutrition.*

basic fundamental. *Keyboarding is a basic skill for secretaries.*

essential needed; required. *Flour and spices are essential ingredients for this recipe.*

integral necessary; essential. *American history is an integral part of the school curriculum.*

key very important; essential. *This is a key concept for students to understand before completing their assignments.*

requisite necessary; required. *The student submitted the requisite records for enrolling in school.*

vital necessary; essential; very important. *The pollution of our environment is a vital concern for all the nations of the world.*

nervous *adj.* excited; not calm. *The kitten grew nervous when everyone crowded around.*

anxious uneasy; worried. *Eloise was anxious about trying out for the varsity volleyball team.*

excitable easily aroused; nervous. *The excitable dog has to be taught to obey commands under all circumstances.*

high-strung nervous; excitable. *The trainer led the high-strung horse back to its stall after the race.*

jumpy easily excited; uneasy. *Dave was jumpy as he waited to learn if his application was accepted.*

overwrought excited; nervous. *The young child was overwrought with fear when the thunder began.*

restless uneasy. *The restless reporters paced the floor as they waited for the news conference to begin.*

tense keyed up; strained. *The student driver was tense about taking the driving test.*

uneasy restless; nervous. *The five-year-old child was uneasy about spending the night away from home for the first time.*

neutral *adj.* not favoring either side. *During two wars, Switzerland remained a neutral nation.*

detached not influenced by others; impartial. *The detached decision of the umpire did not favor the home team.*

fair-minded unprejudiced; just. *The attorney asked the jury to be fair-minded and to consider only the facts when making their decision.*

impartial fair; showing no favor to one side or another. *Judges of Olympic events should remain impartial and rate the athletes on their performances alone.*

objective without bias; impersonal. *Reporters try to present an objective view of a story.*

unbiased not prejudiced; fair. *The committee gave an unbiased assessment of the effectiveness of the city services.*

notable *adj.* 1. worthy of notice. *Writing a book is a notable accomplishment.* 2. prominent; distinguished. *He is a notable physicist.*

distinguished famous; very important. *The distinguished stage actor had never appeared in a movie.*

eminent famous; distinguished. *The eminent poet won the Nobel Prize for literature.*

famous well-known; noted. *That famous athlete endorses only products she actually uses.*

great remarkable; famous. *Abraham Lincoln was a great United States President.*

outstanding well-known; remarkable. *Dr. Salk's polio vaccine was an outstanding contribution to medicine.*

prominent well-known; important; distinguished. *The prominent attorney had lost only one case during her career.*

remarkable worthy of notice. *The remarkable story of the little girl's rescue was featured in all the newspapers.*

renowned famous. *The chef is renowned for his exquisite dishes.*

striking very noticeable. *She bears a striking resemblance to her mother.*

notice *v.* to pay attention to; take notice of; see. *Will Joan notice Barbara's new dress right away?*

detect to find out; discover. *I did not detect any differences in the way the machine was operating.*

distinguish to see or hear clearly. *Were you able to distinguish the last few notes in that song?*

observe to see and note. *I observed the accident from my office window and called the police.*

perceive to observe; be aware of. *He did not perceive the car pulling up beside him.*

sight to see. *The bird-watcher tried to sight the eagle soaring through the sky as it circled its aerie.*

view to see; look at. *Through the kitchen window we could view the children playing.*

numb *adj.* without sensation or movement. *If you don't wear warm gloves, your fingers may become numb from the cold.*

dull not felt sharply; vague. *I had a dull ache in my shoulder from carrying the heavy grocery bags.*

insensitive not sensitive; numb. *My brother seems to be insensitive to both heat and cold.*

nutritious *adj.* providing nourishment. *Apples are a nutritious snack.*

healthful good for one's health. *For a healthful diet, eat foods from each of the major food groups.*

nourishing promoting growth. *What I need now is a nourishing meal and some rest.*

wholesome good for one's health. *Be sure to eat a wholesome breakfast to start your day out right.*

object *v.* to make objection; to protest. *They started to object that it was too cold to play outside.*

demur to show disapproval; object. *The idea of selling the club's building made the president demur.*

disapprove to show or express dislike. *My parents disapprove of violent movies.*

oppose to be against. *The mayor was opposed to the bill the city council passed.*

protest to make objections. *The students wanted to protest the cancellation of the field trip.*

take exception to to object. *The teacher takes exception to our chewing gum in class.*

object *n.* a thing that can be seen or touched. *The little shop had many objects made of china.*

article a particular thing; item. *She unfortunately left several articles of clothing in the locker room.*

item separate thing or article. *How many items did you buy at the supermarket?*

novelty small and unusual object. *My sister bought a novelty as a vacation souvenir.*

thing an object or substance. *Because I like my room to be neat, I always put my things away after using them.*

obtain *v.* to get. *How did he obtain a ticket to the play?*

acquire to get as one's own; obtain. *Kim studied to acquire the knowledge needed to be a competent mathematician.*

gain to come to have; get. *I gain on-the-job experience when I work in the governor's office.*

get to come to have; obtain. *Please get the encyclopedia from the shelf for me.*

procure to get by effort; obtain. *The organization was able to procure funds for their project from the state.*

secure to get; obtain. *Will it be possible to secure tickets for tonight's concert?*

obvious *adj.* easy to see or figure out; clear; plain. *It is obvious that the movie is popular, since the theater is so crowded.*

apparent plain to see or understand. *It is apparent to me that you do not want to go out to dinner.*

conspicuous easily seen. *What do people mean when they say that someone was conspicuous in his or her absence?*

evident easy to see or understand; clear. *That he was a talented musician was evident as soon as he started to play.*

manifest apparent to the mind or eye. *The perfection of the diamond was manifest to the curator.*

plain easy to understand; clear. *Her directions for finding her house were plain to me.*

occasion *n.* 1. a particular happening or event. *Her birthday was a special occasion.* 2. an opportunity; a good chance. *I hope you find an occasion to call us while you are traveling.*

affair any happening. *The governor's ball was a wonderful affair that I will long remember.*

chance favorable time; opportunity. *I didn't have a chance before now to thank you for your generous contribution to our organization.*

circumstance event; occasion. *It was an unfortunate circumstance that made me miss my flight.*

episode a single happening. *Winning the award was a memorable episode in the actress's life.*

event an important happening. *The wedding was the biggest event of the year for the family.*

occurrence event; happening. *The solar eclipse was such an unusual occurrence that I did not want to miss it.*

opportunity a good chance; occasion. *We have the opportunity to travel to Europe this summer.*

offer *v.* 1. to say that one is willing. *We did offer to help Mr. Elliot start his car.* 2. to present as a suggestion. *The President will offer a plan for peace.*

bid to offer to pay. *We expected to have to bid at least $1,000 to obtain the antique vase.*

extend to offer; grant. *The government can extend emergency aid to the flood victims.*

give to offer; present. *The professor gave a lecture titled "Earth's Tomorrow."*

grant to give; confer. *In that tale, a fish can grant three wishes.*

present to offer formally; give. *The Medal of Honor was presented to the courageous soldier in a special ceremony.*

propose to put forward; suggest. *I propose that we delay the meeting until all the information we need is available.*

suggest to propose; offer. *I suggest that the group meet at my house this week.*

tender to offer formally. *She can tender her resignation to be effective in two weeks time.*

opponent *n.* a person or group that competes against another. *Our school's opponent for the game is Deerfield School.*

competitor person or group who competes; rival. *That company is a business competitor of our company.*

enemy person or group that hates or tries to harm another; rival. *The soldier never really knew who the enemy was.*

foe enemy; rival. *I didn't know if Margaret was a friend or a foe.*

opposition any opponent. *The senator takes pride in being in "the loyal opposition."*

rival person who tries to get the same thing as another; competitor. *Angela and Ted are friends even though they are business rivals.*

ordinary *adj.* 1. usual; normal. *The ordinary time it takes to drive downtown is twenty minutes.* 2. not special; average. *Her outfit made her look quite ordinary.*

average usual; ordinary. *The book gave an account of an average day in a small coastal village.*

common ordinary; usual. *Her common response when we ask to stay up late is "No."*

customary according to custom; usual. *Ed did not take his customary route to work this morning.*

general common to many; not special. *The general store offers a variety of goods from fresh fruit to sewing needles.*

habitual done by habit; regular. *Jean is a habitual reader who especially enjoys mystery novels.*

normal usual; regular. *It is my normal practice to read in bed before I go to sleep.*

regular fixed by custom; normal; usual. *Because it was a holiday, we were allowed to stay up past our regular bedtime.*

usual common; ordinary. *Fruit and cheese are my usual afternoon snack.*

partial *adj.* 1. not complete. *We saw a partial eclipse of the moon.* 2. inclined to favor one side. *An umpire should never be partial when he makes a decision.*

abridged shortened; incomplete. *I read the abridged version of the novel.*

biased favoring one side; prejudiced. *Some players thought the referee made biased decisions that affected the game's outcome.*

disposed inclined; partial. *She is more disposed to like traditional furnishings than contemporary ones.*

incomplete lacking some part; unfinished. *The directions I was given were incomplete, so I had a difficult time finding the office.*

one-sided partial; biased. *That driver gave a one-sided account of the accident.*

unfinished not complete. *The road work was still unfinished after six months.*

partner *n.* a person who shares something or joins with another. *The boys were partners on the camping trip.*

associate companion; partner. *Lena is an associate in our firm.*

colleague coworker; associate. *Let me introduce my colleague who will work with you on your project.*

companion someone who goes along with. *Marta is my traveling companion.*

co-owner business partner; associate. *Jason is the co-owner of this restaurant.*

passage *n.* 1. a way used for passing. *The passage led to the back staircase.* 2. part of a writing or a speech. *The passage about whales includes much interesting information.*

aisle long, narrow passage. *Both parents walked the bride down the aisle.*

alley narrow back street; path. *She drove down the alley carefully to avoid the trash cans kept there.*

approach way of reaching a place. *The sidewalk was the only approach to the front of the house.*

entryway a passage for entering. *The building's entryway is a long narrow hall that leads to a set of elevators.*

excerpt passage from a book. *We read an excerpt from one of Scott O'Dell's award-winning books.*

hall passage; entryway. *That hall will lead you to the kitchen and dining room.*

path a passageway for walking or riding. *We rode our bikes on the bicycle path in the park.*

selection portion of a text. *We read a selection about growing up on a farm in Iowa.*

text a short passage; written words. *The speaker memorized the text of his speech before delivering it.*

vestibule passage or hall for entering; entry. *We left our coats on the coatrack in the vestibule.*

pause *v.* to stop for a short time. *He will pause to get a glass of water.*

break off to stop suddenly. *She had to break off the telephone conversation to check the oven.*

cease to put an end to; stop. *The interruptions made the speaker cease his presentation.*

discontinue to put an end to. *After the snow, they had to discontinue train service until the tracks could be cleared.*

halt to stop for a time. *A power outage will halt the use of all electrical equipment.*

rest to pause. *She had to rest for a moment before continuing to read to the class.*

stop to interrupt briefly. *Can you stop at the store on your way home from work to pick up a few items?*

performance *n.* the way in which someone or something functions. *Your performance on the test was very good.*

administration the managing of a business. *The administration of a law firm depends on the caseload.*

execution a carrying out or doing. *The execution of the day's work was her highest priority.*

implementation a carrying out. *The policy's implementation was easier than we thought it would be.*

permit *v.* to let; allow; give consent to. *Please permit me to read your magazine.*

allow to permit; let. *I am not allowed to eat corn on the cob because of my braces.*

authorize to give formal approval. *Were you authorized to sign company checks?*

license to permit by law. *I am licensed to sell real estate in this community.*

sanction to authorize; allow. *Congress can sanction the investigation of one of its members.*

tolerate to allow or permit. *The librarian does not tolerate any noise in the reading room.*

pitiful *adj.* causing emotions of sorrow and compassion. *The injured dog was a pitiful sight.*

miserable poor; pitiful. *The tenement was a miserable place to live.*

sad causing sorrow. *The devastation caused by the forest fire was a sad sight to see.*

sorry wretched; poor. *Due to the sorry condition of the flooded fields, the farmer had to delay planting indefinitely.*

wretched miserable. *For the poor to be living in such wretched housing is a disgrace.*

population *n.* the number of people living in a country, state, town, or other area. *The town's population has greatly increased in the past five years.*

inhabitants persons or animals that live in a place. *The town's inhabitants gathered for the annual spring festival.*

people body of citizens. *The people supported new taxes for education.*

populace the common people. *The tornado warnings were broadcast to the populace by the civil defense.*

public the people in general. *The news conference informed the public of the congressional ruling.*

pose *v.* 1. to hold an expression or position. *The parents and children need to pose for a family portrait.* 2. to present; put forward. *May I pose a question?*

model to pose for an artist or photographer. *He was hired to model clothing for ads in local magazines.*

offer to suggest; propose. *The suggestions offered could help us meet our goals.*

propose to put forward an intention or plan. *One committee member will propose sponsoring a fund-raising event.*

stand to take or keep a certain position. *Early photography required people to stand motionless for a long time.*

Writing Thesaurus

333

position *n.* place; location. *The navigator marked the ship's position on a chart.*

locality a particular place and/or the area around it. *That restaurant is in the locality of City Center Plaza.*

location position or place. *That building is in a bad location because it is not near public transportation.*

site position or place. *Our city had hoped to be the site of the next world's fair.*

situation site; location. *The situation of the castle offered protection from rebel subjects.*

positive *adj.* confident; certain; without doubt. *Gus is positive that his team will win.*

assured sure; certain; bold. *Her assured manner led me to believe that she knew the best way to get there.*

confident having confidence; sure. *Ellen is confident that she answered all the test questions correctly.*

convinced believing; sure; positive. *Convinced that he was better than the competition, Dan felt he would win the race.*

secure sure; certain. *Because of her expertise, Janet knew a promotion to vice president was secure.*

sure free from doubt; certain. *We checked the stock to be sure all the materials we needed were available.*

possibly *adv.* perhaps; maybe. *Possibly we'll finish by noon.*

conceivably imaginably. *The flight could conceivably arrive on time despite the delay in its departure.*

maybe possibly. *Maybe we can meet for lunch sometime next week.*

perchance perhaps. *Call to see if we perchance can still buy concert tickets.*

perhaps maybe. *Since you must get up early, perhaps you should go to bed now.*

probably more likely than not. *We will probably have a history quiz tomorrow.*

practical *adj.* able to be done, used, or carried out. *Her practical solution solved the problem.*

applicable capable of being applied. *"Honesty is the best policy" is a rule that I have found to be applicable to most situations.*

down-to-earth practical; realistic. *Marty's down-to-earth advice helped me handle the situation easily.*

realistic practical. *Because the plan would have been expensive to carry out, it was not a realistic solution to the housing shortage in our community.*

useful helpful; practical. *Expanding the public transportation system would be a useful means of solving the rush-hour traffic problems.*

precious *adj.* having a high price; costing a great deal. *Diamonds are precious jewels.*

costly expensive; of great value. *That costly painting was the only addition the museum made to its collection this year.*

priceless extremely valuable. *The artifacts from the archaeological discovery are a priceless national treasure.*

valuable of worth; having value. *Alphonse's valuable coin collection is always kept in the bank's vault.*

present *adj.* of the time between past and future; current. *Are you busy at the present moment?*

contemporary of the present time; modern. *The class contrasted the works of contemporary poets with those of late nineteenth century poets.*

current of the present time. *Every morning in homeroom, we read the paper and discuss current events.*

modern of the present time. *We are remodeling our kitchen to give it a more modern look.*

up-to-date modern; extending to the present time. *Models in fashion magazines always wear the most up-to-date styles.*

present *n.* a gift. *The present was colorfully wrapped.*

alms money or gifts to help the poor. *Our club collects alms for the poor and distributes them to organizations throughout the county.*

donation gift; contribution. *The senator made a donation of his letters to the Library of Congress.*

gift a present or donation. *This is my Father's Day gift for my dad.*

legacy a gift by will of money or property. *The candlesticks are my grandmother's legacy to me.*

probable *adj.* likely to happen. *The dark clouds and lightning mean that rain is probable.*

impending likely to happen soon; about to happen. *The construction crew worked furiously to meet the impending deadline.*

liable likely. *Be sure to lock the gate, or the dog is liable to run away.*

likely probable. *The teacher asked what the likely results of the experiment would be.*

presumable probable; likely. *The presumable cause of the highway closings was the drifting snow.*

process *n.* 1. a system of operations in the production of something. *Describe the process of canning fresh fruit.* 2. a series of actions with an expected end. *Learning is a continual process.*

course line of action; way of doing. *What is your course of action for completing the project on time?*

mechanism means by which something is done. *The mechanism for winning the election was set into action after the primary.*

method system of getting things done. *The methods used for the cleanup effort proved to be effective.*

procedure way of doing things. *The use of parliamentary procedure ensures that our meetings run smoothly.*

profit *v.* to benefit. *I can profit from your experience.*

benefit to receive good; profit. *The increased taxes will be used to benefit the schools and libraries in the state.*

gain to profit; get as an advantage. *What do you hope to gain by extending the store hours?*

reap to get as a return or reward. *If you exceed your sales quota, you will reap an increase in the percentage of your bonus.*

progress *n.* 1. a movement forward. *The train made steady progress.* 2. development; improvement. *Scientific progress has changed the way we think about the world.*

advance movement forward; progress. *The advances in scientific knowledge help us solve today's problems.*

advancement improvement; promotion. *Technological advancements have changed the way people live, work, and play in our country.*

development growth; process of developing. *Good nutrition is important to a child's physical development.*

expansion process of expanding; growth. *The expansion of the railroads across the United States resulted in greater settlement of the West.*

growth process of growing; development. *The personal computer industry spurred the growth of many software-producing companies.*

headway motion forward; progress. *Our boat had been making headway in the race until the wind shifted.*

improvement better condition or situation. *His program of exercise and diet is responsible for the improvement in his health.*

promotion an advance in rank or importance. *Her promotion to office manager was a result of hard work and dedication.*

rise an advance in rank, power, etc. *He said that his rise to stardom did not happen overnight but resulted from many years of hard work.*

rapid *adj.* fast; quick. *The rapid current carried the canoe down the river.*

fast moving or acting quickly. *The runners kept up a fast pace throughout the race.*

fleet swiftly moving; rapid. *Being fleet of foot, the runner passed us easily.*

hasty in a hurry; quick. *Mom waved a hasty good-bye as she ran to catch the commuter train.*

quick fast and sudden. *The boss's quick reply to my request for vacation enabled me to make arrangements well in advance.*

speedy rapid; fast. *Our class sent a card to our teacher wishing her a speedy recovery from the flu.*

swift very fast. *The express train provides a swift commute into the city.*

antonym: slow

Writing Thesaurus

335

rational *adj.* based on reason; logical. *After thinking it over calmly, Jeff made a rational decision to quit the team.*

judicious wise; sensible. *Sherman made a judicious decision to remain in school and complete his degree.*

logical of logic; reasonable. *It is logical to think that studying hard will help you get good grades.*

reasonable according to reason; sensible. *She had a reasonable excuse for being late to school.*

sane having or showing good sense. *Slowing down is a sane reaction to driving in bad weather conditions.*

sensible having or showing good sense or judgment. *Her ideas for improving the customer service department seemed sensible.*

sound rational; reasonable. *My counselor gave me sound advice about which courses to take.*

rebel *v.* to resist or oppose authority. *The workers wanted to rebel against the unfair demands of their employer.*

defy to set oneself openly against authority. *My brother meant to defy my parents by staying out long after his curfew.*

mutiny to rebel. *The sailors tried to mutiny against the ship's captain.*

protest to object strongly. *We protested the referee's decision without success.*

resist to act against; oppose. *Helen Keller at first resisted all efforts to help her learn to communicate.*

revolt to fight against leadership. *The people revolted against their leaders and called for democracy.*

receive *v.* to get. *You should receive the letter in two days.*

acquire to get as one's own. *I will acquire the deed for the property from my parents.*

obtain to come to have. *If you are able to obtain the needed materials, please let me know as soon as possible.*

secure to get; obtain. *Because he lacked a credit record, he was unable to secure a car loan.*

take to get; receive. *Mom says I don't take criticism very well.*

recess *n.* a brief rest from work. *During the morning, we have a fifteen-minute recess.*

break a short interruption in work. *Michael reads the newspaper during his break.*

pause a brief stop or rest. *The noise of the passing train forced a pause in the debate.*

respite a time of relief and rest. *The cease fire gave the people a respite from fear.*

spell a brief period of time. *Before starting a new project, Lorenzo relaxed for a spell by chatting with a coworker.*

refuse *v.* 1. to turn down; reject. *She might refuse my offer of help.* 2. to be unwilling; decline. *I refuse to let them bother me.*

decline to turn away from; refuse. *I hope you will not decline my luncheon invitation.*

disdain to scorn. *Wanting to be independent, the toddler disdained all attempts to help him put on his boots.*

reject to refuse to take. *The managers voted to reject the proposal to expand the sales force.*

scorn to regard with contempt. *The officer scorned the driver's efforts to avoid a ticket.*

spurn to reject with scorn. *The teen spurned the requests for dates from younger schoolmates.*

regular *adj.* 1. usual; normal; ordinary. *Our regular practice on Sunday is to have dinner in the afternoon.* 2. frequent. *Joe is a regular customer.* 3. occurring at fixed intervals. *We make regular visits to the dentist.*

established set up on a firm or lasting basis. *We have an established Monday morning meeting to discuss the week's activities.*

habitual done by habit; steady. *She is a habitual customer of this restaurant.*

periodic occurring or appearing at regular intervals. *Make sure you take your car in for periodic oil changes.*

recurrent occurring again; repeated. *I have had a recurrent dream that I cannot explain.*

routine a fixed or regular method of doing things. *Brushing my teeth is part of my routine activity.*

unexceptional ordinary; commonplace. *The performance of the football team was unexceptional this year.*

uniform not varying; regular. *The uniform length of time between classes is five minutes.*

release *v.* to let loose; set free. *If you release the door, it will close by itself.*

discharge to release; let go; dismiss. *He was discharged from the army after serving his term of duty.*

excuse to free from duty; let off. *Because of parent-teacher conferences, we were excused from school an hour early.*

exempt to make free; release. *The IRS would not exempt the organization from income taxes.*

free to make free; set loose. *We tried to free the firefly we had caught.*

let go to release; free. *The hostages were let go by their captors.*

let loose to set free; release. *We let loose the injured bird once its wing had healed.*

relieve to take another's place. *I relieved the night-shift nurse from duty at 7 A.M.*

unleash to let go. *She liked to unleash the dog and let him run loose in the park.*

relief *n.* the removal or ease of worry, pain, etc. *Imagine my relief when I remembered the right answer!*

alleviation relief; lessened severity. *The program called for the alleviation of poverty in the United States.*

diversion a turning away; relief. *Tennis is a diversion that takes my mom's mind off her business worries.*

relaxation the relief from work or effort. *For relaxation after school, I take a short walk through the neighborhood.*

reprieve temporary relief. *The postponement of the test day gave us a welcome reprieve.*

respite a putting off; delay; reprieve; a time of relief. *The clearing gave us a respite from the week-long storms that had hit our area.*

rest freedom; relief. *After a period of rest, we were refreshed and ready to begin working on the project again.*

remain *v.* 1. to stay. *We want to remain at home because of the rain.* 2. to continue; to last without changing. *The weather remained warm until the last week of October.* 3. to be left. *All that remains of the old house is the foundation.*

be left to remain. *This chair will be left for the next tenant of the apartment.*

endure to keep up; last. *The pyramids have lasted for ages and are now being restored to make sure they will continue to endure.*

hover to stay in or near. *The small child began to hover near her mother as the guests arrived for the party.*

last to hold on; continue. *The flowers will last for at least a week if you water them.*

linger to stay on; remain. *My cough lingered for days after the other cold symptoms were gone.*

loiter to linger idly. *The students like to loiter in the hall before the bell rings for the start of class.*

reside to live in a place for a long time. *My parents have resided in the same home since my first birthday.*

responsible *adj.* 1. trustworthy; reliable. *A responsible student was chosen to collect the money for the field trip.* 2. required to answer for something. *Who is responsible for turning off the lights when we leave the room?*

accountable liable; responsible. *The clerk was held accountable for banking all receipts.*

dependable reliable; trustworthy. *Vanessa is a dependable baby-sitter.*

liable under obligation; responsible. *Customers are liable for any merchandise they break.*

reliable worthy of trust; dependable. *The reporter's information came from a reliable source in the government.*

unfailing never failing; always ready when needed. *The accountant paid unfailing attention to every detail of the account.*

result *n.* outcome; effect. *He was late to work as a result of a delay in traffic.*

aftermath a result or consequence. *We had a long cleanup effort in the aftermath of the storm.*

consequence a result; an effect. *Being in the play-offs was a consequence of winning our last three games.*

outgrowth a result; an effect. *Organizing the recycling club was a natural outgrowth of our interest in the environment.*

upshot conclusion; result. *The upshot of the meeting was that we would plan a new campaign strategy for the student elections.*

Writing Thesaurus

337

satisfaction *n.* a feeling of being satisfied or contented. *Dan gets satisfaction from doing his job well.*

contentment satisfaction; ease of mind. *Her contentment with the results of the flower show was obvious from her expression.*

fulfillment accomplishment or satisfaction. *I was able to find great fulfillment from my work in the Peace Corps.*

gratification something that satisfies or pleases. *The parents' gratification for all their hard work came in seeing their child graduate from college.*

pleasure something that pleases or gratifies. *It brought me great pleasure to see my photographs displayed in the school hall.*

scarcely *adv.* hardly; barely. *There are scarcely any people awake at five o'clock in the morning.*

faintly dim; not clear. *The deer on the side of the road was only faintly visible to those of us driving in the dusk.*

imperceptibly very slightly. *The flaws in the material were almost imperceptibly noticeable to us.*

slightly a little; scarcely. *I know that area of the city only slightly.*

scheme *n.* 1. a plan of action; a project. *We thought of a scheme for preventing graffiti.* 2. a secret plot. *The scheme to give my mother a surprise party failed when she discovered the birthday cake.*

conspiracy secret planning; plot. *The investigation proved the assassination attempt was not a conspiracy, but rather the action of one person.*

design scheme; plan. *The investor had designs on our company until we reorganized all our operations.*

intrigue crafty dealings; scheming. *The novel focused on the intrigue of international spying.*

maneuver skillful plan, movement, or scheme. *Through a series of financial maneuvers, the employees hoped to purchase the company.*

strategy skillful planning and management. *The coach reviewed the game strategy with us before the start of the second half.*

tactic procedure or method for gaining advantage. *Her game-winning tactic was to keep her opponent running from one end of the court to the other.*

secondary *adj.* not ranking first. *Her primary concern was content, and her secondary concern was style.*

inferior lower in rank, position, or importance. *On the police force, a rank of detective is inferior to the rank of captain.*

minor less important; of lower rank. *The amount of salary increase was a minor issue compared to the need for job security.*

subordinate having less importance; secondary. *My role in helping to prepare for the conference was only a subordinate one.*

subsidiary auxiliary; supplementary. *Workbooks are subsidiary components of the textbook program.*

seize *v.* to take hold of suddenly; grasp; grab. *He seized her hand and shook it eagerly.*

apprehend to seize; arrest. *The jewel thief was not apprehended until the end of the movie.*

capture to take by force; seize. *The English managed to capture Quebec during the French and Indian War.*

catch to grasp or seize. *Try to catch the ball on the fly for an automatic out.*

clasp to hold firmly; grasp. *The child must clasp his mother's hand as they cross the street.*

grab to seize suddenly; snatch. *I had to grab my coat and run quickly so that I would not miss the bus.*

snatch to seize suddenly; grasp. *The thief tried to snatch the purse and run away before the young woman was even aware of what had happened.*

take to seize; catch; capture. *After a short battle, the enemy managed to take the fort.*

senseless *adj.* without meaning; pointless. *Watching that television program was a senseless waste of time.*

foolish unwise; silly. *It was a foolish mistake to leave my bicycle unlocked while I was inside the store.*

inane foolish; senseless. *The inane comment by the celebrity was overlooked by the reporters.*

meaningless without meaning; not making sense. *All of the preparations became meaningless when the conference was canceled.*

pointless without meaning or purpose. *It is pointless to try to reason with a two-year-old who demands to get his own way.*

silly without sense or reason. *Danielle's response to the question was silly because she didn't understand what was being asked.*

unsound not valid; not supported by evidence. *She gave some unsound advice that did not help us achieve our goal.*

antonyms: sensible, meaningful

shield *v.* to protect; guard. *This umbrella will shield you from the rain.*

defend to keep safe; protect. *The Americans were unable to defend New York City against the British in 1776.*

protect to defend; guard. *The dikes help protect the city from flooding.*

safeguard to keep safe; protect. *Every child should be given the vaccine to safeguard against polio.*

screen to protect or hide from. *The protective glasses screen the welder's eyes from the sparks.*

shelter to protect; shield. *The Underground Railroad tried to shelter slaves as they escaped to the North.*

siege *n.* the surrounding of a place for a long time in order to capture it. *The city was under siege for three weeks.*

assault a violent attack. *Wolfe led the British in their successful assault on Quebec.*

attack a use of force or weapons against a person or group. *The Civil War began with the Confederate attack on Fort Sumter.*

blitz sudden, violent attack. *During World War II, Poland surrendered after the German blitz.*

bombardment a vigorous attack. *The troops could not maintain their position during the bombardment.*

incursion a sudden attack. *The Minutemen responded quickly to the news of the British incursion.*

invasion an entering by force of an enemy. *Napoleon's invasion of Russia was not successful.*

onslaught a vigorous attack. *The defenders could not check the onslaught of invading soldiers.*

raid a sudden attack. *The pirates led raids against ships that were returning to Europe filled with gold.*

silence *n.* the absence of noise or sound; stillness. *There was silence while the principal spoke.*

hush a stopping of noise. *A sudden hush fell over the room when the President entered.*

peace a condition of quiet and order. *The peace of the afternoon was broken when the baby woke from her nap.*

quietness state of stillness; silence. *The quietness in the classroom surprised me.*

reserve a silent manner. *His reserve at parties made people think he was unfriendly.*

reticence tendency to be silent. *Calvin Coolidge was a President known for his reticence as well as for his dry wit.*

stillness absence of noise or movement; silence. *The stillness of the night was broken by the ambulance sirens.*

sullenness ill-humored silence. *His sullenness made me uncomfortable, so I left the room.*

antonyms: noise, clamor

similar *adj.* almost but not quite the same; alike but not identical. *The two girls wore similar clothes.*

alike like one another; similar. *Everyone says that my sister and I look alike.*

corresponding similar; alike. *General Grant and General Lee had corresponding roles in their armies.*

matching alike; similar. *The matching patterns complemented the room's decor.*

solemn *adj.* serious; earnest; grave. *He made a solemn promise.*

critical very important; serious. *She had to make a decision that would be critical to her future.*

sedate serious; calm. *His sedate behavior contrasted to my excitement.*

serious earnest; sincere. *He paid serious attention to the report so that he could review the findings with his superior.*

Writing Thesaurus

339

stubborn *adj.* not easily persuaded; having one's own definite idea. *Lee was stubborn and refused to follow my suggestions.*

adamant not giving in readily; unyielding. *Our teacher is adamant about having us turn in all of our assignments on time.*

determined firm; resolute. *She is determined to become a professional skater.*

headstrong stubborn; obstinate; rashly determined. *The headstrong toddler refused to let anyone help her get dressed.*

obstinate not giving in; stubborn. *Theo gave obstinate support to the effort even after it was obvious it would fail.*

opinionated stubborn about one's opinions. *His opinionated comments left little doubt about where he stood on the issue.*

persistent not giving up even in a difficult situation. *Betty was persistent in her efforts even after she broke her ankle.*

tenacious stubborn; persistent. *The tenacious salesclerk did not want us to leave the store without making a purchase.*

willful wanting or taking one's own way; stubborn. *It seems the only word the willful two year old knows is "NO."*

success *n.* a favorable result or outcome; achievement. *Hard work often brings success.*

accomplishment something done with skill, knowledge, or ability; achievement. *Her athletic accomplishments are evident from her many trophies and other awards.*

achievement thing achieved; feat. *She would not rest on the past achievements but continued to strive for excellence in her field.*

fortune prosperity; success. *Obtaining the contract was an unexpected fortune that will help us gain recognition.*

mastery victory; success. *His mastery over his disability is a remarkable achievement that can inspire us all.*

victory success in a contest. *The principal congratulated the team for its victory.*

talent *n.* special ability; natural skill. *She had a great talent for writing short stories.*

aptitude natural tendency; talent; ability. *Grandma Moses did not display her aptitude for painting until late in her life.*

expertise expert skill. *The expertise of a whittler can be seen in the details of his or her carvings.*

flair natural talent. *Alexandra has a flair for giving successful parties.*

genius great natural ability. *Thomas Edison's genius was not evident when he was a boy.*

gift special talent. *Christina's voice was a gift that all opera fans could appreciate.*

knack special skill or talent. *She has a knack for making people feel comfortable.*

tease *v.* to bother or irritate by making jokes, asking questions, nudging, etc. *The sign at the zoo asked the visitors not to tease the animals.*

badger to keep on teasing. *My brother badgered me about my skating until I threatened to tickle him.*

bait to tease or harass. *She tried to bait me into falling for one of her practical jokes.*

banter to tease playfully. *They bantered entertainingly throughout the evening.*

harass to disturb or tease continually. *People get angry if you harass them, even if you do it in fun.*

pester to annoy; vex. *I don't like it when my younger sister pesters me to take her shopping with me.*

tedious *adj.* tiresome; boring. *The politician's speech became so tedious that a few listeners got up to leave.*

boring dull; uninteresting. *The new movie playing at the local theater is boring.*

drab monotonous; dull. *The drab surroundings of our neighborhood made me wish for just one day in a beautiful park.*

dull boring; uninteresting. *The dull plot did not hold our attention for long.*

340

insipid lacking interest or spirit. *The insipid comments of the reporter made me wonder why he was assigned to that story.*

monotonous wearying because of its sameness. *The story line of that program had become so monotonous that I stopped watching it.*

stale not fresh or interesting. *Every time I see him he tells me the same old stale jokes.*

uninspired dull; tiresome. *The performances were so uninspired that I fell asleep.*

wearisome tiresome; tedious. *The wearisome hours of practice make me wish for a vacation from ballet lessons.*

temporary *adj.* lasting for a brief time; not permanent. *While our teacher was ill, we had a temporary teacher.*

passing not lasting; fleeting. *He had had a passing interest in airplanes when he was young.*

short-lived lasting a short time. *The player was a short-lived substitute for the first-string quarterback.*

transitory passing soon or quickly. *Dizziness was a transitory feeling that I had after getting off the ride.*

tenant *n.* a person who pays rent for the use of a house, apartment, or other property. *In that tall apartment building there are several hundred tenants.*

boarder a person who pays for meals and rooms in another's house. *To help pay for their house, my parents always take in a boarder.*

lodger a person who lives in a rented room or house. *College students are lodgers in our house.*

occupant one who occupies or has possession of a place. *The occupant of the apartment is there only through December.*

renter one who rents a place to live. *The renter of this apartment pays extra for garage parking.*

roomer one who rents a room or rooms for lodging. *The college is always looking for homes for roomers.*

thoughtless *adj.* careless; inconsiderate. *It was thoughtless of you to invite only some of your friends.*

careless not thinking; done without thought. *A careless mistake lowered my final grade.*

heedless careless; thoughtless. *The driver of the car seemed to be heedless of the traffic laws.*

inattentive not attentive; negligent. *The inattentive student did not understand the lesson.*

tactless without tact or thought. *Her tactless comment hurt my feelings.*

unthinking thoughtless; careless. *I made an unthinking error on my spelling test that resulted in a lower grade than usual.*

trait *n.* a feature or characteristic. *We all inherit physical traits from our parents.*

attribute a quality or trait. *Blue eyes are an attribute of my family.*

property quality or power of something. *A property of copper is that it conducts electricity.*

quality nature, kind, or character. *The quality of this material is excellent.*

tremendous *adj.* extremely large; enormous. *A tremendous wave rocked the boat.*

colossal huge; gigantic. *The bridge was a colossal structure that spanned the river.*

enormous extremely large. *The package was not only enormous but also so heavy I could not carry it.*

gigantic giant; huge. *The circus featured gigantic elephants in the opening parade.*

huge very big; extremely large. *The earthquake left a huge crevice in the ground.*

immense very large; huge. *In the early 1800s an immense portion of our country was still unexplored.*

turbulent *adj.* disturbed or violently agitated. *The ocean became turbulent as the storm approached.*

boisterous violent; rough. *The boisterous crowd demanded free elections.*

chaotic extremely confused; disorganized. *The hurricane-damaged school was a chaotic mess.*

riotous boisterous; disorderly. *The riotous behavior of the citizens signaled the beginning of the revolution.*

stormy disturbed; violent. *The council meeting ended in a stormy argument over tax assessments.*

unruly hard to control; disorderly. *The unruly student was given two weeks in detention after school.*

violent acting or done with strong, rough force. *The violent storm raged for hours along the coast before it hit the mainland.*

wild violently excited; out of control. *The trapped animal lashed out in a wild frenzy as it tried to free itself from the hunter's net.*

ultimate *adj.* best; greatest. *Chess is the ultimate game of logic.*

extreme very great; very strong; the highest degree. *It was an extreme pleasure to meet the President of the United States.*

maximum largest; highest; greatest possible. *The maximum number of videos that will be distributed is 25,000.*

superior higher in quality; greater; better. *She has a superior command of the English language.*

supreme highest in rank or authority. *Eisenhower was the supreme commander of the allied forces in Europe during the latter half of World War II.*

undercover *adj.* done in secret. *They are conducting an undercover police investigation.*

clandestine secret; concealed. *Early labor unions held clandestine meetings to keep employers from finding out about them.*

covert kept secret; hidden. *The Senate investigated the covert actions of the CIA.*

secretive not frank or open. *She was secretive about the plans for the new company.*

stealthy done in a secret manner; sly. *The stealthy investigation revealed the officer's role in the bribery case.*

understand *v.* to know; comprehend. *Do you understand how a vacuum cleaner works?*

comprehend to understand. *It is difficult to comprehend the effects of the radiation.*

digest to think over for understanding. *I found it hard to digest his comments since I did not agree with them.*

discern to see clearly; perceive. *I found it difficult to discern the truth when so many viewpoints were presented.*

grasp to understand; comprehend. *He grasped the meaning of the event immediately.*

realize to understand completely. *I realized that success was dependent on hard work.*

unpleasant *adj.* not pleasant; disagreeable. *The medicine had an unpleasant taste.*

disagreeable not to one's liking; unpleasant. *I find yard work to be a disagreeable task.*

distasteful unpleasant; offensive. *Her distasteful comments offended everyone in the room.*

various *adj.* of several different kinds; different. *I found shells of various sizes and shapes on the beach.*

distinct different in quality or kind. *The students had distinct abilities and talents.*

miscellaneous not all of one kind or nature. *I filed the memo with other miscellaneous information.*

mixed formed of different kinds. *She gave her mother a gift of mixed nuts.*

sundry several; various. *I selected a pen from the sundry items offered as party favors.*

varied of different kinds. *From the varied selection of recordings, I chose one featuring a jazz pianist.*

visible *adj.* able to be seen. *Because of the fog, the lights were no longer visible.*

apparent plain to see. *The location of the tower was apparent as soon as we entered the forest preserve.*

discernible capable of being seen. *The lights of the city were discernible as we approached the shore.*

distinct easily seen. *The outline of the building was distinct even at night.*

in sight visible. *The ship was in sight of people on the shore long before it docked at the pier.*

perceptible able to be seen; perceived. *The lines on the highway were barely perceptible because of the snow.*

weird *adj.* strange; odd. *The group of people going to the costume party was a weird sight.*

curious strange; unusual. *The two-story gabled house looked curious among all of the ranch homes.*

eerie fearful; weird. *I got an eerie feeling while walking through the empty building after working hours.*

peculiar strange; odd. *Just before the storm, the sky was a peculiar color of grayish orange.*

strange unusual; weird. *She had a strange look on her face when I entered the room.*

wonderful *adj.* excellent; remarkable; marvelous. *What a wonderful sunset we are having tonight!*

fabulous wonderful; exciting. *We had a fabulous vacation when we took the Concorde to Paris, where we boarded the Orient Express.*

spectacular wonderful; grand. *The Fourth of July fireworks display was spectacular last year.*

superb grand; excellent. *We had a superb view of the skiing trails from our chalet at the resort.*

yield *v.* to surrender; give up. *A traffic sign that says "Yield" warns drivers to surrender the right of way.*

give in to admit defeat; yield. *It was not easy for my boss to give in to my demand for fewer working hours.*

relinquish to give up; let go. *To avoid a family argument, I relinquished my claim to the property.*

submit surrender; yield. *Did Antoine submit to his parents' wishes, or did he apply to Temple University instead?*

surrender give up; yield. *The team refused to surrender their lead in the game.*

NOTES

ANNUAL PRETEST/POSTTEST*
Form A

Word	Dictation Sentences
1. **suffer**	No one wants to see another person **suffer** in pain.
2. **customer**	Mr. Chapman treated each **customer** with courtesy.
3. **tablespoon**	Three teaspoons equal one **tablespoon**.
4. **through**	We walked **through** the park instead of around it.
5. **thief**	The word **thief** is a synonym for robber.
6. **siege**	He recovered from a long **siege** of illness.
7. **carpenter**	This cabinet was built by a skilled **carpenter**.
8. **concern**	The change in the schedule will **concern** everyone.
9. **central**	The theme of the story is the **central** idea.
10. **material**	What **material** will you choose to work with for your art project?
11. **inward**	The door swung **inward** toward the kitchen.
12. **afterward**	We went to the movies and **afterward** took a walk in the park.
13. **fashion**	Continue in this **fashion** until you have finished the job.
14. **shelf**	Please put this box on that **shelf**.
15. **magazine**	I subscribe to a **magazine** about computers.
16. **tease**	Don't **tease** the dog, or he might bite you.
17. **resulted**	The contest **resulted** in a tie score.
18. **profiting**	We will be **profiting** from a successful three-day carnival.
19. **knack**	You have a **knack** for saying the right thing at the right time.
20. **isle**	A tiny island is called an **isle**.
21. **connect**	The child learned how to **connect** the dots to form a picture.
22. **error**	The engineer was careful not to make an **error** in her design.
23. **acceptable**	We agreed that the plan was **acceptable** but not exciting.
24. **changeable**	The **changeable** weather at this time of year can ruin a picnic.
25. **irresistible**	The sandwiches were so **irresistible** that we ate them all.
26. **illegal**	Any action that breaks the law is **illegal**.
27. **bandage**	When I accidentally cut my finger, I put a **bandage** on it.
28. **courage**	The diver needed all of his **courage** to make the final dive.
29. **eventful**	We had an **eventful** vacation, but it is nice to be home.
30. **delightful**	The fireworks make the celebration especially **delightful**.
31. **bookstore**	The text for this course is on sale in the **bookstore**.
32. **campsite**	This place near the lake will make a good **campsite**.
33. **approximate**	I did not know the exact number, so my guess was **approximate**.
34. **desperate**	The situation was so **desperate** that nothing seemed to help.
35. **underpass**	That truck is too high to get through the **underpass**.
36. **underneath**	The grass felt cool **underneath** our bare feet.
37. **wondrous**	The Milky Way is a **wondrous** site in the night sky.
38. **nervous**	Do you get **nervous** before taking an exam?
39. **different**	The clown wore a **different** colored sock on each foot.
40. **athlete**	The injured **athlete** was out of action for three weeks.
41. **invention**	The **invention** of the airplane was a major achievement.
42. **consideration**	The teacher took into **consideration** the fact that the students were writing their first research paper.
43. **comedian**	The **comedian** told such bad jokes that no one laughed.
44. **librarian**	The **librarian** suggested that I look for the book on the computer.
45. **attendance**	She received a certificate for perfect school **attendance**.
46. **inheritance**	They used the **inheritance** to buy a new home.
47. **compound**	Try to keep matters simple and don't **compound** the problem.
48. **conduct**	People should **conduct** themselves properly in public.
49. **telegraph**	People used to go to the **telegraph** office to send a wire.
50. **biographer**	The **biographer** vividly recaptured the life story of the famous athlete.

*For more information on using these tests, please see pages Z10–Z11.

ANNUAL PRETEST/POSTTEST*
Form B

Word	Dictation Sentences
1. stubborn	He is very **stubborn,** since he always wants his own way.
2. custody	The keys to the building are in the **custody** of Ms. Nugent.
3. approve	Will you please **approve** our plans for the school play?
4. routine	Some jobs involve variety, while others are **routine**.
5. yield	A **yield** sign directs drivers to allow any oncoming traffic to go first.
6. shield	Sunglasses **shield** your eyes from the rays of the sun.
7. partner	Will you be my **partner** and work with me on this assignment?
8. insert	You can buy a newspaper if you **insert** two quarters into that machine.
9. neutral	Jane would neither agree or disagree, so she was **neutral**.
10. rational	Remain calm and you will find a **rational** solution to your problem.
11. outward	The **outward** push of his arm almost knocked me over.
12. downward	Press **downward** on the handle to open the door.
13. fulfill	To **fulfill** your goal, you usually must have a detailed plan and follow it.
14. golf	**Golf** is a difficult sport to master.
15. phase	When a star enters the mature **phase** of its life, it is called a red giant.
16. arise	I like to **arise** at seven o'clock each morning.
17. resulting	Our efforts kept **resulting** in new challenges.
18. profited	The school **profited** from a successful three-day carnival.
19. knowledge	His **knowledge** of the animal kingdom is remarkable.
20. aisle	The bride and her father walked down the **aisle** of the church.
21. announce	The principal will **announce** the winner of the contest.
22. innocent	The jury found the suspect to be **innocent**.
23. approachable	A good manager demands discipline but is always **approachable**.
24. available	Will you be **available** to attend our meeting tomorrow?
25. antisocial	Since the boy wouldn't talk to us, we felt he was **antisocial**.
26. antifreeze	Dad replaced the **antifreeze** in our car for the coming winter.
27. garage	Our **garage** is large enough for two cars.
28. garbage	The local **garbage** dump is the dirtiest place in town.
29. doubtful	It is **doubtful** that she will arrive on time, since she is often late.
30. forgetful	She is **forgetful** and often cannot remember where she puts her keys.
31. background	The garden will make a lovely **background** for your portrait.
32. throughout	The telephone rang constantly **throughout** the day.
33. delicate	The bride's gown was trimmed with **delicate** lace.
34. moderate	Since her views are not extreme, she takes a **moderate** position.
35. undercover	The detectives used an **undercover** operation to catch the thieves.
36. underground	The earth's water table is an **underground** water supply.
37. fabulous	We all agreed that the fireworks made a **fabulous** display.
38. tremendous	The explosion made a **tremendous** crashing noise.
39. probably	Although he thinks he failed, he will **probably** pass the test.
40. restaurant	My family has dinner in a **restaurant** on special occasions.
41. suggestion	Will you make a **suggestion** about how to complete the project?
42. information	Will I be able to locate the **information** I need in this book?
43. guardian	A child's legal **guardian** is responsible for the child's well-being.
44. custodian	The building **custodian** has come to repair the leaky faucet.
45. performance	Everyone in the audience seemed to enjoy the **performance**.
46. importance	The lawyer advised his client about a matter of great **importance**.
47. compact	Our car is **compact,** yet four adults can fit into it.
48. contract	Most materials **contract** in cold temperatures.
49. paragraph	What is the main idea of this **paragraph**?
50. autograph	We waited to ask the actor for his **autograph**.

*For more information on using these tests, please see pages Z10–Z11.

Scope and Sequence

	GRADE 5	GRADE 6	GRADE 7
Spelling and Phonics			
Beginning and Ending Sounds		15	
Rhyming Words	16, 70, 100	51	
Word Analysis		9, 57, 87, 105	
Developing Oral Language/Speaking Skills			
	T9, T15, T21, T27, T33, T45, T51, T57, T63, T69, T81, T87, T93, T99, T105, T117, T123, T129, T135, T141, T153, T159, T165, T171, T177, T189, T195, T201, T207, T213	T9, T15, T21, T27, T33, T45, T51, T57, T63, T69, T81, T87, T93, T99, T105, T117, T123, T129, T135, T141, T153, T159, T165, T171, T177, T189, T195, T201, T207, T213	T9, T15, T21, T27, T33, T45, T51, T57, T63, T69, T81, T87, T93, T99, T105, T117, T123, T129, T135, T141, T153, T159, T165, T171, T177, T189, T195, T201, T207, T213
Spelling and Thinking/Word Sorting			
Sound and Letter Correspondence			
Short Vowels	32, 36, 38, 41, 228	8, 12, 14, 18, 20, 24, 26, 30, 32, 36, 38–41, 224–228	14, 18, 38–39, 225
Long Vowels	8, 12, 14, 18, 20, 24, 38–40, 224–226	8, 12, 14, 18, 20, 24, 26, 30, 32, 36, 38–41, 224–228	20, 24, 38, 40, 104, 226
Vowel Digraphs and Diphthongs	20, 24, 26, 30, 38, 40, 86, 90, 110–111, 226–227, 235	44, 48, 74–75, 229	
r-Controlled Vowels	62, 66, 68, 72, 74, 76–77, 80, 84, 110–111, 232–234	56, 60, 74, 76, 231	
Consonants, Clusters, and Digraphs	44, 48, 74–75, 104, 108, 110, 113, 170, 174, 182, 184, 229, 238, 247	80, 84, 86, 90, 104, 108, 110–111, 113, 234, 238	32, 36, 38, 41, 228
Homophones and Homographs	25, 49	195	109, 145, 164, 168, 182, 184
High Frequency Words (Words Writers Use)	188, 192, 218–219, 249	170, 174, 182, 184, 247	92, 96, 110, 112, 134, 138, 146, 148, 164, 168, 182, 184, 236, 242, 246
Unstressed Endings	50, 54, 56, 60, 74–76, 230–231	62, 66, 74, 76	194, 198, 218, 219

	GRADE 5	GRADE 6	GRADE 7
Spelling and Thinking/Word Sorting (cont.)			
Special Spellings	140, 144, 146, 149, 200, 204, 206, 210, 212, 216, 218, 220–221, 243, 251, 253	50, 54, 74–75, 98, 102, 110, 112, 200, 204, 212, 216, 218, 220–221, 230, 237, 251, 253	68, 72–74, 77, 104, 108–110, 113, 128, 132, 146, 148, 170, 174, 182, 184, 233, 238, 241, 247
Structural Patterns			
Plurals	158, 162, 182–183, 245		116, 120, 146–147, 239
Inflectional Endings	128, 132, 146, 148, 241	92, 96, 110, 112, 236	
Contractions		45	
Compounds	134, 138, 146, 148, 193, 242	140, 144, 146, 149, 243	26, 30, 38, 40, 227
Prefixes	92, 96, 110, 112, 122, 126, 133, 146–147, 164, 168, 182, 184, 236, 240, 246	92, 96, 110, 112, 122, 126, 133, 146–147, 164, 168, 182, 184, 236, 240, 246	44, 48, 74–75, 85, 122, 126–127, 146–147, 152, 156, 181–183, 206, 210, 218, 220, 229, 240, 244, 248, 252
Roots	13, 31, 61, 85, 97, 139, 157, 169	13, 31, 61, 85, 97, 139, 157, 169	140, 144, 146, 149, 158, 162, 176, 180, 182–183, 185, 200, 204, 212, 216, 218, 220–221, 243, 245, 251, 253
Suffixes	98, 102, 110, 112, 152, 156, 176, 180, 182, 183, 185, 194, 198, 205, 211, 218, 219, 244, 248, 250	98, 102, 110, 112, 152, 156, 176, 180, 182, 183, 185, 194, 198, 205, 211, 218, 219, 244, 248, 250	44, 48, 50, 54, 56, 60, 62, 66, 74–76, 80, 84, 86, 90, 98, 102, 110–112, 188, 192, 218–219, 229–232, 234–235, 237, 249–250
Content Words	116, 120, 146–147, 239		8, 12–13, 38–39, 224
Spelling and Vocabulary			
Word Meaning	9, 15, 21, 27, 33, 69, 81, 87, 93, 99, 105, 123, 129, 141, 153, 159, 165, 171, 177, 189, 195, 201, 207, 213	9, 15, 21, 81, 99, 117, 135, 141, 159, 165, 171, 195, 201, 207, 213	9, 15, 25, 27, 31, 33, 45, 51, 60–61, 63, 67, 69, 72–73, 81, 84, 87, 90–91, 93, 97, 99, 103, 105, 108, 117, 120–121, 123, 126–127, 129, 133, 135, 141, 153, 157, 159, 162–163, 165, 168, 171, 174–175, 177, 181, 189, 192–193, 195, 198–199, 201, 204–205, 207, 210–211, 213, 216–217

Scope and Sequence

	GRADE 5	GRADE 6	GRADE 7
Spelling and Vocabulary (continued)			
Word History	55, 145	25, 109, 133, 175, 181	13, 61, 73, 163, 169, 211
Word Roots	13, 31, 61, 85, 97, 139, 157, 169	13, 91, 163, 199	55, 121, 133, 157, 199
Words From Other Languages	19, 163	31, 49, 85, 169	91
Word Structure	9, 33, 81, 87, 93, 99, 105, 117, 123, 135, 141, 153, 159, 165, 177, 189, 195, 201, 207, 213	21, 45, 57, 63, 87, 105, 123, 141, 177, 195, 207	9, 15, 21, 33, 45, 51, 57, 87, 93, 105, 123, 141, 153, 177, 201, 207
Word Study	13, 19, 25, 31, 37, 49, 55, 61, 67, 73, 85, 91, 97, 103, 109, 121, 127, 133, 139, 145, 157, 163, 169, 175, 181, 193, 199, 205, 211, 217	13, 19, 25, 31, 37, 49, 55, 61, 67, 73, 85, 91, 97, 103, 109, 121, 127, 133, 139, 145, 157, 163, 169, 175, 181, 193, 199, 205, 211, 217	13, 19, 25, 31, 37, 49, 55, 61, 67, 73, 85, 91, 97, 103, 109, 121, 127, 133, 139, 145, 157, 163, 169, 175, 181, 193, 199, 205, 211, 217
Word Clues	15, 51, 73, 91, 117, 127, 135, 171	99, 127, 129, 135, 145, 159, 165, 189, 211	12, 30, 36–37, 48, 54–55, 66, 96, 102, 109, 132, 138, 144, 156, 169, 174, 180, 205, 211
Related Meanings	27, 33, 45, 63, 129	57, 81, 93, 129, 171, 189	21, 49, 57, 69, 90, 117
Words With Similar Meanings	21, 27, 88, 142, 160, 199	27, 33, 45, 51, 69, 73, 81, 87, 93, 153, 171, 177	10, 21, 27, 63, 67, 81, 85, 99, 105, 135, 171, 213
Synonyms and Antonyms	10, 28, 45, 51, 57, 63, 69, 88, 123, 142, 160, 177, 195, 201, 217	63, 69, 93, 105, 117, 123, 135, 153, 157, 201	87, 165, 189, 195, 205
Idioms	37	103	
Eponyms and Toponyms	121, 181	37, 55, 217	19, 97, 193
Spelling and Reading			
Context Clues	10, 16, 22, 28, 34, 46, 52, 58, 64, 70, 82, 88, 94, 100, 106, 118, 124, 130, 136, 142, 154, 160, 166, 172, 175, 178, 190, 196, 202, 208	10, 16, 22, 28, 34, 46, 52, 58, 64, 70, 82, 88, 94, 100, 106, 118, 124, 130, 136, 142, 154, 160, 166, 172, 178, 190, 196, 202, 208, 214	10, 12–13, 16, 18–19, 22, 24–25, 28, 30, 36–37, 46, 49, 52, 54–55, 58, 64, 66–67, 70, 72–73, 82, 84–85, 88, 90–91, 94, 96–97, 100, 102–103, 106, 108–109, 118, 120–121, 124, 126–127, 130, 132–133, 136, 138–139, 142, 144–145, 154, 156–157, 160, 162–163, 166, 168–169, 172, 174–175, 178, 180–181, 190, 192–193, 196, 198–199, 202, 204, 208, 210–211, 214, 216–217

	GRADE 5	GRADE 6	GRADE 7
Spelling and Reading (continued)			
Analogies	10, 16, 22, 34, 52, 58, 82, 94, 124, 130, 154, 172, 178, 196	10, 16, 22, 28, 34, 46, 52, 64, 70, 82, 88, 94, 100, 106, 118, 124, 130, 136, 142, 154, 160, 166, 172, 178, 190, 196, 202, 208	10, 16, 22, 34, 46, 64, 106, 118, 136, 172, 178, 196
Classification	10, 46, 94	16	60, 77, 85, 149, 190, 211, 221
Other Strategies	10, 16, 21, 27, 70, 88, 94, 100, 142, 160, 166, 190, 214	58, 124, 190, 214	16, 28, 34, 51, 58, 82, 88, 124, 136, 139, 145, 160, 166, 172, 190, 205, 208
Spelling and Writing			
Expository Writing	17, 29, 65, 95, T114, 119, 143, 161, 191, 197, 203, 209, 215	17, 35, 59, 71, 107, T114, 125, 137, 155, 161, 173, 191, 209, T222	17, 23, 29, 47, 125, T150, 155, 161, 179, 191, 215
Narrative Writing	11, 23, 47, 71, T78, 83, 101, 125, 131, 167, T186, 191	11, 23, 47, 53, 83, 95, T186, 203	59, 65, 71, T78, 83, 95, 107, 119, 137, 143, 167, 173, T222
Descriptive Writing	T42, 53, 89, 137, 179, T222	29, T42, 65, T78, 101, 131, 143, 215	T42, 131, 197, 209
Persuasive Writing	35, 59, 107, T150, 155, 173	89, 119, T150, 167, 179, 197	11, 35, 53, 89, 101, T114, T186, 203
The Writing Process	11, 17, 23, 29, 35, T42, 47, 53, 59, 65, 71, T78, 83, 89, 95, 101, 107, T114, 119, 125, 131, 137, 143, T150, 155, 161, 167, 173, 179, T186, 191, 197, 203, 209, 215, T222, 258	11, 17, 23, 29, 35, T42, 47, 53, 59, 65, 71, T78, 83, 89, 95, 101, 107, T114, 119, 125, 131, 137, 143, T150, 155, 161, 167, 173, 179, T186, 191, 197, 203, 209, 215, T222, 258	11, 17, 23, 29, 35, 47, 53, 59, 65, 71, T78, 83, 89, 95, 101, 107, 119, T114, 125, 131, 137, 143, T150, 155, 161, 167, 173, 179, T186, 191, 197, 203, 209, 215, T222
Graphic Organizers	T42, T78, T114, T150, T186, T222	T42, T78, T114, T150, T186, T222	T42, T78, T114, T150, T186, T222
Proofreading	11, 17, 23, 29, 35, 43, 47, 53, 59, 65, 71, 79, 83, 89, 95, 101, 107, 115, 119, 125, 131, 137, 143, 151, 155, 161, 167, 173, 179, 187, 191, 197, 203, 209, 215, 223	11, 17, 23, 29, 35, 43, 47, 53, 59, 65, 71, 79, 83, 89, 95, 101, 107, 115, 119, 125, 131, 137, 143, 151, 155, 161, 167, 173, 179, 187, 191, 197, 203, 209, 215, 223	11, 17, 23, 29, 35, 43, 47, 53, 59, 65, 71, 79, 83, 89, 95, 101, 107, 115, 119, 125, 131, 137, 143, 151, 155, 161, 167, 173, 179, 187, 191, 197, 203, 209, 215, 223
Content Connections			
Language Arts	13, 19, 31, 37, 67, 97, 127, 133, 157	19, 25, 31, 97, 109, 127, 157, 163, 175, 181	13, 19, 25, 37, 61, 73, 85, 103, 109, 121, 139, 145, 175, 181, 205

Scope and Sequence

	GRADE 5	GRADE 6	GRADE 7
Content Connections (continued)			
Science	13, 25, 55, 85, 91, 121, 145, 163, 181, 193, 199, 205, 211, 217	13, 31, 37, 55, 61, 97, 121, 133, 139, 145, 169, 175, 211, 217	31, 49, 55, 73, 85, 91, 97, 121, 127, 139, 163, 169, 175, 193, 199, 211, 217
Social Studies	19, 49, 61, 97, 103, 121, 127, 139, 175, 181, 199, 205	25, 49, 67, 73, 85, 91, 103, 109, 121, 127, 157, 163, 169, 193, 199, 205	13, 19, 25, 49, 55, 61, 67, 91, 97, 103, 109, 127, 133, 193, 199, 211, 217
Fine Arts	31, 73, 85, 109, 157, 193, 211	13, 37, 61, 85, 139, 193	163
Math	37, 61, 91, 103, 109, 163, 169, 175, 217	67, 73, 91, 103, 133, 181, 199	31, 37, 67, 133, 145, 157, 169, 181, 205
Health/Philosophy	55, 73, 139, 145	19, 55, 217	217
Grammar, Usage, and Mechanics			
Nouns	67, 114	114	77, 149
Pronouns	114, 150	114	
Possessives	150		
Verbs	42, 78	150	77, 222
Adjectives	186		77, 114
Adverbs	222		77, 78
Prepositions and Prepositional Phrases		78	186
Conjunctions		186	150
Parts of a Sentence	42, 78	114, 222	42, 222
Dictionary/Thesaurus			
Alphabetical Order		159	
Definitions	51, 63, 69, 81, 87, 123, 141, 207	87, 105, 213	21, 105, 165, 177
Phonetic Spellings	9, 21, 27, 57, 105, 129, 135, 141, 159, 171, 189	15, 21, 27, 63, 153, 171	9, 57, 69, 93, 129
Parts of Speech and Inflected Forms	15, 57, 99, 123	57, 93, 123, 177	15, 27, 33, 87, 117, 189
Guide Words	93, 153, 165	9, 51, 129, 141	153
Syllabication	21, 27	15, 21, 63, 153	57
Etymologies and Homographs	45, 117, 213	27, 33, 81, 117, 165, 189, 201, 207	51, 81, 123, 135, 171, 207

	GRADE 5	GRADE 6	GRADE 7
Dictionary/Thesaurus (continued)			
Using a Thesaurus/Synonyms	33, 177, 195, 201	45, 99, 135, 195	45, 63, 99, 141, 159, 195, 201, 213
Base Words		57, 69, 93, 123, 177	87, 189
Electronic Spelling			
Computer Terms	79, 151, 223	151, 223	43, 223
Search Engines	43	43	151
Spell Checker	115	115	115
Graphics	187		187
Internet		79, 187	79
Spelling and Careers			
			T12, T40, T76, T112, T148, T184, T200, T220
Handwriting			
One-Minute Handwriting Hints	T10, T16, T22, T28, T34, T46, T52, T58, T64, T70, T82, T88, T94, T100, T106, T118, T124, T130, T136, T142, T154, T160, T166, T172, T178, T190, T196, T202, T208, T214	T10, T16, T22, T28, T34, T46, T52, T58, T64, T70, T82, T88, T94, T100, T106, T118, T124, T130, T136, T142, T154, T160, T166, T172, T178, T190, T196, T202, T208, T214	T10, T16, T22, T28, T34, T46, T52, T58, T64, T70, T82, T88, T94, T100, T106, T118, T124, T130, T136, T142, T154, T160, T166, T172, T178, T190, T196, T202, T208, T214

Spelling Connections Word List
Grades 1–8

Note: Each word is identified by grade level, unit number, and list designation. Words may be featured more than once per grade or in more than one grade. Words in the targeted grade level are printed in blue.

C	Core List
A	Assessment
LA	Language Arts
SS	Social Studies
S	Science
H	Health
M	Math
FA	Fine Arts
CH	Challenge
P	Preview
PH	Philosophy
PS	Public Speaking
R	Review
WW	Writer's Words

A

a 1-14-C
abacus 7-17-SS
abbreviation 6-29-LA
abdicate 8-7-SS
abilities 7-19-CH
ability 5-29-C
able 4-3-C
aboard 8-2-C
abolish 5-33-SS
about 3-16-C; 4-9-R
above 3-16-C
abridged 7-33-LA
abrupt 8-1-C
abscissa 8-32-M
absence 6-32-C
absent 6-10-C
absolute 7-13-C
absolutely 7-13-C
absolute value 7-29-M
absorb 8-29-S
abstract 7-23-C
absurd 8-28-FA
abundance 8-16-C
abundant 8-16-C
academic 8-15-C
academy 8-15-C
a cappella 8-5-CH

accede 8-29-P
accelerate 7-20-P; 8-7-C
accent 6-1-C
accentuate 8-7-CH
accentuation 8-14-LA
accept 5-23-C
acceptable 6-19-C
acceptance 8-7-C
access 7-5-CH
accessible 7-14-C; 8-23-R
accessory 8-1-C
accident 6-17-C; 7-20-R
accidental 7-24-A
accidentally 7-22-C
acclaim 7-20-CH
accolade 7-20-CH
accommodate 7-5-P; 7-24-A; 8-7-C
accompaniment 7-20-CH
accompany 7-5-C
accomplice 8-1-C
accomplish 7-5-C
accomplishment 7-20-CH
accord 6-11-SS
accordance 7-15-CH
according 7-20-C
accordion 7-20-CH
account 7-20-C
accountability 7-20-P; 8-29-C
accountable 8-23-C
accountant 6-36-A; 8-12-A
accumulate 7-20-P; 8-7-C
accuracy 8-7-C
accurate 6-25-C; 7-20-R
accurately 6-11-P; 7-13-C
accuse 6-5-C
accustomed 7-20-C
ache 4-28-H
achieve 6-8-C
achievement 8-3-C
achieving 6-8-P; 7-10-C
acid 4-32-S
acidic 8-29-S
acknowledge 8-26-C
acknowledgment 8-26-C
acorn 2-31-CH
acoustics 8-13-S
acquaint 8-26-C
acquaintance 8-26-C
acquainted 8-30-A
acquiesce 8-29-P
acquire 5-31-CH
acquisition 8-26-CH

acquit 8-22-SS
acquittal 8-13-P
acre 6-35-P; 7-8-C
acreage 6-21-P; 7-8-C
acropolis 8-15-C
across 3-19-C
act 3-1-C
action 6-29-C; 8-22-R
activate 8-22-C
active 5-5-C
actively 6-11-CH; 8-22-P
activities 6-2-P; 7-19-C
activity 5-29-C; 8-10-R
actor 4-32-P; 5-25-C
actual 7-15-C
actualize 8-22-CH
actually 8-24-A
acute 6-5-C
adapt 7-27-C; 8-1-R
add 2-2-M
addend 4-26-M
addenda 8-9-P
addendum 8-9-P
addition 4-26-M
additional 5-8-CH
additionally 6-11-C; 7-13-R
additive 8-8-M
address 5-31-C
adequate 6-1-CH; 8-14-R
adj. 5-35-CH
adjacent 8-11-M
adjective 4-9-LA
adjoin 8-26-C
adjourn 8-26-C
adjust 8-26-C
adjustment 8-30-A
administer 7-1-P; 8-35-C
administration 8-35-CH
admirable 6-19-P; 7-14-C; 8-23-R
admiration 7-9-C
admire 6-3-P; 7-9-C
admissible 7-30-A; 8-23-C
admission 7-29-C
admit 6-1-C
admittance 6-32-CH
admitted 5-16-P; 6-15-C; 7-29-R
admitting 6-15-C; 8-13-R
adobe 3-9-SS
adolescence 8-30-A
adolescent 8-26-C
adopt 7-27-C
adorable 6-19-C; 7-10-R

B

T357